797,885 Books
are available to read at

www.ForgottenBooks.com

Forgotten Books' App
Available for mobile, tablet & eReader

ISBN 978-1-331-75393-3
PIBN 10230368

This book is a reproduction of an important historical work. Forgotten Books uses state-of-the-art technology to digitally reconstruct the work, preserving the original format whilst repairing imperfections present in the aged copy. In rare cases, an imperfection in the original, such as a blemish or missing page, may be replicated in our edition. We do, however, repair the vast majority of imperfections successfully; any imperfections that remain are intentionally left to preserve the state of such historical works.

Forgotten Books is a registered trademark of FB &c Ltd.
Copyright © 2015 FB &c Ltd.
FB &c Ltd, Dalton House, 60 Windsor Avenue, London, SW19 2RR.
Company number 08720141. Registered in England and Wales.

For support please visit www.forgottenbooks.com

1 MONTH OF FREE READING

at

www.ForgottenBooks.com

By purchasing this book you are eligible for one month membership to ForgottenBooks.com, giving you unlimited access to our entire collection of over 700,000 titles via our web site and mobile apps.

To claim your free month visit:
www.forgottenbooks.com/free230368

* Offer is valid for 45 days from date of purchase. Terms and conditions apply.

English
Français
Deutsche
Italiano
Español
Português

www.forgottenbooks.com

Mythology Photography **Fiction**
Fishing Christianity **Art** Cooking
Essays **Buddhism** Freemasonry
Medicine **Biology** Music **Ancient Egypt** Evolution Carpentry Physics
Dance Geology **Mathematics** Fitness
Shakespeare **Folklore** Yoga Marketing
Confidence Immortality Biographies
Poetry **Psychology** Witchcraft
Electronics Chemistry History **Law**
Accounting **Philosophy** Anthropology
Alchemy Drama Quantum Mechanics
Atheism Sexual Health **Ancient History**
Entrepreneurship Languages Sport
Paleontology Needlework Islam
Metaphysics Investment Archaeology
Parenting Statistics Criminology
Motivational

Fourteen Years a Jesuit

A Record of Personal Experience and a Criticism

BY

COUNT PAUL VON HOENSBROECH

TRANSLATED FROM THE GERMAN BY
ALICE ZIMMERN
(Girton College, Cambridge)

VOLUME II

CASSELL AND COMPANY, LTD.
London, New York, Toronto and Melbourne
1911

ALL RIGHTS RESERVED

CONTENTS

CHAPTER	PAGE
15. A Criticism of the Inner Constitution of the Order: Some General Characteristics	
16. The Criticism Continued: Theory and Practice of the Vows	49
17. The Criticism Continued: Theory and Practice of the Constitutions	105
18. The Criticism Continued: Politics and Confessors	133
19. The Criticism Continued: Court Confessors . .	172
20. Scholastic Years at Wynandsrade, Blyenbeck and Ditton Hall	199
21. The Scholastic Studies	227
22. The Philosophical and Theological Studies of the Scholasticate	246
23. The Attitude of the Order to Learning	270
24. Jesuit Morality	286
25. Jesuit Morality and the State	338
26. Exaeten	369
27. Berlin	399
28. The Tertiate and the End	412
29. General Verdict on the Jesuit Order	423
30. From Then Till Now	447
Index	469

Fourteen Years a Jesuit

CHAPTER XV

A CRITICISM OF THE INNER CONSTITUTION OF THE ORDER: SOME GENERAL CHARACTERISTICS

By the "inner constitution of the Order" I mean the spirit of the Order. Theoretically, it is manifested in the Constitutions of the Order, and, practically, in its activity. Thus the inner and outer are combined, the organism of the Order, with its actual and its historical life, being formed by both.

Criticism will, therefore, extend to the whole of this domain. But, first, some preliminary questions must be answered.

1. Have we the real, and, above all, the complete Constitutions of the Order in the extant editions of the "Institute of the Society of Jesus?" *

A positive answer cannot be given. We can only take what is offered as the "complete" Constitutions in good faith, trusting in the honour of those who issue them, namely, the Jesuit Order itself. Nor is corroboration by another authority of the completeness of the Constitutions, to be found anywhere of course I am only

---

* Prague, 1757; Rome, 1870; etc. The latest edition of the "Institute," published in Florence in 1893, cannot be obtained at ordinary booksellers. When I sought to procure a copy from the Order through the Berlin branch of the Herder firm of publishers at Freiburg i. Br., which is closely connected with the Order, my request was refused. They would not supply me with the latest edition, even for payment.

Fourteen Years a Jesuit

CHAPTER XV

A CRITICISM OF THE INNER CONSTITUTION OF THE ORDER: SOME GENERAL CHARACTERISTICS

By the "inner constitution of the Order" I mean the spirit of the Order. Theoretically, it is manifested in the Constitutions of the Order, and, practically, in its activity. Thus the inner and outer are combined, the organism of the Order, with its actual and its historical life, being formed by both.

Criticism will, therefore, extend to the whole of this domain. But, first, some preliminary questions must be answered.

1. Have we the real, and, above all, the complete Constitutions of the Order in the extant editions of the "Institute of the Society of Jesus?" *

A positive answer cannot be given. We can only take what is offered as the "complete" Constitutions in good faith, trusting in the honour of those who issue them, namely, the Jesuit Order itself. Nor is corroboration by another authority of the completeness of the Constitutions, to be found anywhere—of course I am only

---

* Prague, 1757; Rome, 1870; etc. The latest edition of the "Institute," published in Florence in 1893, cannot be obtained at ordinary booksellers. When I sought to procure a copy from the Order through the Berlin branch of the Herder firm of publishers at Freiburg i. Br., which is closely connected with the Order, my request was refused. They would not supply me with the latest edition, even for payment.

B

thinking of an ecclesiastical authority—which has had an insight into the original documents, the first drafts and editions of the Constitutions. The Order alone tells us, "These are my constitutions and rules." But not even the Order itself has ever stated officially and solemnly, "These are my complete constitutions, my complete rules: there are no others."

Serious doubts arise as to their completeness when we peruse the *Summarium Constitutionum* and the *Regulae Communes**—i.e. those portions of the Constitutions which are supposed to contain a summary, the quintessence of the principles and rules: "A summary (*summarium*) of those statutes which relate to the spiritual direction of our members and which are to be observed by all."

An incoherent mass of matter is to be found here, consisting of fifty-two points and forty-nine rules. Regulations dealing with mere externals stand side by side with others concerned with ascetic discipline. Fundamental rules for the structure and direction of the Society alternate with what is obviously unimportant and transitory. What astonishes us is not so much the lack of arrangement as the lack of coherence. We are sensible of gaps, and involuntarily the thought arises, "Has not something been omitted here and here and here?"

The *Summarium* and the *Regulae Communes* were read once every month during meals from the pulpit of the refectory. The more often I heard them the more strongly I doubted: "Am I hearing something complete or something consciously and intentionally curtailed?" In important and decisive conversations, to be mentioned later, I expressed my doubts to the Provincial of the German Province, Father Jacob Ratgeb. I received the evasive reply: "Leave alone such quib-

* *Inst. S.J.*, II., 70–78.

Criticism of the Inner Constitution

bling. Take things as they come; what lies in the future does not concern to-day."

The Transactions of the fifth General Congregation (1593-1594) afford abundant food for doubt and consideration from this point of view. We know them only from the Decrees published by the Order itself. Incidentally, why has the Order never yet published the complete minutes of even a single General Congregation—and there have been twenty-five of these up to the present time? Space, surely, has not been lacking in its numerous and voluminous works on the inner and outer history of the Order. But even from these Decrees it can clearly be seen that there is intentional obscurity with regard to the Constitutions, so that we have a full right to doubt their completeness when printed and published by the Order.

We find, in the first place:

"Everything in the *Formula Instituti* which was laid before Pope Julius III. and sanctioned by him and his successors, and everything in it referring by way of explanation to our Constitutions is and must be looked upon as the substance of our Institute. And although there is other matter belonging to the substance of our Institute, the Congregation has decided that it need not be discussed at the present time." *

Directly after this we read that a request was made to explain more clearly what are the substantials [of the Institute], and a question was raised as to whether it would not be advantageous to add some examples of substantials, which seemed opportune, to the sentence, "There is other matter belonging to the substance of the Institute." The Congregation consequently determined to amend the Decree.†

The 58th Decree is the result of the amendment:

"The substance of the Institute is, in the first place,

* Decree 44. † Decree 45.

that contained in the *formula* or *regula* of the Society, which was submitted to Pope Julius III. and was confirmed by him and some of his successors; in the second place, that without which the contents of the *formula* could not hold good at all, or only with difficulty, namely · (1) There are some essential impediments to admission; (2) a judicial form need not be observed on dismissal (3) a statement of conscience must be made to the Superior; (4) everyone must be content that anything about him, which has been learnt outside confession, should be notified to the Superior; (5) all must be prepared to show suitable love and charity to one another. And other similar points, the confirmation of which the Congregation has no time to consider at present, especially as the Generals can confirm them when necessary, if they are not confirmed in other General Congregations."

But the seventh General Congregation of 1616 decrees almost in contradiction to the fifth:

"The Congregation decided that it would be more advisable to abstain from the confirmation of other things pertaining to the substance of the Institute, besides those expressed in the *formula*, because it is not possible to express everything in summary. If anybody should feel any doubt, he can apply to our worthy Father [the General of the Order] and learn from him what he ought to think in this respect." *

There is here an evident unwillingness to make known the complete "*substantialia* of the Institute." It is a mere pretext for the seventh General Congregation to say that they cannot be summarised; and there is an avowal of the existence of still other *substantialia* when the fifth General Congregation says that "There is other matter besides."†

* Decree 40.
† See Chapter XIV. for the *Formula Instituti*.

Criticism of the Inner Constitution

The doubt concerning the incompleteness of the editions of the statutes, etc., published by the Order becomes a certainty through the proceedings of the eighth and fourteenth General Congregations.

The Order carefully conceals in its published collections of the Congregational Decrees* the transactions and resolutions of the eighth General Congregation (1645-46) as to an important letter by Innocent X., dealing in eighteen points with comprehensive reforms of the Jesuit Order.

At the fourteenth General Congregation in 1696, the General, Thyrsus Gonzalez, proposed that the Congregation should agree that the past events—*i.e.* the dispute as to the General's attack on *probabilism*—should not again be touched upon. The Congregation decided accordingly, but this important resolution is missing in every official publication of the Decrees.† The editions of the Decrees intended for publicity must not contain anything which could throw an unfavourable light on inner transactions. How frequently may this summarised procedure have taken effect? How can history be written when founded on such "official transactions"?

In the rules of the *Socius* of the Provincial also, allusions are made to secret statutes of the Order, only existing in manuscript form.

"He must take care of the separate archives of the Province of the Order, inasmuch as they contain manuscripts, which are especially important for the direction of the Province." Amongst these books are included, "The book which contains the unprinted regulations (*ordinationes*) by the Generals of the Order binding on the whole Society. The book which contains another kind of unprinted circulars of the Generals." ‡

---

* Prague edition of the *Inst. S.J.*, I., 449-696; Roman edition, I., 139-461.
† For proofs of this see Döllinger-Reusch, *Moralstreitigkeiten*, II., 214.
‡ *Inst. S.J.*, II., 86.

The latter book especially must be characterised as a secret book.

Secret statutes must also be inferred from an utterance of the Spanish Jesuit Miranda, appointed as Assistant to the General, which is contained in a letter written to a friend in 1736, and communicated by the Jesuit Ibañez in his report on the Jesuit state of Paraguay.

"Until I came here [Rome], where I first obtained accurate information about everything, I did not comprehend what our Society was. Its government is a special study, which not even the Provincials understand. Only one who fills the office which I now occupy can even begin to understand it." *

Since Miranda was a Provincial before he was nominated Assistant, he must have understood what he was writing about. Ibañez also mentions unprinted "ordinances, regulations, and letters of the General and Provincials" which doubtless were to be kept secret.†

The words of Don Juan de Palafox, Bishop of Los Angeles, whom the Jesuits hated with a deadly hatred and persecuted even in the grave, are significant in this connection. He says in his famous letter of January 8th, 1649, to Innocent X., to which I must refer again later:

"What other Order has Constitutions which are not allowed to be seen, privileges which it conceals, and secret rules and everything relating to the arrangement of the Order hidden behind a curtain? The rules of every other Order may be seen by all the world . But among the Jesuits there are even some of the Professed who do not know the statutes, privileges, and even the rules of the Society, although they are pledged to observe them. Therefore they are not governed by their Superiors according to the rules of the Church, but according to certain

* *Le Bret Magazin*, II., 458. † *Ibid*, II., 373.

Criticism of the Inner Constitution

concealed statutes known by the Superiors alone, and according to certain secret and pernicious denunciations, which leads to a large number being driven from the bosom of the Society." *

2. Has the Jesuit Order secret instructions, and are the oft-quoted "Monita privata" authentic?

From what has been and must still be said I have not the least doubt that the Order has secret statutes, which it guards carefully. The Jesuit Order merits the designation "secret society" more than any other association.

The question as to the authenticity or spuriousness of the *Monita* cannot be answered so easily and simply.

The *Monita privata Societatis Jesu* ("Secret Instructions of the Society of Jesus") first appeared in print at Cracow in 1612, after they had already been circulated in manuscript form. The editor seems to have been the ex-Jesuit Zahorowski. Almost innumerable editions and reprints in all civilised tongues followed one another. The latest edition was published at Bamberg in 1904.

The importance of the publication follows from the fact that, directly after its appearance, the General of the Order, Mutius Vitelleschi, twice (in 1616 and 1617) instructed the German Jesuit, Gretser, a prominent theologian of the Order, to refute it, and that up to most recent times Jesuit after Jesuit has come forward to repudiate it.†

A few years ago, Adolf Harnack asked my opinion as to whether the *Monita* were genuine or not. I replied

---

* Don Juan de Palafox, *Letters to Innocent X.* (Frankfort and Leipzig, 1773), p. 116 *et seq.*

† *See* Duhr., S.J., *Jesuitenfabeln*, 4th edition (Freiburg i. Br.), 1904, p. 90 *et seq.*

that we had to distinguish between the genuineness of the form and of the matter, and I still hold to this distinction.

The genuineness of the form—*i.e.* that the *Monita* were drawn up by the Order itself in the published text as a secret supplement to the official Constitution of the Order—is hard to prove.

Of the genuineness of the contents—*i.e.* that the *Monita* contain regulations in harmony with the spirit of the Order, whether its author were a Jesuit or an enemy of the Jesuits, whether he wished to write a serious or a satirical work—I am as positive as of the existence of secret instructions of the Order.

But even the genuineness of the form cannot be as easily disposed of as has been done by the Jesuits, and recently, in an especially superficial manner, by the Jesuit Duhr.* In face of the historically indisputable facts bearing on the *Monita,* it only remains to the disinterested and conscientious examiner to pronounce "Not proven" over the genuineness of the form.

Ecclesiastical opinions (those of bishops, Congregations of the Index, etc.) regarding the genuineness are of no value, because they are partial, are prompted by the Jesuits themselves, and condemn them as false without attempting to produce proofs.

It is natural that the Jesuits themselves should deny the genuineness in a flood of refutations. But such denials only merit the belief or unbelief which the denial of every defendant deserves. Only sound proof can turn the scale against the genuineness of the *Monita.* And such proofs have not been produced up to now by the Jesuits. Nor has any convincing invalidation of the facts advanced on behalf of its genuineness been produced.

The advocates of their genuineness rely essentially on

* *Jesuitenfabeln*, p. 91 *et seq.*

Criticism of the Inner Constitution

the fact that the manuscript copies of the *Monita*, upon which the printed edition is based, were to be found in Jesuit colleges. The discovery of such copies in the colleges of Prague, Paris, Roermond (Holland), Munich, and Paderborn is beyond question. The copy in the Jesuit house at Paderborn was found "in a cupboard in the Rector's room" (*in scriniis rectoris**). The manuscript copy at Munich, belonging to the contents of the library of the Jesuit college of this place, which was suppressed in 1773, was only found in 1870 in a secret recess behind the altar of the old Jesuit Church of St. Michael at Munich. It would be a decisive token of genuineness if it could be proved positively that the Prague copy was already there in 1611—*i.e.* before the first printed edition of 1612. J. Friedrich's statement† makes this seem probable, but not certain. What the Jesuit Duhr ‡ writes to the contrary is of no value. It is certain, however, that the discovery in Prague was so disagreeable to the Jesuits that the chief champion of the spuriousness of the *Monita*, the Jesuit Forer, considered it advisable to pass it over in silence in his work of repudiation, *Anatomia Anatomiae Societatis Jesu*. On the other hand, he zealously demonstrated—what no one disputed—that the copy at Paderborn was only brought to light after the first edition had been published. Forer's silence is the more remarkable, as a manuscript note, intended for his book, treats the Prague discovery as a fact.§ The saying that those who keep silence when they could and should speak seem to give consent, comes to my mind in the case of this ominous silence.||

* *Anatomia*, p. 49.   † J. Friedrich, *Beiträge*, p. 8.
‡ *Jesuitenfabeln*, p. 94.   § Friedrich, pp. 9 and 65.
|| Crétineau-Joly, who writes in the pay of the Jesuit Order, has indeed the audacity to designate the discovery of the manuscript *Monita*, in the Jesuit Colleges of Prague and Paderborn as "a base historical lie" ("*un grossier mensonge historique*"). (*Histoire de la Compagnie de Jésus*. Paris, 1844, III., 372, 2.)

I will give a few extracts from the edition in the *Arcana Societatis Jesu*, 1635 (without place of publication), from the manuscript* found by Christian von Braunschweig in a secret drawer belonging to the Rector in the Jesuit college at Paderborn, adding my own remarks.

"What attitude ought the Society of Jesus to take up on re-organisation?" The directions supplied (attainment of the favour of the population through the rendering of services, almsgiving, edifying behaviour for the edification of others) are in absolute harmony with the Constitutions and rules.

"How should the friendship of princes and other great people be gained?" Although the means indicated for ensuring princely favour cannot be verified in detail from the statutes, the whole tendency of the precepts given corresponds with the official "explanation" (Declar. B) to Part 10 of the Constitutions: "Above all, we should retain the goodwill . of temporal princes and great men and persons holding prominent positions." † The practice of the Order also in greeting and receiving princes with a display of magnificence and grandiloquent speech harmonises with what is said on this point.

"What attitude must be taken up by court-chaplains and princely confessors?" The answer suggests a commentary to General Acquaviva's "Ordinance" of 1602. The confessors must seem to exercise reserve in political matters.

"Of their attitude to other religious Orders." Quarrels with other Orders are recorded on almost every page of Jesuit history. They arose mostly because the Society of Jesus, under a pretence of humility (*haec minima societas*—this most humble society) represented itself

---

* Friedrich, pp. 4–32.   † *Inst. S.J.*, I., 130.

as greater and superior in virtue and perfection to all other Orders. The advice given for making good the reputation of highest perfection everywhere is written in the Order's arrogant spirit, of which I shall speak later.

"How may rich widows be kept well disposed towards the Society of Jesus?" The chief directions in this section concern the appointment of Jesuits as confessors and spiritual guides, their interference in household regulation and private affairs, incitations to donations and alms-giving, and correspond to the actual attitude of the Order, which I myself have observed in my home and in many other houses of near relations. Especially the securing of money from wives and widows under the mask of piety (confession and exercises) is a world-wide and ancient malpractice of Jesuit confessors and spiritual guides. The activity of the Jesuit Order in England at the end of the sixteenth and beginning of the seventeenth century affords very interesting examples of this. The English Jesuit, Gerard, relates of himself: "I also received many general confessions; among others that of a widow lady of high rank (Lady Lovel), who for the rest of her days applied herself to good works and gave me an annual sum of 1,000 florins for the Society; another widow (Mrs. Fortescue) gave 700." *

The Catholic priest, William Watson, reports more fully: "In like manner he (the Jesuit Gerard) dealeth with such gentlewomen as the Ladie Louell, Mistresse Haywood, and Mistresse Wiseman, of whom he got so much as now shee feeleth the want of it. By drawing Mistress Fortescue, the widow of Master Edmond Fortescue, into his exercise, he got of her a farme worth 50 pounds a yere and paid her no rent. Another drift he hath by his exercise of cousinage: which is to perswade

* *The Life of Fr. John Gerard* (London, 1882), p. 63, quoted by Taunton. *History of the Jesuits in England* (London, 1901), p. 162.

such gentlewomen, as haue large portions to their marriage, to give the same to him and his companie, and to become nuns. So he preuailed with two of Mr. William Wiseman's daughters, with Elizabeth Sherly, with Dorothy Ruckwood, with Mary Tremaine, with Anna Arundell, and with Lady Mary Percie." * What is said in the *Monita* of "careful excitement of the sensuous faculty" in women and widows does not correspond with reality, from my knowledge of facts.

"Of the means by which sons and daughters of our confessional children are to be brought to a spiritual state." The directions contain nothing which has not been practised hundreds of times. The chapter, "Of the choice of young men for our Society and of the manner of keeping a firm hold on them," is taken from life.

"What attitude should be taken up by our followers in regard to those dismissed from the Order?" The spreading of evil reports, here recommended, about those who have either been dismissed or have withdrawn is an almost regular practice. The advice to ill-treat those to be dismissed and to hinder their advancement after dismissal is confirmed by the practice of the Order. The German Jesuit, Streicher, relates in a confidential letter (now in the State archives at Munich) from Spain, dating from the eighteenth century, "Half a year before dismissal the person to be dismissed is thrown into a dungeon and there reduced (*maceratus*) by a diet of bread and water. Every Friday he is brought, with chains fastened on both feet, by a lay brother into the refectory, and he must scourge himself there [before the others]. Our members have also contrived that no one who has not withdrawn for legitimate and conclusive reasons shall be appointed to a parish or any other benefice." † That this

---

* *Decacordon of Ten Quodlibetical Questions* (London, 1602), p. 89 *et seq.*

† Reprinted from Friedrich, *Beiträge*, p. 73 *et seq.*

Criticism of the Inner Constitution

inhumane treatment was customary not only in Spain is proved by a saying of the Archbishop of Lemberg, Demetrius Sulkow, recorded by Harenberg *· "It is difficult for the persons dismissed [by the Jesuits] to attain to any ecclesiastical dignity . . owing to the antipathy engendered by the Jesuits in the King towards the persons dismissed. It is certain that they wished to dissuade me from appointing any persons dismissed from amongst them to positions in my diocese, and when I asked why, they replied, 'The person dismissed must vanish into some obscure corner, so that he may not mislead others.'"

From my own experience regarding the behaviour of the Order towards dismissed persons, I shall give at least one staggering case further on.

3. Is there a secret class of members existing side by side with the grades of the Order mentioned in the Constitutions? Are there affiliates of the Jesuit Order?

We saw in Chapter V. that the Jesuit Order does not recognise so-called second and third Orders, such as the Franciscans and Dominicans organised among the laity, but that the Marian Congregations might be characterised as third or second Orders of the Jesuits. But however closely the Congreganists may have been connected with the Jesuits, they were not attached to the Order by the bond of obedience. This bond alone constitutes real affiliates, and the Jesuit Order possesses them.

The possibility of affiliates seems to me to be chiefly indicated in two passages in the official "Institute." It is stated in the Constitutions:

"The Society in the broadest sense of the word com-

* *Pragmatische Geschichte des Ordens der Jesuiten* (Halle-Helmstädt, 1760), II., 965.

prises all who owe obedience to the General, also novices and whoever, with the desire to live and die in the Society, places himself in a position of probation for admission into it and to any of the grades which will be discussed." *

And the 129th Decree of the first General Congregation (1558) is as follows:

"May the laity who take the vows in a military Christian Order be admitted into our Order, although it must be supposed that they will not make their profession in our Society? Answer: They may be admitted." †

In the first passage reference is made to those who owe obedience to the General, including novices, and to others who place themselves in a position of probation with the desire to be admitted into the Society. Unless we assume gross tautology, a distinction is drawn between those mentioned in the first place and those in the second by the " and "—*i.e.* those mentioned in the second place, as opposed to those already belonging to the Order, the novices, are "in a position of probation," but do not (yet?) belong to the Society—*i.e.* are consequently affiliates.

The second passage clearly speaks of "laity, who are to be admitted into the Society without making their profession." I acknowledge that the word "profession" may be understood in a restricted sense—*i.e.* in opposition to the vows of the coadjutors; but the possibility of understanding it in a general sense—*i.e.* in the sense of the vows of the Order generally—cannot be denied. We have, then, here also to do with affiliates.

Moreover, the Constitutions openly mention in Part 10 a class of members who might properly be styled affiliates—namely, all those Jesuits who have become bishops or cardinals.

* Constit. V., 1; Declar. A.
† *Inst. S.J.*, I., 170.

Criticism of the Inner Constitution

"He must also vow to God that if ever he is compelled to accept any preferment outside the Society he will at all times listen to the advice of the General for the time being, or of any person appointed by him to take his place; and if he thinks what is so recommended to be desirable, will perform it; not that he who is preferred holds any member of the Society in the place of the Superior, but that he desires of his own free will to be bound in the sight of God to do that which he shall perceive to be best for God's service; and is content that there should be one to set it before him in charity and Christian liberty, to the glory of God and our Lord." *

This regulation is, it is true, directly opposed to the general canonical definitions, according to which a bishop or cardinal is no longer bound by an oath to the superiors of his Order (when he has been a member of an Order), but only to the Pope (*soli R. Pontifici*), but it is for that very reason a particularly striking example of the pertinacity with which the Jesuit Order retains those belonging to it in bondage, in the interests and through the egotism of the Order. Ecclesiastical decisions do not regulate its conduct, but its own interests and extension and the consolidation of its own power.

It will also be observed how skilfully the words chosen conceal their opposition to the canonical law. The Jesuit who has become a prelate has no Superior in the Society —this is not allowed. He only chooses "of his own free will" someone to obey, and this happens to be the General of the Order.

Thus all bishops and cardinals chosen from the Jesuit Order are its affiliates according to the Constitutions.†

Let us, however, disregard what the Constitutions

---

* Constit. X., 1, 6.
† *See* Chapter XIV. for the vow of the professed Jesuits.

say, secretly or openly, regarding affiliates. The historical fact of their existence is clear and unmistakable.

The founder of the Jesuit Order, Ignatius Loyola, made a number of affiliations. Thus the Spaniard, Miguel Torres, whom Ignatius called "the apple of his eye," lived as a man of the world. No one knew that he was a Jesuit and that Ignatius himself had admitted him years previously into the Order. Francis Borgia governed his Duchy of Gandia, living outwardly as a duke, although he had already four years previously made the Jesuit profession with Ignatius's consent. And when Borgia was canonised in 1724 by Benedict XIII., reference to his affiliation was even inserted in the bull of canonisation:

"Whilst still Duke of Gandia he was permitted by our predecessor, Paul III., at St. Ignatius's request, to take the vows with the knowledge of only a few members of the Order. He was granted four years by the Pope to arrange his affairs." *

Ignatius did the same with the rich Spanish abbot, Domenech, and the secular priest, Vergara, who nearly became Grand Inquisitor of Spain whilst still a secret Jesuit. The Infant Dom Luis of Portugal also joined Ignatius's Order as an affiliate.†

We have even a positive theoretical recognition of affiliation by Ignatius. Ex-members of other Orders wished openly to join the Jesuit Order. Ignatius rejected the open union, but caused his secretary, the Jesuit Polanco, to write in general terms:

"I observe that some are joining the Society and helping it according to the talent given them by God, and although they are really not Professed, Coadjutors, nor

---

* *Inst. S.J.* (Prague, 1757), I., 181.

† The evidence is given by Gothein. *Ignatius von Loyola und die Gegenreformation* (Halle, 1895), pp. 359 *et seq.* and 788.

Criticism of the Inner Constitution

Scholastics, they faithfully perform the same duties as these, and may, on their part, possess the merit of obedience." *

In an Italian record, dating from 1617,† regarding the aims of the Society of Jesus and the means of attaining them, we are told:

"That the Jesuits in England had succeeded in appointing an archpriest, who was a Jesuit by vow (*hanno fatto eleggere uno arciprete Giesuita in voto*), and who had persecuted the priests outside the Jesuit Order like a ravening wolf, brought them to extreme distress, and been so successful that almost all the priests in England were Jesuits by vow" (*Giesuiti in voto*).‡

Prince William of Orange forwarded to his ambassador in London, Dykvelt, an intercepted letter from the Jesuits of Liège to the members of their Order in Freiburg-i.-Br., in which it was stated that the King of England, James II., the father-in-law of the Prince of Orange, had become an affiliate of the Jesuit Order. Even Crétineau-Joly did not dare to pronounce the letter apocryphal. He only says, "*Authentique ou controuvée . . . une correspondance dont l'original n'a jamais pu être représenté.*"§ J. Friedrich supplies a valuable confirmation of the affiliation of the English king here reported, in an original letter from the Jesuit Ruga, in London on March 13th, 1687, to the Jesuit Pusterla in Milan, which is to be found amongst the Jesuit papers in the State Library at Munich. || The Jesuit Ruga there says that, at the first audience which he obtained soon after his arrival in England, James II. said to him, "I

---

* Gotthein, *Ibid.*, p. 361

† Reprinted in Döllinger-Reusch, *Moralstreitigkeiten*, II., 376–390.

‡ *Ibid.*, p. 388.   § *Histoire de la Compagnie de Jésus*, 4, 174.

|| *Codex lat. Mon.*, 26,473, f. 311; Friedrich: *Beiträge zur Geschichte des Jesuitenordens* (Munich, 1881), pp. 30, 78; *Abhandlung der kgl. bayerischen Akademie der Wissenschaften*, Class III., Vol. XVI., Part 1.

am a son of the Society of Jesus," and the Queen, " I am its daughter " A few days after this the Queen repeated to him, " It is my ambition to be a daughter of the Society of Jesus."

A document of the seventeenth century, "Instructions for Princes as to how the Jesuit Fathers rule," * speaks openly of affiliation.

" There is a class of secular Jesuits of both sexes, which, with blind obedience, attaches itself to the Society, adjusting all its actions in accordance with the advice of the Jesuits and obeying all their commands. This is mostly composed of gentlemen and ladies of rank, especially widows, also citizens or very rich merchants. Women especially are led on to renounce the world by the Jesuits, who then receive from them pearls, garments, furniture, and revenues. Another class of Jesuits consists of men holding clerical and lay positions, who live in the world supported by the Order and obtain pensions, abbeys, and benefices through it. These must solemnly promise to put on the garb of the Order at the General's command ; they are called Jesuits *in voto*. The Order makes wonderful use of them for the support of its rule. They are kept at courts and near the most prominent people in all kingdoms, so that they may act as spies and give an account of all that is transacted to the General of the Order."

A despatch of the Paris Nuncio of February 8th, 1773, communicated by Theiner,† coincides with this assertion:

" Far from acquiescing in the dissolution of the Jesuits, I know from her [Madame Louise, Carmelite, daughter of Louis XV. of France] that not only is she convinced that the suppression will never come to pass,

---

* Manuscript of the Parisian *Bibliothèque Nationale, fonds italiens*, No. 986.

† *Geschichte des Pontifikats Klemens XIV.* (Leipzig, 1853), II., 321.

Criticism of the Inner Constitution

but also that the Pope has not sufficient authority to carry it out. This is also the opinion which all Jesuit tertiaries secretly propagate everywhere."

Therefore such a well-informed man as the Papal Nuncio recognises the existence of "Jesuit tertiaries" as a matter of course. Since, however, the Jesuit Order does not possess real tertiaries—*i.e.* a third Order, as the Dominicans and Franciscans do—only affiliates of the Order can be understood when the expression chosen by the Nuncio is used.

Saint-Simon also recognises affiliates.

"The Jesuits always have lay members in all the professions. This is a positive fact. Doubtless Noyers, Louis XIII.'s secretary, belonged to them, and also many others. These affiliates take the same vows as the Jesuits so far as their position allows—*i.e.* the vow of absolute obedience to the General and the Superiors of the Order. They are to substitute for the vows of poverty and chastity the service rendered and protection afforded to the Society, and especially unlimited submission to the Superiors and confessor. . . . Politics thus come within their scope through the certain help of these secret allies." *

The Jesuit Lallemant reported in 1642 from Canada that there, with the consent of the Provincial of the French Province, to which Canada belonged, lay members were attached to the Society of Jesus. They took the vow to serve the Jesuit Order throughout their whole life wherever their services were required. The vow was modelled on one which was previously commonly used, with the consent of the General, in the Champagne Province of the Order. It was taken secretly, without outward ceremony, in presence of the confessor. Those joined to the Jesuit Order in this manner received the

* *Mémoires*, 12, 164.

official designation, "*Donnés.*" * This points to a whole class of affiliates.

We also meet with the same arrangement in the English Province of the Order. In the "Records of the English Province," † published by the Jesuit Foley (a lay brother), the following entry is to be found:

"Oliver, George, Rev., D.D., born in Newington, Surrey, on February 9th, 1781; ordained priest in 1806. He was the last survivor of a number of Catholic clergymen, scholars of the English Jesuits, who, though never entering the Society, always remained in the service of the English Province [of the Order] and subject to its [the English Province's] Superiors. . . . He died at Exeter a few years after 1851."

In England, therefore, the institution of affiliates, already mentioned, in 1617, was maintained for nearly two hundred and fifty years—to 1851.

These historical events are so convincing that the secret institution of affiliates must be admitted as an irrefutable fact.

To be sure, the Jesuits still deny the proofs which I have brought forward and which are also known to them, suppress them, and content themselves with an avowal of the existence of affiliates during the first period of the Order. Thus the arch-falsifier, the Jesuit Duhr, who has already been unmasked frequently and will be unmasked yet again, writes:

"A few cases in (*sic*) the difficulties of the first period do not give any right to generalise or speak of an 'Institution.'" ‡

"The few cases of the first period" (which Duhr carefully suppresses, however) are the above-mentioned affiliations of Duke Francis Borgia, Miguel Torres, etc.

---

* *The Jesuit Relations and Allied Documents* (Cleveland, Burrow Brothers and Company), XXI., 293 *et seq.*

† VII., 559.   ‡ Duhr, S.J., *Jesuitenfabeln* (4), p. 921.

Moreover, everything is really admitted by the avowal that there were affiliates during the first period. For what was then possible and actual, "owing to special circumstances," is always possible, and will always be actual when the special circumstances again occur. Their occurrence consequently only depends upon the will of the Superiors of the Order. If they declare that the circumstances have occurred, they have occurred.

4. Are the Constitutions of the Order, and the Jesuit Order itself, authoritatively directed against Lutheranism and generally against heresy?

A distinction must here be drawn between the form and the matter, as in the question of the genuineness or spuriousness of the *Monita*. Ignatius Loyola, when founding his Order and drawing up his Constitutions, can scarcely, indeed, have had Lutheranism and heresy formally in mind. It is certain, however, that the Jesuit Order from its very foundation actually considered the combat with heresy, and especially Lutheranism, to be its chief task. We have the strongest evidence of this.

Urban VIII.'s Bull of Canonisation of Ignatius Loyola in 1623 states:

"God's inexpressible goodness and mercy, which provides for every age in wonderful ways, raised up the mind of Ignatius Loyola . . . when Luther, that horrible monster (*monstrum teterrimum*), and the other detestable plagues (*aliaeque detestabiles pestes*), with their blasphemous tongues,* strove to destroy in the northern regions the ancient religion, with all its sanctity and

---

* What extraordinary expressions (let us take this opportunity of remarking) the Papacy employs, even in its most authoritative proclamations, against the Reformation and the Reformers! Rome is not bound by scruples or dignity of utterance when heretics are in question. Then the most vulgar abuse is in place. It claims as its right not only freedom to abuse, but also to anathematise. I certainly do not recommend that the Papal tone should be imitated by the non-ultramontane party. But we must not marvel too much when this occurs.

its ideal of a perfect life, and to degrade the authority of the apostolic see. This Loyola surrendered himself so implicitly to the guidance and fashioning of the Divine authority . . . that after the establishment of the new Order of the Society of Jesus, which, amongst other works of piety and love, entirely devoted itself, according to its Constitutions, to the conversion of the heathen and the leading back of heretics to the true faith,* he came to a saintly end."

The conclusiveness of this Papal pronouncement is strengthened greatly by a remark of Cardinal Monte, which he addressed to Pope Gregory XV. in the secret consistory in connection with the canonisation of Ignatius Loyola in 1622:

"When in the previous century the devil sowed tares in the well-tilled and prepared field of the Church and tried to undermine religion by Luther's blasphemous tongue in Germany and Henry VIII.'s unprecedented ferocity in England, God's inexpressible goodness and mercy . . . raised up Ignatius Loyola." †

It is explicable, therefore, that Clement XIV. actually states in the Brief, "*Dominus ac Redemptor*," of July 21st, 1773, by which he suppressed the Jesuit Order:

"It is certain that the Jesuit Order was founded . . . for the conversion of heretics."

The official historian of the Order, Crétineau-Joly, who wrote his voluminous work with the material and intellectual support of the Order, also lets slip this admission:

"In the Society of Jesus missions are of secondary importance (*accessoires*). The chief object is . . . the battle against heresy in Europe." ‡

Numerous proofs from the sphere of the Order itself

---

* *Inst. S.J.* (Prague, 1757), I., 119 *et seq.*

† Döllinger-Reusch, *Selbstbiographie des Kardinals Bellarmin*, p. 336.

‡ *Histoire de la Compagnie de Jésus*, I., 318.

Criticism of the Inner Constitution

can also, of course, be produced of the extreme hostility of the Jesuit Order to heresy, even though the Constitutions be not actually directed against it.

Thus, to begin with the founder of the Order, the activity of Ignatius in the interests of the Inquisition is especially noteworthy. He writes, in 1542, to his fellow member, Simon Rodriguez, in Lisbon, that Pope Paul III., at his instigation, has decided to set up a Cardinal's Congregation of the Inquisition. Thus Ignatius Loyola is the intellectual originator of the Roman Inquisition which exists even to this day,* and of its bloodshed. Ignatius also tried his hardest to prevail on Paul III. to consent to the request of John III. of Portugal and establish the Inquisition there on the same lines as in Spain. Indeed, in a letter to the Jesuit Miron, of June 20th, 1555, he declares that he is prepared to place members of his Order at the head of the Portuguese Inquisition, but wishes, so as to keep up appearances, that this should be done at the express command of the Pope.† The matter fell through, however.

The hatred of heretics, and not only heresy, which blazed up in the Inquisition to a bloody persecuting fury, is therefore a pious legacy to Jesuits from their founder. They guard the inheritance carefully and augment it forcibly by putting themselves forward in their writings, from the commencement of their existence to the present day, as definite supporters of the bloody persecution of heretics. I refer to the leading theologians of the Jesuit Order—Tanner, Laymann, Castropalao (seventeenth century); Perrone, Wenig, de Luca, Granderath, Laurentius (nineteenth and twentieth centuries).‡

* *Cartas de San Ignacio* (Madrid, 1874), I., 132, quoted by Druffel; *Ignatius von Loyola an der römischen Kurie* (Munich, 1879), pp. 12 and 38.

† Genelli, S.J., *Leben des hl. Ignatius von Loyola* (Innsbruck, 1848), p. 256 *et seq.*

‡ *Cf.* my work, *Moderner Staat und römische Kirche* (Berlin : C. A. Schwetschke u. Sohn), pp. 146 *et seq*.

Some passages from one of the most outstanding works in Jesuit literature and from the official *Ratio Studiorum* of the Order may still further illustrate theoretically its hatred of heretics, while a historical occurrence and a personal experience may supply practical illustration.

We read in the *Imago primi saeculi*:

" A time ago it was 1617. The Lutherans reckoned this as the centenary of their godless religion, because a hundred years before there appeared the first sparks of the pestilential flame, which afterwards spread quickly, with a hopeless fury, like a storm, first through Germany and then through some neighbouring provinces. Ignatius, whom God in His eternal wisdom raised up to oppose Luther, shall confront him in our work, too. . . . In presence of Ignatius does Luther, the stigma of Germany, the Epicurean swine, the ruin of Europe, the monster who brought disaster on the globe, the outcast of God and man, deserve a centenary jubilee ? * After Luther, false to God and religion, had forsaken the ancient faith, he was joined by a mob of petty schoolmasters, insolent grammarians, degenerate poets, frivolous little Hellenists, drunken orators, and Heaven knows what other ridiculous objects of philosophers and philologists. The dregs of the population, cobblers, dyers, butchers, and weavers followed their example. . . . From all sides streamed together the most vicious people—persons notorious through infamy, condemned by judges, bearing visible brands of shame . . they trampled down everything humane and godly. . . . In front marched Luther, carrying the godless torch which, in the form of an abominable treatise, tried to make all believe that unchastity was more necessary than food, drink, and sleep. . . . This infamous apostate [Luther] led to

* *Imago primi saeculi*, pp. 18. et seq.

battle ignorant persons, who had sprung from foul dens and the lowest dregs, of godless and infamous life, notorious through immorality, harpies of the Holy Scripture. With what an honourable and well-equipped host—really with word and deed—did the Society of Jesus oppose him.* Certainly we do not deny that we have entered into a bitter and eternal struggle for the Catholic religion against heresy. Like St. Jerome, each of us says to-day, 'I cannot agree with you on one point—namely, that I spare the heretics [not " heresy "; *haereticis*, not *haeresi*] and do not prove myself a Catholic. If this is the reason of our disagreement, I can die, but I cannot be silent.' It is in vain for heresy to expect to attain friendship with the Society of Jesus through silence alone. As long as there is life in us, we will bark at the wolves for the defence of the Catholic flock. Peace is out of the question; the seed of hate is innate within us (*Desperata pax est, odii semina innata sunt*). Ignatius is for us what Hamilcar was for Hannibal. At his command, we have sworn eternal war at the altars." †

In the *Ratio Studiorum* the thirteenth " rule for the external students of the Order " is as follows :

" They must not go to public exhibitions, comedies, or plays, nor to executions of criminals, except perhaps of heretics."

This fine injunction remained in force to 1832. Only then—when, indeed, there were no longer executions of heretics—was the permission to Jesuit scholars, boys of tender age, to find edification in executions of heretics cancelled.

The historical event—one of many—was the " Massacre of Thorn," brought about by the Jesuits.

On July 17th, 1724, the Jesuit College at Thorn was destroyed by a section of the students and population. A

* Pp. 550–552. † Pp. 843 *et seq.*

Protestant had not bared his head whilst a procession was passing by, and because a student of the Jesuit college struck off his hat, the fanatical Jesuit scholar was thrown into prison by the Protestant magistrate. This led to a great disturbance, and the destruction of the Jesuit establishment on the following day. The matter came before the high court of justice and the assessorial court at Warsaw; and the president and vice-president of Thorn, Rösner and Zerneke, as well as nine citizens of Thorn, were condemned to death.

This terrible sentence was mainly due to an inflammatory speech delivered to the judges on October 31st by one of the Jesuits.

" ' Oh, thou Mother of God, thou has fallen amongst Tartar heathendom at Thorn. See how the godless trample thee under foot! Thou art no Queen in Poland to the inhabitants of Thorn; rather has a godless and most ignominious insult transformed thee into a wench condemned to the pyre.' The Jesuit recalled to mind the oaths taken by the judges in the Marian Congregations, 'I will never permit anything against thine honour to be done by my subordinates.' * . . . The crucified God entreats and stretches out the hand hacked off by the inhabitants of Thorn, 'Do right and further justice! . . . The head of the serpent must be bruised. I could here speak on behalf of my house, but the wounds of my brothers [the Jesuits], caused by heretical hands, are marks of honour in suffering disgrace for Jesus' sake. I do not ask for corporal or capital punishment; being a priest, I do not thirst for blood.' " †

The further details of the affair show what was really

---

* A very instructive example of the trenchant effect of the Congregations on the public life.

† *Diarius von dem in Thorn a.* 1724, *d.* 17, *Juli entstandenen Tumulte und darau erfolgten Jesuitischen Prozessus*, VIII., 51; *Städtisches Archiv zu Thorn*; Jacobi, *Das Thorner Blutgericht*, 1724 (Halle, 1896), pp. 91 *et seq.* and 173.

Criticism of the Inner Constitution

intended by this hypocritical expression of gentleness on the part of the Jesuits.

To the sentence of death was added the rider: The sentence is only to be carried out if a Jesuit, together with six conjurors from the Polish nobility, shall corroborate on oath the guilt of the accused. This oath was taken by a Jesuit at the command of the Jesuit Rector, and the heretics were put to death on December 7th, 1724, in the cruel manner then customary.

Leaving all non-essentials out of the question, this much is certain—that the lives of nine people, whose offence consisted in the fact that they had not prevented the destruction of a house belonging to the Jesuits, depended on the oath of the Jesuits. The Jesuits took the oath, and the lives of the nine were forfeit.

I put the question, " Who and what are Jesuits ? " They themselves reply, " A band of people following Jesus in a quite special manner, and making His principles their own." The religious and ethical significance of the massacre at Thorn instigated by the Jesuits lies in this question and answer: The strongest antithesis to Jesus Christ, the most furious hate towards " heretics."

A few events connected with the murderous oath of the Jesuits set it in the worst of lights.

The Papal Nuncio, Santini, begged the Rector of the Jesuit College in a letter not to permit the oath to be taken, so as not to be the cause of a ninefold murder. He made this request to the Jesuit Superior by agreement with and at the desire of the Polish Lord High Chancellor, who considered that "such an action would be in keeping with the sanctity of their [the Jesuits'] position." * The letter was placed in the Jesuit Superior's hands in good time, as is shown by his answer, dated

---

* Text of the entire letter: *Leben und Tate Papst Benedikti XIII.* (Frankfort, 1731), I., 714.

December 10th, 1724. Though the "Annual Reports of the College of Thorn," drawn up by the Jesuits, state that it came a day too late, these "Annual Reports" deserve no credence, as they contain entirely uncontrolled Jesuit statements and are also contradicted by the reply of the Rector to the Nuncio's letter. Besides, it is certain that the judges drew the Jesuit Rector's attention, directly before the oath was sworn, to the fact that the Papal Nuncio had advised him against it. But for all that the Jesuit permitted his subordinates to take the oath.

Moreover, a real piece of Jesuit cunning and Roman-ultramontane hypocrisy came to light during and after the act of swearing. When the judicial assembly of Thorn saw the Jesuit with his six conjurors before it, ready to take the oath, attention was drawn to the fact that, according to the canonical law, priests might not assist in a death sentence, and the oath to be taken involved such assistance. The Jesuit Rector replied that he knew the prohibition, but it did not apply here, because the Jesuit whom he had chosen to take the oath was a lay brother —*i.e.* not a priest! *

After the oath, which resulted in torture and death for the nine unfortunate men, the Jesuits, with tears, implored mercy for the condemned. They thereby assumed a real and fitting Inquisitorial hypocrisy, which the Papacy carried on for centuries so as to be able to justify outwardly the noble expression, "The Church does not thirst for blood." †

After the actual drama had taken place, the bearing of the Jesuits remained worthy of the beginning and

---

* With reference to the infamous Jesuit action at Thorn, *cf.* Jacobi, *Das Thorner Blutgericht.*

† *Cf.* my work, *Das Papsttum,* etc., in which I have exposed the absolutely infamous untruthfulness of this Popish entreaty for the life of the heretics condemned by the Popish Inquisition.

Criticism of the Inner Constitution

continuation. Greed for the possessions of the heretics was associated with bloodthirstiness against the heretics.

In the judgment, the excessive compensation of 36,400 florins was awarded to the Jesuits. This was finally reduced to 22,000 florins after the Jesuits had shown themselves very obstinate in their demands. Eight thousand florins were to be paid them in cash, and for the remaining 14,000 florins they received the municipal estates of Lonzyn and Wengorzyn. The estates were only to revert again to the municipality on the payment of 14,000 florins, together with interest at 6 per cent. The estates remained in the Jesuits' hands till the autumn of 1730. The town found it very difficult to raise the 8,000 florins in cash. A merchant, Marianski, advanced this sum to it, taking as security the plate of one of the executed men, the Burgomaster Roesner, and the Jesuits quietly pocketed this sum, which might doubly be termed blood-money. *

This is unsurpassed hate on a large scale. A personal experience may show in what a paltry manner hatred of heresy may be expressed.

When I was stationed in 1889 at Exaeten, as "scriptor," the *Geschichte des deutschen Volkes*, by Johannes Jansen, was read aloud at table. In connection with this the question arose during recreation as to whether we should put the accent on the second or first syllable of the word "*lutherisch.*" I was of opinion (mistakenly, however) that the pronunciation "*lútherisch*" expressed more contempt than the pronunciation "*luthérisch.*" Accordingly, I requested the *Praefectus lectionis ad mensam*, the Jesuit Spiellmann (then chief editor of the magazine *Katholische Missionen*, and a writer of juvenile works which were very much read in Germany), to put a stop to the contemptuous pronunciation "*lútherisch*"

* Jacobi, *Das Thorner Blutgericht*, pp. 137 *et seq.*

during the reading at table. This suggestion was indignantly received; it was considered that the more contemptuously this word was pronounced the better. And from that time onwards, as often as a reader said "*luthérisch*," the "*repetat*" of the Jesuit Spiellmann resounded with especial emphasis. It was desirable that the contemptuous "*lútherisch*" should be drummed into the young scholastics (it was they who read aloud).

THE SPIRIT OF THE ORDER

As the Society of Jesus, the Jesuit Order prides itself on possessing in a quite special manner the spirit of Jesus Christ. The opposite is the case.

Whoever reads the Constitutions of the Order carefully will at once notice how very highly they esteem wealth, rank, prominent position, and, in short, that which is desirable and coveted from a worldly point of view, whereas Christ's teaching stands in sharpest contrast. He designates the lowly, the poor, the small, the insignificant, the despised, as His own.

As I shall deal in separate sections with the arrogance of the Order, its craving after honours and wealth, and similar important points, I will here give only a few selections from the Constitutions in order to illustrate the conflict between the "Society of Jesus" and Jesus.

In the choice of a person for the position of General the man who, as the head of the Society of Jesus, should therefore most resemble Jesus, nobility of birth, the possessions which he had in the world, honours and the like, are considered as desirable qualifications.

Noble birth and riches serve likewise as grounds for admission to the profession of the three vows. Though not expressly mentioned in the Constitutions, both the exponents whom I have to thank for my intimate knowledge of the subject, my Novice-Master, the Jesuit Meschler, and my Instructor during the Tertiate, the Jesuit Oswald, always quoted them at the appropriate point in their instructions.

The Constitutions allow women of rank an exceptional position as compared with those of the middle class.

Finally, the all-permeating spirit of worldly wisdom—of course expressed in unctuous religious form—stands out in the words:

" Above all things, it is necessary to retain the goodwill of the Apostolic See . . . next, that of princes and great men (*magnatum*) and persons holding prominent positions, upon whose favour or disfavour it depends to a large extent whether the way be open or closed for the service of God and for the salvation of souls."*

Such instructions do not exactly breathe the spirit of Jesus Christ.

We have seen already in the description of its educational activity how this worldly, arrogant and selfish spirit influences the conduct of the Order in such things as magnificent buildings and exhibitions, preference for the nobility and contemptuous treatment of poor scholars. We shall encounter it in a still more pronounced form in other domains of the extensive Jesuit field of labour. It is so evident that it strikes all who come in close touch with Jesuits. A remark made by the first Cardinal Archbishop of Westminster, Nicholas Wiseman, the author of the much-read book *Fabiola*, may here be quoted in place of numerous proofs. Wiseman writes to his friend, the Oratorian father, Frederick William Faber, in a confidential letter, dated October 27th, 1852:

" The Jesuits have a splendid church, a large house, several priests. . . . Scarcely was I settled in London,

* Const. X.; Declar. B.

than I applied to their Superior to establish here a *community* in due form of some ten or twelve fathers. I also asked for missionaries to give retreats to congregations, etc. I was answered on both heads, that dearth of subjects made it impossible. Hence, we have under them only a church, which by its splendour attracts and absorbs the wealth of two parishes, but maintains no schools, and contributes nothing to the education of the poor at its very door. I could say more, but I forbear."*

A second characteristic of the Constitutions is their cosmopolitanism. When this point is discussed, the Jesuits reply (and I myself believed for a considerable time in the validity of the answer): " We are no more and no less international than Christianity." This is false and a lie when spoken by Jesuits.

No doubt Christianity desires to spread amongst all nations, but not to deprive any nation of its individuality, nor does it aim at reducing all nationalities to a dead level. This is, however, just the aim systematically pursued by the Jesuit Order. It discourages most severely every national movement and every national peculiarity; and that not only in the case of its own members. The same international levelling effort is brought to bear on the young people entrusted to it for education.

Kink tells us that a national colouring could not be given to Jesuit instruction, if only because the teaching staff of the Order was composed of men from all lands of Catholic Christendom. Although the Emperor Ferdinand I. had commanded, in 1558, that the Jesuits who occupied the two theological chairs [in Vienna] should also have a mastery of the German language, his order was not obeyed. It frequently occurred later on that not even one of the Jesuits teaching at the University

---

* Purcell, *Life of Cardinal Manning* (London, 1895), II., 3.

Criticism of the Inner Constitution

could understand German, and that many government decrees had to be translated into Latin on their account.*

As I have minutely discussed the internationalism of Jesuit instruction and education in previous chapters, I will not go further into it here. I have already quoted the text of the cosmopolitan and unpatriotic rule of the Order—the 43rd of the *Summarium*. This is illustrated in an extremely instructive manner by the secret report of a Visitator† of the Upper German Province of the Order in 1596:

"I do not refer to the party divisions between Catholics and heretics, for the heretics are not worthy of being included under the word 'Christian' [in the rule quoted], because, on account of their faithless life, they oppose Christ and true Christians. Nor do I believe that this rule prevents us from rejoicing at the victory of Catholics over heretics, or forbids us to deplore in our discourses the hostility between Catholics brought about by the heretics. . . To this is due the misfortune that there are some people in our Society who have not a good opinion of the brothers outside our nationality, and who occasionally, in jest and earnest, unkindly censure their customs and their national failings, and cannot bear that such should be sent into this province. This is a very bad fault. It is to be shunned like the plague, and the old confidential intercourse between the different nations is very desirable and should be revived. Formerly there was scarcely a greater ornament of the Society—it was almost a miracle—than that members of such different nationalities should dwell amongst one another on such friendly terms. When this unity ceases, how can we

---

* *Geschichte der kaiserl. Universität Wien* (Vienna, 1854), I., 410.

† A Visitator is a Jesuit commissioned by the General of the Order for the inspection of one or several Provinces of the Order.

speak of a Society, and how can it exist? . . . May those be cut off who disturb this harmony, and rend the seamless mantle of the Society with their poisonous tongues."*

Cosmopolitanism is particularly noticeable in the mixture of the various nations within the individual Provinces of the Order. The German Province, to which I belonged, numbered Danes, Swedes, English, North Americans, Brazilians, Irish, Dutch, Swiss and Austrians amongst its members. I have already mentioned that Alsatians (before 1870) and French Swiss were rectors of the German school at Feldkirch.

The destruction of national sentiment is inevitably connected with cosmopolitanism. To quote from my first little book against the Jesuit Order :†

"Even if we merely conceive the Order as a whole and as what it is meant to be—an organism animated by the same life, the same feelings and the same thoughts—it becomes clear that there can be no question of fostering or even maintaining patriotism. If Germans and French, English and Russians, Poles, Spaniards, Italians, Americans, Swedes, Danes, Hungarians, Japanese and Chinese are to be permeated with the same sentiment, the distinct characteristics which each one of these nations possesses must be suppressed, but it is just in this distinct and characteristic trait that the centre of gravity of patriotism lies.

"It is useless to point to Christianity, which also desires to animate all these national dissimilarities with one spirit and yet does not kill patriotism. In Christianity this one spirit is supernatural, directed towards the world beyond. Christianity unites the nations in an ideal community, and, above all, Christianity leaves each member, the individual Christian, in the place and circumstances in which he was born and bred, and does not mix

---

* Reusch, *Beiträge zur Geschichte des Jesuitenordens : Zeitschrift für Kirchengeschichte*, 1894, XV., 2, p. 264 *et seq.*

† *Mein Austritt aus dem Jesuitenorden* (Leipzig, Breitkopf und Härtel.), 10th thousand, p. 36 *et seq.*

up peoples and nations. But Jesuitism, though also striving after an ideal, and though also aiming at an ideal community, belongs absolutely to this world in its social aims, for nobody could seriously assert that the Jesuit Order would persist as an Order in the world to come. Its methods, therefore, for attaining this temporal ideal of unity are also directed towards this world, *i.e.* even in this world, national, social and political diversities must disappear as much as possible, so far as the members of the Jesuit Order are concerned. The more cosmopolitan the Jesuit, the less attached to native country and home in his feelings as well as in his actions (this point is important), the more indifferently he views the form of government under which he lives, the better he is and the nearer does he approach to the ideal of a Jesuit.

"In this connection, the term which almost takes the place of the word 'patriotism' in the Constitutions of the Jesuit Order is very characteristic. The Jesuit should be animated by universal love (*universalis amor*) towards the Christian nations and princes. And this must be so; it cannot, indeed, be otherwise, if the Jesuit wishes to be what he ought to be.

"It is impressed upon the Jesuit, from his very admission to the Society until the end of his life, that he exists for the world and not for this or that nation. He is made to understand this practically by being despatched to the most dissimilar countries. He goes from Germany to France, America, India, Brazil, Italy and Sweden, and in each he has to accommodate himself as exactly as possible to the existing social and political conditions, and adapt himself to the character and views of the people.

"Such a system may produce forces working with irreproachable uniformity, but not patriots.

"I have already defined patriotism as self-sacrificing love of our native land. By native land, however, I do not only mean the land *i.e.* the fields, woods, mountains and rivers, but above all, the social and political institutions of the land in question, and the ancient and traditional arrangements upon which its inner life rests. A real patriot must love these, too, devotedly. Thus, for example, real patriotism with regard to Germany is necessarily connected with a monarchical sentiment. If within a society the adherence of the members to hereditary and national institutions is diminished by the system then prevailing, their patriotism is also destroyed. If, in spite of this, the individual member preserves true patriotism, he does so in opposition to the system. No further exposition is required to show that the Jesuit system must level away patriotism. So international a Society, consisting of so many heterogeneous national elements must strive for the abandonment of monarchical or republican preferences.

"Besides their chief domiciles which are situated abroad, the German Jesuits have their greatest field of work in lands across the sea, such as South America and British India, which are both republican and monarchical. That state of affairs has nothing to do with their expulsion from Germany. Within this great sphere, comprising such numerous and such vast national and political differences as Europe, America, and Asia, the German Jesuit has to live and work, not as a permanent resident, however, but with the pilgrim's staff in his hand. Now he is in the free North American republic, now in monarchical India, now in Brazil, which is always in a state of political ferment, now he is recalled from any one of these lands to work in the old monarchical European states, as teacher, educator, preacher and superior. He would not be human if he did not lose little by little the old national, patriotic form of sentiment and perception, and gradually assume the universal form of cosmopolitanism."

In presence of these and similar developments, the Jesuit Order makes a great boast of its patriotic activity during the campaign of 1870-71, when the German Province of the Order sent many of its members into the German military hospitals to nurse there, "for love of the Fatherland."

In the first place, there is really no reason to boast of this work of mercy as something unusual. If the "German" Jesuits had avoided giving assistance, it would have been simply disgraceful, and—as they knew very well—they would have damaged their reputation very much. But the patriotic motive for the assistance may well be impugned. The cosmopolitanism of the

Criticism of the Inner Constitution

Order is also displayed in this patriotic work. There were, for example, fifty non-Germans amongst the "German" Jesuits nursing "from patriotic motives," including Swiss, Austrians, Dutch, Luxemburgers and Irish. The statistics which the Jesuit M. Rist has added as an appendix to his vainglorious book, *Die deutschen Jesuiten auf den Schlachtfeldern und in den Lazaretten 1866 und 1870-71*,* reveal this imposing number of "Germans." Now, with the best intentions, we cannot speak of German patriotism in the case of these fifty foreigners, and when amongst one hundred and sixty-nine Jesuits (the number given by Rist) there are fifty non-Germans, evidence is afforded of the innate Jesuit untruthfulness, which extols fifty foreigners in a book entitled, "The German Jesuits," etc.

Rist's book throws at least indirect light on the "patriotic" conduct of the "German" Jesuits in 1866. Whilst the "German" Jesuits were giving free rein to their hate of Prussia in their school at Feldkirch, as I have shown in Chapter VI., the same "German" Jesuits were simultaneously acting as pro-Prussians in the military hospitals at the seat of war. This is double-faced "patriotism."

I do not wish to disparage the nursing activity of the individual "German" Jesuit; protest is only raised against the fact that it is placed to the account of the Order's patriotism. Constitutionally, the Jesuit must know no patriotism, must be absolutely international. Let then the truth be honoured by the Jesuits, and let them not adorn themselves with a word which is not to be found in even the most exhaustive index in the voluminous works on the constitutions and rules of the Order.

The heart of the Society of Jesus (if we may speak of a heart at all) was with Austria in 1866 and with

* Freiburg, 1904.

France in 1870-71, and, therefore, pretty far removed from " German patriotism." This is self-evident, because of the strong Jesuit antagonism for everything non-Catholic ; and my own experiences at Feldkirch and in my home also prove it.

The brutal egotism of the Order, which has already frequently been emphasised, but cannot be emphasised enough, and which manifests itself in everything within the Order, is the main root of Jesuit cosmopolitanism, and also the poison which corrodes patriotism. It is in the interests of the Order to be international and un-patriotic—away, therefore, with the noblest emotions of the natural human heart! But an occasional pretence of such feelings is also in the interests of the Order.

I have already brought forward numerous proofs of this egotism, as manifested in the work of education and the bringing up of the young. Since, however, this side of Jesuit egotism is particularly pernicious because it extends into the world outside Jesuitism, I will supplement the particulars by further historical facts.

Prantl, in his *History of the Ludwig-Maximilian University*, gives a clear statement, based on original documents, of the egotistical intrigues of the Order at the Ingolstadt University during a period of more than two centuries (1550-1773).

The University continually complains, he asserts, " of the greed of the Jesuits in seizing upon everything (*cupido occupandi omnia*)." " Ambition and self-interest came into play always and everywhere when Jesuits were concerned." " The Jesuits did everything in their power to calumniate the professors and vice-chancellor at Munich." " They placed themselves on the same level as the lord of the land, as if he were a mere party to an agreement." " It is of no use even to set precise limits, because this vermin creeps through all the same (*isti caniculi semper subrepunt*)." "They want to share the artistic faculty like the lion in Æsop's fable" The Jesuits are "a restless and domineering race (*inquietum et imperiosum hominum genus*) which seeks to subjugate everything." That zealous Catholic, Professor Giphanius, declares (in a report of 1597): "For some time the Jesuits alone had the ear of the Government and were alone honoured by it, whilst the remainder, no matter how able, were set aside with contempt; whoever desired promotion had to apply not to the Duke, but to the Jesuits, and whoever failed to submit to them not only attained nothing, but had reason to fear that he would be dismissed." On April 8th, 1609, the University directed its attacks against the attempt of the Jesuits to seize upon the entire jurisdiction over the students: "It seemed to be the premeditated plan of the Jesuits to overthrow (*evertendi*) the University and to seize upon the entire control at the expense of the temporal professors." From a memorial "of maturer students" to the Senate of the University on March 28th, 1610 · "The Jesuits tried to ruin the legal faculty, the Jesuit Heiss openly compared the law-students to swine and oxen, and the Jesuit Mayrhofer, in a sermon, called the students of jurisprudence 'sons of corruption and of the devil.'" "They forbade that confession should be made to the Franciscans, and lately some students were expelled because they had attended vespers and a procession at the Franciscan Church." At the end of May, 1610, the University reported to Duke William V.: "The Jesuit craving for rule aims at arrangements such as are to be found in the Jesuit colleges at Dillingen, Graz and Munich; the Jesuit professors only came to the sittings of the Senate when their own interests were in question, and at divisions they supported a particular regulation more in the interests of the Order than in those of the University; they immediately followed up every trivial concession by seeking for another; every remark by the Rector of the University was rejected with the words · 'It is contrary to the Constitutions of the Order, and our Provincial has already decided about it.'" In a memorial of February, 1611, the University complained of "the omnipotence of the Jesuits." "They [the University] had positive proof that the Jesuits only sought to obtain advantage and glory for themselves." "As at Cologne, Louvain, Paris, and Padua, the Jesuits also try to obtain the mastery at Ingolstadt over every one." "Ingolstadt would no longer be an independent University, but a Jesuit College."*

As at Ingolstadt, Jesuit egotism also caused disturbance at the University of Freiburg in Breisgau.

As the Jesuits had the bigoted Archduke Ferdinand, afterwards second Emperor of that name, entirely in their hands, it was easy for them to induce him first of all to found a Jesuit College at Freiburg. From this vantage ground the Order would proceed to take possession of the University. The Archduke issued a letter to the University on August 9th, 1577, stating: "That he purposed to found in his Austrian borderlands [Breisgau] a college of the Society of Jesus which might be incorporated with the University as had been done at Ingolstadt." The University set itself in opposition and replied: " . . . Least of all would the Society of Jesus benefit the discipline, because the youths educated by it are particularly inclined to pride, disobedience and malice, either because they are set free from control too early, or because they are not taught how to use their liberty at the Universities wisely and profitably. Finally, as to the manner in which the fathers of the Society dealt with collegiate affairs, Ingolstadt had supplied proof that peace and

* Prantl, *Geschichte der Ludwig-Maximilians-Universität* (Munich, 1872), I., 230, 248, 250, 252, 253, 258, 351, 356, 357 *et seq.*, 361, 363, 370.

Criticism of the Inner Constitution 41

concord amongst the professors had been disturbed by their admission." The Jesuits achieved their end, however, and after a hard struggle even obtained the supremacy in the Academic Senate.*

The Order also provided egotistically for its material welfare at Freiburg, and this at a time when the country was suffering under the distress of the Thirty Years' War.

The Jesuits caused 16 measures of wine, 20 bushels of wheat, 22 bushels of rye, 6 bushels of barley and 4 bushels of oats to be supplied yearly for their two members of the Senate. They even planned to get the whole income of the University into their hands, "because they could administer it better." In this case, the professorial salaries would be paid by the Order. The plan was unsuccessful. How much its revival was dreaded, however, is shown by a remark in the University records of 1665 : "*Attendite Posteri ; requiescit enim hic ipsorum (Jesuitorum) spiritus, sed non dormitabit*" [Beware, O posterity! The spirit of the Jesuits is reposing, but it will not sleep] † They refused to share in the payment of the war tax imposed on the University. A memorandum of March 10th, 1640, from the University records, reports : "Although a third portion of the contribution is not unjustly assigned to the Jesuits, they have paid none of this up to now, and the University has made everything good. And yet they have enough to reimburse themselves by considerable properties and other means."‡ The amount of means they possessed is shown by the fact that, in 1745, 8,000 florins, which they had once advanced, were returned to them by the University. They stipulated that this should be paid in French or Spanish gold.||

* Schreiber, *Geschichte der Albert-Ludwigs-Universität zu Freiburg i. B.* (Freiburg, 1868), II., 309, 413.
† *Ibid.*, II., 309, 413.
‡ *Ibid.*, II., 428. || *Ibid.*, II., 449.

It is not surprising that at Freiburg also their egotism should have led them away from German and national interests; but the fact is so noteworthy in its singularity that it merits special emphasis.

In the Peace of Nimwegen (February 5th, 1679), Freiburg was yielded up to France and remained French till the Peace of Ryswick (October 30th, 1697). The University had taken refuge at Constance, where it was to be re-established. Louis XIV. wished, however, to have a University in his new acquisition, and the Jesuits willingly offered to help. Although the question as to whether the University was to be an *adpertinens* of the town of Freiburg had been answered in the negative at the Diet of Ratisbon, and it was recognised as a *corpus independens*, the Jesuits opposed themselves to this secretly and openly, even in the sermons in their Marian Congregations, and sent their adroit negotiator, Father Migazzi, to Versailles, where he was graciously received at court and abundantly provided with money. These fathers, therefore, to a great extent attained the establishment, besides the German University at Constance, of a French one (*studium gallicum*) at Freiburg, and the privileges from the former and their establishments in Alsace-Lorraine and Breisgau were transferred to the latter, whereby the Jesuits not only predominated entirely over the secular professors, but enjoyed other prerogatives besides, which they never had and never could have had formerly.*

The state of affairs at the Vienna University presented the same disagreeable picture after the Jesuits set foot there and gradually assumed the power; endless conflict and wrangling on all sides ensued.†

* *Ibid.*, II., 434, from the records of the Syndic of the University, Dr. Rosenzweig.

† *Cf.* Kink, *Geschichte der kaiserlichen Universität Wien* (Vienna, 1854), I., 304 *et seq.*, 323 *et seq.*

Criticism of the Inner Constitution

The Jesuits were only brought within bounds by hard struggles when, owing to Maria Theresa's confidence in him, the Dutchman, Gerhard van Swieten, was called to Vienna in 1745 (first as physician-in-ordinary, then as professor of medicine, prefect of the Court Library and superintendent of the censors.)*

I cannot enter into van Swieten's interesting struggle with the Jesuits, which lasted for years, or into all his remarks about them. It will be sufficient to put before the reader some passages from a memorial to Maria Theresa :

"The Society makes religion its excuse to . . . ensure to itself a profit at the expense of the printer and the bookseller. . . . I have most ample evidence to prove that the real aim of the Society is to enrich itself, and that religion is only a cloak under which it abuses the piety of Your Majesty and your glorious ancestors. . . . I hope that the examples I have brought forward are sufficient to demonstrate the cleverness of the Society by means of which they blandly rob 'externals' and enrich 'our own people.' . . . The Society tries to

* Van Swieten is one of the men best hated and most slandered by the Jesuits, for no other reason than that he was their convinced opponent. A very little reflection must, however, make even the Jesuits realise how baseless their calumnies are, precisely in van Swieten's case. For if Maria Theresa, who, both as woman and Empress, was overwhelmed with praise by the Jesuits, and whose confessors were Jesuits, valued van Swieten more and more as time went on, and trusted him implicitly, it is very plain that he deserved her confidence. It is inconsistent to praise Maria Theresa and calumniate van Swieten; and hatred of the latter can afford the only explanation. Van Swieten was also a good Catholic, whatever the Jesuits might say. He had even been forced to resign his position as teacher in Holland owing to his religion, and, therefore, his opinion cannot be put aside offhand with the favourite saying, "Antagonistic towards Catholicism." Even a man like Kink, who was so favourably inclined towards the Jesuit Order, and, therefore, did not cherish kindly feelings towards van Swieten, acknowledges with regard to his religious attitude: "He exercised practical Christianity and also observed the rules of Catholic worship."

appropriate the profits of 'the externals' for the benefit of 'our people.' "*

Jesuit egotism is shown most unpleasantly in the form of envy and lust for power, by its attitude towards other religious Orders and the secular clergy.

In the first place, Kink gives a full account of the Jesuit feud against the Dominicans in Vienna:

" The pious fathers of the most humble Society of Jesus (*minima societas Jesu*, a term of extreme lowliness which the Jesuits loved to apply to their Order, and under which immeasurable arrogance is concealed) did not rest until an imperial decree of December 2nd, 1656, " excluded the Dominicans for ever from the office of dean,

and refused their opponents [the Dominicans] the personal qualification for academic offices."†

Kink goes on to relate:

' The Franciscans, Carmelites, Augustinians and Benedictines in Vienna gave instruction in Latin and theology in their monasteries in exactly the same way as the Universities, but without the privileges in the matter of conferring degrees, which belonged to the latter alone. In particular, they permitted their scholars to hold public disputations, and that in their churches. This arrangement dated back to the times when the monastic schools were almost the only educational institutions. For this reason, the Vienna University, which had found this custom in existence at its foundation, had never raised a protest against it. However, in 1626, consequently three years after the Jesuits had taken over the philosophical and theological faculty, the Jesuit Order passed a resolution at the consistory to the effect that these public debates were forbidden to the above-named religious orders. The religious orders, however, found a supporter in the papal *legatus a latere*,

---

* Memorandum of December 24th, 1769; complete French original text in Fournier, *Gerhard van Swieten als Zensor: Sitzungsberichte der philosophisch-historischen Klasse der kaiserlichen Akademie der Wissenschaften*, Vol. 24, p. 337 *et seq.* Vienna, 1877.

† *Ibid.*, I., 383 *et seq.*

Caraffa, who, on October 20th, directed the University not to interfere any more with persons and places which were exempt from the academic statutes. In spite of this, the theological faculty soon afterwards refused the printing licence for their *theses disputationis* requested by the Franciscans. As a punishment for this disobedience, the nuncio then commanded that not only were the *theses* to be approved, but that, in addition, all doctors of theology belonging to the Society of Jesus should appear in person at the debates held by the Franciscans. They obeyed, but appealed to the Roman See, which, however, upheld the customs of the religious orders, and in 1627 gave a decision to the same effect as the nuncio: The Jesuits now succeeded with the aid of temporal power where they had failed with spiritual. The religious orders were commanded to cease holding their debates in public and to omit on the *frontispicium* of their printed *theses* the expression *sub praeside*. This command was specially renewed on August 23rd and October 12th, 1725, in the case of the [Benedictine] Scotsmen."*

So far as the secular clergy are concerned, it is a well-known fact that they decline to have the Jesuits as permanent colleagues, however willingly they make use of them as temporary assistants in the cure of souls.

The Order enters into the keenest competition with the secular clergy. It attracts congregations, especially wealthy ones, from the parish churches† into the churches of the Order, and tries, where its feet have become firmly planted, to obtain a mastery over the secular clergy, a mastery which is very oppressive to the subordinates. This endeavour emanates from the general spirit of arrogance and self-seeking in the Order, which tolerates no other gods but itself.

The "ordinary" priest is of inferior value in the Jesuit's eyes; he requires guidance and supervision. He can only be properly shaped by the Jesuit Exercises.

---

* *Ibid.*, I., 415 *et seq.*
† *Cf.* the remarks of Cardinal Wiseman quoted on p. 31.

I have heard Jesuits express this opinion hundreds of times.

This characteristic of the Jesuit Order is as old as itself. On this account there is generally secret strife between Jesuits and the other Orders and the secular clergy, a strife which is only made public in rare instances. Both parties try, in the general ecclesiastical interest, to avoid all din and fury in the warfare.

The "resolutions of confidence" which the secular clergy pass on the Jesuit Order, especially at times of persecution, do not alter this state of affairs. Such resolutions are only passed in the general ecclesiastical and hierarchical interest, and are in reality "an illusive representation of spurious facts." At heart the secular clergy wishes the Jesuit Order at Jericho.

In a work by the English Catholic priest, Dr. Christopher Bagshawe, dating from the first century of the Jesuit Order, we possess a very interesting example of its egotistical attempt to subjugate the secular clergy. A number of Catholic priests were interned in Elizabeth's reign in Wisbeach Castle. They lived on very friendly terms with one another. The position was changed when some Jesuits were also interned there. Bagshawe describes their restless and arrogant activity. It will be sufficient to quote the title of his book:

"A true Relation of the Factions begun at Wisbeach by Fr. Edmunds *alias* Weston, a Jesuit, 1595, and continued since by Fr. Whalley *alias* Garnet, the Provincial of the Jesuits in England, and by Fr. Parsons in Rome with their adherents. Against us secular priests, their brethren and fellow-prisoners, that disliked of novelties and thought it dishonourable to the ancient ecclesiastical discipline of the Catholic Church that secular priests should be governed by Jesuits."*

* *Cf.* Taunton, *The Jesuits in England*, p. 173.

Criticism of the Inner Constitution

My experience also confirms this.

One of the private chaplains in my home, Dr. Pingsmann, afterwards became Canon and Vice-President of the seminary for Roman Catholic priests at Cologne. I remained on friendly terms with him even during my Jesuit period and always visited him when I had to pass through Cologne. A conversation which we carried on as to the possible return of the Jesuit Order to Germany is still very vivid in my mind. On our way back from a walk, we were standing at the entrance of the college for Roman Catholic priests, which had previously been a Jesuit College, when I said jestingly: "We must get in there again." Pingsmann replied, not without vehemence: "We do not want you back at all. Your Order has never yet agreed with us secular priests anywhere." This remark, by a man whom I very much esteemed, made a deep impression on me. I was then in almost complete ignorance of the spirit and history of my own Order. Surprised and startled, I communicated this incident to my Provincial Superior, the Jesuit Ratgeb, and obtained from him (as he placed special confidence in me at that time, a point to which I shall refer later) the characteristic reply:

"My dear Father, Canon and Vice-President Dr. Pingsmann, is a very worthy man, but he has nothing to do with our return. When we return to Germany, the secular clergy will submit to us, as they have done hitherto, though very reluctantly, it is true. Our Order is a very different power from the loosely connected secular clergy. There may be difficulties also for us in the Catholic camp, but no lasting resistance."

The Chancellor of the Paris University, Froment, consequently only states a fact in the history of the Order, and does not utter a slander, when he expresses his opinion as to Jesuit egotism:

"*Uniquement occupés de son agrandissement, les Jésuites ne travaillent que pour eux-mêmes ; leur intérêt règle seul leur prétendue charité. Par intime correspondance, qu'ils ont les uns avec les autres, par la faveur des Grands, dont ils flattent l'ambition, enfin par la prudence des enfants du siècle, dont ils savent faire usage merveilleux, ils trouvent les moiens d'exécuter leurs projets et de se rendre formidables.*"*

This egotism of the Order is not incompatible with individual Jesuit unselfishness, which not infrequently rises to heroism, and I am far from denying it. The individual Jesuit sacrifices himself, with all that he is and has, to the Order. In his case, at least as a rule, the surrender of the personal individuality is made without side or backward glances in his own interest.

Neither do I reproach the Order for possessing the egotism which every association must have, and must give practical proof of having, if it is to exist and prosper at all. But Jesuit egotism extends infinitely further. In its selfishness it has no consideration for others. Jesuit egotism is Moloch-egotism—it eats away the existence, happiness, honour and efficacy of others for its own aggrandisement.

Thus the characteristics of the Society of Jesus and the characteristics of Jesus Christ are in the sharpest antithesis conceivable, and the fundamental opposition is justified—Here is Christ, there is Jesuitism !

* Le Vassor, *Histoire du Règne de Louis XIII.*, I., 1, 61, quoted by Harenberg, *Pragmatische Geschichte*, I., 350.

CHAPTER XVI

THE CRITICISM CONTINUED: THEORY AND PRACTICE OF THE VOWS

I HAVE already shown, whilst discussing the Jesuit "Scheme of Studies," that many rules, and indeed just those which outwardly appear good, are only set down on paper, that they are not observed, and that really, in practice, the Order acts in opposition to them. It manages, however, cleverly to increase its fame by means of these very unobserved rules.

The same remark applies to the Constitutions of the Order—fine words and opposite deeds.

The real reason for this characteristic phenomenon lies in the fundamental Jesuit failing, innate all-pervading untruthfulness.

The panegyrists of the Order, be they Jesuits or others, endeavour to conceal the antithesis between its words and deeds. According to them, the most beautiful harmony prevails, pious words and pious deeds.

I shall thoroughly destroy the apparent harmony and cause dissonances to resound on that great instrument called history, which in trumpet notes will proclaim the truth about the Jesuit Order to every ear that is willing to listen.

Let us turn first to the conflict between the theory and practice of its ascetic discipline, and especially to that part which constitutes the essence of its discipline—the vows.

THE VOW OF OBEDIENCE

Since the vow of obedience is first and foremost concerned with obedience to the Superiors of the Order, there is, of course, no antithesis between theory and practice, so far as this kind of obedience is in question.

But the Order possesses a figure-head in the sphere of obedience, and this is the professed Jesuit's vow of obedience to the Pope. In accordance with this, the Society of Jesus loves to designate itself as the "Flower of the Pope's bodyguard." And in general—*i.e.* so long as the interests of the Order are not opposed—we see that Jesuits do act in accordance with their vow of obedience to the Pope. But where the Pope interferes with Jesuit egotism, he finds in the Jesuits the bitterest and most obstinate adversaries, who, far from fulfilling their vows, do not even render him the ordinary obedience binding on all Christians. The history of the Order is full of such fulfilments of vows. I will submit only a few examples, but they are very striking.

The Jesuit, Thyrsus Gonzalez (afterwards General of the Order), originally a probabilist, recognised the perniciousness of probabilism, and wrote a work against it. He sent the manuscript in 1673 to Rome to the General of the Order, Paul Oliva, for approval. The imprimatur was refused. Gonzalez then applied to Innocent XI., who had just condemned sixty-five lax ethical principles, very many of which originated in the Jesuit Order. The Pope caused Gonzalez's book to be examined, and the examination was favourable. An Inquisitorial decree was thereupon issued on June 26th, 1680:

"By order (*injungendum*) of the Pope, the General of the Order is commanded in no way to permit the fathers of the Society of Jesus to write in favour of lesser probable opinions, and to oppose the views of those who maintain that it is not permissible to follow a less probable opinion when the opposite opinion has been recognised as probable. Also, as regards the Universities of the Society of Jesus, it is the wish of His Holiness that everyone should write in favour of probabiliorism, and should oppose the opposite view [probabilism]. The General must command all to submit to the will of the Pope."*

The assessor of the Inquisition intimated this decree to the Jesuit General on July 8th, 1680, and the General declared he would forthwith obey in all things. The Jesuit General, Paul Oliva, however, was the very one who did not obey. As the Jesuit Gagna reports, Oliva, on August 1st, 1680, drew up a circular which was intended for the whole Order and embodied the Pope's command—it is said to be in the archives of the Order—but it was not forwarded.† For otherwise Gonzalez, as Professor of Dogmatics (*Cathedraticus primarius*) at the University of Salamanca, must have known about it. But it was only in 1693 that Gonzalez heard of the decree issued in 1680, and he himself says, in a written petition to Clement XI., dated 1702, that the Inquisitorial decree and Innocent XI.'s command were not conveyed to the Order.

This disobedience in such a weighty matter is especially important, because it was effected with exceptional cunning. The General of the Order, Paul Oliva, laid the circular drawn up by himself before the Inquisitional Cardinals,‡ in order,|| as Pattuzzi remarks, to make the Inquisition believe in his prompt obedience. Once the belief had been brought into existence, there was no longer any necessity, from the Jesuit point of view, for that which had originated it, namely, the despatch of the circular.

Oliva did indeed issue a circular on August 10th, 1680,

---

* Pietro Ballerini, *Riposta alla Lettera del P. Paolo Segneri*, 1734, p. 349.

† Gagna, S.J., *Lettere d'Eugenio*, p. 611. ‡ Ibid.

|| *Lettere* 2, 595; 6, 218.

which dealt with ethical questions, but no mention was made in it of the decree of the Inquisition of June 26th, 1680.* This circular too was doubtless intended to deceive the Pope. It made it possible to answer in the affirmative the question as to whether a decree regarding disputes on ethical questions had been despatched.

The Archbishop of Vienna, Cardinal Migazzi, in a memorial to the Empress Maria Theresa, dated August 14th, 1761, writes:

"The French bishops only condemned the scandalous book of the notorious [Jesuit] Berruyer after the Papal See had most severely condemned it, and the Pope now reigning [Clement XIII.] had confirmed and repeated the decision made by his most blessed predecessor. In spite of this, the *Patres Societatis* have recently sent this work to Naples to be published, and in Vienna have even recommended it to young people and various other persons who are guided by them." The Archbishop goes on to speak of Jesuit manuals which have been condemned in high places and others recommended in their stead. "But affairs have taken quite a different course since, at Innsbrug and Olmütz, the professors of the Society have continued to use the prohibited books for reading aloud."†

An occurrence related by Gindely should be quoted here, even though it only concerns the egotistical disobedience of the Jesuit Order to a cardinal and nuncio:

"The Jesuits had taken advantage of their position with the Emperor [Ferdinand II.] to set aside the historic right of the Bishop of Prague to the Chancellorship, and request the surrender of the University to their sole authority, and had provisionally attained their object.

---

* Friedrich, *Beiträge zur Geschichte des Jesuitenordens*, p. 85.

† Helfert, *Gründung der osterreichischen Volksschule*, p. 280 (1); complete text in Kink, I., 417 *et seq.*

Theory and Practice of the Vows 53

The Emperor commanded that the adherents of the Bohemian denomination were to leave the University buildings and surrender the same, as well as all other possessions, to the direction of the Jesuits from henceforth. Not only were the Protestants indignant at this measure, but also the Catholics, and especially the clergy, felt uneasy at the thought that the Jesuits were to be sole masters at the University. The Archbishop . . . indeed protested and also communicated his protest to the nuncio, but without avail. His successor, Cardinal von Harrach [a pupil of the Jesuits], who would not agree to the retrenchment of his rights, resolutely continued the battle. The struggle between him and the Jesuits, who would not at any cost let themselves be driven from their position, lasted for over twenty years. It led, on the Cardinal's side, to the bitterest accusations and attacks against the Jesuits, but for all that he was not able to displace them."*

These facts, distinctive as they are for the Jesuit obedience to the Pope, are as nothing compared with the disobedience of the Order, extending over many years and accompanied by open opposition and shameful deeds of violence, in connection with the Malabar and Chinese rites.

In 1702, Clement XI. sent the Patriarch of Antioch, Charles Tournon, as Papal Legate to India and China, in order to settle, with the Pope's authority and to the disadvantage of the Jesuits, the disputes stirred up by the Jesuits about the rites which the Christianised Indians and Chinese had brought over from heathenism and which were upheld by the Jesuits and condemned by all other missionaries. Intense hate of the Legate on the part of the Jesuit Order was the result. To increase his authority, Tournon was made a Cardinal by Clement XI. in 1707. But Tournon's elevation in rank seemed to heighten the fury of the Order, which believed that its standing

* *Geschichte des dreissigjährigen Krieges*, IV., 547 *et seq.*

and power in India and China had been compromised by the Papal decrees. The Jesuits placed themselves, in opposition to the Papacy which condemned them, under the protection of the pagan Emperor of China and invoked his aid against the Papal Legate and against all the remaining members of the Order who obeyed the Pope. On July 24th, 1708, they secured the publication of an imperial edict, which banished all missionaries who, following the command of the Pope, condemned the rites, thus actually making the Jesuits sole owners of the Chinese missions.* Cardinal Tournon himself was brought by force, at the instigation of the Jesuits, in 1707 to Macao, and died in prison there on June 8th, 1710.

It can no longer reasonably be doubted that the Jesuits attempted to poison the Cardinal during his imprisonment, which had been brought about by themselves. The report (*Relazione*) of an eye-witness, Canon John Marcell Angelita, who as Promotor was also the official escort of the Cardinal, with reference to the event,† bears so much the stamp of spontaneity and truth that it must be believed, the more so as the work, in which the report is contained, is in other respects, too, a mine of authentic and rare documents. Amongst them a letter of the Lazarist priest, Antonio Appiani (one of Cardinal Tournon's companions), dated Canton, November 22nd, 1728, deserves special attention.

"For the same reason [because, at the order of the Pope, he condemned the Chinese and pagan rites approved by the Jesuits] the venerable Cardinal Tournon died in imprisonment, wounded to the heart (*accuorato*) For the members of the above-named Order [the Jesuits], because they would not obey the decrees of His Holiness

---

* Wording of the edict in *Memorie storiche della Legazione e morte dell' Eminentiss Cardinale di Tournon, Venezia*, VII., 142 *et seq.*

† Reprinted in *Memorie storiche*, I., 205-232.

the Pope, Clement XI., placed themselves under the protection of the pagan Emperor [of China], and he furthered the stubbornness of the members of the above-named Order by ill-treating the real Catholics who were obedient to the Holy See."*

Whether the expression "wounded to the heart" is an allusion to poisoning, and thus a confirmation of the report, is a question we cannot decide. In any case, Appiani's letter is an eloquent proof of the fact that, even after eighteen years, the remembrance of the intrigues of the Jesuits against the Papal Cardinal Legate, Tournon, was still alive, and caused him to utter sharp words against the "bodyguard of the Pope."

A very important corroboration of the poisoning is to be found in the fact that the Missionary Congregation of the Lazarists, one of the most distinguished missionary societies of the Catholic Church, in a work officially published by it,† has dealt with the report as an authentic document, and refers to the poisoning in most positive terms :

"*Mais pour en revenir à notre douloureuse histoire, il est certain, très certain, indubitable, que la maladie et la mort du cardinal Tournon ont été occasionnées par le poison, que lui ont fait donner les Jésuites.*"‡

J. Friedrich, therefore, on the basis of the report and the corroboration of the *Mémoires*, states the poisoning as a positive fact,§ and H. Reusch, certainly a very careful investigator, speaks of it as "probable." ||

The *Mémoires* also accept as authentic the whole of the remaining contents of the *Memorie storiche*, which are

---

* *Memorie storiche.*, I., 354.

† *Mémoires de la Congrégation de la Mission.* Paris, 1865.

‡ *Ibid.*, IV., 309.

§ *Zur Verteidigung meines Tagebuches* (Nordlingen, 1872), p. 10 *et seq.*, and *Abhandlungen der III. Kl. der K. Bayerischen Akademie der Wissenschaften*, XIII., 2, Abtl, 95. || *Index*, II. (1), 772.

as unfavourable as possible to the Jesuit Order; indeed, they even give in an introduction some information which places the trustworthiness of the *Memorie* beyond doubt

"*Ces faits* [the documents incriminating the Jesuits] *ont été imprimés et publiés en particulier par le Cardinal Passionei dans son ouvrage: 'Memorie storiche dell' Eminentissimo Monsignore Cardinale di Tournon,' qui renferme une partie des documents authentiques conservés dans les archives du Vatican ou de la Propagande et dont la parfaite conformité nous a été attestée par le Préfet des archives du Vatican, le Père Theiner, Oratorien.*"*

What the Jesuits Cornely and Duhr† bring forward against the *Mémoires* of the Lazarists consists partly of untenable calumnies and partly of barren abuse of Friedrich and all those who doubt the innocence of the Jesuits. The audacious attempt entirely to explain away the evidence of the *Mémoires* is especially hollow. The Jesuits Cornely and Duhr triumphantly relate how the General Superior of the Missionary Congregation explained in April, 1872, that the volumes in question of the *Mémoires* (IV.–VIII.) were "contumaciously" published without the contents having been previously examined by him.

I will for once—by way of exception!—believe the two Jesuits' statement that such an explanation exists. But does it then contain even a single word as to the inaccuracy of the contents of the volume published "contumaciously"? It says nothing at all. It is possible to write even the truth "contumaciously." It would have been the business of the General Superior to express an opinion as to the truth or falsehood of the contents, especially concerning the poisoning. His silence about this is a fresh endorsement of the truth of the "report."

---

* *Index*, IV., 126.
† *Stimmen aus Maria-Laach*, III., 279 *et seq.*, and *Jesuitenfabeln* (4), 776–786.

It also seems strange that the General Superior of the same Congregation which published the *Mémoires* should have waited seven whole years after the issue of the work before declaring against the genuineness of the documents contained in them. Moreover, the greatest stress must be laid on the fact that the *Mémoires de la Congrégation de la Mission*, which were so incriminating to the Jesuits, are an official publication of the Lazarist Congregation.* This is evident from the entire character of the work, which is based throughout on letters and documents from the archives of the Order, and is proven to demonstration by the addition to the title-page of every volume, " *à la maison principale de la Congrégation de la Mission. Rue de Sèvres 95.*" The prefaces also of the separate volumes clearly emphasise the official character of the *Mémoires*—e.g., the preface to the second volume:

" *Ce fut pour maintenir dans la Compagnie l'esprit apostolique de nos Pères, que nous eûmes la pensée de publier des rares fragments de leur correspondance que nous possédons encore, ainsi que les biographies de deux ou trois d'entr'eux échappées au désastre qui fit disparaître la plus grande partie de nos archives.*"

A further proof of their official character and credibility is afforded by the *Histoire générale de la Société des Missions Étrangères* (also an official publication of the *Société*) which was published in 1894. For the *Histoire* repeatedly refers to the *Mémoires* and even to the part (Vol. IV.) which is unfavourable to the Jesuit Order, and which contains the report as to Tournon's poisoning. And yet the circular of the Superior of the Missionary Congregation (Lazarist), mentioned by the Jesuits Cornely and Duhr—if it exists at all—must have been known to the author of the *Histoire*. So, in his opinion, the circular does not dispute the contents of the *Mémoires*, but is

* *Congrégation de la Mission*, founded by St. Vincent de Paul.

directed solely against the opportuneness of their publication. Weighty evidence is afforded by the fact that the General Superior of the Missionary Society, Delpech, congratulates "his dear colleague," Launay, in a letter prefixed to the first volume, on his work, especially on his "*exactitude*" and on the "*documents authentiques*" on which it is based. Amongst these *documents authentiques* are included precisely the documents contained in the *Memorie* and in the *Mémoires* which are most incriminating to the Jesuits.

No, the *Memorie storiche* and the *Mémoires* are unassailable sources, but sources from which issue countless proofs of insubordination, and of the open insurrection of the Jesuits against the Pope and his ambassadors (for they persisted in disobeying Tournon's successor, the Papal Legate Mezzafalce, as they had disobeyed him), and also of Jesuit cunning, falseness, passion for calumniation, and malice attaining the limits of crime. Hence it is clear why "the Jesuits so loyally attached to the Pope," who, as their own official historiographer, Cordara—not, I admit, in a work intended for publication—expresses himself, "look down with contempt upon all the other religious associations," do their very best, according to their unpublished axiom, "The end sanctifies the means," to choke up a source which is so tainted from their point of view. For this reason they have attempted to buy up the *Mémoires*, so that copies have become extremely rare. In Germany, for example, there are only two copies, not even complete ones, both of which are at Munich; one (only three out of the eight volumes) at the Court and State Library, and the second (only one volume) at the University Library. The method, which I have referred to already,* of secretly making away with incriminating works must have been employed also in this case.

* Chap. V., p. 189.

Theory and Practice of the Vows

I give, in addition, some documents printed in the *Memorie* and in the *Mémoires*, as an illustration of the "absolute submissiveness to the Pope" of the Jesuit Order.

A letter of Tournon, dated Macao, December 10th, 1707, to the Priest, Fatinelli, in Rome: The Legate complains in the bitterest words that the Jesuits hindered his communication by writing with Rome in every possible way, while, on the other hand, they themselves sent numerous letters and messengers to Europe to bias public opinion against him. The Jesuits sought the protection of the pagan Emperor against the decisions of the Pope, conveyed by Tournon, as to the illegality of the heathen rites, without incurring any of the canonical penalties with which such disobedience is threatened. They had brought about the banishment of the apostolic vicars, Maigrot and Mezzafalce, and of all the missionaries who were not on their side in the question of the Chinese rites. Their opposition to the Papal decree was unprecedented throughout Christendom.* A letter by Tournon, dated Nanking, January 9th, 1707, to the Dominican Croquer: The Jesuits had brought about the ruin of the Chinese Mission through their lies (*menzogne*) and intrigues.† Tournon's remarks regarding the above-mentioned imperial edict of banishment which the Jesuits had procured against all missionaries who had obeyed the command of the Pope —scathing condemnation of the attitude of the Jesuits.‡ Bull of Clement XI., dated March 15th, whereby the Bishop of Macao, who, at the Jesuits' instigation, had opposed the Cardinal Legate, was excommunicated. The noteworthy fact is reported in the Bull that the Cardinal Legate felt himself obliged to place the college seminary and church of the Jesuits in Macao under an interdict.

---

* *Memorie*, I., 169 *et seq.* † *Ibid.*, VII., 118, *et seq.*
‡ *Ibid.*, VII., 200 *et seq.*

The Pope not only does not condemn the measure, but, by connecting the Jesuits with the persecutions to which his Legate is exposed, he clearly refers to them as the instigators.* A letter by Tournon, dated December 27th, 1707, to Cardinal Paolucci, states that: The Jesuits were extremely antagonistic to him; since 1705 they had tried to prejudice the Emperor of China against him; Grimaldi, one of the most influential Jesuits, was doublefaced; the Jesuits incited the Christians against him; they calumniated his companion, the Lazarist priest, Appiani.† A report by Tournon to the Cardinal-Prefect of the Propaganda says that: The hate of the Jesuits against him as the apostolic Visitator extended so far that they caused snares to be laid for him at confession.‡ The missionary priest, Sala, reports that Cardinal Tournon received information through the Bishop of Pekin that the Superior of the Portuguese Jesuits, Pereyra, did everything possible at Court (*faisait tous les efforts possibles*) to have him driven from China.§ From " remarks " by the Secretary of the Propaganda : || The Lazarist priest,

---

* *Memorie*, VII., 67 et seq.   † *Mémoires*, 4, 230 et seq; 254 et seq.

‡ *Ibid.*, 4, 260.

§ *Ibid.*, 4, 296. The report also contains a remarkable passage with reference to the Jesuit mathematician, Adam Schall, a monk of Cologne, who became famous at the Chinese Court. " *Ce Père Schall voulant jouir plus à l'aise des libéralités et faveurs de ce Prince* [the grandfather of the Emperor at the time of this report], *s'était séparé des autres Jésuites et de l'obéissance de ses superieurs, avait pris femme et s'était retiré dans cette maison privée. Après avoir joui des faveurs imperiales il termina tristement sa vie, laissant deux enfants à celle qu'il avait prise pour femme* " (*Ibid.*, 4, 296). What Duhr (*Jesuitenfabeln* (4), 240-244) brings forward against the communication does not sound very convincing. For a confession by Schall regarding other things, a letter of one of his fellow-members of the Order and a audatory remark by the sinologist, Remusat, with reference to Schall's mathematical merit, cannot surely serve as counter-evidence. Schall's portrait has been placed in a window of Cologne Cathedral. But what should the building committee of the Cathedral know of the real history of the Jesuit Order ?

|| In 1726, the Pope, Benedict XIII., had charged the then Secretary of the Propaganda (apparently Dominico Passionei, who later became Cardinal) to annotate a memorial presented to Innocent XIII. by the Jesuits. These comments

Theory and Practice of the Vows 61

Appiani, Tournon's faithful companion, is, for that very reason, persecuted and calumniated by the Jesuits in every possible way; a pamphlet composed and circulated by the Jesuit Superior at Pekin, Antonius Thomas, is especially noteworthy in this connection: "A memorial of the unquenchable hate and the rare talent [for calumny] of the Pekin Jesuits. . . . I will reveal the true cause of the monstrous violation of Christian love and justice [with reference to Appiani]. He has always been the faithful interpreter of the Patriarch [the Papal Legate Tournon]. For this reason he is no longer to see the light. . . The invariable axiom of this 'good community' [the Jesuits] is to do all that is possible, be it just or unjust, to conceal the stains on its honour."*

A letter of Cardinal Tournon to Cardinal Paolucci, of October 27th, 1707 : The whole letter is a denunciation of the Jesuits, who even went so far as to declare openly that he, the Cardinal Legate of the Pope, possessed no jurisdiction. Two or three Jesuits, "who only look with pain upon the rebellion (*la rebellion*) against him of their Superiors and their fellow-members of the Order," were imprisoned and punished by the remaining Jesuits; "they suffer imprisonment, sequestration, insult and a thousand hardships." The Jesuits, especially those in Pekin, were the originators of the opposition against the Papal decree, proclaimed by him, discountenancing the Chinese rites in the Christian churches. "Even if the Jesuits were able, at first, to hide their opposition to the Papal decree

---

are contained in a manuscript comprising twelve volumes from the bequest of the Cardinal-Prefect of the Propaganda at that time, Corsini, *Raccolta di scritture e summari diversi sopra la causa dei P. P. Gesuiti intorno alle Missioni della Cina nella Congregazione di Propaganda*. From this voluminous and authentic collection of documents (at present in the Corsini Library at Rome), the *Mémoires* have reprinted the extracts of chief interest. (*Cf. Mémoires*, 4, 130 et seq.)

* *Mémoires*, 4, 408 et seq.

under the deceitful pretence that the existence of the entire mission in China was at stake, they cannot now any longer conceal the fact that their outrage [on the Papal authority] is premeditated and deliberate. For they publish new books full of teachings which the Holy See has condemned, and the contents of which are more detestable than any published before the condemnation. As a specimen, I am sending you a book translated from Chinese into Latin, which Father Barelli and other Jesuits triumphantly circulate in the capital of Cheh-chiang and show to the mandarins. Through this poisonous seed they destroy the Gospel harvest more than ever, they dishonour the Papal authority in the eyes of the Christians and cause frightful scandal, above all, amongst the heathen, who know what is taking place. . . . Was it necessary to employ such detestable means of provocation in order to maintain their [the Jesuits] damnable manner of proclaiming the Divine Law ? "

The Cardinal then openly accuses the Jesuits of being the authors of his imprisonment in Macao ; he accuses the Jesuit, Emanuel Ozorio, of having intercepted his [the Legate's] letters (*qui est le principal pêcheur de mes lettres*), acting thereby in agreement with the Superior of the Jesuit Mission, Father Thomas Pereyra ; the Jesuits hated the secular clergy ; in their letters they designate the secular clergy as " vulgar persons " (*populace*), an expression which they had also used in presence of the Emperor. " These people [the Jesuits] have no fear of God ; they have intercepted and opened my letters to Rome as well as the bulls for the Bishop of Pekin ; they arm the ecclesiastical and temporal power against me and the missionaries ; they preach by word and example rebellion against the Papal jurisdiction; they declare my instruction to be invalid because I possess no jurisdiction ; they goad on the soldiers who guard me to deeds of violence against

Theory and Practice of the Vows 63

my person, and advise them to strike me if I should attempt to leave my house."*

A circular of the General Superior of the Lazarist Congregation, Bonnet, dated January 1st, 1711, gives a description of the cruel persecutions of the Lazarist priest, Appiani, in China by the Jesuits of that place "*Et M. Appiani emprisonné pendant quatre ans dans la maison des Jésuites, quelles cruautés inouïes n'a-t-il pas endurées de la part de ses impitoyables geôliers? Privé de tout commerce humain, privé même des consolations religieuses, il n'eut jamais la permission pendant quatre ans de célébrer une seule fois la messe; cruauté dont les païens chinois furent eux-mêmes scandalisés.*"†

A letter, dated December 10th, 1707, from the Cardinal Legate, Tournon, to the Papal Nuncio in Lisbon, Conti (afterwards Pope Innocent XIII.), says: "After I had taken the greatest pains to report exactly to His Holiness concerning the distressing events in the Chinese Mission, which had been thrown into the greatest excitement through the violent proceedings of the Jesuits, I now see that my way is everywhere closed for sending further despatches to Rome. The Jesuits make use of the Chinese and Portuguese in Macao, yes, even of the heretical English and Dutch, to intercept my letters. It is really astonishing to see how these fathers send their emissaries in all directions in order to inundate Europe with their false ideas and reports, whilst I am prevented from sending even one to give the Pope and the Holy See the necessary information. . After the Jesuits had been informed last year of the Papal decision, whereby their practice in relation to the Chinese rites was condemned, they appealed with shameless audacity to the [pagan] Emperor without troubling about my prohibition, the ecclesiastical censure and the Papal displeasure with which I threatened them.

* *Mémoires*, 4, 464 *et seq.*, 484, 495 *et seq.*   † *Ibid.*, 4, 520 *et seq.*

They caused several imperial decrees to be issued against Bishop Maigrot, against myself, and, above all, against the Holy See, so as to oppose them to the Papal decisions and to prevent their publication." The Cardinal then describes how one of his missionary priests, Guetty, was tortured at the Jesuits' instigation to compel him to give evidence against him [the Cardinal], and how the Jesuits Pereyra and Barros had been present behind a curtain and directed the procedure.*

A letter by the Cardinal Legate to his brother, dated December 11th, 1707: "I assure you that the Jesuits have not omitted any calumnies or intrigues, that they have indeed made use of devilish devices to blacken me and my actions at the pagan Court. . . . The worst of it is that it is not the heathen who persecute the missionaries and destroy the Mission, but the Jesuits, and they, indeed, do it with sovereign effrontery."†

A report of the Cardinal Legate, dated November 15th, 1707: He relates how the Jesuit, Porquet, disseminates the following dogmas in Canton: "He who asserts that the souls of the dead rest on the altars of their ancestors does not sin against religion; the Pope cannot infallibly settle the disputes concerning Chinese rites; the missionaries are not bound to obey the commands of the Patriarch of Antioch [Tournon, the Papal Legate, had this title] with regard to the Chinese rites; neither the Pope nor the Church can infallibly define whether a thing is an idol."

When an exhortation to retract proved useless, the Jesuit, Porquet, was excommunicated by the Legate, but he took no notice and was supported in this by the remaining Jesuits. "Father Britto [a Jesuit who was canonised in the nineteenth century] told the missionary priest, Giampe, to his face that they [the Jesuits] did not

* *Mémoires*, 4, 522 et seq. † *Ibid.*, 4, 529 et seq.

Theory and Practice of the Vows

recognise the Patriarch either as the legitimate Visitator or as Papal Legate, and they considered his power of jurisdiction invalid."*

Report of the Lazarist priest, Müllener [a German] to his General Superior, Watel, dated December 30th, 1708 · At the Jesuits' instigation, almost all the missionaries who had submitted to the decision of the Pope (*en fils soumis de l'Église*) were banished from China.† A report of the Cardinal Legate, dated 1708, concerning a new imperial decree of June 24th, 1708 : The decree, which was unfavourable to the missionaries obeying the Pope, was published through the influence of the Jesuits, who take up the position that they would rather see the Mission destroyed than that it should be reformed in accordance with the Papal decrees.‡

A peep behind the scenes of the Chinese and Malabar drama, which led to the death of the Papal Legate, Tournon, is also afforded by a remark, not intended for publication, made by the Jesuit Cordara, official historiographer of the Order for thirty-five years. In a most weighty secret report (to be dealt with more fully later), addressed to his brother, Cordara states that Innocent XI. had issued a " very severe decree (*atrox decretum*) against the Jesuits with reference to their behaviour in the Chinese and Indian Mission, which, if it had been published, would have been very bad (*male admodum*) for the entire Society."§

The death of the Pope prevented the publication. His successor, Benedict XIII., who, as Cordara himself says, was entirely in the hands of the Jesuits (*societati addictissimus*) left everything to his favourite, Coscia, bartered

* *Mémoires*, 4, 538 *et seq.*   † *Ibid.*, 4, 549 *et seq.*
‡ *Ibid.*, 4, 562 *et seq.*, 572.
§ *Denkwürdigkeiten des Jesuiten Cordara zur Geschichte von* 1740–1773; Döllinger, *Beiträge zur politischen, kirchlichen und Kultur-Geschichte der sechs letzten Jahrhunderte* (Ratisbon, 1883), 3, 3.

the important official positions for money, and only thought of the enrichment of his family,* abstained from publishing the decree, which reflected disgrace on the Order.

Submission only followed tardily when Benedict XIV., in two bulls quickly succeeding one another (1742 and 1744), reminded the Jesuits, with the greatest severity, of their duty of obedience.†

I have dwelt a long time on the disputes concerning the Chinese rites. But there is no stronger proof than this of the falsity of the Jesuit boast as to the unconditional submission of the Order to Rome and of the unscrupulousness with which the Jesuits work against the Papacy itself when the defence of their interests is in question.‡

From the conduct of the Order also at the time of its suppression by Clement XIV. in 1773, we miss, in spite of all assertions on the Jesuit side to the contrary, the absolute submission to the Pope, which has been solemnly extolled.

In this connection, I can contribute the following from my own experience:

In 1880 Leo XIII. tried to make peace with Prussia, and a hostile feeling was thereby aroused against him in the Jesuit Order. During this time I heard him attacked most violently by my comrades of the Order.

---

* Cordara, *Ibid.*, p. 4.

† *Bullarium Romanum* (Edit. Luxemb., 1748), 16, 230 *et seq.*

‡ I have already called attention to the attempts of the Jesuits, Cornely and Duhr, to represent the Tournon case, and the agitations in China connected with it, as insignificant. Side by side with this misrepresentation must be mentioned the work of another Jesuit, who undertook the whitewashing of the subject more than a century ago, and even to-day is looked upon as a great authority. A *History of the Disputes with reference to the Chinese Rites* was published in 1791 at Augsburg. The author remained anonymous, after the favourite style, but it was soon known that the Jesuit Pray was the originator. The three volumes form a single spiteful pamphlet, teeming with calumnies against the very persons who make the best appearance in the light of history—Tournon, Appiani, Maigrot, etc.

The Jesuits Pachtler and Cathrein were especially reckless in their speech. For instance, it was asserted that the jubilee (of the priesthood) of such a Pope, who watched so badly over the interests of the Church, ought not to be celebrated. The animosity went so far that I felt myself compelled to write to the General of the Order, Anderledy, with reference to the statutory loyalty to the Pope and to ask him to interpose. Characteristically enough, I received no answer, and the ostracism of the Pope continued uninterruptedly. The action of Leo XIII. in bringing about the close of the *Kulturkampf* was at variance with the egotism of the Order, which dreaded lest a truce between Church and State should compel it to retire into the background. Hence the rage against the Pope and the insubordination to the Papal measures.

THE VOW OF CHASTITY

" What pertains to the vow of chastity requires no explanation, it being clear how perfectly it should be observed, namely, by striving to imitate the angelic holiness in the purity both of our mind and body."*

On this regulation in the Constitutions of the Order, the Jesuit Genelli makes the " historic " remark :

" As regards chastity, it deserves to be emphasised . . . that the Society is so immaculate in this respect that its opponents have never been able to prove any assertion against it, although the Jesuits, by living in the world and having intercourse with all kinds of persons, are exposed to the sharpest scrutiny, and their work leads them frequently into temptation and danger."†

It must be freely acknowledged that unchastity has never tainted the Jesuit Order permanently, and that the

---

* Constit. VI., 1, 1 ; *Summar.* n. 28.

† *Das Leben des heiligen Ignatius von Loyola* (Innsbruck, 1848), p. 230.

unnatural restraint of celibacy does not work so destructively here as in so many sections of the Roman Catholic clergy. But it must be stated most distinctly that in this point also Jesuit theory and Jesuit practice are opposed to one another, and that the statements of Jesuit writers, *e.g.* Genelli, with reference to the "angelic purity" of the Order, are untrue. In that very sphere of activity which the Order regards above all others as its domain of glory—the education of the young—the Jesuits have paid their full tribute to sexual humanity. In Chapter VI. I have already touched lightly on this subject, but now I shall deal with it more fully.

Heinrich von Lang, the director of the Bavarian State Archives, gives the following information from papers of the Upper German Province of the Jesuit Order, which are now lying in the Imperial Archives at Munich—*i.e.* reports concerning members of the Order which were sent from the Superior of the Province to the General of the Order in Rome.*

In the first place, Lang gives a complete account of the vicious conduct of the Jesuit, Jacob Marell, towards pupils of the Jesuit establishment at Augsburg. Lang produces original letters of the Jesuits Banholzer, Erhart, and Osterpeutter, dated July 3rd, September 22nd, and December 26th, 1698, which they, in their capacity of confessors, consultors and rectors, addressed from Augsburg to the Provincial Superior, Martin Müller, and in which the abominable details of the doings of their fellow-Jesuit, Marell, are reported.† Lang also prints signed statements by three pupils, Count Oettingen and the two Counts Fugger, who were most frequently misused by the Jesuit Marell.

From p. 26 onwards, in an extract, Lang gives thirty-six "informations" regarding the immoral behaviour of

* *Jacobi Marelli, S.J., amores.* Munich, 1815. † *Ibid.*, pp. 1–22.

Theory and Practice of the Vows

as many Jesuits. The following are examples: Information against Father Werner Ehinger for disgraceful intercourse with a Baron of Ratisbon; against Father Haas at Freiburg for illicit intercourse with two youths; against Father Adam Herler, of Constance, who corrupted seventeen youths; against Father Franz Schlegl, of Munich, for assaults on seven boys; against Father Ferdinand, of Augsburg, for misusing a servant girl; against Father Michael Baumgartner, who, whilst he was sub-regent at Dillingen, entered into an entanglement with a woman of seventy and seduced two girls, one of whom then said, "For shame, what kind of priests are these?" and so on, in one continuous catalogue of similar abominations.

In considering this list of grave offences we must bear in mind that it deals with only one Province of the Order, the Upper German, that the numerous cases happened in the short time between 1650–1723, and that the editor, Lang, Director of the State Archives, declares that he could easily quote "hundreds and hundreds" of such "informations" from the manuscript material at his disposal in the Munich archives. Kluckhohn, who thoroughly searched through the Jesuit papers at Munich in 1874, and gave reports on them before the Royal Bavarian Academy of Science, also confirms the data supplied by Lang.*

Paul Hoffäus, who in 1596 was appointed by General Acquaviva Visitator for the Upper German Province of the Order, and who was one of the most important Jesuits of that time, as the result of his visitation wrote in his Memorial intended for the Jesuit College at Munich:

"It is to be regretted that so many beneficial precautionary measures [for the preservation of chastity] are not always observed, or are observed very carelessly. Feasting (*commessationes*) and

---

* For Kluckhohn's comment, *see* I., p. 207.

frequent visits to single females at their residences take place without necessity. Rendezvous are given in the church for long conversations with women, and there are scandalously long confessions (*confessiones scandelose prolixae*) of women, even of those who frequently confess. Confessions of sick women in their houses are heard without [as the rule prescribes] the presence of a companion who can see the confessor and penitent. Frequently, yes, very frequently, intimacy prevails between two persons [confessor and his female penitent] without any trace of strict repression on the confessor's part. I fear that sweet and agreeable words are exchanged, which are tinged with carnal lust and carnal feelings. Unpleasant occurrences, which lead to apostasy and to expulsions from the Society, teach us what great evils are caused by such transgressions in the case of confessors. Must there not be a strange aberration of intellect and heart when confessors in a free and unembarrassed manner, and without fear of shame, dare to pass many hours joking with women before the criticising eyes of the world, as if they themselves and their penitents were not in any danger from such unrestricted intercourse? It is known and has also reached the ears of the princes [referring to the two dukes of Bavaria] that confessors from amongst our Order have become entangled through such Satanic examples of vice, and have apostatised or been expelled from the Society as evil nuisances."*

This Memorial, to which I shall again refer, affords the more food for thought because it is a secret report and was drawn up only forty-six years after the founding of the Jesuit Order. Consequently, even in its first youth, —*i.e.* at a time in which zeal and the active practice of virtue should still have prevailed—the Order suffered from grave improprieties.

In these cases it is very important to notice that although, formally and directly, the offences of individuals are in question, nevertheless the Order as such is impli-

---

* Printed by Reusch, *Beiträge zur Geschichte des Jesuitenordens: Zeitschrift für Kirchengeschichte*, 1894, XV., 2, 262 *et seq*.

cated because, in these and in other instances, it failed to punish the culprits adequately.

There is no mention of punishment in the above-mentioned "information." In one of the worst cases, that of the Jesuit Theoderich Beck, the Provincial Superior even recommends that clemency should be shown, " because the offences were not publicly known." He acted here quite in accordance with the ordinance already quoted, issued by General Acquaviva in 1595, that immoral actions should not be punished by dismissal when they had led to no open scandal.* How exactly the advice was followed is shown further by the following facts:

A Jesuit, W. K. (he is careful not to mention his name), reported, under date 1st December, 163– (he also does not mention the year), from Rome to the Jesuit Forer at Dillingen that the Jesuit Mena, "an exceptionally clever man, who is sought out by all as an oracle," made a woman, who was his penitent, believe that she might live with him legitimately. He subsequently denounced himself and "died in the Society of Jesus" before the close of the lawsuit which followed. It is related in the same letter of another Jesuit, Azevedo, that "he had only been detected (*nihil aliud fecisse deprehensus*) observing or touching that belonging to a woman which one ought bashfully to keep away from." He also "died in the Society of Jesus."†

THE VOW OF POVERTY

The scope of the vow of poverty (also of the special vow of poverty of the professed Jesuits) is explained by the following passages in the Constitutions:

"Whoever wishes to live in the Society must be convinced that food, drink, clothing and bedding should be

---

* *See* Chapter VI.

† Döllinger-Reusch, *Moralstreitigkeiten*, I., 587 ; II., 305.

of such a kind as appertains to poverty, and that the worst things which are to be found in the house are assigned to him to produce greater self-denial and spiritual development; also in order that a certain equality and a common social measure should be attained. As those who established the Society were specially tried by such poverty and a greater want of bodily necessaries, so those also who follow them must endeavour, by the grace of God, to equal and excel them. . . . Poverty is to be loved as the strong wall of the Order, and, with the help of Divine grace, is to be maintained in its purity as far as possible. All must love poverty as a mother and endure its effects in fitting season, according to a measure of holy discretion; nothing is to be used as an individual possession, and they must also be ready to beg from door to door when obedience or necessity requires this."*

And with reference to the gratuitous performance of the work of the Order which is connected with poverty, the Constitutions say:

"All who are under obedience to the Society should remember that they ought to give gratuitously what they have gratuitously received, neither demanding nor receiving pay, or alms, by which masses, or confessions, or sermons, or lessons, or visitations, or any other duty of all those which the Society can render according to our Institute, may appear to be remunerated. . . . Also they must not, although others are allowed to do so, accept any pay or any alms for masses, sermons, lessons, or administration of sacraments, or for any other pious work which the Society may carry out in accordance with its Constitutions, as recompense for such services, from any other person than from God (for whose service alone they are to do everything)."†

* *Exam. gen.*, IV., 26; *Summar.* 23, 24.
† *Constit.* VI., 2, 7; *Examen generale*, I., 3; *Can.* 1, *Congreg.* 5; *Summar.* 27.

Theory and Practice of the Vows

Only on one point, which is to be discussed minutely further on—the interference of the Jesuit Order in politics—is the opposition between Jesuit theory and Jesuit practice so sharp as in the case of poverty. We may [say at once that Jesuit poverty is communistic wealth.

Apart from actual business associations, there is scarcely any non-religious society which strives so intently and with such considerable success after possessions and riches as the Society of Jesus, a name which, in just this connection, is a cruel mockery. But amongst the religious bodies, the so-called spiritual Orders, the Jesuit Order occupies a supreme and exceptional position through its "poverty."

I will give some personal recollections first of all.

No doubt I have felt, as the Constitutions of the Order express it, "the effects of poverty." The already described dormitory and living arrangements during my novitiate, which continued throughout the scholasticate, afforded full opportunities for the practical experience of poverty. Bedding and clothing were, if not exactly mean in the strictest sense of the word, far from any suggestion of opulence. A palliasse which was frequently very hard, coarse bed-linen, a small blanket and a narrow and short bedstead formed my nightly couch for years. The clothing was outwardly, it is true, generally clean. As regards, however, the cleanliness underneath, *e.g.* the cleanliness of the undergarments, there was none, since, for example, one and the same pair of trousers was worn next to the skin for years, and shirt and stockings, in spite of perspiration and in spite of scanty washing and rare baths, were only changed once a week. Thus I also experienced the uncleanliness which is frequently, but not necessarily, connected with poverty.

But two points must be noted in the case of these

"effects of poverty," and they are not the only ones, as I shall show. In the first place, it was a poverty brought about by force of circumstances. The German Province of the Order was obliged, while established abroad (in Holland and England) after its expulsion from Germany, to cut its cloak according to its cloth; it could not immediately have everything in good order. And in the second place, this effect of poverty, to which still others were added according to necessity (threadbare or torn clothing) are the tests imposed on the individual to prove his contempt for the world, his obedience, his constancy, etc. They are not phenomena which develop from the attitude and from the spirit of the Order. Thus even the meagre "effects of poverty," regarded from religious and ascetic points of view as characteristic of the Order, are still further reduced. Hence I have a perfect right to disregard these things in describing the poverty which I personally endured.

In other respects I have learnt to know the poverty of the Jesuit Order as easy living, based on wealth, and even luxury, combined with a spirit of intense eagerness for money and gain.

It is obvious that an Order which clothes and feeds thousands, and in many instances lodges them in magnificent and spacious buildings, must be rich, very rich. The revenues, from which the enormous sums for maintaining the members, houses and churches of the Order are derived, point to a capital of many millions. I saw this clearly from the beginning. But I came to see other things clearly as well.

The material foundation of the Order, safeguarded by an enormous fortune of millions, was not the only, not even the most marked, feature of opposition to its theoretically ascetic and religious foundation—*i.e.* to Jesus Christ's vow of poverty. We find it in the daily life and

Theory and Practice of the Vows

in the habits of the Order of the Society of Jesus in certain circumstances.

The daily fare at dinner and supper is very good and very abundant, incomparably better than that of the secular priests and even most comfortably situated and well-to-do families of the middle class. The Jesuit Order knows no trace of poverty in eating and drinking.

The "poor" Jesuit daily eats a dinner consisting of soup and two meat dishes, with suitable additions and stewed fruit, and a supper consisting of a meat dish or other hot food, and he drinks good beer with this. On festival days, according to their importance, several dishes, amounting to five or six, are served, and wine is supplied besides the beer. In the English Jesuit houses (Ditton Hall, Stonyhurst, London, Liverpool and Manchester) I have enjoyed meals which must be characterised as very well cooked, sumptuous dinners,* at which neither oysters and champagne, nor pastry, poultry and game, nor even the after-dinner cigarette with coffee and liqueurs were lacking.

Was the meal of which Christ and His company partook before His passion and death, the picture of which frequently adorns the refectories of the Society of Jesus, of the same nature?

The "magister meals" constitute a special kind of feast. Every three months, or even more frequently, the Jesuits appointed as *magistri* in the different colleges have special festivities with a meal at which things are done in great style. From a purely human point of view, I am quite capable of appreciating such recreation, spiced with

---

* Such feasts are called D*uplicia ;* they are divided, according to their importance, into D*uplicia secundae*, *primae* and *primissimae* (*sic !*) *classis*—a division which, it is important to notice, has been copied from the Liturgy, which classes the feasts of the Church under *festa simplicia* and *duplicia*, and these again under *duplicia secundae* and *primae classis*. The designation *duplex primissimae classis* for specially sumptuous meals is Jesuit Latin, or rather Jesuit dog-Latin.

pleasures of the table, in the course of a hard and monotonous professional life. But the purely human point of view is by no means that which is accepted by the Society of Jesus; it takes to itself very emphatically the ideal of Christly perfection and asceticism, and such feastings are out of place for the wearers of the soutane and biretta.

A true Jesuit peculiarity may be added. It is that the good living, expressing itself in luxurious meals and feasting, is most carefully kept from the laity. In their eyes the Jesuit appears as the poor, mortified member of an Order which is very much in want of support and alms. The liberality of the unsuspecting public would receive its deathblow if it got wind of such things.

An event during my stay at the Jesuit college in Holland, Blyenbeck, where I studied philosophy as a scholastic from 1881–1883, shows to what serio-comic situations such secret proceedings frequently lead.

One fine summer afternoon my uncle, Baron Felix von Loë (Centre Deputy and founder of the Catholic National Union), came over the moor from his estate at Terporten, situated on the other side of the neighbouring Prussian border, as he frequently did, to visit his friend, the Jesuit Joseph Schneider (author of an " official " work on Indulgences), who was stationed in Rome as Consultor of the Congregation of Indulgences, but was spending his holidays at Blyenbeck. It was just the time for a " magister meal," and Father Schneider as a distinguished guest took part in it. A great dilemma occurred! I was called to the Rector, and requested to entertain my uncle in the meantime and explain to him that Father Schneider could not be spared just then " owing to urgent business." About an hour later, Father Schneider appeared with a face rubicund from eating and drinking, and in a very cheerful frame of mind. He repeated the excuse about important business. I suffered torture, partly owing to the untruth with which we had regaled my uncle, and partly because I was afraid that Father Schneider's evident cheerfulness might cause the "urgent business" to appear in a somewhat curious light.

From this may be deduced the value of the constantly repeated pitiful complaints made by the Order in newspaper articles and elsewhere with reference to the "bread of exile" which it is compelled to eat.

The country-houses of the Order, officially named "villas," are peculiarly characteristic of Jesuit poverty. The Order seeks to acquire country-houses, frequently at great expense, in the neighbourhood of its colleges, where every Thursday the inmates of the colleges, fathers and scholastics, may be recuperated by good air, good food and all kinds of active games. This is certainly an excellent arrangement from the point of view of health and the care of the body. It may reasonably be doubted, from the knowledge revealed to us in the Gospels of the Christly spirit of poverty, whether it is in accordance with the spirit of poverty of a Society of Jesus. Notwithstanding the exile in which the German Province of the Order lived in Holland and England, the wealth of the Order was sufficient for the expensive purchase and support of such villas. Thus, the novitiate house at Exaeten had its villa at Oosen on the banks of the Maas, and the college at Wynandsrade had its villa at Aalbeck.

On journeys, the "poor" Jesuit travels second class. I was accustomed to travel third class as long as I believed in the Jesuit Order. When I went with other comrades, I found it rather difficult to persuade them to use the lower class.

The Jesuit father (not the brother) has his own spacious room, not luxuriously but comfortably furnished, with bed, writing-table, standing-desk, chairs, *prie-dieu*, bookcase and stove.

Consequently it is not to be wondered at—and this is also an effect of Jesuit poverty—that when Jesuits, brought up in such comfort, become through exterior events the possessors of a large income they incline towards prodigality. For example, the Jesuit Cienfuegos, who was made Cardinal, "made an enormous display," as his fellow-Jesuit, Cordara, the historiographer of the Order, tells us. This "poor" member of the Order wasted over 70,000 gold florins yearly in dissipation as Imperial ambassador at Madrid and holder of the rich archbishopric of Monreale.*

It is a fair question then : "Where does poverty come in when the exterior life of the Jesuit is so comfortably, even luxuriously appointed ?" And, further, "Are there not many amongst the Jesuits who are struck by the antithesis of the Constitutions of the Order and the actual life, and who, as a result of these thoughts, doubt whether they are really in the Society of Jesus, that Jesus who entered the world in exceeding poverty, passed through it in exceeding poverty, and left it in exceeding poverty?" Of course, there are many whose spirit of idealism and aversion from the world takes offence at the "poor" things offered for their use and enjoyment by the Jesuit Order. I belonged to this number. I frequently expressed my trouble and doubts to my Superior, especially during the novitiate. I received the stereotyped reply.

"Our poverty does not consist in privation, but in our aloofness in the midst of possessions ; also especially in the fact that we do not call anything our own amongst the objects with which we are surrounded and which we use. Every pencil, every piece of paper, every book, every pen and every sheet of note-paper, our food, the rooms and the clothes which we use, have to be asked for;

---

* Cordara, S.J., *Denkwürdigkeiten;* Döllinger, *Beiträge*, 3, 3.

we are possessors, or masters, of nothing. Hence we are poor."

A sentence uttered by my Novice-Master, afterwards my Provincial, the Jesuit Mauritius Meschler, also throws interesting light on this poverty. When I once, at the Annual Statement of Conscience, expressed my misgivings as to the sumptuous feasts, he said:

"But, dear brother, are only the wicked to enjoy the good things of this world? Has not God also created them for the righteous?"

I was not then quick enough at repartee to answer him with the saying of Christ, who certainly also belonged to the "righteous":

"The foxes have holes, and the birds of the air have nests; but the Son of man hath not where to lay his head."

It does not strike anyone, who believes in the authority and piety of the expositors, that such explanations are humbug and devoid of the Evangelical spirit; indeed, they gradually lull the ascetic and religious conscience to sleep. The individual considers that he and the Order are poor, whilst he lives a very comfortable life on the interest of the Order's millions and enjoys in a duly "detached" manner the good things of this world.

I repeat that Jesuit poverty is in reality communistic wealth, not Evangelical poverty.

I have also had experience in various ways of the famed gratuitousness with which the Jesuit carries out his spiritual work (sermons, hearing of confessions, giving of exercises, and saying mass).

During my third probationary year, the tertiate, which I passed at Portico in England (near the manufacturing town of St. Helens), we tertiaries were sent on Sundays into the neighbouring parishes to help the priests, at their request, in preaching, hearing confessions and saying mass.

The "gratuitousness" of such assistance comes very forcibly to light. Our rector and tertiate instructor, the Jesuit Oswald, carefully selected from amongst the requests submitted those which promised to be most lucrative. He openly stated that he preferred to decline absolutely requests which did not promise, besides the allowance for travelling, at least one pound sterling!

This instance of the application of the principle is the more noteworthy because it belonged to the tertiate period, *i.e.* the highest stage of the Jesuit training, and because the very man who was appointed by the Order to instruct us in the Constitutions of the Order and initiate us into its spirit proclaimed this principle with reference to "gratuitous" money-making.

The Order charges high fees for Exercises, popular missions, festival sermons and masses for souls. It prefers to give Exercises to rich and noble people, because the donations, too, are rich and noble. When I gave Exercises in 1889 to a number of noble ladies at Münster, I received 500 marks (£25) for my exertions, which only lasted three days. The Procurator of the Province, the Jesuit Caduff, accepted the money with pleasure, and remarked facetiously that I seemed able to give profitable Exercises. I never brought back less than 300 marks (£15) from the castle of Count D.-V., in Westphalia, where I often went to preach, hear confessions and say mass. At the death of my father, my mother gave from two to three thousand marks (£100–£150) to the Order for saying masses for the dead. I have already stated how, in all probability, the Order also received a considerable portion of my mother's fortune through the agency of the Jesuit Behrens.

Such and similar occurrences might be multiplied a thousandfold, and an idea can be obtained through them of the productive source of revenue for the Order

Theory and Practice of the Vows

which springs from the gratuitousness of its spiritual aids.

So much regarding Jesuit poverty from the limited history of my personal experiences. I will now deal with the larger history of the Order's poverty.

Here also stress must be laid on the fact that the defection from the rules drawn up in the Constitutions is observable even in the early youth of the Order. The Jesuit *primitiae spiritus*, the first fruits of the spirit, are degenerate already, and the high-sounding, ascetic theory of the Order is in sharp antithesis to them.

In the already mentioned secret report of the Upper German Province of the Order, by the Visitator, Paul Hoffäus, appointed by General Acquaviva, we find, under date 1596:

"We have swerved aside, we have fallen away violently, indeed, from the first form of poverty. We are not content with necessary things, but desire that all shall be comfortable, plentiful, diverse, profuse, rare, select, elegant, splendid, gilded, precious and luxurious. I can only think with shame and pain of how many thousand florins have been expended here [in Munich] in latter years for the maintenance and the embellishment of the college, as if we were not poor members of an Order, but courtiers and spendthrifts. Woe to those who have brought about and devised this damnable and accursed expenditure to the corruption of our religious poverty. This is the more to be regretted because the corruption has already become a habit which can no longer be exterminated unless the axe is placed at the root. There is not a trace left of the poverty of our fathers. Everything is done in grand style."*

It is praiseworthy that the officials in the Order raised their voices in warning. But this did not help matters. The evil spread. And when the whole is surveyed, when we observe the continually increasing gigantic riches of

* Reprinted in Reusch, *Beiträge*, p. 262.

the Order and see innumerable examples of its remarkable commercial aptitude for money-making, the not unjustifiable doubt arises: "Are not the warning voices of officials only raised *pro forma, ut aliquid fecisse videantur?*" Be that as it may, the historical life and behaviour of the Order gives the lie to its theoretical warnings.

As the pseudo-mysticism of the Jesuit Order is an inheritance from its founder, Ignatius Loyola, so its pseudo-poverty and its notable acquisitiveness are characteristics handed down from the founder.

Ignatius Loyola instructed the Jesuit Laynez, appointed by himself confessor to Duke Cosimo de Medici, who afterwards played an important part at the Council of Trent, and became Ignatius's immediate successor in the generalship of the Order, that "he was to 'insinuate' [this was the expression used by Ignatius] to the Duke's wife, who was to be confined shortly, that she should act in the same manner as the Queen of Portugal had acted before her confinement, namely, make a settlement of 500 gold florins on the Jesuit College.*

These 1,000 gold florins obtained from two princesses during childbed travail have themselves, as it were, become reproductive—they have produced a million future generations. The "insinuation" of the founder of the Order has remained a model for all later "insinuations," at the death-bed, in confessionals, etc., and thus the Order has heaped up possessions on possessions.

K. von Lang points out† that the Upper German Province of the Jesuit Order received in the years 1620–1700 alone through "insinuations," 800,000 florins. Amongst these are single sums of 15,000, 32,000, 56,000, 92,000 and 117,000 florins. In 1718 a member of the

---

* Druffel, *Ignatius von Loyola an der römischen Kurie* (Munich, 1879), p. 18 *et seq.*

† *Geschichte der Jesuiten in Bayern*, 1819, p. 57.

Theory and Practice of the Vows 83

Peutinger family bequeathed 100,000 florins to the Jesuit College at Ellwangen. From about 1700 onwards, the donations in the Upper German Province were only noted down in the secret books. The size of the sums—which were frequently gigantic for that period—was to remain concealed.* The yearly fixed revenue of the Upper German Province, which consisted of 583 persons, amounted in 1656 to 185,950 florins, according to von Lang's† minutely verified documents. To this should be added many thousands through gifts, donations, fees for masses, etc.

It was especially Duke William V. of Bavaria who laid the foundation for the wealth of the Upper German Jesuits. He endowed the Jesuit College in Munich with a yearly income of 2,675 florins, and to this were added the tithes from Ainling and Edenhausen to the amount of 3,000 florins, and the monastery of Ebersberg, with all its revenues and landed property.‡

He met their endeavours to get the most popular places of pilgrimages into their hands by building them a college at Altötting. He presented them, moreover, with the abbeys of Biburg and Mönchsmünster, and contrived, in spite of the opposition of the district, and against Papal decrees, that the Jesuits connected with the foundations should become members of the Bavarian prelacy, and should receive a seat and vote in the Diets.§

The predilection of this duke for the Jesuit Order was so boundless that there was a general complaint that the avarice of the Jesuits would eventually devour the whole of Bavaria.

William's example was imitated. His princely neigh-

---

* Lang, *Ibid.*, p. 58. † *Ibid.*, p. 158 *et seq.*

‡ Sugenheim, *Baierns Kirchen und Volkszustande im 16. Jahrh.* (Giessen, 1842), p. 317 (2).

§ F. Stieve, *Briefe und Akten zur Geschichte des 30 jahrigen Krieges*, IV., 414.

bour, the Archduke Leopold, Prince Bishop of Passau, a boy of fourteen, endowed the Jesuit College at this place with 30,000 florins.

Thus it is explicable that on the suppression of the Jesuit Order in 1773 the Upper German Province possessed a gigantic landed property which was distributed as follows:

To the college at Munich belonged: the monastery of Ebersberg with the priory of Erding, Aham, the domain of Pfaffenhausen with Tondorf, Eugenbach, Hornbach, Holzhausen, Wolfshausen and Rännerzbach; to the college in Ingolstadt: Mönchsmünster with fifty-eight farms, Biburg with Leitenbach and Rozenhausen of ninety-one farms, the estate of Randeck and Essing, the manors of Prunn, Stockau, Oberhaunstadt, Oberdolling with Hellmansperg; to the college at Landsberg: the manors of Vogach, Pestanagger, Winkel and Zangenhausen; to the college at Amberg: the Abbey of Kastell together with the manors of Engenreut, Hofdorf, Heymaden, Garstorf, Gebersdorf; to the college at Ratisbon: the monastery of St. Paul, the manors of Gieselshausen, the tithes and dues of Kalmünz, Lengenfeld and Holzheim; to the college at Straubing: the manor of Schierling; to the college at Landshut: the estate of Niederding; to the college at Burghausen: the tithes of Märkel and Seibelsdorf; to the college at Feldkirch (Vorarlberg): the tithes of Frastanz and the pasturage of Streichenfeld; to the college at Neuburg: the monasteries of Berg, Neuburg, and Echenbrunn; to the college at Augsburg: the domain of Eitenhofen, the manors of Kissingen and Mergethau with the laundry at Lechhausen; to the theologica seminary at Dillingen: Lustenau; to the college a Eichstätt: Wittenfeld and Landershofen; to the colleg at Bamberg: the estates of Sambach, Winden, Stetbach Leimershof, Hohengüssbach, Knetzgau, Merkendorf, Sand

Theory and Practice of the Vows

hof and the vineyard of Ziegelang. The Imperial Commission found assets of more than three millions in the college at Ingolstadt.*

When the Austrian State officially estimated the wealth of the Order directly after its suppression, it amounted to 15,415,220 guldens, for Bohemia, Moravia, Silesia and the remaining German-Austrian hereditary lands. But this does not seem to have been nearly all. For the President of the Imperial Exchequer reports, under date of August 16th, 1782, that more than 120,000 guldens of "Jesuit gold" had been discovered at Genoa, and more than eighteen millions were supposed to be lodged in the Order's name in Holland, four millions of which belonged to Austria. The President even learnt the names of the banks at Frankfort which had negotiated the payment of the interest. But the further levy arranged by the Bethmann† firm led to no results.‡

The following facts from the same period throw the Jesuit wealth into bold relief:

The Bohemian and Austrian Chancery Court reports, under date of April 28th, 1781, that of the outstanding claims of the Jesuits on private individuals, 3,214,000 guldens have already been collected, 2,674,939 guldens were converted into ready money, and, in addition to this, 381,654 guldens earnest money would be collected.

The Emperor (Joseph II.) considered it "unseemly" that the State as an assignee of the Jesuits should have private debtors, and privately advised Prince Schwarzenberg, who was placed in sad difficulties through the notice to redeem this outstanding debt, to sell one of his estates

---

* From the documents quoted by Lang, *Geschichte der Jesuiten in Bayern*, p. 205 *et seq*.

† The fifth German Chancellor, von Bethmann-Hollweg, is descended from a member of this banking firm.

‡ Hock-Biedermann, *Der osterreichische Staatsrat*, 1760–1848 (Vienna, 1879), pp. 67, 444.

in the German Empire so that he might pay the proceeds into the Austrian Government Credit-bank and thus liquidate the debt contracted with the Jesuits.*

On May 25th, 1647, John Palafox, Bishop of Los Angeles, wrote to Pope Innocent X. :†

* Hock-Biedermann, *ibid.*, p. 521.

† The evidence of Bishop Palafox (who died in 1659 when Bishop of Osma, in Spain) is especially unfavourable, and is consequently contested by the Jesuits with all manner of culumnies. Palafox lived and died in the odour of sanctity, so that his beatification was instituted and almost completed. Therefore the Jesuits, fighting as is their wont by means of falsifications and misrepresentations, have tried to discredit his letter directed to the Pope, from which the above quotation has been taken. But the authenticity of the letter is guaranteed, apart from other proofs, by a decree of the Congregation of Rites, dated December 16th, 1760, in which, amongst the writings of Palafox, these two letters are also mentioned, and it is said of them, as of the remaining writings: "They contain nothing against religion and good morals, nor do they contain any new, strange doctrine opposed to the general belief and custom of the Church." The Congregation announces at the same time that, after the examination of his writings, the beatification of Bishop Palafox could be continued (Décret rendu dans la cause de l'Église d'Osma, p. 30. Rome: *De l'Imprimerie de la Chambre Apostolique*, 1760. In a collection belonging to the Court and State Library in Munich: Jes. 832). This official document is of the greatest importance also in connection with the contents of the letters. For the Congregation of Rites could not possibly declare that the letters were "not opposed to good morals" if they had not become convinced after minute examination that they contained nothing slanderous and untrue. When, therefore, Duhr (*Jesuitenfabeln*, p. 640 *et seq.*), who, moreover, carefully keeps this important decree secret, asserts most positively: "A number of his [Bishop Palafox's] assertions are in disagreement with known facts and are accordingly shown to be untruths," he makes an audacious attempt to deceive, which is not improved by the fact that Duhr refers to "remarks" (*animadversiones*) by the *Promotor Fidei* in the proceedings in regard to Bishop Palafox's beatification. For it is the business of the *Promotor Fidei* to raise difficulties from all available quarters against a beatification, and that is why he is also called the *advocatus diaboli*, the devil's advocate. Moreover, this quotation by Duhr requires to be explained. As I could not find the remarks of the *advocatus diaboli* at any German library, I begged the Intelligence Bureau for German Libraries in Berlin to ask Duhr in which library the remarks could be found. Duhr replied that they were private property. Thus I am deprived of the possibility of verifying them. And until Duhr produces the work itself, I must place a note of interrogation after his quotation. I have already caught Duhr tripping in regard to many of his quotations, and shall do so again, no doubt. The accuracy of the contents of the letter is, moreover, supported by the fact that, on account of the remonstrance of the Jesuit Order, Rome caused an examination to be carried out, with the result that Innocent X. decided in three briefs (May 14th, 1648, November 19th, 1652, and May 27th, 1653) in favour of the Cardinal and against the Jesuits. These briefs were so embarrassing to the Order that it tried to divert their influence

Theory and Practice of the Vows 87

"Most Holy Father,—I found almost all the wealth, all immovables and all treasures of this Province of America, in the hands of the Jesuits, who still possess them. Two of their colleges have 30,000 sheep, without counting the small flocks ; and whilst almost all the cathedral churches and all the Orders together have hardly three sugar-refineries, the Society alone has six of the largest. One of these refineries is valued at more than half a million thalers, and this single Province of the Jesuits, which, however, only consists of ten colleges, possesses, as I have just said, six of these refineries, each one of which brings in 100,000 thalers yearly. Besides this, they have various corn-fields of enormous size. Also they have silver mines, and if they continue to increase their power

in a truly Jesuitical way. It smuggled into the bullarium (Lyons edition of 1655, 4 vols.), directly after the briefs, a document (*Processus et finis causae Angelopolitanae*) of which the essential part is as follows : " Decisions in favour of the Fathers of the Society [of Jesus] from the accompanying brief." The ruse was discovered, however, and the Congregation of the Index censured this volume of the bullarium by means of a decree of August 3rd, 1656, " until it was cleansed from the additions " (*donec expurgetur ab adjectis*). In two further decrees (July 27th, 1657, and June 10th, 1658), the resolutions interpolated by the Jesuits were emphatically designated as such " additions." (Reusch, *Index* II., 485, 495.)

A second Jesuit trick must also be reported in the Palafox matter. When, as has already been mentioned, Bishop Palafox's beatification was proposed, the Jesuits vehemently opposed it. The proceedings continued, however, in the usual slow fashion. Then, in 1765–1770, there appeared pseudonymous and anonymous writings, most probably by Jesuits, which designated as suspect the works declared by the Congregation of Rites to be blameless in regard to dogma and morals. The nuisance increased so much that the Congregation of the Index was obliged to put an end to it by means of a decree, dated September 10th, 1771. At the same time, it again confirmed, at the Pope's command, the earlier decrees in favour of the orthodoxy of Palafox's works and enjoined silence on the *Promotor Fidei* (*advocatus diaboli*), (*ibid.*, 495 *et seq.*)

Nothing is to be found of all these important facts in the " historical " statement by the Jesuit Duhr. He brings forward, as has already been mentioned, an unverifiable and unfavourable expression of the *advocatus diaboli* and lays stress upon the assertion, which has already been proved untrue by Arnauld, that Palafox has described his letters as written *ab irato* (*ibid.*, p. 643). The confession, not, of course, intended for publication, which the official historiographer, the Jesuit Cordara, makes in a report regarding the intrigues of his Order against the beatification of Palafox is very interesting : " If John Palafox had obtained the heavenly honours [the canonisation], the letters, which he is supposed to have addressed to Innocent X., would doubtless have reflected disgrace on the Society [of Jesus] . . . The Jesuits tried, with good reason, but not perhaps in a very well-considered manner, to hinder the case of Palafox." (*Denkwürdigkeiten* : Döllinger, *Beiträge*, 3, 29.)

and wealth as excessively as they have done up to now, the secular clergy will become their sacristans and the laymen their stewards, whilst the other Orders will be forced to collect alms at their doors. All this property and all these considerable revenues, which might make a sovereign powerful, serve no other purpose than to maintain ten colleges. . . . To this may be added the extraordinary skill with which they make use of and increase their superabundant wealth. They maintain public warehouses, cattle fairs, butchers' stalls and shops. They send a part of their goods by way of the Philippine Islands to China. They lend out their money for usury and thus cause the greatest loss and injury to others."*

One of Palafox's colleagues, the Bishop of Maragnon, Gregorio de Almeida, complained, in 1679, that the Jesuits yearly snatched 40,000 gold ducats from him.†

With reference to the wealth of the Jesuits in China in the seventeenth and eighteenth centuries, the records of the *Missions Étrangères* of Paris (the oldest Catholic Missionary Society existing to-day) contain interesting information

"*Les Jésuites ont trois maisons à Pékin. Chaque maison a, dans un commerce usuraire, la valeur de cinquante ou soixante mille taels. Chaque tael vaut au moins quatre livres de notre monnaie de France. L'intérêt de l'argent à la Chine est ordinairement de trente pour cent. Les Jésuites prétendent qu'ils n'en prennent que vingt-quatre, ou, ce qui ne vaut pas mieux, deux pour cent par mois. Le calcul du profit est facile à faire. Le capital de 60,000 taels pour chaque maison fait pour les trois maisons ensemble un total de 720,000 livres et la rente d'environ 80,000 liv. pour nourrir onze ' pauvres religieux.' Mais ce profit n'est rien comparé au profit du commerce de vin, d'horloges et d'autres industries, avec lesquelles ces Pères amassent des*

---

* *Don Juan Palafox, Briefe an Papst Innozenz X.* (Frankfort and Leipzig, 1773), pp. 7-9.

† Evidence given by Friedrich, p. 40.

Theory and Practice of the Vows

trésors immenses, qui les rendent beaucoup plus riches dans les Indes que le roi de Portugal.

As the Lazarists (founded by St. Vincent de Paul) reprinted these data in the official history of their Congregation,* we have evidence as to the truth of these facts from two of the most distinguished Catholic Missionary Societies, who, owing to their activity in China and India, knew quite well what they were writing about.

In the same place,† the Lazarists also publish the text of several previously mentioned usurious agreements (*contrats usuraires*) which the Jesuits had concluded, partly with Christian and partly with heathen Chinese, and which the Papal Legate in China, Cardinal Tournon, had declared to be null and void, for the very reason of their usurious character, threatening ecclesiastical punishments in case of repetition.

The sums with which the Jesuit Order had to do at the time of its suppression are shown by a remark of the Jesuit Cordara,‡ that Cardinal Marefoschi, who was nominated by the Pope as Commissioner of Enquiry of the Jesuit *Seminarium Romanum*, had discovered that an item of 500,000 scudi had not been entered at all.

In short, the wealth of the Jesuit Order was and is so notorious, that Crétineau-Joly,§ the fanatical defender of the Order, in the face of undeniable facts, was obliged to admit that the wealth of the Jesuit Order in France amounted to fifty-eight millions in the middle of the eighteenth century. Neither the property of the missions in the colonies nor the alms and gifts were included in this gigantic sum, as he mentions specially. But experience shows that the alms and gifts amount to a considerable

---

* *Mémoires de la Congrégation de la Mission* (Paris, 1865), 4, 239.

† *Ibid.*, 4, 240 *et seq.*

‡ *Denkwürdigkeiten :* Döllinger, *Beiträge*, 3, 49.

§ *Histoire de la Compagnie de Jésus* (Paris, 1845), 5, 275 (1).

total yearly, and that the property of the missions was enormous, so that many millions must be added to the fifty-eight. The number of French Jesuits who enjoyed the interest on these millions was then scarcely more than four thousand.

The fact of the great wealth of the Jesuits is therefore firmly established. A certain piquancy is added by the way in which the Order acquires its millions.

It follows two paths to reach this goal. The one is apparently spiritual and religious, and we encounter on it the Jesuit as Preacher, Director of Exercises, Confessor and Spiritual Director. The other path is the usual way of all business people.

I have already indicated repeatedly the profitableness of the first way, which bears the official designation "gratuitous service" in spiritual affairs. I can also confirm from personal experience how well trodden and profitable is this road.

In this connection I give a few further characteristic passages from the history of the Order.

The English Jesuit, Gerard, says of himself:

"I also gave a retreat to two fine young men who were brothers, who both came to the resolution of entering the Society. . . . Before his departure (the elder), among other almsdeeds, he gave to the Society eleven to twelve thousand florins. My host (Henry Drury) bestowed nearly one-half of his goods upon the Society."*

The particulars are supplemented by information given by the Catholic priest, William Watson, about 1599–1600.

"Father John Jerard (Jesuit) caused Henry Drurie to enter into this exercise; and thereby got him to sell the Manor of Lozell in Suffolke, and other lands to the value of 3,500 pounds, and got

* *The Life of Fr. John Gerard* (London, 1882), from Taunton, p. 162.

Theory and Practice of the Vows

all the money himselfe. Two others had the exercise giuen them at that time by Fr. Jerard: vz. Maister Anthony Rowse and Edward Walpole, of whom he got 1,000 pounds each. . . . He dealt so in like manner with Maister Iames Linacre, from whom he drew 400 pounds. He also received from Edward Huddlestones 1,000 under pretence of the said exercise, and he hath drawne Maister William Wiseman into the said exercise so oft, as he hath left him now very bare to liue."

Watson also reports the same of other wealthy people.*

Abundant details regarding the commercial and business road are available, and I will select a few of them:

M. Martin, the manager of the French Trading Company at Pondicherry, says in his Report:

"It is an established fact that, next to the Dutch, the Jesuits carry on the greatest and most successful trade in the East Indies. They surpass the English and other nations, even the Portuguese, in this respect. They have carried on this [the trade] to such an extent that Father Tachard alone owes the Trading Company [at Pondicherry] more than 160,000 piastres, *i.e.*, more than 450,000 French livres. You have been able to observe that the 58 bales which belong to these fathers, and the smallest of which was as large again as one of those belonging to the 'French' Trading Company, were distributed among all the ships of the squadron [which Louis XIV. had sent to the East Indies under Admiral du Quêne] and were not filled with rosaries or *Agnus Dei* or other weapons which would be characteristic of an apostolic consignment. These are the fine and good wares which they bring out from Europe to sell in this country, and they import as much as they can get on the ships at every outward sailing."†

The agreement between this information, given by a merchant holding a trustworthy position, and the

* *Decacordon of Ten Quodlibetical Questions*, 1602, p. 89 *et seq.*

† *Voyages de Mr. du Quêne*, III., 15: in Harenberg, *Pragmatische Geschichte des Ordens der Jesuiten*, II., 543 *et seq.*

above-quoted statements of the Lazarist priests and the missionaries of the *Missions Étrangères* is noteworthy.

We also encounter Jesuit trading on a large scale in the Island of Martinique.

The commercial transactions of the Jesuit Lavalette in the Island of Martinique resulted in the bankruptcy of the large mercantile house of Lioncy and Gouffre at Marseilles. The General of the Order, Centurione, caused 500,000 livres to be paid as partial compensation to the mercantile house by the French Provincial of the Order, the Jesuit de Sacy. But the half-million could not avert the ruin of Lioncy and Gouffre. The Jesuit de la Marche, who was sent as Visitator by the Order to Martinique, was also obliged to acknowledge that Lavalette had been drawn into illicit commercial transactions. Lavalette's liabilities amounted to 2,400,000 livres in 1761. In 1762 the Jesuit Order took up eighty-six of the bills put into circulation by Lavalette amounting to more than one million. By way of counterbalancing the Lavalette case, the Order had recourse to a method which it had frequently made use of, and which was almost always efficacious in face of the credulous multitude. It caused a certificate of good conduct to be drawn up with reference to his spiritual zeal, his success in the education of the young, his zeal in preaching, hearing of confessions, etc., by the Bishop of Marseilles and numerous inhabitants of the town (for the affair had caused the greatest stir in Marseilles). But such artifices had no effect on the Parliaments of Aix and Paris, and in August, 1762, they condemned the Order to pay one and a half million livres.

The Jesuit Soullier, who tries to cloak Lavalette's offence and that of the Order by every possible means, was obliged to admit these facts.*

---

* Soullier, S.J., *Les Jésuites à Marseille* (Marseilles, 1899), p. 179 *et seq.*

Adrien Artaut gives an excellent description of Lavalette's cunning methods:

" *En quelques années il [Lavalette] dota la maison [des Jésuites] de la Martinique d'un fonds dont a estimé le revenu annuel, peutêtre avec un peu d'exagération, à 280,000 livres. . La nature de ses opérations n'est pas encore complètement connue, mais il ressort des discussions qu'elles ont soulevées, que ce religieux arriva à diminuer, dans une proportion énorme, le charge qui grevait les retours de la Martinique sur France. . . . Dès que les récoltes de la Mission devinrent trop importantes pour trouver acquéreur sur place, le P. Lavalette se vit obligé de les envoyer en France où on les vendait pour le compte de cette Mission. . . . Le P. Lavalette, combinant l'avantage de la Mission et celui des colons, offrit de délivrer sur ses correspondants de France, chargés de la vente de ses récoltes, des traites à valoir sur le net produit de ces récoltes et de délivrer ces traites au pair. En d'autres termes : pour mille livres reçues à la Martinique, le P. Lavalette faisait payer mille livres en France ; et cependant les mille livres reçues à la Martinique n'en valaient en France pas plus de six cent soixante-six. . . . Les traites étaient données à des échéances très éloignées. . Les produits coloniaux se vendaient en France à de bons prix, ce qui permettait de perdre un peu pour réaliser tout de suite ce prix. Enfin, les conditions avantageuses mêmes auxquelles ces traites étaient offertes, inspirèrent d'abord de la méfiance aux colons, qui n'en prirent, en premier lieu, que pour de faibles sommes, et à qui le P. Lavalette n'en remit jamais que pour une partie de la valeur de ses envois. Il resta donc toujours une partie de cette valeur à remettre directement de France et, pour le retour de cette partie, très considérable avant que les traites du P. Lavalette eussent acquis la vogue dont elles jouirent par la suite, l'intelligent administrateur combina une opération toute contraire qu'il épargnait aux colons : il se fit renvoyer le solde de la valeur de ses envois en espèces qui gagnaient aux Iles cinquante pour cent. L'ensemble de ces combinaisons permettait, on le voit, au P. Lavalette de délivrer, à peu près sans perte, des traites au pair de Martinique sur France.*"*

---

* Georges Roux, *Un Armateur Marseillais* (Paris, 1890), p. 132 *et seq.*

Evidently the Jesuit Lavalette would have played a prominent part in any corn exchange, option business or banking-house.

It is, of course, untrue that the Superiors of the Order knew nothing of Lavalette's affairs, and had not sanctioned them, as the defenders of the Order, with Duhr at their head, assert. How could it have been possible, under the perfect system of control, for the Superiors to know nothing for years of their subordinate's important and extensive affairs which involved France's largest banking houses? No, the Superiors remained silent so long as all went well and advantageously for the Order. And in this case silence certainly means consent.

The "Records of the House" (*historia domus*) of the Jesuit College at Colmar from 1698–1750,* published by Julien See and M. X. Mossmann in 1872, are especially instructive, because they afford us interesting glimpses into the business activity and business ability of the Order. The glimpses are the more interesting because the Records, not being intended for publication, contain uncoloured information. Almost every page gives accounts of purchases, sales, revenues, legacies, gifts, financial law-suits, etc., etc. The entries connected with material profit or loss are much fuller than those relating to spiritual and religious matters. Characteristic "kindnesses" towards other Orders also come to light. I will give a few instances:

From 1720: "*Cette Résidence accepta une petite fondation, que le Sr Benoist Singler de Turgheim et le Sr Medinger et sa femme, ses beaupère et belle-mère firent en la ditte année au profit de la Résidence.*" A long lawsuit with the relatives, who were prejudiced to the Jesuits' advantage, was connected with the *fondation*. In this, an assertion was made by the plaintiffs' lawyer: "*que les Jésuites étoient des hérédipets, des furets de succession, des fabrica-*

† *Mémoires des R.R.P.P. Jésuites du Collége de Colmar.* Geneva, Paris, Colmar.

Theory and Practice of the Vows 95

teurs des deux actes, dont était plainte et qu'il étoit temps d'avertir le public d'être en garde contre ces sortes de gens." The lawsuit concluded with an *accommodement, que le dit Collège (de Colmar) accepta pour le bien de la paix, et depuis il a vendu du vin provenant de la dite succession, au moyen de quoy il en a aquité plus de mille écus de dettes, de manière que de sept mille francs deübs par le défunt, il reste encore quatre mille livres et plus à payer au Collège de Strasbourg, tant en capitale qu'en intérest.*"*

From 1727: It is reported with satisfaction that *un marchand luthérien de Strasbourg* was *assez simple* to rent for sixty livres yearly an unused cellar belonging to the Jesuits, which had never brought in anything previously, and *son bail est pour 9 ans et sera avantageux au Collège*.† The above-mentioned lawsuit regarding the *fondation Sr Benoist Singler* reappears, but *on a trouvé que nous possédons la quantité de vignes, préz, terres labourables, jardins, contenus dans l'acte de la ditte donation.*‡ *Au mois d'Aoust de cette année on a loué les deux gros tonneaux qui étoient vuides, en sorte que le loyer de la cave est présentement de 228 livres.*§

From 1729: (If gain or loss were in question, the Jesuits made short work of it.) *Après avoir averti la ménagère de Turchheim que nous voulions finir avec elle, nous avons loué le petit jardin et le pré dont elle jouissoit, ce qui produit au Collège une rente de 21 livres.*∥ In July two advantageous purchases of houses were concluded *sous un nom emprunté*, and as *Monsieur le Stätmestre Charlepaur, un luthérien*, also endeavoured to get the houses, the sale was effected *en secret et au plus tot.*¶ The following entry shows how versed the Jesuits were in money-making: *La Demoiselle Dupuy, surnommée la Flamande, étant morte en 1727 après nous avoir donné 400 livres par son testament: le Père Beaujour pris des mesures en arrivant*

* *Mémoires*, pp. 47, 48. † p. 66. ‡ p. 69 *et seq.* § p. 70. ∥ p. 72. ¶ p. 74.

à Colmar pour être payé de la ditte somme, mais le Sieur du Puy n'étant pas en état d'y satisfaire en donnant de l'argent, on a tiré de luy des toiles et autres marchandises pour la valeur de la somme en question."*

The following remark is characteristic of the followers of Jesus: *Il y a longtemps que nous souhaitons de vendre du vin en gros par le moyen des gourmets de cette ville, mais enfin nous avons réussi cette année et nous en sommes redevables à Mr. Müller, Stätmestre, qui a engagé les gourmets à nous rendre service en nous faisant vendre nôtre vin aux Suisses.†*

From 1730: Under date of May 29th, it is reported that three fields at Vintzenheim had been let on lease, and the tenant *doit nous donner chaque année trois sacs de beau froment bien vanné et bien nettoyé, soit que les terres se reposent ou qu'elles soient ensemencées en orge et avoine.* These very favourable terms for letting, which held good in all circumstances, were confirmed, although it is reported of the three fields *deux étoient en friche et le troisième cultivé à grands frais et peu de profit.* The tenant was therefore regularly cheated.‡

The following is an instance of "Christian friendliness": The Dominicans had placed carts at the Jesuits' disposal free of charge, so that the vineyards of the Jesuit College might be prepared, *ce qui nous a épargné au moins 40 livres.* In return for this friendliness, the Jesuits prevented the Dominicans from taking foreign pupils.§ A Christian spirit also pervades the following: As the winter was severe, the Jesuits applied to the town for a consignment of wood. They received it in the form of 10 *cordes de bois.* But the Capuchins also seem to have received wood: *il est surprenant que les Capucins aient 30 cordes de bois chaque année et nous seulement douze.*‖

From 1731: *Le 6. du mois de May nous avons fait*

---

* *Mémoires*, p. 74. † pp. 78, 79. ‡ p. 81. § pp. 95, 126. ‖ p. 96 *et seq.*

acquisition de deux schatz [a square measure] *de terre labourable au canton dit Logelweg, ban d'Ingersheim, moyennant la somme de cent livres et trois livres de tringelt (Trinkgeld). Les raisons qui nous ont porté à faire cet achapt sont :* 1. *que ces deux schatz sont voisines des* 4 *autres que nous faisons planter en vigne ;* 2. *qu'il y a huit noyers dans les dittes deux schatz, lesquels noyers auroient donné beaucoup d'ombrage à la nouvelle vigne ;* 3. *que ne faisant pas cette acquisition, il auroit fallu fair une séparation entre l'autre propriétaire et nous, ce qui auroit couté considérablement.** . . . *Au mois d'Aoust de cette année nous avons appris que Mademoiselle Chauffour avoit fait son testament, et qu'elle nous avoit légué* 600 *livres. Pendant le mois de Décembre le P. Beaujour a veu la copie du testament de Mademoiselle Chauffour, où elle augmente son leg pieux de* 600 *livres, ainsi, si ce testament subsiste, nous toucherons après sa mort la somme de* 1,200 *livres.*†

From 1736: *Feu Madame Marguerine a légué à notre Église, pour orner le Saint-Sacrement,* 29 *perles fines.*‡

The Capuchins were also forbidden, at the instigation of the Jesuits, to take foreign pupils. This right, which brought material advantages with it, was reserved to the Jesuits.§ *Dans un temps auquel les vignes étoient fort recherchées à cause du prix excessif du vin,* the Jesuits sold a part of their vineyards for 1,272 livres *pour placer l'argent plus utilement ailleurs.*‖ Purchase of vineyards for 840, 640 124 livres.¶ Testamentary dispositions in favour of the Jesuits to a not insignificant amount.** Through the adroitness of their Rector, the Jesuits obtained gratis from different communities 460 *arbres de sapin non ordinaires mais extraordinairement longs et gros.* The whole was valued at 1,600 livres.†† Madame la Dauphine presented

---

* *Mémoires,* p. 99.   † pp. 107, 108.   ‡ p. 114.   § p. 114.   ‖ p. 115.
¶ pp. 117, 120.   ** p. 129 *et seq.,* pp. 132, 136, 143.   †† p. 135.

1,000 thalers to the college at the request of her confessor, the Jesuit Croust.* Favourable letting of vineyards, which did not bring in much,† etc., etc.

In 1762, the Chapter of Spalatro presented a memorial to the Venetian Senate in which it complained bitterly of the " intrigues and violence " of the Jesuits, who tried to seize upon everything

"Besides the handsome allowance which is settled on them from the public treasury for the maintenance of two missionaries, they have seized 2,000 ducats which fell to them as a legacy. The late Archbishop Bizza has also provided for them by another legacy of 8,000 sequins. In addition to this they possess several houses. They have let other houses; they have some properties in the Spalatro district, and still more important ones on the Island of Brazza. Consequently things have gone so far that three or four strangers [the Jesuits] are much better off than many spiritual communities, and especially than the Chapter of Spalatro, which consists of sixty persons and has a revenue of not more than 160 sequins."‡

The greed and covetousness of the Jesuits are brought out in a strong light through events in a German town:

A bitter and continuous feud had begun between the Jesuits and several Orders [shortly after the capture of Magdeburg in the Thirty Years' War] because, contrary to the text of the Edict of Restitution, the churches and Church property, which were refused to the Protestants, were not returned to the former possessors, these very Orders, but were taken possession of by the Jesuits who had no legal right to them. The Premonstrants, as well as the Benedictines and Cistercians, had had to suffer from the deeds of violence of the Jesuits. They saw how these sheltered themselves under the favour of the Emperor, who, in order to stamp out heresy the more effectively, would have preferred to transform all

* *Mémoires*, p. 141.   † p. 142.   ‡ *Le Bret Magazin*, 1, p. 188.

Theory and Practice of the Vows

the old monasteries into Jesuit colleges, academies and seminaries.*

Jesuit acquisitiveness frequently assumed such forms that even Popes intervened.

Urban VIII., in the Constitution *Ex debito* of February 22nd, 1622, forbids all members of Orders, " also those of the Society of Jesus," to carry on commerce. Clement IX. renewed this prohibition in the Constitution *Sollicitudo pastoralis* of June 17th, 1669, again calling special attention to the " Religious of the Society of Jesus." He lays stress on the fact that many from the above-mentioned Orders, consequently also from the Society of Jesus, had, in spite of the ecclesiastical laws, carried on commerce and had evaded the instructions of Urban VIII. by means of subterfuges and pretexts.†

It is noteworthy here that, whilst the remaining Orders are only mentioned in a general way (Mendicants and non-Mendicants), the Society of Jesus is specially mentioned and not less than nine times.‡

Two lawsuits of recent times reveal the avarice of the Jesuits and the roundabout ways in which they satisfy their rapacity in exactly the same hideous forms :

From May 13th to May 16th, 1864, the trial, which at the time agitated the whole world, of Benedict de Buck, accused of having threatened to kill the Belgian Jesuit Lhoire, was held at the Brussels Assizes. After the first few hours of the proceedings, however, it was no longer

* K. Wittig, *Magdeburg als katholisches Marienburg: Historische Zeitschrift* 1891, vol. 66, p. 60.

† *Acta Sanctae Sedis*, VII. (1872), 319 *et seq.*

‡ Duhr tries to soften down the special mention of the Jesuit Order when he writes (p. 645) that, according to Papal privileges, " the Society of Jesus was not understood in certain prohibitions, even if these had to do with all the spiritua Orders, unless specially mentioned." Duhr does not see that, if this is really as he says, the special mention of the " Society of Jesus " by Urban VIII. and Clement IX. is a convincing proof that the Jesuit Order had had an active share in commercial and financial operations. For otherwise, on account of the Papal privileges, it would not have been mentioned.

the accused, de Buck, who stood in the dock, but the Jesuits Lhoire, Hessels, Bossaert and Franqueville. They were convicted of having induced the millionaire, William de Boey, who died in Antwerp in 1850, to make a will which handed over his estate of millions to the Belgian Jesuits, unjustly passing over de Boey's poor relations (the de Bucks) and appointing a sham heir, the lawyer Valentyns, who was attached to the Jesuits and almost unknown to the testator. The accused, de Buck (who had uttered the threat in a rage at his unjust disinheritance brought about by the Jesuits), was acquitted, and the accusing Jesuits left the Assize Court branded as legacy-hunters.*

A lawsuit which took place in July, 1890, at Straubing, in Bavaria, likewise ended disadvantageously for the Jesuits. Personal recollections are connected with this:

In 1881, during my stay at Wynandsrade, my fellow-scholastic, Brother Karl Ebenhöch, died there from inflammation of the lungs. He had been my "guardian angel" during my postulancy at Exaeten. I therefore obtained permission to help in nursing him. I was a witness of his hard death-struggle and death. He repeatedly cried out during his last hours: "Mother, the money! Mother, the money!" The cry sounded to me so strange and weird that I made known my uneasiness to the Rector, the Jesuit Hermann Nix. He eased my mind and explained everything away by ascribing the cry to "inexplicable hallucinations of delirium." I only learnt after my departure from the Order that a lawsuit had taken place in 1890 before the jury at Straubing, in which the widowed mother of the late Karl Ebenhöch, Babette Ebenhöch, the Catholic priest of Kronungen, Johann Hartmann, the Jesuit, Hermann Nix, and a sum

* *Cf.* the pamphlet, *Der Jesuitenprozess in Brüssel.* Cologne and Düsseldorf, 1864.

of 66,000 marks had played the leading parts. The priest Hartmann was condemned to three years' imprisonment and ten years' loss of civil rights for inciting to perjury, and Frau Ebenhöch, whom Hartmann had incited to commit perjury, was acquitted. It appeared from the documents of the action that Frau Ebenhöch's son, the Jesuit Ebenhöch, who died in my presence, had inherited a sum of 66,000 marks from his grandmother. It was stated in the will that if the heir died without issue, the inheritance should pass to two aunts, his mother's sisters-in-law. The accused woman did not at first reply to the President's question as to what had become of the money after her son's death. And thus the President ascertained that the money had not come to the two aunts, but had been handed over to the Jesuits in Holland. Finally, the accused declared that 36,000 marks out of the 66,000 had been given back to her by the Jesuits. The two aunts sued for the delivering up of the inheritance for which the accused was responsible. The proceedings disclosed that Frau Ebenhöch had obtained the advice of the Jesuits, and especially that of the Jesuit, Hermann Nix, as to her action in the case. Letters from this Jesuit, but without any signature, dated from Ditton Hall, in England, where Nix was then the "spiritual father," *i.e.* the spiritual director of the theological scholastics, were found in Frau Ebenhöch's possession. The participation of the Jesuit Nix also follows from the letters of the priest Hartmann, who had induced the accused woman to make false affidavits as to her fortune. Nix is not called by his proper name in these letters, but "Mr. Dittonhall" (his place of residence in England), or "Mr. Widnes" (the Ditton Hall post town), and the remittances of the Jesuits to Frau Ebenhöch are mentioned as "the sending of pictures." A legal document drawn up in the Jesuit Nix's presence was read aloud in which young Ebenhöch bequeathed his wealth to the Jesuits. The priest Hartmann, who lied at the opening of the case, admitted finally with tears that he had only lied " because he had believed it to be his sacred duty not to expose the Jesuits." To the President's question as to whether the Jesuits, and especially the Jesuit Nix, were consequently at the bottom of the matter, Hartmann began a reply, but then stopped short. No doubt this was a reply.*

When the dying Ebenhöch's cry, " Mother, the money! " sounded in my ears, I had no idea of the story behind it, which was to be unfolded a few years later in the Assize Court of Lower Bavaria. I believed the statement of the Jesuit Nix, the chief culprit in the lawsuit, that the dying man had spoken in " inexplicable hallucinations of delirium."

All that has been said with reference to the wealth and the money-making of the Order and the love of luxury which sprang from it is confirmed by the strictly private *Memoirs* written by the Jesuit Cordara and so frequently quoted. Döllinger has brought this important document to light from the dust of the archives at Munich:

" Many reproach the Society with avarice and an extravagant lust for wealth. It caused a stir that the Society should be provided with such large revenues, and that in a short time its wealth should have reached and even surpassed that of the old Orders."

And its historiographer, for Cordara was this for thirty-five years, can give no other answer to the accusation than:

" That which is attributable to the piety of the faithful was imputed to the avarice and cunning of the Jesuits."†

Cordara therefore acknowledges the wealth of his

---

* The documentary account of the lawsuit, with its previous history, is to be found in the writing: *Der Jesuiten-Sensationsprozess des Pfarrer Hartmann von Kronungen verhandelt vor dem Schwurgerichte in Straubing.* Barmen, 1891.

† *Denkwürdigkeiten:* Döllinger, *Beiträge,* 3, 66.

Theory and Practice of the Vows

Order, but he traces back its origin to the "piety of the faithful," and abstains from saying that the "piety" was, as we have seen, largely stimulated by the "insinuations" and the "gratuitous" aid of the Jesuits.

Cordara's account of a conversation he had with the King of Sardinia is still more plain and incriminating:

The King told him that two things had been specially harmful to his Order—its boundless wealth (*divitias immodicas*) and its predominance over the other Orders. I replied · "This may be so (*id ita esse fortasse*). And so far as the wealth is concerned, I have frequently admitted that, although many colleges suffered from want, the whole Society might be called rich and opulent (*divitem et opulentam*)."*

Cordara, it is true, lays stress on the poverty and the simplicity of life of the individual Jesuits in opposition to the admitted wealth and luxury of the whole Society. But the results are poor. For he cannot unwrite the words which he sets down in a spirit of complaint and blame a few pages further on regarding the effeminacy and luxuriousness of individual Jesuits, of the "apostles," as he sarcastically calls them :†

". . Many of our 'apostles' wished for a quiet and inactive life under the shade of the colleges; they believed that they had worked very hard when they had spent the whole morning in hearing the confessions of a few pious women (*mulierculae*). . . . Many of them, after preaching once a week to a pious congregation of noblemen or merchants, devoted the rest of their time to the care of their bodies or to reading, or else spent it in intercourse with friends or unprofitable conversation. I myself have known 'apostles,' who not only shunned all labour and trouble, but were

---

* *Denkwürdigkeiten :* Döllinger, *Beiträge,* p. 35 *et seq.*

† To the King's reproach with regard to the Jesuit predominance over other Orders, Cordara replies by referring to the tyranny of the Dominicans, who as Inquisitors, had at their disposal against their antagonists "the dungeon and executioner" (*carceres lictoresque*).

more effeminate than women; who thought themselves very ill-used if they had to forgo their morning chocolate or their after-dinner nap, if they were deprived at any time of food or sleep. And yet these were men whom birth and education had not accustomed to luxury; on the contrary, they had from youth upwards received a hard, even a harsh training. Their effeminacy was acquired in the Society of Jesus."*

I will conclude this chapter with an amusing and doubtless true story from the satirical pen of Saint-Simon:

"When a fleet from India was unloading at Cadiz, eight large cases came to hand labelled 'Chocolate for the Most Venerable Father General of the Society of Jesus.' The cases were so exceedingly heavy as to cause curiosity as to their contents. They proved to be large balls of chocolate, the weight of which aroused suspicion. A ball was broken open, and gold was found concealed inside, covered by a layer of chocolate of the thickness of a finger. The Jesuits were informed of the circumstance; but these cunning politicians were very careful not to claim this valuable 'chocolate.' They preferred losing it to confessing."†

* *Denkwürdigkeiten:* Döllinger, *Beiträge*, p. 64 *et seq.*
† *Mémoires*, II., 433, 434.

CHAPTER XVII

THE CRITICISM CONTINUED: THEORY AND PRACTICE OF THE CONSTITUTIONS

Vows are more or less common to all Orders; it is the constitutions which show the special characteristics of each. So, too, in the case of the Jesuit Order. My intention is to show the great discrepancy between the theoretical excellence of the Jesuit Constitutions and the actual life and work of the Order.

It is, of course, impossible to refer to all the facts in question; a few important items must suffice.

THE ARROGANCE OF THE ORDER

The Constitutions overflow with humility; the glory of God is everything, the glory of the Order nothing. And indeed a Society of Jesus should be founded on humility. But it is only on paper that humility is the basis of the Society of Jesus. Its life and work are characterised by a spirit of unlimited arrogance. Though the Constitutions constantly refer to the Jesuit Order as " our poor little Society " (*minima societas*), in word and deed it assumes the rank of the greatest, the *maxima societas*, whose glory fills the world, and in comparison with which all else is small and mean. " God, I thank thee that I am not as other men are . . . or even as this publican." These hard and haughty words of the Pharisee express the real but unwritten motto of the Jesuit Order. Their current motto, "Everything to the greater glory of God" (*Omnia ad majorem Dei gloriam*), proclaimed aloud wherever they set foot, and graven in gold and stone on all their works, appears in the light of history to be a mere false pretence under the cloak of religion.

Hard words these, and before I attempt to justify them by the acts and declarations of the Order itself, I will make way for a man whose judgment on the Jesuit Order is of the first importance and whose heart was full of love and enthusiasm for it.

I refer to the Jesuit Cordara, of whom I have spoken before. For thirty-five years, up to the suppression of the Order in 1773, he held one of the most important positions, that of historiographer to the Order, which gave him official knowledge of everything, even the secret reports. After the suppression of the Order, Cordara published Memoirs, in which he raises this among other questions: "Why did God permit the suppression of the Jesuit Order?" Here is his answer:

"It is doubtless true that we had also grown accustomed to condoning numerous crimes according to human fashion. (*Multa etiam inter nos admitti consuevisse humano more crimina pro non dubio habendum.*) It may also be assumed that a special stain attached to the Society, which excited the wrath of God against us. Let us examine its nature more closely, although the Divine judgment be dark and far from human comprehension: The investigation will lead us, if not to positive, at least to probable conclusions. . . . I presume that it [the Society of Jesus] appeared holier than it was, in any case not of such holiness as is required by the Constitutions and the sacredness of our duties. . . Our churches were splendid, and their adornment expensive. The festivals of the saints were celebrated with pomp and splendour. But was it solely for the sake of religion, or rather to show off our power? This is hidden from men, who only see the exterior, but not from God, who proves hearts and reins. . . . I have often wondered why it was that with us any transgression against chastity was so severely punished, whereas our Superiors were so mild and indulgent towards other transgressions of a more grievous nature, such as backbitings, slanders, and revilings. And I believe that it was not because the former were worse and more displeasing to God, but because, if they had become known, they might have obscured the power and glory of the Society.* The sin of pride is secret. It creeps into good actions, so as to be hardly distinguishable from virtue. But God, Who seeth in secret, is not deceived. . . . Nothing is more hateful to God than pride. Nothing rouses His anger more or provokes Him to vengeance. God resists the proud, and gives His grace to the humble. But if we do not wish to deceive ourselves, we must confess that our community has suffered much from this disease. Our novice-masters filled us with this spirit when they impressed on our tender minds so great an estimate of the Society. They represented admission to the Society as an incomparable gift, a benefit of God, than which there could be no greater. They tell anecdotes of those who preferred the habit of the Society to tiara and purple. It is in vain that they afterwards combat pride after having sown such seeds of it. With this same spirit the youths are inspired during their studies, as no authors are praised except Jesuits, no books prescribed but such as are written by Jesuits, no examples of virtue quoted but such as are represented by Jesuits, so that these poor youths are easily convinced that the Society of Jesus excels all other Orders in learning and holiness. And some weak-minded persons even believe that everything praiseworthy done in the world was done under the auspices of our Society. This opinion, adopted in youth, the majority do not abandon in later life, and I know some old men who still continue to live in this delusion. And I confess that I myself was thus deluded for a long time. And all the external circumstances favoured this pride and arrogance. The magnificence of the buildings, the splendour of the churches, the pomp of the festivals, the favours of the populace inspired us with pride. Wherever we turned our eyes, we met with occasions for pride. . . . Then there was the

* Cordara's words are a valuable testimony to the fact that the Ordinance of General Acquaviva, not to punish breaches of chastity if they have not given rise to public scandal, is generally observed.

great multitude of our flatterers, who spoke to us almost solely about the superior merits of the Society and the defects of other Orders. . . . There were certain differences, too, between the Society of Jesus and the other Orders, so that the main body of Jesuits believed that they had nothing in common with members of other Orders and considered them as greatly inferior. . . . Another source of pride within the Society was the noble rank of many Jesuits. As all [Jesuits] treated one another as brothers, even those who were not of the nobility seemed to acquire that rank, and were regarded outside the Order as aristocrats. . . . The entire Society of Jesus, at least in Italy, was permeated by irrational pride, and but rarely a Jesuit gave precedence to a member of the nobility. Even our lay brothers regarded themselves as noble, and on this account better than members and priests of other Orders. I may quote here an occurrence, true, though almost incredible, which happened to me when I was staying for my health at the country house of the Roman College at Albano. One of our lay brothers named Jarolfo was there as manager of the country house and other property belonging to the *Collegium Romanum*. Although himself the son of a peasant, he was much honoured by the villagers as the superintendent of great possessions and treated almost as a prince (*dynasta*). He told me that at some festivals he was invited to the banquets of the Franciscans, and boasted that on such occasions the seat of honour usually occupied by the superintendent of the monastery was given to him. I reproved him gently, and tried to make him understand that he should take precedence of lay brothers, but not of priests, which latter was not seemly. To which he replied in irritation (*stomachans*) : ' As if lay brothers of our Society were not equal to the priests of other Orders.' So much superior our people deemed themselves to those of other Orders. The majority of Jesuits believed that they had nothing in common with other Orders, and considered them as greatly inferior to themselves . . . Of these differences [between other Orders and the Order of the Jesuits] the Jesuits boasted, and held them as marks of distinction and deemed themselves above all other monks. . . . All this [the merits of the Dominicans] most of our people either ignored or deprecated, and considered themselves equal or superior to the

Dominicans; their opposition they declared to be creditable to themselves, and whatever could break the power of this most powerful Dominican Order, and obscure its reputation, they attributed to their own glory. On all other Orders they looked with something approaching contempt. They were continually bragging of their Bellarmin, Suarez, Sirmond, Petavius [famous Jesuit authors], and boasted the more insolently of the merits of these others, because they themselves, having little or no knowledge of the history of literature, believed that hardly one other first-class author existed besides those mentioned. . . . I have known few among my fellows, who preferred foreign [non-Jesuit] preachers or scholars to their own, but many who despised and ridiculed them. Another more subtle kind of pride I seem to have recognised in that immaculate chastity of the members so much extolled by the multitude, and I do not know if God has not been provoked by this very pride to desire the destruction of the Society. Chastity was highly valued by the Jesuits; they basked in its splendour, they boasted of being distinguished by it from other monks. I have often heard them say that much that was disgraceful was spread abroad about other Orders, many bad examples were set by them, but that nothing of the kind happened among the Jesuits. By means of such talk they were not only tempted to secret vainglory, but they took occasion in consequence to lord it over other Orders, and to despise these latter as the scum of humanity. They did not consider that the boast of chastity is as nothing in God's eyes if love be not added unto it, and that in the Gospel those virgins were called foolish who had not the oil of love in their lamps. They did not consider that before God humility is worth more, and is more excellent, than chastity."*

To these words, so full of emotion and religious feeling, I need add nothing of my own. It will suffice to quote a few more facts from the Order's endless record of arrogance.

It was revealed to Saint Mary Magdalene of Pazzi that God in heaven delighted so greatly in two saints, that it was as if there were no other saints in heaven

* Cordara, S.J., *Denkwürdigkeiten*. Döllinger, *Beiträge*, 3, 64-74.

beside them; these were St. John the Evangelist and St. Ignatius Loyola.*

The Jesuit Ludovicus Mansonius, Provincial of the Neapolitan Province, a particularly prominent member of the Order, reports that Christ had appeared to the sainted virgin Johanna ab Alexandro, a penitent of his confessional, on the seventh of June, 1598, in the Jesuit church at Naples, and had said to her:

" I desire that everyone should love the Society [of Jesus] specially, because it is My Society, and I constantly bear it in My heart, and cannot allow that a member thereof should suffer from any greater fault. . . Know also, O My daughter, that as long as My Society continues, and I desire that, being named with My name, it should continue to the end of the world, I require this one thing of its members, that they walk in My footsteps."†

In the discussion on the surrender of the Carolinian Academy at Prague to the Jesuits, the Order declared:

" No one could watch more carefully or conscientiously over the maintenance of the Catholic Faith in the kingdom, no one could distinguish more accurately and safely between true and false doctrine, finally no one could better train the young in piety and good conduct, than the Society of Jesus, which disregarded all earthly gain or profit, and was wholly consecrated to virtue and religion." ‡

The Jesuits Höver and Miller write ·

" The reputation of the comparatively new Society of Jesus began just at that time to spread more and more. Its founder,

---

* See Döllinger-Reusch, *Moralstreitigkeiten*, II., 350.

† *Ibid.*, I., 529, and II., 346. The "revelation" on the retaining of the name—Society of Jesus—is a favour "from Heaven" to Sixtus V., who, having resolved to alter the name, died suddenly in 1590, and perhaps also a warning "from heaven" to his successors not to expose themselves to a similar fate. *Comp.* Hübner, *Sixte-Quint* (Paris, 1870), II., 54, 55.

‡ Tomek, *Geschichte der Prager Universität* (Prague, 1849), p. 253.

Saint Ignatius Loyola, had recently been beatified by Paul V.; the fame of Francis Xavier, the Apostle of India and Japan, filled the Catholic world. Peter Canisius was considered the 'hammer of heretics' in Germany; Spain was proud of her Duke of Gandia, the humble holy Jesuit Francis Borgia; Laynez, and Salmeron had distinguished themselves in the Council of Trent as extremely learned theologians; Aloysius and Stanislaus were venerated as examples to the young, and 'angels in the flesh'; Bellarmin and Suarez were quoted by all people of culture. News penetrated to Europe from Japan, India, China, and the rest of the foreign missions of the splendid successes of Jesuit missionaries. From England came reports of the glory of their preachers and martyrs, of a blessed Father Edmund Campian, Garnet, Parsons, and so many others. Germany boasted, besides the blessed Father Canisius, of a venerable Johannes Rem, and of many other notable preachers and great men. The schools and universities of the Jesuits vied with the best establishments of Europe. . . . When Donna Arsilia Altissimi heard the funeral bell of the Roman College in the morning of the 13th of August, she said to her two daughters : 'A Jesuit must have died just now; come, let us pray for his soul.' They knelt down at the altar of their private chapel, and (to quote her statements on oath): 'With Victoria and Anna I desired, beads in hand, to say the *De Profundis* for the dead, but; strange to say, the *Te Deum* rose to my lips instead. I tried for a second, third, and fourth time, but never could utter the *De Profundis*. Then my daughter Victoria tried, but she could not say it either, but said against her will : 'Glory be to the Father, and to the Son, and to the Holy Ghost.' We marvelled, and said to one another: 'A great saint must have died in the College.' In the afternoon we went to the Church of the College, and found an enormous crowd of people in it. There we heard that a young Belgian Father [the Jesuit Berchmanns, canonised by Leo XIII.] had died in the odour of sanctity. . . .

"On August 14th, 1621, at four o'clock in the morning, the Jesuit lay-brother, Thomas di Simoni, was favoured with the following revelation : He saw heaven open. From a lofty, shining throne of clouds he beheld Mary, Queen of Angels, descending to him. Two princes of heaven carried her on a splendid throne.

One of them was robed in a white surplice. As he was on the other side of the Queen of Heaven, the lay brother could not see his face, but he thought it must have been St. Aloysius [also a Jesuit]. The other was Johannes Berchmanns in the habit of the Jesuits."*

The bombastically boastful words of the Jesuit Löffler, quoted in Chapter V., on the Marian Congregations, are applicable here too, also the arrogant "revelations" as to the predestination of all Jesuits to salvation and above all a literary monument of pride, self-erected by the Order.

The work, *Imago primi saeculi Societatis Jesu*, "A Picture of the First Century of the Society of Jesus," appeared in 1640 at Antwerp. On account of their unbounded arrogance, its contents gradually grew extremely unpleasant to the Order. How much this work was felt to be an incubus by the Order was proved by the communication made by Gerhard van Swieten to Maria Theresa on December 24th, 1759, according to which the Order was trying to buy up all the copies at high prices.

"*Le 'saeculum primum societatis' est tel que la Société [de Jésus] rachepte tous les exemplaires à grand prix pour anéantir la mémoire, s'il fût possible. . . . Ce livre fera toujours la confusion de la Société.*"†

To this day the Jesuits try to represent the "Imago" as "essays of young scholastics," or, as the Jesuit Duhr expresses it, merely "a poetical and rhetorical festival oration."‡ The attempt is thoroughly dishonest.

The mere outward form of the folio volume published by the then famous Plantin Press (Balthasar Moretus), almost 1,000 pages, typed and illustrated with obtrusive

---

* *Leben des heiligen Johannes Berchmanns* (Dülmen, 1901), p. 50 f, 190 f, 194.

† Contributed by Fournier, Gerhard van Swieten als Zensor : *Sitzungsberichte der philosophisch-historischen Klasse der Kaiserlichen Akademie der Wissenschaften*, v. 24, p. 454.

‡ *Jesuitenfabeln*, p. 560.

luxuriousness, such that Crétineau-Joly is forced to admit "*le luxe de la typographie et l'art de la gravure,*"* contradicts the repeated assertion of Jesuits as to "mere exercises in style of young scholastics." "Mere exercises" are not published in such luxurious garb. Indeed the title-page states that the Flemish-Belgian Province of the Order had "designed" the "picture": *Imago . . . a provincia flandro-belgica . . . repraesentata*, and in the *Imprimatur* of January 8th, 1640, the Jesuit Johannes van Tollenare, Provincial Superior of the Flemish-Belgian Province, says:

"After three theologians of our Society had revised the book, 'A Picture of the First Century of the Society of Jesus,' drafted by the Flemish-Belgian Province of the Order of the same Society."

The portentous volume is, therefore, the description of the life and work of the Society of Jesus, *officially* drafted by one of its Provinces and presented to the Society on the special occasion of the centenary celebration of the Society of Jesus.

In these circumstances it would be absolutely impossible to speak of insignificance in connection with the *Imago*, even if its authors had been really "young scholastics." For the prestige they lacked would be amply supplied by that of the three theologians who were commissioned by the Provincial to examine the work and who passed it for press. Above all, there would be the important prestige of a whole "Province," which adopted and published the contents of the work as its intellectual property.

But the Jesuitical evasion as to the scholastic authorship may be refuted from the work itself. For the very preface states that the work had been composed and published by very busy men (*conceptum, compositum ab*

* *Histoire de la Compagnie de Jésus*, 3, 471.

hominibus occupatissimis), an expression utterly inapplicable to scholastics, and on page 24 it says that the strenuous occupation of the authors consisted of preaching, teaching of various branches of knowledge, and performance of the other offices of the Society. But such occupations are not for scholastics.

These words of the *Imago* were naturally known to the Jesuit Duhr. Yet he writes untruthfully of " poetical and rhetorical festival orations " and of the " poetical and rhetorical effusions of the Jesuits and Jesuit students " which had been " collected " in the *Imago*.*

Through the irony of history, however, Duhr was given the lie by one of his own Order. The Jesuit Bremer confesses, in his small Church Lexicon,† that the author and designer of the *Imago* was no less a person than the chief hagiographer of the Order, the Jesuit Bollandus, whose name is on the gigantic work *Acta Sanctorum*. Let us, however, assume Duhr's gross prevarication to be true. If young scholastics had really collaborated in the work, this would render its significance the greater. For the deduction would be that the contents of the *Imago* are the genuine embodiment of the true Jesuit spirit, that spirit in which the young scholastics of the Order have themselves been trained, that spirit which is fostered in them by the Order itself from the first hour of their novitiate, as the Jesuit Cordara has so well described it.

Besides, the written work of students is submitted to the strictest supervision and examination by their superiors. And if the spirit of the *Imago* had not been the genuine spirit of the Jesuits, how could a whole Province with its head have backed the young students, and have imprinted on their work the official stamp of its approval ? No ! the magnificent volume, *Imago primi saeculi Societatis*

---

* Duhr, *Jesuitenfabeln*, pp. 506, 507.
† *Kirchliches Handlexikon* (Munich, 1907), I., 685.

The Constitutions

Jesu, is a Jesuit product, the genuineness and originality of which it would be hard to match, and it is, therefore, of the first importance in forming an estimate of the Jesuit system. It is true that the estimate must be based on the point of view of religious asceticism.

The Order of the Jesuits is a religious Order. It even professes to be a prominent type of what the Church of Rome calls " the state of an Order, state of Christian perfection "—so prominent as to consider itself justified in taking to itself the name of the Founder of the Christian religion, the ideal of Christian perfection, the name of Jesus Christ. But the essential characteristics of Jesus are humility, absence of self-aggrandisement, of all self-praise, all vainglory, or boasting of His own actions.

From this point of view of Christ, an estimate of the *Imago* and the spirit which produced it must be condemnatory. Not the spirit of Christ is expressed in it, but the anti-Christian spirit of what Catholic asceticism, in strongest aversion, calls " the world." Most substantial pride, vain arrogance, immeasurable ambition abound in this centennial volume. Spiritual pride it was, that cardinal sin against which the Scriptures so specially warn Christians, which alone indited the composition of the *Imago,* so exclusively and so emphatically indeed that, even if the work had been the product of a secular society, not obliged to follow ascetic principles in the description of its actions, the excess of self-glorification displayed in it would still be loathsome and revolting.

In the first place, let us look at the illustrations of the *Imago*

The title-page displays, in the figure of a virgin, the Society of Jesus enthroned on the back of Chronos, the God of time. Above it are floating angels, holding crowns of victory with the inscriptions: To the teacher (*doctori*), the martyr (*martyri*), the virgin (*virgini*). On lofty columns there are two angels blowing trumpets, whence issue scrolls with the words · " Loyola embraces a hundred years," and " May he encompass the whole world." Six shields, borne by angels, represent the birth of the Society of Jesus, the spread of the Society over the whole earth, the Society as benefactress of the world, the Society growing famous through persecutions, the Society loved by Belgium (referring to the publication of the *Imago* by the Belgian-Flemish Province). Like the frontispiece are the illustrations of the text. Under the superscription: " The Society of Jesus," is a picture of the sun shining on the globe; below this the verse of the Psalm: " And nothing is hid from the heat thereof."* Under the heading: " Prophecy for the coming century of the Society of Jesus," a picture of Noah's Ark† floating on the waters. Under the heading: " The Society of Jesus spread over the whole globe fulfils the prophecy of Malachi: ' For from the rising of the sun even unto the going down of the same, My name is great among the Gentiles; and in every place incense shall be offered unto My name, and a pure offering,' " the two hemispheres are represented.‡ Under the heading: " The Society spreads the faith over the whole world," a picture of four trumpets resounding from clouds, below which is the verse of the Psalm: " Their line is gone out through all the earth."§ Under the heading: " Conversion of kingdoms and provinces by the Society of Jesus," a picture of the globe suspended and floating freely from an elaborate pulley, with an angel turning the lever; below this: " Give her a foothold and she will move the earth," and below a bombastic poem on this gigantic feat of " the descendants of Loyola."|| Under the heading: " The Society equipped for missions," a picture of lightning darting from clouds, and splitting rocks, below this a verse from the book of Job: " He

* P. 43. † P. 51. ‡ P. 318. § P. 320. || P. 321.

The Constitutions

sendeth lightnings, that they may go, and returning say unto him, Here we are."*

Under the heading: "The Indian Missions of the Society," a picture of an angel with a bow and arrow, standing between the two hemispheres; below this: "One sphere does not suffice."† Under the heading: "The Society's task is to act and suffer strenuously," a picture of a bull standing between ploughshare and sacrificial altar; below this, "Ready for either."‡ Under the heading: "The Society exhausts itself without remuneration in the service of its neighbour," a picture of a fountain with sevenfold jet; below this the words from Isaiah: "Ho, everyone that thirsteth, come ye to the waters buy without money and without price."§ Under the heading: "Congregation of the Blessed Virgin," a picture of the Milky Way, extending across the nocturnal sky; below this: "The way to the Heights."‖ Under the heading: "The Society by precept and example shows the way to salvation," a picture of three angels holding torches with flames uniting into one; below this the words: "The light itself enflaming giveth light, though lightened for others."¶ Under the heading: "Education of Boys," a picture of an eagle teaching her young to fly; below this the verse of the Scriptures: "As the eagle sheweth her young to fly."** Under the heading, "The Society trained to fight during a whole century," a picture of a strong arm, proceeding from the clouds, holding a flag rent by the storm; below this the words: "It hath beauty greater than its own."†† Under the heading: "The Society is in vain attacked by its enemies," a picture of a crowd of men wearing fool's caps aiming arrows at the sun; below this: "No arrow hits the sun."‡‡ Under the heading: "The frequent fastings of Ignatius enduring for several days,"

---

* P. 324. † P. 326. ‡ P. 453. § P. 455. ‖ P. 464.
¶ P. 466. ** P. 470. †† P. 564. ‡‡ P. 565.

a picture of a bird of Paradise flying across desert lands, below this: "He lives on little, because he is close to heaven."*

All these pictures are explained by long poems, overflowing with complacency and self-righteousness.

The poems suggest the text of the work, which is composed of poetry and prose. Setting aside the poetry, I will proceed to give specimens of the prose: The Preface declares Jesus to be the sun, and the Order of the Jesuits the moon; it also remarks that it is useless to supply the Preface with a date, as this is naturally suggested by the universal rejoicing at the centenary jubilee of the Society of Jesus. Still, the authors seem to have been somewhat afraid of the accusation of vainglory, and they therefore say "modestly" · "Our work could not be under suspicion of conceit, as though we wished to praise ourselves or our own. The Society is wholly the work of God and not of men. We glorify God's work. Has He not often commanded that His works should be extolled with the highest praises? Nor need we keep silence concerning the praise of our forefathers for fear of sounding our own. Those whom God has employed as helpers and labourers in so great a work could not be omitted from our presentment; their merits are new, divine benefits declared merely as a public thanksgiving."

The conclusion is in harmony with the introduction. When the praise of the Society of Jesus had been continuously proclaimed for 949 folio pages, we read on page 950: "If we take into account the merits of the Society and the desires of its members, much yet remains to be said. But, in order to bring it to a conclusion, let us greet it [the Society of Jesus] with the words of most eminent men, but recently written or spoken." Then follow laudatory comments by Popes and other persons.

* P. 715.

The work is divided into six books. The synopsis at the end of the preface gives an excellent general impression of the arrogant spirit pervading the whole, as a short sketch of the contents of each book, based on a passage of Scripture referring to Christ, institutes a comparison between the Jesuit Order and a definite period in the life of Christ: "Who being in the form of God . . made Himself of no reputation, and took upon Him the form of a servant," and was born a beggar in a stable. Thus the first book will show how Ignatius, a descendant of the highest nobility, became a beggar, and as a result this "poor little Society" was founded. After the birth of Christ we are told of Him: "'Jesus increased in wisdom and stature, and in favour with God and man.' Following in His footsteps, we shall describe in the second book the growth of the Society," etc., etc.

The first book is preceded by an introduction, consisting of seven dissertations. They contain this passage: "Those who have died in the Society of Jesus have fulfilled a century, for age is not measured by the length and number of years, but wisdom is better in men than grey hairs."* The first book describes "The Birth of the Society." "When that monster of the universe, that fatal plague, Martin Luther, had cast out all religion from his mind, and had divested himself not only of the garb of religion, but also of all its external forms, even the fear of sin . . . did not the warrior Ignatius face him in the arena?"† As Christ Himself, so also the Jesuit Order was foretold by the prophets.‡ Jesus Himself is the true founder of the Society. "It is evident that the Society of Jesus is distinguished as to time only from the community of the Apostles. It is not a new order, but only a renewal of that first religious community whose one only founder was Jesus."§ The name "Society of

* P. 35.   † P. 55.   ‡ Pp. 59–64.   § Chap. III., p. 65.

Jesus" was revealed to Ignatius by God Himself.* "By no other means is chastity so much endangered as by the other sex, which often, without any participation of its own, weakens resolution, shakes firmness and suddenly precipitates the highest virtue into the abyss."†

The subject of the second book is the growth of the Society. In ten chapters, four discourses and eighteen poems,‡ with bombastic self-glorification, the spread of the Order of the Jesuits over the whole world is traced to the Order's intrinsic merit. Fifteen pages are filled with funeral orations (*elogia sepulcralia*) on Ignatius and his first disciples, which vie with one another in arrogant expression.§ The third book describes the actual work of the Society. In preaching, instruction and education, the Jesuit Order attains the most excellent results. By its means morality and piety have been restored, its charity is unlimited.‖ The successful activity of the Jesuit Order in the confessionals is described and praised in these frivolous words: "How crowded they are everywhere! How often has the industrious zeal of our confessors been insufficient for the number of penitents. Crimes are now redeemed more cheerfully and eagerly than they were formerly committed. . . . The majority wash off their sins almost as soon as they have burdened themselves with them."¶ The chariot of God described by the prophet Ezekiel foreshadows the Jesuit Order, "as any honest critic may easily recognise."** The noble spirit of the Jesuits (*generositas*) is eloquently praised.†† Through the sagacity of its members, the Jesuit Order resembles the eagle. . . . Equipped with wisdom, virtue, mental qualities, sagacity, and industry, they distinguish truth from falsehood; they examine, perceive, and understand everything, nor do they occupy the

Chap. IV.   † P. 92.   ‡ Pp. 204–330.   § Pp. 280–295.
‖ Pp. 331–400.   ¶ P. 372.   ** P. 401.   †† P. 403.

The Constitutions

lowest place in the arena of art and science. All that is flourishing in the humanities, all the intricacies of philosophy, all the hidden things in Nature, all the difficulties in mathematics, all the mysteries of the Godhead shining in darkness would be proclaimed by their works, which fill great libraries, though I were to pass them over in silence."* This self-praise continues for another seventy-four folio pages of prose and verse.†

The fourth book deals with the tribulations of the Order‡; these are unmerited; their chief cause is the hatred of the wicked against the Jesuits. On the slanders directed against the Order: "The Son of Man came eating and drinking [the Society of Jesus came after the example of its leader, contenting itself with ordinary food and raiment] and they say: 'Behold a glutton, a drunkard,' the Society is soft, luxurious, effeminate."§

The fifth book revels in a display of honours gained by the Order of the Jesuits.‖ One chapter (the fifth) is filled with miracles wrought by Jesuits. The next chapter describes the heroic virtues practised in the Order. The eighth chapter proves from special "revelations" that everyone who dies a Jesuit goes to heaven. "It is the privilege of the Society of Jesus that Jesus Himself comes to meet every dying Jesuit."¶ The ninth chapter enumerates the honours shown to the Order of the Jesuits by Popes, kings and princes. In the tenth chapter the list of honours is continued by quotations from panegyrics on the Jesuits by famous men, among them a bishop: "O sacred Society, formerly not sufficiently known or appreciated by me, thou excellest the pastoral staff, mitres, cardinal's purple, sceptres, empires and crowns!"**
It is significant that this fifth book, which extols the honours of the Jesuit Order, contains nearly the

* P. 406 et seq.   † Pp. 406-480.   ‡ Pp. 481-580.   § P. 559.
‖ Pp. 581-727.   ¶ Pp. 648, 649.   ** P. 667.

largest number of pages (147) of the six books of the *Imago*.

The sixth book, extolling the glorious achievements of the Flemish-Belgian Province of the Order, which concludes the work, displays to the last the same arrogant spirit and hatred of Luther. On page 937, the Belgian lion is depicted with the Jesuit emblem on its breast, inscribed all over with the names of Belgian-Flemish Settlements of the Jesuits. Below the picture is a poem, entitled: " The sun [*i.e.* the sign or emblem of the Jesuits] on the Belgian lion." Here is a verse of this poem:

" He [the Belgian lion] bears Loyola's emblem graven on his breast. Greeting from afar with bowed neck the divine [Ignatius], he rejoices to lick his sacred feet."

Enough of quotations. Those given are not forced and far-fetched passages, but real, ordinary samples.

Whoever has struggled through this folio volume, so full of hatred for those of different faith, and above all, of endless self-praise, of pompous prayers to God, Christ, and Mary, all to the tune of " We Jesuits are specially favoured, holy, perfect," of boasts, of exploits, and good works accomplished by the Jesuit Order, while realising at the same time that it is all meant to be a picture of the essence and history of the " genuine associates of Jesus " (*genuini Jesu Socii*), must needs recall the words of Jesus:

" Take heed that ye do not your alms before men, to be seen of them . . . Therefore when thou doest thine alms, do not sound a trumpet before thee, as the hypocrites do in the synagogues and in the streets, that they may have glory of men . . . let not thy left hand know what thy right hand doeth. . . . And when thou prayest, thou shalt not be as the hypocrites are; for they love to pray standing in the synagogues and in the corners of the streets, that they may be seen of men."*

* Matt. vi. 1-5.

"So likewise ye, when ye shall have done all those things which are commanded you, say, We are unprofitable servants: we have done that which was our duty to do."*

In the light of these and similar words of Jesus Christ, the hollowness, nay falsity, of the "Picture of the First Century of the Society of Jesus" must appear as obvious and clear.

The magnificent volume of the *Imago* supplies overwhelming testimony to the correct opinion of the comparatively honest Jesuit Cordara, who from his orthodox Christian point of view saw in the suppression of the Jesuit Order a judgment of God on their arrogance and pride · "for God resisteth the proud."†

THE RELATION OF THE ORDER TO WOMEN

In the Constitutions and history of the Order there are two chapters on this subject which almost contradict one another.

While Jesus and His disciples stood in simple and natural relationship to women, and innocently admitted them as followers and helpers, the Society of Jesus takes up a position towards women which in theory is distorted and unnatural, and in practice selfishly exploits them.

In theory it sees in woman the dangerous and intellectually inferior sex, to be surrounded by danger signals and warnings; in practice it treats her as a docile creature, easily influenced, whose devotion is of high value to the Order.

The theory contained in the Constitutions of the Order is thus expressed:

* Luke xvii. 10. † I. Pet. v. 5.

" Jesuits are not to undertake the regular cure of souls for nuns or other women, but they may on occasion (*semel*) hear confessions of nuns, of one convent for some special reason." * In hearing confessions of women they should be severe rather than familiar. If obliged to speak to women outside the confessional, it should be in a public place and with downcast eyes. If any priest be sent to women by his Superior to hear confession, or for some other purpose, the companion assigned to him by his Superior [generally a lay brother] is to be in a place where he can see both parties, so long as the priest may be engaged with the women, but out of earshot of any secret conversation, so far as the place admits of this; if it does not, the priest is to be careful that the door should remain open, and that the meeting should not take place in a dark spot.

" The cure of individual souls, especially of women, should not be undertaken by our members.† When they [lay brothers] accompany our priests on visits, especially to women, they are to observe carefully what rules are prescribed for priests. Besides, they ought to know that they are obliged on their return to report to the Superior without being questioned by him, if [during the visit] these rules have been in any way disregarded." ‡

He [the Superior] is not to allow our priests to visit women nor to write to them except in an urgent case, or in the hope of great results, and even then he is only to allow it to experienced and prudent men.§ The rule, that the companion of a priest visiting women or hearing their confessions should report to the Superior, if Rule 18 [presence of the companion during the visit or confession] has been observed, is to be maintained so strictly that the Superior is to impose on the companion omitting the report a penance of three scourgings, besides one in public. In case of repetition, the matter should be reported to the General, who will then consider if such persons can remain members of the Order.||

* Constit. VI., 3, 5.   † Rules 16–19 for the Priests.
‡ Rule 72 for the Superior of Professed Houses, and Rule 70 for the Rector.
§ Rule 5 for Lay-brothers.
|| From an epistle of General Acquaviva, Nov. 13th, 1607. *Inst. S.J.*, II. 308 *et seq.*

The Constitutions

"Our members (*nostri*) should know that not only priests, in going to women for the purpose of confession or for other reasons, should strictly observe Rule 18 on the continual presence of the companion, *i.e.* that so long as they are engaged with the women the companion is to be where he can see them, but not hear what is to remain a secret; but that all lay brothers are under this law, whether they themselves visit women or accompany others of our people . . . And the companions should know that they must report to the Superior anything that may have occurred contrary to this rule and ordination without being questioned by him immediately on their return.*

"If the place where the sick woman is lying is so small that the companion of the confessing priest cannot be present, the former must report to the Superior immediately on his return [that the confession of the sick woman had been heard without the companion's presence], and the Superior should consider if the Father should go to this place a second time, or if, as I [the General of the Order, Acquaviva] should be more inclined to think, the care of the invalid should be left to the parish priests."†

As regards the advancement of their spiritual life, *e.g.* by Exercises, women are placed in a line with uneducated people (*rudibus*). The particular meditations (of the Spiritual Exercises) are to be set before women in church, and in doing this great care must be taken that no suspicion or offence may arise. For this reason it may be well to give the points of meditation to women not in writing but verbally, lest people should think there was an exchange of letters. If anything has to be given in writing, it should be done quite secretly.‡

An ugly spirit meets us here. It is, of course, in the first instance, the general ultramontane spirit, already noted, which estimates and judges woman only as an "immediate occasion for sin." But here also we meet with a

* *Monita generalia*, 3. *Ibid.* II., 215.
† *Instructio III. pro Confessariis Societatis*, II., 285.
‡ *Directorium*, 9, 16; *Inst. S.J.*, II., 435.

striking speciality of the Jesuits: to the general sexual contempt of women the Order adds as its own specific a certain social classification.

In a secret instruction by General Mercurian to the Provincial Superior of the Upper German Province, the Jesuit Hoffäus, quoted by Döllinger-Reusch* from the Jesuit manuscripts in the State Archives at Munich (confiscated on the suppression of the Order in 1773), we read: "Women of rank, who must, however, at least be baronesses (*haec facultas ad eas, quae sunt infra statum Baronissarum extendenda non est*), may enter colleges of the Society of Jesus. But care should then be taken that steady matrons, and not young ladies (*adolescentulae*) should be the companions of the lady of rank."

"Most carefully," writes another General of the Order, "familiarity with women of poor or low estate (*familiaritas tenuiorum et ignobilium feminarum*) should be avoided, as they are more exposed to suspicion and danger."†

An "instruction" of the sixth General Congregation of the year 1608 is still more explicit. The interesting words show how skilfully rigid theory may turn into indulgent practice when the transformation seems desirable for the advantage of the Order:

"Since custom has decreed, to the loss of much time and spiritual advantage, that visits and greetings should be exchanged [with women], we deem it necessary to give definite instruction as regards the strict observance of the rule on not visiting women. Certainly we may but rarely hope for great advantage therefrom except in cases of necessity (*e.g.* illness, mourning, death, or some religious ceremony). But as the customs of the Society, and the benefits received, and a certain discourtesy implied by refusing these, do not permit that visits to women should be forbidden to all

---

* *Moralstreitigkeiten*, I., 250.

† Instruction of General Acquaviva, Jan. 1st, 1604. *De Spiritu ad Superiores*, c. 5 *de castitate*. *Ibid.* II., 272.

our members, a certain modification [of the rule] is required. At present we think it most appropriate that regard should be paid not only to the persons to be visited, but also to those of our members who are to pay the visit. Three conditions are necessary in order that a woman be found worthy (*ut digna existimetur*) of being visited by our people. In the first place, she must be a person of rank and distinction (*persona nobilis et primaria*); for there is no need to show special courtesy to all pious women of whatever estate they be, as such may be sufficiently helped and instructed in our churches in confession and pious discourse. Secondly, the woman in question must have uncommon merit as regards services rendered the Society. Thirdly, the act of courtesy must be welcome to her husband or her relations."*

This division of the female sex into aristocratic and non-aristocratic women, and the different treatment based upon it, may be traced back to the founder of the Jesuit Order, Ignatius Loyola, and is thus an original characteristic of the Jesuits. In confidential communications on himself, dictated to his amanuensis, the Jesuit Gonzalez, we read · "He [Ignatius] said : 'We must behave prudently, and have no intercourse with women, except with those of very high rank "† (*nisi essent admodum illustres*).

And now to pass from theory to practice.

There we find that Jesuits very soon and very generally break through the wire fencing drawn by their Constitutions round women, and show no prudence at all in their intercourse with them. I have already quoted, in speaking of the theory and practice of the vows of chastity, the accusing testimony of the Jesuit Hoffäus, the Visitator of the Upper German Province. To this may be added as still more weighty, because founded on a still more universal knowledge of things pertaining to the Order, the complaint of General Acquaviva in a circular epistle to the whole Order, dated December 21st, 1605:

* *Instructio III. pro Confessariis Societatis*, 1, 9; II., 286.
† *Acta S.S.*, Julii 7, 653.

"Lay-brothers [who accompany visiting priests] should be exhorted that, on returning home in the evening, they must report to the Superior if the rule [concerning the manner in which women are to be visited] has been neglected by the priest or any other for any reason whatever, and those who show themselves to be less conscientious in this should be treated with severity, and their confessors should be exhorted to reprimand them sharply, if they do not observe this rule. . . . As regards hearing confessions [of women] in church, the Superiors are charged to have the confessionals erected in exposed places and in such a manner that confessors may, as it were, be companions one to another; the Superior should also occasionally investigate if the confessionals have not perchance been moved from their position, and if the gratings are still intact and narrow."*

Especially this last remark, on the confessionals not being displaced and on the gratings being intact and narrow, forces us to the conclusion that there were gratings which had been damaged and widened for unmistakable purposes.

An enlarged grating seems to have existed between the English Jesuit Garnet, whose acquaintance we have already made, and his penitent, Lady Anne Vaux. Passages from letters of the lady to the Jesuit seem, at any rate, to point to an earthly rather than heavenly love, and in any case their tone contrasts strongly with that prescribed in the Constitutions of the Order. Thus Lady Anne signs on one occasion: "Yours and not my own, A.V." And furthermore: "To live without you is not life, but death. O that I might see you!"†

I have spoken already of the extent to which the exploitation of rich women, especially in England, was carried. Rich and aristocratic women were and are special objects of the spiritual care of the Jesuits, in spite of all

* Inst. S.J., 307, 308.
† Jardine, *A Narrative of the Gunpowder Plot* (London, 1857), p. 177 et seq.

decrees and ordinances of their official Constitutions, though women of low degree are neglected in accordance with the Constitutions of Ignatius Loyola, whose reference to "women of very high rank" has been already quoted. History reports that Elisabeth Roser, a Spanish lady, who had bestowed many benefits upon him during the early times after his conversion, was curtly rebuffed by him, when he began to aim higher; and when she demanded back money she had lent he broke with her altogether, saying with emphasis that the Society had no dealings with women. At the same time, however, he was in close intercourse with Margaret Duchess of Farnese, daughter of the Emperor Charles V. He became her father confessor, and assigned to her his most distinguished associate, the Jesuit Laynez (his successor as General of the Order) as travelling companion to Genoa, when the duchess went to greet her imperial father there. And he himself baptised her twins born in 1541.*

The activity of Jesuit confessors at the courts of princes, to be treated in detail in the next chapter, is chiefly directed to princesses.

This historically established attitude of the Order is confirmed by my personal experience. I need only recall to memory what I experienced in the house of my parents, in so many families of relations and friends, and later on during my own membership of the Order.

My mother, as a woman of rank, was a continual object of Jesuit attention, which received outward expression in a diploma, signed by General Anderledy, in which she was endowed with "all the graces and dispensations of the Order." The Jesuits Behrens, Wertenberg, Hausherr, Meschler followed one another in uninterrupted succession for decades, till her death in 1903, as directors and

---

* See Druffel's *Ignatius von Loyola an der römischen Kurie* (Munich, 1879), pp. 9 and 36.

father confessors. My dear, good mother! How completely she surrendered herself to Jesuit influence in the best of faith and with voluntary self-sacrifice. She obeyed her Jesuit advisers like a child. How trustfully she heaped benefits upon them and gave liberally of the goods of this world to her "disinterested" spiritual directors! I am filled with anger and bitterness when I remember how Jesuitism inveigled and exploited this remarkable woman.

Many other women, relations of mine, fared similarly.

The soul of my sister Antonia was completely enslaved by the Jesuits Behrens, Brinkmann and Hausherr, as was that of my aunt Countess Therese von Loë (*née* Countess Arco-Zinneberg) by Hausherr. The Jesuits Behrens, Löffler, Meschler, Fäh, Schäffer, frequented the castles of the Rhenish Westphalian, Silesian, and South-German Catholic nobility, and everywhere it was rather the lady than the lord of the manor that submitted to Jesuit direction. The noble families of Droste-Vischering, Galen, Fürstenberg, Geyer, Matuschka, Waldburg-Wolfegg, Metternich, Oberndorf, Loë, Stolberg, and others were and are linked to the Jesuits by their womenkind.

When I myself, on completion of my ascetic and scholastic training, entered on my work as member of the Order, it was the obvious intention of my Superiors to take advantage of my many aristocratic connections, and without my own repeated, energetic opposition I should have doubtless turned into an "aristocratic ladies' confessor."

When I had to give Spiritual Exercises to a number of ladies of rank in 1889 or 1890, I found out how little the Constitutions of the Order, as to the way in which Exercises are to be given to women, are observed in the case of ladies of rank. They were not given in either church or chapel as required by the rule, but in the ballroom of the splendid Erbdroste Manor at Münster in Westphalia.

The Constitutions

The avoidance, nay refusal, of the pastoral care of nuns emphasised in the Constitutions is humbug also. There is no Order which exercises a more comprehensive and systematic influence over nuns, or stands in closer connection with them, than the Jesuits. Even those nuns who ought naturally to turn for direction to the monastic orders of their own name and spirit, such as the various orders of Franciscan nuns, receive their ascetic and pious training from the Jesuit Order. Only the Dominican nuns form an exception. The old antipathy between the sons of St. Dominic and the sons of St. Ignatius is after all too strong. Otherwise the Jesuit is the constant guest of nunneries. The number of Exercises he gives, of confessions he hears there, is legion. During the short period of my work in the Order I was employed a good deal in the nunneries of England, Holland, and Germany. This work is much sought after; the good nuns take excellent care of the father, and show their gratitude abundantly in coin of the realm for the pious services rendered gratuitously. Violent outbursts of jealousy are not infrequent among the Jesuits who, according to their Constitutions, decline the pastorate of nuns, on account of real or imaginary poaching on their special preserves in a nunnery. I may quote a tragi-comic experience of my own. In the summer of 1892, when I was studying in the Royal Library at Berlin (which sealed my resolution to leave the Roman Catholic Church and the Jesuit Order), the well-known Jesuit Tilmann Pesch, the Gottlieb of the notorious Hamburg Letters, was there at the same time. I was staying with the Grey Sisters in the Nieder Wallstrasse, and he I do not know where. One day at noon, while I was sitting at dinner, Pesch rushed into my room and heaped abuse on me, accusing me of wishing to give Exercises to the Ursuline nuns in the Lindenstrasse, which he himself had intended to do. As I was absolutely innocent, I wrote to my Superior at that time, the Jesuit Frink at Exaeten and complained seriously of this foolish exhibition of jealousy. In his answer, the Rector tried to find excuses on the score of "peculiar temperament."

The following anecdote will show how well these nun-shunning Jesuits fare among them:

The Jesuit Meschler was travelling with several French Jesuits from Rome across the Alps, after the General Congregation of 1883. In some town in the north of Italy—I believe it was either Milan or Turin—they spent the night. But the French Jesuits did not stay with members of their own Order according to the statute,* but, as Meschler told me, in the beautiful nunnery of the Sacred Heart. Of course, they were more comfortable there.

In the light of all these facts, it was truly Jesuitical for Ignatius Loyola to ask Paul III. to deliver himself and his Order from the spiritual direction of women and nuns,† and for the Order to persist in the pretence: "We exist not for women and nuns, but for men!" It would be more honest to add: "But women and nuns exist for us."

* *Regulae peregrinorum*, 11.

† Genelli, S.J., *Leben des heiligen Ignatius von Loyola* (Innsbruck, 1848), p. 262.

CHAPTER XVIII

THE CRITICISM CONTINUED: POLITICS AND CONFESSORS

THERE has been no more constant reproach against the Jesuit Order, and hardly any that the Order itself has repudiated with greater moral indignation, than that of political activity, in contravention of the Constitutions and the destination of the Order, which is declared emphatically to be not of the world, but devoted exclusively to the salvation of the soul.

In a letter to the *Courrier Français*, in Paris, in 1847, Johannes Roothaan, General of the Order, still declares with an air of most ingenuous sincerity ·

"Politics are absolutely foreign to the Society. It has never joined any party, no matter what its name. The purpose and vocation of the Order is greater and loftier than any party: . . . Slander may delight in spreading false assertions accusing Jesuits of taking part in political intrigues. I have yet to be shown that even a single member of the Order entrusted to my care has offended in this respect against the very definite rules of the Order."*

And, indeed, whoever innocently peruses the Constitutions would be inclined to believe the simple, straightforward-sounding words of Roothaan. For they state, as plainly as could be desired:

" As our Society, established by the Lord for the propagation of the faith and the salvation of souls, can fulfil its purpose under the banner of the Cross for the benefit of the Church and the edifica-

* Ebner, S.J., *Beleuchtung der Schrift des Dr. Joh. Kelle : Die Jesuitengymnasien in Oesterreich* (Linz, 1874), p. 536.

tion of our neighbour through the spiritual service and weapons peculiar to it and its Constitution, it would injure these and expose itself to great dangers by putting its hand to worldly concerns or affairs of politics and the State. That is why our fathers have very wisely ordained that we who serve God should not become involved in things from which our vocation must shrink. And as our Order, especially in these dangerous times, is in bad odour in many places, and with various princes (the maintenance of whose love and favour should be counted as a service to God, as our Father Ignatius of sacred memory believed), perhaps through the fault of some, or through ambition, or indiscreet zeal, whereas the odour of Christ is needful for fruition, the Congregation has decided that even the appearance of evil must be avoided, and the accusations repudiated, even those arising from false suspicions. Therefore, our people are forbidden emphatically and earnestly by this present decree to engage in these public affairs, even if invited or tempted to do so, or to let themselves be moved by entreaties or persuasions to deviate from the Institute of the Order. The *Patres definitores* have also been charged to indicate the most effective remedies for this disease."*

" By virtue of sacred obedience, and under penalty of ineligibility for all offices and dignities, and loss of the right to elect and be elected, our people are forbidden to meddle with the public and worldly affairs of princes which concern the State, or to presume to be charged with things political. The superiors are strictly charged not to allow our members to interfere with such things in any way. If they perceive that some are thus inclined, they are to report them as soon as possible to the Provincial, so that he may remove them from their posts, if there is opportunity or danger of their becoming involved in such affairs."† Similar prohibitions are repeated in Canon 12 of the fifth General Congregation, and in the *Monita generalia*, 18.‡

Yes, indeed! If the Jesuit Order were not permeated by an abysmal contradictoriness founded on conscious insincerity, as I have already so frequently pointed out.

---

* Congreg. 5, Decret. 47, *Inst. S.J.*, I., 254 *et seq.*
† Congreg. 5, Decret. 79, I., 269.   ‡ I., 485; II., 217.

To the non-political programme of its Constitutions, and the non-political declaration of its General, uttered in the deepest note of conviction, are opposed as weighty accusations the political actions or rather factions of the Order, almost from the first year of its establishment.

Not the "welfare of the souls" of men, so piously placed in the foreground, is the purpose of the Jesuit Order; its aim always and everywhere, in detail as in general, is: *Government of the individual, the family, the State, attainment of a definite influence on the current affairs of the world. And that is why the Order is intensely interested in politics.*

Until 1773, the year of its suppression by Clement XIV., the Jesuit Order intervened decisively and assiduously, but as much as possible in secret, in the politics of almost all European countries. And in the genuine ultramontane and Jesuitical spirit, the Order cloaked its political activity with religion by establishing from the beginning of its labours the institution of princely confessors, an institution —I emphasise this word as expressing an organisation— which, though in the sharpest imaginable contrast to the Constitutions of the Order, furnishes almost immeasurable leverage to Jesuit lust of power.

Since the restoration of the Order by Pius VII., in 1814, its active political power has not even distantly approached that of former centuries. Though the striving for it has remained the same, the circumstances are altered. Constitutionalism is not suitable soil for royal confessors, and many courts, where Jesuit confessors used to hold their evil sway, have vanished from the scene (*e.g.* France, the Bourbon Courts in Italy, the Episcopal Principalities of Germany and Poland).*

* One Jesuit confessor of princes, in miniature (as regards the Court, not the Jesuit), has appeared in the nineteenth century, the Jesuit Beckx (afterwards General of the Order), who, with his fellow-member, Devis, played the part of such Jesuits as Lamormaini, La Chaise or Tellier, at the little court of the last reigning

By no means always, but rarely, indeed, have the politics of the Jesuits been skilful, still less successful. Failure upon failure must have been entered in the political log-book of the Order, until at last it fell a victim to its own politics. Still the question is not whether the Jesuits were clever or clumsy politicians, but only whether and to what extent they took part in political conflicts in spite of their Constitutions and the oft-repeated solemn assurances to the contrary.*

As I am not writing a history of the Jesuit Order, I shall give no connected, complete description of its political activity. I shall present extracts, snapshots, from the course of the Order's existence, extending over nearly four centuries, but in such abundance that a complete estimate may be formed.

Neither shall I touch on the question, whether and how the Order, in its vastness and intricacies, could have avoided political activity. We are only concerned with the fact, which is, moreover, naturally evolved from its system, of its political activity, and with the irreconcilable contrast between this fact and the assertion laid down by the Order itself as a principle regarding its avoidance of politics.

For this contrast contains a huge amount of untruthfulness and hypocrisy, and as both these failings characterise the essence of Jesuitism—the system, not the individual—their exposure is of special value in a characterisation of the Order.

Duke of Anhalt-Köthen, converted to Catholicism at Paris in October, 1825. And possibly, even probably, the twentieth century may show us in Austria, always greatly blessed with Jesuits, another confessor of princes in the grand old style drawn from the Jesuit Order, when the Archdukes Francis Ferdinand and, still more, Francis Salvator, with their wives, who are wholly devoted to the Jesuits, ascend the throne of the Habsburgs.

* The political and general ability of the Jesuit Order has been enormously overrated. In a final estimate I mean to show that the power and danger of the Order result less from ability and superior skill in applying its various means than from other circumstances.

My long list of political facts and documents is prefaced by a caution against political activity proceeding from the Order itself and, moreover, from a part of the Order where facts were accurately known. But there is this to be said about the caution: it was not sincere, as I shall prove. It was meant to save appearances only.

In his treatise on "Remedies for the Cure of Diseases of the Soul" (*Industriae ad curandos animae morbos*), incorporated in the "Institute" of the Order, General Acquaviva speaks of "the worldly and insinuating spirit of the courtier seeking the familiarity and favour of strangers" (*saecularitas et aulicismus insinuans in familiaritates et gratiam externorum*).

This paragraph was addressed to the numerous Jesuits who, as the counsellors of princes, obviously had influence on political affairs. The General does not straightway forbid the acceptance of such positions, although they are contrary to the Constitutions of the Order, but after some general ascetic counsels as to how the danger of the worldly spirit of the court might be obviated, Acquaviva says, with inimitable cunning and equivocation:

"They [*i.e.* members of the Order occupying such positions at temporal courts] are to be exhorted to a wise reserve; they are to suggest (*suggerant*) that in some things princes should apply to other members of our Order, or to persons outside it, according to circumstances, so that it may not appear as though our members directed everything" (*ne videantur nostri omnia movere*).*

This caution is easily understood, seeing that even in a confidential letter of June 6th, 1579, General Mercurian writes to the Jesuit Mengin, the confessor of Duke William of Bavaria: "The other day a father wrote to me that a man of great distinction had said to him: 'Your people would do well, and it would be much to the

* *Inst. S.J.*, II., 358.

Society's credit, if they kept within their [pastoral] limits.'"*

Thus, but a few decades after the institution of the Order, its interference in politics had assumed such dimensions that responsible men felt obliged to protect the religious prestige of the Order, at least in the eyes of the public, from the unconstitutional and worldly political activity of numerous members. These cautions were of no avail, if only because they were not inspired by a serious desire to check the abuse. General Acquaviva, in particular, played a double part, as we shall see.

And now to give instances of the political activity of the Jesuits.

In the latter part of the sixteenth century we meet the Jesuits Stanislaus Warsewicz and Anton Possevin as political agents at the court of John III. of Sweden. Possevin went about in Stockholm in splendid clothes and wore "costly headgear with a black silk veil, more like a courtier or the ambassador of a prince than the member of an Order." Having received the King into the Catholic Church, he returned to Austria and Rome in May, 1578, with many commissions for the Emperor and the Pope. These concerned partly family and partly public affairs, and were addressed to the Emperor, the Kings of Poland and of Spain, and to the Pope. Possevin had tried in every possible way to bring about friendly and peaceful relations between King John and the Emperor and the Kings of Poland and Spain, in order, by the protection of these powerful rulers, to shield him from internal and external attacks by Protestant princes, and at the same time to inspire him in this way with courage and confidence in the fulfilment of his sacred enterprise [the Catholicising of Sweden].

* Duhr, S.J., *Die Jesuiten an den deutschen Fürstenhöfen des 16. Jahrhunderts* Freiburg, 1901), p. 62.

Politics and Confessors

Nor had John failed to supply Possevin with the requisite documents for the establishment and confirmation of these friendly relations with the above-mentioned courts. Even the affair of the Neapolitan inheritance had taken a happy turn, owing to the endeavours of Possevin and the Bishop of Mondevi, Papal Nuncio in Poland. Possevin was also to urge it again, and if possible to achieve its success with the assistance of the Pope and the above-mentioned Powers. Of many things Possevin had to treat in the name of the King with the Emperor [Rudolph II.].*

A letter addressed by Father Haller, Rector of the Jesuit College at Graz, to General Acquaviva, June 11th, 1598, is literally a political report:

"For many years there have been disputes between Bavaria and Austria, especially with the Emperor. . . . As regards our people, I doubt if they are quenching this fire with the requisite love and wisdom. Father Viller acts to the contrary. . . . Both parties have their adherents, who report from their party point of view, and thus add fresh fuel to the quarrel. As the matter is submitted to our people by these reports, there is a danger that the advice to test the truth of the reports be not given. . . . But because the cause of Christianity in Germany is obviously much concerned in the union of the two parties, and the great influence of members of the Society of Jesus on princes and their councillors is well known, it would be well worth the Society's while to try with greater zeal than before, and with every means at its disposal, to bring about this reconciliation, especially at Prague, Vienna, Munich and Graz."†

The Father Viller here mentioned was one of the most active political Jesuits in Austria. The following two passages from letters help to characterise him; one from a letter of Archduke Charles to his mother, dated

---

* A. Theiner, *Schweden und seine Stellung zum heiligen Stuhl. Nach geheimen Staatspapieren* (Augsburg, 1838), I., 497, 498.

† Duhr, *Die Jesuiten an den deutschen Fürstenhöfen*, p. 46.

Rome, the 29th of May, 1598, and the other from a letter by Viller to the Spanish Ambassador de San Clemente. The first passage.

"To Sper [Bavarian Agent in Rome] I have not said a word, but the Reverent Nuncio, the tutor and my *father confessor* [the Jesuit Viller] have given him a piece of their mind."*

The second passage:

"As the Archduchess Maximiliana was dead, he [Viller] recommended for marriage with the son of the King of Spain her younger sister of thirteen, Margaret, who was eligible in every respect."†

The Jesuit Blyssem, Austrian Provincial, was also one of the political councillors of the Styrian Court. On the 16th of April, 1580, he reports from Vienna to General Mercurian:

"Before Christmas I was summoned to Graz by Archduke Charles, and had various discussions with him regarding his person, and the general position of things. Then he begged me to stay till Easter, so that what he had begun so successfully should be confirmed. Your Reverence may see from a few points quoted here that my stay was not in vain."

The "few points" concern the difficult position of the Archduke respecting "the Turk and his obdurate heretical subjects."‡

Regarding the interference of the Jesuits with respect to the Protestants and the Augsburg Confession of Faith, we must not lose sight of the fact that these points were eminently political. As regards the Turkish question, it is obviously of a political character, though perhaps not for the Jesuits. For in a note to the Jesuit Viller, sent by Archduke Ferdinand on a political embassy to Rome, General Acquaviva characterises "Proceedings against the Turks" as not pertaining to politics.§

---

* Hurter, *Ferdinand II.*, 3, 582.
† Duhr, *Die Jesuiten an den deutschen Fürstenhöfen*, p. 47.
‡ *Ibid.*, p. 58.   § *Ibid.*, p. 51.

Politics and Confessors

We shall see how the Jesuit Caussin, father confessor of Louis XIV. of France, utilises this principle of Acquaviva's to justify his position. In the winter of 1581-82 Blyssem returned to Graz in order to assist the Archduke during the sessions of the Diet ·

"Although I much dislike travelling because of the dangers which I know from former experience and therefore dread, yet I cannot disappoint the pious prince or the councillors who so greatly desire it. I shall, therefore, render assistance, as I did last year, but only in things referring to God, conscience and holy religion " *

In the end everything was ranged under the heading of " God, conscience, holy religion," as indeed everything can be ranged under it. In his " Instruction to Confessors of Princes," to be discussed later, General Acquaviva simplifies matters still more by indicating " conscience " as the only limit to their actions.

The equivocations of the Jesuit Blyssem are distinctly and hideously evident in a confidential report to the General Acquaviva, dated February 28th, 1582.

Blyssem repudiates interference with military or political questions, as subjects unsuitable for a confessor; while in the same breath he tells of having worked out a report on the military and political question, if and how the fort of Graz could be manned against the Protestants, but that " the document was written in the third person and without the name of the author "; at the end of this document, actually written by him, but apparently and in the eyes of the public anonymous, " he had, as a final conclusion, given his own opinion." This conclusion read as follows :

" Affairs of war are to be discussed with warriors, and princes, and men of the world who are versed in such things, and not with members of the Order: The profession of the Jesuits does not

* Duhr, *Die Jesuiten an den deutschen Fürstenhöfen*, p. 60.

extend to such discussions, on the contrary it absolutely forbids them."*

Thus the Jesuit who meddles in politics is safe on all sides. He himself has composed a military and political report, but so that the authorship is not to be identified, and, moreover, he repudiates his own document by reference to his profession as a Jesuit.

In the second part of his report Blyssem gives the means to be employed by the Archduke in order to save the Catholic religion. These means are anything but religious.

Surrender of the arsenal and artillery to the Catholics; gradual and unobtrusive increase of soldiers in the fort; appointment of Catholic officials; favours to Catholics; treaties with Catholic princes; expulsion of preachers from the towns; prohibition of heretical sermons; pastorates, and schools in Graz, etc.†

Duhr, the Jesuit of the twentieth century, reporting these "non-political" practices of his fellow member of the sixteenth century, is not in the least offended by them. For him also all this was regulated by conscience. But when Duhr adds: "These counsels of Father Blyssem are quite in harmony with the valedictory decree of the Reichstag of 1555,"‡ he makes it plain to everyone not trained as a Jesuit that there is absolutely no domain to which "pastoral" counsels might not extend. Further reports of the Jesuit Blyssem to Rome grew so "non-political" that the author found it advisable to employ pseudonyms. The Nuncio is called *Substitutus*, the Archduke *Bedellus*, the Provincial (Blyssem himself) *Examinator*, the General of the Order *Rector Academiae*, the Pope *Promotor*, the Estates of the Realm, *Eruditi*.

On the 20th of March, 1580, Blyssem reported to the General of his Order on his intervention in the negotiations

* Duhr, *Die Jesuiten an den deutschen Fürstenhöfen*, p. 62.   † *Ibid.*, p. 63.
‡ *Ibid.*, pp. 63, 64, 65.

Politics and Confessors

with the Estates, concerning the separation of the other Estates from the cities. This report also ends with the typical assurance · " I refrain from all political advice, and only discuss what belongs to my office," *i.e.* what concerns conscience.

What a very elastic conscience! Even the Jesuit Duhr, at the end of his description of the " pastorate " of Blyssem at the court of Graz, allows this admission to escape him:

" The Jesuits might expect at the court of Graz a greater interest in the real field of their activity, the moral and religious life of the court, than in the political measures against the refractory Protestants."*

The quarterly reports of the Jesuit College at Braunsberg, in Ermeland, of March, 1565, contain the following:

" In February there began in the presence of the King the session of the Comitia of the Kingdom of Poland, in which two of our priests took part, one accompanying the Nuncio of the Pope, the other the Cardinal [Hosius].† In May, 1606, the Jesuit M. Mairhofer, Rector of the Jesuit College at Munich, wrote to Duke Maximilian of Bavaria on the re-election of a prince-abbot of Fulda. The letter, founded on a secret report of the Jesuit Rector of Fulda, is so political that Mairhofer himself thinks it well to emphasise:

" I beg that this letter may be kept secret, for it would be taken very ill of me and of us all [the Jesuits], if we interfered in political affairs, as indeed only *suspecti vel qui non longe respiciunt* (suspicious or shortsighted people) will say."‡

---

* Duhr, *Die Jesuiten an den deutschen Fürstenhöfen*, p. 68.

† Published from the original deposited in the archives of the Cologne Parish of the Assumption of the Virgin Mary, by Karl Benrath. *Die Ansiedelung der Jesuiten in Braunsberg*, p. 71.

‡ For the whole letter, from an original MS. in the State Archives at Munich, see Stieve, *Briefe und Akten zur Geschichte des dreissigjährigen Krieges*, V. 931.

It is a very remarkable fact that the Jesuits delegated to Rome for the General Congregation of the Order by every Province were also political agents. Thus the General Congregation, a purely religious institution according to the Constitutions of the Order, became the centre of far-reaching political intrigues.

Steinberger reports that the Electors Maximilian I. of Bavaria and Anselm Kasimir of Mayence charged the Jesuits Lorenz Forer and Nithard Biber, delegated by the South German Province of the Order in 1645, to the eighth General Congregation in Rome, with commissions and instructions in order to induce Pope Innocent X. to promote a separation of France from Sweden, and to support Germany with money and troops. Innocent was so unpleasantly impressed by this Jesuit importunity that he addressed a serious warning to the General Congregation: to beware lest anyone should interfere in worldly matters.*

Under Henry III. of France, whose murder by Jaques Clement was glorified by the Jesuit Mariana, the Jesuit Matthieu was a chief promoter of the League of the Guises. He was active in Rome, Paris, and Madrid. The heads of the League employed him repeatedly as political ambassador, especially in treaties with Philip II. of Spain.†

As the Jesuit Cordara reports, the Jesuit Caballius was the ambassador of King Joseph I. of Portugal to the Pope.‡

From the manuscripts deposited in the Court Library at Vienna, *Litterae annuae S.J. Provinciae austriacae* (Annual Reports of the Austrian Province of the Society of Jesus), of 1615–1771, Krones quotes some interesting details of the political activity of the Order in Hungary before and after the Peace of Tyrnau-Linz in the year 1647. At

---

* *Die Jesuiten und die Friedensfrage bis zur Nürnberger Friedensexekutionshauptrezess*, 1635-1650 (Freiburg, 1906), p. 100 *et seq.*

† Grégoire, p. 301.   ‡ Döllinger, *Beiträge*, 3, 18.

the Hungarian Election and Coronation Diet in 1655 the Jesuits sought with all their might and cunning the repeal of the decrees of 1606 and 1608, which were unfavourable to them:

"The Austrian Provincial Bernhard Geyer consulted with the Catholic leaders on the means of carrying out this difficult enterprise . . . this was the secret plan of campaign: First, ways and means must be found in order to prevent the delegates of the counties from letting directions hostile to Jesuits prevail, and from speaking in that sense during the Diet. On the other hand, it was important to guide the decisions of the monarch in the proper direction. The Provincial undertook to do the latter. Father Geyer painted to the monarch the dangers of heresy, and received from him the most welcome assurances. The General of the Order, Goswin Nickel,* did not spare petitions to the royal councillors and the Catholic magnates of Hungary. But the most effective measure was the influence brought to bear on the delegates of the Diet and above all on the so-called 'mixed Compilation Committee,' for the compilation of objects of treaty. . . . Pope Alexander VII. sent his Nuncio to Pressburg for the furtherance of the desires of the Jesuits [settlements and the possession of landed property for the Order] to explain to the monarch there how friendly the Church of Rome was to the Order and the interests of Catholicism. In the printed annual report of the Order of 1651 there is a remark actually expatiating on the profit to be derived from the Order for government purposes. It is too significant not to find a place here. 'The Secretary of State of the Crown of Sweden,' it says, ' a wise and not unlearned man, did not hesitate in the presence of twenty selected magnates to make the assertion that the Austrian dynasty had nothing more excellent or useful in its realms and provinces than the Society of Jesus. For with its help the Emperor could keep the nations conquered by him in faithful obedience with a mere sign, and direct them at his will.' The Report inserts the remark that the 'Order did not learn this without a blush of modesty'; in any case, it took good care to divulge this equivocal

* The only German General besides the present General of the Order, Francis Xavier Wernz.

praise. But it would be a mistake to consider the Jesuits in the State of Austria in the light of disguised agents of the Viennese Government, as grateful tools and supporters of monarchical interests, with which the Order was determined to rise or fall. In the great structure of the ruling Order, which extended over all parts of the world, the Austrian Province (including Hungary) formed only a part, one link in the mighty chain, the end of which was in the hands of the central administration—the generalship. The fathers of the Austrian Province also served the one common purpose: the authority and power of the Order in the denominational life of the Catholic world. Thus it would be much more justifiable to make the assertion that the Order of the Jesuits had used the Austrian and every other dynasty as a means for its comprehensive purposes. It served the dynasty as far as it benefited itself by doing so. And no unprejudiced person following the history of the development and activity of the Society of Jesus could deny that the chief aim of its ambition was pre-eminence in the world of Catholic Orders."*

When the Polish throne had become vacant through the abdication of King John Casimir of Poland, Duke Philip Wilhelm of Neuburg and Jülich-Burg and Prince Charles of Lorraine applied for it. The Polish Jesuits worked for the latter; for the former in particular his confessor, the Jesuit Joh. Bodler. A few months before the election, which resulted eventually in the choice of neither the Duke nor the Prince, but the Pole, Michael Wisniowiecki, Bodler wrote on the 14th of January, 1669, to his fellow member Servilian Veihelin, Rector of the Jesuit College at Munich. His strictly confidential letter affords a profound insight into the political activity of the Jesuits and their cunning and duplicity:

"Recently," it states, "a letter from Prince Auersperg, Imperial Prime Minister for the Duke of Neuburg, had come to Neuburg. As Auersperg could have no inkling that his letter would be sub-

* Krones, *Zur Geschichte des Jesuitenordens in Ungarn* (Vienna, 1893), pp. 8, 9, 11, 18 *et seq.*

mitted to the Jesuits he had spoken freely and bitterly about them. On account of Auersperg's bad handwriting, which only the Jesuit Carlius [the English Jesuit Carly] could decipher, Duke Wilhelm had given the letter to the Jesuits. He [the Jesuit Bodler] was sending him [the Jesuit Veihelin] a copy of a passage from Auersperg's letter, but it was exclusively meant for him alone, 'for you see how careful we [Jesuits] must be, lest our prince [the Duke of Neuburg] or the other [the Prince of Lorraine] should learn that matters which at their urgent request were to have been kept secret have been read by and made known to us.'"

The important passage from Auersperg's letter was as follows:

"The *dilatio electionis* would not benefit Lorraine either. I am for dismissing Isola's [Baron L'Isola] secretary. These and other people are serving the Duke of Lorraine, and this might easily have caused the rumour that your Excellency was not in favour here [in Vienna]. Your Excellency need not think that it would be in his Majesty the Emperor's power to prevent the *Patres Societatis* from working in a different direction, partly as confessors, partly as Polish Jesuits. It is their way—how long they may succeed in it God knows—in all *promotionibus*, that some work for one party, some for the other, so that they should earn thanks and benefit, no matter how it may turn out. If your Excellency now, when there is perhaps still time, would complain of it to the General [of the Jesuits] it may have the effect of recommending all *cautelas ne sic pateat*, but *in toto non esset remedium*. Your Excellency has not deserved it of them [the Jesuits], and the more they interfere with worldly affairs, the worse they come off, as can be seen in Spain, and I am sorry for the Society, which did so much good in the first century."

The Jesuit Bodler continues:

"So much for Auersperg. Father Gabriel [Riddler] has translated this into Latin and thinks of sending it to the General [of the Order]. Having read these and other similar communications, our prince continues in kindness to us, but is eagerly trying to find out what reason induced our *patres* to work for his rival."

The General might perhaps be induced to forbid the Polish Jesuits their machinations. The Duke wanted to send Father Riddler to Prague:

"None of us approve of this plan, neither do we see what he could accomplish there, especially as the Duke seems to require of him, what he now condemns in Father Richard, the confessor of the Duke of Lorraine, and in the Polish Fathers. I hope Father Gabriel will speak to the Duke about this journey, or at least that the Duchess may do so, as she wishes to keep Father Riddler here for her own sake (*sui solatii causa*). . . . I am writing this, not only that you should know what is going on, but also that you may help me with your advice. I have hitherto kept silence on the matter as one that does not concern me, but now, if the matter ends less favourably for the Society, which is sure to be the case if the Duke's hopes are not fulfilled, I may possibly be reproached for not having written to the General more carefully and in detail, seeing I was familiar with the course of events. I have written to him once, but thought afterwards that further reports could be of no use."*

It cannot be denied that those who try to promote religion by force of arms and political revolution are taking part in politics. Indeed, these violent religious politics are a fundamental principle of the Jesuits. Of this we have a striking testimony. A report on affairs in Scotland, sent by the Papal Agent at Brussels, Monsignore Malvasia, in 1596, to the Secretary of State of the Papal Cardinal Aldobrandini, says:

"The Jesuits consider as one of their established axioms (*assioma stabilito*), confirmed by the authority of Father Parsons [one of the leading English Jesuits], that the Catholic religion [in England and Scotland] can only be restored by force of arms. For the property and revenues of the Church, which have in the meantime been distributed among heretics and have passed through many hands already, cannot be recovered in any other way. They

* Reusch, *Beiträge: Zeitschrift für Kirchengeschichte* (1894), Vol. II., p. 268.

[the Jesuits] believe that only the arms of Spain may be used to bring about this event. They [the Jesuits], no matter whether from Rome or anywhere else, come to these parts with this idea, which has been firmly impressed upon them by their Superiors."*

Perhaps Malvasia was thinking of an event which caused this Jesuit principle to be made known a decade earlier. In September, 1584, the vessel in which the Jesuit Creighton was going to Scotland, furnished with secret instructions, was captured by the English, and Creighton taken to the Tower of London. On his capture he tore up a document, and tried to throw the pieces into the sea. They were collected again, and the Catholic priest, Thomas Francis Knox, member of the Oratorian Congregation founded by St. Philip Neri, and thus a trustworthy witness, published this interesting document for the first time a few years ago in his *Records of English Catholics*. It is sufficient to quote the following from a number of things enumerated which Creighton is to accomplish:

" Lastelie and especially to depose her Matie [Queen Elizabeth] and set up the Scottish Queene [Mary Stuart], which indeede is the scope and white whereto all this practise dothe level."†

In the confessions made by Creighton in the Tower, and also published literally by Knox, the " aim and end," and the means to attain them, are very plainly expressed. Pope Gregory XIII., Philip II. of Spain, and the Duke of Guise are mentioned, with the number of troops to be furnished by each, as chief promoters of the " religious " scheme. There was even an exact estimate among the papers of the " non-political " Jesuit as to the number of soldiers required for the conquest of England. Since 1581 or 1582 the Jesuit Parsons had been in close touch

* Bellesheim, *Geschichte der Kathol. Kirche in Schottland* (Mayence, 1883), II., 466.
† Thomas Francis Knox, *Records of English Catholics*, II., p. 426 *et seq.*

with the Duke of Guise, who in his turn was completely in the hands of the French Jesuit Matthieu. Guise was one of the worst political intriguers of his time, and tried to promote in every way the deposition of Queen Elizabeth of England and the raising of Mary Stuart to the English throne. In this endeavour, supported above all by Philip II. of Spain, which also aimed at the assassination of the odious " heretic,"* Guise was eagerly helped by the two above-mentioned Jesuits. Especially Parsons pursued the cause most zealously with Philip II., whose confidence he had gained.

There is no direct proof that Parsons and his French brother-member Matthieu promoted the murder-plot. But there is a very suspicious passage in a letter of Parsons to his General, Acquaviva, dated Rouen, September the 26th, 1581, in which he strongly advocates Mary Stuart's rights to the throne and then, speaking of Elizabeth, uses the words: "When she who now reigns is destroyed: *Extincta ista quae nunc regnat.*"†

An indirect and convincing proof of Parsons' knowledge and approval of the murder-plot is the fact that its chief promoters, the Duke of Guise, Philip II. of Spain, the Papal Nuncio in Paris, and the Cardinal Secretary of State in Rome, were Parsons' confidants, so that it would have been a matter of impossibility for the Jesuit going to and fro and mediating between these persons to have remained ignorant of a plot which had been hatching for years.

A sidelight on the political activity of the Jesuits is thrown by the report of Mendoza, the ambassador of Philip II. to the King, saying that: The Jesuit Creighton had promised the Duke of Lennox 15,000 men for the war in Scotland.‡ Mendoza adds, however, that Creighton

* *Cf.* my work, *Das Papsttum*, etc., 201–204.

† Taunton gives the most important part of this interesting and wholly political letter, pp. 89, 90.

‡ S.S.P. (Simancas), III., No. 255. Taunton, p. 97.

might have made the promise "entirely on his own initiative," which is all the more suggestive of the vast "religious" activity of the Jesuits.

Under the pseudonym of Richard Melino, the Jesuit Parsons was sent to Rome in 1583, with secret instructions by the Duke of Guise, in order to induce the Pope to give money for the enterprise against England; troops were to land in several ports, and the English Catholics were to unite with them.*

Parsons† is also the author of two political pamphlets which, under the cloak of religion, demand the dethronement of Elizabeth · "An Admonition to the Nobility and the People of England and Ireland concerning the present wars made for the execution of his Holiness' sentence [Deposition by the Pope of Elizabeth] by the high and mighty Catholic King of Spain," and "A Declaration of the Sentence of Deposition of Elizabeth, the Usurper and Pretended Queen of England." Like a true Jesuit, Parsons tries to pretend that his friend, the subsequent Cardinal Allen, was the author of these pamphlets.

The Catholic priest Taunton sums up Parsons' highly treasonable plots in these words:

"The party to which Parsons attached himself had given themselves wholly to furthering the Spanish King's schemes, and the Jesuit became one of the most earnest workers. Fortunately, among the Spanish State papers of the period there has been preserved a document which puts Parsons' position in a perfectly clear light. On 18th of March, 1587, he produced a paper entitled 'Considerations why it is desirable to carry through the enterprise of England before discussing the succession to the Throne of that

---

* Teulet, *Relations politiques avec la France et l'Espagne*, V., 308.

† So as not to be disturbed in his political activity Parsons used the following pseudonyms: Robert, Perino, Ralph, Stefano Cornelio, Ottaviano Inghelberto, Richard Melino, Marco, Mercante, Rowland Cabel, John Howlett, Redman Giacomo Creletto, Signor Hamiano, Eusebius. (Taunton, *History of the Jesuits in England*, London, 1901), p. 48 (2).

country, claimed by His Majesty'; and the document is of sufficient value to be quoted *in extenso*, for it shows Parsons, who as a Jesuit was supposed to be particularly devoted to the Pope's interest, engaged in deceiving both him and the unfortunate English Catholics in the interests of the King of Spain."*

Taunton copies the document *in extenso*. The Jesuit coolly discusses Philip II.'s prospects after the strongholds of England and Scotland had fallen into his hands, and he calmly takes the death of Mary Stuart into his political and military calculations. Of himself Parsons speaks in the document only as Richard Melino, one of the many pseudonyms under which he concealed his political activity. In 1593 Parsons went to Spain to the court of Philip II., and there continued his intrigues with great zeal. In the following year, 1594, appeared the worst of his political writings—of course, again without his name—"Conference on the next Succession to the Crown," which was so hostile to Elizabeth that its mere possession was declared high treason by Act of Parliament. For a long time the Jesuit Order tried to deny the authorship of Parsons, but it is undoubtedly his work.†

During his residence in Spain Parsons issued another political treatise: "Principal Points to facilitate the English Enterprise." In this, after proposing that "the English exiles in Flanders should make constant raids, summer and winter, on the English coast ." he says:

"Finally, the great point which ought to be considered first is to obtain very good information from England of everything that is being done or said by the enemy. . . . An attempt may now be made to amend matters, as Father Henry Garnet, Provincial of the Jesuits, writes that trustworthy men may be obtained in London who will get their information at the fountain-head in the Council, and they themselves will provide correspondents in the

* Taunton, p. 116.
† Compare *Historia Societatis Jesu*, by the Jesuit Jouvency, p. 138.

principal ports, who will keep advising as to the warlike preparations."*

Parsons' political and warlike intrigues are also evident in a report of the Spanish Council of State to King Philip II., dated July 11, 1600:

"The Queen of England will not live long, and the English Catholics beg your Majesty to declare yourself in the matter of the succession. . Your Majesty's decision may be conveyed in confidence to the Arch-priest and General of the Jesuits in England, so that it may be published at the proper time. . . . The answer to be given to Father Parsons may also be left to the Duke [of Sessa, ambassador in Rome]. We here are of opinion that Parsons may be told, as was before resolved, that your Majesty would nominate a Catholic sovereign as the successor of Queen Elizabeth."†

Under James II. of England (1685-88) the Jesuit Order exercised an almost unlimited influence. Among the tools of the Order were the King's confessor, the Jesuit Warner, who was also Provincial of the Jesuits in England, and above all James's favourite, the Jesuit Edward Petre. Of him Macaulay says: "Of all the evil counsellors who had access to the Royal ear, he bore perhaps the largest share in the ruin of the House of Stuart."

To avoid entering into too great detail about the Jesuit Petre, I will only quote some extracts from the reports of the Tuscan Ambassador in London, Terriesi, quoted by Taunton from MSS. in the British Museum:

"Writing to the Grand Duke (22nd July, 1686) he says: 'Let your Highness prepare to hear continually fresh news of this country both as to its temporal and spiritual affairs; for the King seems determined to push forward in matters of religion as far as he can. And the Jesuit Petre, who governs him, is the man to force him to extremes without a thought as to the consequences. He says

* Taunton, pp. 448, 449.
† *Ibid.*, p. 276, from Cal. S.S.P. (Simancas), IV., 665.

plainly that Protestants believe ' that the Jesuits are at present the *primum mobile* of the government.' "

" Writing 30th December, 1686, he says : ' The Jesuit Father Petre rules His Majesty's mind more than ever. '

" Writing 15th August, 1687, Terriesi says : ' The report they [the people] circulate, ascribing all the trouble to the Jesuits' counsel, by which they say His Majesty is completely governed, is most intolerable to the King. Yet I believe it in a great measure to be a calumny ; still, as His Majesty has the Jesuits so constantly with him, it causes suspicions, which will be worse if Father Petre becomes Cardinal, as it is said the King certainly wishes. . . ' "*

The Jesuit Petre attained to the height of his political activity on November the 11th, 1687, when James II. made him a member of the Privy Council. As Privy Councillor Petre took an oath of allegiance, which would naturally suggest some scruples from a Catholic point of view.† But that is where the use of the Jesuit maxim, " The end sanctifies the means," would come in.

Petre accepted his political office by express permission of the Provincial of the English Province, the Jesuit Keynes, and with the silent consent at any rate of General Gonzalez himself. A letter, dated January 8th, 1688, from the General to the English Provincial does certainly express " surprise " that Petre should have been allowed by the Provincial to accept an office " implying interference with matters forbidden by the statutes of the Order," but it does not contain a word of blame, let alone a command to relinquish the office.‡ The letter ends with an assurance that the General would consult his assistants on the matter. As Petre retained his office undisturbed even after this consultation, it may be concluded that it ended in approval of Petre's political office. This conclusion is all the more justified as, if there had

* Taunton, pp. 448, 449.
† *Cf.* Michaud : *Louis XIV. et Innocent XI.* (Paris, 1882), 2, 113, 118.
‡ Crétineau-Joly, *Historie de la Compagnie de Jésus*, 3rd edition, 4, 148.

been the slightest sign of disapproval, the Jesuit authors would certainly have pointed it out. But they have maintained a profound silence.

Taunton concludes his account of the Jesuit Petre with these trenchant words:

"It is the custom to speak sternly of Petre's foolhardy conduct, and to accuse him of ambition. I think historians have not, as a rule, understood the full position of the case. Petre has been made the scapegoat for others. I do not wish to extenuate his responsibility for the catastrophe; but I do think the chief blame rests on other shoulders. If he were free from ambition, who then were the ambitious men? Petre, like a good Jesuit, was in the hands of his superiors *perinde ac cadaver*. It was therefore the superiors of the Society who were the ambitious men. They and they alone are primarily guilty of the fall of the Stuarts. Hitherto they have escaped, while Petre has borne the opprobrium. The General, the Provincial and the Confessor are the real culprits. If, as we know, from a letter dated 3rd March, 1688, the Provincial had, without the leave of the General, allowed Petre to accept the office of Privy Councillor, still the General tolerated it. Considering that they knew all about the man, and yet left him in this position; considering that they allowed him to take the oath and become a Privy Councillor, who can now say that they were not the ambitious men? The *libido dominandi* eats into a Society as well as into persons, and more easily where the individual gives up all personal ambition and makes the Society his all in all."*

The historians of the Order do not speak of Petre and his political doings unless absolutely obliged to do so. They mostly prefer to ignore the existence of a Jesuit Petre; that is to say, they pass him over in absolute silence. In modern times the Jesuit Duhr is conspicuous for such silence. In his voluminous work of 975 pages, *Jesuitenfabeln*, published in a fourth edition in 1904, Petre is only mentioned once in a superficial remark (p. 674), though thirty pages are devoted to the court

* Taunton, pp. 460, 461.

confessors of the Order and their doings, but Petre does not exist for him.

This silence of Duhr's is all the more striking, considering that eighteen years before (1886-87), in the *Zeitschrift für Katholische Theologie*, he attempted the defence of Petre in long articles. And in 1904 not a word of such defence, not even a reference to it. Duhr must have had a feeling that it would be best not to reopen the topic of Petre.

From Duhr's defence of 1886-87 we may report as curiously characteristic that it is almost exclusively restricted to refuting the reproach of Petre's having aspired ambitiously to the dignity of a cardinal; this was impossible, he asserts, since Petre, as a professed member of the Society of Jesus, had taken a vow not to aspire after such dignities. Duhr ignores almost completely the far more serious reproach of political activity, also forbidden by the Constitutions of the Order, and seals his very extensive defence of his fellow-Jesuit Petre with this assertion:

"There are no facts nor authentic, irrefutable conclusions to justify the accusation brought against the Jesuit Petre. But if incontestable proof should be brought against Father Petre, there would be absolutely no reason why we should hesitate to recognise it, for it would be no more reasonable to reproach an Order of the Catholic Church for having one wicked member than the company of the Apostles on account of one Judas. In any case, truth must prevail."*

That is Duhr all over, or rather the Jesuit spirit. The facts, that for years Petre exercised unlimited political influence, that he officially held a political post involving work contrary to the statutes of the Order, as even the General was obliged to confess; these facts, and authentic, irrefutable conclusions drawn from them, exist. And yet

* *Zeitschrift für Kathol. Theologie, Jahrgang,* 1887, p. 232.

he clamours for facts to justify the accusations. Jesuit and ultramontane authors in general know their public.

The comparison between the Order of the Jesuits and the company of the Apostles, among whom there had also been a Judas, is also characteristic. There we have, first of all, the genuine Jesuit arrogance: The company of the Apostles = the Order of the Jesuits. Well, why not? The Order of the Jesuits is the Society of Jesus. But then there is a suggestion of confession and resignation in the reference to Judas; after all, the Jesuit Petre may possibly have been a Judas. How strange, then, that the Superiors of the Order always gave this Judas the highest praise and entrusted him, even after he had played his political, his "Judas" part in England, up to his death in 1699, with the most important offices, as Duhr himself reports!* In this way the likeness to Judas extends really to the Superiors of the Order, and the above-quoted opinion of Taunton is thus confirmed.

Seeing the numerous ways—and there will be more still—in which Duhr's truth has been unmasked, his emphatic word in conclusion: "In any case the truth must prevail," need hardly be discussed.

After all, Crétineau-Joly is more honest than the Jesuit Duhr. This is what he says about Petre and the Order's toleration of the latter's position of political power:

"Petre took a position contrary to the statutes of Saint Ignatius, and the rest of the Jesuits raised no objection, or else, which is very improbable, the document was lost."†

It is true that the Jesuits raised no objections, but they tried to make up for this in another way. Their sixteenth General Congregation in 1730, when Petre's political

---

* *Zeitschrift für Kathol. Theologie*, Jahrgang, 1886, p. 682.
† Crétineau-Joly, *Histoire de la Compagnie de Jésus*, p. 172.

activity was at an end, issued a decree, the 26th, which says :

"If Jesuits are claimed for political work by any sovereign, they must declare that their Constitutions forbid their interference in such matters."*

Thus the Order had saved its principles in the case of Petre, and had officially disapproved of a practice it had known and tolerated. The Order would, if necessary, save appearances.

A pendant to the Jesuit Petre is found in the seventeenth century in the Minister of State and Jesuit, Eberhard Nidhard, in Spain, characterised tersely by the Ultramontane *Historisch-politische Blätter* (surely an unimpeachable source) as : "Soldier, Jesuit, Professor of Philosophy, Confessor and Preceptor at the Viennese Court, Father Confessor to the Queen of Spain, Spanish Minister of State, Inquisitor-General, Spanish Ambassador in Rome, Archbishop, Cardinal—that is, in brief, the biography of the Austrian Jesuit Eberhard Nidhard."†

The Venetian Ambassador at the Court of Madrid Marino Zorzi, states in a report to the Signoria, of April, 1667, that Nidhard "ruled the Spanish Monarchy."‡

The fact that the Jesuits took an active part and were a moving force in the political and military troubles of the Thirty Years' War hardly requires to be proved. Gfrörer says :

"After the Jesuits had fully established themselves under the two childishly weak successors of the Emperor Maximilian II., and had, as it were, become masters of the House [of Austria], they carried forward openly their great political schemes. It was no longer a question of merely winning a few provinces by cunning, but of subjugating by force of arms the whole of Germany and,

---

* *Inst. S.J.*, I., 397.
† *Historisch-politische Blätter*, vol. 98, p. 139.
‡ From the Reports of the Embassy, *ibid.*, p. 143.

Politics and Confessors

through Germany, Protestant Europe, and of suppressing the Reformation. They intended to bring about an enormous revolution. If the Jesuits themselves and their ambitions are not merely to be taken as products of the period, the Thirty Years' War is the work of their Order. The princes and kings who fought for the Catholic cause in this terrible struggle played the parts assigned to them by the Jesuits. . . . The most important part in this far-seeing plan was reserved for the Imperial House. Unconditional satisfaction of their lust of power was the bait thrown by the Jesuits to the House of Habsburg. These princes were led to imagine Germany at their feet . . . and were flattered in the ancient claims of this dynasty to rule the universe, which had been revived since the union of the Spanish and Austrian inheritance in one House. But first the Jesuits had to procure an emperor suitable to their plans, for what was to be done with men like the Emperor Rudolf II., like Matthias? They found him in the person of Ferdinand II. . . The establishment of a military force independent of the Emperor, under the command of the Duke of Bavaria, alongside of the imperial sovereign, was not merely a natural result, but rather the work of a profound, far-seeing policy. Because Wallenstein's gigantic genius tore this fabric to pieces, and tried to imprint on the Thirty Years' War a purely imperial character, he was bound to fall. That artful calling into the ranks of the Bavarians and the fall of the Duke of Friedland were the work of the Jesuits."*

This general opinion is confirmed by many a fact taken from the history of the Order. On the 19th of June, 1618, the Jesuit Rumer, Rector of the Jesuit College at Passau, wrote a letter to the Jesuit Lamormaini, Rector of the Jesuit College at Graz (who soon after became Father Confessor to the Emperor Ferdinand II.), which gives proof positive of the activity of the Jesuits in urging on the war·

"I hear that an army is being raised for your Imperial Majesty against the Bohemians. If this matter should lead to war, I may

* Gfrörer, *Geschichte Gustav Adolfs* (Stuttgart, 1837), p. 339.

hope for good results soon. But if it leads to concord, I fear we shall be left out, as we were at Venice. The Estates will certainly not accept us unless obliged to it by force. There has never been a better opportunity for depriving the Bohemians of all privileges injurious to religion and the Royal charter than now."*

The Jesuits of Münster were also eagerly devoted to politics. Fathers Schücking, Cörler and Mulmann were specially prominent.

In the garden belonging to the House of the Order the Catholic ambassadors held their preliminary meetings. During his sojourn in Münster, one of the most distinguished among them, Gaspar de Bracamonte y Guzman, Count of Peñaranda, the principal Spanish ambassador, built for himself in the neighbourhood of the college a house which he presented to the Fathers on his departure in 1648. In spite of their rigid principles the Fathers managed to get on very well with the non-Catholic statesmen also · " *suaviter in modo, fortiter in re.*"†

Jacob Balde, the famous Jesuit composer of odes, entered at the same time from Munich into political relations with the French ambassador Avaux, at Münster. These he immortalised by dedicating the Ninth Book of his *Silvae Lyricae* to the representative of France.‡

One of the most interesting proofs§ of the active share of the Jesuit Order in the Thirty Years' War is the following fact, drawn from the depth of the State Archives of Munich after a hundred and sixty years :

From an official estimate of January, 1729, made by the Provincial Procurator of the Upper German Province of the Order of the Jesuits, Father Bissel, it appears that at the

---

* *Apologia oder Entschuldigungsschrift auss was für unvermeidlichen Ursachen alle drey Stände des löblichen Konigreichs Boehaimb sub utraque ein Defensionwerk anstellen müssen* (Prague 1618), pp. 81, 394.

† Steinberger, p. 54.   ‡ *Ibid.*, p. 48 *et seq.*

§ I shall bring forward other proofs later, in discussing the activity of Jesuit confessors of princes.

time of the Thirty Years' War the Order advanced large sums to the Catholic League :*

The German Province had lent 262,208 guldens, the interest on which in 1729 amounted to 302,271 guldens 18 kreuzers; the College at Liège 200,000 guldens, for which in 1729 interest of 130,833 guldens 9 kreuzers was due; the Cologne College 29,250 guldens for which the interest in 1729 amounted to 30,000 guldens. The sum total of capital advanced plus interest amounted accordingly to 954,562 guldens 27 kreuzers. To his estimate the Jesuit Bissel adds this remark:

"I shall not reveal this to others [of the Order], so that our people may not tell strangers. For this might bring mischief and ruin on our establishments."

Thus the estimate was strictly private and only meant for the Superiors. The Jesuit Duhr, trying to hide the fact that the Jesuits had anything to do with the Thirty Years' War, though referring to the Catholic League, of course says nothing of the Order's great money loans to the League.†

On the relations of the Jesuits to the French League at the end of the sixteenth century the Jesuit Prat, who characterises the League as a revolutionary movement, admits:

"The Society of Jesus supplied it [the League] at first with a few eager partisans, while other members were on the royal and legal side. But eventually, led by the directions of their General [Acquaviva] and by the example of Sixtus V., they kept in the background. . Henry III. . . . demanded the presence of Father Auger at his court, and that all the members of his Order should openly range themselves on the Royal side. Being informed of the complaints and wishes of the King, Claudius Acquaviva at first proceeded to treat with the French ambassador in Rome.

* J. Friedrich, *Beiträge*, p. 16. Here is also the documentary evidence from the Jesuit Papers in the State Archives of Munich.
† *Jesuitenfabeln*, pp. 151, 16L.

Then he entrusted Father Maggio with the task of explaining to Henry III. the reasons for the measures [taken by the Order] of which the King had complained."*

So the amusing anecdote which Saint-Simon tells of the 1692 campaign is probably no mere invention.†

"*Il arriva une chose à Namur, après sa prise, qui fit du bruit. . . . On visita tout avec exactitude Lorsque, dans une dernière visite après la prise du château, on la voulut faire chez les Jésuites, ils ouvrirent, toute en marquant toutefois leur surprise, et quelque chose de plus, de ce qu'on ne s'en fioit pas à leur témoignage. Mais en fouillant partout où ils ne s'attendaient pas, on trouva leurs souterrains pleins de poudre dont ils s'étoient bien gardés de parler : ce qu'ils prétendoient faire est demeuré incertain.*"‡

The participation of the Jesuits in the revolution in Portugal in the middle of the seventeenth century, through which John IV. of the House of Braganza came to the throne, has been so clearly proved that even the Jesuit Ravignan could not but admit it ·

"It was the only time, so far as I know, that the Religious of the Society took part in a political revolution that overthrew one throne in order to put another in its place." ‖

Ravignan tries to extenuate the awkwardness of the

* *Recherches historiques et critiques sur la Compagnie de Jésus en France du temps du P. Coton,* 1564–1626 (Lyon, 1876), I., 65 *et seq.*

† Saint-Simon is very inconvenient to the Jesuits as a witness. The Jesuit Duhr disposes of him for his readers with the following words : " Lavallée [editor of Madame de Maintenon's Letters] charges the Memoirs of the Duc de Saint-Simon, which have been exploited in an anti-Jesuit manner, with blind hatred and deliberate untruthfulness." This is a piece of genuine Jesuitical misrepresentation. Lavallée does not dream of discrediting Saint-Simon's Memoirs as a whole ; indeed he constantly refers to the Memoirs in explanation of passages in Madame de Maintenon's Letters. In the passage quoted (inaccurately, too) by Duhr, Lavallée speaks exclusively of Saint-Simon's antipathy for Louis XIV. and Madame de Maintenon, without saying a word against the general trustworthiness of the Memoirs.

‡ *Mémoires* (Paris, 1873), I., 12.

‖ *De l'Existence et de l'Institut des Jésuites* (Paris, 1855), p. 238.

fact by saying that the Portuguese Jesuits had acted here rather as Portuguese than as Jesuits, an evasion which might serve in similar cases for all countries in which Jesuits live and support thrones. Georgel, Secretary of the French Embassy in Vienna, tells us how great was the general influence of the Jesuits in Portugal:

"At court they were not only directors of conscience to the Princes and Princesses of the Royal Family, but the King and his Ministers consulted them on affairs of importance. In the government of State or Church no office was bestowed without their approval or influence, so that the high clergy, the aristocracy, and the people vied with each other for their mediation and favour."*

Even Pombal had to bow at least once to the preponderant influence of the Jesuits. At one time he seems to have planned marrying the Princess de Beira to the Duke of Cumberland, and thus uniting Portugal to England. Surely a political enterprise! Who was it that thwarted this plan successfully? The Jesuit Order. Thus reports Maréchal de Belle-Isle,† and Crétineau-Joly is bound to confirm him.

I have mentioned already the fact and the reason why the Jesuits have been less prominent politically since the restoration of their Order than formerly. But even during the comparatively short period of not quite a hundred years numerous political intrigues and actions were set on foot by the Order.

In the diary of Manning (afterwards Cardinal), written during his second stay in Rome (after his secession to the Church of Rome), November, 1847, to May, 1848, the following passage, dated December 5th, 1847, occurs:

"Broechi told me that the Jesuits are able and excellent in their duties as priests, but that their politics are most mischievous;

Mémoires pour servir à l'Histoire des Évènements de la Fin du 18 *Siècle* Paris, 1817), 1, 16.
† *Testament politique*, p. 108, and Crétineau-Joly, 5, 176.

that if a collision should come with the people the effect would be terrible; that they stick to the aristocracy, *e.g.* to the Dorias, the Princess being a Frenchwoman; that no day passes but they are there. The people call them Oscuri, Oscurantisti."*

In 1866 and 1870–71 I was too young to be able to judge of the political activity of the Order in those stirring times, but the events at Feldkirch and in my family circle, which, as I have already shown, was completely under Jesuit dominion, prove the strong political partisanship of the Order for Austria and France. The extensive influence of the Order and its traditional habit of political intrigue justify the conclusion that its anti-Prussian and anti-German sentiments may have led to actions, or in any case to desires.

But I was old enough to judge of subsequent events.

In 1883–87, when I was studying theology as a Jesuit scholastic at Ditton Hall, in England, I was sent several times for a short stay to the Continent for various purposes of no special interest. During one of these journeys (I forget in what year) I spent the night in the Jesuit College at Canterbury, where some of the Jesuits exiled from France had settled. The Rector was the renowned Jesuit du Lac. He treated me with great candour, and told me with many details, which I have forgotten, how zealously he had been working in France for General Boulanger; that he had collected large sums of money for the " Deliverer of France " from the Legitimist nobility; " *la sale et impie République* " would have to be overthrown by Boulanger, whom God (!) had elected, and " *le drapeau blanc royal* " hoisted once more. These words sounded strange in my ears from the lips of so responsible a person. I should have thought them stranger still if I had known who and what *le brave Général* was (but I never caught sight of a newspaper), and that the qualifying

* Purcell, *Life of Cardinal Manning* (London, 1895), I., p. 364.

epithets "*sale*" and "*impie*" used by du Lac of the Republic applied particularly well to Boulanger.

There was a significant epilogue to this conversation at Canterbury. In a letter to General Anderledy, well known to me from my youth, I felt bound to report to him the political activity of the Jesuit du Lac; other matters too were dealt with in this letter. Anderledy replied to all, omitting only what concerned du Lac and Boulanger. Later I understood the reason for this omission. The General of the Order, who may also have placed his hopes on Boulanger, did not wish to interfere with du Lac's political doings.

Ever since the establishment of the Centre Party in Germany it has always been closely connected with the Jesuit Order. Theologians of the German Province were often consulted by parliamentary members of the Centre. The leader of the Centre, Lieber, was a frequent guest in the German Jesuit Colleges on the Dutch frontier (Exaeten, Wynandsrade, Blyenbeck). The Provincial, Jacob Ratgeb, used to go to Hanover for important consultations with Windthorst. Once he returned in a state of great annoyance, and in his vexation at Windthorst's "prudence" he allowed these words to escape him: "If Windthorst is not willing, we shall go ahead without him." I never learnt to what the cunning Guelph's unwillingness may have referred. In 1889, at Windthorst's desire, and under the pretext of study and pastorate, two Jesuits were sent to Berlin for permanent residence. I was one of the two, and the other was Jacob Fäh, formerly Rector of Feldkirch, and chief editor of *Stimmen aus Maria-Laach*. I shall recur again to my stay in Berlin. Here, in connection with politics, I can only say that Windthorst and the other Centre leaders made us very welcome. In the lobby of the (old) parliamentary buildings I had a long conversation with Windthorst, in which he said emphatically that the question of the return of the Jesuits, and of the territorial independence of the Pope (the Papal States) must always remain in the foreground. Later on, up to Windthorst's death, another Jesuit, Victor Frins, was his constant adviser in Berlin. In the discussions on the new civil code (*Bürgerliches Gesetzbuch*) the celebrated Jesuit Lehmkuhl played a great part as an inspirer of the Centre Party. August Reichensperger also held lively intercourse with the German Jesuits. His name recalls to me a serious yet diverting "political" occurrence.

In the summer of 1882 August Reichensperger visited the Jesuit College at Blyenbeck. In his honour an open-air picnic was held. Pütz, the Rector, made a speech on the guest of the day, in which he mentioned the exile of the Jesuits from Germany, and the hope of their speedy return with the aid of the Centre Party and its glorious leader Reichensperger. August Reichensperger answered very pleasantly, but with reference to the exile said, almost literally: "Those who plunge into politics as deeply as the Jesuit Order must put up with the occasional political consequences of the plunge." Tableau ! The faces of the surrounding fathers (for we scholastics stood apart) grew long and aghast at this candour. On the very same evening the Rector joined us young Jesuits during recreation, and tried to blot out the impression made by Reichensperger's words. He said Reichensperger had been brought up on Gallo-Josephinian ideas, and a little youthful infection was still in him, and that was why he repeated things he had heard in former days; but the Jesuits had never interfered in politics.

After the expulsion of the Jesuit Order from Germany, the German Province of the Order settled not only in Holland and England, but also in Denmark. Very soon the Jesuits succeeded in converting the widow of the Danish multi-millionaire and press magnate, Berling, proprietor of the great Copenhagen paper *Berlingske Tidende,* to Catholicism. With this lady's money the Jesuit College at Ordrupshoj, near Copenhagen, was built, being in the North what Feldkirch is in the South. It is naturally impossible to ascertain how far the Jesuit influence extended to the *Berlingske Tidende,* and through it to politics.

The Catholic Princess Waldemar of Denmark, daughter of the Duke of Chartres, was also in the hands of the German Jesuits of Copenhagen and Ordrupshoj. Her intense hatred of Germans may doubtless be ascribed to Jesuit influence, apart from her French descent. It is well known that it was Princess Waldemar of Denmark who, in 1887, manipulated matters so as to place the forged documents against Bismarck in the hands of the Tsar Alexander III. Considering the simultaneous political activity of the French Jesuit du Lac, and the influence of the " German " Jesuits in Copenhagen on the French Princess Waldemar of Denmark, it is not a very romantic supposition to connect the origin of the forged anti-Bismarck documents, which almost caused a war, with the Jesuit Order.

An interesting and instructive medley of the political proceedings of the Jesuit Order is spread before us, sufficient to mark the striking contrast between Jesuit words and deeds in this important point also. It only remains to show the road by which the Order is enabled to enter the political arena in the most effective and, at the same time, the least conspicuous manner. That road is confession. For centuries the Jesuit Order supplied nearly all Catholic princes and politically influential men with confessors. Their pastoral work presents vistas of quite enormous activity, comprising in their motley but systematic variety the whole of Europe.

In the beginning of the eighteenth century the Duke of Saint-Simon writes :

"*Les Jésuites maîtres des cours par le confessional de presque tous les rois et de tous les souverains catholiques terribles par la politique la plus raffinée, la plus profonde, la plus supérieure à toute autre considération que leur domination, soutenue par un gouvernement dont la Monarchie, l'autorité, les degrés, les ressorts, le secret, l'uniformité dans les vues, et la multiplicité dans les moyens en sont l'âme.*"*

But the Jesuits do not admit Saint-Simon's testimony. Well! a few decades later it was borne out by a man whom they could hardly set aside as a Jesuit-hater or misinformed. The Jesuit Cordara admits in his Memoirs:

" Nearly all kings and sovereigns of Europe had only Jesuits as directors of their conscience, so that the whole of Europe appeared to be governed by Jesuits only : *reges ac principes prope omnes Europae solis Jesuitis utebantur conscientiae arbitris, ut soli jam Jesuitae tota dominari viderentur Europa.*"†

Therefore, *Habemus confitentem reum*. The Order of the Jesuits governing Europe through its confessors of sovereigns stands here convicted before us : the official Constitutions forbid the acceptance of the office of confessor of a sovereign. The fortieth decree of the second General Congregation of 1565 runs thus :

" Since it was proposed to appoint for the illustrious Cardinal of Augsburg [Otto von Truchsess] a theologian of our Society to be his father confessor and also join his court, the Congregation has decided not to appoint any of our people either to a sovereign or any other lord of the Church or State, to attend his court or reside there in order to fulfil the office of confessor, theologian, or any other office, except for the very short period of one or two months."‡

Is this strict prohibition meant to refer back to the

---

* *Mémoires* (Paris, 1873), 7, 132 *et seq.*
† Döllinger, *Beiträge*, 3, 72.
‡ *Inst. S.J.*, I., 188.

founder of the Order himself, Ignatius Loyola, who, scarcely twenty years before, by virtue of holy obedience, *en virtud de santa obediencia*, appointed Fathers Le Jay, Pollanco and Pelletier as confessors to the Dukes Hercules of Ferrara and Cosimo de Medici, and had placed Fathers Gonzalez and Miron as confessors at the disposal of the King of Portugal ? * Hardly ! This decree, too, is nothing but a paper to save appearances prudently produced by the Order, to be shown in case of necessity and soothe the minds of the public. The calculated deceit of the strict prohibition is almost proved by the action of the fifth General of the Order, the Neapolitan Claudius Acquaviva.

Not very long after the decree was issued, in 1602, Acquaviva drew up an Ordinance in which he gives precise instructions for confessors of sovereigns, and passes over the previous "strict prohibition" with the truly Jesuitical phrase of : "The greater glory of God."

"If the Society [of Jesus] can no longer escape such an office because, for various reasons, the greater glory of our Lord God seems to require it, then care should be taken as to the choice of suitable persons, and the manner in which they carry out their duties, so that the sovereign should derive benefit, the people be edified, and the Society sustain no injury thereby."†

Then, after apparently strict injunctions (in Notes 4–7) that the father confessor should not engage "in exterior or political affairs," and not let himself be employed as "censor of ministers and courtiers," all this is again made possible in another way in Note 8 in the shape of an exhortation to the sovereign:

"The sovereign should listen with equanimity and patience to whatever his father confessor should think fit to suggest (*sugge-*

* *Cartas de S. Ignacio de Loyola* (Madrid, 1874), I., 326 ; II., 65 ; III., 173.
† *Inst. S.J.*, II., 225.

rendum) to him daily according to the voice of his conscience. For as a prominent person and a sovereign is concerned, it is fitting that the priest should be allowed to suggest what he considers good for the greater service of God and the sovereign, and not only with regard to such things as he might know from him [the prince] in the character of penitent, but also with regard to those which he might hear elsewhere (*quae hinc inde audiuntur*), requiring a remedy, for the removal of oppression, the lessening of annoyances frequently arising from the actions of the ministers, contrary to the wish and will of the sovereign, whose conscience may be oppressed by the harm done, and the duty of making provision against it."*

So the confessor is to suggest [*suggerere*] to the sovereign whatever his conscience may dictate to him [*quidquid dictante sibi conscientia*]. It is obvious that an opening is thus provided for the most pronounced political influence. Thus we see, for instance, that the Jesuit Caussin, Father Confessor to Louis XIII. of France, wrote to General Mutins Vitelleschi:

"If he dissuaded the king from an alliance with the Turks, it would not be interfering with politics; for the question whether an alliance with the Turks should be permitted was not a political one, but a matter of conscience."†

A letter from General Caraffa, of May 23rd, 1648, to the Rector of the Jesuit College at Münster, Gottfried Cörler, cunningly points to "conscience" as the road by which the official prohibition regarding interference with politics might be evaded. This confidential letter is all the more interesting because Caraffa refers in it to an encyclical, published by himself, against interference with politics:

" . . . As regards my encyclical that our people should not meddle with affairs of war or peace, I did not mean thereby to

Inst. S.J., II., 226.
† *Tuba Magna*, II., 310.

Politics and Confessors

prevent our people in the confessional from directing the consciences of those turning to them with doubts, but only from dealing with such affairs outside the confessional."*

As the Jesuit House at Münster, to which the letter was addressed, was just then a chief hotbed of political activity, Caraffa's duplicity (for his letter is the essence of duplicity) is of particular significance, and was probably particularly effective.

We have seen already, and shall see more clearly still, what a great part the "conscience" formula, introduced by the Generals Acquaviva and Caraffa, played in the political doings of the Order, how it is applied again and again when Jesuit confessors of sovereigns desire to represent their political influence as unpolitical.

* *See* Steinberger, p. 199, for Latin text.

CHAPTER XIX

THE CRITICISM CONTINUED: COURT CONFESSORS

ACQUAVIVA, that Machiavelli in Jesuit garb, not satisfied with an equivocal official "Ordinance" destined to be enrolled in the Constitutions of the Order, also issued a secret Instruction for the Confessors of Sovereigns.

This secret Instruction was published by the Benedictine Dudik, himself a strict Catholic, in his *Archiv für Oesterreichische Geschichte** from the manuscripts of the Court Library at Vienna.† It is composed throughout in the form of questions, as Dudik expresses it, "as a Confession Mirror for Sovereigns."

"From the questions," says Dudik, "the purpose at which the Jesuits aimed through their father confessors may be clearly perceived, namely, the supremacy of the Catholic Church, such as a Gregory, an Innocent, or a Boniface aspired to obtain."‡

Here are some questions from the "Instruction":

Whether he [the father confessor] tried skilfully to find out himself, or through trustworthy, zealous, and wise men, how the ministers, magistrates and judges discharged their offices; whether he had discreet and able men at hand through whom, by searching the lives of citizens (*explorans*), he could inquire into (*inquirat*) the source of their income, their expenditure, and if they had entered into forbidden contracts; whether he [the prince] had hampered the Inquisition; whether, when called on to

---
* Vol. 54, p. 234.   † MS. Chart. Sign., 11,821.   ‡ Vol. 54, p. 234.

execute its sentences on heretics, he had refused to do so; whether he had carried on an unrighteous war; whether he had broken his princely oaths; whether he had disobeyed the Pope and Prelates of the Church?*

The Jesuit Order—it should be here noted—is the only one of all the monastic Orders which has official and secret Instructions for the Confessors of Sovereigns. I was, therefore, more than justified in designating the Confession of Sovereigns as an institution of the Order.

Very characteristic and significant for the fundamental attitude of the Order towards the confession of sovereigns is this circumstance:

The Generals Goswin Nickel (a German) and Mutius Vitelleschi issued the following orders in official letters of February 23rd, 1641, and November 28th, 1654, both addressed to the Provincial of the Upper German Province:

"When sovereigns require a Jesuit's opinion on any subject, the Jesuit in question is to report the matter to his Superior, who is to lay it before several Jesuits for discussion. The resolution formed after this consultation is supplied to the Jesuit who has been consulted by the sovereign."†

This Ordinance, which is in the first instance concerned with the confessors of sovereigns, could only have the result doubtless intended by the Generals, that it was just the most important matters (those that required a second opinion) which were not kept secret between

* The publication of the secret Instruction is exceedingly inconvenient to the Jesuit Duhr. He passes over this significant document in a mere footnote, mentioning it casually, and just where he ought to have discussed it he misleads by hushing it up. (*Die Jesuiten an den deutschen Fürstenhöfen des 16 Jahrhunderts*, Freiburg, 1910, p. 6.) In the *Jesuitenfabeln* (4 Ed., p. 100) Duhr also displays the same disingenuousness; he quotes from Dudik a passage from a letter of General Vitelleschi, in which the Imperial Father Confessor in Vienna, the Jesuit Lamormaini, is referred to Acquaviva's official *Ordinatio*, but passes over the secret Instruction in silence.

† From the manuscript papers of the Jesuits published by Döllinger-Reusch, from the Archives at Munich. *Moralstreitigkeiten*, I., 650.

sovereign and confessor, but came to the knowledge of the General of the Order, and could thus be utilised by him in his general calculations and measures.

This is clearly expressed in letters by the Jesuit Caussin, Father Confessor of Louis XIII. of France, to General Vitelleschi. Caussin, who appears to have been an ingenuous man, objects to being expected to report to the Superiors of the Order the confidences made to him by the King, and the discussions he held with him.

'I am reproached for not seeking advice of my Superiors on the matters I discuss with the King. . . . But I know from Thomas [Aquinas] that, according to natural, human and divine right, matters of confession are to be kept secret. . . . What law or what constitution of the Society [of Jesus] is there that bids the Father Confessor report to his Superiors on the affairs of his penitents ? . . . Is the King's conscience to be revealed to as many persons as there are Consultors in our Houses ? "*

Thus Caussin was of the opinion, and he must surely have known, that the Ordinance of his Superiors contained an invitation to violate the secret of the confessional.

We have already seen that the Order disregards the secrecy of the confessional in the case of its own members. But here the secrecy of the confessional, which according to general theological doctrine every priest is bound to preserve even at risk of death, is set aside on principle by the Jesuit Order for the furtherance of its own political ends. The Jesuit Caussin opposed the demand of his Superiors. Other Jesuit confessors of sovereigns behaved differently. For instance, a great deal has been written in controversy about the betrayal of the confession of the Empress Maria Theresa. But it appears to be an established fact that either a genuine confession or a

* The letter is published *in extenso* in *Liberius Candidus, Tuba Magna*, Edit. 4 (Strassburg, 1760), II., 329 *et seq.*, and in part in Döllinger-Reusch, I., 651.

strictly confidential communication made by the Empress to him, as her spiritual director, was reported by the Jesuit Campmüller to his Superiors in Rome. No contradiction such as, for instance, that made by the Jesuit Duhr* can affect the gist of the matter. It is positively absurd that Duhr, in order to contradict it, refers to his own researches in the Archives at Vienna and Simancas, and states that there he had found nothing about a " betrayal of confession." From what we know of Duhr's researches, we are positively compelled to disbelieve him. But even if nothing were to be found in Vienna and Simancas, what proof could that be in contradiction of the fact ?

The rest of Duhr's counterproofs are just as unconvincing. They may be summed up in the silence preserved on this matter by Arneth, Maria Theresa's biographer, and a statement made by him in answer to a letter from Duhr, that in "his researches in the Archives" he had learnt nothing about the matter. These assertions and purely negative proofs are opposed by positive and permanent testimonies.

Canon Ginzel, of Leitmeritz Cathedral, a strictly orthodox Churchman, reports :

" On this affair, Dr. Jacob Stern, Royal and Imperial Court Chaplain at the time of Maria Theresa, living in retirement as titular provost of Ivanzia at Hetzendorf, near Vienna, who had a very extensive knowledge of current events, told the author (in 1830) as follows : ' The urgent representations made by the Bourbon Courts to Theresa on account of the suppression of the Jesuits had not remained entirely without effect on her.
Then one day the Abbot of St. Dorothea (his name I have forgotten) came to Theresa and handed her a paper written by her Father Confessor, the Jesuit Campmüller, containing one of her recent confessions. Its main contents are said to have been her

* *Jesuitenfabeln* (4), pp. 40-68.

scruples as to the recent partition of Poland. Theresa now voted for the suppression of the Society and is supposed to have reported to Ganganelli this violation of the seal of confession, as a reason for not allowing the Jesuits to remain in her dominion.' "*

These recollections of a Court Chaplain of Maria Theresa, told to Ginzel himself, who, as the latter points out, "had a very extensive knowledge of current events" and was, therefore, still in the enjoyment of his mental faculties, are doubtless of great significance, not lessened by Duhr's derisive remarks about "the old gentleman."

Another remark added by Ginzel still further assists in clearing up the point in question:

"On the other hand, we must note that the scruples which the august lady . felt with regard to the partition of Poland were very openly expressed before all her counsellors, and if the Father Confessor wrote down such scruples, he did not violate the seal of confession, inasmuch as they had not been uttered in confession only."†

What the Jesuit Campmüller had reported to Rome about his Imperial penitent need not have been a confession in the strictest sense of the word. But it was a breach of confidence of the meanest kind if Campmüller passed on what the Empress had put before him as her spiritual director, in the shape of questions and doubts, no matter whether she communicated similar questions and doubts to her "counsellors."

Thus Campmüller seems to have acted strictly according to the decree of Mutius Vitelleschi, who did not literally speak of genuine "confessions" either, but of "points requiring another opinion." The partition of Poland may surely have been a point that might cause Maria Theresa to turn to her spiritual director in order to obtain his opinion.

* *Kirchenhistorische Schriften* (Vienna, 1872), 2, 231.
† *Ibid.*

Court Confessors

An equally strong proof is furnished by the testimony of the Imperial Russian Professor and General Superintendent of the Lutheran Congregations at St. Petersburg, Dr. Ignatius Fessler. Fessler is one of the most remarkable and sincere personalities of the eighteenth and nineteenth centuries, whose experiences and adventures are not sufficiently known. In his interesting book, *Reminiscences of a Seventy Years' Pilgrimage,* he says:

" The Professor at the University of Vienna, whom I venerated most of all, and who loved me like a father, was Josephus Julianus Monsperger, a hale old man of seventy-nine, a Jesuit formerly *tertiae professionis*, and consequently initiated in the secrets of the Order. The Rector of the Professed House in Vienna had been obliged to go on a journey, and had charged him to clear up the rectory and to have it cleaned. A picture had then attracted his attention; he had taken it off the wall, in order to look at it in a better light. Meanwhile he had noticed in the place where the picture had been hanging a small closet which appeared to him suspicious; he noticed and pressed a spring, and the door flew open. Among a mass of papers his glance fell on a case with the superscription: ' Confessions of the Great and Powerful.' He opened it, and found Confessions of the Empress, the Archdukes, Archduchesses, several Ministers and other persons of high rank. . . . So Monsperger frequently informed me."*

The Jesuit Duhr tries to get the better of this testimony by talking of " romantic embroidery," and by " proving " that Monsperger had held no position in the Professed House at Vienna, and that the journal of that House did not mention a journey of the Rector's in the year 1764. Still, he does not dare to attack Fessler's trustworthiness.

Voltaire also reports in a letter to the Duc de Richelieu, a " betrayed confession," and says that the Jesuit

---

* Fessler, *Rückblicke auf eine siebzigjährige Pilgerschaft* (Breslau, 1824), pp. 166-168. In consequence of this discovery, Monsperger left the Order of the Jesuits and became Professor of Oriental Languages at Vienna University.

M

d'Aubanton, Confessor to Philip V. of Spain, had told the contents of a confession of the King's to the Duke of Orleans, and that the Count Fuentes and the Duke of Villa Hermosa held proofs of this.*

Unfortunately Voltaire does not give these proofs. But the fact corresponds with the sketch of d'Aubanton made on the strength of long acquaintance by Saint-Simon.

We will now turn our attention to the work of individual Jesuit confessors of sovereigns. Here also a few extracts will have to suffice. The Jesuit Maggio, Father Confessor of the Emperor Rudolf II., by means of a memorandum and by verbal representations, sought to induce the Emperor to proceed with the utmost severity against the Protestants. It is obvious that, considering the conditions of the time, shortly before the outbreak of the Thirty Years' War, this was strong and decisive interference in politics. The Jesuit Duhr,† who takes good care not to communicate Maggio's documentary memoranda which are at his disposal in the Secret Archives of the Order, does not, of course, see anything touching politics in his fellow Jesuit's action, neither does Maggio himself, who is naïve enough to utter a strong warning against interference in politics when writing to General Borgia in March, 1571.

It is evident that the double face and even double conscience, assumed officially a few years later by the Jesuit confessor of sovereigns, in accordance with General Acquaviva's Instruction, began to manifest itself even then in its main features.‡ Only a few months later this duplicity appears distinctly in a report to Rome of the Jesuit Emerich Forsler of the 21st of May, 1571:

---

* *Œuvres*, Edit. Beaumarchais, 6, 79.

† Duhr, *Die Jesuiten an den deutschen Fürstenhofen des 16. Jahrhunderts*, p. 18.

‡ *Cf.* Sacchini, S.J., *Hist. Societ. Jesu ad ann.* 1571, nr. 139.

"The relations of our Father Stephan to Archduke Charles [Governor of Graz, son of King Ferdinand] are quite confidential; on the most important matters the Archduke asks and receives his advice, and thinks so highly of him that he wished to admit him to the public Council (*publicum consilium*), when religious matters would be discussed with the Estates of the Realm. This I have forbidden; he is only to help privately as much as possible, in a prudent and discreet manner."*

Dudik shows† that the Jesuit Lamormaini, the confessor of the Emperor Ferdinand II., was the originator of the Decree of Restitution of March 6th, 1629. Still more interesting is his proof, that the election of Ferdinand II.'s son as king, in August 7th, 1636, at Ratisbon, can be traced back to the Jesuit Lamormaini. The Senate of Hamburg wished to reward the merits of the Jesuit in this indubitably political affair by a present of 1,000 thalers. Lamormaini wisely declined for himself, but induced the Senate to turn over the sum to the Jesuit Heinrich Schachtin, who was secretly at work in Hamburg.

As principal adviser of the Emperor Lamormaini had also a considerable share in Wallenstein's fate. Under the presidency of the Emperor a "secret council" was held on January 24th, 1634, in Prince von Eggenberg's house, when the Duke of Friedland's fate was decided. As the Jesuit Lamormaini could not be present the Emperor sent Bishop Anton Wolfrath to him, in order to inform him of the resolutions and to get his opinion. "The Vienna Bishop," writes the Emperor to the Jesuit, "will communicate to your Reverence a matter of the greatest importance and that under the strictest seal of conscience or confession."‡

This is in agreement with Gindely's report about the meeting of the College at Ratisbon, in July–August, 1630, at which Wallenstein's first deposition was discussed:

* Duhr, *Die Jesuiten an den deutschen Fürstenhöfen*, p. 25.
† P. 243 *et seq.*   ‡ Dudik, p. 244.

"It now depended only on the opinion of two persons [for the Electors had already decided against Wallenstein] who had the greatest weight with the Emperor [Ferdinand II.] and whom he considered almost more than Eggenberg, namely the Empress and [the Jesuit] Lamormaini. . . Lamormaini threw the whole weight of his prestige into the balance against Waldstein.* It cannot be doubted that he did this, not on his own initiative, but by the instructions of the General of the Jesuits, who in his turn was only carrying out the directions of the Pope. The Spanish Cabinet held the opinion that the Confessor alone had clinched the matter and that without him the Emperor would have retained his general. Three years later and, moreover, several months before the murder at Eger, when Lamormaini warned against Waldstein's plots and requested the Spanish Ambassador at Vienna, the Marquis of Castaneda, to call the Emperor's attention to the danger threatening him, Philip IV. forbade his ambassador to interfere in any way. 'Lamormaini,' says the letter of the Spanish King to Castaneda, 'is the cause of the present dangerous situation; he advised and brought about the dismissal of the Duke of Mecklenburg [Wallenstein], and if he speaks to you again, you are to tell him that he himself is the cause of all the trouble.'"†

A very telling document in proof of the Jesuit Lamormaini's political activity is the report written with his own hand, on September 18th, 1630, to Ferdinand II. on the proposals which the Elector of Bavaria had made to him (Lamormaini) on his attitude to the Winter-King. "This matter also concerns conscience and religion": these words conclude Lamormaini's expositions. Besides this the report deals with stationing of troops in Pomerania and Silesia, and filling the posts in the highest law-courts in Speyer and Vienna, which are reproached with dilatoriness.‡ Even the Catholic historian, Steinberger, who is strongly

---

* The older and more correct spelling.

† Gindely, *Waldstein während seines ersten Generalats* (Leipzig, 1886), 2, 291 *et seq.* For the letter of the Spanish King Gindely quotes the *Archive of Simancas*, *Philip IV. to Castaneda*, dated 19th September, 1633.

‡ For wording of the report, *see* Dudik, p. 337 *et seq.*

in favour of the Jesuits, says of Lamormaini and his relation to politics :

"At the Imperial Castle at Vienna, the well-known Father William Germain Lamormaini exercised a pretty extensive influence on his Imperial penitent (*filius spiritualis*), Ferdinand II. The Emperor followed the advice and judgment of his Father Confessor, as the sheep follows the shepherd, and in order to safeguard his conscience in every direction he initiated him into everything, even the most insignificant trifles. As regards Father Lamormaini's political views, his position concerning the Mantuan succession and in the discussions preceding the Treaty of Prague, added to his semi-French descent [Lamormaini came from Luxemburg], seem to justify the supposition of the Spanish statesman that he favoured France."*

It was universally said that Lamormaini had caused the so-called Mantuan War of Succession. A very tortuous letter from Lamormaini, addressed to the King of Spain with the object of diverting the suspicion, failed in its endeavour.†

Forty-one confidential letters from the Emperor to the Jesuits Becanus and Lamormaini, published by Dudik,‡ show in how many directions the confessors were occupied, and within what vast limits matters were considered "questions of conscience." Even on the appointment of court-marshals and on lawsuits their opinion was taken. But mostly it is questions of high politics which the Emperor places before them: the state of affairs in Hungary, Bohemia and Silesia, the influence on certain Electors. There are frequent cautions from the Emperor to treat the documents sent for perusal as strictly confidential. For Tilly also the Jesuit received imperial commissions. For the Emperor's brother, Archduke

---

* *Die Jesuiten und die Friedensfrage in der Zeit vom Prager Frieden bis zum Nürnberger Friedensexekutionshauptrezess*, 1635-1650 (Freiburg, 1906), p. 15 *et seq.*

† Dudik, pp. 245-248.   ‡ Pp. 256-278.

Leopold, the Imperial Confessors undertook considerable money transactions, etc., etc.

A truly servile dependence on the Jesuits in private and public affairs is revealed by these letters from the Emperor and the Archduke.

Gindely describes this dependence in detail. In one instance, however, the influence of the Jesuits failed, although it was brought to bear at high pressure. This was creditable to the Emperor and a disgrace to the Jesuit politicians.

"At that time [1635] it might have been possible for the Emperor to prevent France from taking any further part in the German disputes, by purchasing this favour with the surrender of Alsace. If he decided on this sacrifice he would have no need to treat with Saxony or to surrender Lusatia to that Power. In Rome it was desired that the Emperor should satisfy the French claims; Pope Urban VIII. wanted in this way to make France more powerful, and to snatch Lusatia from the hands of the Protestants. At that time Lamormaini received an Instruction from Rome to influence the Emperor in this sense, and to represent to him the recovery and reconversion to Catholicism of Lusatia as a work pleasing to God, for which Alsace might be sacrificed. But, however much Lamormaini might try, this time all his exhortations availed him nothing."*

To the Emperor Ferdinand the Jesuit's advice was so indispensable that when Lamormaini was ill, he sent the Prince of Eggenberg to him and begged for his opinion. Thus Khevenhiller's Annals proclaim the truth in saying that:

"Lamormaini tyrannised over the Emperor and the Princes, and the Emperor was so completely in his power that not the Emperor but the Jesuits reigned supreme."†

Through Lamormaini's influence, foreign Jesuits were also set to work for the Emperor.

---

* Gindely, *Geschichte des dreissigjährigen Krieges*, p. 14 et seq.   † II., 595.

Court Confessors

In December, 1619, Ferdinand II. sent Count Wratislaw von Fürstenberg to Louis XIII. in Paris in order to induce the King to help. At first all attempts were in vain. Finally he [Count Fürstenberg] succeeded in winning over the Royal Confessor, the Jesuit Arnoux; the latter had probably received directions from Rome to act in Ferdinand's interest; in any case he undertook the task. At Christmas he put it to the King as a duty to assist the Emperor, who was oppressed for the sake of religion

In the evening of the same day the Royal Private Secretary repaired to Fürstenberg's house and brought him word that not only the King but also the Ministers had been won over to active support of the Emperor.*

This explains the remark of Gustavus Adolphus: "There are three 'L's' I should like to see hanged: the Jesuit Lamormaini, the Jesuit Laymann, and the Jesuit Laurentius Forer."†

On the part of mediator between Spain and France played by the Jesuit Coton, Father Confessor to Henry IV. of France, Coton's fellow-Jesuit Prat writes:

"*Persuadé qu'une alliance entre la France et l'Espagne aurait de grands avantages pour l'Église, et qu'elle imposerait aux puissances hérétiques de l'Europe, il avait toujours eu soin de ménager un rapprochement entre ces deux couronnes, si longtemps ennemies. . . . Le projet du P. Coton abouti enfin . . . au mariage de Louis XIII. avec Anne d'Autriche.*"‡

In a letter to Louis XIV. Fénélon attacks the Jesuit La Chaise, the all-powerful confessor of the King:

" Your Father Confessor is not vicious, but he shuns sterling virtue and only loves worldly and licentious people. He is jealous of his prestige, which you have raised to an unlimited height.

---

* Gindely, III., 6, quotes an original report of Fürstenberg's to the Emperor dated Dec. 24th, 1619.

† Dudik, p. 248. ‡ *Recherches*, etc. (Lyons, 1876), III., 199, 200.

184 Fourteen Years a Jesuit

Never before did a King's Father Confessor alone appoint bishops and decide all questions of conscience. You, Sire, are the only person in France who does not know that he [La Chaise] is ignorant, that his mind is narrow and uncultured. The Jesuits, too, despise him and are indignant at his giving in to the ambitions of his family. You have turned a member of an Order into a Minister of State ; he knows neither people nor things, and falls a ready victim to any who flatter him and give him presents."*

Especially interesting are the remarks of Madame de Maintenon, scattered in numerous letters, on this Father Confessor of her Royal lover. They do not throw a particularly favourable light on his character, or that of the Jesuits in general. Yet no one could dispute that Madame de Maintenon had undeniable powers of observation, and an interest in the Jesuits in general and La Chaise in

* Grégoire, *Histoire des Confesseurs* (Paris, 1824), p. 363 ; Lavallée, *Correspondance générale de Mme. de Maintenon* (Paris, 1866), 4, 45 *et seq*. As regards Grégoire, the tactics of the Jesuits are very clear. Wherever Grégoire reports something in favour of a Jesuit princely confessor he is quoted in full ; if he reports anything unfavourable it is suppressed, or Grégoire is called " Grégoire the undiscerning." Of course, the Jesuit Duhr is particularly great at this double-faced use of Grégoire. For instance (in the *Jesuitenfabeln* (4), p. 69), Duhr quotes a few words of praise by Grégoire on the Jesuit Arnoux, Confessor of Louis XIII. of France, but suppresses the following intervening phrases : " In the year 1621 Father Arnoux was dismissed from his office as confessor to the King. . . . At first he looked and spoke with resignation, but instead of congratulating himself on being exempt from an office which must always be a burden in the eyes of piety, he appeared to take his dismissal as a disgrace. Details told by Gramond prove that the confessor's bitter grief was to be seen in his behaviour, and that he still strove ambitiously to recover his lost position. So hard is it (as a historian says) for monks who have been employed at court to shake off its chains. In order to return to his position, Arnoux engaged in intrigues in which the true spirit of the Society [of Jesus] was revealed, as on their own confession they are like a lion to those who fear them, like a hare to the courageous " (pp. 332-334). Duhr is careful also not to tell his readers the general opinion expressed by Grégoire on Jesuit confessors. " The Jesuit confessor at court was in a sense the Agent of the Order, so as to work in its interest, to slander and ruin those who thwarted or appeared to thwart its ambition. . . . Among the Jesuit confessors of princes some are justly to be praised. But the virtue of the individual does not represent the spirit of the community into whose secrets the confessors were initiated, and who in several countries, especially in France, Spain, and particularly in Portugal, brought the sovereigns under their rule, and thus governed the people for the benefit of their Society." (Grégoire, pp. 336, 426 *et seq*.)

particular. The letters are addressed to the Archbishop of Paris, and belong to the period of 1695–1700. Here are some specimens :

"Do not attempt to cure Père La Chaise, or to teach him moderation on the principle that the pious are of no use . . . this principle of the good Father's [Madame de Maintenon frequently speaks sarcastically of La Chaise as "*bon père*"] is universally known, you may openly discuss it with him. Do not feel in honour bound to tell him that he in particular ought to be the protector of piety, instead of saying that we are all of no use, just because I love good people and he cannot bear them. . . . Father de la Chaise has been to see me . . . he was gay and free in his manner, and his visit was more like an insult than an act of civility. (*Sa visite avait plus l'air d'une insulte que d'une honnêteté.*) The Jesuits make war on us openly on all sides, and those who wish for peace are to be pitied. . . . It is your place to defend the cause of the Church and the Bishop of Meaux [Bossuet], which Father La Chaise attacked in speaking to the King. By the way in which the King spoke to me this evening, I doubt less than ever that you should speak to Father La Chaise about Confessors.
I want you to make the Jesuits feel that you have given them up, and that your consideration for them is forced. Perhaps you will spare them, they will grow still more bitter against you . . . although my head is in a sad state to-day, I cannot help relieving my feelings to you about all the mischief that the good Father [La Chaise] has achieved with the King. . Father La Chaise wants to set right the harm he has done in the matter of Father Poisson, but he has more talent for evil than for good, and the reason is that his intentions are not honest. He complains greatly to the King of not being included among the [newly to be appointed] bishops. Such speeches remove the impression of kindness; and I was malicious enough to tell him straight out that he need not be the enemy of the bishops, because he was not of their number.
   On Sunday I saw Father Bourdaloue [a Jesuit and celebrated preacher in Paris], who expressed to me the sorrow of the Society [of Jesus] at my appearing not to love them, on account of the estrangement between me and Father La Chaise. I answered

that it was not my fault, and that I was ready to meet any advance on their part."*

I have dwelt so long on Madame de Maintenon and her relations to the Jesuit La Chaise, because the Jesuits try to make the public believe that her unfavourable opinion of him was mainly based on " forgeries " by the Calvinist La Beaumelle. The testimony of the genuine letters of Madame de Maintenon is suppressed by the Jesuits.†

The Jesuit La Chaise was followed by the Jesuit Tellier (or Letellier) in the post of Confessor to Louis XIV. His influence on the King and his policy was so great that even Crétineau-Joly admits that " Letellier dominated (*dominait*) Louis XIV."‡

Saint-Simon, who was personally acquainted with the Jesuit Tellier, draws a vivid picture of him:

" Till then Father Tellier was quite unknown to the King. He only knew his name, which, with five or six other Jesuit names, was on a list drawn up by Father La Chaise of those who would be suited to succeed him. Tellier had passed through every grade of the Society, having been Professor, Theologian, Rector and Provincial Scriptor. He had been commissioned [during the dispute about the Chinese rites] to defend the creed of Confucius. . . .

* Lavallée, *Correspondance générale de Madame de Maintenon* (Paris, 1866), 4, 52, 89, 151, 154, 161, 179 *et seq.*, 310. The statement about the Jesuit Bourdaloue is also worthy of note. In the pulpit he played the part of the stern penitential preacher who attacks the loose morals of the court ; in the boudoir of the former mistress and future wife of Louis XIV. he sued for her favour towards his Order.

† The Jesuit Duhr deals in truly Jesuitical fashion with the doings of his fellow-Jesuit La Chaise (*Jesuitenfabeln* (4), pp. 674–681). The seven pages he devotes to him are filled with timid elusion of the subject, an attempt to discredit sources that are unfavourable to La Chaise. But Duhr evades the real task which he should have attempted, to justify La Chaise's conduct as the confessor of a king who was mastered by his passions. He says : " We cannot here discuss the question whether any reproaches can be brought against this Jesuit and of what nature ; our only object is to clear away some of the fabulous deposit (*sic*) which has accumulated about this confessor in such masses that his person has become almost mythical " (p. 674). We should imagine it was just these reproaches which were in question.

‡ Crétineau-Joly, 4, 451.

He was a zealous partisan of Molinism [system of the Jesuit doctrine of grace which derived its name from the Jesuit Molina], and desired to erect the new dogmas of his Order on the ruins of the antagonistic opinions. Educated in such principles and initiated into all the secrets of the Order, because of the genius which the Order discovered in him, he had, ever since entering it, lived only for the realisation of the principles of the Order, believing that for the attainment of this end everything was permissible. Of severe intellect, always on the alert, a foe to all frivolity and social pleasures.

All moderation was hateful to him, he only tolerated it under compulsion, or with the prospect of thus more surely attaining his goal. . . . His life was a hard one from inclination and habit.

Formed by the principles and policy of the Society of Jesus he was thoroughly false, deceitful and malicious, concealing himself by a thousand folds and windings . . . scoffing at the most formal agreements if it no longer suited him to abide by them, and passionately pursuing those with whom they had been made. He was a terrible man, aiming at revolution both openly and secretly. . . . His outward appearance promised nothing else, and it kept its promises. If met in a forest, he would have inspired terror; his face was sombre and false; his eyes were wicked, penetrating and crooked. That such a man, who had dedicated his body and soul to the Order, who knew no other nourishment than its deepest secrets, and no other God but the Society . . . was in all other respects coarse, ignorant and insolent, knowing neither courtesy nor moderation, is not surprising. He had completed his training in the principles of the Order at Rome, and the Order had been compelled to send him back to France on account of the sensation caused by his book [on the Chinese rites] which had been placed on the Index. When he visited the King in his cabinet for the first time after his introduction, Bloin and Fagon were present. Fagon, leaning on his stick, closely watched his expression and movements. The King asked him whether he were related to the Le Telliers (a family of the old nobility). The Father bowed. ' I, Sire, related to the lords of Le Tellier ? Far from it. I am a poor peasant's son, from Normandy, where my father was a farmer.' Fagon, whom nothing escaped, turned to Blois and said, pointing to the Jesuit : ' What a villain ! ' (*Quel sacre !*). Nor was he mistaken in this strange judgment on a confessor. This Tellier had put on the manners and gestures of a man who was afraid of his position, and only accepted it out of obedience to his Order. I have dwelt in such detail on this new confessor, because he was the originator of those amazing storms under which even to this day State and Church, education and doctrine, and so many good people are suffering, and because I have a more immediate and exact knowledge of this terrible personality than anyone else at court."*

Saint-Simon also tells us with what perseverance Tellier sought his society, because he knew of the great influence which Saint-Simon possessed with the King and the Dukes of Berry and Orleans.† He concludes his account of Tellier with the words:

"He (Tellier) saw the King an old man and a Dauphin in his first childhood. His task with the King was an easy one for he doubtless remembered the legacy of Father La Chaise, I mean the strange counsel which he gave him. He preferred to leave everything to the Jesuits rather than irritate them and expose himself to the chance of a dagger."‡

Saint-Simon also gives a character sketch of the Jesuit Bermudez, Confessor at the Court of Madrid, in connection with which we may note that Saint-Simon, during his stay at Madrid as French ambassador, had a good deal of intercourse with Bermudez.

"Bermudez, a Spaniard to the core, hated France and the French, and was secretly devoted to the House of Austria and connected with the whole Italian cabal."§

The predecessor of Bermudez in the office of Confessor to the King was his fellow-Jesuit d'Aubanton, who played the same important political part in Spain as his co-Jesuits, Caussin, Coton, La Chaise, Tellier, etc., in France, and

* *Mémoires*, p. 240.   † Pp. 240 and 9, 231.
‡ Pp. 9, 431.   § Pp. 19, 133.

Becàn, Lamormaini, etc., at Vienna. D'Aubanton, formerly Assistant to the General in Rome and, as Saint-Simon asserts, the author of the bull *unigenitus* directed against the Jansenists, which caused so much trouble and disturbance, had succeeded the Jesuit Robinet as the King's Confessor.*

"*Ce changement de confesseur,*" says Saint-Simon, "*fut un grand et long malheur pour les deux couronnes*" (France and Spain).

The importance which d'Aubanton attached to himself and his position as the King's Confessor, and the value set by the Order on the appointment of one of its members, may be gathered from an interesting communication of d'Alembert's.†

D'Aubanton had induced Louis XIV. to arrange that Philip V. of Spain should take a Jesuit confessor, in the first instance d'Aubanton himself. And the regular appointment of a Jesuit as the King's confessor in Madrid was laid down, owing to the influence of the Jesuits, as an essential condition of a good understanding between France and Spain, in a secret article in the Treaty of Peace of 1720.‡

One of the most adroit political agents of his day was the Jesuit Monod, Confessor of the Duchess Christine of Savoy, daughter of Henry IV. of France. Her husband, Victor Amadeo I. of Savoy, often made use of Monod for diplomatic missions. His biographer, Raimond, says of him in the *Biographie universelle* :

"Monod ruled over Paris, Madrid, Rome and Turin. Cardinal Richelieu recognised the danger of Monod, who had combined with his fellow-Jesuit Caussin, the Confessor of Louis XIII., and succeeded in bringing about the banishment of both Jesuits from court."

* *Mémoires*, 11, 110.   † D'Alembert, *Œuvres* (Paris, 1805), 10, 57.
‡ *Cf.* Döllinger-Reusch, I., 102.
§ Grégoire, *Histoire des Confesseurs*, pp. 193, 194.

Very discreditable was the part played by the confessor of Duke Charles IV. of Lorraine, the Jesuit Cheminet.

"He supported the Duke in his desire for a separation from his wife, to whom he had been married for twelve years, in order to marry a Mademoiselle de Cantecroix. And this though he was also confessor to the Duchess! Rome decided in 1664 against the amorous Duke and the accommodating Jesuit."*

A marked hostility to Germany characterises the political activity of the Jesuit Vervaux, under Maximilian I. of Bavaria.

Vervaux was Maximilian's confessor and, as Steinberger admits, "may be regarded as the type of an accommodating court theologian." In the spring of 1645 he was sent, with the cognisance and approval of his Superiors (as is shown by a letter addressed by the Provincial of the Upper German Province, Nicasius Widmanns, to the Head of the Jesuit Professed-House in Paris), by Maximilian to Paris to pave the way for an understanding between France and Bavaria. Vervaux set out on this distinctly political embassy under the *alias* and with the outward appearance of Chevalier Baptiste de Clorans, on March 3rd, 1645. On April 5th and 11th Clorans-Vervaux had interviews with Mazarin which, however, led to no result, and the Chevalier Jesuit returned to Munich on May 22nd, without having accomplished his purpose.†

Two years later Vervaux composed a report for his penitent Maximilian I., in which he once more advocated an alliance with Bavaria and France, on the ground that it was lawful, honourable, and necessary. The document ends with the words:

"If the matter turns out well, the Austrians and

---

* Grégoire, *Histoire des Confesseurs*, p. 181.

† For details and documentary proofs, *see* Steinberger, *Die Jesuiten und die Friedensfrage*, pp. 41-75.

Spaniards will show honour to those whom they used to despise, and take up a more suitable attitude."

This clearly shows that it was not with a view to conquering the Protestant Powers that the Jesuit Vervaux desired the alliance between France and Bavaria, and that this was not a question of religious denominationalism, which would have made the opinion of a confessor seem natural. No, this Jesuit was intervening in actual politics; and the Jesuit proposal was even directed against Spain and Austria, Catholic Powers.*

That the princes did not always select Jesuit confessors of their own free will, but were often driven by threats to surrender these influential posts to this powerful Order, is evident from a communication made by Maréchal, physician-in-ordinary to Louis XIV. of France.

Maréchal informed the Duke and Duchess of Saint-Simon that the King had told him the following: The Jesuit La Chaise, for so many years his confessor, had urged upon him (the King) shortly before his death to choose his next confessor also from the Jesuit Order. He was influenced, he said, in making this request only by his desire for the King's interests. He (La Chaise) knew his Order well, and although the many slanders spread abroad about it were untrue, yet he could only repeat that " he knew his Order well, and on that account implored the King to accede to his request; the Society was very widely disseminated and composed of the most various persons, for whom it was not possible always to be responsible; he besought the King not to drive the Society of Jesus to extremities, for it was easy to play him a nasty trick (*un mauvais coup*)." Saint-Simon adds: "It was the consideration of this power of the Order which induced Henri IV. to favour the Jesuits. . Louis was not superior to Henri IV.; he was careful to bear in mind

* Steinberger, *Die Jesuiten und die Friedensfrage*, p. 97 *et seq.*

the revelations of Father La Chaise, and avoided exposing himself to the revenge of the Society of Jesus by choosing his confessors from outside their ranks. He wished to live and to live in security. He therefore commissioned the Dukes of Chevreuse and Beauvillier to inquire with all due precautions which of the Jesuits he had better take as his confessor."*

Not infrequently the Order encountered difficulties, in instituting the appointment of princely confessors, from the bishops, who were not always in agreement with the *morale aisée* of the Jesuit directors. But the Jesuits managed skilfully to set aside the difficulties. A particularly striking instance of this occurred in the case of one of the numerous Jesuit confessors of Louis XV. of France, who, doubtless, was in special need of a legitimised *morale aisée*. The Archbishop of Paris, Cardinal de Noailles, refused the jurisdiction of the King to the Jesuit de Lignières, so that Lignières would not have been able to absolve the King.† What action was taken by advice of the Jesuit ?

"*Le roi se rendit à Saint-Cyr, qui dependoit du diocèse de Chartres, où il fut confessé par le père de Lignières, et, pour soustraire celui-ci à la jurisdiction du Cardinal de Noailles, on l'envoya à Pontoise, qui était alors du diocèse de Rouen. On obtint ensuite un bref du Pape qui permettoit au roi de choisir pour confesseur tel ecclésiastique qu'il voudroit, pourvu qu'il fut approuvé par l'ordinaire, en déclarant que le roi ne devoit être reputé d'aucun diocèse particulier.*"‡

---

* *Mémoires*, 6, 238 et seq.

† In order that a priest, even if a member of an Order, may hear confessions he must be "approved" by his diocesan bishop and equipped with jurisdiction. The priestly consecration alone (*potestas ordinis*) does not entitle him to hear confessions; to it must be added the *potestas jurisdictionis* of the ecclesiastical authorities.

‡ *Mémoires de la Régence* (La Haye, 1737), 3, 153. Grégoire, p. 119.

Court Confessors

If we assume that Jesus Christ did really institute confession, what would He have said to such confession and absolution on the part of His Society ?

And now a word as to the material position of the Jesuits who acted as princely confessors.

The Jesuit confessor of the King of France received an annual salary of 6,854 livres, of which 300 went in the upkeep of a carriage. Whenever the confessor dined at court a banquet of six courses had to be served him.* Louis XIV. had presented to his confessor, the Jesuit La Chaise, a beautiful country-house as a place of retirement. It stood on the spot where is now the celebrated cemetery, which takes its name, Père La Chaise, from the Royal Confessor. The Jesuit d'Aubanton, Royal Confessor at Madrid, drew a salary of 4,000 livres.†

I may conclude this section with a few quotations, partly from Jesuits themselves, partly from other persons, regarding Jesuit politics and the confessors of princes.

A very interesting insight into the views of the Order as to the spiritual direction of princes is afforded by a secret report of the Visitator of the Upper German Province of the year 1596, the Jesuit Paul Hoffäus :

"The present Pope too [Clement VIII.], speaking, as is piously believed, in the words of God, whose Vicar he is on earth, has publicly reproached us with interfering in the affairs of princes and states, and trying in a measure to rule the world according to our views. That is why the last General Congregation [the fifth, 1593-94] has bidden us by the strictest decrees ‡ to keep aloof from such matters. And if we do not at last become wise, frightened by so many evil consequences, it is to be feared that we may some day feel the avenging hand of God, to our far greater injury. True, it is said that our confessors, who are the spiritual counsellors of princes, should be more leniently judged in this respect. Yet they

---

* *Journal historique de Trevoux* (Verdun, April, 1709), p. 247.
† Saint-Simon, *Mémoires*, 16, 205.   ‡ Decret. 47, 79 ; *cf.* p. 133, 134.

ought to know that it is a question here of a prohibition in the Constitutions and in the decrees of the above-mentioned Congregations, and also consider that the permission is only accorded to them by a dispensation, assuming that both parties receive the dispensation and not one only. But such a dispensation must only be moderately and prudently used, so that no evil consequences may ensue for the Society and, which is of most importance, that greater spiritual benefits, which should be undertaken to the honour of God and the salvation of our neighbour, may not be hindered. Would that the confessors might carefully observe the words of the dispensation, which perhaps refers only to doubtful cases, where it is not sufficiently certain whether the matter touches the conscience but little or not at all, while it is possible that the wish of our General [Acquaviva] is that our people should take no part at all in purely political matters, or only in cases when a prince is in grievous sorrow, or would be greatly distressed or offended if his confessor were to refuse his services in a particular case. Further, as intervention in worldly affairs is so much opposed to our Institute that we cannot but fear that God will refuse His aid to our deliberations on these matters, and our counsel might therefore direct the prince to the wrong road, it seems advisable that the confessors, as far as is possible, should refrain from lightly urging the prince to this or that course without the advice of the Superior of the Order, and that they should rather urge him first to seek advice from his own counsellors before he invites our members to give their advice. Else the prince's counsellors might be justified in imagining that politics were conducted according to the views of the Jesuits, and that they were only consulted *pro forma* without any result, which would be wounding to them and also injurious to us. I do not say this in order to entangle the confessors and lay snares for them, but rather to warn them not to enter too securely and freely into temporal discussions, but with a certain wholesome fear and moderation, and rather avoid such matters, as far as this can be done in seemly fashion and without giving offence."*

* From Reusch, *Beiträge zur Geschichte des Jesuitenordens: Zeitschrift für Kirchengeschichte* (1894), p. 265 *et seq.* Reusch rests his statements on unpublished documents in the State Archives at Munich, to which he had access in the original

The Jesuit Viller also speaks some plain words, which throw a strong light on the attitude of the Jesuit Order towards the office of princely confessor.

Viller, Father Confessor of Archduke Charles of Styria, was one of the most influential Jesuits of Austria; for many years he filled the most important posts in the Order—those of Rector and Provincial. Because of the great favour he enjoyed at court, he had many envious enemies, who denounced him secretly to the General. He defended himself in several long and outspoken letters. On June 8th, 1598, he wrote to the Jesuit Duras, German Assistant to General Acquaviva:

"In the early days of our Society we all rejoiced if one of us found favour with a prince, and our efforts were directed towards the end of winning the favour of princes. Now there are some who are angry and envious if any one is in favour and labours with good result. Under the pretence of virtue they show zeal for the discipline of the Society and are filled with envy."*

In a letter addressed by the Jesuit Francisco Antonio, Confessor to the Empress Maria, wife of Maximilian II., to the General Mercurian, on April 30th, 1576, we read:

"There is not a bishop, ambassador, or lord who would not desire to have some Jesuits in attendance; the door [to the princely courts] which is closed by the vows after profession, appears in a fashion to be reopened in this way. For there is no lack of those who seek after such posts with princes, and this leads to many abuses. In the first place they grow accustomed to a certain liberty, which is little in harmony with our rules. . Finally, there is little spiritual advantage to be gained by it: it leads to ill reports about the Society, as people notice that our members tolerate considerable abuses at the courts or else refuse to see them, only because they desire to enjoy this liberty and honour."†

* Duhr, p. 45.
† Duhr, who gives an extract from this letter (in *die Jesuiten an den deutschen Fürstenhöfen des 16ten Jahrhunderts*, Freiburg, 1901, p. 16), describes it as a "somewhat one-sided exposition." Its contents would probably appear even

In a letter to Leschasser, of March 27th, 1612, Paolo Sarpi reports:

"Many as were the intrigues which they [the Jesuits] stirred up against us [*i.e.* Venice, from which territory the Jesuits had been expelled], they cannot be compared with those which they have set on foot in Constantinople. For there they are doing all in their power to stir up the Turks against us."*

A manuscript report by Leibnitz, of August 28th, 1682, contains this passage:

"*Dans quelques jours nous reprendrons cette matière où nous verrons combien il est peu à propos que les Ecclesiastiques se mêlent des affaires d'Estat, et principalment les Jésuites, qui sont aujourd'huy si puissans, qu'il leur est forte aisé de pancher la balance du costé, qu'ils croyent le plus a leur bienséance, et ce costé est apparamment celuy de la France, à laquelle il est évident que ces bons pères veuillent sacrifier le trône imperial, en quoy peutestre ils réussiront, si on continue à les consulter et à les croire à la cour de Vienne.*"†

The following is from an Italian manuscript preserved in the Bibliothèque Nationale in Paris: ‡ "Instruction to princes as to the manner in which the Jesuits rule" ·

"As among the reports which the Provincials send in there are also some which deal with the character, inclinations and intentions of the various princes, the General and his Assistants in Rome are placed in a position to survey and judge of the political

---

more one-sided; *i.e.* they would throw an even stronger light on the Jesuit pursuit of the office of confessor at princely courts, forbidden by the Constitutions, if Duhr had published the letter in full, and not in an extract, which doubtless was garbled.

* Le Bret, *Magazin* (Frankfort, 1773), 3, 542. "The Magazine for the use of political and ecclesiastical history as well as of ecclesiastical law of Catholic princes in respect of their clergy," by Johann Friedrich Le Bret (Frankfort and Leipzig, 1773-78), 10 vols., contains a number of valuable and rare documents on the history of the Jesuit Order.

† Onno Klopp, *Die werke von Leibniz* (Hanover, 1866), V. 169 *et seq.*

‡ *Fonds italiens*, No. 986.

state of the world and to regulate the attitude of the Order in accordance with its own interests. In particular, the confessions, which a great many of the Catholic nobility and many Catholic princes make to the Jesuits, are a means of procuring for the Order a knowledge of important matters, an object for which princes have to pay large sums to ambassadors and spies, but which now only costs the Jesuits the money for postage. In the same manner they also learn the disposition of the subjects and know which of them are well-disposed to the princes and which are not. .

In Rome the Jesuits constantly swarm around the cardinals, ambassadors and prelates, and inquire about everything that occurs or is about to occur, and try to turn it to their own advantage, so that events of importance often have an entirely different issue from that which the princes desire. The greater part of the business of Christendom passes through their hands. They prevailed on Gregory XIII. to order all legates and nuncios to take Jesuits as their companions and confidants. Jesuits who are taken into the confidence of a prince seek advice immediately of the General about matters of importance and follow his directions."*

Macaulay sums up his judgment in these words:

"They glided from one Protestant country to another, under innumerable disguises, as gay Cavaliers, as simple rustics, as Puritan preachers."†

Crétineau-Joly, who writes in the pay of the Order, takes up a peculiar position. He cannot deny the enormous influence of the Jesuit Order on the political conditions of Europe. But he discovers a theory of justification.

"In the intention of Loyola politics were certainly excluded from his institution; but in the sixteenth century all matters of the court and diplomacy, and even the wars, had a religious basis. The Jesuits were, therefore, compelled to intervene in political and social movements." ‡

From Huber, *Geschichte des Jesuitenordens* (Munich, 1873), p. 101 *et seq.*
† Macaulay's *History*, Chap. VI.   ‡ Crétineau-Joly, 2, 175.

And feeling that he has thus cleared the way, he boldly bears testimony to the gigantic political power of the Order.

"Colbert, Louvois, Seignelai, Pontchartrain, and Croissy, the Ministers of Louis XIV., were encompassed by the counsels of Father Antoine Verjus [a Jesuit]; the Marshal of Luxemburg and Villars sought his opinion in affairs of importance; the Count of Crecy, the French ambassador at the German Reichstag, did not wish to be the only one deprived of the illumination of the Jesuits [*lumières*]. He besought Louis XIV. to obtain for him this diplomatic helper (*cet auxiliaire diplomatique*) from the Superiors of the Order, and accordingly Father Verjus was instructed [by his Superiors] to repair to Germany. There the breadth of his intellect and the moderation of his character soon won for him the regard of Catholic and even Protestant princes. Baron von Schwerin, ambassador of the Elector of Brandenburg, Grote, the Hanoverian ambassador, both zealous Lutherans, were among his best friends. . . . The most celebrated parliamentarians [of France] followed the pious counsels of [the Jesuit] Jean Crasset." *

Ibid., 4, 468 *et seq.*

CHAPTER XX

SCHOLASTIC YEARS AT WYNANDSRADE, BLYENBECK AND DITTON HALL

I PASSED my time as a scholastic of the Society of Jesus (a name, as I have shown, but little suited to the Jesuit Order) in the colleges at Wynandsrade, Blyenbeck (in Holland), and at Ditton Hall, in England. I will deal shortly with this period of seven years, 1880–87.

Notwithstanding the variety of times and places, there is nothing but uniformity to record about the external part of the life. I was surrounded everywhere by the same daily routine and customs. Life in the Jesuit Order, especially during the training (*i.e.* the scholastic period), goes on like absolutely regular and even clockwork. To the scholastic the days from four in the morning to nine at night are identical—religious exercises, studies, recreation; recreation, studies and religious exercises always follow each other at exactly the same intervals.

I do not wish to find fault with this; rather the contrary. Uniformity and regularity are desirable during the training of members of every profession, if they are to be qualified for prominent positions. Still no other calling, not even that of a soldier, is as regular and uneventful as that of the Jesuits. In all other professions some time and space are available for individual activity and for freedom, since no other calling aims at destroying the personality of the individual. But the Jesuit Order is determined to transform the whole man into the whole

Jesuit; hence the suppression of all freedom, even in external matters. Even recreation, which would seem to be necessarily connected with liberty and individuality, is used for compulsion and restraint. For the Superior arranges exactly with whom every one is to associate either during the two daily recreation hours after dinner and supper, or the two weekly walks. The scholastics are not allowed any freedom in choosing their companions. Here also the system of *turmae* prevails. They are also strictly forbidden to abstain from recreation, although real recreation might frequently be found in doing so.

This inflexible uniformity of the external life, which knows hardly any exception, and which divides the scholastic's year 365 times into mathematically equal parts and particles, is a means, gentle yet irresistible, of killing personal individuality. The polishing and planing of the personality which is set up in the novitiate with intensive force, transforming human beings into easily and noiselessly rolling balls, is also active in the scholasticate. For, since the balls are living, it is possible that angles may grow out again. Anything of the kind must be prevented. Hence the perpetual motion of the evenly working machine of exterior Jesuit life.

Another result of this system which is advantageous to the Order must be mentioned. The continual occupation under constant and strict supervision, the absolute lack of really free time in which individuality may realise and assert itself, essentially restrict free thought. There is no time for pondering over doubts and difficulties which the life of the Order may suggest. Consequently opposition to the Jesuit system cannot develop. Minutely regulated activity overrides obscurity, doubt and opposition.

The studies which I had to pursue also belong to the exterior life of this period. They were the Humanities and Rhetoric at Wynandsrade (1880-81), Philosophy at

Blyenbeck (1881–83), and Theology at Ditton Hall (1883–87). I shall deal with them separately.

My inner life within this rigid frame was stirring enough. In spite of everything, I had not become a "ball" during my novitiate. I had retained my individuality; it had maintained its ground against all the levelling discipline. But, just because of its strength, it exposed me to the severest pain, though in the end it led to the joy of freedom after long and hard years of struggle.

My Rector at Wynandsrade was the Jesuit Hermann Nix, the same who played so ugly a part behind the scenes in the Hartmann-Ebenhöch trial.

In reality, it is not the duty of a Jesuit Rector to be the regular spiritual guide of his subordinates; the spiritual father (who at Wynandsrade was the Jesuit Eberschweiler) was there for that purpose, but Nix took upon himself this function, at least so far as we scholastics —and especially I myself—were concerned.

I laid bare my soul to him and unreservedly submitted myself to his guidance. And it is due to the Jesuit Nix that I did not even then leave the Order, but rather pursued the thorny path with greater firmness. Again and again, by day and by night—for the struggle continued even at night, with unflinching constancy and untiring patience— this I willingly grant—he strove to bring my self-asserting ego under the yoke of a delusive belief in Church and Order. Again and again he pointed out the great and shining goal—the glory of God—when I wished to forsake the holy calling, and from my own religious idealism he forged the chains to fetter me to the Jesuit idol. How I hate him, this typical Jesuit—warm-hearted and cold, idealistic and prosaic, gentle and harsh, pious and godless, conscientious and utterly unscrupulous, passionate and coldly calculating. He, who was neither a Master of the Novices nor even a spiritual Father, fastened the burden of the

Jesuit life so firmly upon me that the knot held for fourteen years. Nevertheless, I must thank him on two scores.

All the energy latent within me was awakened and guided by him to definite action. To his teaching I owe the skill and strength, which I have been obliged to draw upon so frequently up to the present day, to overcome apparently insurmountable difficulties. And—most important of all—should I have been capable of fighting against Ultramontane Rome and Jesuitism with thorough knowledge, and thereby performing a work of enlightenment for mankind, if I had left the Order at Wynandsrade after a novitiate of two years? Never! I should again have become what I was previously, and what millions are to-day—a Catholic who devoutly, although perhaps not without inner difficulties, jogs along on the appointed path. Above all, this book, which throws light and truth on the Jesuit Order, would have remained unwritten had it not been for the Jesuit Nix. Consequently I thank him, notwithstanding my hatred.

When I passed in July, 1880, from the novitiate at Exaeten into the scholasticate at Wynandsrade, there was indeed considerable uneasiness within me, but on the whole I stood with firm feet on the trodden path of the Order. This was soon, almost suddenly, changed at Wynandsrade.

A profound change took place on November 13th, 1880, almost in one night, with the taking of the vow. It was not that I objected to the wording of the vow. Far from it! I wished to be poor, chaste and obedient. But the uneasy feeling which had already frequently troubled me, that the Jesuit Order was not what it appeared to be, and that there were dark abysses under my feet, took possession of me with a power previously unknown. Two forces now began a hard conflict within me.

The Ultramontane Jesuit point of view which had

been fostered in me by inheritance and training gave its verdict, which was powerfully strengthened by family tradition and religious beliefs, in favour of the Order. Nature rose in opposition to it. I wanted to believe in the goodness of the Jesuit Order, and to maintain undisturbed the ideal picture formed of it from the first years of my childhood, but I could not. The voices sounding from Church and family, belief and tradition, raised no living echo in my innermost soul. Doubt and oppression lived there because they were natural. Such tormenting conditions arose for soul and body that words may not even suggest them. The life of the spirit and the nervous system suffered severely. Not that I became confused in thought or neurasthenic. But, in spite of clearness of thought, strength of will and outward peace, there arose in me an agonising tumult which caused every chord of my soul and every fibre of my body to tremble. For weeks—for months, indeed—I did not sleep. My bed became a rack of indescribable misery. The hours from nine at night to four or five in the morning, in which I was defencelessly exposed to the inner conflict without possibility of outer diversion—for I was strictly forbidden to seek relief by getting up and occupying myself with other things—were hours of torture in the worst sense of the word. And then the long day lasted from four in the morning to nine at night, and all the time I was obliged to fulfil my duties under constraint. Nobody must notice anything of my inner suffering; I had to be equable, even cheerful. The cries and the bitter weeping of my tortured soul had to be suppressed. Certainly I found some help in the prescribed occupations. But of what kind were they? I, a man of twenty-eight, having passed my matriculation and law examinations and done some practical legal work, sat on the form with boys of eighteen, did Latin and Greek exercises, wrote compositions, and learnt grammatical rules and poems like a pupil of the second class.

And this was not all, not even the worst.

Along with my doubts about the Order arose doubts in connection with my religion and my Church. That which years before had vaguely troubled me, and years later was the real cause of my leaving the Order, then appeared for the first time in clear form.

For if my belief in certain dogmas of the Roman Catholic Church, and thus in the Church itself, had not given way previously, I should never have left the Jesuit Order, but should have sought and found strength, through belief in the Church and the support of her judgment that the Order was good, to sacrifice my judgment and my desires, and by trampling my individuality under foot, have followed in the path of the Order to the end. But when the rock of the Church crumbled under my feet, naturally the Jesuit erection founded on it also collapsed.

I have mentioned in the first part of this book the difficulties and terror which the dogma of the Real Presence of Christ in the Sacrament had caused me even in childhood, and how, later, my belief in the doctrine of the Church regarding the Virgin Mary and her adoration also received a rude shock. These two dark clouds again appeared on my religious horizon at Wynandsrade simultaneously with the doubts about the Order.

Only those who know from personal and practical experience the intimate connection of these particular doctrines concerning Christ and the Virgin Mary with Catholic feeling, and the manner in which they form the pivot of the Catholic faith, can estimate the awfulness for a Catholic heart when they begin to totter and fall. It is no exaggeration to say that the sun seems to be extinguished when these religious stars begin to fade.

Scholastic Years

I shall deal with the difficulties concerning the sacrament of the altar when speaking of my stay at the Ditton Hall Theological College, because they are closely connected with formal theology, but I will say at once what is necessary about the Virgin Mary and her adoration. For, although the Virgin Mary and her adoration are also connected with dogma, and are consequently also conceptions of formal theology, scholarly theology has abandoned them more completely than other religious doctrines. They have really passed over into the popular consciousness, into everyday Catholic sentiment, so to speak.

In the Catholic Church the adoration of the Virgin has assumed forms which not only directly and manifestly contradict the position occupied by Mary in the Scriptures, but have also become so unlovely in themselves and so unreligious that their continuance—indeed, their continually increasing grotesque developments—can only be explained by the general suppression of intellect and judgment which broods like darkness over the high and low Ultramontane Catholic world.

Now this adoration of the Virgin and the work of its further development lie in the peculiar domain of the Jesuit Order. In the course of time it has led to a fearful development of a pseudo-religious and pseudo-mystical nature. And even to the present day the Jesuit literature dealing with the Virgin is a collection of the most extravagant doctrines and assertions, and, above all, of the wildest devotional practices and miraculous stories. I have already, in previous chapters, cited examples of the ascetic practices of the Marian Congregations in honour of the Virgin.

The following dates from the time when the Order was in its prime, shortly before its suppression:

In the middle of the eighteenth century the Jesuits held a service at Munich in honour of the Virgin Mary's comb. A poem and a portion from a sermon regarding the Virgin's hair will illustrate the service —

Gott der alle Häärlein zählet,
Hat ihm diese auserwählet,
Mir seynd diese wenig Häärlein
Werther drum als alle Perlein.

Absolons goldgelbe Locken,
Schätz ich mehr nicht, als die Flocken,
Er selbst gilt bei mir sehr weing.
Ist ja nur ein Eichelkönig.

Doch Maria deine Locken,
Mich zu deiner Lieb anlocken,
Schönste Jungfrau, deine Strehnen
Pfleg ich allzeit anzuflehnen.

Wie im Hohenlied zu lesen,
Seynd der Brauthaar Pfeil gewesen,
Ich befiehl mich deinen Haaren,
Die dem Gespons so angenehm waren.

Steh uns bei in allen Gefahren
Deck uns zu mit deinen Haaren,
Führe uns an deinen Locken
In die Stadt, wo alle frohlocken.

From the sermon: "A janizary, living in Constantinople, had such thick hair that no bullet was able to injure him. The hair of our dear Lady resembles this janizary's hair. Come, therefore, dear Christian, if thou wilt be bulletproof, here into the Hair Chapel of our dear Lady. Hide behind the miraculous hair of the Mother of God and the bullets of thine enemies will not harm thee. Thou wilt stand in the middle of the storm of bullets, as though encased in a woollen bag, if thou art a servant of Mary's hair, for Mary's hair shields her janizaries."*

The Jesuit Pemble published a booklet of the Virgin Mary, "*Pietas quotidiana erga S. D. Matrem Mariam,*" in which, amongst other things, he recommends the following devotional exercises in her honour :

" We should say at all hours : ' Holy Mary, make us gentle and chaste ' ; scourge ourselves or box our ears and offer the blows to God through Mary's hands ; always carry a picture of the Mother of God on our breast ; write or grave Mary's holy name on the breast with our fingers, if not with a knife ; kiss Mary's name whenever it occurs in reading ; cover ourselves over modestly at night so that Mary's chaste eyes may not be offended ; lie between Christ's wounds and Mary's breast and draw thence as much grace as possible ; desire rather to be out of the world or in hell if Mary had not lived ; keep our eyes so in check as not even to see a bare calf or toe on lying down or getting up ; beat the breast eleven times—eleven thousand would be more devout—possibly with a stone in the hand, in remembrance of the eleven thousand virgins, worshippers of the Virgin Mary, who followed in the train of St. Ursula [which eleven thousand virgins are still honoured in Cologne] ; hang a rope round the neck and recognise ourselves as vassals of the blessed Virgin ; eat no apples, because Mary remained free from the sin of eating an apple [in Paradise] ; pray to Mary that she may give us a pleasant dream of herself." †

Such "religious" aberrations, which are even now expressed in hundreds and thousands of "pious" Jesuit monstrosities, had always been difficult for me to digest, notwithstanding my Catholic belief in the Virgin Mary. In

---

* From the collected works of A. v. Bucher, I., 87, 88.
† *Ibid.*, I., 144 *et seq.*

the Jesuit Order this food was set before me again in various shapes.

The Jesuit Hermann Nix had a special reverence for the Virgin Mary. He frequently said that this was derived from his patron saint, the blessed Hermann Joseph, a monk of Cologne, who lived in the Middle Ages, and had become distinguished through a specially intimate relation with Mary. Wynandsrade was extremely rich in pictures and statues of Mary, sickly sweet productions of no artistic value. Our thoughts and senses were directed to Mary in every possible way. Orations were made in her honour, poems had also to be composed, even by such as, for example myself, had no trace of a poetic gift. This superfluity of cant regarding the Virgin re-awakened my old contradictory spirit. The pictures of distorted and turbulent piety which I had observed at such places of pilgrimage as Kevelaer, Lourdes, Einsiedeln, again arose before me. They all appeared to me impious and unwholesome. But since the Jesuit Order—indeed, the Church herself—defended these things, I appeared to myself wrong-headed and wicked on account of my contrary feelings, and severe conflicts ensued.

What attitude did my spiritual guide, the Jesuit Nix, take towards these inward conflicts? I have already said that he helped me over these difficulties. But how?

Firstly, the ancient and simple pacifying method, which has been resurrected and developed by the Jesuits, was employed with masterly skill by this man, who was ready for any emergency: "All these things are temptations of the devil; he grudges you your happiness and the certainty of Heaven, which he himself has lost."

Consequently Satan was conjured up. Difficulties and misgivings concerning Faith and the Jesuit Order, which originate in the creed and organisation of the Order, do not exist and may not exist. The wickedness of our own nature and the promptings of a personal devil are the sole sources of all religious revolt. I repeat what I have already said: What do not the Roman Church and its Orders owe to the devil, that great ultramontane sheep-dog? The keeping alive of the belief in the Prince of Darkness is literally a vital matter for ultramontane Rome. Hence the enormous, yearly increasing, ultramontane Catholic devil-literature, with all its absurd superstitions.

Naturally the fear of the devil also took effect in my case, the more so as Nix deepened it by all kinds of hints and tales of his own activity and that of other Jesuits in succouring souls obviously attacked by the evil one.

Nix, who was so clever in religious and psychological matters, combined two other influences with the infernal one: the appeal to my idealistic nature, which was made by indicating the glory of God, and the goading on of ascetic pride under the disguise of religion, which ensued through dwelling on the thought that only those chosen for high and great purposes are exposed to such attacks: the gold of holiness must be extracted in the crucible of suffering.

In my state of mind at that time no more was required. I issued so triumphantly (really, so overcome) from the battle that my nature, like a well-trained dog, obeyed for years. A single effort of the will sufficed to quell my strongest resistance. I marched forward over a field strewn with the corpses of natural feelings and judgments.

Nix must have informed the General of the Order of my victory, for towards the end of my stay at Wynandsrade I received a letter from the General, old Father Beckx, in which he expressed himself as greatly pleased with my "progress in virtue."

The year at Wynandsrade was given over to ascetic

practices owing to the struggle just described. I could not do enough in the way of self-conquest, denial of personal inclinations and humiliations.

A lay brother suffered from consumption, combined with a tormenting cough, and he had not the strength to expectorate the mucus. I asked permission to be with him a good deal, and frequently removed with my finger the clogging mucous masses from the patient's mouth and pharyngeal cavity. The school routine, with its tasks, etc., was an abomination to me. But no real pupil of the second or first class carried out his schoolboy tasks more zealously than I, although I was twenty-eight years old. I begged frequently for permission to perform kitchen-service, which was particularly exhausting because it shortened considerably the already scanty recreation time. The ancestral seat of my family, Hoensbroech Castle, is situated quite close to Wynandsrade. Strangely enough, I had never been there. I had an ardent desire to see the fine structure, the cradle of my race. I intentionally avoided going even into its vicinity during our walks until the Jesuit Nix, having heard of this, commanded me to go there. A sacrifice of my life which I attempted at Wynandsrade also deserves to be mentioned. The Jesuit asceticism (in common with the general ultramontane asceticism) recognises and commends the sacrificing of the individual's life for that of another in peril when it is more precious than his own; *i.e.* God, " the Lord of life and death," is begged to take the offered life and permit the other to continue. The conditions for this heroic act are that the sacrifice takes place with the spiritual guide's permission, and that the victim is then in a condition of grace, *i.e.* not burdened with grievous sins. Now, during my stay at Wynandsrade, a literary light of the German province, the Jesuit Kreiten, was seriously and, as it was said, hopelessly ill. My fearful spiritual troubles caused me to think of death as a deliverance. I consequently begged the Jesuit Nix for permission to offer myself as a sacrifice for the patient, as I had learnt during the novitiate period might be done. I received the necessary permission and an injunction to offer my life to God at the next Benediction (an evening service at which the monstrance with the consecrated host is exposed). Words cannot express the ardour with which I offered myself, and the earnestness with which I begged God, Who was present (as I believed) in the host, to take my poor life, spare me superhuman struggles, and permit me (as I thought) to enter into the certainty of eternal life. But I am still alive. I will return to this event when discussing my present relation to belief in God and His providence.

I underwent bodily discipline also; I scourged myself and, with the permission of my spiritual guide, Nix, wore a penitential girdle more often during my time at Wynandsrade than at any other period of my Jesuit life, although my body endured enough mortification owing to the continual sleeplessness arising from inner struggles.

The most severe discipline I underwent was due to the prohibition to give any outward hint of my inner suffering. Letters to my mother and others had to speak of happiness and contentment with my calling, whilst the feeling of despair inwardly tormented me. During visits which I received a few times, owing to the nearness of some relations—my mother also visited me there—I had to hide the tumult of my soul and its torment under a cheerful aspect and calm manner. When such an attitude seemed to me insincere, Nix's stereotyped reply was, "All that you are experiencing of despair and disgust is not due to yourself. The sensations are due to the devil. Your better self recognises its happiness and rejoices in it." Even to-day I shudder with horror when

I think of the "happiness" and the "joy" which I then felt.

On account of its ascetic and religious aspect, I must here briefly touch on an event, the already-mentioned pilgrimage to the relics at Aix-la-Chapelle, which occurred during my stay at Wynandsrade.

I passed a dreadful night before the day on which the pilgrimage was made; my body and soul were almost in a state of collapse. I supplicated the Jesuit Nix to allow me to remain at home. "No, certainly not; the relics will help you." I knelt, stood, and sat for hours with the other scholastics in the burning sun amongst thousands of pilgrims gazing, with prayer and song, up at the gallery of the Cathedral of Aix-la-Chapelle, where the relics were shown by turns—Christ's swaddling clothes, a vest belonging to the Virgin Mary, etc. Verily "out of the depths" in the fear and distress of my soul have I cried to the Master and His saints. I shed tears of the bitterest misery in face of the relics. Fool that I was! My remedies did not lie in the legendary rags, called the sacred relics of Aix. My remedy would have lain in the determination to free myself from the yoke which inherited and cultivated superstition had placed upon me. But how could I make such a resolution at that time when my understanding was still in bondage? The Jesuit Nix praised me after my return; the pilgrimage would draw down God's most bountiful blessing upon me!

I am not carrying on any religious controversy in this book. But for that very reason I propose to write a word about the irreligion of the system of pilgrimages and relics. Such disorder and deception should be whipped with lashes and scorpions out of every society calling itself Christian. What Rome teaches her believers in this respect is no better than what draws the Tibetans to their Dalai-Lama and Taschi-Lama. Loretto, Rome, Trèves,

Aix-la-Chapelle, Lourdes, etc., with their relics and miraculous pictures, are on the same level of human aberration and religious degradation as Lhasa, Taschi-Lumpo, and the Buddhist temples of the Indo-Chinese.

Christ once said, " But the hour cometh when the true worshippers shall worship the Father in spirit and in truth. God is a spirit: and they that worship Him must worship Him in spirit and in truth." When will this time come which was foretold two thousand years ago ?

The Jesuit Nix gave the annual eight days' Exercises just before I and the remaining scholastics of my year left Wynandsrade. An instruction connected with them may be mentioned, which strongly exposes the arrogant and egotistical Moloch spirit of the Order.

Nix wished to show what thankfulness and, consequently, what self-sacrifice we owed the Order. It fed, clothed, supported and taught us. It invested us with respect, threw open to us the doors of the highest circles of society, for a Jesuit was held in honour everywhere; in short, we owed what we were and, still more, what we should be to the Order; consequently it was our duty, etc. The theory seemed to me very disputable. For, apart from the fact that I—the consideration was not inspired by pride—should have been respected in the world without the Jesuit Order, it occurred to me that, in return for the nourishment, clothing and lodging which the Order gave us, I and the others sacrificed our body and soul, indeed our whole being—will, understanding and feelings—unreservedly, and that what the Order gave us was amply counterbalanced by this sacrifice. I expressed my thoughts to Nix, and received the answer, "Dear brother, you forget one thing: God, Who has called you and the others for all eternity to the Jesuit Order, has only given you body and soul, understanding and will, that you may employ these gifts in the service of the

Order. Through God's predestination, your body and soul are, therefore, not so much your property as that of the Order." My mind was satisfied with this answer. This is a striking proof of my spiritual narrow-mindedness at that time.

In the summer of 1881 I went to Blyenbeck, which my father had placed at the disposal of the Jesuit Order after its banishment from Germany. I was to study philosophy there for two years.

It was with a strange sensation that I crossed the threshold and court of the ancient castle where in my childhood and youth I had stayed so frequently, and whence I had gone for happy rides and taken part in many delightful hunting parties. I was to live there no longer as the son of the house, in the best rooms, but as a brother of the Society of Jesus, one amongst thirty or forty, high up under the roof, exposed to summer heat and winter cold, as at Exaeten, and with five, six, and even more to share rooms which, even through their outer decorations, stucco ceilings and baroque chimney-pieces, reminded me of other things than the life of the Order and of a scholastic.

I did not find it easy to accustom myself to so completely altered a situation and to live as a member of the Order, who had renounced the world, in the same place where I had previously ruled as the son of the house and given myself up to pleasure. Every walk in the vicinity, which abounded in woods and heaths, was full of memories for me: here I had amused myself with my brothers and sisters on horse and foot, had played " robbers and police " with them; there I had shot foxes, here snipe, there rabbits, and here roebuck. It required considerable determination to banish the pictures which arose and to let bygones be bygones. But this was done. And I can also testify to the fact that, in the face of these difficult relations, I consistently and resolutely showed the earnest desire, combined with self-sacrifice to follow the ideal which I still perceived in the life of the Order and the Society of Jesus. At Blyenbeck my Superior, the Jesuit Miller, also informed me that he had told the General, in the secret "second catalogue," "that I had made good progress in virtue and was a *homo spiritualis*, a man aiming at spirituality."

During the second year of my stay at Blyenbeck I had to make the *abdicatio bonorum*, renunciation of property.

According to the statutes of the Order,* the renunciation of property should really be made during the second year of the novitiate, and only custom, at least in the German Province of the Order, had made it usual for this act to be performed in the fourth year.

I renounced my fortune for religious poverty with complete resignation. Fortunately, only resignation of the right of enjoying and disposing of property is connected with this first act of renunciation; complete renunciation of property is only connected with the taking of the last vows. I was consequently able, after leaving the Order, to receive back at least a portion of my property from my eldest brother, in whose possession it had remained.

I also took my first step on the way to the priesthood at Blyenbeck, as I received, from an Indian bishop staying there on a visit, with the remaining scholastics of my year, the so-called four minor ordinations (*ordines minores*). Since the "minores" are only a first step to the sacrament of priestly consecration, and impose no obligations on the consecrated person, I can pass over the consecration ceremony. I did not even receive the outer sign of the four ordinations, the tonsure on the back of the head, for I had already had a natural tonsure there for years.

* Exam. gen., IV., 2; Constit. III., 1, § 7, 25.

I finished my philosophical studies at Blyenbeck in July, 1883, and was sent to Ditton Hall, in England, to study scholastic theology for four years.

Wynandsrade and Ditton Hall, the beginning and end of my scholastic period, were of decisive importance for my inner life. At Wynandsrade false asceticism succeeded in strengthening me in my wavering religious views; at Ditton Hall the old difficulties, increased by new ones, arose with greater violence. I there fought the dreadful fight which inflicted lasting wounds (in the Jesuit ultramontane sense) on my soul. Through these the heart-blood of my inherited and acquired Catholic life gradually flowed until there was no longer any left, and I had to search out the way to new life.

I have only unhappy recollections of Ditton Hall. It was internally and externally a hell to me.

The ugly house is situated in a hideous neighbourhood, surrounded by large chemical factories (Widnes, St. Helens, etc.), which destroy all vegetation for miles around with their poisonous fumes. In summer and winter the dead trees stretch out their withered branches like ghosts into the murky air which, black and dirty through smoke and thick vapour, is but rarely illuminated and warmed by the sun. When the west wind was blowing from the factories (as was usually the case), the house was filled with an unwholesome odour mingled with soot. On our walks we saw hardly anything but factory squalor, and the paths we trod were black with slag and coal. By way of comfort for the prevailing depression and repulsiveness, we were informed that infectious diseases and harmful bacilli and bacteria could not get a hold there. Headaches and throat troubles occurred frequently, however. I suffered from almost chronic hoarseness.

The outer hell might have been endurable. But the inner one!

Scholastic Years

In the first place, I must recall my Superior at that time, for he made the hell as hot as possible for me.

A change of Rectors occurred a few weeks after my arrival at Ditton Hall. The former Rector, the Jesuit Hövel, was chosen as assistant to the General of the Order in 1883 at the General Congregation sitting at Rome, and the Jesuit Wiedemann took his place as Rector of Ditton Hall. Gossiping, mean, revengeful, suspicious, vain, crafty and thoroughly false, he had every characteristic which enables a Head to render life miserable to his subordinates. The antipathy was mutual; but whilst I endeavoured honestly to recognise and respect in this person, repugnant to me from the very bottom of my soul, the "Superior placed over me by God," he gave free rein to his aversion. One must know the absolute dependence of the Jesuit subordinates upon the Jesuit Superior to estimate what a jealous Superior, furnished in addition with all the idiosyncrasies just mentioned, means to his subordinates — what it means, for example, to be obliged to make a Statement of Conscience to such a man. I met with nothing but disparaging words of contempt from this Jesuit when I conscientiously opened my soul to him, and spoke of the waters of affliction and despair which had crept up and threatened to engulf my reason and my will, and when I laid bare the almost indescribable pain within me. I was conscious of his mistrust everywhere. I had always pursued my studies with indefatigable application, and continued to do so at Ditton Hall. Wiedemann accused me of idleness, and tried to make others share his opinion of me. I hate the Jesuit Nix; the Jesuit Wiedemann does not deserve as much. With his miserable paltriness and hollowness, he deserves contempt. I do not believe, indeed, that my course of development would have been retarded lastingly through any influence whatever, and that anything would have prevented me from standing where I stand to-day; but if a better man than the Jesuit Wiedemann had had the guidance of my soul during the four years of my theological training, the severance effected later from the Order and Church would perhaps have taken place more quietly and with less bitterness.

In spite of his aversion to myself, the Jesuit Wiedemann exploited me and my worldly connections when Jesuit interests came into question.

One of my fellow-scholastics, Brother Cecil Longridge, had been an English artillery officer in India before he entered the Order. He retained a liking for artillery problems, such as the science of projectiles, and, in spite of dogmatics and moral theology, he was particularly interested in the construction of a new cannon on the wire system. Wiedemann sent for me one day and charged me to write to my cousin, General von Loë, who was then the General in command of the 8th Army Corps at Coblence, send him Brother Longridge's constructional drawings, and beg him to have them tested by experts. Perhaps, Wiedemann said, there might be something in the idea, which would be very advantageous to the Order. I was to write the letter quite on my own initiative, so that there should be no suspicion that the Order as such had any interest in the invention of the cannon. Some months later I received a friendly answer from Walter Loë saying that he had had the matter looked into, but it did not seem to be practical. Possibly further details regarding the Jesuit cannon are to be found in the records of the office of the commanding General at Coblence. Unless I am mistaken, the cannon was then offered to the English War Office with the same negative results.

My theology course brought the priesthood within appreciable distance, and with my theological studies came the duty of allowing myself to be submerged in the dogmas of the Church. Then, on a sudden, there gaped beneath my feet the abyss, into the sinister darkness of which my eyes had already glanced fugitively, though kept back hitherto from closer observation by my well-disciplined will.

The essence of the Roman Catholic priesthood, its mystically religious climax, lies in the power of transforming bread and wine into the body and blood of Jesus Christ. Through this power the priest is the originator of "the true, actual, and real presence of Christ in the altar sacrament."

The belief in the lasting presence of Christ in the consecrated host preserved in the tabernacles of Catholic churches is one of the most potent sources of Catholic piety; millions derive from it daily vital energy and strength in bodily and spiritual troubles. And, indeed, for the individual who believes that he may have intercourse and conversation with the all-good and all-powerful God as with a friend present in the body, the sorrow of life loses much of its weight. It is not, however, this belief—which rests like a transfiguring gleam over the life of the Catholic Christian, and can give no why or wherefore concerning the presence of Christ in the host, but takes the presence for granted without making difficulties—of which I speak here. The dogma which terrified me was that which sought a foundation in theological scholarship for the belief in the real presence of Christ.

The dogmatic teaching of the Church, which is, however, unknown in its details to the mass of believers, is as follows :—

1. After the priest's words, which he pronounces in the name and, as it were, the person of Christ over bread and wine (generally only during Mass), "This is My body" and "This is the cup of My blood," the nature and substance of bread and wine disappear, and the

nature and substance of Christ's flesh and blood take their place (transubstantiation). The "accidents" of the bread and wine (form, colour, smell, taste, and weight) remain, however, so that the human senses can perceive no change. The senses only perceive bread and wine as before, although in reality there is no more bread and wine present.

2. The entire body of Christ (skin, hair, nails, bones, all the limbs and also the genitals) is present in the consecrated host, and consequently (*per concomitantiam*) also the blood; and the whole amount of Christ's blood is present in the consecrated wine, and consequently (*per concomitantiam*) also the whole body of Christ.

3. The whole body and all the blood of Christ are not only in the entire host and the whole amount of wine, but also in each separate part of the bread and wine, so that when consecrated bread and consecrated wine are divided into thousands of particles and small drops, the whole body and all the blood of Christ are present in every particle and every little drop, and that without fresh words of consecration, but only through the physical process of division.

4. Mastication of Christ's body in the mouth of the receiver is consequently also impossible, because a fresh body of Christ occurs simultaneously at every division, whether it occurs through the teeth or by other means.

5. Although a natural decomposition of the consecrated bread and the consecrated wine is impossible, since the substances of bread and wine are no longer present, the consecrated host and consecrated wine are nevertheless also subject, like other food, to the natural laws of decomposition, so that, in the recipient's stomach, for example, the decomposition of the swallowed host and the swallowed wine takes place in exactly the same manner. The substance of the flesh and blood of Christ

Scholastic Years

disappears at the commencement of the decomposition and the substances of bread and wine again take its place.

6. Consecrated bread and consecrated wine have the same action as ordinary bread and wine, although the substances of bread and wine are no longer present, so that we may satisfy our hunger with consecrated bread, *i.e.* with Christ's flesh, and become intoxicated with consecrated wine, *i.e.* with Christ's blood, as with other bread and wine.

7. The priest retains the power of consecration permanently, and it cannot be alienated from him. No sin, not even apostasy, can take it away, so that I still retain this miraculous power. In addition, the priest is not fettered by time and place in exercising his extraordinary power; it is also at his command when desired outside Mass. Every priest can consequently transform all the supply of bread in every baker's shop, and all the supply of wine in every wine-store, into Christ's flesh and blood, provided that the bread-shops and wine-stores contain natural bread and natural wine, and that the words of consecration be spoken in or immediately outside the shop or store, consequently not at any considerable distance from either.

This miraculous sacerdotal power is also illustrated by "facts." I will only relate two stories, which were current during my theological term of study. During the French Revolution a priest apostasised, but was beheaded in spite of this. In his rage, and with blasphemous design, he changed the bread of all the bakers' shops which he passed in the Parisian streets on his way to the scaffold into the body of Christ. A priest addicted to wine, who could not forgo his early morning drink, transformed an entire cask in his wine-cellar into the blood of Christ, so as to be able to drink out of it before Mass without breaking the strict rule not to partake of anything before Mass. For the consecrated wine, owing to the fact that it is no longer wine but Christ's blood, does not belong to the things which may not be taken before Mass or Communion.

This is the essential purport of the dogma of the " real presence of Christ in the altar sacrament." " This is an hard saying; who can hear it ? " has seemed to me to apply to this doctrine ever since I came to know it.

I need not dwell on the seven points named above to make it clear why fear—indeed, horror—seized me as to their contents, and that finally unbelief supplanted fear and horror. Is this supposed to be the meaning of that sweet memorial feast, which Christ instituted at the last meal He took with His disciples ? Was that breaking of bread and proffering of the wine cup supposed to have such a brutal meaning ?

The nearer the day approached on which I was to be equipped with this priestly power, the more violent became my opposition and the more dreadful my spiritual anguish. When the Bishop of Liverpool really consecrated me and twelve fellow-scholastics to the priesthood in July, 1886, in the Ditton Hall church, scepticism had already seized the best part of my soul, and I allowed the ceremonies of the consecration to be enacted over me whilst in a condition impossible to describe. In vain I told the trouble of my soul to my spiritual guide. It was always the same: " It is the devil who is tempting you; you must disregard all this."

How I suffered when, a few days after my ordination, I read my first Mass in the old castle of my ancestors, Blyenbeck, whither my superiors had sent me, before the whole of my family (mother, brothers, sisters, and other relations) ! I had even hastened to old Father Oswald, who happened to be at Blyenbeck, and whom I then trusted, on the previous evening and in the morning just before the commencement of Mass, and described my anguish of conscience with bitter tears—truly tragic tears. He also could only lay the blame on the devil. So, in reality, I approached the altar driven by the "devil," and "transformed" bread and wine into the body and blood of Christ.

For six whole years I bore the burden of this priesthood with continually increasing anguish. Nevertheless, I tried to carry out even the hardest duties of a priest connected with the dogma of Christ's real presence. I will only give one very striking example.

According to the doctrine of the Church, it is the duty of the priest to swallow the consecrated host when he observes that it is getting decomposed—possibly owing to dampness in the tabernacles, or for other reasons—if he is not positive that it is already quite decomposed, and consequently that Christ is no longer present in it. When I was hearing confessions before reading Mass one morning in a parish where I was assisting in the priestly duties, as I so often did, a woman confessed she had not swallowed the host on receiving the Communion just before, because the thought of also swallowing Christ's genitals had been too dreadful; she had spat the host into her prayer-book; it was still there. After I had tried in vain to persuade her to swallow it, it seemed to me that I could do nothing else but swallow the expectorated host myself. I told the half-distracted woman to leave the prayer-book with the host behind when she went from the confessional. I then took the host, saturated as it was with saliva, and pressed into a pulpy mass, from the prayer-book and swallowed it, together with that which I consecrated at the Mass I read directly after.

This incident also illustrates the troubles caused amongst believers when the pious but vague belief in the presence of Christ in the host begins to be supplanted by a knowledge of dogma.

Two other fundamental doctrines of the Roman Catholic belief troubled me during my theological course —the doctrine of the Holy Trinity and the doctrine of original sin.

The doctrine of the Trinity is an absurdity tinged with Buddhism and Hellenism, and the dogma of original sin caused by the fall of Adam and Eve is also an absurdity combined with anthropomorphic and crude conceptions.

It was a long time before I attained to such recognition. But once I had done so, it became, and is still, incomprehensible to me why every clear and religiously disposed person does not discard both these doctrines.*

It is outside the scope of this book to go into these "thoroughly Christian" dogmas and expose their absurdity. It is sufficient for me to affirm that the doctrines of the Trinity and original sin became the outlets through which I passed from ultramontane Jesuit night and bondage to light and liberty.

There is still one peculiarity of the scholasticate in particular, and of the whole Jesuit existence in general, to be mentioned.

The Jesuit scholastic is kept in complete ignorance regarding the history and mission of his Order. He does not know, and must not know, that great abuses have occurred within the Jesuit Order. He only hears praise and glorification; only light, and no shade, is shown

* I have been obliged to write this word of renunciation of Catholic dogma so as to explain the breaking down of my belief. I do not intend to discuss religious polemics. On the contrary, it is necessary that I should explain that I condemn wrangling of the kind when it occurs in an unlovely and wounding form, as it does only too frequently. Every religion and every Christian belief has cause to utter a *mea maxima culpa* in face of reason and humanity, owing to the wilderness of absurdities surrounding their dogmas and customs; the Catholic religion is by no means the only culprit in this respect.

him. He lives in complete ignorance of facts. He has entered with the firm belief in the supermundane character of the Order and in the almost divine nature of its foundation; and this delusion is kept alive in him. We may excuse the fact that attacks by adversaries are not given him to read, although such concealment does not point to honourable dealing and confidence. But even admonishing and warning voices from within the Order itself, which we have found and shall still find making themselves audible at every period, must not reach his ear. He hears only the bombastic, vainglorious, official stories of the Order, which are stories but not history. I am positive that even the suppression of the Order by Clement XIV. would be concealed if it were possible. As it is impossible, it is put down as an aberration on the Pope's part.

I can give a striking example from my own experience of wilful exclusion of historical truth in regard to the Suppression:—

Once, when performing the duty of reader in the refectory, the Rector, the Jesuit Miller, gave me the third volume of Döllinger's *Beiträge* just published, in which the *Memoirs* of the Jesuit Cordara were contained, with the observation that the *Memoirs* were to be read at dinner, and I was consequently to study them, *i.e.* familiarise myself with the contents. Scarcely half an hour later, before I had found time to glance at the book, I was called to the Provincial's Socius, the Jesuit Kurte, who informed me, by order of the Provincial, that Cordara's *Memoirs* were not to be read, and I was to return Döllinger's book to the Rector. The Rector received me with visible embarrassment, murmured something about a "mistake" having occurred, and took back the ill-omened book. Cordara had, as we know, written with great love for his Order, but candidly on the causes of its suppression. We scholastics must remain in ignorance of the frank recognition of abuses by such a prominent Jesuit as Cordara.

The same thing happens with Jesuits as with most ultramontane Catholics. As they hear nothing of the infamous actions and grave offences against religious, political, social and intellectual life of the Papal system,* so in like manner the Jesuits do not hear of the great faults and deficiencies of their Order. And as hundreds, indeed thousands, of books and writings radiate the undimmed glory of "godliness" over and around the Papacy, so do innumerable Jesuits spread the same glory around their Order. Fawning flattery, as far removed from truth as the poles from one another, forms the daily food of Loyola's disciples.

So long as the Jesuit looks upon this artificial light as the real light of history, he considers himself wicked and corrupt if he doubts the excellence of his Order, and he applies to himself pitilessly and effectually the theory of the temptation of the devil, which has become incorporated into his body and blood, as soon as his own reason and natural understanding raise their voices. It is generally only an accident that opens his eyes a little and lets him see facts in their true light. I must speak later of the accidents which tore the veil from my own eyes.

At the present time it seems incomprehensible to me that I could have lived for years in such implicit faith. At that time implicit faith and blind and naïve belief constituted the very air which I and my fellow-scholastics breathed.

One of the worst of the many crimes committed by the Order against its members is that it not only conceals the truth regarding its own history, but deceives them with "historical" untruths.

* *Cf.* my work, *Das Papsttum*, etc.

CHAPTER XXI

THE SCHOLASTIC STUDIES

THE scholasticate, as its name indicates, is the young Jesuit's period of study, divided under the headings of the Humanities, Philosophy, and Philology.

All studies are based on the official *Ratio atque Institutio studiorum Societatis Jesu.**

One criticism of this Scheme of Study has already been given in Chapters IV. and V. There I showed how backward and unmindful of the requirements of the times are the school instruction and education of the Jesuit Order, based on a Scheme of Study which has continued unaltered from the sixteenth to the nineteenth century (1832). I have also shown that the "improvements" introduced in 1832 cannot be described as a real advance or suitable adaptation to the requirements of modern times. How can a Scheme of Study dating from 1599, which still holds good in 1910, and was for the first time after two hundred and thirty-three years subjected to a few additional and trivial alterations, pretend to the very slightest value?

We must not, however, forget that its value is by no means to be appraised according to its effect on the outside world or in the sphere of knowledge. The Jesuit Order has only one criterion for its institutions: the interests of the Order. This " gauge " is also the foundation of the Scheme of Study, and, judged by this, its value

* *Inst. S.J.* (Romæ, 1870), II. 469-549.

is inestimable. For in its Scheme of Study the Jesuit Order possesses a powerful implement with which to guard its members from enlightenment, and contrives that it shall reach them only in such measure as is necessary and useful for the purposes of the Order.

I.—THE HUMANISTIC STUDIES

My personal experiences in the college at Wynandsrade and at the Jesuit educational institution at Feldkirch show the methods adopted in the humanistic studies of the Order, and how the pupils are allowed, after an absolutely inadequate training, to be appointed at their institutions to teach the young pupils entrusted to the care of the Order. Attention was also called to the important fact characterising the " humanism " of the Jesuits, that the Order does not of its own initiative give a thorough professional training in scholarship to the pupils intended to teach humanistic subjects, but only when compelled by external circumstances (*i.e.* the imperative decree of the State that teachers shall have undergone a professional training in philology and passed examinations in it) to comply with this most primary requirement of humanistic training. This demand became a matter of life or death to the Order. They made a virtue of necessity, swallowed the hateful command under compulsion, and sent their scholastics to university lectures on philology. But for State interference the Order would have continued to adhere to its own " philological " methods.

I have also dwelt briefly on the fruits of Jesuit scholarship, but it still remains to answer the general question: What has the Jesuit Order accomplished in scholarship since its beginning? The result is an absolute blank, and only the untruthful Jesuit boastfulness could speak of " achievements," and even brag of them. Is it, indeed, an achievement if here and there a Jesuit succeeds in writing a serviceable book on philology, if a Greek or Latin classic is edited by a Jesuit with not unserviceable annotations?

The Jesuit Order has existed for nearly four hundred years; for nearly four hundred years it has frequently had excellent human material to mould by its curriculum, which lays special stress on the humanities. What, then, is the result of this four hundred years' activity? The list of those Jesuits and their works worthy of mention in the history of scholarship would not fill more than half an octavo page. No great men, no pioneers, no reformers are to be found among them; they are but average scholars, such as may be met with by the hundred at universities and colleges, with this difference only, that universities and colleges produce many eminent as well as average scholars.

Involuntarily the Jesuits emphasise this discreditable fact by their ceaseless boasting, if at any time or place any Jesuit does achieve something in the domain of scholarship. The Jesuit Balde with his Latin Odes, the Jesuit Fox with his Commentary on Demosthenes' *de Corona*, and a few others, are the stock pieces continually produced from the "philological" Jesuit storehouses which have been four hundred years in filling. Does not this throw a strong light on the miserable poverty of these storehouses?

The primary cause of the whole worthlessness of Jesuit scholarship is revealed by the fact that the Constitutions of the Order expressly define humanistic studies as mere auxiliaries to theology, not as independent pursuits: "Because theoretical and practical theology requires a knowledge of the Humanities, Latin, Greek, and Hebrew, the requisite number of competent professors in these subjects are to be appointed." *

* Const. IV., 12, 2.

These few remarks, with the criticisms in Part I., will suffice to place in their true light the methods and results of the philological studies of the Jesuit Order.

But "Rhetoric" too is included among the humanistic studies of the Jesuits. This name is given to the highest of the classes for the humanistic training of the scholastics. On this I must make a few comments, not because theoretical and practical training in eloquence offers any peculiar features, since it corresponds to that principal branch of Jesuit activity, its preaching labours, but because in the "Rhetoric" class classics too are read, and the attitude of the Order towards the vernacular classics there finds expression. That is why I must once more discuss this point, so characteristic of the Jesuit spirit and of its influence on its young pupils. In consequence of its international character the Jesuit Order holds aloof from all national literature. This fact is quite obvious from the wording of the *Ratio* and from all Jesuit writings on education. But the aversion of "German" Jesuits to German classics is especially keen, and amounts to blind hatred, displayed in brutal fashion.

In illustration I quote the utterances of two "German" Jesuits, both of whom, though for different reasons, enjoy considerable reputation in German Catholic circles, and who exercise a profound influence on those many millions.

The Jesuit Baron Ludwig von Hammerstein, one of the most prolific and widely read popular authors of Catholic Germany, says, in his work *Das Preussische Schulmonopol mit besonderer Rücksicht auf die Gymnasien* :—

"In modern schools, as has been said before, enthusiasm is naturally centred on the German classics and on the intellectual sphere in which they move. Goethe claims the first place among them. And what is the ideal that is held up to the youth of

Germany in Goethe ? Goethe himself shows it us in the description which he gives of himself and his doings in the character of Faust :

> *Ich bin nur durch die Welt gerannt,*
> *Ein jed'Gelüst ergriff ich bei den Haaren ;*
> *Was nicht genügte liess ich fahren,*
> *Was mir entwischte liess ich ziehen.**

"So this is Goethe ! How he 'seized every pleasure' may be seen by the catalogue of his wanton loves, which he pursued as a boy, as a youth, after his marriage, and as an old man of over eighty years, with married and unmarried women, choosing his victims among factory girls, barmaids, actresses, pastors' daughters, noble spinsters, etc. In this sense he wrote in his *Zahme Xenien :*

> *Ich wünsche mir eine hübsche Frau,*
> *Die nicht alles nähme gar zu genau,*
> *Doch aber zugleich am besten verstände,*
> *Wie ich mich selbst am besten befände.*

"Such is Goethe ! Such is the ideal brought before our schoolboys nowadays. . . . The best known only of his love adventures supply a whole catalogue. Gretchen, Friederike, Lotte, Charlotte von Stein, Corona Schröter, Christiane Vulpius, Minna Herzlieb, etc. Such, then, is Goethe, the man who occupies the post of honour among the heroes of our literature, this the hero whom the Minister of Public Instruction, von Gossler, holds up to the reverent admiration of the young, this the poet whose most valuable poems 'it should be a national duty for every man of culture to retain in his memory as an imperishable treasure,' a duty which lies on the schools to accomplish. This is the man whom Dr. Falk, Minister of Public Instruction, recommends, not only as a model of language and style, but as a teacher of 'true Christian, national and humane education.' This, then, is the man who is to inspire the hearts of the young Prussian scholars with enthusiasm. No wonder, then, that unbelief and immorality prevail at those schools. Of course, nothing is further from my mind than to depreciate the excellence of some of Goethe's poems. On the contrary, I prize this excellence; but I maintain that what is beautiful and fascinating in Goethe

---

* *Faust*, II., Act V.

makes him more dangerous and pernicious as an ideal for youth. No one will drink poison offered in a basin filled with dish-water or soap-suds, but poison in a beaker of wine of Cyprus or Muscatel is dangerous, and all the more so if the wine is offered by a competent judge as an ideal potion, the partaking of which is supposed to be the 'national duty of every person of culture.' This is the case with Goethe, the principal ideal of the modern school.

"I will also devote a few short remarks to his colleagues Schiller and Lessing. Schiller is at any rate a less unsuitable ideal to set before the young than Goethe; still, I cannot regard even him as suitable. His *Räuber* and his *Fiesco* will, to say the least, not instil conservative principles into the youthful mind, nor yet *Tell*, with its glorification of tyrannicide. It is well known that Schiller also passed through a phase of laxity in regard to the seventh commandment. Youth will hardly be fired with enthusiasm for Christianity and pure morals by hearing Schiller exclaim in his *Götter Griechenlands* :—

> *Da ihr noch die schöne Welt regieret,*
> *An der Freude leichtem Gängelband,*
> *Selige Geschlechter noch geführet,*
> *Schöne Wesen aus dem Fabelland!*
> *Ach, da euer Wonnedienst noch glänzte,*
> *Wie ganz anders, anders war es da!* etc.

"This, indeed, sounds rather more alluring than the precepts of the Cross and the Crucified. . . . Thus Schiller viewed the Christian moral law and Christian monotheism! Those who are versed in German literature know well enough that such utterances are not isolated. Certainly Schiller could strike other chords in the human heart, but he is on that account no less dangerous an ideal to set before the young. The man who won their hearts by the 'Song of the Bell,' or 'Wallenstein,' will seduce them all too easily from the paths of faith and Christian morality by his *Räuber, Kabale und Liebe, Götter Griechenlands*, and such like.

"With regard to Lessing, I observe that *Emilia Galotti*, with its atmosphere of libertinage, and *Minna von Barnhelm*, with its love dalliance, are more suited for the training of novel-heroes, blasé worldlings and idlers, than serious and high-principled youths. Nor is Lessing's passion for gambling exactly a qualification for an ideal. . . . How utterly opposed to such ideals appear those of the old school! Whilst Lessing hungers after gold to gratify his gambling propensity, a St. Francis of Assisi elects extreme poverty. Whilst Lessing endeavours by his writings to undermine Christianity, a St. Francis Xavier, by his apostolic preaching, wins whole kingdoms for Christ and Christian morality. Whilst Goethe welds his life into a chain of excesses, a St. Benedict throws himself among thorns, to overcome the temptations of the flesh by self-inflicted suffering. Which of these two ideals was chosen with truer pedagogic discrimination, that of the ancient schools of the Church, or that of the modern secularising schools of the State? Schiller and Goethe are valuable supporters of Lessing in his active attempts to undermine all Christianity, all faith. Schiller says: 'What religion I follow? Not one of those that you name. And why none? From love of religion.'* Schiller thus renounces all existing objective religions, Christianity in particular, of whatever denomination. Before he had reached the age of thirty, he was completely estranged from Christianity, and had familiarised himself with the pantheistic doctrines of the Jew, Baruch Spinoza. Religion furnished him with neither results nor convictions concerning supersensual matters, and even in relation to morality he held it to be a mere substitute for general virtue, and valued it in proportion to its effect and not for its intrinsic worth. . . . And Goethe? Goethe is anything we please as occasion arises—or, rather, as his epicurean humour suggests—*i.e.* he is really devoid of all religious convictions whatever. If any special obloquy is to be heaped on Catholicism, Schiller can supply it with his *Don Carlos*, his *History of the Thirty Years' War*. So too Lessing, who in his *Nathan*, in the famous dialogue between the Patriarch and the Templar, sets a flattering portrait of the Catholic priesthood and Catholic morality before the Catholic, Protestant and Jewish pupils of a German gymnasium.

"Thus Goethe, Schiller and Lessing are the three most brilliant stars in the modern German classical firmament—stars held up

* "*Welche Religion ich bekenne? Keine von allen,
   Die du mir nennst. Und warum keine? Aus Religion!*"

to the grateful veneration of the pupils. The heroes of the second class mostly resemble them." *

To the same category as the Jesuit Hammerstein belongs the Jesuit Baumgartner. Baumgartner, a Swiss, is considered the great literary authority of the Order: poet, essayist, critic, especially appointed by the Order to carry on classical research. If the Jesuit Hammerstein is a popular writer who shouts his tirades against the German classics into the ears of the masses, the Jesuit Baumgartner (according to the Jesuits and German Catholics) is the "æstheticising, subtle critic who lays before the reader the clarified results of his researches in his monographs on Lessing, Schiller, and Goethe." Thus his opinion on the classics marks with special significance the attitude of the Jesuit Order towards the heroes of our literature.

I quote specimens of Baumgartner's criticisms from two of his works, *Goethe und Schiller. Weimars Glanzperiode*, and *Der Alte von Weimar*. Both appeared as so-called "supplementary pamphlets" to the Jesuit periodical, *Stimmen aus Maria-Laach*. Thus the Jesuit Order, which publishes the periodical, has identified itself closely with these writings:—

". . . To whomsoever the Odes on Laura may have been addressed, whether to the widow of Captain Vischer, in whose house Schiller lived, or to some other similar muse, such poetry, combined with other circumstances, presupposes a fairly wild and dissolute life. In Mannheim, Schiller drifted into the immoral life of the actors there, so that subsequently the experiences of stage life in Goethe's *Wilhelm Meister* were no novelty to him, but rather came home to him as personal reminiscences. At the same time he fell in love with Margaretha, daughter of the bookseller Schwan, and entered into such passionate relations with Charlotte von Kalb that finally he even urged her to a divorce. In Bauerbach he

---

* *Das Preussische Schulmonopol*, pp. 56–59, 73–81.

wooed with foolish passion another Charlotte, the daughter of his benefactress, von Wolzogen ; in Dresden a Fräulein Arnim captivated him. In Weimar he openly renewed his *liaison* with Frau von Kalb, whilst simultaneously he thought of marrying a daughter of Wieland, and his double love for the sisters Lengenfeld was not exactly straightforward, until at last he won Lotte for his wife. Certainly this was a sufficient number of adventures for a space of ten years.

" One of these attachments Schiller himself later called 'a wretched passion,' and thereby stigmatised the character of his youth as a succession of errors. Not much weight is to be given to the virtuous tirades in his early dramas when, while still a student at the Karlsschule, he repeatedly extolled the Duke's mistress, Franziska von Hohenheim, in the most extravagant manner, as the 'ideal of virtue,' though the young man knew who that Franziska was. Whilst young Goethe was inclined towards softness and effeminacy, young Schiller appears wilder, more passionate and impetuous. Still, he did not squander so much time in endless sentimental correspondence with women, and never lavished such boundless thoughts and energy on the female sex as the spoilt darling of Frau Aja. . . . No more than Goethe, did Schiller possess any deep religious and philosophical culture. . . . He had never thoroughly studied the philosophy of Aristotle and Plato, not to mention that of the Middle Ages, of Descartes, Bacon, or Leibnitz. The religious impressions and the pious faith of his childhood were almost entirely lost in the whirl of his stage life. He was a freethinker. The Catholic Church was yet more of an unknown country to him than Spinoza. His literary store of ideas dated no further back than the shallow literature of the illuminati of those days : the periodicals, novels, plays of a literature which was still entirely under the influence of Rousseau, Voltaire, Diderot and the rest of the 'philosophers.' Schiller certainly studied history in an eclectic spirit, just as he happened to require matter for his dramatic projects or for essays on other subjects. At Bauerbach he had to make the best of the books which the librarian, his brother-in-law, Reinhold, procured for him ; in Mannheim his theatrical worries entirely absorbed his necessary leisure. Not until he was in Dresden and Leipzig did his studies somewhat gain in breadth and depth.

Then he began to read Kant seriously, and investigated more detailed works on the Thirty Years' War and the revolt of the Netherlands. But even there his studies were not those of a scholar, calmly investigating truth, but rather of a literary hack, who rummages about for spicy historical matter in order to fill his 'review' and earn his fee." *

"However much Goethe's real merits demand acknowledgment, they must not be exaggerated, as is only too often done. His brilliant intellectual gifts, his physical strength and his length of life, his favourable surroundings—all these were gifts not of his own bestowal. He had for years allowed them practically or almost entirely to lie fallow, or else squandered them on unimportant matters. The establishment and moulding of modern classical literature is not his work. The arduous, difficult pioneering was accomplished by others, in the first instance by Klopstock and his disciples, Wieland, Lessing and Herder. Goethe himself received his most fruitful and momentous impulses from Herder. Even talents of a lower order, like Lavater and Merck, influenced him powerfully. Lenz, Klinger, and the other poets of the *Storm and Stress* gave him considerable impetus. Wieland and Knebel had a stimulating influence on his work up to the last. When, absorbed in Court and State affairs at Weimar, he had almost entirely devoted himself to the writing of prose, it was Schiller who recalled him to the realm of poetry, and to a great extent he owes his second prime to this stimulating intercourse.

"In reality Goethe produced but few really classical prose works; these are the four novels: *Werther's Leiden, Wilhelm Meister's Lehrjahre, Die Wahlverwandschaften* and *Wilhelm Meister's Wanderjahre.*

"Even if a torso, a fragment, may betray the hand of a master yet the full productive power, the genius and industry of the artist, can only be manifested in the perfected, finished masterpiece. In the case of Calderon and Shakespeare, it is not necessary to collect fragments: their rounded and perfected works of art occupy many volumes. Not so with Goethe. With him the small and fragmentary occupies as much space, at times even more, as the great and important.

* *Goethe und Schiller. Weimars Glanzperiode*, pp. 36–38.

"Nor are *Stella* and *Clavigo* works of genius. *Egmont* is a historical tragedy swamped by a love story; *Götz*, in spite of the far-reaching influence which it exercised on the history of literature, is an unsuccessful imitation of Shakespeare. Even the three versions of the latter show the intrinsic weakness of the tragedy. *Mahomet* and *Tancred* are Voltaire's property, not Goethe's. During the eighty-two years of his life, despite his great genius, Goethe produced only three genuine, superb, intellectually great, artistically perfect dramatic works: *Iphigenie, Tasso, Faust*.

"Of the longer epics, one only is perfect: *Hermann und Dorothea*. *Reinecke Fuchs* is a mere compilation; *Achilleis* a feeble fragment. There still remain the elegies, epigrams and aphorisms, the *Westöstlicher Divan*, the ballads and lyrics. Of these last more than a third are occasional poems, far more than a third love poems. The D*ivan* again is more than half love poetry. If on the one hand we set aside the didactic poems, on the other hand the erotic, not much remains: God, the World, the Fatherland, Art, History—in fact, all that is ideal—receive but scant treatment. · : . The prevailing fundamental principle of this poet, with all his brilliant gifts, is not inspiration emanating from above, nor aspiring thither; not the Christian ideal, but the mighty Eros of pagan antiquity, a love of life, a lust for enjoyment, that takes no thought of God and eternity; a sensual love, portrayed in its full vernal magic and youthful charm, as well as in the gloomy storm, the dreary disillusionment it leaves in the human heart after a brief delight.

"There can hardly be a doubt about this in respect to Goethe's lyrical work. Apart from a small fraction, it is one continuous love song, chanting the bliss and rose of love in all its phases, in every harmony and melody, key and modulation. The elegies carry the theme to the boundary-line, where realism ceases to be attractive; his diary and the *Walpurgisnacht* go far beyond. The four novels deal with the same theme in a wider frame. Ardent love yearnings, joys, woes—'the atmosphere of a woman's man,' to quote Fr. Vischer—pervades the whole with sultry oppressiveness. *Faust* is heavily charged with the same atmosphere, for it is on Gretchen and Helen only that all Faust's thoughts and desires are concentrated. Tasso is a love dreamer like Faust and Werther.

Even *Hermann und Dorothea* is not exempt from that erotic atmosphere. In Goethe's hands, *Götz* finally becomes a drama of adultery, *Egmont* a love tragedy; Achilles himself is a love-sick enthusiast. In the *Grosskophta* seduction, and in *Stella* bigamy, are presented in detail; in *Pandora* the foolish ecstasy of an old man in love is extolled. In his youthful carnival's jests the poet's passion finds vent in coarse ribaldry, in his musical plays it undulates gracefully in charming duets, in his Marienbad elegy and at the end of *Faust* it even endeavours yearningly to dally its way into heaven. . If he happens to be reading Rousseau, he raves about nature; if it is Voltaire, of civilisation; if he reads Spinoza, he obtains an intuition of God which enables him to see in each separate existence the universal whole; if he hears of Leibnitz, he sees Monads everywhere; and if it is Aristotle, the Monads become Entelechies: But nowhere do we meet with a clear, matter-of-fact definition of Nature, knowledge and God, intuitive apprehension of God and the real meaning of Monads and Entelechies. Goethe made just as much fun of Kant's Categorical Imperative as of Fichte's Ego and Non-Ego; and Schelling's little book on the Kabirs was more interesting to him than his natural philosophy. He was no more a consistent follower of Spinoza than of Schelling or Hegel. He abhorred not only all philosophical idealism, but any system whatever. . . . His poetry, seen in the light reflected upon it by his life, appears a mere glorifying of the most commonplace material existence, petty vanity, foolish stage adventures and love affairs, egotistic self-admiration and sensual love of enjoyment; it shows no comprehension of the life of nations, of the sublimity of divine revelation and of the Church, no trace of fear or love of God, such as inspired the minstrels of the Middle Ages. This egotistical demigod no longer stands before us alone, but surrounded by a whole swarm of adoring followers, who have long ago rent asunder all the diplomatic cobwebs of mystery in which the old man draped himself, who deify his sensual love songs as the highest and truest poetry, his realism as the loftiest outlook on life, his paganism as purified 'Christianity,' his unpardonable moral aberrations as ideals of life, who recommend the very essence of his errors as the highest development of our national culture to be studied and copied by all.

" . . . Surely the danger to religion and morals lurking therein needs no further exposition. Goethe's poetry and life speak for themselves. Even if conscientious teachers expound but a very limited selection of his works, this offers but slight protection, as his works are in universal circulation, are obtainable everywhere in cheap classical and popular editions, in elegant drawing-room volumes elaborately bound, in the most splendid *éditions de luxe*. His songs are sung, his dramas acted, his heroes and heroines, he himself and the whole galaxy of his loves are to be met with in every shop-window. It is not necessary to learn a new or an old language in order to understand his poems. His ideas and ideals seldom go beyond the comprehension of the most commonplace public, and should this be the case, there are numerous commentaries at hand which enlarge upon his love affairs under pretence of philological erudition. Invested with the authority of the greatest classical poet, and regarded as the benefactor and glory of the nation, he makes his way into all circles; with his bewitching charm, like the Pied Piper of Hamelin, he draws all hearts to him, especially those of women and youth. He never preaches unbelief and immorality as boldly, as audaciously as Voltaire, Wieland or the modern French realists, but always veiled, gently, insinuatingly, alluringly, in an apparently innocent form, always with an admixture of what is good and true, what is partly good, partly true. He undermines the faith and morality of the young without their realising the seduction. If the venom of his pagan principles is not to penetrate further and further, it is indeed time that all those who have any influence on the education of the young should take this danger seriously to heart, and unite their forces to check it.

" Above all, it is evident that the reading and study of Goethe must again be restricted in accordance with the principles of truly Christian pedagogics, which lays more stress on religious and moral training than on beauty of form, style and language. The school cannot and must not take part in the modern hero-worship of Goethe, if it is to retain its Christianity. It must, on the contrary, rectify the erroneous ideas which are necessarily engendered by that cult. All precautions, all anthologies, all expurgated school-editions are of no avail if the author of *Iphigenie*, etc., is overwhelmed with praise from a misunderstood patriotism or æsthetic over-estimation; if instead of a better authority Eckermann's *Gespräche* and lines from Goethe are everlastingly quoted, even for the most commonplace occasions; if all æsthetic and all poetic theory is to be based on Goethe; if he is continually compared with Dante, Shakespeare, Calderon, and the young are solemnly given to understand that as a poet he has left all the former poets far behind him; that ' our Goethe ' is the greatest poet, the man of most universal knowledge, the zenith of all civilisation. And yet Goethe did not know enough scholastic theology and philosophy for the mere comprehension of Dante's *Divine Comedy;* he has not written a single tragedy which as a stage play can stand comparison with the masterpieces of Shakespeare and Calderon.

. Instead of incessant eulogy, let us tell the young plainly how low Goethe stands as a man, how hollow and superficial was his outlook on life, how immoral and pernicious were his principles, how small his importance as a naturalist or art critic. Let us tell the young how, after thirty years of foolish wanderings, he turned to Aristotle's *Poetics*, and as a man of fifty, to the greatest benefit of his poetic development, at last studied those rules on art which have for centuries constituted the basis of Poetics at all Catholic educational establishments. Let us lay before the young the restless, fragmentary labours of young Goethe, the enormous harm done to him by the frittering away of his energies. Let us show them the weaknesses and defects of Goethe's poetry, as contrasted with that of the ancients, of Shakespeare and Calderon. There is hardly a quotation from Goethe that could not be replaced by one from the ancient classics or from the best Catholic writers.*

" Why always Goethe, Goethe—nothing but Goethe ? After all, what does it profit the Seven Sacraments if this Privy Councillor of Weimar, consort of a dance-loving Christiane Vulpius, considered them beautiful, without believing in them ?

" What avail his sketches of the Flight into Egypt if they only serve to introduce our youth into the unclean society of Wilhelm Meister ? What good sayings has he ever uttered about the ancients, about the Bible, about religion, art, literature and life that cannot

* Probably from the *Poets of the Society of Jesus.* See Chapter V.

be found more correctly, purely, very often better and more beautifully stated by Catholic thinkers, poets, artists and writers ? Why do we refuse credence to the most conscientious Catholic scholars and scientific inquirers till Goethe and Eckermann have given their blessing ? . . . The Church has never proceeded against works of polite literature with that severity which she is wont to exercise against strictly theological and philosophical works of erroneous and hurtful tendency. Goethe's works have never been placed expressly and distinctly on the Roman Index. They were left to its general regulations, as the Popes of the Renaissance once left the works of Boccaccio, Valla, Beccadelli and Poggio, to the conscience of the individual. This, however, does not amount to a free passport for Goethe's works. Apart from numerous passages which sin grievously against the requirements of Christian discipline and morals, they are thoroughly leavened with the most dangerous errors by which our modern times are affected, and which the Vatican Council has expressly repudiated in its binding decrees. That rationalism, pantheism and religious indifference in which all Goethe's poetry has its roots, and which is clearly enough displayed in his prose writings, has been eternally branded by the Church herself. But few of his works are untouched, or nearly so, by these errors, though they appear but rarely in outspoken form ; the great majority of his writings are steeped in them in a most attractive and alluring fashion, and are thus fully calculated to trivialise and obscure religious ideas, and to weaken and undermine Christian faith. The clear vision, faith and steadfastness of every individual will modify this influence in very different ways. . . . It will be a great gain for real Christian education when we revert from an almost idolatrous cult of the great poet to a sober, sensible and just appreciation of his life and works, when we know him as he actually was, and do not esteem him beyond his deserts."

" . . . Youths and men will no longer accept a Werther, a Wilhelm Meister, a Faust as types of the true German spirit, but as the poetical forms of a morally decadent period. They will then compare the spurious universality of Goethe with the real universality of Catholic learning, and will be easily convinced that an Angelo Secchi [a Jesuit] understood more of the property of light and of the unity of natural forces, a Raphael Garruci and a de Rossi more of Christian art, a Reichsperger and Pugin more of the laws of Gothic architecture, a Jannsen* more of German character, history and national spirit, and a Peter Cornelius and Eduard von Steinle more about Raphael and Italian painting, a Joseph von Görres more about Mysticism† and German folklore, a Friedrich von Schlegel more about universal literature, a Lorinser more about Calderon, a Cardinal Wiseman more about Shakespeare than Johann Wolfgang Goethe, Heinrich Meyer, Wilhelm Riemer, Peter Eckermann and all the rest, together with the comet-like tail of philologists and critics.

"When this glittering Goethe meteor is no longer considered a universal lodestar of real world-philosophy, wisdom and knowledge, we shall once more be able to recognise and show honour to other constellations in the firmament of German literature."‡

It is hard to know whether to marvel most at the inferior understanding revealed in these Jesuit appreciations of Lessing, Schiller, and Goethe, or at the hatred which casts forth poison against great minds because they illumine humanity with their light, and thus remove it from Jesuit influence.

Whenever we open Baumgartner's bulky Goethe-monograph, the same passion for disparagement, the same calumniating malice, are manifested. I quote a few examples:—

"It is most characteristic of Goethe that in this play [Shakespeare's *King John*] he was but little interested in its great political, ecclesiastic and patriotic motives, nor in the passionate and powerful male characters, nor in the pathetic characters of Queen Eleanor and Constance, but especially in the two affecting scenes with Prince Arthur; not in the light of a harmless, unfortunate prince, as conceived by Shakespeare, but as a girl in boy's clothes— Christiane Neumann. 'The whole play now hung upon her. She

---

* The notorious Ultramontane fabricator of history.

† Görres wrote a half-crazy book on Mysticism. *Cf.* my work, *Das Papsttum in seiner sozialkulturellen Wirksamkeit*, I. 235-245.

‡ *Der Alte von Weimar*, pp. 271-278, 281-284.

acted well. But when Hubert approached with the tongs to put out the prince's eyes, she did not show enough terror. On this, the manager, Goethe, tore the tongs from Hubert's hands, rushed at Christiane, and made such terrible eyes at her that she fainted. Now, Goethe himself was frightened, knelt down before her, and when she recovered consciousness gave her a kiss.' This is the chief scene during nearly forty years of stage management described in a glorified light in all books on Goethe, even in histories of literature. It is a striking proof of the profound contrast between the virile and universal genius of a true dramatist like William Shakespeare and the lyrical adorer of maidens, Wolfgang Goethe, who was more interested in the caress than in King John and all the Kings of England, Ireland and Scotland put together."

Of Goethe's attitude towards the French Revolution, the Jesuit says:—

"And Goethe? Goethe felt embarrassed. As a true disciple of Rousseau and Voltaire, as a decided non-Christian and pagan, he could not in common consistency but approve of the thorough and complete abolition of the old order of things, the guillotining of kings, the old nobility, the priests, the abolition of honour and the other remnants of the Seven Sacraments, the secularisation of the whole of life, with a view to the speedy occupation of Europe with Greek republics, with the greatest possible number of gods, *hetaerae*, philosophers and poets, painters, sculptors, intellectual enjoyment and artistic delights. This was his religion and the view he took of life. But, as an ordinary Frankfort citizen, he wanted at the same time to eat and sleep in peace; as a Weimar Privy Councillor he desired an increase rather than a decrease of salary; as the friend of a Duke, he preferred seeing him crowned to seeing him decapitated. The French Republic was not organised on the model of Periclean Athens, but according to the uncomfortable military rule of Roman agitators, triumvirs and tyrannicides. Not poems, but proscription lists, were issued. Olympic games were not held, but heads were cut off. The freethinkers in Paris were not content with taking an unwedded Vulpius into their houses, and having her little boys christened by a gentleman who scarcely believed in Christ himself, simply to throw dust in people's eyes; they preferred to guillotine people who objected to such things, to pocket their money, and to remodel the world. That would not do at Weimar. All violence was odious to the Privy Councillor. Who would read his *Tasso*, if there were no more duchesses and Court ladies? Who would shed tears over his *Werther*, if the world became so callous and unfeeling?"

Even Goethe's affecting lines to Schiller's memory serve Baumgartner to asperse the object of his hatred·—

" The contrast which Schiller offered to the prevailing tendency in Weimar was certainly indicated in a subsequent verse, but it was amiably neutralised by the reflection: ' He was ours '—it was a cunning stroke of policy. For thus Schiller was for ever bound to the triumphal car of his former rival."*

I must, however, say a word in defence of the Jesuit Baumgartner against himself, *i.e.* his publications in disparagement of Goethe and the other classics. These ugly judgments are not altogether his innermost convictions. Baumgartner's undeniable poetical talent had led him to a considerably higher estimate of the " Old Man of Weimar," and he had put this conception into writing, but was compelled to publish a different version, the one prescribed by the censorship of the Order.

In 1887, after the conclusion of my theological studies at Ditton Hall, I was transferred, in the capacity of scriptor, to Exaeten, where the editorial staff of the *Stimmen aus Maria-Laach* was quartered at the time. The Jesuit Joseph Fäh was editor-in-chief and also Vice-Rector of the whole establishment. Fäh told me one day that, according to the censor's verdict, Baumgartner had concluded his monograph on Goethe with a too favourable general estimate; that the manuscript had been returned to him (Baumgartner was at the time at the

* *Goethe und Schiller*, pp. 82-83, 118-119.

college of Blyenbeck) with the intimation that the criticism on Goethe must be considerably altered in an unfavourable direction. I asked, in surprise, " But will Baumgartner do it ? " Fäh answered, " Of course he will." And he did.*

This occurrence shows two things : the hatred of the Jesuits for Goethe and the power of Jesuit censorship and Jesuit obedience. Not in vain do the Constitutions of the Order prescribe blind obedience.

* I know Baumgartner well. I was with him at Exaeten for a long time. He is the typical example of the transformation Jesuit training can effect in a man of real ability. When quite young, on leaving the Jesuit College of Feldkirch, he entered the novitiate of the Order. He would have distinguished himself, had he been able to develop freely in accordance with his individuality. But the Jesuit machine trimmed him, castrated him in mind, will and disposition. Thus his mental powers were broken, and worse : he became a zealot, a man who directed his rancour against all that is beautiful and true in nature and humanity, while inwardly yearning after it, in spite of his invectives. Poor fellow !

CHAPTER XXII

THE PHILOSOPHICAL AND THEOLOGICAL STUDIES OF THE SCHOLASTICATE

PHILOSOPHY and theology, rightly understood, are separate, independent branches of knowledge (*Wissenschaften*). But philosophy, in the Jesuit sense, is altogether dependent on theology, is even its "handmaid" and "servant": "The professors of philosophy [says the eighth canon of the third General Congregation] are to teach philosophy in such a manner that it becomes the handmaid and servant of true scholastic theology, which is commended to us by our Constitutions: '*Ut verae theologiae scholasticae, quam nobis commendant Constitutiones, ancillari et subservire faciant.*'"* Therefore I shall treat in the same section of Jesuit philosophy and theology.

First, a few words as to the outward form of these studies.

The philosophy course generally lasts for three years, though there are some exceptions. Every year there is an examination of half an hour, and at the end of the third year a final examination of an hour's duration on the whole of philosophy. Only those who "surpass mediocrity" in this examination (*mediocritatem superaverint*) enter on the four years' course of "scholastic theology" known as the "Major Dogma." Those who do not pass the final examination must content themselves with the three years' course, known as the "Minor Dogma." Every

* *Inst. S.J.*, I., 477.

year of theological study also ends with an examination. The examination of the fourth year (*examen rigorosum*) lasts two hours. This examination decides whether those who possess "virtue surpassing mediocrity" are afterwards to take the degree of " professed " or only that of " spiritual coadjutor." If the candidate is to become a " professed " the examination must show that he has attained " that degree of thorough philosophical and theological knowledge which will qualify him to teach both subjects satisfactorily."*

All examinations are oral; they are conducted by four examiners under the presidency of the Rector or the Provincial, who must swear to fulfil their duty conscientiously and to disclose their verdict only to the General of the Order and the Provincial,† for entrance into the books designated for the purpose.

If anyone possesses " conspicuous gifts for ruling or preaching " (*illustria gubernandi concionandive talenta*) the " insufficient knowledge " (*doctrina impar*) shown in the examination may be overlooked. This decision is exclusively in the hands of the General of the Order. Also " excellent knowledge of classical and Indian languages " may, if the General consider it advisable, atone for the deficiencies in philosophy and theological knowledge.‡

In the philosophy year, logic and ontology (the science of being) are studied. The second year's course includes natural philosophy (*i.e.* a medley of miscellaneous matter belonging to the domain of natural science, decked out with philosophy and styled cosmology, including miracles with their criteria), and psychology (simplicity, spirituality, immortality of the soul, its connection with the

---

* Rules 17 and 19 for the Provincial.
† Rule 19, 12 for the Provincial; Congreg. 12, Decret. 22.
‡ Rule 19, 10 for the Provincial; Congreg. 6, Decret. 15.

body, its difference from the animal soul). The third year's course comprises ethics (natural morality) and natural theology (theodicy). In the last two years there are also a few lessons on chemistry, physics, botany, and astronomy. Instruction and achievement in these branches of science hardly correspond to the work done in the middle and higher forms of a gymnasium. When I studied philosophy at Blyenbeck, "lectures" delivered by the Jesuit Epping on astronomy were anything rather than scientific. We laughed a good deal, slept not a little (the lessons were early in the afternoon), and profited accordingly.

In the case of theological studies the system is not quite so hard and fast. The two professors of theology —generally there are no more—arrange among themselves, with the permission of the Principal and the Prefect of Studies, how the theological subject matter shall be distributed over four or, as the case may be, three years.

Together with the scholastic—*i.e.* speculative—theology a two-years' course on moral theology (*casus conscientiae*) is given. This is an extremely important—I might almost say all-important—branch of Jesuit study, by which the young Jesuit is trained for practical life, and especially for his work in the confessional.

The pupils receive the summary of the lectures in the form of hectographed "codices." No notes are taken during lectures. Neither are text-books used except for moral theology, where the *Theologia moralis* of the Jesuit Lehmkuhl is the text-book in use.

What has been imparted in the lectures is elaborated and impressed upon the mind by regular disputations. Great importance is attached to these. The ordinary disputation, of one hour's duration, held several times a week, is called a "Circle" (*Circulus*). Every Saturday a more important debate, "*Sabbatina*"—short for *disputatio sabbatina*—is held. The "*disputationes men-*

struae," held five or six times a year, are attended with special solemnities. The Rector of the House appears at the head of the other Fathers, and so does the Provincial, if he happens to be in residence. Whereas in the "Circle" and "Sabbatina" the defenders and opposers are chosen in advance, and only a few theses (mostly those gone through immediately before) are selected for debate, in the "Menstruae" the proposers are only nominated by the Prefect of Studies at the outset of the debate (everyone is expected to be prepared), and the theses to be defended extend over a wider field.

The form of all disputations is the same. The defender announces the thesis, defines the *status questionis*—*i.e.* explains what the thesis asserts and what it does not assert—and states the arguments for its correctness in syllogistic form. In theological theses the proofs are generally of three kinds. 1. From the Holy Scriptures (*ex s. scriptura*). 2. From reason (*ex ratione*). 3. From pronouncements of the Fathers of the Church (*ex s. s. Patribus*). Thesis, *status questionis*, and arguments are committed to memory as literally as possible from the "Codices." When the defender has concluded his final argument, the opposer attacks the thesis. And now begins a verbal dispute in strictly scholastic-syllogistic form between defender and opposer, until the defender either succeeds in solving the difficulties or breaks down in the attempt. If he fails, he is, as the scholastic slang has it, "in the sack" (*in sacco*), and the professor presiding at the disputation intervenes to save the threatened thesis. At the "Menstruae" the invited Fathers also take part in the debate.

Sometimes, though rarely, "public performances" (*actus publici*) are organised, *i.e.* one person supports a number of theological and philosophical theses against opposers from among the secular clergy or the priests of the Order. No such ceremony took place during my period of study.

Some, whom the Order wishes to train more fully for some special service, pass through a *biennium* in theology, philosophy, or one of the kindred branches of knowledge (Exegesis, Church Law, Church History), after the four years' course.

In all lectures and disputations the use of Latin is compulsory.

And now as to the spirit of the studies.

As regards philosophy, let me first refer to what I have already quoted from the Constitutions of the Order, from the Scheme of Studies, and from decrees of the General Congregation as to the fundamental standpoint adopted by the Jesuit Order in philosophy. Unswerving adherence to the peripatetic system of Aristotle (who died 322 B.C.) —again solemnly declared in 1883!—with partial application of this system even to questions of natural science, and a re-endorsement of resolutions passed by the General Congregations of the Order in the eighteenth century (1706 and 1751) in favour of the Aristotelian system

The argument for this adherence to Aristotle is very characteristic :

"That philosophy must be followed because it is more useful to theology."*

From this Aristotelian standpoint, it is self-evident that the whole of modern philosophy must be sorely neglected. Minds like Descartes, Leibnitz, Spinoza, Kant, Hegel, Fichte, Schelling, Schopenhauer, E. von Hartmann, etc., are disposed of by inadequate theses. A few syllogisms, and a Kant, a Descartes, etc., fall to the ground.

Here once again I keenly regret that when I left the Order I left behind all my manuscript notes. From the "Codices" of my period of Jesuit study a clear and

* Congreg. 23 of the year 1883; Decret. 15.

Studies of the Scholasticate 251

instructive description might have been given of the treatment allotted to the study of modern philosophy by the "modern" Jesuit.

The works of modern philosophers were not placed in our hands. The few details concerning them in our "Codices" represented for us the sum total of their publications. The reference libraries at our disposal contained exclusively the works of Jesuit writers. It is the same here as with the piety and asceticism of the Order · Jesuits, Jesuits, Jesuits, and nothing but Jesuits!

I feel ashamed and indignant when I remember that when I was thirty years old I used to be content with the ill-concocted dilution which the Order served up to me as the quintessence of the labours of these great thinkers. Kant especially was treated with a superficiality that surpassed everything. I only made this great man's acquaintance when I was staying in Berlin in 1888, on a mission for the Jesuit Order. There, free from police supervision, I plunged deeply into the study of his works. He became my chief liberator, who enlarged my innermost thoughts, and opened a new and unknown horizon to my ideas. How I apologised to him for having thought so poorly of him when I was a Jesuit-Scholastic! But the fault was not mine!

Peter Beckx, General of the Order, in his official letter of July 15th, 1854, to Count Leo Thun, Austrian Minister of Public Instruction, draws a picture, both pertinent and vested with supreme authority, of the Jesuit attitude towards any development of philosophy later than that of the ancients or the Middle Ages:

"How can we place reliance in philosophy as it has shown itself in our days, how can we with any confidence expect to gain from it knowledge and a basis for truth, when its four great schools, which under Kant, Fichte, Schelling and Hegel by turns subjugated the whole of Germany, finally melted away into pure (*sic*) atheism, and were abandoned one after the other, and at the same time—to say nothing of religious and political degeneration—have left behind them a state of doubt, uncertainty and almost universal confusion, in which men continue their contention, but without appearing to understand one another's meaning?

"What has caused this state of things? Simply this: The ground which was wrested from true philosophy by the aforementioned four schools has not been recovered, and men, either not understanding the real cause of the evil or not wishing to admit it, seek it ever along fresh paths, thus falling from one error into another. The truly Catholic Universities were always agreed and clear as to the basis of philosophy [the Aristotelian system]."*

And twenty years later the Jesuit Ebner characterises in an official controversial treatise against Joh. Kelle, Professor at the University of Prague, the whole of modern philosophy by the scornful words:

"Futile vagaries, confused ideas, foolish arrogance and charlatanism clothed in boastful, empty phrases in a repulsive, unintelligible jargon; systems as hostile to sound sense as to God and Christianity, all of which really tend towards materialism and pantheism, and which perhaps have recently reached their climax and, it is to be hoped, their conclusion, in the absurdities and blasphemies of that monstrous abortion, the 'Philosophy of the Unconscious'" (*Philosophie des Unbewussten*).†

The following facts, too, speak for themselves: Piccolomini, General of the Order, issued a decree in 1661, for "the higher studies," which to this day is found unaltered in the official edition of the Constitutions of the Order. In it is stated

"The Prefect of Studies is to see to it that the Aristotelian definitions of origins, causes, nature, the motion, and the *continuum*, the infinite, are accurately explained, and that natural philosophy

* *Monatsblatt für Kathol. Unterrichts- u. Erziehungs-wesen.* 12 Jahrg. Münster. P. 294.
† *Beleuchtung der Schrift des Herrn Dr. Johann Kelle: Die Jesuitengymnasien in Oesterreich.* Linz, 1874. Pp. 595–596.

is thoroughly discussed according to the Aristotelian arrangement: In Aristotle's *de Caelo*, the nature, properties and influence of the heavens on the sublunary bodies, are not to be omitted. In the first book on generation, the Aristotelian doctrine on generation and corruption is to be thoroughly studied."

To an inquiry sent by the Province of the Upper Rhine, Gonzalez, General of the Order, under threats of a heavy penalty, pronounced against the introduction of " new philosophical ideas " into the schools of the Order.*

His successor, Tamburini, prohibited thirty propositions from the works of Descartes and Leibnitz.† Up to the year 1832 Aristotle was the text-book used for the entire three years' course in philosophy.‡

What spirit, then, prevails in theology ? That of the medieval scholastics, in particular the spirit of Thomas Aquinas, prince of scholastics, who died in 1274.

The Second Rule for the Teacher in Theology, as stated in the *Ratio Studiorum*, is :

" In Scholastic Theology our people are to follow strictly (*omnino sequantur*) the teaching of St. Thomas; they are to regard him as their own teacher (*eumque ut doctorem proprium habeant*), and do their utmost to inspire the students with enthusiasm for his teaching."

This order, dating from the year 1599, is even surpassed by the 15th Decree, issued in 1883, by the twenty-third General Congregation of the Order:

" Our most holy master, Leo XIII., having a few years ago commanded through an encyclical *Aeterni Patris* how the studies of Christian schools under the guidance of the Angelic Doctor [*Doctor Angelicus* is the official designation of Thomas Aquinas] are to be brought back to the wisdom of ancient times, the Society of Jesus, for the first time since the issue of the encyclical assembled at a General Congregation, considers it advisable to give an

---

* *Monum. Germ. paed.*, 9, 122.
† *Ibid.*   ‡ *Ibid.*, 16, 464.

unequivocal token of its filial obedience and consent by a public and solemn declaration. In the conviction, therefore, that it could do nothing more agreeable or more conducive to the fulfilment of the wishes of his Holiness than to establish anew what has long ago been confirmed to the same effect by our ancestors, the Congregation decides by the motion of the Very Venerable General that: what was ordered by our holy Father Ignatius in his Constitutions (IV., 14, n. 1), and by the fifth General Congregation in the 41st and 56th Decrees, is to remain in full force—namely, our people are to regard St. Thomas in all respects as their own teacher and are to be bound in duty (*teneantur*) to follow him in Scholastic Theology."[*]

One point here is specially noteworthy ·

Whilst the *Ratio* of the year 1599, in the same rule[†] which sets up Thomas Aquinas as a prominent authority, makes this reservation: "It is not to be understood from this that we may never deviate from him in any single point"; the decree of the Congregation of the year 1883 drops this reservation, and changes the more lenient expression of the *Ratio* into a binding law:

"They [the Jesuits] are to be bound to follow him [Thomas Aquinas] in Scholastic Theology": *eumque in scholastica theologia sequi teneantur.*

One word about the encyclical on which the decree of the Congregation is based. It is that of August 4th, 1879, in which Leo XIII. commands the revival of philosophy and theology in the spirit of the Scholastic School, and designates Thomas Aquinas as the leader they are to follow:

"Among scholastic teachers, Thomas Aquinas, prince and master of all, is by far the greatest. . There is no department of philosophy which he has not treated with perspicuity and thoroughness. . . He was successful both in overcoming all

---

[*] *Monum. Germ. paed.* 2, 118.
[†] Rule 2 for the Professor of Theology.

errors in the past, and in providing victorious weapons against all errors that may arise in ages to come."

After quoting the eulogies of Thomas Aquinas by earlier Popes, he continues thus:

"A crowning glory which no other Catholic theologian shares with him was conferred on him, when the Fathers of the Council of Trent, in the very hall where they were assembled, commanded that, together with the Holy Scriptures and Papal decrees, the *Summa* [St. Thomas's principal work, entitled *Summa theologica*] should be laid on the altar, so that counsel, proofs and solutions might be drawn therefrom. . . . Civil society also would gain much in peace and security if a healthier doctrine, more in harmony with the orthodox faith as set forth in the works of St. Thomas Aquinas, were taught at their academies and schools. We earnestly exhort you all, reverend brethren, for the promotion of all knowledge, to reintroduce the golden wisdom of St. Thomas, and to propagate it as far as possible. . . ."

This declaration, as we have seen, gave the Jesuits a pretext for promulgating anew, in more stringent form, the old decree of the Order concerning the preservation of St. Thomas's spirit in philosophy and theology. But there is yet more! Papal encyclicals and decrees of the Congregations of the Order are identical; they have one and the same origin—the Society of Jesus. For the "German" Jesuit, Joseph Kleutgen, is the author of the encyclical *Aeterni Patris*. This I was told by the Jesuit Meschler when he was Provincial of the German Province. This is a significant proof, not only of the fact that Jesuit theology is firmly rooted in the *Summa* of the Monk of the Middle Ages, but also of the unobtrusive but mighty power which the Jesuit Order exercises on the Papacy. It writes to all the "Patriarchs, Primates, Archbishops and Bishops of the Catholic world who live in grace and unison with the Apostolic Chair" [invariable heading of all Papal Encyclicals]; it points out the path to be followed by Catholic theological studies in all countries; thus the Order is the greatest obstacle to modern evolution of Catholic thought. And doubtless the encyclical concerning the revival of philosophy and theology according to the principles and precepts of Thomas Aquinas is not the only one signed by the Pope which was composed by the Society of Jesus.

If I blame the Order for their rigid adherence to Aristotelian philosophy and Thomistic theology* I would in no way underrate the great intellects of Aristotle and Thomas Aquinas.

Both are conspicuously eminent—the heathen Greek even more than the Christian Monk—among the intellectual heroes of all ages. Both were creative geniuses, who stimulated and deepened the human mind. And however narrow was the field for which Aquinas worked, he was an Ultramontane Catholic in the narrowest sense.† In this field he has dug shafts and piled up heights which, considered from the standpoint of metaphysical-ultramontane speculation, are admirable. But we are not

---

* In order to guard against quibbling, I observe that the expression "Thomistic" is not used here in the sense of "Thomism," but as the definition of a form of theology which, like the Jesuit theology, acknowledges Thomas Aquinas as its leader and chief teacher. By "Thomism" is understood the interpretation put upon the words of Thomas Aquinas by his commentators (Cajetan, Soto, Melchior Canus, etc.). To "Thomism" in its narrowest sense, i.e. the "Doctrine of Grace," attributed to Thomas by his interpreters, the Jesuits have opposed Molinism (so called after the Jesuit Molina), which also refers its "Conception of Grace" to Thomas Aquinas. Both doctrines are unworthy of an ideal conception of God.

† The ignorance prevailing even in highly cultured non-Catholic circles with regard to Thomas Aquinas as a narrow, Ultramontane theologian is shown by a speech of the well-known Dr. Friedrich Naumann at the Protestant Congress at Bremen in September, 1909. Naumann, speaking on liberalism in religion and politics, represented Thomas Aquinas as a theologian of liberal opinions, whom, however, the Roman Church of to-day, with diplomatic cunning, honoured as her own, and thus kept up the appearance of large-mindedness, while the Protestant Church repudiated many evangelical liberal theologians with hurtful shortsightedness. From this estimate of Thomas (I heard it myself) it seems to be impossible that Dr. Naumann can ever have looked into a single one of the Dominican's works.

concerned with the individual greatness of the Stagirite and Aquinas, but with the circumstance that an organisation with pretensions to intellectual and scholarly vitality, the Jesuit Order, continues to draw its supplies of knowledge and learning from sources which flowed hundreds, nay thousands, of years ago, and that by this retrograde direction of mind it shows itself hostile to progress and uncompromisingly refuses to tread new paths.

Certainly the Order has one good excuse: it is ultramontane, therefore progress in knowledge is impossible for it, as for the whole ultramontanised Catholic Church of which it forms a part. But, if *est ut est aut non est* explains and excuses everything from the Jesuit's point of view, the world which is neither Jesuit nor Ultramontane cannot accept this excuse in passing an objective judgment on the Order; it is compelled to say: Your principles are indeed necessary to yourself and your own existence, but in themselves they are retrograde and contain the negation of living scholarship.

I have already pointed out the great importance attached by the Order in its theological and philosophical school work to the scholastic-syllogistic method. And rightly! For this form is more than a form, it is the outward and visible sign of the spirit prevailing in Jesuit studies.

The 13th Rule for the Teacher of Philosophy in the *Ratio*, even the "new" one of 1832, runs thus:

"At the very outset of their studies in logic, the young people [scholastics] must be trained to feel that nothing is more disgraceful in the disputations than any deviation from the syllogistic form, and the teacher must insist with special force on the strict observance of the laws of the disputation and the prescribed alternation of attack and defence."

From the *Manual on Logic for the Use of Schools,** by

* *Logica in usum Scholarum* (Freiburg, 1893), p. 96.

the Jesuit Frick I quote a specimen of a disputation, in Latin however, for this sort of thing cannot be translated without almost destroying its effect. First, the "*Defendens*" proposes the thesis, stating the arguments in favour:

Defendens: "*Scepticismus universalis, ut doctrina repugnat. Probatur: 1. ex ipsa assertione scepticismi; 2. ex principio contradictionis.*

The "*Defendens*" having explained the arguments, the "*Objiciens*" begins his work:

Objiciens: '*Scepticismus universalis, ut doctrina non repugnat. Probatur: Qui saepe fallitur, nullam fidem meretur. Atqui ratio saepe fallitur. Ergo nullam fidem meretur.*"

The "*Defendens*" repeats the Syllogism of the "*Objiciens*," an follows it up with his "distinctions," and thus the disputation is set going:

Qui saepe fallitur nullam fidem meretur: distinguo majorem: *qui fallitur per se:* concedo majorem; *qui fallitur per accidens:* subdistinguo majorem: *non meretur fidem, nisi quand error ille accidentalis excludatur:* concedo majorem: *quano exclusus est:* nego majorem.

Atqui: *ratio saepe fallitur:* contradistinguo minorem: *ratio fallitur per se et in evidentibus:* nego minorem: *per et in no evidentibus:* transeat minor.

nulla, fidem meretur: distinguo consequens: *fidem in evidentibus:* nego consequens; *in non us:* subdistinguo consequens: *nisi constet de iis legitimitate:* transeat consequens: *si constet: consequens*

Objiciens: '*Atqui ratio fallitur per se:* ergo *nulla stinctio.*"

The "*Defendens*" repeats the *subsumptio* of the "*Objiciens*":

Defendens: '*Atqui ratio fallitur per se:* nego minorem subsum tam."

Objiciens: "Probo minorem subsceptam *humana essentialiter est fallibilis*; atqui quod ratio essentiale est, illi per se et semper inerunt: ergo ratio e per se et semper fallibilis."

After again repeating the worc of the the "*Defendens*" continues:

"*Ratio humana essentialiter est fallibilis*. distingu majorem: ex essentia rationis est, ut quod falli per accidens vel ex defectu evidentiae alicujus rei, concedo majorem ex essentia rationis est, ut possit etiam falli per se, i.e. sin conditione requisita evidentiae: nego majorem; atqui quo rationi essentiale est, illi per se et semper conveniet; concedo minorem; ergo ratio est per se et semper fallibilis: distingu consequens: per se et semper communicabiles ad extra semper possit: nego consequens: per se et semper conveniet rationi, i sit talis, quae per accidens errore possit, concedo consequens."

The syllogistic-formalistic characteristics of the disputation, conspicuous in the terms *distinguo, subdistinguo, transeat, concedo* and the like, I have marked by different type. If we realise that his formalism holds sway in the Jesuit schools evening after evening, year after year, we shall understand how these mechanical ossified forms gradually produce a similar rigidity of the intellect. The apparent gain in clearness and certainty from the numerous short distinctions is acquired at the cost deeper and more living comprehension of the debated. With the aid of three, four or even fi "distinctions," the number does not matter, **pupil is ready** at a moment's notice to dispose of th difficult problems. In order not to seem unjust, I purposely given an instance of a disputation in which distinctions and the syllogistic form really lead to a cle and correct result, which could, however, have bee attained just as quickly and clearly without the scholast paraphernalia, *i.e.* the inconsistency of absolute scepticism the Jesuit Frick, I quote a specimen of a disputation, in Latin however, for this sort of thing cannot be translated without almost destroying its effect. First, the "*Defendens*" proposes the thesis, stating the arguments in favour:

Defendens: "*Scepticismus universalis, ut doctrina repugnat.* Probatur: 1. *ex ipsa assertione scepticismi;* 2. *ex principio contradictionis.*

The "*Defendens*" having explained the arguments, the "*Objiciens*" begins his work:

Objiciens: "*Scepticismus universalis, ut doctrina non repugnat.* Probatur: *Qui saepe fallitur, nullam fidem meretur.* Atqui *ratio saepe fallitur. Ergo nullam fidem meretur.*"

The "*Defendens*" repeats the Syllogism of the "*Objiciens*," and follows it up with his "distinctions," and thus the disputation is set going:

Qui saepe fallitur nullam fidem meretur: distinguo majorem: *qui fallitur per se:* concedo majorem; *qui fallitur per accidens:* subdistinguo majorem: *non meretur fidem, nisi quando error ille accidentalis excludatur:* concedo majorem: *quando exclusus est:* nego majorem.

Atqui: *ratio saepe fallitur:* contradistinguo minorem: *ratio fallitur per se et in evidentibus:* nego minorem: *per accidens et in non evidentibus:* transeat minor.

Ergo: *nullam fidem meretur:* distinguo consequens: *non meretur fidem in evidentibus:* nego consequens; *in non evidentibus:* subdistinguo consequens: *nisi constet de ratiocinii legitimitate:* transeat consequens: *si constet:* nego consequens.

Objiciens: "Atqui *ratio fallitur per se:* ergo *nulla distinctio.*"

The "*Defendens*" repeats the *subsumptio* of the "*Objiciens*":

Defendens: "Atqui *ratio fallitur per se:* nego minorem subsumptam."

Objiciens· "Probo minorem subsceptam: *ratio humana essentialiter est fallibilis;* atqui *quod rationi essentiale est, illi per se et semper convenit;* ergo *ratio est per se et semper fallibilis.*"

After again repeating the words of the "*Objiciens,*" the "*Defendens*" continues:

"*Ratio humana essentialiter est fallibilis:* distinguo majorem: *ex essentia rationis est, ut possit falli per accidens, sel ex defectu evidentiae alicujus objecti,* concedo majorem; *ex essentia rationis est, ut possit etiam falli per se,* i.e. *sub conditione requisita evidentiae:* nego majorem; atqui *quod rationi essentiale est, illi per se et semper convenit:* concedo minorem; *ergo ratio est per se et semper fallibilis:* distinguo consequens: *per se et semper convenit rationi ut actu errare possit:* nego consequens; *per se et semper convenit rationi, ut sit talis, quae per accidens errare possit:* concedo consequens."

The syllogistic-formalistic characteristics of the disputation, conspicuous in the terms *atqui, distinguo, subdistinguo, transeat, concedo* and the like, I have marked by different type. If we realise that this formalism holds sway in the Jesuit schools evening after evening, year after year, we shall understand how these mechanical ossified forms gradually produce a similar rigidity of the intellect. The apparent gain in clearness and certainty from the numerous short distinctions is acquired at the cost of a deeper and more living comprehension of the questions debated. With the aid of three, four, or even five or six "distinctions," the number does not matter, a Jesuit pupil is ready at a moment's notice to dispose of the most difficult problems. In order not to seem unjust, I have purposely given an instance of a disputation in which the distinctions and the syllogistic form really lead to a clear and correct result, which could, however, have been attained just as quickly and clearly without the scholastic paraphernalia, *i.e.* the inconsistency of absolute scepticism.

But if we now imagine this method applied to dark and abstruse questions of philosophy and theology, in which scholasticism abounds, the result, instead of enlarging our comprehension, is mere wordy warfare and dreary verbosity. The combatant who disposes of the best equipped arsenal of distinctions—and in this respect the wealth of scholasticism is amazing—comes off victorious; he "resolves" the difficulties, and "defends" the thesis. But neither the solution nor the defence advances our comprehension by a single hair. *Formaliter, materialiter, essentialiter, accidentaliter, potentialiter, actualiter, abstracte, concrete, entitative, terminative, reduplicative, simpliciter, absolute, relative, virtualiter, secundum quid:* these are but a few of the literally endless terms on the disputation list, which professors and students have at their disposal, and on the skilful choice of which depend a successful solution and defence. Such expressions as *potentialiter nego, actualiter concedo, entitative transeat, terminative concedo, virtualiter subdistinguo,* or other similar distinctions, suffice to solve every problem of theoretical knowledge of theology in heaven and earth, and to refute all the works of Spinoza, Kant, Schopenhauer, Nietzsche, and the rest.

This barrenness and lack of progressive spirit which have characterised scholasticism from its first origin to the present day are due not so much to the rigidity of ecclesiastical dogma—since the dogmas that have been defined during the last thousand years might be counted on the fingers of one hand—as in the rigid, formalistic, syllogistic treatment which ecclesiastical philosophy and theology have received in the scholastic schools. In this form, hermetically sealed and reeking with the musty smell of centuries, the first conditions of life—air and light—are lacking.

Is it not a remarkable circumstance, alone sufficing to condemn this formalism, that all further development in philosophical and theological thought was and is accomplished outside the syllogistic form ? Within this brazen tower of scholasticism revolve, mechanically set in motion by syllogisms, the ancient, petrified distinctions on the pointed axis of a *concedo, transeat, nego, subdistinguo*. The stream of life flows past this structure.

Perhaps we might apply the words of Mephistopheles to the scholastic syllogistic disputations:

> "For just when the ideas are lacking
> A word may prove most opportune."*

Then there is another point: the use of the Latin language for all lectures and disputations.

However much and rightly we may value the strictly logical structure of the Latin language, and however justly we may find in it a suitable aid for scholarly international intercourse, still it cannot be doubted that the exclusive use of Latin for philosophical and theological speculation must have the effect of hindering and benumbing the spirit of research. Free, living and fructifying thought is only possible in the mother tongue, *i.e.* in a form that is most easily and naturally handled, and the same applies to the expression of the thought. Those who use a dead language to express their innermost and deepest cognition, must at once renounce the possibility of any true and complete development. They castrate it at birth. The free development of cognition requires a living pliant form capable of development. Scholastic philosophy and theology make use of a dead language because they themselves are dead, *i.e.* incapable of development, because they abide motionless by the standpoint of hundreds, even thousands, of years ago (I refer to Aristotle and Thomas Aquinas); and they abide by it because, among other reasons, they make use of a dead language. It

* Goethe. *Faust*, I.

is impossible to express philosophical and theological life in Latin. To translate Kant or Fichte, Schleiermacher or Biedermann, to say nothing of the moderns, into Latin is a contradiction in terms. Only where nothing can be added or taken from the doctrine, only where the stream of time has not forced the Middle Ages aside, is Latin a suitable mode of expression, as is the case in the language of inscriptions on monumental tombstones.

Besides these fundamental limitations to philosophical and theological research and systematic checks on the mobility of the intellect, the Jesuit Order has a considerable number of Special Regulations, all with the same aim to fetter intellectual freedom, and cultivate exactly the same knowledge in all members of the Order. The production of "silently revolving and smoothly rounded balls" is also the main aim of Jesuit scholarship.

The most important of the regulations are these:

"In accordance with the teaching of the Apostle, we should be of one mind, and, so far as is possible, also use the same utterance. Differences of doctrine are not to be allowed either in word, in public pleadings, or in written works. Yes, even difference of opinion in practical matters, which is apt to prove the mother of discord and foe to the union of will, is to be avoided, as far as possible. But union and mutual conformity are to be most sedulously cultivated, and nothing opposed to these must be tolerated."*

"Without consulting the Superiors no new questions (in philosophy) are to be proposed, nor yet any opinion which is not at any rate based on some good authority; nor should anything be defended which is contrary to the traditional philosophical principles and the general opinion of the schools. Those who are disposed to innovation or to free thought must be removed from the teaching office without hesitation."†

"Since novelty or difference of opinion may not only hinder the very aim which the Society has set before itself to the greater

---

* Summ. Const. n. 42. Const. III., 1, 18.
† Cong. 5. Decret. 51. *Inst. S.J.*, I., 253.

glory of God, but also cause the very existence of the Society to totter, it is necessary to check by definite legislation in all possible ways intellectual licence (*licentiam ingeniorum*) in the introduction and pursuit of such opinions."*

"Even in the case of opinions about which Catholic Doctors (Professors) are not agreed among themselves [where there is freedom of opinion] care must be taken that there should be conformity [lack of freedom] in the Society itself."†

"No one should teach anything which is not in conformity with the spirit of the Church and tradition, or which could in any way lessen the faith and zeal of true piety. . No one should defend an opinion which the majority of the learned judge to be contrary to the accepted doctrines of the philosophers or theologians or the general opinion of the schools. . In the case of questions which have already been treated by others, no one should follow new opinions, nor yet should new questions be introduced concerning matters in any way connected with religion or of any great importance, without first taking counsel with the Prefect of Studies or the Superiors. Care should be taken that the philosophy professors take to heart the directions in the eighth canon of the third General Congregation.‡ For the attainment of this end it will be of great assistance if by means of careful selection only those are admitted to teach philosophy and theology . . . whose obedience and submissiveness are evident, and that all who are not so disposed . . . be removed from the teaching office and utilised in other occupations."§

"Since it is not infrequently doubtful whether or not any doctrine is new [and therefore must not be taught], and whether anything differs from the usual school interpretation, which might lead to difficulties between the Prefect of Studies [who has the chief direction of the studies] and the Professors, this rule is laid down : If the Prefect of Studies opposes a doctrine . the Professor must follow the view of the Prefect and may neither teach nor defend the doctrine in question, until the Superiors, to whom the matter must be submitted, have given their decision. If the

---

* Rule 54 for the Provincial: *Inst. S.J.*, I., 43.
† Const. III., 1. Declar. O. *Inst. S.J.*, I., 43.
‡ P. 246.
§ Instruction of General Acquaviva: *Monum. Germ. paed.*, 4, 12 *et seq.*

Professor abides by his opinion the Rector should secretly take the opinion of three or four learned fathers; if these, or the majority, decide that the Prefect is in the right, the Rector is to see to it that the Professor submits absolutely (*omnino*), and similarly in the opposite case. But that no suspicion may rest on the decision of the fathers, only such fathers are to be chosen for this purpose who are in no way addicted to new doctrine, and who are equally well disposed to the Prefect and the Professor. If the Rector has no such fathers at his disposition, he should apply to the Provincial Superior, so that he may in the manner described ask counsel of some such fathers. If even this is of no avail, and if the differences of opinion [in a matter of scholarship!] cannot be reconciled, it rests with the Superior to punish those who are at fault in the matter."*

Finally, the panacea for preventing any individuality in scholarship, any step on a new path, is the strict and comprehensive literary censorship at the disposal of the Order.

" The eleventh General Congregation in its 18th decree already laid down the severest penalties (deprivation of office, forfeiture of the right to vote and stand for election) for those who published books without permission. Under the heading of 'books' are included pamphlets, single sheets and anything (*quidquid*) which attains publicity in print."†

For works on dogma four censors are requisite; for exegesis, church history and philosophy, three; for all other books, pamphlets, or articles, two. Not only the text, but also the preface and title of a work must be submitted to the censor. Besides the general censors in Rome, special censors are appointed for every Province; they are to realise to the full the great importance of their office.‡

Finally, General Peter Beckx, on May 11th, 1862, issued a comprehensive Instruction, which presents the present theory and practice of the Jesuit literary censor-

---

* Ordinance as to the Higher Studies: *Inst. S.J.*, II., 557.
† *Inst. S.J.*, I., 350; *cf.* Const. VII., 4, 11.
‡ *Regulae Revisorum* gen. reg., 1, 2, 15. *Inst. S.J.*, II., 71 *et seq.*

ship, without, however, modifying the above-quoted rules. The most important points in this *Ordinatio* are:

1. Every one who desires to publish anything must first submit it to the Provincial that he may judge whether its publication would be advantageous. 2. The Provincial is to report to the General about it. 3. If the Provincial approves it he is to hand it on to the censors. 4. The censors are to be appointed by the Provincial; they are to be anonymous to the author of the work and he to them. 5. The censors must carefully observe the rules of the Roman general revisionists. 6. Books on the Constitution of the Society of Jesus, its rights and privileges, as well as those which the General may reserve for his own censorship, may only be published after being approved by special censors appointed by the General. 7. If the censors are unanimous in their opinion that a work may be published, "because in their opinion it surpasses mediocrity appreciably in its own particular kind" (*quod mediocritatem in suo genere non mediocriter superare censeant*), the Provincial must at once give his consent to the publication. If the censors fail to agree, the Provincial is to refer the matter to the General. 8. The censors are to report their decisions to the General and Provincial. 9. The censors should note anything which, in their opinion, should be altered, and should emphasise what in their opinion are essential and what unessential alterations. 10. The comments of the censors may be communicated to the author (without giving their names). 11. Anything which any member of the Society of Jesus writes, whether anonymously or under his own name, whether a thesis, preface, letter or dedicatory epistle, title, superscription, must be submitted to the censorship. 12. Similarly with articles in newspapers or periodicals. 13. If a grievous calumny is circulated against the Society of Jesus the local Superior may, if the Provincial cannot be consulted,

give permission for its refutation, but this must first be read through by two suitable fathers. 14. The Provincial may entrust to the Local Superiors the examination of the announcements, etc., published by schools. 15. New editions and also translations must be submitted to the censorship. 16. No publishing contract may be concluded until the whole work has been submitted to the censor.*

Nearly all books published by Jesuits bear the *imprimatur* of the Order in the form of a special permit signed by the Provincial. For special reasons this may be omitted. The wording of the Jesuit *imprimatur*, at any rate in the German Province, is invariable, *e.g.* :

" Since the work with the title *Biology and Theory of Evolution*, third edition, composed by Erich Wasmann, Priest of the Society of Jesus, has been examined by some revisers of the same Society, commissioned for the purpose, who approved its publication, we accordingly give our permission that, provided it seem good to the persons concerned, it should be printed. For purposes of authentication this document, signed by us and provided with our official seal, may serve. Exaeten, July 29th, 1906. Father Karl Schäffer, S.J., President of the German Province of the Order."

My reason for reproducing the *imprimatur* of this particular work is that it is not theological but scientific, and that its author, the Jesuit Erich Wasmann, on the strength of this work claims a place in the ranks of scientists who pursue free research. But the very first page of his book shows plainly the extent of his " free " research ; it is the censors and the Provincial of the Order, *i.e.* theologians, who have to decide whether the biological investigations are to be published or not.

As with this book so with all others, no matter whether they treat of history, art, mathematics, astronomy, botany, zoology, physics, or any other subject. Before they can appear, the red or blue pencil of the theological censor

* *Inst. S.J.*, II., 253 *et seq.*

does its work, and the Provincial, who usually knows next to nothing of secular learning, decides whether the manuscript is to be published or not. Indeed, my own Provincial Superiors, the Jesuits Hövel, Meschler, Lohmann, Ratgeb, had only received the philosophical and theological training of the Order.

In answer to the objection that the Society is bound to act thus in order to maintain its internal solidarity, since liberty of thought and teaching would be centrifugal forces tending to its destruction, I say: True, but unity and uniformity in thought and teaching brought about by law and the threat of punishment combined with a strict censorship, are the grave of all true striving after knowledge, and admit of no free, continuous development of human cognition. Where learning is made to serve purposes which lie outside its scope, its exercise cannot produce true knowledge. But in the Jesuit Order everything is made to subserve the ends of the Order, above all the learning which, regarded from without, seems to be cultivated with such zeal. And one of the chief ends is the strengthening of its own inner life, the extension of its power, the deepening of its influence over men, and eventually the strengthening of the Roman Church, with all its claims to temporal and political dominion. But crudely biased learning is not learning at all, even if (as I must show later) individual achievements of individual Jesuits may and do have scholarly value. But these are exceptions to the rule; their scholarship is good, not because, but in spite of their being Jesuits; they are but accidents in the domain of learning.

But the Order knows no mercy when the scholarly achievements of members do not fit into its own framework of learning. Then the censorship and punishment do their worst.

In the years 1890 and 1891 I was myself book-censor

(*censor librorum*) for the German Province, a position which may testify to my reputation for learning in the Order. I am therefore exactly informed of the methods of Jesuit censorship. When the interest of the Order is opposed, not the smallest regard is paid to personal freedom, nor to the established results of scientific investigation or individual ability. The censorship deletes and the author submits; the punitive authority punishes and the culprit remains dumb.

In the last year of my theological studies one of my fellow-scholastics, a man of superior gifts, who was specially interested in natural science, the Jesuit Breitung, wrote an article for the Jesuit organ, *Zeitschrift für Katholische Theologie* (published at Innsbruck) about the Deluge. Breitung maintained the ethnographic universality of the flood, *i.e.* that all persons then in the world perished except Noah and his family, but in accordance with the results of geological and palæontological research, he abandoned its geographic universality, *i.e.* he admitted that not the whole earth but only the whole of the inhabited earth was flooded. The article had passed the Provincial censorship, but found no favour at Rome with the head censor of the Order; it was a "new doctrine subversive of the Scriptures." (Galileo's teaching was also "new and subversive of the Scriptures.") The General Anderledy issued a decree which condemned the theory of the geographical limitation of the Deluge. When Breitung had ended his studies he was not allowed to devote himself to natural science, as had been universally expected on account of his special gifts and preliminary studies, but was appointed teacher in the lowest classes in the College of Ordrupshoj, in Denmark. There he was "harmless." What scientific work he now carries on I do not know.

A few years later the Belgian Jesuit Hahn, Professor of Natural Science at the College at Arlon, had published a book on the Spanish Saint Teresa a Jesu, and had come to the conclusion that some remarkable phenomena in the life of this nun, which had hitherto been regarded as miraculous and tokens of divine grace, were of a hysterical character. His book had actually been "crowned" by a Spanish Catholic academy. But Rome here again thought differently. The book was censored, and the Order removed its author from his scientific professorship.

One of the most celebrated theologians of the Order at the present day is the Jesuit Domenico Palmieri. He too came into conflict with the censorship in his theological researches—I forget what was the point in question, certainly not one which was established dogmatically, *i.e.* "infallibly" by the highest ecclesiastical teaching authority—and in consequence he had to resign his chair.

And now a word as to my own studies which were crowned with success. All my examinations in philosophy and theology were passed satisfactorily, even the last *examen rigorosum* of two hours' duration. In theory we were not supposed to know anything about the results of examinations, but usually something leaks out, and besides, the Provincial Superior, Jacob Ratgeb, informed me that I had passed the last examination, accordingly all the previous ones also, "very well," and that I was *in via ad Professionem*, on the road to the grade of professed. I had therefore "attained that degree of philosophical and theological culture which suffices for teaching both subjects satisfactorily."

I allude to my scholarly qualification within the Order because, very soon after I left it, doubts on the subject were publicly strewn about, originating in Ultramontane Jesuit sources, which, of course, found the readiest credence. For what tales are not told and believed of an "apostate"? The *Kölnische Volkszeitung*, doubtless inspired by Jesuits, even went so far as to hint at insanity. *Ecrasez l'infame!*

CHAPTER XXIII

THE ATTITUDE OF THE ORDER TO LEARNING

THIS attitude has really been sufficiently characterised in the previous section. But as the Jesuit Order makes special claims to learning, and as even in the non-Ultramontane world this view is widely spread, a further consideration of the subject from other, more general points of view seems justified.

Of course the principles which the Roman Church sets up in regard to its conception of knowledge and freedom of research are also the principles of the Jesuit Order.

These principles are expressed in innumerable official Papal utterances, of which I shall only quote a few of the more modern ones.

1. Provincial Council of Cologne (tit. 1, c. 6) (especially confirmed by the Pope). 2. A letter of Pius IX. to the Archbishop of Munich of December 21st, 1863. 3. Syllabus of Pius IX., of December 8th, 1864. 4. Vatican Council of the year 1870. 5. Constitution of Leo XIII., *Officiorum ac munerum* of January 25th, 1897. 6. *Motu proprio* of Pius X. of December 18th, 1903. 7. Syllabus of Pius X. (against Modernism) of September 8th, 1907.*

All these manifestoes are included, so far as their contents are concerned, in the "infallible" pronouncement of the Vatican Council:

---

* For the wording, see my book, *Die Katholisch-theologischen Fakultäten im Organismus der preussischen Staatsuniversitäten* (Leipzig, Breitkopf u. Härtel), pp. 22–38.

The Order and Learning

"If anyone asserts that human knowledge should develop so freely that its assertions, even when they are opposed to revealed doctrine, are to be regarded as true and cannot be condemned by the Church, he shall be excommunicated."*

These Roman principles as to learning find their practical application in the Index, the rules of which were remodelled in 1900 by Leo XIII. and suspended as a Damocles' sword over the whole output of Catholic learning.

To this must be added Rome's final right of decision in so-called dogmatic facts (*facta dogmatica*) and dogmatic texts (*textus dogmatici*), by which vast domains of historical knowledge are withdrawn from free research.†

But even the silent recognition of the bondage of all knowledge assumed by the authoritative Roman doctrine did not suffice the Jesuit Order. It therefore declared, in the 12th decree of the 23rd General Congregation of 1883 :

"Since in such a mass of errors, which steal in everywhere and in our own day have frequently been condemned by the Roman See, it is to be feared that some of our own members, too, may be attacked by this plague, the General Congregation declares that our Society is to abide by the doctrine contained in the encyclical *Quanta cura* of December 8th, 1864, of Pius IX., and reject, as it always has rejected, all errors rejected by the Syllabus of this same Pope. But since some Provinces [of the Order] have demanded the particular condemnation of so-called Liberal Catholicism, the General Congregation gladly accedes to this request, and earnestly entreats the Venerable Father General to have a care that this plague is by all means averted from our Society."‡

Thus the Order solemnly gave its consent to the destruction, initiated by Rome, of teaching and learning. Thus from its very inception Modernism (under the name

---

* Sess. 3, c. 4, *de fid. et. rat. can.* 2.

† *Cf.* my work *Die Katholisch-theologischen Fakultäten im Organismus der preussischen Staatsuniversitäten*, pp. 39-46.

‡ *Monum. Germ. paed.*, 2, 117.

of Liberal Catholicism) was outlawed, and how this sentence of outlawry was carried out has been seen in our own day by the tragic fate of the Jesuits Tyrrell and Bartoli.

The attitude of the Order to learning furnishes the contents of a book, published at Innsbruck with the *imprimatur* of the Order and the ecclesiastical authorities by the Jesuit Dr. Josef Donat, Royal and Imperial Professor at the University of Innsbruck, in the year 1910, *Die Freiheit der Wissenschaft, ein Gang durch das moderne Geistesleben*. There is nothing of any novelty in the book, nor is it singular of its kind, but it contains the old opposition to free research, the old submission to the Roman censorship in the newest forms :

"Those who acknowledge the Christian [*i.e.* Catholic] conception of the world, cannot accept this freedom of thought and knowledge [just characterised as freedom from the Syllabus and Index]. Here [in opposition to the Church] is the true reason why thousands, in whom Kant's autonomy in thought has become the veritable sinew of their intellectual life, will not hear of any guidance by revelation and the Church. They can no longer endure the idea of letting their reason unhesitatingly accept the truth from an external authority [the Papacy]. . . . It is not knowledge which the Church attacks, but error; not truth, but the emancipation of the human intellect from submission to the authority of God, which comes forward under the disguise of scientific truth. . . . If it is an infallible dogma, which is opposed [to a scientific result], the believer soon finds the conflict springing from his investigations at an end. For he knows then the value of his hypothesis, that it is no true progress, but error. . . . Thus the philosophical errors of the present day are almost invariably opposed to infallible dogmas, for the most part fundamental doctrines of the Christian religion. These are the title deeds, on the strength of which revelation and the Church impress on the investigator the duty not to set his own opinions in opposition to religious doctrines, because no opposition can continue between faith and reason. . . . If the Catholic investigator finds his scientific opinion in opposition

The Order and Learning

to a not infallible declaration [*e.g.* the decision of a Roman Cardinals' Congregation, as in the case of Galileo] he will maintain an impartial attitude and once more test his views in the sight of God. If he is compelled to admit calmly to himself that his views are not so convincing as to hold their own in face of so high an authority, directed by the Holy Spirit, he will humbly renounce the natural satisfaction at being allowed to retain his opinion, remembering that true wisdom is convinced of the fallibility of human reason and is ready and willing to accept instruction from a God-directed authority. . . . Everything that is good and profitable in modern knowledge remains untouched by the Syllabus; it only attacks what is anti-Christian in our time and our leading ideas. It is not the freedom of knowledge which is condemned, but that liberal freedom which shakes off the yoke of belief. The ecclesiastical book-legislation [the Index] consists mainly of two factors: firstly, the preventive censorship; certain books must be subjected to examination before publication: secondly, the prohibition of books that have already appeared. . . . Catholic scholars who have any knowledge of the supernatural mission of their Church will surrender themselves with humble confidence to its direction [in matters of knowledge]. . . . Those who are convinced that even in our generation the Christian faith is the noblest inheritance handed down from the past, and one which it is essential to maintain, will raise no objection if the Church does not withdraw even before men like Kant, Spinoza, Schopenhauer, Strauss [in the application of the power of the Index]. . . . Ranke's *History of the Popes* has been placed on the Index, because it disparages the constitution and doctrines of the Catholic Church, not because it speaks the truth about the Popes."*

This exposition is prefaced by the Jesuit author, in unconscious irony and absolute failure to grasp its meaning, by Goethe's saying—and after all, why should not Goethe be quoted on behalf of Syllabus and Index?—

---

* Donat. *Die Freiheit der Wissenschaft, ein Gang durch das moderne Geistesleben* (Innsbruck), pp. 63, 88 *et seq*, 123, 128 *et seq.*, 193, 207, 209, 213. In this last passage, then, the Church claims dominion even over history.

"*Vergebens werden ungebundene Geister*
Nach der Vollendung reiner Höhe streben:
Wer Grosses will, muss sich zusammenraffen,
In der Beschränkung zeigt sich erst der Meister
Und das Gesetz erst kann uns Freiheit geben."*

A pendant to the teaching of the Austrian Jesuit is supplied by the German Jesuit Hilgers, who in an extensive work, 638 pages, large octavo, published in 1904, on *The Index of Forbidden Books*, sets forth the necessity and utility of this Roman censorship and its supervision of learning, especially in our own day. On the compelling power of the Index, Hilgers writes:

" By the republication of the Index in the year 1900 the Church has not only opportunely adapted its legislation to the needs of the age, but also, in the consciousness of its right and duty, proclaimed it to the whole world, and impressed it afresh on Catholics of every nation. All Catholics of all lands will feel in conscience bound faithfully to observe these laws, as the tenor of this constitution distinctly requires, and a further decree of the Congregation of the Index still more expressly commands. . . . The justification and utility of the preventive censorship is to be sought in the divine teaching and pastoral office of the Church, like that of the prohibitive censorship. This ecclesiastical measure manifests itself not only as the love of a mother for the faithful, but also as paternal precaution in face of authors and writers, who are by it prevented from sowing tares. . . It is forbidden under the severest penalties even to offer dynamite for sale. Is it excessive severity if the laws of the Church admonish booksellers that all forbidden books may only be offered for sale after seeking the easily granted ecclesiastical permission, and may only be sold to those persons of whom the sellers may reasonably assume that they demand them for a lawful purpose ? . . We may, therefore, surely assert that men of learning such as professors of theology and history [philologists have already been mentioned] are as much

---

* From one of Goethe's sonnets.

bound as others to seek a dispensation from the prohibition of books from the ecclesiastical authority."*

As already shown there is nothing either new or remarkable in the utterances of these two Jesuits. On the contrary, it would be new and remarkable if Jesuits did not speak thus, for these are the views demanded by the Ultramontane clerical point of view. But no further proof is needed to show that they are incompatible with free research; and it was for this reason that I quoted the utterances of Donat and Hilgers.

But is not all this in opposition to the great activity the Jesuit Order actually displays in the domain of knowledge? There is no other Order of the Roman Church which effects so much in the sphere of learning, and many Jesuits have achieved notable success in various subjects. Jesuit theory may therefore be directed against knowledge, but Jesuit practice is on her side.

The answer to this objection brings out in even sharper light the innate constitutional ignorance of the Order.

Where among the innumerable Jesuit writers (the Jesuit *Sommervogel* fills several quarto volumes with their names and works) is one to be found who in that domain of knowledge, which more than any other is the test of free, creative thought, philosophy, has produced a single new idea or even opened out a single fresh vista? In spite of whole libraries of folio volumes on philosophy written by Jesuits, we find here a vacuum, which speaks more eloquently than any arguments. No Jesuit has ever gone beyond scholasticism and Thomas Aquinas. The bulky works of a Suarez, Sanchez, Becanus, Molina, de Lugo and, to mention the most recent, a Tongiorgi, Palmieri, Liberatore, Kleutgen, Pesch, Frick, Lehmen, are nothing but endless repetitions and variations on the philosophical

* Hilgers, *Index der verbotenen Bücher* (Freiburg), pp. 25, 42, 43, 51.

ideas of the twelfth and thirteenth centuries, which in their turn are the outcome of Aristotelean thought. Whether the Jesuit work on philosophy has appeared at Rome or Madrid, Paris or Lisbon, in Germany, Belgium, or England, whether it dates from the sixteenth, nineteenth, or twentieth century, the contents, in spite of all differences of form and language, are everywhere the same. This sterility, this complete lack of creative intellectual power, is enforced with iron necessity, by the position which the Order in its Constitutions assigns to philosophy. As we have already seen, it is the handmaid, the servant of theology; and Jesuit-Ultramontane theology is essentially stationary and incapable of development. For how should or could the handmaid rise above the mistress; how could she go along a road of her own, when she is bound by blind obedience and innumerable directions to the girdle of her employer? I repeat: For the learning of an organisation its attitude to philosophy (if it is at all concerned with it) is the test, since it is the branch of knowledge which depends most on the original activity of the intellect. Tried by this test, Jesuit learning does not approve itself true metal, at any rate not of its own prospecting. It is "ancient" wisdom (as the twenty-third General Congregation expressed it), in the best case in a new dress, usually without even this.

For theology matters are even simpler. It goes along "fixed highroads" towards goals unchangeably set up at the beginning. Here certainly neither freedom nor learning is to be found.

The same may be said of all branches of knowledge, which, either actually or by the fiat of Rome, "are connected with philosophy and theology": ethics, sociology, economics. There too we may see books of enormous size but the smallest actual achievement. There too the Jesuit revolves in a circle, the centre of which is the authority, and its circumference the thought of past ages. True, he understands how to draw modern circumstances and things into this circle, above all by wide reading and a genius for quotation to give his works an appearance of scholarly research and genuine learning (and here the German Jesuits Cathrein and the brothers Tilmann and Heinrich Pesch have been particularly successful), but closer examination shows that the "modern" writers on ethics, economics and sociology move along in ancient grooves and have only given a modern equipment to the vehicle of their learning.

Now for the other branches of learning and the liberal arts. There is none which the Jesuit Order has not approached, and there are several which it has helped to advance. They are at work in astronomy, mathematics, geology, palæontology, Assyriology, zoology, botany, biology, physics, optics, acoustics, chemistry, philology, literature, history, language, art in all its forms, archæology, and a twentieth-century Jesuit, Balthasar Wilhelm, S.J., has even written on aeronautics.* On many of these domains they move with apparent freedom, examine and bring to light new results, and thus work apparently in a scholarly manner.

The cause of this apparent intellectual freedom lies, in the first place, in the subjects themselves, which are for the most part (*e.g.* astronomy, mathematics, botany, art, archæology, optics, acoustics, physics, chemistry) not at all or not so much dependent on philosophy and theology; the "ancient wisdom," to which everything must be referred back, hardly exists here, and accordingly a Jesuit is comparatively free in his researches and able to bring to light new and good results. Even in the domain of secular and ecclesiastical history Jesuit principles leave some scope for detailed research. And therefore here

* *Die Anfänge der Luftschiffahrt.*

too we meet with conspicuous Jesuit achievements. I recall a large number of smaller biographies, articles in learned reviews, and above all great collective works, *e.g. The Acta Sanctorum*, the Collection of Councils by the Jesuit Labbe, the *Collectio Lacensis*, etc. But in estimating the scholarly value of such achievements, we must never forget (1) that they are all writings with a special aim, and have not originated in independent, unprejudiced research, but with the object of serving the Church and the Order and defending " Catholic truth "; and (2) that every one of them, single articles as well as folio volumes, must pass the censorship of the Order before it can be published.

There is a very general opinion, widely spread but incorrect, that the Jesuit Order has achieved great things in the domain of knowledge. If we realise how long the Order has existed and the many thousand members it has had in the course of centuries, drawn from the best classes of the population and, therefore, with natural abilities, and the privacy in which they work, and compare the result achieved in these conditions, so propitious for learning and study, they appear but meagre, in spite of some signal achievements.

The Order has never at any time been a real promoter of learning, still less has it helped to open up new paths. The very opposite is the case; for, taken as a whole, it has always served as a drag on the advancement of knowledge. On this point the testimony of history coincides with that of scholars. Thus Kink, the historian of the University of Vienna, who is anything but anti-Jesuit, admits:

" Another mistake they made in their methods of instruction was their dependence on scholasticism, to which they gave the reins more and more. . . . In the professorial chairs this was particularly remarkable; especially after the Society had gained undisputed hegemony over the other orders and the secular clergy, the comfortable security of exclusive possession and the removal of all control, if only from psychological reasons, were an inducement to effeminacy and a hindrance to further advance, when the impulse from without was lacking. And as they had admitted scholasticism into their midst, the abuses, which are as it were inborn in this method, made way, at first imperceptibly, then gradually more clearly and markedly. Among these was an unfaithful dialectic, which delighted in setting up and opposing abstruse theories and with dogmatic stubbornness rejected every simple reconciliation, and sometimes appealing to the party spirit of the whole community, adhered to the pronouncement once made, or even in some cases by skilful tacking sought to avoid submission to the higher authority. . . At last they were even reproached with relaxation in their system of ethics and conduct of discipline; so that authoritative voices were raised, which though not hostile in principle asserted that, so far as their educational work was concerned, they had not been able to resist degeneracy."*

In a memorial of November 5th, 1757, to the Empress Maria Theresa, van Swieten says·

"Facts have shown that the studies at the University [of Vienna] were in an unsatisfactory condition, since the Society had been incorporated with it. . . . It is consequently clear that it has not attained the goal which the two Emperors [Ferdinand I. and II.] had set before them. On the contrary, all the Universities which came under Jesuit rule have fallen into decay: Graz, Olmütz, Tyrnau are striking instances. It would certainly have been far better if the University had never been united with the Jesuit Order."†

Maria Theresa herself had no very high opinion of Jesuit learning. When the Court Commission of Studies, in 1775, proposed to her the foundation of an Academy of

* Kink, *Geschichte der kaiserlichen Universität Wien* (Vienna, 1854), I., 414-420.
† *Ibid.*, I., 490.

Science, suggesting that a beginning should be made with three Jesuit teachers, Hell for Astronomy, Scharfer for Physics, Mako for Mathematics, along with Professor Jacquin, she said:

"I could not make up my mind to begin an *académie des sciences* with three ex-Jesuits and a professor of Chemistry, however excellent. We should make ourselves ridiculous in the eyes of the world. . . . I do not consider the Abbé Hell strong enough; and it would repay neither the time nor the trouble to found something even worse than the existing academies."*

A vivid picture of the inferior scholarship of the Jesuit Order at the University of Freiburg i. Br. is afforded by Schreiber. He quotes from the records subjects chosen for disputation by the Jesuits in the course of a good many years:

On September 17th, 1621: How was it possible for the head of Symmachus, unjustly put to death by him, to appear to the Arian King Theodoric in the head of a boiled fish? Through what power or grace was Boethius able to carry, in his hands and actually speaking, to the nearest church the head which the King had struck off? What was the nature of those cauldrons into which this Theodoric was cast after his death by Pope John and Symmachus? and how was their heat maintained? On April 26th, 1623: Was the corpse of the Emperor Julian thrown out of the earth by natural forces? On June 12th, 1623, thirty-six magistrands disputed on the questions: Whether there was a place of descent to Hades, and where it was situated? Whether the worms that gnaw the bodies of the damned can live in fire through natural power? Whether it was probable that springs were heated and metals melted by hell fire? On September 7th, 1629 · Whether this was a probable deduction: He devotes no

---

* From the Archives of the Royal Imperial Commission on Studies, quoted by Kink, I., 510.

care to his clothes, therefore he is a genius. On July 23rd, 1658: Who was the Promotor who conferred the degree of magister on the Virgin Mary? Is the cloak with which Mary covers those whom she protects the mantle of philosophy? Was the lightning which consumed the wheel on which St. Catherine was to be torn a natural phenomenon? On July 13th, 1711: Is the philosopher or the poet in greater danger of lying? On January 29th, 1729: Does the divining-rod discover treasure by natural means? Does the ointment of arms (*unguentum armarium*) heal the wounds of the absent by natural sympathy? Why does the blood of a murdered man boil when the murderer approaches him? On August 17th, 1743: Were the conditions of the present day foreseen by Aristotle and proclaimed by the comet of the previous year? *

However much allowance we may make for the taste of the age and the "red tape" which enwrapped all learning, we cannot but condemn the bad taste and ignorance of such disputation themes. While the Jesuits were regaling themselves and their pupils with such fare, the rest of the world, in which Kepler, Galileo, Newton, Leibnitz, Descartes, etc., were living and working, had long ago left behind these monstrous absurdities. Even some of the students revolted against such "knowledge"; for the minutes report that on July 4th, 1743, Frehner, an aspirant for the doctorate, "threw St. Barbara with her questions at the feet of his examiner [the Jesuit Ebner], with an expression of contempt."†

A personal experience may serve to show the spirit that prevails even in the most learned circles of the Jesuit Order. Once, at Exaeten, during the mid-day recreation, we were discussing the story of the Creation. I expressed the opinion that geology and palæontology clearly proved

* *Geschichte der Albert Ludwigs Universität zu Freiburg* (Freiburg, 1868), 2, 421 *et seq.* † Schreiber, 2, 425.

that the world with its flora and fauna had taken not a few days, but periods of considerable length, to come into being. I was indignantly contradicted by the Jesuit Lehmkuhl, the moral-theological celebrity of the Order; in his view the strata, petrifactions, etc., were no disproof of the six days' creation, for God could have introduced all these, without their having had any previous existence, into the interior of the earth. And when I asked whether he would also include coprolites among the works of God's creation he gave a decided affirmative. Moreover, he denounced me to the Rector for " liberal opinions."

There is one peculiarity of Jesuit learning as to which I desire to say a few words. Knowledge without objective truth (if, indeed, there be such a thing) and without subjective truthfulness is impossible. The investigator must reproduce as he finds them the results of his investigations which he recognises as true, whether they prove agreeable to him or the opposite. If he alters or adapts them to fit in with definite aims or his own religious or political attitude, he is guilty of falsification.

But Jesuit knowledge, in every domain where the interests of the Order and the Roman Church are concerned, is an unscrupulous and skilful falsification. A weighty accusation, but in view of the facts completely justified.

In proof I will bring forward only one instance, which, in view of its importance, may count as a test case—the work of the German Jesuit Duhr. This single instance will suffice, because Duhr is the officially appointed historiographer of the German Province. The archives of the Order are at his disposal, and his numerous historical works on the Order have been approved by its censorship. His work may therefore be regarded not as that of an individual but of the Order, representing the history of the Order as written and circulated by the Order itself.

Again and again, both in this book and in my work

on the Papacy,* have I convicted Duhr of untruthfulness and falsification.

The Munich historian, Sigmund Riezler, deals very severely with Duhr, again and again convicting him of misrepresentation and untruthfulness.†

The *Jesuitenfabeln*, so frequently quoted in this book, supply particularly abundant material for estimating Duhr's love of truth. I will give a few instances :—

In order to disprove the genuineness of the *Monita Secreta*, Duhr ‡ emphasises the opposition between Chap. IV. of the *Monita*, on the political activity of Jesuits and the official Instruction of General Acquaviva to the confessors of princes, which apparently prohibits political activity. Duhr does not mention that besides this " official Instruction " there is also a secret one, which contains very different directions. This silence is the more significant as Duhr refers to Dudik for Acquaviva's official Instruction, while it is just Dudik who made public the secret Instructions.

Duhr has a special preference for quoting the Austrian historian Gindely; but he suppresses everything unfavourable that Gindely says of the Jesuits. A particularly striking instance is the false impression created by this means as to Gindely's opinion of the position and influence of the Jesuit Lamormaini in his character of confessor to the Emperor Ferdinand II. By means of a long quotation from Gindely, Duhr " proves " the beneficent and purely religious character of Lamormaini's influence on the Emperor. But he omits Gindely's verdict on Lamormaini's share in the first deposition of Wallenstein, as also Dudik's revelation from sources in the archives as to Lamormaini's decisive influence on his second deposition.§

* *Das Papsttum in seiner sozial-kulturellen Wirkshamkeit.*
† *Historische Zeitschrift.* New Series. Vol. 48, pp. 245-256.
‡ *Jesuitenfabeln*, p. 100.   § *Ibid.*, 845 *et seq.*

In dealing with the Gunpowder Plot, planned with the complicity of the Jesuits, Duhr does not even mention Jardine's standard work, *A Narrative of the Gunpowder Plot*. Probably because, as shown in a previous chapter, Jardine quotes from the records much that is unfavourable to the Jesuit Garnet, Provincial of the English Province.*

In the chapter "Ignatius Loyola founded the Jesuit Order for the extirpation of Protestantism," Duhr adduces all manner of proofs to show that the Jesuit Order was not founded against Protestantism, but omits the very significant passage from the bull of Pope Urban VIII. (1623), which decrees the canonisation of Ignatius Loyola. This omission is the more noteworthy, since a bull of canonisation is one of the most important Papal documents. But that is the very reason for omitting it. This sort of thing must be kept from Duhr's circle of readers.†

In order to set the charitable disposition of the Jesuit Order in as favourable a light as possible, Duhr falsifies the original text of an ordinance for the professed house at Vienna in 1635. While the words of the Ordinance ‡ are "concerning the remains of the food to be distributed at the door of the professed-house of the Society of Jesus at Vienna to poor students" (*de reliquis ciborum*, etc.), Duhr gives as a literal quotation in quotation marks: "Concerning the distribution of food, etc." The word "remains" would have weakened the impression of benevolence.§

---

* *Jesuitenfabeln*, 1–33.   † *Ibid.*, 295.   ‡ *Mon. Germ. paed*, 16-245.

§ Duhr, 380. Falsifications of the text are a very common Jesuit means of embellishment. The English Jesuit Foley was commissioned by the Order to publish eight large volumes of Records, which furnish a collection of documents concerning the Jesuits in England. The Catholic historian, Taunton, says of this work in the preface to his *History of the Jesuits in England*, p. viii.: "Foley's value consists almost as much in his omissions as in his admissions. And I am bound to remark that I have found him at a critical point quietly leaving out, without any signs of omission, an essential part of a document which was adverse

The Order and Learning

This anthology, incomplete as it is, illustrative of the love of truth evinced in the writings of Duhr, will be most suitably concluded by a quotation from Duhr himself:

"Falsification remains falsification, and is always reprehensible, even when it is intended to attain or sanctify the most sacred ends."*

"If we find an author untrustworthy in one particular, we are bound in the first instance to regard as correspondingly untrustworthy all his statements that fall under this heading."†

The Jesuit Duhr is a type. As is he, so are they all. No dependence is to be placed on works or documents published by Jesuits. The Jesuit axiom, "The end sanctifies the means," is the first principle of Jesuit authorship. The end, the [defence of the Order and its glorification, sanctifies every falsification.

---

to his case." And Taunton supplies the proof for his weighty accusation on p. 313," where he gives in full the account of the conversation between the Jesuit Oldcorne, imprisoned in the Tower on a charge of high treason, and Garnet, restoring Garnet's admission of avowal of treason " quietly omitted by Foley, who, though professing to quote Gerard, gives no signs of omission."

* *Geschichte der Jesuiten in den Ländern deutscher Zunge* (Freiburg, 1907), Preface, p. v.

† *Jesuitenfabeln.* 4th ed., p. 785.

CHAPTER XXIV

JESUIT MORALITY

ARE we really justified in speaking of " Jesuit morality " ? Is not that to which we apply the term the very same as the official morality of the Ultramontane Roman Catholic Church ? Both questions may be answered in the affirmative, and it is this very affirmation of two seemingly contradictory statements that accentuates most markedly the reality, danger and power of the conception designated as Jesuit morality.

There is no other domain in which Jesuitism has succeeded so completely in forcing its domination on Catholicism as that of Moral Theology. The development which the practice of the confessional, *i.e.* the domination of the private and public life of Catholics by means of the confessional, has attained since the end of the sixteenth century within the Church of Rome— and it is the practice of the confessional which is concealed under the term Moral Theology—has been mainly brought about by the moral theologians of the Jesuit Order. The present-day Catholic morality is penetrated throughout with Jesuit morality.

This important fact is most strikingly expressed by the circumstance that the greatest authority on Moral Theology in the Romish Church, Alfonso Maria di Liguori (died 1787), whom Gregory XVI. canonised in 1839, and Pius IX., in 1871, honoured with the rank and dignity of a doctor of the Church, was merely the commentator of the moral theologians of the Jesuit Order, especially the two most influential, Busenbaum and Lacroix.*

"Liguori's teaching," says the official historian of the Order, Crétineau-Joly, "is identical with the teaching of the theologians of the Society [of Jesus] His canonisation was, therefore, the justification of the casuists of the Society, and especially of Busenbaum."† And the Jesuit Montezon triumphantly asserts: "The teaching of the Jesuits was solemnly declared by the Church to be secured against all censure by the verdict passed on the moral theology of Liguori at his beatification. For even if the Jesuits were not expressly named in the proceedings the verdict is directly concerned with their theology, which the venerable Bishop [Liguori] had adopted as his own. *Nihil censura dignum* (Nothing deserving of censure or offending against faith and morals is to be found in the moral-theology of Liguori), thus says the decree [of the Congregation of Rites, of May 14, 1803], and afterwards another Roman tribunal [the holy *poenitentiarie* of July 5, 1831] declared that every confessor might without further examination abide by all the decisions of Liguori. That is a complete and solemn apology for Jesuit doctrine."‡

Thus it appears that the assertion constantly repeated and put forward as a screen, that there is no such thing as Jesuit morality, and that the morality of the Order is that of the Catholic Church, is but apparently true. The real truth is that the morality of the Jesuit Order has become the morality of the Catholic Church.

Just as Ultramontanism for a clear thousand years (since the days of Gregory VII.) has dominated Cathol-

* For further details about Liguori and his dependence on Jesuit morality, see my book *Das Papsttum*, etc., II., pp. 70-157.

† Crétineau-Joly, 6, 231.

‡ Sainte-Beuve, *Port Royal*, I., 526: Döllinger-Reusch, *Moralstreitigkeiten*, I., 356

icism in the domains of dogma, ecclesiastical polity and general culture, so Jesuitism, which is Ultramontanism raised to a higher power, has for four centuries dominated the morality of Catholicism.

A specially convincing proof of this domination has been afforded by a declaration, made by the professors of the priestly seminary at Mayence in the year 1868, in favour of the moral theology of the Jesuit Gury, which says :

" We will only record the circumstance that this textbook is in use at numerous educational establishments in Germany, Italy, France, Belgium, England and North America."*

How this domination began, gained a firm footing and maintained it to the present day, cannot be set forth here. At any rate it exists, and the stages on its triumphal progress are the moral theological works of the Jesuits (quoted in alphabetical, not chronological, order) : Amicus, Azor, Ballerini, Burghaber, Busenbaum, Cardenas, Castrapalao, Coninck, Escobar, Filliuci, Gobat, Gury, Haunold, Hurtado, Lacroix, Laymann, Lehmkuhl, Lessius, Lugo, Mazotta, Moya, Palmieri, Reuter, Sabetti, Sanchez, Scaramelli, Schmalzgrueber, Stoz, Tamburini, Valentia, Vasquez, Vogler, Voit, Zaccaria, and many others.

I must content myself with extracts from works on Jesuit morality. For a more detailed account, especially as regards Probabilism, Casuistry and Confession, I must refer my readers to the second volume of my book on the Papacy. The quotations are, of course, selected with a view to a characterisation of the Jesuit Order, *i.e.* I shall set forth those moral-theological dogmas of the Order which will assist the recognition of its fundamental conceptions of morals and ethics, and in order as far as possible

* *Darmstädter Allgemein. Kirchenzeitung* (1868), No. 41.

to comprise everything in one chapter, I use the words Morals and Ethics in their widest acceptation.

I intend here to give no extracts or disquisitions relating to the seventh commandment and marriage. This unpleasant subject, so rendered by Jesuit moral theology, has been treated in detail in the work above quoted.*

Love and marriage, the most glorious sources of human happiness and human perfection, have been overspread with slime and filth by the spiritual direction and moral theology of the Jesuits. The natural human and, on that account, noble sexual life has been degraded by their moral theological examinations, and because this was and is done under the shelter of Christianity, Christianity too was degraded. A man who by his own confession was versed in sexual perversion, Ludovico Sergardi, afterwards Roman Cardinal and the friend of Alexander VII., bears testimony thus:

"Moral theology has attained to such a pitch that it is necessary to warn uncorrupted youths against having anything to do with it, lest they entangle themselves in shameful snares and become victims of unchastity. For what abominations do not the moral theologians set before the public! Among all the brothels of the Suburra, there is none which might not be called chaste compared with the contents of these books. I myself, who was a leader of immoral youths and often desecrated my years by unchastity, confess that on reading Sanchez [one of the leading moral theologians of the Jesuit Order, whose chief work on Marriage is to this day a classic in the Order] I found myself blushing on more than one occasion, and that his writings have taught me more abominations than I could have learnt from the most brazen of prostitutes. Ovid, the past-master in the Art of Love, Horace the daring, and Tibullus the libertine, if compared with Sanchez, seem fitted to preside over an educational establishment for young ladies. For

* *Das Papsttum*, etc., II., 229-410.

in their case the witty expression, at any rate, conceals the wickedness, but in Sanchez unadulterated libertinism and uncovered lust range at will."*

I shall preface my extracts from Jesuit treatises on fundamental questions of morals and ethics by criticisms of Jesuit morality uttered by men whose knowledge of the subject and good Catholic sentiments are beyond suspicion. The only non-Catholic among the number is Leibnitz. His importance as a personality, a connoisseur and not unfriendly critic of the Jesuit Order justify his admission here.

I shall also quote Jesuit critics on the morality of their Order, since their opinion on this matter is obviously of special value.

From Abbé de Rancé, founder of the Trappist Order, and an intimate friend of Bossuet:

"The morality of most Molinists [Jesuits, so called after the Jesuit Molina] is so corrupt, their principles are so opposed to the sanctity of the Gospels and all the rules and exhortations which Jesus Christ has given us by His words and through His saints, that nothing is more painful to me than to see how my name is used to give authority to opinions which I detest with my whole heart   What surprises as well as grieves me is that in regard to this matter the whole world is dumb, and that even those who regard themselves as zealous and pious, observe the deepest silence, as though anything in the Church were more important than to maintain purity of faith in the guidance of souls and the direction of morals. . . . Unless God takes pity on the world and subverts the zeal which is applied to destroying right principles and replacing them by wrongful ones, the evil will continue to increase and we shall soon see an almost universal devastation."†

Rancé also relates how the Jesuits revenged them-

* Ludov. Sergardii, *Orationes* (Lucca, 1783), p. 205. D.-R., I., 117.
† *Lettres de A. J. Le Bouthillier de Rancé*, published by B. Gonod (Paris, 1864), pp. 358–365, from Döllinger-Reusch, I., 113 *et seq.*

selves for his judgment on their morality, and thus supplies a fresh condemnation of Jesuit morality:

"Every day brings me fresh experience of the injustice and violence of those persons known as Molinists. They shrink from no calumny which may serve to destroy my reputation. . . . Their false moral principles allow them to utter against me all the calumnies inspired by envy and passion."*

The Papal Nuncio at Vienna, Francesco Buonvisi (afterwards Cardinal), wrote on May 6, 1688, to the Abbot Sfondrati:

"I do not like to see him [the Emperor Leopold I.] surrounded by these little foxes [the Jesuits], who ruin everything by probabilism, saying that in certain cases it is permitted to follow the less probable view, reserving to themselves the right to advise the prince to follow this on the pretence that the weal of the State requires it, in order to prevent greater evils."†

The Augustinian monk, Giovanni Berti, says:

"They [the Jesuits] play various parts; one in the pulpit, another in the confessional, one in the professor's chair, another in China. In the pulpit they are disciples of Poemi, in the confessional of Guimenius [the pseudonym of the ultra-lax Jesuit Moya], in the professorial chair of Molina, at court of Varroda, in Europe of Mascarenhas, in China of Le Tellier, not to say of Confucius. As occasion requires they are now zealous priests, now lax moralists, now quarrelsome scholastics, now followers of Machiavelli, now apparent Christians, now open idolaters."‡

Cardinal Aguirre, in a letter dated April 26, 1693, writes to the King of Spain:

". . . It is a question of the boundless liberty with which many modern writers, especially Jesuits, allow very lax opinions

* *Lettres de A. J. Le Bouthillier de Rancé*, p. 355.

† *Memorie per servire alla storia politica del Card.* Fr. Buonvisi (Lucca, 1818), 2,238. *Ibid.* I., 105.

‡ *Lettera di Fra Guidone Zoccolante* (1753), p. 51. *Ibid.* I., 106.

to be printed and also teach and apply them practically. Alexander VII. condemned forty-five of these opinions, Innocent XI. pronounced sixty-five dangerous and scandalous, and finally Alexander VIII. condemned two, one as heretical, the other as erroneous and subversive of morality. The General [of the Jesuits, Thyrsus Gonzalez], in order to counteract this evil, has ordered a book to be printed in Germany, which Innocent XI. has frequently called upon him to publish. But his subordinates, instead of showing gratitude and trying to amend, have taken up arms against him. Some of them declare that he is a Jannsenist—a shameful calumny, since he has no dealings whatever with the condemned principles of Jannsen, and has indeed combated them in his book most emphatically. . . It is a matter of common knowledge that many Jesuits have also applied the epithet 'Jannsenist,' to Pope Innocent XI., who condemned so many of their lax opinions. They apply the same epithet to all the many learned and pious prelates, doctors and writers who have written against their lax morality."*

The Dominican Concina, whom even the Jesuit Cordara calls a righteous man, says:

"For more than a century and a half Christian morality has had to endure the onset of bad doctrines. This method permeates the whole of casuistic theology, and inflicts fatal wounds on almost every part of its body. Not content with perverting written law, it has almost wiped out all trace of that inscribed by nature in the heart of man. . . . There is nothing too lax, unjust, or shameful, not to say godless, for them to represent through the medium of unlimited probabilism as pious, decent and holy. That is the worst of all evils, the pestilential source which brings ruin to souls. . . . They have found a middle road, not quite a broad way, so as not to call forth any involuntary alarm, nor yet straight and narrow, thus pandering to the evil inclinations of men, reconciling the world and the Gospel and transforming rough roads into

* For the Spanish original, see Patuzzi, *Lettere* 6, LXXXII. For an Italian translation, Döllinger-Reusch, II., 115 *et seq.*

smooth ones. This middle road has probably carried more souls to hell than the broad way."*

Johann Adam Möhler, Professor at the University of Tübingen, and unquestionably the greatest Catholic theologian of the nineteenth century, author of the rightly renowned *Symbolik*, writes:

" Moral theology has sustained a specially deleterious influence through them [the Jesuits]. The reason whose very essence it was to distinguish, to resolve the infinite into a number of finite magnitudes, could not truthfully and with clear, decisive vision face the infinitely holy principles of Christian morality. It split up everything into individual cases and, therefore, treated morality as mere casuistry; and as the infinite power of moral and religious inspiration was not sufficiently regarded, everything was gradually transformed into cunning calculation as to the manner of acting in individual cases, which often really meant the best method of disguising our own egotism from ourselves. Probabilism took an important place in Jesuit morality, *i.e.* the maxim that of two possible courses in a particular case, the one based on the weaker arguments may be chosen, instead of teaching how to follow the holy sense, the inward Christian impulse in a free and cheerful spirit . . . . casuistry is atomism of Christian morality. . . . This method of treating Christian morality often had a poisonous effect on the innermost being of Christian life. Religious depth, stern and holy morality and strict Church discipline were undermined by it. And as it was characteristic of them to transform the inner being into mere externals the Jesuits also conceived of the Church as primarily a state . . . they threatened to excavate, as it were, the whole Church, to rob it of all power and inward life. The tendency of Jesuitism was also unquestionably very dangerous for the Church, and it was necessary to put a check on its efforts. . . . Although the suppression of the Jesuit Order was a work of violence and accompanied by the most crying injustice, it need not be regretted on historic grounds. The Order belonged to a past age, and in

* *Theologia christiana dogmatico-moralis* (Romae, 1749-51), dedication to Pope Benedict XIV.

spite of the change of circumstances continued its activity according to the old fashion. It was, therefore, impossible for it to intervene beneficially in the newer age."*

Reinhold Baumstark, for many years leader of the Baden Catholics in the Second Chamber at Carlsruhe (who died in 1900), wrote of the influence of Jesuit morality on the confessional:

"Jesuitism has transformed the confessor of the Catholic Church, *i.e.* the priest, to whom every Catholic must confess his sins at least once a year before receiving the Easter communion, into the spiritual director, *i.e.* that priest who, in the confessional and outside it, directs and governs the whole conduct of the individual not only from the point of view of what is permissible or sinful, but also from that of expediency, prudence and results. . . . His whole life is gradually surrounded and dominated by it [the intercourse with the confessor introduced by the Jesuits]; outward obedience to law, irreproachable conduct and piety are strongly in evidence, but that which constitutes the chief, indeed sole worth, of a man—his free self-direction, inward piety and real moral personality—is destroyed in this fashion."†

Leibnitz characterises Jesuit morality in the first place as · "*Cette morale ridicule de la probabilité et ces subtilités frivoles inconnues à l'ancienne Église, et même rejettées par les payens.*" Then he continues:

"*On voit en Europe qu'il y a en a souvent entre eux qui sont pleins de petites finesses, qui ne seraient pas approuvées parmy les honnestes gens du grand monde. Je croy que leurs enseignments d'école et leurs livres de morale contribuent beaucoup à gaster l'esprit des novices et de leurs jeunes gens.*"‡

---

* From a lecture dictated by Möhler in 1831, at Tübingen, communicated by the Lucerne Canon and Theological Professor, J. B. Leu, in *Beitrag zur Würdigung des Jesuitenordens* (Lucerne, 1840), pp. 23–29.

† *Schicksale eines deutschen Katholiken* (Strassburg, 1885), 2nd edition, pp. 85 *et seq*, 147, 148.

‡ Rommel, *Leibniz und Landgraf Ernst von Hessen-Rheinfels, Ungedruckter Briefwechsel* (Frankfort-a-M., 1847), I., 279, 280.

Jesuit Morality

Among the testimonies against Jesuit morality from within the Order, the first place is due to the General Thyrsus Gonzalez.

Gonzalez, the thirteenth General of the Order (1687–1705), for many years waged a heroic war against the bad morality of his Order as incorporated in probabilism and its excrescences. The most influential of his subordinates organised revolt upon revolt against him, and strove by open and secret attacks, calumniation and intrigues, to make his life and position unbearable, until at last they drove him out of his mind.*

The story of Thyrsus Gonzalez forms one of the by no means uncommon sections of the history of the Jesuit Order, in which, instead of the much-vaunted "sacred" and "blind" obedience to the Superiors, brutal disobedience prevails, and the disaffection stirred up by the Order's egotism and greed for rule gives way neither to General nor Pope; for Gonzalez, too, acted in agreement with Pope Innocent XI. and under his orders.

Here, as everywhere, when the dark sides of the Order's history are concerned, the official historians of the Order try to distort and hush up the matter. Thus, *e.g.* the Jesuit de Ravignan, who wrote his book *De l'Existence et de l'Institut des Jésuites* (Paris, 1855) by command of the Order, in dealing with the struggle of the Order with the General and Pope, which was waged with the utmost virulence, only says:

* The Jesuit Bonucci bears testimony to the fact that Gonzalez was driven out of his mind by his subordinates. In a confidential letter of September 9, 1719, published by Pietro Bigazzi as an interesting contemporary document (*Miscellanea storica e letteraria*, Firenze, 1847). Bonucci writes referring to the great annoyances to which the successor of Gonzalez, Tamburini, had also been exposed by his Jesuit subordinates, says: "He will be the second General in our time to be driven out of his mind (*e questo sara il secondo Generale che a giorn nostri avevero fatto impazzire* (*cf.* Döllinger-Reusch, I., 265). The "first" Genera driven out of his mind "in our time" can only refer to Gonzalez.

"Many of the Order's theologians have attacked probabilism; the strongest condemnation of the kind known to me is that written by one of our Generals, Thyrsus Gonzalez. Many other of our members have approved of probabilism."*

It is only when we begin to study the historical material relating to probabilism† that we come to realise how untruthful are such utterances in consciously suppressing the truth.

Gonzalez relates that Innocent XI. said to him on the occasion of his first audience that his (the General's) task must be to divert the Society of Jesus from the precipice (*a praecipitio avertere*) into which it seemed about to fall, by trying to adopt as the doctrine of the Order the laxer view as to the use of probable opinions. "The Pope also commissioned him to summon a prominent Spanish Jesuit to Rome as Professor at the *Collegium Romanum*, to teach the stricter morality approved by Gonzalez himself."‡ And this statement was repeated on oath by Gonzalez as a witness at the Beatification of Innocent XI.§

As Gonzalez clearly expresses his assent to Innocent's declaration, and as, moreover, his whole life and work were devoted to extirpating the lax morality of his Order, his testimony bears the crushing weight of the voices of a "beatified" Pope and a General of the Order, whose office of itself enabled him to know the condition of the moral teachings of his Order.

The Jesuits, too, must necessarily feel the weight of their General's words. On this account they not only

---

* P. 152.

† Döllinger and Reusch, in their *Moralstreitigkeiten*, so frequently quoted supply almost complete material.

‡ Concina. *Difesa*, 1, 28; *Sac. Rituum Congregatione Em. et Rev. D. Card. Ferrario, Roman. Beatificationis et Canonizationis Ven. Servi Dei Innocentii Papæ undecimi. Positio super dubio an sit signanda commissio introductionis causae in casu* (Romae, 1713), p. 180, printed by Döllinger-Reusch, I., 132 (2).

Ibid.

Jesuit Morality

keep them as secret as possible, but they do not even shrink from representing as false the statements made on oath by their General.

"They assert that it is certain that the Pope maintained a purely passive attitude in this matter; the words placed in his mouth by Gonzalez could never have been spoken by him."*

The real reason for the resistance of the Jesuit Order to a reform of its morality and its obstinate adherence, in spite of Pope and General, to its lax probabilism, is worth noting. It is the lust of dominion which, like a red thread, runs through the whole of Jesuitism and its history, which here, too, allowed the end to "sanctify the means.".

H. Noris, Consultor of the Congregation of the Inquisition, and afterwards Cardinal, in a letter addressed to the Grand Duke Cosimo III. of Florence, in 1692, gives as the view of the Jesuits:

"The doctrine of their General [Thyrsus Gonzalez] was dangerous to the efficacy of the Society; for as they [the Jesuits] were confessors to so many great princes in Europe, so many princely prelates in Germany, and so many courtiers of high rank, they must not be so severe as their General desired, because if they wished to follow his teaching they would lose their posts as confessors at all the courts."†

It would be impossible to exceed the severity of the judgment passed by the Jesuit, Michael de Elizalde. He was a friend of the Jesuit Cardinal Pallavicini, who calls him one of the greatest theologians of the Order,‡ and was Professor of Theology at Valladolid, Salamanca,

* *Ibid.*, I., 135, and II., 163.
† The interesting letter is printed by Concina, D*ifesa* 2, and Patuzzi, *Lettere* 6. Döllinger-Reusch, I., 176.
‡ *Lettere del Card. Sforza Pallavicini* (Rome, 1848), 2, 35; 3, 229.

Rome and Naples. He composed a work on Probabilism approved by Pallavicini, which, however, failed to attain the Imprimatur of the Superiors, and he was actually threatened with the severest penalties by General Paul Oliva. His work appeared first in a mutilated edition, but six years later, after his death, was republished *in extenso* with the title, *De recta doctrina morum* (Friburgi, 1684). Elizalde's polemics are directed against the theologians Diane and Caramuel, but chiefly against his fellow Jesuits Escobar, Tamburini and Moya. He summarises his views on Jesuit morality thus:

"Recently I looked through a summary of morals in severa volumes. I sought for Christ, but found Him not. I sought for the love of God and our neighbour, but found them not. I sought for the Gospel, but found it not. I sought for humility, but found it not. But if we read in St. Paul or any other apostle or saint, we find the very opposite; everywhere Christ, love, humility, holiness abound. These two doctrines, therefore, are in no way connected, and stand in no relation to one another. The Gospel is simple and opposed to all equivocation; it knows only yea, yea; nay, nay. Modern morality is not simple, but makes use of that equivocating probabilism, using yea and nay simultaneously, since its rule is the probability of mutually contradictory statements."*

In a memorial sent to Clement XI., in October, 1706, the Jesuit Camargo tells of the experiences which he and others had of Jesuit morality when conducting popular missions in Spain:

"How many contradictions, dangers and difficulties I and all the others experienced who, in the direction of conscience, reject the common rule of probabilism so universally diffused throughout Spain, God alone knows, and it sounds incredible. Morals have grown so lax that in practice scarcely anything is regarded as

---

* *De recta doctrina morum*, 1, 8 qu 7, § 2 : Döllinger-Reusch, I., 150.

not permitted. . . . Not only among the people, but also among confessors, preachers and professors does the opinion prevail, that we commit no sin, if we believe while acting that we are acting rightly, or do not think that we are acting wrongly, or are in doubt about the matter. . . . I know not through what mysterious or, at any rate, terrible decree of God it has come about that this moral doctrine, which is so hateful to the Apostolic See and so contrary to Christian morality, has found such favour among the Jesuits, that they still defend it, while elsewhere it is scarcely tolerated, and that not a few Jesuits believe themselves bound to defend it as one of the doctrines of the Order. . It is regrettable that the enemies of the Society can, without untruth, reproach it as being the only apologist for probabilism, which is the source of all laxity and corruption of morals, and has been condemned almost expressly by the Apostolic See, and even promote and spread it with zeal."*

That the Jesuits Elizalde and Camargo were persecuted and grievously calumniated by their fellow-Jesuits for their candour,† is a matter of course to those who know Jesuit ways. Cardinal Manning and Abbé de Rancé also had experience of this peculiarity of the "Society of Jesus," which is doubtless based on the command of Jesus, "Love your enemies . . . do good to them that hate you," as have countless others before and after them.

The Jesuit André complains in a letter:

"Every day I hear the casuists of our Order maintain that a king is not bound to abide by a treaty which he has only concluded in order to bring to an end a war which has turned out to his disadvantage. I hold the opposite opinion. I stand almost alone among a crowd of persons who pretend to be religious. Neither law nor gospel is binding in matters of State—an abominable doctrine!"‡

* Printed in Concina, D*ifesa*, 2, 60: Döllinger-Reusch, I., 265-266.
† *Ibid.*, I., 56.
‡ Charma, *Le Père André*, 2, 358; Döllinger-Reusch, I., 104, 105.

The Jesuit La Quintinye, to whose piety and purity of morals his General, Paul Oliva, bears testimony, after vainly directing protests to his superiors, addressed himself on January 8, 1679, to Innocent XI.

He says that during the last fifteen years he had repeatedly written to former Popes about the sad conditions that prevailed in the Society of Jesus, to which he had belonged for more than thirty years; but he did not know whether his letters had ever reached the persons to whom they were addressed. His complaints dealt with—1. The moral doctrines prevailing in the Society of Jesus, which had already been condemned by many bishops and popes. 2. The practice of the Jesuits in the direction of souls based on this doctrine. 3. The means adopted by the Jesuit superiors to compel the subordinates to adopt their moral doctrines. 4. The cunning which the Jesuit superiors employed to prevent the Papal decrees against the lax Jesuit morality from being made known to the subordinates. They assured the Pope of their intention to obey, and the Jesuit General publicly called upon his subordinates to prove their obedience; but secretly and in private letters they admonished them to abide by the lax moral doctrines condemned by the Popes.*

Two Jesuit voices raised on behalf of Jesuit morality really bear testimony against it; but for that very reason and on account of their boastful tone, they furnish proofs of special strength.

The Jesuit Le Roux says:

" Ivenin [an opponent of the Jesuits] thinks it may be deduced from their teaching that a man who, for forty years, has led a godless life and then received the sacramental absolution by mere attrition [penitence from fear of punishment], and immediately after loses his reason through a fatal illness, has a right to ever-

* Döllinger-Reusch, I., 57-61 and II., 1-19, where the documents are printed.

Jesuit Morality

lasting bliss, although he never, not even at the end of his life, loved God. That we unhesitatingly admit."*

And in the *Imago primi Saeculi* it is stated in praise of Jesuit morality that:

"Now [in consequence of the activity of the Jesuits] sins are atoned more speedily and eagerly than they were formerly committed; nothing is more common than monthly or even weekly confession; most people have scarcely committed a sin before they confess it."†

Everything which can be said against Jesuit morality may be summed up in the fact that several Popes, especially Alexander VII., Innocent XI., and Alexander VIII., found themselves compelled to condemn in solemn manifestoes a number of really monstrous maxims of this morality, which were actually taken from the works of some of the leaders in moral theology.

Truly the bodyguard of the Pope took little notice of the condemnation, but "proved," also through its leaders, that most of the condemned maxims were not understood by their Jesuit authors in the sense on which the Papal condemnation was based; therefore they might calmly go on teaching them.

For a detailed account of this masterpiece of Jesuit obedience and Jesuit power of exposition I must refer to my work on the Papacy.‡

FUNDAMENTAL PRINCIPLES OF JESUIT ETHICS AND MORALITY

1. **Untruthfulness.**—I have repeatedly emphasised the fact that part of the essence of Jesuitism is an all-pervading untruthfulness. It is a subtle poison, which exercises its

---

* Döllinger-Reusch, I., 80. † *Imago*, p. 372. ‡ II., 444 *et seq.*

power to kill truthfulness, faith and loyalty throughout the whole organism of the Order.

The Order's system of government, built up on mutual supervision, secret reports, espionage, denunciation, is opposed to all human and Christian simplicity and candour, and necessarily begets mistrust, suspicion, and at last conscious and unconscious untruthfulness.

Thus the Constitutions of the Order prepare the ground, on which the moral theological doctrines as to the permissibility of mental restriction, of every kind of equivocation, of half and three-quarter truths, easily take root and shoot luxuriantly upward. These doctrines are the flesh and blood of the Jesuit body, and are more or less the ethical and moral base of the individual Jesuits.

To what an extent Jesuitism has lost all sense of truth, is shown in startling fashion just where it appears to come forward against untruth and lies. Thus the Jesuit Delrio, Professor of Theology at the Universities of Salamanca and Graz, writes·

"It is an article of faith that a lie (which deserves the name) is in itself something morally bad. Yet consider: it is one thing to say something false and another to hide something true, by making use not of a lie but an equivocation. The utterance of a judge at Liège was both cunning and permissible, who said to a stiff-necked witch, who denied all accusations, that if she spoke the truth sufficiently he would, as long as she lived, provide from his own or public means food and drink for her every day and see to it that a new house was built for her, understanding by 'house' the wooden [scaffolding] with the bundles and straw on which she would be burnt. Other [permissible equivocations] are cited by Sprenger [a Dominican]: They should treat the guilty person with greater honour than is customary, and admit respected persons, whom he would not suspect, to intercourse with him. These may discourse about various alien matters, and finally advise him with confidence to confess the truth, promising that the judge would show him mercy and they would act as intermediaries. The judge should then come and promise to let mercy prevail, understanding by this, —for himself or the State, for the preservation of which everything that is done is an act of mercy. The judge might also say to the accused that he was giving him good counsel, and a confession would be of great advantage to him, even in saving his life. For this is most true, if understood of eternal life, which is the true life."*

And this encouragement of infamous lying in trials when life is hanging in the balance is passed unhesitatingly by the censor of the Order, who, moreover, in the case of Delrio's work, was one of the most famous Jesuits of the sixteenth and seventeenth centuries, Oliverius Manäraus, who justifies his imprimatur " by the judgment of weighty and learned theologians of the Order." And, what is more, a Jesuit of the twentieth century, Duhr, who has become sufficiently well-known to us, praises his fellow-member of the Order, Delrio—

"Because he severely attacks the judges, who wish to make the witches confess by means of false representations and lies."†

Consequently, even to the present day, Jesuitism— for Duhr's work, too, passed the Order's censorship— does not find any falsehood or inaccuracy in the disgraceful craftiness and lies of the judge at Liège, and in the counsel of the Jesuit Delrio.

With such a conception of "lying," it is no wonder that we find the most prominent moral theologians of the Jesuit Order putting forward preposterous doctrines with regard to equivocation.

* *Disquisitionum magicarum libri sex* (Coloniae, 1679), p. 768.

† *Die Stellung der Jesuiten in den deutschen Hexenprozessen. Vereinsschrift der 'Görresgesellschaft zur Pflege der Wissenschaft im katholischen Deutschland"* (Cologne, 1900), p. 44.

The Jesuit Cardenas says:

"Sanchez [a Jesuit] mentions two kinds of ambiguities which he declares to be perfectly admissible. In the first place, if I make use of words which are in themselves ambiguous and apply them in one sense whilst the listener believes I am applying them in another sense. If there is no sufficient reason for concealing the truth, the use of such ambiguity is unlawful, but not untruthful. Thus, for example, if some one has killed a Frenchman (*hominem natione gallum*), he can say, without lying, that he has not killed a '*gallum*,' if he takes this word in the sense of 'cock.' To this class must also be referred the ambiguity in the case *non est hic*, *i.e.* according to the way it is understood: he *is* not here, and he *is* not *eating* here. That Innocent XI. did not condemn this use of ambiguity is certain. For he only condemns ambiguity connected with mental reservation, which means that something is added mentally. But in the cases of ambiguity quoted above nothing is added mentally, because the different significations (*gallus, est*) lie in the words themselves. The second kind of permissible ambiguity arises when the words in themselves are not ambiguous, but assume another meaning owing to the conditions of place, time and persons. Thus it is related of St. Francis that when on one occasion robbers, who had passed him, were pursued by the officers of the law, he replied to their questions as to whether the former had gone that way by saying 'They have not come here,' at the same time putting his hands into his sleeves. And this reply was perfectly truthful, for the robbers had not passed through his sleeves. He could also have put his foot on a stone and said, 'They have not gone through here,' because they had not gone through the stone. There is no mental reservation in this case, because, through his placing his foot on the stone, the words in question ('come through,' 'gone through') related to the stone. In this class are also included those words which have only one meaning in themselves, but are ambiguous, without mental reservation, according to the different way in which they are used. Thus, for example, the word 'know,' which really signifies certain knowledge, is also frequently used for defective knowledge. On the other hand, 'ignorance' means lack of certain knowledge, but is frequently used for the lack of any knowledge. Consequently, if someone has heard from another person that Peter committed a theft, and replies on being asked, 'I do not know,' *i.e.* 'I have no infallible knowledge of it,' he is not lying. Suare and Lugo [the chief theologians of the Jesuit Order] also give the following example: 'A man who has only a loaf, which is necessary for his subsistence, answers the person who asks for one truthfully when he states, 'I have none,' for he really has none which he can give, and he is asked in this sense. By these different ways of making use of ambiguity which we have quoted as permissible, all pangs of conscience and doubt are removed. Thus, an adulterous woman, when questioned by her husband regarding the adultery and threatened with death, may reply without falsehood and without mental reservation, 'I have not wounded your honour,' for 'wounded' means a material wounding, which cannot be applied to honour. She may also deny her adultery by taking this word in the sense in which it is frequently used in the Scriptures, namely, as idolatry. Any one who is questioned by the police concerning the whereabouts of a criminal, can give St. Francis's reply, which we have already cited. Whoever is asked by the judge on oath how much he has of a certain commodity, which is unjustly taxed at too high a rate, may swear that he has a considerably smaller quantity of it than he really has, and it can be shown in many ways that this is no perjury. In the first place, when he swears that he has, for example, twenty pitchers of oil, he does not deny that he has more, but speaks the truth, saying that he has twenty pitchers. Secondly, he may swear that he has not more than twenty, because he speaks the truth so far as the judge, who only asks as to the amount of oil which ought to be taxed, is concerned. As, according to the hypothesis, the tax is unjustly high, it is quite true to say that the person does not possess more, adding [mentally] than must be taxed."*

The Jesuit Laymann:

"Ambiguities are not lies. Ambiguities are modes of expression with a double meaning, one of which, that conveying the truth,

* *Crisis theologica. Venetiis* (1710), IV., 120 *et seq.*

the speaker has in view, and hence does not lie, even when the person addressed interprets the words in the other sense, which is incorrect, and is thus deceived. For the speaker does not practise the deceit on the person addressed, but only permits it. . . . Although it is a probable view that every promissory perjury is a deadly sin, the opposite view is more probable. . Although an ambiguous oath is no perjury when there is just cause for concealing the truth, and is even exempt from all moral wrong, it is to some extent a false oath and not permissible when there is not just cause. Three assertions are implied by this thesis:—
1. An ambiguous oath is no perjury, because one sense of the ambiguous expression is correct, according to the hypothesis; consequently, whoever confirms this sense with an oath does not commit perjury. Indeed, when an expression is really not ambiguous, but when it has in itself or in the circumstances only one meaning and that the false one, no perjury is committed when the person under oath does not intend to emphasise this false sense, but another, which does not correspond with the words sworn by him. An oath is only false when God is called upon as a witness for something false; but he who swears in the above-mentioned manner does not call upon God on behalf of the false sense which he refers to outwardly, but on behalf of the truth which he retains inwardly."

Laymann admits, it is true, that he who swears thus utters a lie and usually commits a grievous sin. He then continues:

"2. That an ambiguous oath is no sin, can be proved in the same way. For one interpretation of the ambiguous expression is true, and it can consequently, if necessary, be confirmed with an oath. . It follows from clause 2 that he who has returned a loan may swear before a court of justice, if he has no other proof, that he has never entered into any agreement for a loan, adding to himself, such that he should have to return the loan twice. Covarruvias, Azor and Suarez declare this view as probable. He who has been induced under severe threats, or without the inner wish, to bind himself, and has said to a woman, 'I will marry you,' may, when asked by the judge about the matter, deny on oath that he has spoken such words, understanding the oath to mean that he has voluntarily agreed to marry her. He who is asked under oath if he has come from a place which is falsely supposed to be infected with the plague, may swear that he has not come thence, saying to himself, ' from the plague-infected place.' "*

The Jesuits Ballerini and Palmieri :—

" The general teaching of the theologians is that for a just cause ambiguity and equivocation are permissible even when under oath. And, in fact, when ambiguity is used, that which is manifested outwardly corresponds with the inner meaning of the person under oath, and hence the truth necessary for the oath is present. The listener is deceived, it is true, but we only admit that he misleads himself. A person is permitted to swear falsely aloud when an addition is spoken softly, provided that it is evident that an addition has been made, although the meaning of the addition is not understood."†

The Jesuit Lehmkuhl, whose *Moral Theology* is taken as the basis of instruction for the confessors designate in numerous seminaries for Roman Catholic priests in Germany, France, Italy, Holland, and elsewhere, says :

" Lying is always sinful. . . . But mental reservation is frequently free from falsehood ; consequently [*sic !*] it is occasionally permissible and necessary and occasionally not permissible to make use of it. Under mental reservation is understood the keeping back of the sense of the words or its mental definition. This may occur in different ways :—1. If the words themselves have different meanings according to their interpretation, so that the speaker must give them a particular meaning. 2. If the words have not a double meaning in themselves, but may be taken in a sense different from the obvious one through conditions of place, person and time. For example, the expression, ' I do not know,' may admit the

  Theologia moralis. Liber quartus, tract. 3, cp. 14. Edit. Monach., 1625, II., 165, 174, 176, 177.
  † *Opus theolog. morale, Prati*, 1892, II., 415, 418.

meaning in certain circumstances, 'I do not know so that I can communicate it.' 2. If the words can neither have such a meaning in themselves nor through special conditions, but can only have another signification through mental addition; for example, if anybody, on being asked whether he has been in Cologne, replies, 'I was there,' and says to himself, 'in spirit.' The last manner of speaking, which only consists of mental reservation, is never permissible, but is untruthful. The two other ways are permissible in suitable circumstances, for in whatever way the words are spoken —and they must be considered along with the circumstances—they express the real meaning which the speaker mentally intended, even though not clearly and definitely. The speaker intends, however, that the full meaning shall not be understood by the person addressed, and herein he is justified, and it is admitted that they may perhaps even be wrongly understood. Consequently, a part of the truth is concealed, which, for just reasons, may and must frequently occur. . As often as I use in permissible fashion any reservation not exclusively mental, I may, according to the importance of the occasion, swear even with this reservation."*

Lehmkuhl's instructive remarks regarding calumniation also belong here. On the authority of Liguori and the Jesuit Busenbaum, he declares that it is a deadly sin—

"To call a priest or a pious member of an Order a liar, whilst it is a pardonable sin to accuse a soldier, who lives a freer life, of philandering or vendetta. Nor is it very sinful to relate similar or analogous offences of one who is already notorious in other respects; for example, to say of one who is known as a drunkard that he quarrels with his wife, or of a robber that he has committed perjury. . . . Who would consider it a serious calumny to say that an atheist is considered capable of secretly committing any crime (*quaelibet crimina*)?"†

* *Theologia moralis. Edit.* 6. 1890, I., n., 772, 773.
† *Ibid., n.* 1178, 1179.

Jesuit Morality

The Jesuit Gury:

"Anna had committed adultery; she replied first of all to her husband, who was suspicious and questioned her, that she had not broken the marriage bond; the second time, she replied, after she had been absolved from the sin, 'I am not guilty of such a crime'; finally, the third time, because her husband pressed her still further, she flatly denied the adultery, and said, 'I have not committed it,' because she understood by this, 'such adultery as I should be obliged to reveal,' or 'I have not committed adultery which is to be revealed to you.' Is Anna to be condemned? Anna can be justified from falsehood in the threefold case which has been mentioned. For, in the first case, she could say that she had not broken the marriage bond, because it was still in existence. In the second case, she could say that she was innocent of adultery, since her conscience was no longer burdened with it after confession and the receiving of absolution, because she had the moral certainty that this had been forgiven. Indeed, she could make this assertion on oath, according to the general opinion and that of Liguori, Lessius, the Salmanticenses, and Suarez. In the third case, she could, in the probable view, still deny having committed adultery in the sense that she was obliged to reveal it to the husband."*

Such theories have been practically utilised in the Jesuit Order from early times. Some historical occurrences which have become famous will serve as examples.

The Jesuit Garnet, Provincial of the English Province of the Order, made use of equivocation, as he himself writes in a letter "to the Fathers and Brethren of the Society," so as not to be convicted of participation in the Gunpowder Plot in the examination before the Commissioners.† Garnet says, in a letter dated March 20th, 1606:

---

* *Casus conscientiae*, I., 182 *et seq.* (Parisiis, 1892), 8th edition.

† Text of the letter in Jardine: *A Narrative of the Gunpowder Plot* (London 1857), p. 203 (1).

"In cases where it becomes necessary to an individual for his defence, or for avoiding any injury or loss, or for obtaining any important advantage, without danger or mischief to any other person, there equivocation is lawful. Let us suppose that I have lately left London, where the plague is raging, and on arriving at Coventry, I am asked before I can be admitted into the town whether I come from London, and am perhaps required to swear that I do not: it would be lawful for me (being assured that I bring no infection) to swear in such a case that I did not come from London; for I put the case that it would be very important for me to go into Coventry, and that from my admittance no loss or damage could arise to the inhabitants."*

Garnet acknowledged in a letter to his accomplice, the Jesuit Greenway, that he knew of the Gunpowder Conspiracy from the conspirator Catesby's confession, and that he was obliged to impart his information (he made this confession to the court of justice in a "declaration" written in his own hand). The letter was intercepted, and the Commissioners questioned him as to the existence and contents of the letter. Garnet replied, "upon his priesthood that he did never write any letter or letters, nor send any message to Greenway since he was at Coughton; and this he protested to be spoken without equivocation." A few days afterwards, on being shown his letter to Greenway, and asked how he could justify his falsehood, he boldly replied, "that he had done nothing but that he might lawfully do, and that it was evil done of the Lords to ask that question of him, and to urge him upon his priesthood when they had his letters which he had written, for he never would have denied them if he had seen them; but supposing the Lords had not his letters, he did deny in such sort as he did the writing of any letter, which he might lawfully do."†

Jardine, the keen-witted investigator of these cir-

* Jardine, *Ibid.*, p. 233 *et seq.* † Jardine, *Ibid.*, p. 244 *et seq.*

Jesuit Morality

cumstances, criticises, on the strength of the still extant minutes, the Jesuit Garnet's attitude before the tribunal:

"He had denied all knowledge of the Plot until betrayed by the conferences with [the Jesuit] Hall, and he denied those conferences until he plainly perceived that he only injured himself by so doing; and when afterwards abashed and confounded at the clear discovery of his falsehood, he admitted to the Lords that 'he had sinned unless equivocation could save him'! From the beginning to the end of the inquiry, he had acted in strict consistency with the principles he now acknowledged, never confessing any fact until it was proved against him, and never hesitating to declare palpable falsehoods respecting matters which tended to inculpate himself and affirm them by the most solemn oaths and protestations."*

And this is the man of whom Professor Buchberger, the editor of the *Kirchliches Handlexikon*,† which was episcopally approved, writes · "Garnet was a man incomparable in knowledge and saintliness" This is another proof of the great extent to which the official Roman Church adapted itself to the morals of the Jesuits.

The Jesuit Gerard relates ·

"They [the Commissioners] asked me then whether I acknowledged the Queen [Elizabeth] as the true governor and Queen of England. I answered, 'I do acknowledge her as such.' 'What!' said Topcliffe, 'in spite of Pius V.'s excommunication?' I answered, 'I acknowledge her as our Queen, notwithstanding I know there is such an excommunication.' The fact was [the Jesuit continues] 'I knew that the operation of that excommunication had been suspended in all England by a declaration of the Pontiff till such time as its execution became possible."‡

The Catholic theologian, Taunton, rightly remarks on

---

* Jardine, *Ibid.*, p. 237. † Munich, 1907, I., 1594.
‡ *The Life of Fr. John Gerard* (London, 1882), p. 225.

this cynical and naïve utterance : " It shows what reliance can be put upon some of the protestations of allegiance."*

The shameless inaccuracy of the Jesuit's reply reflects, of course, more on the Papacy than on Jesuit morality. For Gregory XIII., a special friend of the Jesuits, had indeed authentically interpreted the Bull of deposition of his predecessor, Pius V., in the manner indicated by Gerard, and had entrusted the "interpretation" in an audience of April 14th, 1580, to the Jesuits Parsons and Campian, who were journeying to England.†

The Jesuit, Robert Southwell, directed the daughter of his host, in whose house he lay concealed from the sheriff's officers of Queen Elizabeth of England, that she should reply " No," to the question as to whether Robert Southwell were in her father's house, and confirm the reply with an oath. In order to make the " No " correct, she was to think, " He is not in my father's house so that I am bound to tell them."‡

The attitude of the Parisian Jesuits with regard to a book by their fellow-Jesuit, Santarelli, *Tractatus de haeresi, etc.*, affords a specially striking example of the ability of the Jesuits to say "Yes" and "No" about the same circumstance. This book, which was published in 1625, with the approval of the General, Vitelleschi, taught the usual doctrine of the Order regarding the Pope's supremacy over kings and princes, and defended the view that the Bull, *Unam sanctam*, which dogmatically established this doctrine, was not suspended by Clement V.'s Brief, *Meruit*, published in favour of France. The Parisian Sorbonne condemned the book. On March 14th, 1626, the French Parliament cited the Provincial of the Jesuits at Paris

---

* *The Jesuits in England*, p. 165.

† *The Jesuits' Memorial*, p. XXVI., and *Harleian Miscellany*, 4th edition, II., 130.

‡ Taunton, p. 168.

and six other Fathers to appear before the bar so as to question them about the book. I quote from the minutes of the case:

" ' Do you approve of Santarelli's bad book ? ' 'On the contrary, we are ready to write against it and contest all that he says.' ' Do you not know that this wicked doctrine has been approved by your General in Rome ? ' ' Yes, but we here cannot help this indiscretion, and we blame it most emphatically.' ' Do you believe that the Pope may excommunicate and depose the King, and release his subjects from their oath of allegiance ? ' ' How should the Pope excommunicate the King, the eldest son of the Church, who would certainly do nothing which would render it necessary ? ' ' But your General, who has approved the book, considers that its contents are correct; do you differ in opinion ? ' ' The General, who lives in Rome, can do nothing but approve that which the Roman Curia has sanctioned.' ' And your own conviction ? ' ' Is quite different.' ' And what would you do if you were in Rome ? ' ' We should act in the same manner as those who are there.' "*

Louis XIV.'s confessor, the Jesuit La Chaise, writes to the Jesuit Petre, the political favourite of James II. of England, in a letter dated March 7th, 1688:

" One of your Assisting Fathers of that Kingdom (which was Father Parsons) having written a book against the succession of the King of *Scots*, to the Realm of *England*, Father *Creighton*, who was also of our Society, and upheld by many of our Party, defended the Cause of that King, in a Book intituled, *The Reasons of the King of Scots, against the Book of Father* Parsons ; and tho' they seemed divided, yet they understood one another very well, thus being practised by Order of our General, to the End, that if the House of *Scotland* were excluded, they might shew him, who had the Government, the book of Father *Parsons ;* and on the other Hand, if the King happened to be restored to the Throne, they

* Reusch, *Der Index*, II., 351, 352.

might obtain his Good Will, by shewing him the Works of Father *Creighton*: So that which Way soever the Medal turn'd, it still prov'd to the Advantage of our Society."*

Whether the letter is genuine in this form is uncertain. But we are certain of the existence of the two mutually contradictory works by the Jesuits Parsons and Creighton mentioned in it,† and in this fact lies the proof of the equivocation of the Order which is expressed in a typical manner in this letter. And this is the point. The letter—in case it is not genuine—would then be, like the *Monita secreta*, a sharply pointed, satirical exposure of Jesuit double dealing.

On December 24th, 1613, the Jesuit Adam Contzen, Professor of Theology at Mayence, suggested in a letter to the Jesuit Cardinal, Bellarmin, that a *Supplicatio* to the King of England, or to the Dutch States-General, should be written in the name of a Protestant preacher, showing the necessity for a Calvinistic council, in order to divert attention from a letter directed against Pope Paul V. (demonstrating that the choice of the Pope was simoniacal, consequently invalid).‡

The Jesuit, Hugo Roth, also pretended that he was a Dutch Calvinist in his anonymous work, *Cavea turturi structa*, published in 1631, against the Dominican Jacob Gravina. In a letter addressed to the Jesuit Forer he says it would not be well that he (Roth) should be known to be the author, because it would lead to a popular scandal if it were known that members of the Orders attacked one another.§

---

* *Collection of Papers Relating to the Present Juncture of Affairs in England.* Third Collection, p. 27. London, 1689.

† Sommervogel, S.J., *Bibliothèque de la Compagnie de Jésus* (Bruxelles-Paris, 1895-1900), 6, 303; 9 (Supplément), 148.

‡ Döllinger-Reusch, *Moralstreitigkeiten*, I., 550, and II., 262.

§ *Ibid.*, I., 584; II., 309.

Jesuit Morality

Specially characteristic of the Jesuits was their attempt, towards the end of the sixteenth century, known as "The Douai Knavery" (*la fourberie de Douai*), to destroy the Catholic Theological University at Douai, which displeased them because it had a tendency towards Jansenism.

A professor at Douai, P. de Ligny, became implicated in a secret correspondence. The writer of the letters, who pretended to be the Jansenist leader, Antoine Arnauld (he always signed himself as Antoine A. and had the answers sent to Brussels, which was then Arnauld's place of residence), severely attacked the Jesuits, and warmly took up the cause of the Jansenists. The aim of the correspondence was to unmask Ligny and the other professors as Jansenists. The object desired was achieved and Louis XIV. deprived the Professors Laleu, Rivette, Ligny and Malpaix of their office, and banished them to different parts of France. The cunning correspondent, "who had rendered such a signal service to religion," was not, however, Antoine Arnauld, but a Jesuit, probably the Jesuit Lallemand who, as Sainte-Beuve* reports, when an old man, still boasted "*avec jubilation, qu'il avait imaginé, filé et conduit à la fin, qu'il se proposait, la fameuse fourberie de Douai.*"

The "Fourberie de Douai" created great commotion. All respectable people were unanimous in its condemnation. Leibnitz pronounced upon it, saying:

"The deceit in the Douai case is very wicked and a very bad example. In legal parlance it may be designated as *stellionatus* (artful deception). But, in spite of everything, I do not believe that the Jesuits will gain much by it; for if, as seems probable, the matter is taken up further in the courts of law, the handwritings will be compared, and it will easily be seen that the handwriting is not that of Arnauld, and the Jesuits of Douai will be forced to say how they obtained the documents. Besides, the intrigue bears

* *Port_Royal*, 5, 464.

several marks of falsehood, so that I cannot see the use of such a cunningly contrived p[ie]ce of roguery, except to cause alarm among the ignorant. . . . [D]o not believe that these controversies [the affair at Douai] can [be] laid to the charge of the Roman Catholic religion; the failings [o]f human nature are only too well known, and the Jesuits have [g]iven too many proofs of their vindictive character to be consid[er]ed exempt from human passions. Doubtless their general superior ought to express their strong disapproval of those who have ca[rri]ed out the affair at Douai, which was a very dishonourable busines[s] (*chose forte malhonneste*) . . . But it seems that two consideratio[ns] restrain the Superiors (although they must be exceedingly displea[s]ed, as I readily believe). In the first place, they think that their [?] punishment would damage the reputation of the Society [of Jes[u]]; secondly, they have such a bad opinion of the so-called Jans[en]ists that they rejoice over the matter as a service rendered to t[he] Church, although they do not approve of all the circumstances. [Leibnitz thus clearly reproaches the Jesuits with their observanc[e] of the principle 'The end sanctifies the means.'] If I were [in] place of these Superiors, I would make amends to Arnauld."

The Jesuits th[em]selves, however, thought very differently on the subje[ct] of "making amends," as the abovementioned remark [o]f the chief culprit, the Jesuit Lallemand, shows.

Arnauld himsel[f] tried to obtain the "amends" by p[ub]l[is]hing several complaints" against the Jesuits. It [is said] in one of [t]hese ·

[app]eal to you my right reverend Fathers. . . . It only [remains for] me to cit[e] you before the tribunal of all honest people [who] are [?] already so indignant about the rascality of [?]nauld, so [t]hat if nothing else can avail to shame you public inf[a]my may, at any rate, compel you to change

dated Sept[em]ber 12th and October 9th, 1691, to Landgraf Ernst [R]heinfels: *Rommel, Leibniz und Landgraf Ernst von Hessen-Rheinfels* [1]847), II., pp. [3]06 and 326.

your attitude. . . . There is only one ay for you to save the honour of your Society, show honour t God, and acknowledge that all those of your Society who have teen part in this wretched intrigue have acted very badly."*

The Jesuits also tried by a cuning trick to disarm the Dominican Concina, one of the keenest opponents of their moral teachings. Such a tistworthy witness as the Jesuit Cordara gives an accoun of this:

"Whilst the struggle against the Juits raged thus [chiefly stirred up by Concina], a violent work sddenly appeared from a secret place of publication with the title 'oncina's Recantation, in which Concina, repenting of his misdeeds, withdrew his accusations against the Jesuits, accused himself o wicked malignity, and unmercifully reproached himself with 1any infamous actions. Nobody doubted but that a Jesuit was th author of the pamphlet, which was immediately circulated throug the whole city [Rome] and was eagerly read on account of its sarical wit."†

Is it surprising that this false nd treacherous spirit which pervades the manuals of mral theology and the "glorious" history of the Order hould also make its way into the daily life of the Jeit? Ever since my suspicions were aroused, in the secon year of my novitiate, regarding the Order's secrecy, concealment and avoidance of the light, they never ceased to distuo me; and numerous experiences proved to me that, in he Society of Jesus, Christ's saying, "Let your commuication be Yea, yea; Nay, nay," is not observed, but tat the words of the genuine Jesuit are full of secondary meanings and reservations. My mistrust of the uprigtness of their words and deeds became insurmountably rong as time passed,

---

* *Seconde Plainte de M. Arnauld aux R. R. . P. Jésuites,* from Arnauld, 31, 453 *et seq.*; for the evidence concerning the false Arnauld " *cf.* Reusch, *Beiträge zur Geschichte des Jesuitenordens* (Munich, 394), pp. 169-195.

† *Denkwürdigkeiten,* Döllinger, *Beiträge,* 3, 10.

several marks of falsehood, so that I cannot see the use of such a cunningly contrived piece of roguery, except to cause alarm among the ignorant. . . . I do not believe that these controversies [the affair at Douai] can be laid to the charge of the Roman Catholic religion; the failings of human nature are only too well known, and the Jesuits have given too many proofs of their vindictive character to be considered exempt from human passions. Doubtless their general superiors ought to express their strong disapproval of those who have carried out the affair at Douai, which was a very dishonourable business (*chose forte malhonneste*) . . . But it seems that two considerations restrain the Superiors (although they must be exceedingly displeased, as I readily believe). In the first place; they think that their punishment would damage the reputation of the Society [of Jesus]; secondly, they have such a bad opinion of the so-called Jansenists that they rejoice over the matter as a service rendered to the Church, although they do not approve of all the circumstances. [Leibnitz thus clearly reproaches the Jesuits with their observance of the principle 'The end sanctifies the means.'] If I were in place of these Superiors, I would make amends to Arnauld."*

The Jesuits themselves, however, thought very differently on the subject of "making amends," as the abovementioned remark of the chief culprit, the Jesuit Lallemand, shows.

Arnauld himself tried to obtain the "amends" by publishing several "complaints" against the Jesuits. It is stated in one of these ·

"I appeal to you, my right reverend Fathers. . . . It only remains for me to cite you before the tribunal of all honest people in the world, who are already so indignant about the rascality of the false Arnauld, so that if nothing else can avail to shame you the fear of public infamy may, at any rate, compel you to change

* Letters, dated September 12th and October 9th, 1691, to Landgraf Ernst von Hessen-Rheinfels: Rommel, *Leibniz und Landgraf Ernst von Hessen-Rheinfels* (Frankfort, 1847), II., pp. 306 and 326.

your attitude. . . . There is only one way for you to save the honour of your Society, show honour to God, and acknowledge that all those of your Society who have taken part in this wretched intrigue have acted very badly."*

The Jesuits also tried by a cunning trick to disarm the Dominican Concina, one of the keenest opponents of their moral teachings. Such a trustworthy witness as the Jesuit Cordara gives an account of this:

"Whilst the struggle against the Jesuits raged thus [chiefly stirred up by Concina], a violent work suddenly appeared from a secret place of publication with the title *Concina's Recantation*, in which Concina, repenting of his misdeeds, withdrew his accusations against the Jesuits, accused himself of wicked malignity, and unmercifully reproached himself with many infamous actions. Nobody doubted but that a Jesuit was the author of the pamphlet, which was immediately circulated through the whole city [Rome] and was eagerly read on account of its satirical wit."†

Is it surprising that this false and treacherous spirit which pervades the manuals of moral theology and the "glorious" history of the Order should also make its way into the daily life of the Jesuit? Ever since my suspicions were aroused, in the second year of my novitiate, regarding the Order's secrecy, concealment and avoidance of the light, they never ceased to disturb me; and numerous experiences proved to me that, in the Society of Jesus, Christ's saying, "Let your communication be Yea, yea; Nay, nay," is not observed, but that the words of the genuine Jesuit are full of secondary meanings and reservations. My mistrust of the uprightness of their words and deeds became insurmountably strong as time passed,

---

* *Seconde Plainte de M. Arnauld aux R. R. P. P. Jésuites*, from Arnauld, 31, 453 *et seq.*; for the evidence concerning the "false Arnauld" *cf.* Reusch, *Beiträge zur Geschichte des Jesuitenordens* (Munich, 1894), pp. 169-195.

† *Denkwürdigkeiten*, Döllinger, *Beiträge*, 3, 10.

especially in the case of five influential Jesuits who were my Superiors — Meschler, Nix, Ratgeb, Hövel and Pütz.

Words cannot express what a subordinate, especially one who is so absolutely dependent as a subordinate in the Jesuit Order, suffers in an atmosphere of falsehood, which surrounds him and emanates from his superiors. And this suffering was not felt by myself alone. Others, too, were oppressed by its weight. Only very rarely, and then but casually, did one of us dare to speak to another of his feelings. For both alike have the right and the duty to report everything they hear to the Superior. In the Jesuit Order, there are no friends to whom we can confide cares and mental anguish without fear of betrayal. The Constitutions of the Order have made breach of confidence a law. And yet I once heard a complaint of the untruthfulness which pervaded the Order made in a most affecting manner by a fellow-Jesuit, a dying one, it is true, who had nothing more to hope for and nothing to lose.

In 1889 or 1890, the Jesuit Niemöller died at Exaeten of consumption. I frequently visited him, and he spoke to me confidentially. Once he said to me in a hoarse, rattling voice: " Do you know what has been the hardest thing in the Order, what has caused me the severest spiritual tortures? The feeling of being surrounded by a system which is full of reservation. But we must believe that our judgment is mistaken," he added hastily, " for the Church has certainly approved the Jesuit Order with its theory and practice." I did not reply to the poor man, because the authority of the Church, to which he could still cling, had already begun to totter in my estimation. For years this " authority " had also prevented my condemnation of Jesuit untruthfulness.

One afternoon—it must have been in 1887 or 1888—

I was in the library at Exaeten. A report had spread amongst us that the neighbouring estate of Oosen, which is situated on the Maas, had been bought by the German Province of the Order as a place for recreation. Whilst I was there, the *Socius* of the Provincial Superior, the Jesuit Pütz, entered. No one could give more positive information, so I asked him if this report was founded on truth, *i.e.* whether the estate had been bought, or would be bought. He replied without hesitation, "No, what are you thinking of?" On the following day, it was announced that Oosen had been bought, and the purchase was actually legally concluded in the morning of the day, on the afternoon of which the Jesuit Pütz, who knew exactly the fact of the purchase, had so definitely denied it.

I have already mentioned the mental reservation which the Jesuit, Cardinal Franzelin, advised me to employ on taking the official oath when I entered the Prussian State service, and how deceitfully the Jesuit Superior at Blyenbeck (unfortunately I also had a share in this) kept a "magister meal" secret from my uncle, Baron Felix von Loë.

All these are small passages from daily life—I could easily multiply them—which, owing to their insignificance and frequency, show especially clearly the extent to which untruthfulness has become incorporated in the flesh and blood of the Jesuit. He no longer feels that restrictions, reservations, and the like are dishonourable, and that they offend against faith and honesty. The "classic moral theologians" of his Order teach that they are permissible; members of the Order, to whose "virtue" and "saintliness" the history of the Order calls special attention, practise "knaveries" and make use of mental reservations; why then should such teachings and examples not be followed in daily life?

2. The End Sanctifies the Means.—I may be mistaken, but in my view it is here we find the deepest shadows over Jesuit morality.

The oft-quoted maxim, " The end sanctifies the means," does not occur in this abrupt form in the moral and theological manuals of the Order. But its signification, *i.e.* that means in themselves bad and blameable are "sanctified," *i.e.* are permissible on account of the good ends which it is hoped to attain through them, is one of the fundamental doctrines of Jesuit morals and ethics.

It is well known that many violent disputes have raged about this maxim. The Jesuit Roh offered a reward of 1,000 florins to anyone who could point it out in the moral and theological writings of the Order. The matter was not decided. In April, 1903, the Centre deputy, Chaplain Dasbach, repeated Roh's challenge at a public meeting at Rixdorf, increasing the sum to 2,000 florins. I took Herr Dasbach at his word, published the proofs from Jesuit writings, which appeared to me convincing, in the magazine *Deutschland*,* edited by myself, and called on the challenger, Herr Dasbach, to pay the 2,000 florins. He refused. I sued him for payment at the County Court at Trèves (Dasbach's place of residence). The court pronounced that the matter was a betting transaction, and that the money could not be recovered at law. On appealing against this to the High Court of Appeal at Cologne, my case was dismissed on March 30th, 1905, on the ground that the passages brought forward from Jesuit authors did not contain the sentence, "The end sanctifies the means," either formally or materially. My counsel advised against applying for a revision at the Supreme Court of the Empire, as the facts of the case would not be discussed there, only technical errors in the previous judgments.

* July, 1903.

Jesuit Morality

I have given the main points of the Cologne judgment in the *Zeitschrift für Kirchengeschichte*,* with my comments, and there also expressed the well-founded supposition that in essential points it was composed with the assistance of Jesuit theologians. But even this judgment contains the sentence, "Whatever we may think of the morality manifested in these cases," etc.

All the proceedings, with the quotations (Latin and German) from the writings of the leading moral theologians of the Jesuit Order, have been given in detail in my work, *Der Zweck heiligt die Mittel*, an ethical historical examination, together with an *Epilogus galeatus*,† to which I refer the reader.

I will only submit a few passages here :—

The Jesuit Becanus says:

"Is it an offence if a person advises another to do the lesser evil so that he may abstain from the greater ? Or, as others put the question, is it permissible to advise the lesser evil so as to prevent the greater ? In particular, may I advise Peter, who wishes to commit adultery, to commit a simple sin of unchastity, so that the adultery may be prevented ? Likewise, may I advise a man who wishes to steal the whole treasure to be satisfied with a part ? Some believe that it is not permissible, for we must not do evil that good may come, as the Apostle says in the Epistle to the Romans, iii. 8, or, which is the same, ' It is not permissible to make use of a bad means so as to attain a good end'; thus it is not permissible to steal money so as to give alms from it ; it is not permissible to lie so as to convert some one to the Catholic Faith. Others are of the opposite opinion, as Dominicus Soto, Sylvester (Prierias), Navarrus, Adrianus, and Johannes Medina en Vasquez . . . To this is added a proof based on reason : It is permissible to advise Peter, who is determined to sin, to commit a more trivial sin without designating the object of the lesser sin. And yet the result of this advice is that, while he was previously determined

* Vol. 27, p. 339 *et seq.*
† Third Edition (Berlin, 1904), C. A. Schwetschke und Sohn.

to commit adultery, he is now advised rather to commit a simple act of unchastity. This latter point of view must be thus understood: If I saw Peter disposed and absolutely determined to commit adultery so as to satisfy his desires, and I was not able to dissuade him from his design in any other way than by advising him to commit a simple act of unchastity in place of the adultery, it would be permissible to advise the latter, not inasmuch as it is a sin, but inasmuch as it prevents the crime of adultery, which would otherwise have been committed. Augustinus also speaks in this sense when he says that both murder and adultery are sins, but, for all that, if a man be determined to commit one of the two, he should rather choose adultery than murder. I say the same of the thief or robber, who is determined to steal from Peter his whole stock of gold articles. For, if I cannot prevail on him in any other way than by the advice to be satisfied with half, it is permissible to advise him to commit the lesser theft so that he may abandon the greater. The reason is that he who advises thus does not injure Peter, but rather renders him a benefit; he contrives so that Peter retains half his possessions, which he would otherwise have lost entirely."*

The Jesuit Castropalao says:

"Does a man commit a sinful offence if he offers another an occasion for sin or does not remove the occasion offered although he could do so? If you do not remove the opportunity for sin, with the intention that the other should sin, it is clear that you yourself sin on account of the evil intention. It remains doubtful whether you are excused from the sin, if you were prompted by some good purpose. The motive may be either that the person in question may be caught committing the sin and punished, or that he may be reformed, or that you secure yourself from harm. If you act from any of the above reasons, you do not apparently approve the sin of the other person, but permit it. But as to this we must say that if you merely permit the sin of the other so that he may be detected and punished, then you yourself sin, for there does not seem sufficient reason to justify such a permission. The

* *Opera omnia. Mogunt.* 1649, *Partis secundae tract,* 1, c. 27, qu. 4, p. 396 *et seq.*

punishment is not a worthy aim in itself, because it can only be imposed when the sin has been committed; indeed, if you, before the sin has been committed, desire the punishment for the sin, it implies a silent consent to the sin itself. This is the opinion expressed by Medina . . Sanchez . . . and Bonacina. They say, for instance, that guards by concealing themselves so as to extort a very heavy fine from travellers who have unlawfully passed the frontier are guilty of a deadly sin, which is very hard. But if you permit another to sin so that he may be detected and reformed, it is allowable, and it follows from what we have said when treating of admonition on the sixth point; for the reform of the sinner, which is confidently expected, seems to be sufficient reason for permitting the commission of the sin. Besides the above-named theologians, this doctrine is held by Navarrus . . ., Navarra . . ., Valentia . . ., and Sanchez, who again cites Bonacina . . ., Molina . . . and Joh. Sanchez. . . . But the prospect of reform must be almost certain, for only then can the hope of permanent and radical improvement make up for the permission of the prospective sin. In the second place, I say that you may permit a sin so as to make your position secure. For these reasons, a married man, when he suspects his wife of adultery, or is secretly aware of it, may take witnesses with him so that he may prove the adultery and may bring about the divorce. As the husband suffers the greatest injury through the wife's adultery when he is forced to live with her, he may, to avert this wrong, and as no other practicable way of doing so is presented, except permitting the sin and confirming it by witnesses, permit it and call in witnesses. Navarra, Sanchez, Bonacina and Molina hold this view. The difficulty arises, is it permissible, for the purpose named, to offer the sinners the opportunity for the sin? A common opinion negatives the permissibility, for this does not only entail permitting a sin, but co-operating in its perpetration, and Emmanuel Sa. . . ., Sanchez . . . and Bonacina hold this view. Hence, as Bonacina and Sanchez reason, the husband is not allowed to come to terms with his wife that she may make an appointment with her lover, who seeks to violate her chastity, fixing time and place, not in order that the adultery may be committed, but in order that the latter may be caught in his wicked design. For such an agreement is a tacit, indeed, an express consent to the proposed adultery, which is not permissible. Peter Navarra considers it permissible, however, though only in rare cases, to offer sinners an occasion for sin. It may be said as a proof of this: In the first place, an occasion for sin may be presented by a passive medium. This, for example, is the case when the father, who wishes to catch the son who is stealing, leaves the key in the money chest as if through forgetfulness, or places coins in a place where the son can easily take them and then be convicted of the theft; then, I say, the father performs an indifferent action. Sanchez and others hold the same opinion in this case. In the same way a woman does not seem to sin when she, in presence of a seducer from whose importunity she cannot defend herself, uses an ambiguous expression which the seducer takes as consent, but which is in reality no consent on her part. When she says, for instance, to the seducer: 'I agree, if you come at this time and hour, the door will be open,' the expressions are indifferent, and although they are considered by the seducer as a consent to the adultery, this is not the case. Consequently, it is allowable for her to express herself in this way, because she has a sufficient reason for the equivocation. Granted, moreover, that the expression might appear to the seducer as a consent to the adultery under given circumstances, yet it is no consent when the matter is well considered; for such an expression is frequently used, not in order that the adultery may be committed, but so that he who secretly designs it may be punished. The woman does not say, 'I agree to your carrying out your wicked design,' but only, 'I agree to your coming to-night.' These words may not only denote that he should come for adultery, but just as well that he should only come to receive his punishment, so that she may rid herself of his attentions and defend her honour. . . . Does a man commit a sinful offence who advises a person about to commit a serious sin to commit a less serious one? . . . It is certainly permissible to suggest a smaller offence to some one who is quite determined to perpetrate a serious one, so that he may be prevented from committing the greater. For example, you may urge one who wishes to commit sodomy to commit a simple unchaste act; and you may point out to one who wishes to commit a murder and then to steal, how to obtain money through usury; for by this indication you do not directly tempt the person either to unchastity or to usury, you only point out the way in which the greater sin may be avoided, and although the way is morally wrong, you do not induce the other to follow it, but you only say that this is the way to avoid the greater sin, which is true. This is the view of Covarruvias, Cajetan, Valentia, Sanchez, Lessius and other theologians to be mentioned later. The difficulty, therefore, begins when the question is whether it is permissible expressly to advise anyone who is determined to commit a grievous sin and persuade him to commit the lesser sin, when he cannot be restrained in any other manner. The first opinion teaches that it is permissible in this case, for you do not persuade the other absolutely to commit the lesser sin, but only on the hypothesis that he wishes to commit the more serious sin. In case he wishes to commit the more serious sin, however, it is right to persuade him to be satisfied with committing the lesser sin, for by this his own cause and God's are fitly protected. Consequently you do not sin. This is what is taught by Sanchez, who cites others besides, Lessius . . ., Rebellus . ., Molina . . ., Bonacina ., and Vasquez. . . . The second view teaches that it is in no case permissible to recommend the lesser sin to him who wishes to commit the greater. For the recommendation of the lesser sin is still a counsel to sin: a comparative presupposes a positive. But to advise something which is unlawful is not permissible. Moreover, free choice of the lesser sin is never permissible, even when it is made by one who is ever so determined to commit the greater sin. Consequently the advice to do this is never permissible. Advice to do something which is in itself not allowable can never be permitted. This is the view of the theologians Cajetan, Covarruvias, Sylvester, Emanuel Sa, Valentia and Conrad Summenhart. In this matter, I believe that the first point of view is correct if he who is advised to commit the lesser sin and persuaded to do so is already prepared not only to commit the greater sin, but also the lesser. For then we do not advise the commission of the lesser evil, but the omission of the greater; also, we do not determine the sinner to commit the lesser sin, but rather deter him from the perpetration of the greater. This is clear from the following example: Peter is determined to kill Francis in order to rob him; he wishes to commit the murder, and you persuade him to be satisfied with wounding. In giving this advice you wrong no one : you do not injure Peter, because you take care that his soul is not stained with so many crimes ; nor yet Francis, because you manage his business advantageously. It follows from this that you are allowed not only to advise Peter in this case to commit the theft, but also to help materially in the act, because you do not help in an act which is not permissible in itself and wicked, but which is rather good and honest so far as you are concerned, being committed with the tacit and assumed consent of the owner of the property who, it is supposed, in order to escape death, has given you permission to aid in the theft, so that his death is prevented by this assistance. This is the view of Sanchez, Bonacina and Vasquez."*

The Jesuit Voit says:

" In regard to the knotty question whether it is a sinful offence to recommend a lesser sin to one who would otherwise certainly commit a greater, Valentia and Sa reply that it is not permissible, for even the smaller sin remains a sin, consequently to advise it always remains something bad in itself; Laymann, Dicastillo and others reply with a distinction. If the lesser evil is comprised in the greater, and the greater evil cannot be prevented otherwise, it is permissible to advise the lesser evil, because then the lesser sin is not advised and suggested, but it is only intended that he who is determined to commit the greater sin shall abstain from committing a part of it. It is not permissible, however, to advise the lesser evil when it is by no means contained in the greater evil— for example, to advise one who is determined to commit a murder to get drunk—for that means to cause him to commit a sin which he had by no means intended to commit. In the former case, that evil is not directly advised, but it is chosen as a means for preventing the greater evil. Sanchez and other weighty theologians declare it to be permissible to recommend the lesser evil, although it is not contained in the greater, because then also the evil is not recommended as such, but only as a means of hindering the greater evil. . . . He who does not remove the occasion for sin [though

* *Operis moralis pars prima*, tom. 1, pp. 476–478. Ed. Lugd., 1669.

it is in his power] to the end that the person should be detected, amend and repent, does not sin, because this action is not designed to lead into sin, but to permit a sin as a means for the prevention of many sins." *

It follows from these passages:

1. That the recommending of a lesser sin, the presenting of an opportunity and the inducement to commit it, is morally permissible if it is done in order to prevent a greater sin. 2. That the prevention of the greater sin is clearly and distinctly designated as a "good end." 3. That as the recommendation to sin, no matter how small it may be, is in itself bad, Jesuit morality sets up the principle that a "means" in itself bad (advising, presenting of an opportunity for the lesser sin) is morally permissible, and is "sanctified" by the "good end" (prevention of the greater sin).

That this is the substance of the above moral and theological principles cannot be contraverted by any subtleties. On the contrary, the subtleties which the Jesuit Becanus, etc., employ to veil this result, make it even clearer to every person endowed with healthy judgment. And it is just these subtleties which show in an unparalleled way the unhealthiness of Jesuit moral feeling, and justify my assertion that the darkest shadows in Jesuit morality are here to be found.

3. Tyrannicide.—Juan Mariana, a celebrated Jesuit and an "ornament" of his Order, has defined with unprecedented candour and minuteness of detail the doctrine of the lawfulness of the murder of princes (not only tyrants) in his book *Concerning the King and his Education* (*De rege et regis institutione*), published in 1599 at Toledo. The

* *Theolog. moral.* Edit. Lugdun, 1850, I., 402, 406.

book bears the imprimatur of the Order, dated "Madrid, December 2nd, 1598"·

"I, Stephan Hojeda, Visitator of the Society of Jesus for the Province of Toledo, give, under the power of special authority from our General, Claudius Acquaviva, permission that the three books, *Concerning the King and his Education*, written by Father John Mariana, of the same Society, may be published, because they have been previously sanctioned by learned and distinguished men of our Order."*

The sixth chapter of the first book says:

"A noble monument has been recently erected in France which shows how important it is that the people should be pacified. Henry III., King of France, lies there murdered by the hand of a monk, and the charm of the knife has been thrust into his entrails. This is an ugly but memorable spectacle calculated to teach princes ['*principes*,' not '*tyrannos*'] that godless, hazardous enterprises do not remain unpunished. . . Jacques Clément . . studied theology at the college of his Order, the Dominican. When he, in answer to his question, had been told by the theologians that a tyrant could justly be killed . he went into the camp on July 31st, 1589. On August 1st, which is dedicated to the chains of the Apostle Peter, after reading Mass (*sacris operatus*), he obeyed the summons of the King, who was out of bed but not

* The approval of Mariana's doctrine by the censorship of the Order has caused so much annoyance to the Jesuits that they keep it as secret as possible. Thus, for example, the Jesuit Cathrein, a learned luminary of the German Province, specially emphasises the official approval of Mariana's book, but suppresses its approval by the Jesuit Order (*Moralphilosophie*, II. (4), 671 (Freiburg, 1904)). Here is a still more significant circumstance. When I wrote the work *Warum sollen die Jesuiten nicht nach Deutschland zurück?* in 1891, under compulsion of obedience to the Order (as I shall presently show), I mentioned the imprimatur of the Order in discussing Mariana's book. The Jesuit Ratgeb, at that time Provincial, requested me to omit this passage: "Why should we," was the gist of his comment, "put weapons into our enemies' hands?" Reusch charged me with the sin of omission in the *Deutscher Merkur*, and only then did the Jesuit Ratgeb consent to the reinsertion of the passage—*i.e.* the mention of the Order's imprimatur—in the second edition of my work, on the ground that the fact had now been made known and it would no longer be advantageous to suppress it.

completely dressed. During a conversation, he drew nearer to the King, apparently to present a letter, and inflicted a deep wound in the vicinity of the bladder with a knife hidden under medicinal herbs. What magnificent presence of mind! what a glorious action! . . . The courtiers who rushed in covered him [the monk] with wounds. . . . He [the monk] bought the liberty of his country and nation with his blood; he rejoiced exceedingly in spite of blows and wounds. He won a great name through the murder of the King. . . . Thus died Clément, France's everlasting glory, as most people believe. . . . Opinions differ as to the monk's act. Whilst many praise him and consider him worthy of eternal renown, others, distinguished by discretion and learning, blame him: It is not permissible, they say, for any man on his own authority . . . to kill a king deposed by the nation. . . . And they confirm this with many proofs and examples. . . . This is what those teach who espouse the cause of the tyrant. But those who espouse the people's cause can bring forward as many and as weighty proofs. It is certain that a king may, if the circumstances require it, be cited before their tribunal by the community from which he derives his kingly authority, and, if he scornfully rejects the remedy, may be divested of his princely rank. . . . We also see that, from ancient times, those who have murdered tyrants are held in honour. . . . I observe that philosophers and theologians agree as to the fact that a prince who has taken possession of a state by arms and violence, without right and without the consent of the nation, may be deprived of life and power by anybody (*a quocunque*). As he is an open enemy and wrongfully oppresses the country and has the nature and name of a tyrant in truth and reality, he may be removed by any means (*amoveatur quacunque ratione*) and be deprived of the power of which he has forcibly possessed himself. . When a prince enjoys his power by consent of the people, or by inheritance, his oppressions and whims must be borne as long as he chooses to infringe those laws of honour and morality to which he is bound as a person. For princes must not be changed lightly   . . But if he brings ruin on the state   this must not be overlooked in silence. But first the method of deposing such a prince must be carefully considered. . .   The most practicable and safest method seems to be to authorise the public assembly to determine in general conference what is to be done. . . . If the prince then amends, I consider that he must again be reinstated and stronger measures need not be adopted. If he refuses the remedy, however it is permissible to deprive him of his power after judgment has been passed upon him. . . . And if the state cannot defend itself in any other way, it is permissible, according to the law of self-defence and on a man's own authority, to kill the prince, who has been declared an open enemy, with the sword (*ferro perimere*). And this authority is possessed by every private individual who seeks to aid the state, abandoning all hope of impunity, at the risk of his own salvation. You ask what is to be done when the authority of the public assembly [of the Estates] has been suspended, as may frequently occur. In my opinion, the matter remains the same . . . and he who, in accordance with public wishes, tries to kill the prince has, in my opinion, not acted wrongly. This is adequately confirmed by the evidence which I have already brought forward against the tyrants. Consequently it is only the question of fact (*questio facti*) which is disputable, *i.e.* who should be regarded as a tyrant; the question of justice (*questio juris*) is clear that a tyrant may be killed. . . . It is well for princes to consider that, if they oppress the State and become unbearable through their vices and moral infamies, their life hangs in the balance, and that it is not only lawful to kill them, but even honourable and glorious: . . . If all hope [of the prince's reformation] has disappeared, and if the State and the sacredness of religion are in danger, who is so devoid of wisdom that he cannot acknowledge that it is right to shake off tyranny by means of the law and by weapons ? . . . This is my opinion founded on sincere conviction, and since, being human, I may be mistaken, I shall be thankful if anyone can advance anything better. I close the discussion with the words of the tribune, Flavius, who, convicted of participation in the conspiracy against Nero, and asked why he had forgotten his oath, replied, ' No soldier was more faithful than I at the time when you deserved to be loved. I began to hate you when you became a matricide, wife-murderer, racer and incendiary.' A soldierly and brave spirit ! "*

* *De rege et regis institutione,* pp. 65-80.

Jesuit Morality

In Chapter 7 Mariana asks the question, "Is it permissible to kill a tyrant by poison?" He writes:

"It is a glorious thing to exterminate the whole of this pestilential and pernicious race [of tyrants] from the community of mankind. Limbs, too, are cut off when they are corrupt, that they may not infect the remainder of the body; and likewise this bestial cruelty in human shape must be separated from the State and cut off by the sword. . . . The question is only whether a public enemy and tyrant may also be killed by poison and deadly plants. This question was addressed to me a few years ago by a prince in Sicily when I was teaching theology there. . . . In my opinion, it is not permissible to mix either an injurious medium or poison in food or drink. But there is one reservation [killing by means of poison is permissible]: if the person to be killed is not obliged to drink the poison, but the poison is applied from outside without the co-operation of [the person to be killed]. Thus, for example, if the poison is so virulent that a chair or dress besmeared with it has the power to kill."*

Consequently Mariana has not only "tyrants, usurpers" in his mind, as is asserted by Jesuits, but also legitimate princes (*principes*) who rule "tyrannically."

The attitude of the Order towards Mariana's teaching is extremely instructive.

The approval of his doctrine by the censorship of the Order, based on an examination by "learned and important" theologians, has already been mentioned. Only seven years after the publication of the book does General Acquaviva seem to have found fault with the contents in a letter to the French Province of the Order. But the censure is made in such a general manner and without mentioning any name, that it cannot positively be shown to be directed against Mariana.

* *Ibid.*, pp. 81-85. The Jesuit Cathrein had the audacity to write opposite these plain words of Mariana's, "But only by open violence [may a tyrant be killed, according to Mariana], not by poisoning, as Mariana emphatically adds later" (*Moralphilosophie*, II. (4), 672 (1)).

Again and again I must repeat that the Jesuits rely on the blind credulity of their readers. And, indeed, how easy it would have been for the General of the Order, if he had really wished to condemn and censure Mariana's teaching, to have expressed his condemnation and censure in an effective manner, and checked the further circulation of the book.

Instead of this, a reprint of Mariana's book was issued at Mayence (*typis Balthasaris Lipii, impensis haeredum Andreae Wechelii*) in 1605. And it cannot be doubted that this was published with at least the tacit consent of the Jesuits, who were then almost omnipotent at Mayence. Indeed, the omission of Mariana's most disgraceful words regarding the murderer of Henry III. (" France's eternal glory"), an omission which, as Reusch pertinently indicates, " would scarcely have been suggested by the Protestant publisher,"* renders the conclusion as to the co-operation of the Jesuits in the new edition almost inevitable. Even the Jesuit Duhr admits that it may be " possible that the changes in the Mayence edition are due to a Jesuit."†

Consequently the words of Isaac Casaubon, addressed as far back as 1611 to the Jesuit Fronton Le Duc, remain unanswered and unanswerable :

" . . . Wechel's Successors are merchants, and do not pretend to any literary knowledge. They were informed by a Jesuit of high standing that Mariana's book, printed at Toledo and approved, was to be issued in a complete edition for the public weal. They were not expected to do anything except defray the cost of printing ; they were not to trouble about anything else, because the book was to be published at Mayence by the Fathers of the Society of Jesus. They did as they were bidden. Wechel's Successors

---

* *Beiträge zur Geschichte des Jesuitenordens* (Munich, 1894), p. 7.
† *Jesuitenfabeln* (4), p. 739.

supplied the money, as requested, and the Jesuits managed everything else."*

The murder of Henry IV. by Ravaillac followed on May 14th, 1610. A storm of indignation arose in France against Mariana's doctrine, the Parisian Sorbonne had his book burnt by the public executioner, and only then did the Order, in the person of its General, Acquaviva, oppose the doctrine. But even this opposition which, as circumstances show, was due solely to opportune reasons, presents so much that is characteristic of the Jesuits that we are justified in doubting whether it was meant seriously.

In the first place, Acquaviva issued a letter on July 6th, 1610, which threatened with the most severe punishment all those belonging to the Order who defended the permissibility of tyrannicide. (Here, too, Mariana is not named.) It is a striking fact that this threat was not sent to Spain, where naturally the greatest impression had been made for the previous twelve years by Mariana's book, nor yet to the remaining Provinces of the Order, but only to France, obviously to appease the bitter anger which prevailed there against the Order owing to the murder of the King. On August 14th, 1610, Acquaviva wrote to the remaining Provinces of the Order in a different key and without the threat of punishment.†

Meanwhile, the indignation against the Jesuits caused by Mariana's teaching continued to increase, and troubles of every kind came upon the Order from every side. Finally, Acquaviva caused a third letter, dated August 1st, 1614, four years after his first letter, to be sent to all the Provinces, repeating the threat of punishment contained in the first letter, which had only been sent to Paris.‡

---

* *Casauboni Epistolae*, Edit. 2 (Magdeburg, 1666), p. 728 *et seq.*
† *Monumenta Germ. paed.*, 9, 43 (3).
‡ *Ibid.*, 9, 47.

This threat was then also inserted in the Constitutions of the Order : *

"In virtue of holy obedience, under pain of excommunication, ineligibility to hold any office, privation of ecclesiastical office and other punishments at the will of the General, it is commanded that no person belonging to our Society shall presume to assert publicly or privately, in lectures or in counsels, and still less in books, that any person (*cuique personae*) is permitted under any pretext of tyranny (*quocunque praetextu tyrannidis*) to kill kings or princes, or to contrive their death : *praecipitur . , ne quis . . . affirmare praesumat, licitum esse cuique personae, quocunque praetextu tyrannidis, Reges aut Principes occidere, seu mortem eis machinari.*"

But this "severe" decree is probably the most cunning piece of deception which has ever been published officially concerning an important matter. For under the prohibition accompanied by the heaviest punishments, "that it is not permitted to any person under any pretext of tyranny to kill kings or princes," is concealed the permission that certain persons, under certain pretexts of tyranny or in face of "real" tyranny, are allowed to do so. In addition the perfect tense *licitum esse*, instead of the present *licere*, should perhaps be rendered "has been permitted," in which case it is possible that the whole decree, together with its punishments, only refers to the past, so that a prohibition of the doctrine of tyrannicide for the present and future is not contained in the decree.

Thus the opposition of the Order to Mariana closed with a piece of real Jesuitical equivocation. Where clearness and exactitude of expression were necessary and easy, after fifteen years of vacillation, words were chosen which do not absolutely exclude the permissibility of

* *Inst. S.J. Censurae et praecepta hominibus Societatis imposita* (Edit. Romæ, 1870), II., 51.

tyrannicide in certain circumstances (*e.g.* in cases of "real" tyranny) for the present and future.*

The following facts also throw a curious light on the subject of Jesuits and tyrannicide.

When, after the attempt by John Chatel, a pupil of the Jesuits at Clermont, to murder Henry IV. of France, on December 27th, 1594, a domiciliary visit was made to the Jesuit college of that place, such incriminating documents were found in the possession of the Jesuit Guignard that he was put on his trial and was hanged on January 7th, 1595. The Jesuit Prat, the historiographer of the Order for the period between 1564-1626, can find nothing to bring forward in defence of his fellow-member† but: "*Les auteurs du temps s'accordent si peu sur la nature de ces pièces qu'il n'est pas possible de la conclure de leurs récits.*" He was obliged to admit, however: "*Il est cependant probable que le P. Guignard, en qualité de bibliothecaire (!), avait la collection des écrits de toute sorte qui avaient été publiés sur le meurtre de Guise, sur le crime de Jacques Clément* [the murderer of Henry III. extolled by the Jesuit Mariana]."

---

* The Jesuits try to reason away the offensive wording of the threat. The means adopted for this purpose are not very skilful. They assert that (*see* Duhr, S.J., *Jesuitenfabeln* (4), p. 741 (3)) not *cuique personae*, but *cuicunque personae* stood in the original text of the decree, and that *cuique* is a "printer's error." But this "printer's error" is to be found in two editions of the Constitutions officially published by the Jesuits themselves and declared to be "authentic," namely, the Prague edition (1757, II., 5) and the Roman (1870, II., 51). According to Duhr, it is true, the word used in the newest edition of the Constitutions of 1893 is *cuicunque*. The Order refused to let me look at this edition, which cannot be obtained through booksellers. But even if the statement about the remarkable "printer's error" is correct, this does not alter the sense of the passage in question. Whether we should read *cuique* or *cuicunque personae*, in both cases the translation is, "Any person has been permitted," etc. The ambiguity consequently remains. The Jesuits Prat, Schneemann, Duhr and Reichmann do their best to place the attitude of the Order towards Mariana in a better light by means of all kinds of "historical data." Reusch puts aside these efforts with the remark, "The data here collected may be shown as partly false, partly inaccurate, and partly undemonstrable" (*Beiträge*, p. 9), and proves his verdict.

† *Recherches, etc.* (Lyons, 1876), I., 1888.

Paolo Sarpi states* that, after the murder of Henry IV., a Jesuit had extolled this deed as meritorious from a pulpit in Prague. And Sarpi adds the characteristic words: "Even if the French Jesuits deny that they approve of the doctrine [Mariana's], I do not believe them, even if they swear it; they try to deceive God by some equivocation, mental subterfuge, or silent reservation."

A "memorandum," dated April 1st, 1606, signed by the Governor of the Tower, Sir William Waad, and by two other witnesses (W. Lane and J. Locherson), reports concerning the Jesuit Garnet, who was confined in the Tower owing to his participation in the Gunpowder Plot: "Garnet doth affirm, that if any man hath or should undertake to kill His Majesty, that he is not bound to confess it, though he be brought and examined before a lawful magistrate, unless there is proof to convince him." †

It is certain from the testimony of the Duke of Aveiro and the Counts of Atougouia and Tavora (all three of whom were executed as accomplices) that the Jesuits, especially the Jesuit Malagrida, by instigation and advice, had a share in the attempted murder of King Joseph of Portugal (September 3rd, 1758). Amongst the papers belonging to the Jesuit Malagrida, one was found addressed to the Lady-in-Waiting, Anna de Loreña, and sent back by her to the writer, in which, months before the perpetration of the act, reference is made to it.‡

Nor was Mariana's doctrine without influence on the Jesuit education of the young. In 1760, the Jesuit Longbois made his pupils compose an essay which bore

---

* Letter dated June 22nd, 1610, to Leschasser, Le Bret, *Magazin*, 2, 318.

† Jardine, *A Narrative of the Gunpowder Plot* (London, 1857), p. 238 (1).

‡ Heeren und Ukert, *Geschichte der europäischen Staaten*: Schäfer, *Geschichte von Portugal* (Gotha, 1854), V., 281 *et seq*.

the heading, " Brutus encourages himself to murder Cæsar," in which the sentence occurred, " Shall I kill Cæsar ? He is the Emperor . . . yet a tyrant : *Brutus ad caedem Caesaris se hortatur. Caesarem interficiam? Est imperator sed tyrannus.*"*

* Reusch, *Beiträge*, p. 57.

CHAPTER XXV

JESUIT MORALITY AND THE STATE

THE Jesuits, though not the authors, are the most energetic champions and propagators of the doctrine of the indirect supremacy of the Church (Papacy) over the State.

Since the two greatest theologians of the Jesuit Order, Bellarmin and Suarez, reduced this doctrine, inclusive of the right of the Pope to depose princes, to a properly articulated system, it has been a *rocher de bronze* of Ultramontane Catholic dogmatics and canon law, until at length the Syllabus of December 8th, 1864, and the Encyclicals of Leo XIII. and Pius X. raised it from the sphere of theological opinions to the height of a dogmatically established doctrine.* And this promotion is the work of the Jesuit Order.

No matter what dogmatic, canonical or moral-theological books by Jesuits we open, we encounter in all the indirect power of the Church over the State. The subject is so important that I will cite numerous proofs. I will begin with the present General of the Jesuit Order, Francis Xavier Wernz, a German from Würtemberg :†

"The State is subject to the jurisdiction of the Church, in virtue of which the civil authority is really subordinate to the ecclesiastical and bound to obedience. This subordination is indirect,

* *Cf.* my book, *Rom und das Zentrum* (Leipzig, Breitkopf und Härtel), p. 16 *et seq.*
† *Jus Decretalium* (Romae), 1898–1901.

Jesuit Morality and the State

but not merely negative, since the civil power cannot do anything even within its own sphere which, according to the opinion of the Church, would damage the latter, but rather positive, so that, at the command of the Church, the State must contribute towards the advantage and benefit of the Church."*

"Boniface VIII. pointed out for all time the correct relation between Church and State in his Constitution *Unam sanctam*, of November 18th, 1302, the last sentence of which [that every person must be subject to the Roman Pope] contains a dogmatic definition [a dogma].† The legislative power of the Church extends to everything that is necessary for the suitable attainment of the Church's aims. A dispute which may arise as to the extent of the ecclesiastical legislative authority is not settled only by a mutual agreement between Church and State, but by the infallible declaration or command of the highest ecclesiastical authority."‡

"From what has been said [namely, that the Pope may only make temporal laws in the Papal States], it by no means follows that the Roman Pope cannot declare civil laws, which are contrary to Divine and canonical right, to be null and void.§ The theory, which calls the Concordats Papal privileges, whilst denying the co-ordination of State and Church, assumes the certain and undoubted doctrine that the State is indirectly subject to the Church. This opinion is based on the Catholic doctrine of the Pope's irrevocable omnipotence, in virtue of Divine right, the valid application of which cannot be confined or restricted by any kind of compact." ||

"As it not infrequently occurs that, in spite of attempted friendly settlement, the dispute [between Church and State] continues, it is the duty of the Church authentically to explain the point of dispute. The State must submit to this judgment."¶

"The most celebrated pronouncements of Pius IX. are the encyclical *Quanta cura* and the Syllabus of December 8th, 1864. There is no doubt that the encyclical *Quanta cura* is an *ex cathedra* pronouncement of the Pope, and is thus infallible. But the Syllabus can also rightly be named a definition *ex cathedra*, although the certainty as to this is less clear than in the case of the encyclical

---

* *Jus Decretalium*, 15 et seq.   † *Ibid.*, 29.   ‡ *Ibid.*, 105.
§ *Ibid.*, 147. || *Ibid.*, 216.   ¶ *Ibid.*, 223.

Quanta cura. Since, however, both documents have received the assent of the bishops, they have both become the certain and infallible rule of conduct."*

The central organ of the Jesuit Order, the *Civilta cattolica*, published for more than fifty years at Rome,† says

" The aim of the civil community or of the State is exclusively temporal happiness. But this is subordinate, in the human being who has an immortal soul, to eternal happiness, to which the Church and the Church alone can lead. In the case of a human being who is both a Christian and a citizen of the State, the duty to obey the Church stands higher than the duty to obey the State, for God must be obeyed rather than man. Consequently the authority of the State is subordinate to the authority of the Church. But the subordination of the State to the Church is not only commanded by reason. This is also the general teaching of the Fathers and Doctors of the Church [the *consensus theologorum*].
Finally, Pope Boniface VIII. expressly teaches in his dogmatic bull *Unam sanctam*, in which he compares the two powers with the two swords mentioned in the Gospel, that the temporal power must be subordinated to the ecclesiastical. . . That which apparently belongs to the domain of the State, such as purely civil and political affairs, is completely assured against all danger of encroachment on the part of the ecclesiastical authority. It is true that the line of demarcation cannot always be clearly discerned at the points of contact. But even here a dispute between State

---

* *Jus Decretalium*, 354 *et seq.* It is very remarkable that the leading Centre organ, the *Kölnische Volkszeitung* (*Literarische Beilage*, 1901, No. 52, p. 399 *et seq.*), bestows great praise on the work of Wernz, calling " its programmatic statements [and the statements given as illustrations are doubtless ' programmatic'] modern in the best sense of the word."

† The *Civilta cattolica* is the recognised mouthpiece of the Vatican. Pius IX. gave it this character in a brief of February 12th, 1866, so that the *Civilta cattolica* could write of itself, " We are not, it is true, the originators of Papal thoughts, and it is not according to our inspirations that Pius IX. speaks and acts, but we certainly are the faithful echo of the Roman See " (Supplement to the *Allgemeine Zeitung* for November 19th and 20th, 1869). Leo XIII. and Pius X. stood and stand in closest relation to the *Civilta cattolica*.

and Church is not permissible. For, since the former is subordinate to the latter, the Church must always settle the dispute which has arisen after courteous remonstrances and reasonable discussions, and the State has no more right to oppose its decision than a lower court of justice to resist the decision of a higher. The Christian principles as regards the relation of the Church to the State are contained in the saying of Thomas Aquinas, ' The temporal power is subjected to the spiritual as is the body to the soul ; and consequently it is no usurpation when a spiritual superior interferes in temporal affairs. A distinction must be made here between three kinds of concerns. In the first place, the purely spiritual, such as public worship, the administration of the Sacraments and the preaching of the Word of God ; these, of course, stand exclusively under ecclesiastical authority. Secondly, the mixed concerns, as, for example, marriage, burial and charitable institutions ; these stand under the power of both, but so that the ecclesiastical authority occupies the higher place and intervenes directly in order to amend and annul anything which the civil laws may have ordained in these matters in opposition to the Divine or canonical laws. Finally, the purely temporal concerns, such as the army, taxes and the civil laws. Although these stand directly only under the civil power, they may indirectly [*ratione peccati*] also fall under the ecclesiastical jurisdiction if, for instance, the laws connected with them promote immorality, or are in any way injurious to the spiritual welfare of the nation. In this case, the laws issued by the civil power may and must be revised by ecclesiastical authority, and rendered void. For it is the duty of the ecclesiastical authority to prevent public sins and to remove the obstacles in the way of eternal salvation. . . . Catholicism asserts the necessity of that harmony which follows from the subjection of the State to the Church. . No distinction must be drawn between individuals and the State ; both have the same duty : the ruler does not live for himself, but for those whom he rules. Consequently, he must so arrange his business that it is in accordance with the necessities and the prosperity of his subjects, and does not hinder but promote the fulfilment of their duties and the attainment of the aim which they have as human beings. If, then, their needs and welfare and the voice of duty necessitate submission and obedience to the Church, the ruler cannot overlook this in the arrangement and guidance of the social life of his subjects. Obviously this holds good in every State, even though the ruler should be heterodox; how much more so where he is a Catholic!

"'The Church is a real kingdom, the kingdom of God on earth, of which Christ is the invisible and the Pope the visible monarch.

It is the duty of every person to be a subject of this kingdom. Every person baptised is, consequently, more subject to the Pope than to any earthly ruler.

"'The Church is not subordinate to the State, but the State is subordinate to the Church. . . . Hence it may amend and annul the civil laws and the temporal decisions of the courts if they are contrary to spiritual welfare; it may check the abuse of the executive power and of armed force, or command the use of the same when it is necessary for the defence of Christian religion. The tribunal of the Church is higher than the civil; the higher tribunal may revise the affairs of the lower, but, on the other hand, the lower cannot in any way revise the affairs of the higher.'"*

The doctrines of the "German" Jesuits of the present time are of special interest. Those of the German General of the Order have been given already, and I will add the opinions of others to his.

The Jesuit von Hammerstein writes: †

"Some superiority of the Church over the State is consequently indisputable; on the other hand, any supremacy of the State over the Church is but an illegal usurpation. But of what nature is that hegemony of the Church? How far does it extend? By what standard is it measured? We reply: The Church has the right, even where statesmen are concerned, 'to bind and to loose all things,' as far as the mission of the Church regards such a 'binding and loosing' as desirable after judicious consideration of the circumstances; *i.e.* all spiritual affairs of States are directly subordinate to the Church, and all temporal indirectly so far as

* Ser. 7, Vol. 5, pp. 139, 148, 276, 280, 647; Vol. 6, p. 19; Ser. 6, Vol. 7, p. 27; Ser. 7, Vol. 6, pp. 291, 301.

† *Kirche und Staat*, Freiburg, 1883.

they are affected by the direct mission of the Church.*
The system which we acknowledge touching the fundamental conception of the Christian and social structure is consequently that of the indirect power of the Church in temporal matters. We not only maintain that this is the more correct view, but simply the correct and only true one.† . . . The Church need not concern itself with temporal matters, but with the incorporation of the temporal (as of the subordinate and individual) into the spiritual. For incorporation is necessary, and no other kind than this is valid.‡ . . . We may thus sum up the entire dominion of the Church (the outer as well as the inner): The Church stands above the State, directly in spiritual, indirectly in temporal or, more accurately, in mixed affairs, *i.e.* in such as, besides their temporal character, have also a sufficient spiritual bearing as far as this extends.§ . . . In virtue of its teaching office the Church possesses the power in case of necessity to define the boundaries between Church and State, for it lies directly within its province to establish the plenary power specially conferred on it by revelation and to instruct the nations on the subject. By this means, however, the task is also indirectly imposed of defining the limits of the political jurisdiction. Not only the relation between Church and State, but also the relations of States to one another and to their dependents are subject to the doctrinal judgment of the Church.|| . . If a State thinks it ought to wage war against its neighbour, it is a peremptory demand of the conscience that it should previously remove any doubt as to the legitimacy and permissibility of the war in some way or other, and if the subjects desire or are compelled to take part in the war they must likewise be clear as to the permissibility of their course of action. If they cannot themselves remove the doubt, it is the duty of the parties concerned to apply for enlightenment to that authority [the Papacy] which Christ has established for the religious instruction of nations.¶ . . . The priests are bound to observe the civil laws so far as they do not contradict the holy canons or are not incompatible with the sanctity of their spiritual status. But they are not subject to the civil laws *quoad vim coactivam*, because they cannot be cited before the temporal but only before the ecclesiastical tribunal for the violation of these laws. Priests can

* P. 117.   † P. 120.   ‡ P. 123.   § P. 125. || P. 133   ¶ P. 134.

only be punished by a temporal judge if the Church hands them over to the temporal arm for some just cause."*

The Jesuit Laurentius writes:

" The rights of the Church with regard to the State, as at present claimed by the Church, are contained in the scheme of the Vatican Council concerning the Church. . . . What was proposed there corresponds well with the teaching of the indirect authority (*cum doctrina de potestate indirecta bene conveniunt*). After rejecting the false doctrine concerning the origin and nature of the civil authority, the scheme sets up the Catholic doctrine concerning the civil authority. It teaches that . . . the judgment concerning the rule of conduct in as far as it is possible to determine questions of morality, permissibility or unlawfulness, belongs, even as regards the State and public affairs, to the highest teaching office of the Church."†

The next quotation is from the Jesuit Lehmkuhl. I have already spoken of Lehmkuhl's importance as a moral-theological authority. Lehmkuhl and his teachings have, however, also a political significance. For it is an interesting fact that, in discussing and voting on the civil code, the Centre Party was guided by the directions of the Jesuit Lehmkuhl; and there seems no reason why it should not again apply to Lehmkuhl as its adviser in other cases also.‡

* P. 141.

† *Institut. juris ecclesiastici* (Freiburg, 1903), p. 643, 644.

‡ Hermann Oncken published in his book, *Rudolf von Bennigsen* (Munich, 1909), a letter by the leader of the Centre party, Karl Bachem, addressed to Bennigsen on July 6th, 1896, in whch Bachem states that in the " Compromise " which the Centre had arranged with the other parties with reference to the civil code, the collaboration " of the German Jesuits, especially of their most prominent authority, P. Lehmkuhl, was of the first importance. In the other discussions, too, concerning the marriage law," Bachem relates further, " we have always enjoyed the disinterested advice of the Jesuits, and if we have succeeded in finding a way enabling the Centre in the final vote to approve the great national work . . . the Jesuits have done outstanding service to our side." Bachem demands as compensation, because " the Jesuits, in an extremely important matter, have

Jesuit Morality and the State

In a commentary on the civil code,* Lehmkuhl minutely criticises Germany's most important code of laws from the point of view of the Divine and ecclesiastical law, and declares there are many things in it which, from the standpoint of the Church's supremacy over the State, must be rejected.

"Because civil law and the natural and ecclesiastical law clash on several points, the Catholic cannot conscientiously avail himself of all the rights which the civil code confers on the citizens of the State; the spiritual director and confessor must in certain circumstances impose a duty which the civil code does not set up."†

This mobilisation of the forces of the spiritual directors and Catholic lawyers (for we must not forget the Union of Catholic lawyers) against the civil code has spread far and wide, for even in 1900 Lehmkuhl's *Commentary* had reached its fifth edition.‡

Lehmkuhl writes in his *Moral Theology*:

"It is evident that an oath taken in accordance with the civil law and constitution can never be binding with reference to laws which are contrary to the Divine or ecclesiastical law. Indeed, if there is a controversy between the State and Church at the time when the oath is required and civil laws are issued or emphasised which are directed against God and the Church, it is not permissible to swear except with reservation and the omission of these laws. But if these [anti-ecclesiastical] laws are, as it were, buried in the codes, although they have not been expressly pronounced invalid

again so brilliantly proved their patriotic attitude," Bennigsen's assistance in the matter of the suspension of the entire Jesuit law, which Bennigsen refused. Germany consequently owes its civil code "in the first instance" to the Jesuits, and especially to the Jesuit Lehmkuhl.

* *Das Bürgerliche Gesetzbuch des Deutschen Reichs nebst Einführungsgesetz*, Freiburg, 1900.

† *Ibid., Vorwort*, p. vii.

‡ Further information as to Lehmkuhl's verdict is to be found in my book, *Moderner Staat und Römische Kirche* (Berlin: C. A. Schwetschke und Sohn, 1906) pp. 80-88.

by the State, it is not then necessary to add such a protest expressly, as the person who takes the oath must reasonably so understand the sense of the oath that it only applies to valid laws. Kenrick and Sabetti [Jesuits] teach the same for America. The same may be said about every oath of allegiance and the military oath; they must also be understood in like manner in ordinary circumstances. Consequently, if a soldier is commanded to do something which is so obviously wrong as to require him to refuse obedience, or if he, through his officer's fault, is exposed to spiritual dangers, it would be better to desert from military service than be exposed to such immediate occasion for sin; the obligation of his oath need not prevent him from being permitted or, under some circumstances, even compelled to leave the colours. Indeed, if anyone is forced to become a soldier [*e.g.* in all States where conscription prevails], it must be considered whether the compulsion were just, or whether the oath be invalid owing to unjust compulsion, or whether it involved an important reason for mental restriction or dissimulation in swearing. . . . The obligation of the oath [*i.e.* of any oath] can be directly removed by the ecclesiastical authority, namely, by the power of the Pope and the bishops, or by others legally delegated in accordance with the will of the Pope."*

But the strongest incitement to the disregarding of civil laws is afforded by the Jesuit Lehmkuhl in his *Conscience Cases*:†

"The priest Remigius, who had been banished from his native land by laws relating to ecclesiastical policy, nevertheless frequently returns in disguise, even for pleasure, exercises spiritual functions and rejoices over the fact that he breaks the laws with impunity. When the functionary Paul, a pious Catholic, hears this, he takes no action, but he is scandalised at the fact that Remigius does not observe the laws issued by the legitimate power, and begs him,

* *Theologia moralis*, I., n. 411, 421, 423, 6 Edit. Friburgi, 1890.

† Moral theology calls imaginary occurrences, which it uses as foundations for the instruction of confessors, "conscience cases" (*casus conscientiae*). The "Conscience Cases" of the Jesuits Gury and Lehmkuhl are best known and most widely circulated.

Jesuit Morality and the State

through a friend, to discontinue such proceedings in future in order that he may not be obliged, should Remigius be denounced to him, to punish him according to his office and conscience. Remigius sends him a jesting reply to the effect that he fears neither laws nor fines; if a fine should be imposed upon him, he has a key at his disposal with which he could open Paul's money chest so as to take from him the money to pay it; if he should be condemned to imprisonment, he has arms and weapons with which he could defend himself. The questions are: 1. How must these laws and penalties be judged? 2. Did Remigius act rightly, or was Paul right to take offence? 3. May Remigius carry out in earnest what he has threatened in jest?

"I reply to the first question that it does not follow that because such laws have been issued by the legislative power they are proper laws. Else we must also call the edicts issued by Diocletian against the Christians proper laws. It has been stated above that, according to the doctrine of St. Thomas Aquinas, it is essential to the existence and comprehension of a law that it should be a reasonable regulation, issued by those who are devoted to the care of the community, and that it must be promulgated. If only one of these conditions is lacking, it is no law; in case of uncertainty the presumption is in favour of the legitimate legislator. Now in the case of these laws, most of these conditions, not one alone, are lacking. They are in truth and reality not reasonable regulations because, for numerous reasons, they are not just, because they violate the superior right of the Church, the right of the priest and the right of the Catholic nation; indeed, they may perhaps even attempt to urge the priest to commit a dishonourable and forbidden action. They do not proceed from a person who is devoted to the care of the community, consequently not from the legitimate authority. For care for religious matters and for the religious community is not incumbent on the State. Consequently the authority has even less legitimacy than if the French Government wished to make laws for the German Empire. If the laws are invalid as prohibitory laws, then the penalty inflicted by them is not legally imposed, but is unjust, *i.e.* these laws are null and void as penal laws.

"To the second question I reply: Remigius is not guilty of

any transgression of the law; for an invalid law is no law. Consequently, whether he returned to his native land for the sake of recreation or to bring spiritual help to others, he did not transgress the law. Therefore his pleasure in the non-payment of the fine is completely free from objection; the rather that the joy at violating this law, which is in itself invalid, is not morally blameworthy. Paul's vexation is consequently unfounded. Generally also such a manner of dealing [as that of Remigius] should not be a cause of offence to Catholics, but rather of edification. If Paul, owing to his faulty education, does not understand that which even uneducated people understand, he must be taught better. Paul unjustly threatens to inflict fines. He has acted rightly up to now by overlooking the matter, because it is not only no duty, but even unpermissible, to carry an unjust law into effect. But he may admonish Remigius and beg him to give up coming back in this way if possible, or to act carefully, so that he (Paul) may not be involved in any difficulties.

"To the third question I reply: This question may take the following form. Is not Paul, if he imposes the fine upon Remigius, obliged to refund it, as a violation of justice has taken place? May not Remigius oppose an attempt at arrest? The first question must be answered in the affirmative if Paul's treatment is objectively unjust, has produced a result and is theologically very sinful. Now Paul's deed is objectively unjust; it produces an actual effect as soon as Remigius is obliged to pay, and there can be no doubt as to the theological sin. Paul, however, may be excused owing to subjective ignorance. In such a case, it is true, he would not himself be obliged to refund; but Remigius, in demanding to be refunded, need not assume this good faith on Paul's part. Although it would be better for Remigius to fall back upon the chief offenders, namely, upon the originators of the unjust law, for repayment, he may yet betake himself to any person immediately concerned in the wrong, especially if the other persons can only be reached with difficulty. A distinction must be drawn in the second question. As the cause for which Remigius is punished is evidently unjust, and this is clear to every reasonable person, his defiance, if conducted without bodily injury to the officials, is not blameworthy, if it is successful. If its failure could be anti-

Jesuit Morality and the State

cipated, or if it would give rise to offence, it would be better to abstain from it. Armed defence, or bodily injury to officials would, as a rule, not be permissible, mainly because it would occasion greater evil and popular disturbances. If, therefore, Remigius were to make use of arms and weapons, not to inflict wounds, but only as a threat, he might easily be acquitted of all guilt."*

Lehmkuhl was attacked by a Catholic critic on account of this "case." In the preface to the second edition of his "Conscience Cases" he replies thus:

"I am blamed because I have permitted a priest, who is expelled by laws which are in themselves invalid because they have no power over spiritual affairs, to disregard these laws even without an imperative reason. But this blame has only strengthened me in my opinion, because I see that it is absolutely necessary to expel that most pernicious opinion from the people, that even unjust and godless laws must be obeyed so long as their neglect is not enforced by a higher law. This opinion lessens the authority of the Church and strengthens tyranny. It must be maintained absolutely that such laws, issued by a usurping power, possess neither of nor in themselves any binding power; but that, if they were ever to be binding, this is only by chance so that greater evil may not arise. Therefore, those who violate such laws, when there is no danger that greater evil will ensue and, as in our 'case,' seek to return to their country for pleasure, are morally right if they do it in an honourable and temperate manner; if they act in an intemperate manner, they are guilty of intemperance, but not of law-breaking."†

TOLERATION, RELIGIOUS EQUALITY AND DENOMINATIONAL PEACE

The hatred expressed in the *Imago primi Saeculi*, in the first half of the seventeenth century, of all those who

---

* *Casus conscientiae*, I., *casus* 22, 2. Edit. Freiburg, 1903.

† *Ibid.*, Preface, p. vii.

hold heterodox views, has remained the key-note of the entire pastoral activity of the Jesuit Order.

"Peace is out of the question. The seed of hate is innate within us; Ignatius is for us what Hamilcar was for Hannibal. At his command we have sworn eternal war [against the heretical wolves] at the altars."*

An enormous mass of books and pamphlets against "heretics" and "heresy" has been published in the course of time by the Jesuit Order. Most of them are tuned to a note in which rage and vulgarity are mingled.

Time and custom have tempered many things. But tolerance, religious equality and denominational peace have never found acceptance among Jesuits. The Jesuit Order regards these foundations of the modern civilised State as symptoms of decay in the structure of the Christian social order. And even at the present day wherever the opportunity offers, especially under the favourite cloak of anonymity, it still spits out poison and gall against all who are not Ultramontane Catholics.

The present General of the Order, Francis Xavier Wernz, says :†

"The Catholic Church undoubtedly considers all religious communities of unbelievers and all Christian [non-Catholic] sects absolutely illegitimate and destitute of every claim to existence. Duly baptised members of non-Catholic Christian sects are formal rebels against the Church if they obstinately persist in their errors. For through baptism they are subject to the absolute and eternal control of the Church. It is, therefore, a grave error to believe that the different Christian sects—for example, the Anglicans, Lutherans, members of the Russian Orthodox Church, etc.—are legitimate parts of some universal Church, and are, as it were, joined to the Catholic Church as sister-churches. . . . The Catholic

* *Imago primi Saeculi*, p. 843.
† *Jus Decretalium* (Romae 1898), I., 13, 52, 113.

Church alone possesses a real ecclesiastical law objectively and subjectively; what is sometimes so designated in the case of other religious communities, whether of unbelievers, Jews, heretics or schismatics, is only an apparent ecclesiastical law (*jus putativum*); it is therefore not permissible to deal in one and the same book with the ecclesiastical law of Catholics, schismatics and Protestants.

. According to Divine right, all duly baptised Catholics, schismatics and heretics, are subject to ecclesiastical law, even against their wish or without their consent."

The Jesuit Lehmkuhl writes :*

"The Catholic Church insists, and has pronounced in recent times through several Popes by solemn decrees,† that it is an erroneous, perverse and absurd assertion, springing from the muddy sources of indifferentism, that liberty of conscience is the individual right of every person. . . . Freedom of cult can at best be regarded as a lesser, perhaps even a necessary evil, so as to avoid greater ones. . . Inasmuch as by the word 'cult' or denomination, an organised society with definite religious aims, which is not in harmony with the [Catholic] Church, is understood, the principle naturally holds good that the denominations separated from the Church have no justified existence; they have no social rights. . . . If denominations separated from the Church are to be regarded as legitimate subjects, it is only in so far as their general aim is to worship God in some way, but not in so far as they are especially Wesleyans, etc. In their concrete form they are characterised by an aim which is godless and false, and consequently falsifies human nature and its claims. In this respect, therefore, they can never attain a jot of true right and true legitimation, even should all kingdoms of the world unite in their favour. . . . It is useless to object that the various sects separated from the Church do not pursue such unnatural aims as heathen superstitions with their many-headed monstrosity. This may be so. But even if the

---

* *Gewissens und Kultusfreiheit : Stimmen aus Maria-Laach*, 1876, pp. 195, 255, 257, 258, 266, 406, 534, 536.

† Gregory XVI., *Mirari vos* of August 15th, 1832, and Pius IX., *Quanta cura* of December 8th, 1864.

error, to which they adhere in good faith, promotes the general aim of the worship of God, good faith and even unmerited error in no way remove from the specific character of the separate sects as such the taint of objective illusion and consequent objective illegitimacy. If good faith sufficed for the creation of an objective and real right, all manner of things might be justified. We are far from instituting a comparison here; but good faith may possibly exist even in the thieves' caste in Madura. . . . It is the duty of the State to be Catholic. A Catholic State and a Catholic prince must always regard the denomination deviating [from the Catholic Church] as an evil."

The Jesuit von Hammerstein says:

"The State, unless it desires to rebel against that power to which it owes its entire authority, must be Catholic, or, if it is not, must become so. We consider it a misfortune that in the delirium for freedom of 1848 and the following years complete civil rights were bestowed upon the Jews." "We regard as a regular and healthy condition that in which the entire population without religious schism acknowledges the [Catholic] Church founded by Christ. . . . On the other hand, we regard as an abnormal condition that in which a large portion of the inhabitants are not Catholics The emancipation of all cults—liberty of worship —should never go beyond the requirements of the individual case. . . . In case of doubt [as to the granting of liberty of worship], enlightenment must be sought from those to whom Christ said, 'He that heareth you heareth Me.' A monarch, even a constitutional one, must, before he signs a law, regarding the admissibility of which he is not absolutely certain, seek instruction, not only from a theologian present at court, but conformably to the importance of the matter [the granting of liberty of worship], from the highest doctrinal authority on earth, whose duty it is to decide in matters of religion and morals, the Vicar of Christ. . Religious equality is a morbid condition which may be required by circumstances."*

* *Kirche und Staat* (Freiburg, 1883), pp. 81, 83, 180–182.

Jesuit Morality and the State

The Jesuit Cathrein says:

"Objectively amongst all Churches the Catholic Church alone has the right to existence, because it alone is the true one. Consequently a Catholic government in an entirely Catholic land must not permit the public exercise of other religious creeds, otherwise it violates the right of the Church. It is not as though a government had to decide what is true or false, revealed or not revealed, but because it has the guarantee of the infallible ecclesiastical authority. And as, according to God's purpose, all governments and peoples should be Catholic, there ought to be only one religious cult on earth, namely, the Catholic, so that all humanity should form one great religious family under the Roman Pope, the Vicar of Christ. . . . But this is an ideal aim which is far from being realised. Actually at the present day in almost all countries different religions are found side by side in peaceful possession. What, then, should be the attitude of a Catholic government in a land with an entirely mixed population towards the different religious creeds? We say a Catholic government advisedly. For a government founded on principles of religious equality must afford the same civil protection to all publicly acknowledged creeds. But a Protestant government must, from its own religious point of view —that of freedom in individual judgment—let its subjects decide which of the Christian religions they wish to embrace. If, nevertheless, Protestant governments frequently persecuted those whose faith was different, this only proved that they were not in earnest in regard to freedom of judgment. Stress was only laid on freedom of individual judgment so long as it could be used against the existing ecclesiastical authority. Besides, a government can only tolerate one particular religious creed and exclude others, if it is absolutely certain of the correctness of the one and the falseness of the others. But, apart from the evident truths founded on reason as to the existence of God, the reward of good and evil in the next world, etc., and some of the fundamental truths of Christianity, a government cannot attain this conviction of itself, but only through the medium of an infallible, supernatural doctrinal authority. A Catholic government can count upon this, but not a Protestant. Is it then permissible for a Catholic government to accord complete freedom of public worship to the different Christian or even heathen (Mohammedan and Jewish) creeds if so many and such different denominations come within its sphere of power? Our answer is Yes, as soon as these can no longer be prevented from existing without occasioning great evil. True, the non-Catholic creeds have no right to existence in themselves; and unity in the true religion is so great a benefit for the State itself that all efforts should be made to maintain it. This, however, becomes morally impossible when once several religious communities have gained a firm footing in a land and cannot be opposed without occasioning greater evil. And, what is more, the Catholic government may even, for very pressing reasons, permit the adherents of other creeds to worship publicly and protect them in this as in their other civil rights. This is civil toleration which must be distinguished from religious toleration. A Catholic of profound conviction and religious education, be he king, minister, mayor or rural policeman, can afford religious tolerance to no adherent of other religions; but the Catholic government may and must afford and practise civil toleration where it has become a necessity."*

The extreme limit of toleration, the killing of heretics, also finds a place in the armoury of Jesuit morals and ethics.

I will pass over the teachings of the most prominent Jesuits of the seventeenth century (Bellarmin, Tanner, Laymann, Escobar, Castropalao, etc.)† and will here only put together a few of the remarks of "modern" Jesuits.

The Jesuit J. L. Wenig, Royal and Imperial Professor, and in 1866 Rector at the University at Innsbruck, says:

"The passing of the sentence of death upon heretics was at any rate not unjust, as the crime of heresy can only be meetly atoned for and entirely prevented from injuring the ecclesiastical

---

* *Moralphilosophie*, II. (4), pp. 563 *et seq.*

† They are to be found in my book, *Moderner Staat und römische Kirche* Berlin: C. A. Schwetschke und Sohn, 1906), pp. 141 *et seq.*

and civil community by capital punishment. . . . We have seen that the ecclesiastical Inquisition cannot agree with the modern ideas as to toleration, enlightenment and humanity, but, for all that, I cry, 'Long live the ecclesiastical Inquisition!' For these ideas are not only unchristian, but also unreasonable, while the mission of the Church which, through the Inquisition, watches over the purity of dogmatic theology and ethics, is divine and consequently independent of the spirit of the age and of circumstances."*

The Jesuit de Luca says:

"First of all the Church merely excommunicated, then imposed fines, then banished, and finally, though only under compulsion, proceeded to capital punishment. For, since heretics scorn excommunication and fines, and if sent to prison or exile, infect others, the only effectual remedy is to send them prematurely to their own proper place. . . . Theologians are so certain that the Church has the right ' at least indirectly ' [through the State as bailiff] to pass sentence of death that some most severely blame those who dispute the right of the Church to inflict capital punishment. Suarez [the chief theologian of the Jesuit Order] says it is a Catholic doctrine that the Church may punish heretics with death."† . . . "It is the duty of the State to punish the heretic with death at the direction and by the order of the Church; it cannot deliver the heretic handed over to it by the Church from this punishment. Capital punishment is not only incurred by those who have apostasised as adults, but also by all who obstinately adhere to the heresy imbibed with their mother's milk. Where this punishment exists, it is incurred by all apostates to heresy, even if they wish to become reconverted, as well as by all who remain obstinate when reproved for heresy."‡ . . . "Heretics and apostates who previously belonged to the Church may be forced by the Church, through bodily punishment and even capital punishment, to return

---

* *Über die kirchliche und politische Inquisition*, 1875, pp. 65, 72, 74.
† *Institut. juris eccles. publici*. Romae, 1901, I., 143, 145.
‡ *Ibid*., I., 143, 145, 146, 261 *et seq*.

to the true faith. This is what all theologians to-day teach in accordance with St. Thomas Aquinas."*

In the *Kirchenlexikon*, the Jesuit Granderath undisguisedly defends the justice of capital punishment.†

He declares that the punishments for heresy—banishment, confiscation of property and death—appear heavy at the present time, "partly owing to the sentimental objection to severe requital of crime, peculiar to our age, and partly to an incorrect estimate of the crime of heresy."

And the Jesuit Laurentius writes in another part of the *Kirchenlexikon* :

"If the Church excludes all those who have taken part in executing a death sentence from service at the altar, it does not follow that this punishment cannot also be inflicted by it. That the Church has really the power, in her own right, to pass sentence of death for severe offences against religious law, has frequently been asserted, but the necessity for such a power cannot be proved, and this authorisation does not clearly follow from Revelation. The Church has contented herself with handing over the culprit to the temporal arm with a request to spare the life of the condemned."‡

The Jesuit Order also gives, as officially as possible, a very significant emphasis to its consent to the capital punishment of heretics, which would scarcely be credited were we not in possession of the authoritative proofs. In its *Ratio Studiorum*, the Jesuit Order permits boys entrusted to it for instruction and education to attend "executions of heretics" :

"They [the pupils] must not go to public exhibitions, comedies, or plays, nor to executions of criminals, except those of heretics." ‖

---

* *Institut. juris eccles. publici. Romae.* I., 270. † V. (2), 1445 *et seq.*

‡ XL. (2), 1827. I have already shown in detail in my book, *Das Papsttum*, etc., I. (5), 180–201, that this "request" was a preposterous piece of malice practised for centuries by the Papacy.

‖ *Inst. S.J.*, II., 541.

Jesuit Morality and the State

It was not till the year 1832 that this sentence, clearly designating the execution of heretics as an edifying spectacle for scholars, was removed from the *Ratio Studiorum*, not because the Order condemned the practice, but "because these words might give offence in various places: *expunguntur haec verba, quia offenderent in variis regionibus.*"*

These are the rigid fundamental principles of Jesuit intolerance, leading at last to bloodshed. A few examples of sectarian persecution will enable readers to complete the picture.

Here also I refrain from quoting Jesuit literature of the sixteenth and seventeenth centuries. It presents vulgarity and filthiness to the full. But neither did people speak nicely on the opposite side, and the polemic bitterness of Jesuitism may be explained and excused by this. I shall quote from Jesuits of the present time.

The Jesuit Tilmann Pesch, who died in 1899, was one of the great literary writers of the German Province. The Jesuit review, *Stimmen aus Maria-Laach*,† to which he was a very zealous contributor, and the Jesuit Reichmann extol him in fulsome fashion as scholar, writer, Jesuit and preacher:

"This is not the place to estimate his full importance and greatness, and perhaps the time has not yet arrived for this."‡

The book, *Christ oder Antichrist, Briefe aus Hamburg*,‖ is Pesch's sectarian and polemic masterpiece. It appeared, according to the favourite Jesuit custom, under the pseudonym Gottlieb. The bulky volume (955 pages) is one long vulgar defamation of Protestantism and the personality of the Reformers, especially Luther

---

* *Monum. Germ. paed.*, 16, 503.   † 1889, Part 10.
‡ Reichmann, S.J., *Briefe aus Hamburg* (Berlin, 1905), 5th edit., preface.
‖ Berlin, 1905, 5th edition, *Verlag der Germania*.

"A historical description of Luther must include an illustration—a summary one, it is true—of the fact that the reforming principles of the great man imply not only the overthrow of political order and of Christian family life, but also the collapse of the entire moral order. Fortunately, the nations which embraced Lutheranism had retained enough conservatism from the pre-Reformation period to preserve them from experiencing all the consequences of Lutheran teaching. Here, too, it is impossible for me to give all the data from Luther's words and works which would demonstrate this characteristic of the Lutheran work of reformation. I will content myself with a little, but this little is quite sufficient for the establishment of facts. I say therefore—and I am not afraid that my assertion will meet with opposition from any thinking person—that he who, in the most unequivocal manner, declares all good works to be sins, who repeatedly clearly and distinctly invites people to sin, *i.e.* to every violation of the Divine command and injury to the conscience, who denies the freedom of the human will, who blusters at every opportunity against the value of human reason, who not only fails to oppose superstition (to which, indeed, many uneducated classes of the people are often unfortunately only too much inclined), but promotes and adopts it, who teaches and practises the principle that the end can sanctify bad means, I say that he who teaches thus and brings forward such teachings consciously and prodigally may be rightly designated as a rebel against the entire moral order. Now, according to the most conscientious and learned criticism, all this is to be found in Luther's writings. And up to the present time no one has been able to disprove this result of learning. Only one thing is certain, that Luther also sometimes wrote the very opposite.* Whoever reads Luther's writings will be surprised to find how frequently and decisively the Reformer brings into prominence the indomitableness of brutal desire in human beings ; men must succumb helplessly to every attack of sensuality. Neither vows nor marriage bonds are to be respected. . . . The case appears in another form when the Reformer continually repeats that all human beings without exception have succumbed to the sin of unchastity and always and everywhere used every opportunity to give free rein to all promptings

---

* *Christ oder Antichrist*, p. 25 *et seq.*

of sensuality. . I am convinced that to all who move in circles animated by Christian life and thought such assertions appear like declarations from another world, a world of morass and misery. And the question intrudes itself: What prompted a man who professed to be a Reformer of the Christian Church, the chosen tool of the thrice holy God, to a view so low and so degrading to mankind? The question provokes a reply which absolutely annihilates the Reformer, if we note the numerous passages in Luther's writings in which he declares in plain words that it is absolutely impossible to overcome the brutal passions. In Luther's opinion, man's vocation does not lie in the sphere of reason —indeed, reason is in his eyes a 'fool' and the 'devil's mistress'— but in that of animal nature. Man's merit, like that of every tree and every animal, lies in being exceedingly fruitful.*

"In the first place, it is acknowledged to be a fundamental dogma of the entire Lutheran system that it is impossible for man to observe any Divine law. . . . It is a necessity, according to Luther's teaching, that every person should sin. In the second place, Luther declares that a Christian may disregard all the Ten Commandments. . . . Like Calvin, Luther also teaches that God has condemned some who did not deserve it, and destined many to condemnation before they were born; he thus incites people to sin, and calls forth all their vices; whatever we do is not done of our own free will, but through necessity. . . Finally, in the third place, the warning against good works follows quite logically, and the repeated invitation to break the commandments and commit sins, particularly to sin in order to annoy the devil.†

"I have just mentioned the temptations to suicide to which Luther, as he himself testifies, was exposed. This reminds me of a few remonstrances which Pastor Walther addressed to me in his missive with reference to my account of the last hours of the Reformer of Wittenberg. I purposely abstained from a more minute exposition for the simple reason that, according to my conviction, from the data which are available up to the present time nothing more can be said about it. Concerning the last moments of his life (referring to the writing, *Wider das Papsttum zu Rom vom Teufel gestiftet*), I said that even Luther's prayer consisted of curses;

* *Christ oder Antichrist*, p. 243 *et seq.*   † *Ibid.*, p. 245 *et seq.*

Regarding Luther's death, it only states that his soul was demanded of him on that night . And, again returning to Luther's death, Pastor Walther gives at the close of his missive a peaceful and extremely edifying picture of the dying Reformer as furnished by Luther's partisans, Jonas and Coelius. For my part, I wish from the bottom of my heart that the poor man had ended a life racked by awful remorse with sincere repentance and had died a holy and godly death. But if Walther expects me to accept the information given by Jonas and Coelius, without further consideration, as the statement of a true event, and see in the impenitent Reformer a dying saint, I think this is, to put it mildly, asking rather too much. I, for my part, also possess an account of Luther's decease, and one which is essentially different. According to this narrative, Luther—to put it shortly—had spent the evening at a cheerful drinking-party, and then feeling sick, was conducted to his room by Count Mansfield's servants; next morning he was found hanging to the bedpost and dead. The true details were kept secret from Luther's friends for obvious reasons, and the rumour was circulated that the great man died a godly and edifying death. For my own part, I attach no importance to this narrative. But what would Pastor Walther say if I expected him to accept this report as the only one corresponding with the truth? Not only he, but his liberal colleagues also, would reject such a demand with righteous indignation. And yet, if Luther, in an evil moment through weariness of life, had given way to the promptings of suicide which he had himself admitted, this would, from the liberal Protestant point of view, by no means be regarded as so terrible. Suicide is quite compatible with the modern ideal of life."*

* P. 357 *et seq*. The Jesuit Reichmann, who has re-edited Pesch's violent book, remarks at this point that the untenability of the account of Luther's suicide has been proved "meanwhile." But he quietly permits the infamous calumny to remain in the text. For it has the desired effect on the readers in spite of the proof, and this is the more certain as none of the proofs are given. It is evident from the following that Pesch wished to implant the belief in Luther's suicide in the historical consciousness of the Catholic people: Once when the Sub-Agent of the Cologne priestly seminary, Dr. Pingsmann, paid me a visit at Blyenbeck, I was walking in the garden with him and Pesch. The latter told us that he had proofs of Luther's suicide; though not absolutely decisive, that did not matter; if rightly presented, the effect on the people would still be to make them believe the fact. Some years later, as we observe, he did " present them rightly."

Jesuit Morality and the State

This huge volume, full of slander and provocation, which on account of its high price could not attain to a wide circulation, did not suffice Pesch and the German Province, of which Pesch was, of course, the instrument. The poison of sectarian strife must penetrate to the masses. Accordingly the Jesuit Pesch and the German Province of the Order originated an undertaking, existing to this day, which is systematically occupied in poisoning the wells and stirring up denominational hatred at a low price—the *Flugschriften zur Wehr und Lehr*, published at Berlin by the *Germania*.

Ever since the appearance in the year 1890 of the first of these pamphlets with the title *Luther and Marriage*, by Gottlieb (pseudonym for the Jesuit Pesch), thousands of these little "green leaflets" have appeared year after year, at 12 pfennigs (1¼d.) a piece, and been scattered broadcast among the Catholics of Germany. Almost all are attuned to a note of violent and spiteful attack on Protestantism. The style is coarse. Here is an instance:

"When the chieftain of the Evangelical Alliance goes on the warpath it is in the eyes of his peoples an event which resounds throughout Europe; the Ultramontanes are seized with panic, and they feel just exactly as in the past the American backwoodsmen must have felt at the news that the Indian chieftain Two-Strikes or Sitting Bull was dancing the war-dance and sharpening his scalping-knife. . . . Doubtless these tactics have advantages which must not be underrated. In the first place all the geese in the Evangelical Alliance will stretch out their necks and break out in a cackle of admiration; what a hero is our Willibald (Professor Dr. Beyschlag)! His rest and recreation after the labours of the term and the festivities in honour of his seventieth birthday consist in the moral annihilation of a Roman Bishop and as an interlude breaking the bones of the whole Catholic Church. And how gracefully he does it! He plays with poor Dr. Korum like a cat with a mouse!"*

* *Die Segnungen der Reformation,* p. 66.

And the coarse style is matched by the contents:

"Every moral licence, every lapse of morality, in Catholicism signifies a perversion, a falling away from Catholic principles. But if once we accept the Protestant principle of 'evangelical freedom' it is only thanks to a most lucky lack of logic if the most serious consequences do not result in the social and moral domain. In the French Revolution French excitability with iron consistency deduced the consequences from the principles of the Reformation. Alas! for us, if German thoroughness should enter on such paths! But what did the Protestants do? They annihilated the three Gospel counsels. . . . To the husband they said: 'The claims of passion are no more bound to give way before the sanctity of the marriage vow than before the vow of chastity.' They whispered into the ears of all men: 'The animal instinct is untamable and unlimited, and justified in all its claims.' . . . All moral excesses, which according to the reports of the societies for promoting morals in all our large Protestant towns are threatening the ruin of the German nation, are absolutely permissible according to the principle, the immediate consequences of which were described by Luther.*

"There is perhaps no other dogma to which Luther remained so faithful during the long period of his reforming activity as this: To have two or more wives is good, but it is better and more advisable to be content with one; this was his philosophy of life in youth and age, which he preached by word of mouth and in writing, at table and in the lecture hall, only not from the pulpit, and to which he never proved unfaithful even in evil days in spite of all attacks. . . . The only logical conclusion to be drawn from the secret Gospel of Luther, Bucer, Melanchthon and other Fathers of Protestantism is that every Protestant is to have as many wives as he pleases, either by dispensation of his consistory or confessor. If we also consider that according to the common Christian and Protestant doctrine men and women have the same rights and duties it follows that a Protestant woman too has the right to have as many husbands as she pleases. This would be logical, but at the

---

* Leaflet No. 80, Professor Beyschlag's *Anklagen gegen den Bischof von Trier,* pp. 1, 27.

same time a very bad thing. The fact cannot be altered even by Luther's maxim: 'Sin boldly and believe even more boldly.' Another logical consequence of the dogma of universal priesthood and Luther's clear pronouncements is that every Protestant can supply his own dispensations and spiritual counsel, so long as he can excuse it before his own conscience and the Bible. Thus we should by perfectly logical means have reached the standpoint of the Berlin roués and prostitutes. Now let some one say that these are not bad Protestants! Is not every logical Protestant necessarily a bad Protestant?"*

The spiteful spirit which pervades the whole of these *Flugschriften* is very clearly expressed in the confession openly set down in leaflet 51–52:

"It is useless to say that we must not offend the convictions of those who hold a different faith. In our view this is only a trick of the devil's, mere ill-applied courtesy and consideration. Such reserve neither serves the cause of truth nor the true welfare of our Protestant brethren."†

PRACTICAL APPLICATION OF JESUIT MORALITY

The many thousand Jesuit confessionals and the many millions of penitents who confide their souls to Jesuit guidance, are the field where Jesuit morality is practically developed. It is a domain of which, although I know it intimately, since I was myself at work on it, I can obviously not speak. I will however quote some historical instances.

Le Bret, in his *Magazin*, gives an extract from a book

---

* *Katholische und Protestantische Sittlichkeit*, pp. 27 *et seq.*

† P. 86. Besides the Jesuit Tillmann Pesch, the originator of the whole undertaking, the Jesuits chiefly occupied in the composition of leaflets were, as long as I remained in the Order, Reichmann and von Hammerstein. As a rule they, like Pesch, wrote anonymously or pseudonymously. Further details about the *Flugschriften* may be found in my pamphlet *Die deutschen Jesuiten der Gegenwart und der konfessionelle Friede* (Berlin: A. Haack).

entitled *Difesa del giudizio iformato dalla Santa Sede Apostolica:*

"When in the year 1624 the Venetian fleet conquered Scio, the victorious General, Antonio Zeno, gave orders that all the Turks should be driven out of the island. About three hundred renegades, whom everyone knew to be Mohammedans, because they had openly professed this religion, took refuge in a mosque and begged for mercy on the ground that they were Christians. The General, surprised, sent Father Carlini, a Dominican, at that time Vicar-General in the Levant, but now Archbishop of Napoli di Romania, to question them about their religion. They cried aloud that they were really Christians. They were for the most part women, who in order to be able to marry Turks, had openly adopted the Mohammedan religion. But having repented their fault they solemnly recanted before the Jesuits, and were permitted by them to continue openly to profess the Mohammedan religion, go to the mosques, and take part in Mohammedan observances, while the Jesuits administered the sacraments to them in secret. When this was reported to the General, he caused the women to be confronted by the Jesuits to whom they had referred, especially Father Lumaca, who had taken the chief part in instructing them. And, in fact, the Jesuits did recognise the greater part of the women as their penitents. These simple people were accordingly pardoned. But a severe reproof was administered to their instructors for not remembering Christ's saying, 'He who denies Me before men, him shall I also deny before My heavenly Father.' I do not appeal to dead witnesses: the worthy prelate of Napoli di Romania, who transacted this matter by public command, is still alive, and can testify of it to any one who desires. Other witnesses, too, are the Archbishop of Corinth, Bernardino Cordenos, the Archbishop's secretary, Antonin Gavazzi, Prior of the Monastery of SS. Giovanni e Paolo at Venice, the Dominican Maria Ferro and Angelus Bevilacqua at Venice, who all testify on oath to the truth of these events.

"When in 1606 Paul V. was at war with Venice, and the Jesuits, on account of their advocacy of the Pope, were driven out of Venice, they tried by every possible means to injure the 'heretical' Republic:

They stole disguised into Venetian territory, and advised the women to refuse to perform their conjugal duties, and the sons to deny obedience to their fathers until the Republic had given way. At Constantinople they stirred up the Turks to war against Venice."*

Louis Sotelo, a Franciscan and Bishop, who was burnt at Foco in Japan, in August, 1624, on account of his faith, wrote in January of the same year from his prison at Omura a letter to Pope Urban VIII., which contains the bitterest reproaches against the Jesuits:

"Although he had been sent from Rome to Japan as Bishop, they had tried to hinder his mission; owing to their fault the Church in Japan was in a deplorable condition, because they would allow no other priests or members of orders but themselves to work there, though the thirty Jesuits could not suffice for the whole of the large territory. They circulated slanders about other missionaries, and forbade the believers to admit them into their homes, although this was a season of persecution. The Jesuits did all in their power to destroy the effect of such testimony. It seemed to them best to deny the truth and genuineness of the letter, and they quoted the statement of a certain John Cervicos as to the inaccuracy of the facts there stated, as well as of Fra Peter Baptista, who maintains that the signature was forged and that not only was it not the hand of his colleague, Fra Louis Sotelo, but did not even resemble it. Unfortunately, however, Dr. Cervicos and Fra Peter Baptista were still alive, and both protested against this statement attributed to them by the Jesuits. One of them proved n writing and swore before a notary and witnesses on October 10, 1628, that the words put in his mouth by the Society [of Jesus] were shameful lies, and the other revoked the doubts which he had at first expressed as to the signature of Fra Louis, and insisted that, after a more careful examination, he believed it to be genuine, and also believed that of the holy martyr to be authentic and worthy of the writer."†

* From letters of Paolo Sarpi in Le Bret, *Magazin*, I., 427 *et seq.*, and III., 542.
† Gioberti, *Il Gesuita Moderno*.

In 1759 the Jesuit Mamachi set the boys in one of the classes of the Jesuit College at Toulouse a composition on this subject:

"Heroes at times commit crimes which are favoured by fortune. A fortunate crime ceases to be a crime. A man whom France now designates by the shameful name of robber will be styled an Alexander if he is favoured by fortune"*

Anselm Feuerbach, quoting from the documents, reports the confession of a Catholic priest, Franz Riembauer, who on November 2, 1807, at Ober-Lauterbach, in Bavaria, murdered his former cook in the most cruel manner. She had borne him a child, and was threatening to denounce him

"When I met the Eichstadt woman at Ratisbon [so Riembauer confessed in November, 1817, to the examining judge at Landshut] she declared her intention of never leaving me. . My honour, my position, my public credit, everything that was of necessity dear and sacred to me, was threatened by the woman's arrival at Ober-Lauterbach. I thought to myself: What shall I do if she comes after all? Then I remembered the principle laid down by Father Benedict Stattler [a Jesuit] in his *Ethica Christiana*, which permits the taking of another's life if there is no other way of saving our own honour and good name; for honour is a greater good than life, and we have the same right of defence against a person who threatens our honour as against a robber. On considering this principle, which Professor Stattler had also formerly expounded to us young theologians in the course of his instruction, I decided that it applied to my case and accepted it as a *dictamen practicum*.† I said to myself: My honour will be

---

* From Reusch, *Beiträge*, pp. 56, 57.

† The principle laid down by the Jesuit Stattler, which fortified the Pastor Riembauer in committing the murder, runs thus: "It is permissible to avert a grievous disgrace by killing the unjust adversary, if no other means are available; if the disgrace has already been incurred, it is not permissible to avenge it by murder, unless there is no other way of making him amend, while there is great

ruined by this wicked person if she comes to Lauterbach and carries out her threats; I shall be removed by the Consistory, shall forfeit my property, and gain an ill name throughout the diocese. Although even at that time I meditated on Stattler's principle and thought it applicable to my case, it was then no more than an idea and I had not yet considered the mode of execution."*

Such are the ethics and morals, the toleration, religious equality and denominational amity taught, both theoretically and practically, in the course of Moral Theology, which the young Jesuit must attend for two years.

My professors of Moral Theology were the Jesuits Frins (afterwards counsellor to the Centre leader Windthorst) and Stentrup. Frins gave expression to his opinion of Protestant morality by emphatically declaring his conviction that every young Protestant girl was morally ruined by the age of fifteen. Another of his utterances was that he could not understand how a married couple could look each other in the face without blushing. Stentrup taught Moral Theology in the narrowest sense of past ages. Progress, civilisation, and the modern state were an abomination to him.

The discussion of Conscience Cases which takes place in all the Houses of the Order once a fortnight, in the presence of all the Fathers and also the Superiors, gives an actuality to Moral Theology during the whole of a Jesuit's life; and it is intended to supply a standard for his duties as spiritual director. At Exaeten, the only house in which I was stationed for any length of time

danger that he will renew the accusation. . . . A grievous calumny may not as such be averted by the previous murder of the calumniator, unless it is clearly oreseen that the unjust calumniator will find credence for his calumny, and there is also no other means of warding off the calumny and re-establishing his injured honour " (*Ethica Christiana communis*, III. (3), 1889–1893).

* *Aktenmässige Darstellung merkwürdiger Verbrechen* (Giessen, 1829), II., 86 *et seq.*

after the end of my scholastic studies, the Conscience Cases were under the direction of Lehmkuhl, some of whose principles I have already quoted. Lehmkuhl, the classic authority in the domain of Moral Theology, is one of the most distinctive types of Jesuitism in the bad sense of the word that I have ever met. Not in the sense of being himself bad; on the contrary, he took the greatest pains to lead a pious and virtuous life in the Jesuit acceptation of these terms. But for that very reason the Jesuit system had taken complete possession of him; the revaluation of moral and ethical conceptions which it contains was incorporated in him.

Another characteristic of Jesuit Moral Theology deserves emphasis. Lehmkuhl, the great authority on Moral Theology, who had a hundred solutions at hand for every case, and in the two volumes of his work on Moral Theology dissects virtue, sin and temptation anatomically into their final components, was in his own person helpless in face of sin and temptation. He was literally devoured by scruples, and afraid at every step of offending God; he confessed, sometimes more than once, every day. At the same time he defended, with a perfectly calm mind, all the enormities which have been discussed in the domain of mental restriction.

Nowhere is the saying of straining at a gnat and swallowing a camel more applicable than in the case of Jesuit morality.

CHAPTER XXVI

EXAETEN*

THE *Examen rigorosum* concluded my scholastic training. Usually this is immediately followed by the Tertiate, the third year of probation (*tertius annus probationis*), which forms the outward conclusion of the ascetic training. I was not, however, sent direct to the Tertiate, but first to Exaeten as a Scriptor.

Nine years had gone by since I entered Exaeten as a postulant, seven since I had left it to begin my scholasticate.

During this time the house had undergone a complete transformation. The novitiate had been transferred from there to Blyenbeck, and the philosophate from Blyenbeck to Exaeten. The German Province had also collected most of its writers there, and finally Exaeten had become the headquarters for the publication of the two periodicals so widely read in Germany, *Stimmen aus Maria-Laach* and *Die Katholischen Missionen*.

These thoroughgoing internal changes had resulted in considerable external alterations: A stately college, with roomy corridors, libraries, and a large and splendid

---

* On two occasions, apart from my novitiate, I was stationed at Exaeten: immediately after the conclusion of my studies, 1887-8, and after my Tertiate, 1889-92. I shall condense the most important events of these two sojourns in one chapter, if only because in my lack of written notes I am unable, after the lapse of twenty-three years, to state exactly from memory which belonged to the first and which to the second sojourn.

chapel, had been added to the old, confined Novitiate House (*Domus Probationis*).

If Exaeten appeared to me new and strange, I, too, entered it as a newcomer and a stranger. Indeed, the transformation which the birthplace of my Jesuit life had undergone was but a weak reflection of the change that had taken place in me.

Full of belief in the Catholic Church, and therefore full of confidence in the Jesuit Order on which she set so great a value, I had crossed the threshold of Exaeten nine years before. Not with youthful lightheartedness—it was only with violent and heavy struggles that I attained the resolution to leave the world and to serve God in poverty, chastity and obedience as a disciple of the Society of Jesus. But a firm belief in the truth of that which had been brought to maturity in me through the atmosphere of my home and the powerful example of an honoured father and a beloved mother, had induced me, not to silence my nature and my deepest individual feelings—that would have been impossible—but at any rate to trample them down, and with the sword of religious idealism in one hand, I had won my way to the entrance of the Order, hoping, with the trowel of prayer and mortification in the other, to erect the tower of Christian perfection which from my earliest childhood had been set before me, through centuries of traditional vision, as a shining sanctuary.

But how had the glory of this tower faded away! Its very foundations were shaken when, after the completion of almost a decade in the Order, I again entered the place where with eager, never-resting effort I had first put in my spade in the endeavour to build it.

The will of the Superior had designated me as a writer (*scriptor*). In the first place, I was to assist with the editing of the papers *Stimmen aus Maria-Laach* and *Die Katholischen Missionen*. The chief editor of these periodicals was the Jesuit Fäh, a Swiss, who also presided over the whole college as Vice-Rector, representing the Rector, Hermes, who had fallen ill, and soon afterwards died.

That Fäh became my superior in a twofold capacity was both fortunate and unfortunate for me. Fortunate, because in him I found a man who, in spite of two decades of Jesuit training—for Fäh had entered the Order very young, straight from the Jesuit School at Feldkirch—had preserved his humanity, who himself could speak a candid word, and understand one when spoken by others; unfortunate, because this very characteristic of his postponed the process of development which was driving me to burst the bonds of the Order, and so hindered my taking the final step. Fäh also boasted in a strong degree what I was already beginning to lack: belief in the Church and its authority as directing the Jesuit Order. True, he once said to me in an hour of sadness, when in distress at being suddenly transferred from Berlin to Brazil:

"If I did not believe in the divinity of the Church which has given its sanction to the Jesuit Order, I should long ago have left it, and should not submit to such harsh commands."

This remark set me thinking. It served me as a support when the divinity of the Church fell in ruins before me, long after I had recognised that the excellence of the Order was a mere delusion.

Among Jesuits who have attained a literary reputation, my more immediate comrades (*Socii*)* at Exaeten were Langhorst, Baumgartner, Lehmkuhl, Beissel, Spillman, Frick, Tillmann Pesch, Cathrein, Epping, Dressel, Dreves,† Pachtler, and Pfülf.

* Socialism may boast that it has given its members the same official designation: comrades, *Socii*, as the Jesuits have used for several centuries.

† Guido Maria Dreves, the celebrated hymnologist, was the son of the poet Lebrecht Dreves, a convert to Catholicism. Dreves, my fellow-pupil at Feldkirch, was an original man of singular gifts. In the autumn of 1909 I accidentally read

With none of these did I enter into any close relation. Indeed, the rule of the Order does not tolerate such intimacy, but I had a good deal of intercourse with all of them during our daily recreation and our walks. None of them, with the exception of Baumgartner, was gifted beyond the average; all, even Baumgartner, had completely lost their individuality in the sense of intellectual originality. The knowledge of some of them was varied, but even this variety was levelled away by the formal uniformity of training and purpose.

During my residence at Exaeten I was drawn towards the Provincial of the German Province, the Jesuit Ratgeb—or rather he was drawn towards me. Evidently he desired to train me to higher things.

The Jesuit Order knows exceedingly well how to exploit advantages of birth, family relations, and the like; its contempt for such worldly things is a mere pretence. It knows very well how great a value such things have for its work among mankind. This work, and nothing else, is concealed under the motto of the Order *Omnia ad majorem Dei gloriam*.

When such outward advantages are combined in any individual with "virtue which exceeds mediocrity" and "knowledge sufficient for teaching philosophy and theology satisfactorily," this individual is specially adapted to render great services to the Society of Jesus. And such an individual was I for a long time in the eyes of my Superior. For many years, during the many "Statements of Conscience" which I had to make to my Superior, I was told that I was making good progress and should become a very useful tool for the service of God. When

in a South German paper that he had died as a secular priest in the neighbourhood of Munich—he must, therefore, have left the Jesuit Order. With his strong individuality he never really belonged there. His bigoted mother, who was body and soul under Jesuit dominion, and lived at Feldkirch as a widow till her death, induced him to enter the Order—her fortune probably went the same way.

Exaeten

my scholastic training was concluded, and a year afterwards my ascetic training also, this general and theoretic recognition of my utility took a distinct and particular direction, and it was the Jesuit Ratgeb who gave it this form, through special marks of confidence. One of these, my mission to Berlin, will be treated in the next chapter. Others may be mentioned here.

In regular long conversations Ratgeb instructed me in the method of government of the Jesuit Order. Sometimes he came to my room for this purpose, on other occasions he let me come to him. They were informal discussions in which many subjects were treated which, however, all clearly had the aim of initiating me in the true nature of Jesuitism. For a long time—before the final collapse of my Catholic religious edifice—I had been a docile pupil, *i.e.* I followed the expositions of my Provincial with zeal and interest; but then I became so indocile that the confidential conversations ended somewhat abruptly, and with a sharp discord. From that time the Jesuit Ratgeb disliked me as much as he had formerly favoured me. Two of these notes of discord may be emphasised:

Our conversation had turned on the relation of the Jesuit Order to the Papacy since the restoration of the Order by Pius VII. in the year 1814. With one exception, Ratgeb pronounced a favourable judgment on the successors of Pius VII., Leo XII., Pius VIII., Gregory XVI., Pius IX., and Leo XIII., *i.e.* he regarded them as friends to the Order— for a true Jesuit has no other standard of judging matters of ecclesiastical or secular history and personalities than that of friendship or opposition to the Order. The exception was Leo XII. Why this Pope was supposed not to have been well disposed to the Jesuits I could not clearly understand from Ratgeb's utterances, but two things were startlingly clear: the hatred with which the influential Jesuit judged the anti-Jesuit Pope, and the calm determination with which he expressed the necessity of getting rid of such opponents. Ratgeb's words, which were indelibly impressed on my memory, were these: " Do you think that it is impossible to get rid of Popes who oppose the interests of the Order ? "

I could only understand his words in one sense, and my terror at their meaning must have been expressed in my face, for after a penetrating look into my eyes, Ratgeb suddenly passed on to a different subject.* I am thoroughly aware of what I am writing here; but the words I heard, and the impression they made upon me, are facts.

Here is a second note of discord: Ratgeb had been enlarging on the influence of the Order at royal courts and on prominent persons; he let drop the names of the Jesuits Lamormaini, Vervaux, La Chaise, and others. There was something peculiarly observant in his glance as he said to me:

" Will you accept the post of tutor to the sons of the Austrian Ambassador in Paris ? "†

Abruptly I answered, " No," and abruptly I was dismissed by the Provincial. That was the end of our intimate conversations. I had a feeling that the offer of this post was a test. Ratgeb, who was no longer quite sure of me, wanted to know whether I was suited for higher things. How matters really stood with me at that time—that the Jesuit system had become a horror to me, and the Catholic Church a mere ruin, that my gaze and will were fixed on a separation from both—of course he could not guess.

In my place another Jesuit received the post of tutor

* Leo XII., as a matter of fact, died suddenly after only three days' illness, on February 10th, 1829. *Cf.* Wiseman, *Recollections of the Last Four Popes.*

† The Austrian Ambassador in Paris was Count Hoyos Sprinzenstein, whose three sons at that time were between eleven and fourteen years of age; one of them is now Secretary to the Legation at the Austrian Embassy in Berlin.

refused by me, which, of course, was made to serve the political influence of the Order.

Here is another proof of confidence. In the summer of 1889 the Provincial Ratgeb sent me with the Jesuit Tilmann Pesch to Mayence, to take part in a political conference to be held there in the house of a Bishop, Dr. Haffner.

There were present: Windthorst, Prince Löwenstein (now a Dominican), the Bishops of Mayence and Trèves (Dr. Korum), the chief editor of the *Germania*, Dr. Marcour, the deputies Lieber and Racké (who was murdered at Christmas, 1908, by his own son); my uncle, Baron Felix von Loë; and three Jesuits, I, Tilmann Pesch and Frins (the future legal adviser of Windthorst in Berlin). A great social-political and " apologetic " undertaking was to be founded. The exchange of opinions was very lively. Windthorst, a cunning politician, and legal assistant to the Protestant Duke of Cumberland, represented the milder tendency towards persons of a different faith. Bishop Korum of Trèves and the Jesuit Pesch were in favour of sharp and extreme measures, and let fall characteristic remarks. Thus, for instance, when Professor Dr. Beyschlag of Halle and his activity against the Roman Church were under discussion, Pesch asked : " Is there no means of attacking him in his private life ? " Very typical of ultramontane Jesuit fighting methods ! The discussion, which led to no definite result, lasted many hours. But for all that, there in Mayence the idea of a fighting denominational organisation which should help to win members for the Centre Party took shape, and was finally realised in the " National Union for Catholic Germany." And the Jesuit Pesch who, in spite of the great assistance of Korum, Bishop of Trèves, had not succeeded, owing to the opposition of Windthorst in calling into being an " apologetic " Union of Agitation, soon afterwards began on his own account to stir up denominational hatred in his *Flugschriften zur Wehr und Lehr.* In this he was most willingly supported by the Berlin paper *Germania,* which undertook the publication of the venomous review, and carries it on to the present day. The then business manager of the *Germania,* who called himself "Director," a certain Max Muschik, who, unless I am mistaken, soon afterwards had to make himself scarce on account of his "directorial" activity, also took part in the Conference.

As yet I have said nothing about the *vita communis* in the Order—the manner of our daily common life. I do not refer to the external arrangements, which found expression in the daily routine, but rather to its inner character, the tone of the intercourse, the relation of the individuals to one another, and so forth.

Since a Jesuit's day contains only two periods of recreation, an hour after dinner and another after supper, and as with few exceptions walks take place only twice a week, while at other times the rule prescribes silence for the whole of the day, and visits in different rooms are only allowed by special permission of the Superior, there is but little opportunity for personal social intercourse and for the exercise of the virtues—natural and "supernatural"—which it calls forth.

In general, it may be said that the tone in these common recreations was good and cheerful. Serious disagreements, and marked unpleasantness and enmities, were exceptional. All tried to accommodate themselves to one another. Still, the virtues which manifest themselves in the common life of the Jesuits are in no respect greater than those manifested in any good family life. On the contrary, they are far less, for the Jesuit has only twice a day, for a short time, the opportunity of exercising these virtues — amiability, pleasantness, adaptability, self-sacrifice and unselfishness—while in a well-ordered family they have to be exercised all day long, from morning till night. But in one respect the life in the Jesuit and other Orders is exactly on a par with the secular life so greatly despised by the members of the Order. Human weaknesses, such as envy, dislike and friction, are to be found here as there.

During my membership of the Order I only witnessed one case of excess, or rather its consequences, during the recreation hours. A Jesuit returned from one of his frequent excursions in a state of considerable intoxication, and as the evening recreation happened to be in progress, he shared in it in a more than " animated " condition. It was a most unpleasant scene, the more unpleasant since the person in question, even when sober, was a noisy chatterbox. I never heard that this serious excess on his part was reprimanded by the Superior, as should certainly have been done. I have not mentioned this circumstance in order to throw stones at the Order or the particular Jesuit, but only to prove the evident fact that the sanctity of the life in the Order does not exclude considerable excesses. This Jesuit was one of the most distinguished writers of the German Province.

What does not the ordinary Catholic layman behold in the Jesuit Order—and indeed in all Orders ! And how very different is the reality within their walls !

They—by " they " I mean Catholic circles who see in the Order " the highest state of Christian perfection "— form most exaggerated conceptions of the perfection of its members. In reality they are, and remain, human beings. Only the strict seclusion which they have erected as a wall between themselves and the rest of the world, enables them to produce the impression of something superhuman and specially holy. The virtue of the members of an Order which is surrounded and guarded by hundreds of rules and fences, which knows itself watched at every

step by Argus eyes, and thus has scarcely an opportunity for stumbling and falling, is on that very account far less genuine and robust than the virtue of the man of the world who, in the midstream of life and its temptations, has to preserve it by fighting.

The life of men and women in Orders is easy and pleasant when once the first conflict caused by the parting from family and home is passed, and for many this parting does not even occasion a conflict.

While the Christian of "lower grade," the "man of the world," as he is contemptuously called by the members of the Order, is consumed with anxiety as to the sustenance of himself and his family, the men and women in Orders live a life of ease; everywhere their house is built, their table spread, their bed prepared*; and the quaint irony of the circumstances consists in this—that their house, table, and bed are prepared for them by the charitable offerings of the men of the world who "stand far below them in perfection," and are troubled by all the cares of life.

If only the laity knew the real state of things as regards the convents and their inmates, then no reform by the spiritual authority, nor restrictive legislation by the temporal, would be needed to call forth a truly Christian evangelical perfection in the numerous settlements of the Order, or to bring the parasitical existence of so many hundreds of them to a well-deserved end.

But there is one really dark side to the Jesuit common life.

The system of supervision and espionage which permeates the Order, the mutual denunciation declared to be a rule and duty, make innocent intercourse and comradeship and friendship absolutely impossible. This last,

---

* From this freedom from care and anxiety I must exempt the nursing orders. They impose severe duties in hospitals and asylums on their members, and often demand heroic sacrifices from them. But here too we may say that countless secular male and female nurses do the same.

indeed, is expressly forbidden. One Jesuit does not show himself to his fellow-Jesuit as he is, but rather as he would like to appear. He has no friend to whom he may freely open his heart. Thus members of the Jesuit Order never approach one another closely, and therefore Jesuit common life knows nothing of intimacy, in which consist the savour and sweetness, the refreshment and strength, of human intercourse.

Discipline prevails in the Jesuit Order, in spite of all human failings and the very comfortable life led there. This discipline is above all manifest in the promptitude with which a Jesuit lets himself be sent hither and thither —literally from one end of the earth to another, sometimes from one day to another. Here readiness for sacrifice and self-denial are displayed in an amazing fashion; every difficulty is overcome, health and life are sacrificed without the slightest demur. Still, even here there is a "but"; I do not wish in any way to minimise the undeniable heroism of the Jesuits, but has not every profession its self-sacrificing and courageous heroes? Are there not "martyrs of science" as there are martyrs of faith, and have not hundreds and thousands of soldiers spilt their heart's blood as readily for the flag as a missionary for the Cross? If all those are to be canonised and beatified who have held high their ideals in a life of renunciation and sacrifice, or who have sealed with their blood their endeavours and convictions, there would not be room in the world for the necessary altars, on which would stand the images of men and women of all professions, among them hundreds and thousands of such as were not Christians at all, who believed neither in God nor a future life. Therefore, with all due recognition of the heroism shown by Jesuits, and other religious orders too, the rest of the world, believers and unbelievers alike, may say to them, "We too have our heroes."

It is owing to the narrow education of Catholics that they know scarcely any martyrs and saints except their own; indeed, they object to the expression "martyrs of science." This was my case too for several decades; but when, in later years, I saw before me the heroism of humanity, independent of religion and creed, in heroic men and women, when I observed the numbers of those who had sacrificed themselves for purely human objects and aims, then the haloes around the ecclesiastical saints and martyrs began to pale, and from thence forward I saw in them only men who, like many thousands of others, had sacrificed themselves for their ideals. The comprehension of this truth helped me greatly in my separation from the Church and the Order.

Let us, then, allow the Jesuit Order its heroism, but let us give it the place that it deserves, side by side with the millions of heroic men and women of all professions, all nations, all religions, and even of no religion.

Besides my literary labours, of which I shall have to speak later, I also undertook pastoral work at Exaeten—or, rather, from this place as a centre. In this respect, too, I enjoyed the special confidence of my Superiors. Confession, preaching, giving Exercises, missions, conferences (learned and religious discourse), in short, the whole domain of Jesuit spiritual direction was open to me.

I will give some details. Missions (popular missions) are exercises for the masses. Their momentary but very transitory effect on the people is immense, and in particular the confessionals are besieged. I took part in an unusually large mission at Gelsenkirchen in 1889 or 1890. Fourteen Jesuits were literally occupied day and night; from early morning—four o'clock—till eleven or twelve at night, they heard confessions. The whole town was in a state of feverish excitement. This religious fever and nervous excitement are special characteristics of a mission. That they also have good effects cannot be denied, but the manner in which these are produced is absolutely opposed to the simple religious spirit of the Gospel. Everything is suggestion—there is no inward and personal contemplation. Externals prevail.

A typical example of the external character of the spiritual direction peculiar to Jesuits is related quite ingenuously by the Jesuit Rist.*

In a report to his Superiors the Jesuit Sarrazin there relates how, when at Erfurt in the winter of 1870-71, he prepared a French prisoner for death:

"All admonitions had been in vain. At last the Jesuit sent word to the sick man, through the Sisters of Mercy, that by acting thus he was providing for himself a funeral without the attendance of a priest.

"'What! A priest would not then follow my corpse?'

"'Certainly not; none would be allowed to accompany you.'

"'Well, then, you may go quickly and fetch the priest.'

"On the very same evening he received the Last Sacraments, and was thus prepared for death, which followed a few days afterwards."

Such conversions, through purely external means such as the absence of a priest at a funeral, are in complete accord with Jesuit moral teaching, as expounded, for instance, by the Jesuits Le Roux and Slaughter:

"Ivenin thinks that it results from our teaching that a man who has lived a godless life for forty years can, by mere 'attrition' (penitence through fear of eternal punishment) receive the sacramental absolution, and

* *Die deutschen Jesuiten auf den Schlachtfeldern und in den Lazaretten*, 1866 und 1870-71.

immediately afterwards lose his reason through a fatal illness, and yet have a right to everlasting salvation, even though he never loved God, not even at the end of his life. To this we unconditionally assent."*

"It may happen that a man attains salvation who has often transgressed all God's commands, and has never fulfilled his first command of love—that is, if he receives the Sacrament with mere attrition, and dies immediately afterwards."†

The contrast between Christianity and Jesuitism can scarcely be more clearly demonstrated. But it is comprehensible that such practice and theory produce great spiritual results, the duration of which is, however, in proportion to the crumbling nature of its foundation.

Thus, as in the case of the Exercises, sermons on death, the judgment and hell are the real centres of gravity of the missions. By these the hearers are belaboured most effectively, and converted through fear.

For the spirit in which the missions are often conducted, a passage from a letter by the Jesuit Johannes Gastel, of March 25, 1685, from the South American Mission, is characteristic :—

"With a view to avenging the death of the abovementioned Fathers [three Jesuits had been murdered by the Caribs, near the Orinoco], fifty Portuguese soldiers and four hundred Indian bowmen will soon be sent out to kill as many of the Caribs as possible. There is no better method for subduing the savagery of barbaric nations than to drive out tyranny with tyranny, and to inspire fear, so that they may not attempt anything similar in future."‡

The Jesuit Aloysius Pfeil also relates a circumstance

---

* Le Roux, S.J.

† Slaughter, S.J. Quoted by Döllinger-Reusch, L, 80.

‡ From the Jesuit papers in the State Archives. Friedrich, *Beiträge*, p. 38.

which reveals a similar lack of the religious and Christian conception of the missionary vocation.

"At that time Portuguese and Indian troops were sent out from San Luiz de Potosi to subdue the tribe of the Tramambases, who inhabit the interior of Maragnon, to Christ and the King of Portugal, if they did not surrender of their own free will. The faithful soldiers who marched into battle were accompanied by Fr. Peter Luiz."*

That the Jesuit missions were conducted in the same spirit, as regards heretics, is a matter of course, but it is also strikingly demonstrated by a letter from the Jesuit Bobadilla, one of the first comrades of Ignatius Loyola, to the Roman King Ferdinand:—

"But Bobadilla had never been so inwardly glad and happy as when he beheld the Spanish and Italian cavalry who had come to Germany for the Smalkaldic war, for these were the true instructors to convert the heretics."†

An interesting communication is made by the Jesuit Mundwiler in a treatise on the Jesuit von Waldburg-Zeil, of the noble house of Zeil, who had attained great celebrity in Germany as a popular missioner:

"The General, Johannes Roothaan, who had been expelled from Rome, summoned the Jesuits scattered throughout Westphalia to a conference in Cologne in the year 1849, when he was on a journey from Trèves to Belgium. There were present, besides the General Roothaan and his companion, the Jesuit Villefort, the Jesuits Minoux, Behrens, Devis, Joseph von Klinkowström, Stoppar, and Burgstahler. Count Joseph zu Stolberg-Stolberg, founder of the St. Boniface Union, himself an ex-Jesuit, also took part in the discussions. They resulted in the decision to revive the Popular Missions, and at the call of the General, Father Roothaan, and the Provincial,

* From the Jesuit papers in the State Archives. Friedrich, *Beiträge*, p. 38.
† The letter is quoted by Druffel, *Beiträge zur Reichsgeschichte*, I. 20.

Father Minoux, the following Jesuits went as missioners to Germany: Ketterer from England, Max von Klinkowström from Australia, Roh from Belgium, Hasslacher from France, Anderledy and Pottgeisser from America.

"The Jesuit residences at Cologne, Bonn, Coblence, Mayence, Münster, Paderborn, Ratisbon, Gorheim, which became centres of the missionary network spread over Germany, also owe their origin to the Cologne conference of the year 1849."*

And in spite of the expulsion of the Jesuit Order from Germany in 1873, the Jesuits continue to the present day in the most various parts of the Empire to carry on their missions undisturbed, and in this way to perform one of the most effective pieces of work conducted by the Order.

I gave Exercises to schoolboys, students, gentlemen, ladies, girls, nuns, in private houses and educational establishments; and in spite of my youth in the Order, I was even designated to give Exercises in the priestly seminaries. The insight I thus obtained into all the circumstances of ultramontane Catholic life, even on its political side, was extremely instructive. But, on account of their religious and confidential character, they cannot be reproduced.

One circumstance in connection with the Exercises (though not given by me) I can communicate, as it was long ago made known to the public. It shows how the essentially religious Exercises may also be utilised for political purposes. It also contains a characteristic picture of Jesuit sentiment.

The Federal Deputy and President of the Senate, Dr. Petri, wrote, on March 17, 1895, to the publisher of the *Deutscher Merkur:* "Shortly before the Convents Debate in the Prussian Lower House I received a letter from the Chief District Judge, F. Beck, dated from Heidel-

* Georg von Waldburg-Zeil, S.J. (Freiburg, 1906), p. 77 *et seq.*

berg, May 4, 1875, of which the original is at your service, which contains the following passage:

"'The Jesuit Roh, in 1851, when directing Exercises at St. Peter's (in Freiburg), said: "Our ultimate aim is to overthrow the Hohenzollerns—keep that before your eyes. And if you betray it, it will be denied. The convents and ecclesiastical associations will know how to solve this problem."'"

This was told me by Pastor Napper, who had heard it himself, and pledged his word of honour to its truth.

The only disproof of this credible and well-testified utterance of the Jesuit Roh consists in a statement made by the Episcopal Chancellery in Freiburg, which, however, does not bear on the matter:

"In the minutes (!) nothing is to be found about this expression; in view of § 15 of the Prussian Constitution, and the disposition of Frederick William IV., there was not the shadow of an excuse for any expression to the effect communicated; there was no such person as a Dr. Napper, only one called Nopper, who had, however, on one occasion expressed himself as unfriendly to popular missioners, and, therefore, there could scarcely be a less dependable witness for the Chief District Judge Beck than this man."

Everywhere and always I tried to give my best to the people who turned to me in their religious difficulties—little as that may have been. But even when my belief was no longer Catholic I endeavoured to maintain the faith of others. As long as I outwardly bore the character of a Jesuit and priest, I had to give those who turned to me, trusting in this character, that which was due to my seeming, and to what they saw in me. That I regarded as my duty.

Only twice in the very last period of my outward adhesion to the Order and the Church did I act differently.

On those occasions I allowed the man in me, and not the scholastic theologian and Jesuit, to find utterance—in relation to a woman who had murdered her child, and a student.

The murderess, who had many years previously, out of shame and despair, killed an illegitimate, prematurely born child, incapable of life, directly after its birth, and whose action had remained undiscovered and without consequences to others, desired, being urged to it by her confessor, to give herself up to justice. Meantime she had contracted a happy marriage, and her denunciation of herself would have brought great suffering and trouble on her own and her husband's highly respected families. I brought her to see that the destruction of this premature birth, which was incapable of life, was no great sin, and that the self-denunciation required by her confessor would have been an absolute crime.*

I freed the student of his belief in an everlasting hell, which was torturing him into despair. Farther on I shall return to this inhuman and irreligious "dogma."

Many a confession have I heard in Germany, Holland, Belgium, England. Obviously I cannot give details here, but a general remark may not be out of place.

Ultramontanism under Jesuit direction has collected for itself out of the religious conception of confession a powerful means for subduing to its own service Catholics of all classes in every relation of life—private and public—

* Many persons may perhaps disapprove of my decision that the murder of this illegitimate child, incapable of life, was no great crime on the mother's part. I could give very good reasons for my opinion, but I avoid doing so, as I have not mentioned this case as a specimen of my ethical and moral views, but only to show that in the last period of my priestly and Jesuit labours the human being who thought freely, if perhaps mistakenly, was beginning to oust the dogmatically trained, unfree Jesuit. The demand of the confessor for self-denunciation is, however, not to be set to the account of ultramontane Catholic moral teaching, but rather to the individual fanaticism and folly of the priest in question; still it shows what harm the influence of an uncritical, inexperienced, and fanatical confessor may bring about.

for its own secular and political aspirations after dominion. That piety also is developed in confession and spiritual consolation supplied is a matter of course, else indeed the confessionals would soon stand empty. But the religious effect of confession has become a secondary matter, although the confessing masses are not aware of it. Its main end is the influencing of men—citizens, politicians, and others.

Reinhold Baumstark has given an effective description of the disastrous influence of the Jesuit Order in this respect.*

And yet, non-religious as confession has become through the methods by which it is carried on, though it actually has become the centre of a state within a state, it yet remains and must remain a *noli me tangere*. The Jesuit Order knows this, and on this knowledge rest the exploitation of confession and spiritual direction for its own governing ends. The final aim of all its missions, exercises, conferences, and prayers, is confession. In this it possesses a lever with which it can move the world, in the first instance the ultramontane Catholic world, along its own lines.

This Jesuit exploitation of confession is as old as the Jesuit Order itself. For this we have the very competent testimony of Pope Clement VIII. (1592–1605):

"I should like to know what they [the Jesuits] do every day for three or four hours in the confessional, with persons who confess every day. I cannot help inferring from their proceedings the truth of the reproach brought against them, that they use confession as a means for obtaining knowledge of events taking place in the world."†

To my great joy, still vivid within me, I may say that I myself, in spite of the Jesuit ultramontane training, never became a Jesuitical ultramontane confessor. I also

---

* *Cf.* my work, *Das Papsttum*, etc., II., 512 *et seq.*
† From J. Friedrich, *Beiträge*, p. 49.

confined confession, as far as possible, to the actual statement of sins; I never tried to use it for penetrating into family and private affairs. All such revelations on the part of penitents were stopped by me with the remark "The object of confession is the statement of sins."

In other respects too I was an un-Jesuitical confessor. The frequency of confession, carried by Jesuitism beyond all bounds, was energetically combated by me.

Weekly, even daily confessions, have transformed Jesuit piety, and even more the desire of the Order to obtain the rule over men, into a far-spread abuse. The commands of the Church only lay down the duty of confessing once in the year, and are far from advising daily confession. Even though I did not advocate a single annual confession, I did my best to stop too frequent confessions. They are injurious: they make men terribly dependent on their confessors for their religious life, and they foster the whole race of scruple-mongers and bigots who do so much harm to themselves and others.*

I was also employed in spiritual direction within the Order. For a long time I had the office of "giving" to the lay brothers the points for their daily morning meditation. This means that I set the subject of meditation before them, and expounded it. I enjoyed my intercourse with these simple people, and I believe that my manner, too, was congenial to them.

It is one of the most characteristic traits of the Jesuit Order that it deliberately tries to maintain its lay brothers in a state of "simplicity"—that is, in as great a state of ignorance as possible. The Constitutions lay down, in two places:

"The lay brother [*coadjutor temporalis*] is not to learn more than he already knew before he entered the Order."†

---

* *Cf.* my remarks on children's confessions in Chapter II.

† Exam. gen., VI. 6.

"None of those who are admitted for the purpose of domestic offices are to learn reading or writing, or, if they have learned already, to continue their studies."*

It is evident that the Order does not wish to expose those on whose regular and daily work the security and regularity of its outward life depend to the "dangers" of education, which might perhaps introduce unrest into the ranks of these useful serfs.

Another not unimportant spiritual office which was allotted to me was that of confessor at the renewal of vows.

Every Jesuit, until he takes his last vows, whether as formed coadjutor or as professed, must twice a year (usually in February and June) renew his vows. The renewal (*renovatio votorum*) is preceded by a *Triduum* with special spiritual exercises and a general confession covering the period since the last renewal.

For this half-yearly office, special extraordinary confessors are appointed, so that at any rate twice in the year there is a possibility of unburdening the conscience to another than the regularly appointed confessor. Of course, the extraordinary confessor is bound to seek from the Superior the right of absolution for "reservation cases" which may be confessed to him, or else to direct the penitent to seek absolution for his reserved sin from the Superior. Thus the Order here too, in spite of apparent slackening of the reins, maintains control at any rate over the more serious lapses of its members.

But my proper office at Exaeten was, as I have already said, that of Scriptor.

I served my apprenticeship from the lowest stage. I had to correct proofs, and write trial articles, which underwent correction, and so on. For this good training I am sincerely grateful to the Order. But

* Reg. comm. 14.

that I was a good pupil may give the Order less cause for gratitude.

Very soon I was set to independent and scholarly work. Church history, especially that of the Popes, was to be my special subject, and it corresponded in every way to my inclinations.

With what a high conception of the purity, even divinity, of this history did I approach my task! I never suspected at that time that this study would have such terrible consequences for me: the collapse of my faith, its abandonment, separation from Church, Order and the whole of my past life. I call these consequences terrible. For although I recognise the great value that they were in my life, and though I appreciate the light that they kindled within me, yet the conflict I had to endure and the sufferings I had to bear were terrible, and the remembrance of things past, irretrievably lost, is, in spite of all that I have gained, a lasting and ever-painful open wound.

It is impossible to forsake sanctuaries, honoured for decades out of the depths of a believing soul, to burst through bonds which from the home of childhood upwards have been twined round youth and manhood, without the bitterest suffering. And yet I thank the fate, though it seems to have been a blind one, that led me, by the hand of the Jesuit Order, to the road which at last brought me freedom.

Two stages on this road to freedom were of special importance—Brussels and Berlin.

The Jesuit Fäh, my two-fold Superior, sent me to Brussels in order that I might there, with the assistance of the Bollandist Library,* carry on more exact studies in the history of the Papacy than the literary resources

* The Bollandists are, in a sense, a literary republic within the Belgian Province of the Jesuit Order, with their own library and their own establishment; but, of course, they are subject to the general Constitutions, rules, and Superiors of the Order, like all other Jesuits.

at Exaeten would have rendered possible. I also received permission to use the public libraries of the Belgian capital.

In the Jesuit de Smet, at that time Superior of the Bollandists, I found an amiable and ever-ready guide in my studies. That he, as I firmly believed, was a sceptic in no way detracted from his human excellence.

My time at Brussels was but short, but I made good use of it, and the study of historical works, which were not written from the ultramontane Catholic standpoint, but dealt with Church and Papacy in a free spirit, from a purely scholarly point of view, was a revelation to me. At the age of thirty-eight I read such works for the first time! Such things then existed? The Papacy and Church could be approached from another side? Their history consisted not only of light, but even of darkest shadow?

Such questions and thoughts stormed in upon me like a flood, and caused walls to totter which had hitherto blocked out every view of the "other side" of the "Divine" Church and the "Divine" Papacy.

On my return to Exaeten, I hinted to the Jesuit Fäh some of the impressions I had received. The serious character of the impressions made on me at Brussels cannot have been quite clear to him—perhaps on account of my very guarded report—for he only made a few casual remarks about "temptation" and "struggle." But very soon temptation and struggle came my way through his agency, though in a very different manner from that meant by Fäh.

One day he said to me: "Windthorst wishes the question of the Papal States to be brought forward again; in the first place, the *Laacher Stimmen* are to publish articles on the subject, showing the necessity of the Papal States for the freedom of the Pope. Afterwards the articles are to appear as a pamphlet; set to work at once, and write the articles. Unlimited space will be at your disposal in the *Laacher Stimmen*."

When I received this order—for an order it was—a tumult had already broken out within me, for my reason and will were fighting on this very subject of the Papacy. Even the dogmatic religious difficulties to which I have before alluded had fallen into the background before the questions: Is the Pope the Vicar of Christ? Is the Papacy of divine origin? Is it an infallible guide in religion and morals? Whether Christ is actually and really present in the consecrated host is a matter of enormous importance for the religious life of the Catholic Christian, and especially of the priest; but, after all, it is a question of faith. But whether the Papacy has played that particular part in the world, whether in religion and morals in the course of centuries that blessing has proceeded from it which its divine origin and its divine mission would of necessity demand—these are questions of history to be solved by historic means.

And I had already looked too deeply into ecclesiastical and Papal history in the Brussels libraries to be able to give a cheerful and unhesitating assent to these questions.

Therefore the order to defend the Papacy, and defend it as a divine institution, which would suffer wrong if it did not also receive the position of a temporal sovereign with territorial possessions, was a hard one for me. I tried to evade the task by pointing to others of better ability and more learning. Fäh, who could be very curt on occasion, would listen to no excuse, and said: " Do you write the articles, and say no more about it."

I lacked the courage to reveal my inner thoughts—it was fortunate that I did, else I should not stand to-day where I do stand—and I wrote the articles. But how? I could say nothing from my own convictions. I therefore took what others had written on the subject. It is only the arrangement that is my own. These articles, and the pamphlet afterwards, received a great deal of praise. Windthorst, the intellectual author of my production, frequently expressed to me at Berlin his especial appreciation, and the leader of the Centre Party, Dr. Porsch, told me one day at the dinner table of the Berlin Catholic Provost, Jahnel, that at the General Assembly of Catholics at Buchum, the lecturer on the Papacy, Baron von Wendt-Gevelinghausen, had spoken about my Church and State pamphlet.

Even more distressing to me was a second literary task.

My Provincial, the Jesuit Ratgeb, commissioned me to write a pamphlet in defence of the Jesuit Order, with the title, *Why should the Jesuits not return to Germany?* This was after my stay in Berlin. The collapse of my religion had already taken place, and the necessity of leaving the Order and the Church was pressing upon me. In this mood I was to become the official apologist of the Order! I did what I could to escape from this truly terrible command. Ratgeb had told me how effective it would be, if a member of the German nobility belonging to the Jesuit Order were to write this pamphlet. I, therefore, begged him to pass me over, and entrust the work to one of the Jesuits, Prince Radziwill, Count Stolberg-Stolberg, Baron von Hammerstein, or Baron von Geyer-Schweppenburg, who had been much longer in the Order than myself. In vain—I was said to be the best fitted. Here, again, I dared not reveal myself. I should never have attained to liberty, as I shall explain later. So I accepted, an unwilling slave to obedience, and a hypocrite in my own eyes. And yet I did not want to be a thorough hypocrite. I transported myself back to the years of the novitiate, when I still believed in the excellence of the Order. And I wrote from my heart the faith that I then had, the ideal of the Order which at that time I had seen before me. I brought about their resurrection, and described them in words. Thus the pamphlet became a confession *d'outre tombe;* a gruesome grave, in which my faith and youthful ideals were mouldering, lay like a dark abyss between the writer and that of which he wrote.

And yet the pamphlet was a piece of hypocrisy. The compulsion in which I was placed explains, but cannot fully justify, my self-deception. I had to choose between writing and retaining the possibility of freedom, or not writing and continuing to lead perhaps a long life in servitude and the most painful captivity.

Before anyone throws a stone at me, he should first find himself in a similar situation, and then cast it, if he still can.

A third and longer pamphlet written by me was called *Christ or Anti-Christ.* It was a result of my stay in Berlin. It was this sojourn that brought me freedom, but it was only long afterwards that I cast off my deep-rooted, because inherited, dogmatic opinions—for instance, the dogma of the metaphysical divine humanity of Christ (the doctrine of the two natures, God and Man). At that time I did not realise that the most prominent Protestant theologians denied this " fundamental dogma of Christianity," and I thought this denial anti-Christian. And, therefore, in this pamphlet, the composition of which was specially advocated by the Superiors of the Order, I collected passages from all the Protestant theological works in which the divinity of Christ was denied, and opposed to them the traditional proofs of Christ's divinity.

One piece of literary work which I was specially urged to undertake I did refuse, and I am still glad I did so. The Jesuit Tilmann Pesch desired that the Provincial should make me his collaborator in his *Flugschriften zur Wehr und Lehr.*

Exaeten

The personality of Pesch, and still more the harshness of his denominational polemics, were so repugnant to me that, even at the risk of having a black mark set against my name, I declined outright, and even acquainted the Provincial Ratgeb with the reason for my refusal.* He made no answer, but Pesch never forgave me for refusing him.

As long as I remained a Jesuit, my literary labours were highly appreciated, both in the Order and outside. Scarcely had I left the Order than they were depreciated by the same persons who had hitherto praised them. This, of course, is the Jesuit ultramontane fashion; there is but a short interval between " Hosanna ! " and " Crucify him ! " as indeed is the case everywhere.

However, I am quite ready to join myself in the depreciation. The writings of my Jesuit period are poor, both in matter and form. Indeed, they could not be otherwise. For they were composed at a time when all religious enthusiasm was quenched in me, when doubts were gnawing at my religious convictions, and they were written in part against my own conviction, under the influence of Jesuit obedience and distressing outward circumstances. What good thing can flow from such a source ?

Soon after I left the Order I publicly repudiated my Jesuit writings, in particular those about the Papal States and in defence of the Order. And I had a right to repudiate them, for I was not morally free when I wrote them.

I must say another not unessential word about my pamphlet, *Why should the Jesuits not return to Germany?*

So far as the facts and historical aspect are concerned, it is very superficial, and full of objective untruths. Still,

---

* Instead of me, Pesch appointed another amanuensis, the Jesuit Reichmann, who is still carrying on his denominational and quarrelsome activity—anonymously and pseudonymously.

the fault was not mine, but the Order's, which, as I have already shown, most carefully conceals the truth about itself and its history from its members and adherents. All that I quote there in defence of the Order is taken from Jesuit writers, and at that time I did not myself know how they falsify the truth. I only came to know the real history of the Order after I left it. Had I known it before composing my pamphlet in its defence nothing —not even the prospect of the most serious consequences —would have kept me from refusing the commission to write it. True, even at that time I had already broken with the Jesuit Order, but on account of my own experience, and because the religious Catholic belief in me had begun to weaken, not because I knew its history. Among a thousand Jesuits there are not two who know it.

To the interesting experiences of my Jesuit period of literary activity belongs the following:

In the year 1889 appeared the work, *History of the Moral-Theological Disputes in the Roman Catholic Church since the Sixteenth Century, with Contributions to the History and Characterisation of the Jesuit Order based on Unpublished Documents*, and published by Ignatius von Döllinger and Fr. Heinrich Reusch,* which supplies a whole arsenal of pointed weapons against the Jesuits. It caused great excitement in the Order. It was feared that disastrous consequences would ensue. The Jesuits, Tilmann Pesch and Pachtler, wanted to write a refutation. They said such attacks could not remain unanswered. The facts revealed must be " set back into their right light." In a conversation between these two Jesuits and the Provincial Ratgeb, at which I was present, the matter was discussed in detail. Ratgeb gave the wise counsel : " Do not answer

Geschichte der Moralstreitigkeiten in der römisch-katholischen Kirche seit dem 16ten Jahrhundert, mit Beiträgen zur Geschichte und Charakteristik des Jesuitenordens auf Grund ungedruckter Aktenstücke bearbeitet und herausgegeben von Ignaz von Döllinger und Fr. Heinrich Reusch.

it; a refutation would give the book importance and a wider circulation, and would draw the attention of the Catholics to it. The arrangement and style of the book are so cumbersomely dreary [very unfortunately Ratgeb was right] that it will lead a neglected existence in libraries, and do us no injury." Ratgeb prophesied truly, and I must make the shameful confession that I only studied the book and recognised its value after I had left the Order.

In Exaeten too I had a second proof of the ridiculous prudery which everywhere scents immorality and temptations to break the seventh commandment (in spite of the official moral-theological studies of sexual things).

A Catholic artist had been commissioned to paint a picture of the patroness of Christian philosophy, St. Catherine of Alexandria, which was to hang in the chief study of the young philosophers of the Order. The picture arrived, and the Provincial, the Jesuit Lohmann, invited some of the Fathers, among whom I was one, to a preliminary view. It was painted in a very "pious" style—in the style of Deger's Madonnas. The face was young and pretty, but expressionless. The Provincial was greatly dissatisfied. He said that she was too pretty and too young. The sight might prove a temptation to the young scholastics; and so St. Catherine had to put up with a few additional strokes of the brush, which made her appear older and not quite so pretty.

A horrible experience, which also throws a strong light on the Christian love of humanity and our neighbours evinced by the Jesuits shall conclude my reminiscences of Exaeten. During my theological studies at Ditton Hall, one of my co-scholastics, Joseph Kreutzer, was dismissed from the Order. His dismissal caused a great sensation. Brother Kreutzer, with whom I had studied philosophy, had always appeared to me a good and zealous member.

We never heard any details about the cause of his dismissal, only general unfavourable comments were spread about him. Then suddenly Kreutzer appeared in the parish of Exaeten, at Baexem, and from there often came to the Consulting Room at Exaeten, to consult with various Jesuits. He had particular confidence in me, though why I do not know. He acquainted me with the history of his troubles. He had been wrongfully dismissed —he had done no wrong. The Superiors, in particular the Provincial, at that time the Jesuit Lohmann, and his Socius, the Jesuit Pütz, had treated him with great harshness. He was now alone in the world, without any means, and on the brink of despair.

As the Jesuit Pütz was also at Exaeten as Socius of Lohmann's successor, the Provincial Ratgeb, I went to him and informed him of Kreutzer's circumstances, and begged his assistance. Pütz would not hear of it. He said Kreutzer had brought his sad fate upon himself. The Order had acted very generously towards him; nothing more could be done for him. When I informed Kreutzer of this, in another and last conversation, the poor fellow was overwhelmed by a storm of despair and discouragement. A few days later he cut his throat with a razor, and bled to death, in a room in the poor village inn where he was staying. He was put away in the churchyard at Baexem as a suicide. A few weeks later I was passing the churchyard with the Jesuit Pütz, and I begged him to go to the neglected grave and say a prayer over the unfortunate departed. His answer was a curt negative.

CHAPTER XXVII

BERLIN*

FROM the lonely Dutch moorland to the cosmopolitan stir of the German Imperial capital !

When in the beginning of May, 1888, after a walk with the Jesuit Spillmann through the corridors at Exaeten, I was returning to my own room, I received an order to go at once to my Provincial, Father Ratgeb. He communicated this astonishing piece of news :

"You and Father Fäh are to go at once to Berlin, until further notice. Father Fäh will live in St. Hedwig's Infirmary, you with the delegate of the Prince Bishop, Provost Jahnel, who has given his consent to this. The object of your Berlin residence is to prepare the ground for a permanent settlement. Whether, and to what extent, you will at once be able to practise any spiritual care there, depends on the goodwill of the Provost and of the Prince Bishop of Breslau, Dr. Kopp. You must, therefore, try to be on good terms with both these personages. In order that your stay in Berlin may lead to no annoyance with the police and other authorities, you are to be matriculated as a student at the University. What lectures you attend is left to your own decision, but I desire that you should occupy yourself in detail with Protestant theology, in order to be able to combat it in your writings. You are to place yourself entirely at the

---

* In Berlin too I was twice stationed as Jesuit—1888 and 1892. For the reason for which in the previous chapter I recorded the events at Exaeten under one heading, I shall do the same with my Berlin sojourns.

disposal of the leaders of the Centre, and especially Windthorst, who approves of our plan, but without in any way intruding upon them. There is to be no relation of Superior and subordinate between Father Fäh and you—all important steps must be discussed by both of you. You are to send me regular reports. I have also another commission for you personally, which requires a good deal of skill. I have been informed by the General that the Prince Bishop Kopp is annoyed with the Jesuits, because he believes that they are opposing his appointment as Cardinal. You are to write to the Prince Bishop that you are commissioned to inform him that we German Jesuits should be very glad to see him made Cardinal, and that you are ready at any time to bring him the expression of our respectful and friendly sentiments. Further [Ratgeb added this at the end as a mere detail], you are first to go to Schurgast, in Upper Silesia, to your relation, Baron Otto von Ketteler, who is dying and desires to confess to you; and after that you are to perform the marriage ceremony for your brother Clement. Meantime, Father Fäh will precede you to Berlin."

Such, not literally but as to their content, were my instructions as a Jesuit ambassador to Berlin. I was greatly agitated by the whole commission. It was a very striking and honourable mark of confidence on the part of the Order. Was I to reply to it by revealing my inner troubles? After a short deliberation I decided "No." I had a human right to attain a clear decision about the doubts that were troubling me, and only the freedom of study in Berlin could bring me this clearness.

I brought consolation to my former fellow-pupil at Mayence, Otto von Ketteler. I performed the marriage ceremony for my younger brother Clement with the Baroness Kunigunde Raitz von Frenz, in the Chapel of Castle Kellenberg, near Juliers, before a large assembly of relations, and then I entered the ancient and ugly Provost's house in Berlin [at the present time there is a stately new building], behind St. Hedwig's Church, where an attic, into which came wind and rain but very little light, was assigned me as a dwelling-place.

Soon I was on good terms with Provost Jahnel, whom I learned to value as an intelligent, energetic man, and an organiser of the first rank. He was not exactly well disposed to the Jesuits, but Fäh and I got on very well with him. He had no objection to candid speech.

True, he afforded us little opportunity for our pastoral activity.* Fäh had to minister in the newly founded pastorate of the Sacred Heart in the Schönhauser Strasse, and I in the parish of Wicksdorf.

Every Saturday evening I went out there, heard confessions, celebrated High Mass, preached and catechised, and returned on Sunday evening to the Provost's house. We also helped with confessions occasionally in St. Hedwig's Church. Besides that there was a pastorate of nuns, which was very uncongenial to me, at St. Hedwig's Infirmary, the Grey Sisters of the Niederwall Strasse, and the Ursuline nuns, in the Linden Strasse.

We always kept in touch with the Centre Party. Windthorst was especially amiable. The deputies, Baron von Franckenstein, Dr. Lieber, Count Praschma, sen., Count Conrad Prensing, Count Galen, sen., frequently visited us, and we were often their guests at the Kaiserhof. On great occasions we always had particularly good places in the President's Tribune of the Imperial and Prussian Parliaments. But apart from occasional discussions about political matters and questions of the day, we were not

* Provost Jahnel visited me again in 1897—two years after my marriage, in my Berlin house at the Kurfürstendamm. He made no attempt to convert me, but only expressed his regret at the step I had taken. He remained over an hour in animated conversation with me. I greatly regretted his early and unexpected death.

employed in politics. We were, in the first instance, only to prepare the ground.

I had some very interesting conversations with Dr. Lieber, leader of the Centre. He had temporary quarters with the Grey Sisters in the Niederwall Strasse, where I also lived on the occasion of my second stay in Berlin. We often dined together there, and we spent many evenings in my room or in his. The insight which Lieber afforded me into his methods of thought and action was not exactly edifying. He was an intriguer and a thoroughly pushing man. It was a matter of annoyance to him that there were other leaders besides himself in the Centre Party, and it was not his fault that he did not become the sole leader. The most important of the numerous conversations was that in which he described to me his relations to Windthorst, and in characterising Windthorst let fall the remark that the unscrupulous Guelph, after the celebrated speech at Cologne on the 6th February, 1887, in which he expressed his views on the intervention of Leo XIII. in the matter of the Septennate, had said:

" On that occasion I lied myself out of the difficulty with the help of God."

The details, including my own regret at an indiscretion I had committed, and the wording of a statement of Lieber's in the *Germania* of February 20th, 1896, which referred to it, are given in my book, *Rom und das Zentrum*.

At that time Lieber was circulating very zealously a pamphlet printed for private circulation, in which he attacked his colleague of the Centre, Racke. He handed me several copies, with the commission to send them to my Provincial Superior.*

* Lieber, in his declaration, speaks of reminiscences which he had composed, and which were perhaps to appear later. If this were to happen, I should find myself compelled to publish some of Lieber's letters as a complement to the reminiscences. Some of them are addressed to me, and some to a lady, who gave them to me, unasked, for my free disposal.

My commission to the Bishop of Breslau was executed in the following manner:

I wrote to him what the Jesuit Ratgeb had said to me, and asked him whether I might call on him for further explanation. Kopp answered from his castle of Johannisburg in a very diplomatic manner. The difficulties with the Jesuit Order had never been as great, he said, as my Superior seemed to assume. Everything was now in order, so that further steps would be superfluous. And in fact in the year 1893 Kopp attained the goal of his ardent desires and energetic efforts—the Red Hat—and thus became Cardinal by the grace of the Pope and the Jesuit Order.

The main interest in my Berlin stay was concentrated in the University and Library, that is to say, in my studies.

After matriculating (Fäh, who had not passed a school-leaving examination could only attend as a " hearer "*), I entered my name for Adolf Harnack's " History of Dogma " and Friedrich Paulsen's " History of Modern Philosophy." I refrained from entering for any other theological and philosophical lectures; I wished to acquaint myself with Protestant theology by means of private study.

It has often been asserted that Harnack's lectures caused my secession from Rome. That is incorrect. Harnack and his lectures did not make the smallest impression on my development. I admired his learning, but I was amazed at the ignorance of Catholicism which he frequently evinced, as did also many other University Professors. Harnack did not supply me with a single thought or impulse which could have hastened the separation from my past, far less suggested it. Nor do I think that Harnack is a man who will have a permanent influence. For that—paradoxical as it sounds—he is too clever.

---

* Only persons who have passed the School-leaving (*Abiturienten*) Examination of a State High School can be matriculated as members of the University. Others may attend as guests (hearers). This is known as *hospitieren.—Translator.*

He sees things in too many colours, and from too many points of view. His nature is too conciliatory and, therefore, he delights in theses and antitheses, and in seeking to combine contradictions in a "higher third." For detailed research and minute accuracy Harnack's method furnishes a model, but it has no influence in determining the further development of religious theology. In detailed research Harnack leads the way, but he is no pioneer in his conception of life.

If, therefore, I cannot include the theologian and scholar Harnack among my liberators—and, indeed, was often in later life obliged to oppose him violently in this his double capacity*—I remember with gratitude and pleasure the kindness of the man Harnack, which I also experienced in his hospitable house.

Friedrich Paulsen's lectures were an æsthetic pleasure, both in form and matter. Two visits, also, which I paid to Paulsen in his quiet home among the pine woods of Steglitz, brought me many interesting and stimulating experiences. But even then I perceived what I long afterwards expressed to Paulsen himself, that he was essentially a bookworm, who saw and judged the world and its events only from the standpoint of his student's existence, and not in the light of facts. Paulsen too had no direct or determining influence either as a personality or teacher.

The man who did exercise a powerful influence over me was Heinrich von Treitschke, and it was just his course of lectures for which I had not entered.

My Provincial Ratgeb had, it is true, left me a free hand in the choice of lectures, but his intention was that I should only attend theological and philosophical courses. Had I informed him that I wished also to hear Treitschke's

---

* *Zeitschrift*, März, 1907; 2 Februarheft, pp. 338-349; *Adolf Harnack über den Katholizismus.*

Berlin 405

historical lectures, it would have led to explanations which I desired to avoid.

So I chose the road of somewhat extensive " visiting."*
On the very first occasion I heard a diatribe of Treitschke's on the hereditary hostility of Papal Rome towards Germany. The eloquence of his language, though at first difficult to follow, and the passionate patriotism of his irresistible attacks on the foes of his country and enlightenment, carried me away. His burning patriotism kindled in me the yet glowing fire of German sentiment, which for the last decade had been smothered under the ashes of Jesuitism, and now blazed forth once more in a bright flame. Again and again I felt drawn to his lecture room. Ten or twelve times, at least, I must have heard Treitschke without paying my scot.

It is such men that we need in our University chairs, to assist us against Rome and everything Romish, against the foes of civilisation and Fatherland. It is not a clarified knowledge, which is colourless and characterless, but knowledge of flesh and blood, knowledge expressed with individual and daring convictions, which can educate an upright generation.

Besides my public lectures from Harnack and Paulsen, and far exceeding them in importance for me, were my private studies in my attic in the Provost's house, and in the reading room of the Royal Library. I may say that I there made an exhaustive study of the whole newer Protestant theology and philosophy.

Among the philosophers Kant was my leader, whom I now first learned to know in his true character. Through Kant I attained to a recognition of the autonomy of reason, and its right to self-direction. Kant confirmed me infallibly in the consciousness, which had been long, but timidly, dawning within me, of the right and duty of

* *Hospitieren.*

conducting research, free and independent of faith in authority, of being not a mere child in leading strings, but a thinking human being, even in face of the things of the other world. What miserable superficialities my Jesuit Philosophy Professors had repeated to me about Kant's "unemployable" because "illogical" *Critique of Reason!*

If Kant was a liberator of my reason, Schleiermacher, Rothe and Biedermann became my liberators in the domain of religious theology.

I learned to understand the conception of religion, and to value it, apart from ecclesiasticism, and even in opposition to it; I learned to know the Churches for what they are—diseases incidental to religious development; I began to understand that there are no principles or formulas of faith, nor yet can be; that the name of dogma conceals a mass of fabulous and absurd theories (*e.g.* original sin, the Trinity); that "salvation" cannot be accomplished by blood, not even by the blood of a "God-Man," but by self-purification; I saw that Christianity was not a hieratical organisation, but individual life.

Two other liberators I must also mention with gratitude, neither of them theologians, Ranke and Gregorovius; both showed me the Papacy in its historical, not in its pretended "Divine" aspect; both inspired me to special studies on the social and civilising aspect of the Papacy, which caused me to realise that, though the Papacy is a prominent institution of historic importance and power, it it still thoroughly human, and burdened, like every other long-lived human institution, with an enormous mass of religious and moral error of the most serious nature, the traces of which, in the course of centuries down to the present day, have caused not only blessing and civilisation, but also ruinous destruction and brutal ignorance.

I also learned to know the Ultramontane Papacy and indeed Ultramontanism in general, as a political abuse of the Catholic religion. I came to know that the Vicars of Christ, in spite of their religious vocation, had gradually become political sovereigns, and continue even to the present day to put forward this claim, absolutely contrary to the doctrine of Christ. Of course, all this was not as clear in my mind at that time as it is when I set it down to-day. My Berlin studies were the beginning, the dawn, of my later clear recognition; they set in motion what was not built up into a mountain, but at first produced a huge abyss which swallowed up all the faith which had accumulated in me for forty years. But I crossed over the abyss, and found my way to heights of world conception worthy of a human being.

The consciousness of the entire sacrifice of one dogma was completed even during my Berlin residence, and strangely enough it was one of my pastoral experiences that brought about this sacrifice.

A student lamented to me that the dogma of everlasting punishment was driving him to despair. This confession of his removed the last check on a resolution that had long been seeking consummation in me. I told him that the belief in everlasting hell was blasphemous, and this one word of deliverance also delivered me from my belief in hell.

Further than this and to the actual denial of hell and a personal devil I did not attain at that time; at any rate, I did not express this opinion, and probably scarcely acknowledged it to myself. It was only the formal breach with the Church and the Order which effected this too.

What did I not suffer from the dogma of eternal punishment, and what have not many millions of souls suffered from it! And yet in the whole history of religion, including the pre- and non-Christian religions, there is no doctrine so brutally blasphemous as this, just on account of its " Christian " premises.

The "Christian" God as the Catholic-Ultramontane, and in part also the orthodox evangelical, dogmatics describe Him, becomes so odious a Being that a reasonable man must turn away with horror from such a God. If there is such a God, then the deepest pessimism and hatred of God is the only thing possible for us, His pitiable creatures, and I confess that from such a God I would not even wish to accept heaven. He would be a hell-God—worse even than the Prince of Hell himself.

For let us realise the Christian doctrine of God and His hell, and the doctrine of the "Divine Grace" required for the avoidance of hell

(1) The All-knowing, All-good, and All-powerful God, although He foresaw that millions, even milliards, of people would suffer the everlasting pains of hell, yet created the human race, without any compulsion from without or within, and thus Himself, by His own free act, inaugurated the population of hell.

(2) The All-knowing, All-good, and All-powerful God acts in a Divine manner at the procreation of each individual human being by introducing the soul into the embryo, although He foresees that millions of people, called into being by Him, also of His own free will, will become everlastingly wretched in His hell. It is in His power to make the individual act of procreation of no effect by not creating the human soul, but He does create it, with the consciousness and the knowledge: "This soul, which is completely innocent of its earthly existence, which unasked receives its life from Me alone, will become everlastingly wretched, will suffer nameless tortures for ever in the flames of Hell, produced and maintained by Me; therefore, I create a being for everlasting torture." But still He creates it.

(3) No human exertion, however great, can deserve of God the "grace" to resist the temptations of sin, which

will cast him irretrievably into hell. The "effective grace" [*gratia efficax*] which alone enables him to overcome sin, is an absolutely free gift of the All-wise and All-good God, Who refuses it, although, being all-knowing, He knows that this refusal must signify everlasting hell for the man.

What judgment should we pass on a man who would permit even one human being, whose fate lies in his hand, to be wretched in body and soul throughout his whole life? All the rest of mankind would trample such a wretch to pieces. And yet the good God holds the fate of all men so completely in His hand that every other state of dependence is insignificant by comparison. For men are His creation, called into being by Him, unasked, and maintained in being.

Indeed, a man condemned to hell by this "God" might cry into His face: "It is You who should be in hell, not I, for You called me into life unasked, although You foresaw that I should end in hell. It was You who refused me Your grace, although this alone could have saved me from hell."

The dogma of hell is, more than any other, a "priest's dogma"; that is, a dogma invented by a priestly caste, who desired to maintain mankind in fear for its own dominating ends.

Another pastoral labour, the deliverance of a woman from a position of disgrace, in which several of my relations generously assisted me with large sums of money, became many years later, after my breach with Rome, a source of great trouble for myself and my brave wife,* but unfortunately the inviolable seal of confession keeps the whole locked safely from the public gaze.

I shall be easily believed when I say that my whole soul was in a state of turmoil during my Berlin residence. My sleepless nights began again. I suffered so much that

---

* *Cf.* my pamphlet, *In eigener Sache und Anderes* (Berlin, H. Walther), pp. 17, 18.

when I returned to Exaeten, in September, my emaciated appearance and my prematurely grey hair attracted attention. But I still struggled against taking the last step and separating myself from my inherited religion. The deeply rooted doctrine, again and again impressed upon me during my life in the Order, of the diabolical origin of religious doubts had even yet not quite perished within me. Above all, the terrible thought of a separation, and the almost complete impossibility of carrying it out, stood before me like a threatening spectre, and an impassable wall seemed erected before my eyes.

My family is one of the oldest and most respected of the Catholic families of Germany, and for centuries has been one of the mainstays of Catholicism. I had an old mother, and brothers and sisters who, with sincere fidelity, clung to their inherited religion, and to whom I was bound by strong and tender bonds of love. That I was a priest and a Jesuit was in their eyes and those of all my relations an honour and a blessing. The suffering I should cause them by my separation from the Church and the Order gave me a sensation of horror. Further, I was no mere faithful layman—I was a priest, the member of an Order. Thus chains were fastened about me which could not be unloosed, but only burst asunder. What scandal should I not occasion to the Catholic world and my family name and my former position, if I fell away from grace ! The weight of these thoughts, and their power in checking my final resolution can only be understood by those who have been in a similar position, who, with equal enthusiasm, equal readiness for sacrifice, have adhered to Catholicism and Jesuitism.

The effect on me of these internal struggles may be shown by two circumstances ·

A little daughter of my elder brother Wilhelm died of diphtheria in July, 1888. When I received the telegram with the news of her death, I prayed, with bitter tears and on my knees, to the soul of the child—for at that time I still believed that she could hear me—to obtain from God that I too might die, and thus be saved from ruin, for at that time I regarded as ruin that which lay before me.

I myself fell seriously ill with diphtheria, as the result of confessing an invalid suffering from this disease. I thought that the fulfilment of my wish was near, and I prayed earnestly to God that my illness might lead to death.

But I lived on, and I submitted to the decree of a God whose "kind and Fatherly providence" was still one of my dogmas. But I wished to leave Berlin, and to adopt the last means of subduing, if possible, the turmoil within me. I therefore begged my Provincial, Ratgeb, to send me to the Tertiate. There, in the quiet of a renewed novitiate, the decisive struggle was to be fought to an end. Ratgeb consented to my wish, and in October, 1888, I began my "Third Probationary Year" at Portico, near the English manufacturing town of St. Helens. It was a probationary year in a very different sense from that understood by the Constitutions of the Order. For in it I made trial of my faith.*

* In my place, the Jesuit Frins went to Berlin. He became Windthorst's theological and political legal adviser, and retained this position until his death. My Berlin companion, the Jesuit Fäh, remained more than a year longer in the capital; then suddenly very much against his wish and will, he was transferred to Brazil. What the Order desired to attain when it sent Fäh and me to Berlin was in fact achieved, and since then numerous Jesuits have been active in Berlin. Their headquarters are at St. Hedwig's Infirmary, in the Grosse Hamburger Strasse. From this centre they carry on the work of their Order in a comprehensive and truly Jesuitical, *i.e.* untruthful, fashion, in spite of the Jesuit Law. In order to be able to " work " undisturbed, they assume the title of " Professor " or " Doctor " without having the least right to either, and in this wrongful assumption of false titles they are strongly supported by the Central Organ of the Centre Party—the Berlin *Germania*. It publishes innocent announcements, such as: Professor (or Doctor) So-and-So will give an address here or there, or preach a sermon, or give exercises. But these professors or doctors are Jesuits. Sometimes six and more of these professors and doctors are working at the same time in Berlin.

CHAPTER XXVIII

THE TERTIATE AND THE END

THE Constitutions of the Order make frequent mention of the Tertiate.*

As the novitiate lays the foundation for the structure of Jesuit asceticism, so the Tertiate is to supply the coping-stone of the building, after the conclusion of the long years of study. The Tertiate is essentially a repetition of the novitiate. It is, therefore, officially designated "Third Probationary Year" (*Tertius annus probationis*), while the novitiate consists of the first two probationary years.

All the exercises and experiments of the novitiate are repeated in the Tertiate. The chief experiment—the Exercises extending over four weeks—are there intensified by the midnight meditation, omitted in the novitiate out of consideration for the youth of the novices and the sleep they require.

The daily instructions given by the Instructor (the official title of the Director of the Tertiate) deal with the Constitutions and the history of the Order.

In my introduction I mentioned that when I left the Order, I left behind the valuable notes I had made on these instructions. The instructions, however, were only valuable in as far as they contained explanations of the Constitutions, the so-called Institute of the Society of Jesus, and even there they concealed more than they

* Exam. gen., I., 12, 18; IV., 16; V., 2—1; X., 7. Cong. VIII., Decret. 9. Cong. XVI., Decret. 34, etc.

The Tertiate and the End

revealed. All that they provided of the history of the Order was one huge falsification.

We learned nothing about the inward conflicts, nothing of the abuses which originated in the Order, nothing of its contradiction between words and deeds. The history of the Order was set before us as one great tale of glory, free from stain and reproach.

The Instructor, and also Rector, of the House was the Jesuit Augustine Oswald, whose truly Jesuitical love of gain I have already characterised.

As all Tertiaries are priests, we were utilised a great deal for pastoral work, such as preaching and hearing confessions. Thus I obtained an instructive insight into the religious and social conditions of England. The conditions in the great towns (I speak chiefly of Liverpool and Manchester) were, at any rate at that time, terrible. On the one hand, magnificent churches, equipped with excessive luxury; on the other, terrible misery, both social and religious. Drink caused frightful havoc, and not only in the lowest and lower classes of the population. I was curiously impressed, too, by the systematic exploitation of religion for financial objects. There were, for instance, the charity sermons, where matters were arranged as in a theatre or concert room. The prices of the seats in the church varied according to their position, from 6d. to £1, or even higher, if a particularly celebrated preacher was in the pulpit. The Jesuit Bernard Vaughan, of whom I had seen more than enough at Stonyhurst, was in great request for charity sermons.

In the residences of the English Province (Portico and Ditton Hall, though situated in England, belonged to the German Province of the Order) I was also frequently occupied in pastoral work, and thus had an opportunity of confirming interesting observations no longer new to me; first, the excellent fare in eating and drinking of the poor Jesuits, and, secondly, the completeness of Jesuit obedience.

At that time the Jesuit Anderledy was General of the Order. He often took very strong measures against abuses. He was particularly anxious to limit luxurious living, and to suppress independent action, which the English Jesuits, in particular, were inclined to adopt. For both these reasons the "German General," as the Swiss Anderledy was called, was hated in the English Province. Once at dinner in the Jesuit residence at St. Helens, when port and claret were circulating, and loosening men's tongues, I heard the most spiteful expressions used about Anderledy—*e.g.* "I wish the man would die soon," which, indeed, did happen.

Here, too, I encountered what appears so often in the history of the Order: theoretical submission, blind obedience to the Superior, who represents God (Pope and General), practical disloyalty as soon as the Vicar of God causes any annoyance.

I had entered the novitiate full of idealism, the strength of which carried me over opposing difficulties, and my idealism had drawn its strength from my firm belief in the divinity of the Catholic Church.

I entered the Tertiate devoid of all idealism, and wounded to death in my belief. But I entered it with the honestly taken resolution if possible there to win back my faith, and through it my idealism.

In accordance with this resolution I worked, suffered and prayed in the Tertiate. Yes, indeed, I prayed. More urgent pleading is seldom sent upwards from the depths of any human soul. For the horrible alternatives stood in dreadful clearness before my eyes day and night. Either I succeed in fighting down my doubts, *i.e.* recognise them as error and temptation, and then I remain, not only a Catholic and a Catholic priest, but also a Jesuit, because in that case the favourable judgment which the Church pronounces on the Jesuit Order can and will cover my own unfavourable judgment; or, I do not succeed, *i.e.* the doubts are transformed from temptations into truths, into certain recognition; and then I must leave the Church and the Order, must put off my faith and my priesthood.

The troubles I then experienced were dutifully revealed in the Confessions and Statements of Conscience to my Superior and spiritual Director, but even here I did not reveal their real background and true character. I did not tell them that the doubts were no longer merely cruel and grievous temptations to me, but that I had already begun to see in them the truth. I did not tell, in particular, that enthusiasm for the Order was completely extinguished within me, and that my remaining or not remaining in it depended on the fate of my doubts. It was insincerity, or rather a lack of complete sincerity. But even a man unjustly imprisoned does not reveal to his jailers the means of his liberation. Speech and openness would have been forged into locks and bolts which would have made my departure impossible.

And then!—this much was clear to me, even at that time. The Jesuit handling of confession and Jesuit Statement of Conscience are wrong. For confession exists only for the purpose of declaring sins, and the Order has no right to lay bare men's souls by the Statement of Conscience. My silence was therefore justified and comprehensible, from a religious and human standpoint.

When in July, 1890, my Tertiate was at an end, I too was almost at the end of my struggle. Work, suffering, and prayer had produced no change of disposition. My doubts had grown almost into certainty. I left the peaceful house of Portico with the consciousness that the breach must and would be accomplished—that the end was close at hand.

THE END

For more than two years afterwards I still stood at the edge of the precipice, wandering to and fro beside it, and stumbling, before I could summon up determination to take the leap, not into the gulf below, but right across it to the other side where, separated by the deep chasm, I could set firm foot on new ground in a new world.

I refrain from trying to give a psychological explanation of this long hesitation. Perhaps it is altogether inexplicable, and one of the unintelligible things which arise from the lowest depths of the soul, uncomprehended even by the individual himself.

The elements of a possible solution of this apparently insoluble riddle are to be found in the forty years of my Catholic, Ultramontane and Jesuit past, in the thought of my family, and the effect of my exit on the Catholic world; and finally, in my fear of the step to be undertaken, which at that time appeared to me a leap in the dark. For the new land of which I have spoken, on the other side of the abyss, was at that time scarcely perceived by me. True, I longed for it, but I had not yet a hopeful belief in the possibility of reaching it and still less any clear comprehension of its nature.

On some sides I shall be reproached with having so long continued to play the hypocrite by living outwardly as a Catholic and a Jesuit and priest, while inwardly I no longer possessed the religious basis for these three offices.

In the first place, I reply, special spiritual experiences are not so simply disposed of, and it is not possible to take a calendar and watch in one's hand, and determine the day and the hour when Catholic thought and sentiment were finally dismissed, and the opposite views adopted all ready-made. The road of knowledge always winds in curves and spirals, like the mountain roads, which cross steep passes and climb up to mountain summits. Many years after my breach with Rome had been accomplished, I still discovered in myself Catholic views, and I found it difficult to uproot them from my mind. Our mother's milk remains long with us. Home and education are powerful forces, and fourteen years' membership of the Jesuit Order is an iron clamp which seizes on the innermost depths of the soul.

Even when the will to loosen all bonds and hindrances has long existed, the hesitation as to the time and mode of loosening them is not hypocrisy, but lack of clearness and explicable consideration.

Further, I reply, hypocrisy is a matter which I alone have to settle with my own conscience. It concerns no one else at all. For no one has been in any way wronged by my action. My duty towards others was, as I have already shown, performed up to the last, even though I was a hypocritical priest and a hypocritical Jesuit. For others I was to the very last that which I seemed to them to be.

What this long hesitation cost me I need not say, nor, indeed, can I. The cry of a despairing soul, resounding through thousands of years: "Out of the depths have I cried unto thee, O Lord. Lord, hear my voice!" was constantly on my lips during that last period. And how earnestly I sent it upwards—how I cried and prayed! Words fail to describe the misery in which I lived.

And yet there was no one to whom I could tell my sufferings! For, as I have already explained, silence as to my inner struggles was necessary, else the possibility of freedom would have been cut off. I am absolutely certain that, had I spoken, the gates of a lunatic asylum would have closed on me for life.

During my connection with the Order, numerous members of the German Province disappeared behind the walls of a lunatic asylum in Belgium, close to the little town of Diest, near Louvain. The institution, the name of which I have forgotten, belonged to a fraternity of "Brothers of Mercy." There was no State control over admission, and thus no difficulty in the way of disposing of inconvenient individuals.

This fact is not altered by the circumstance that many Jesuits leave the Order without being interfered with. My case was a different one. I was a priest; and I wished to leave, not only the Order, but also the Church. Even silent acquiescence in this twofold apostasy would have greatly injured the Order, especially on account of the name which I bore, and the respect that I had already attained in wide Catholic circles. The Jesuit Order has never been soft-hearted, and in order to maintain its reputation, it shrinks from nothing; its ethical principles would have found no objection to declaring me insane on account of my opinions, and the logical consequences would have resulted: that conveniently open Belgian lunatic asylum would have housed me for the rest of my life. Such prospects for the future were bound to close my lips.

It was, therefore, impossible for me to leave the Order in a so-called legitimate fashion; that is, to ask for dismissal in the usual manner. Only the illegitimate road remained open.

For this road I required the means of subsistence, and was obliged to have money. In spite of the vow of poverty and the renunciation of fortune, I was still, even according to canonical right, the owner of my share of our patrimony, which was managed by my elder brother. Legally I was therefore entitled to a fortune, and I was certain of its actual possession for the future, but for the moment I could not touch my property; for the day I revealed myself to my family, the Order would at once have been

The Tertiate and the End 419

acquainted with it. Besides this, as my mother and family were so well disposed to Ultramontanism and the Jesuits, they would have made the greatest difficulties, and a long-drawn-out conflict would have resulted, to which at that time my nerves were not equal. The explanation with my family, as well as the financial arrangements, could only take place after the decisive step had been taken.

Three accidents came to my aid.

When the Jesuit Fäh, with whom, as far as was possible in the Order, a kind of friendly relation connected me, was transferred to Brazil, he begged me to collect some money from relations and acquaintances to purchase books for the Brazilian Settlement. Some hundreds of marks (between 400 and 500) had been collected by me, and I had deposited them, as I was bound to do, with the Procurator of the German Province, the Jesuit Caduff. This sum I must now make use of. As I was certain that I could repay it afterwards out of my own fortune, I felt myself entirely justified in using it in my necessity. Certainly I did it with a necessary lie, by telling the Jesuit Caduff that I was now able to buy books with that sum. Without this lie I should not have got the money. But I never even came into the position of having to use other people's money. The second accident enabled me to put my hand on my own.

I was ordered to Blyenbeck, in order to hold a discourse in the little town of Goch, on the Lower Rhine, situated quite close to that place. It was my last public appearance in Catholic circles, by the side of Lieber, the leader of the Centre Party. I found it difficult enough. But it appeared to me a fortunate circumstance. For Blyenbeck was my father's property. There was my brother's exchequer, where I could draw money from my own property which was standing at my brother's account;

this could be taken into consideration afterwards when we settled our accounts, and subtracted from the total belonging to me; which, as a matter of fact, was done. But now I already had the money collected for the Jesuit Fäh. I dared not give it back to the Procurator. My inner excitement and disturbance were so great that the slightest circumstance and the smallest intervention might lead to the discovery of my condition and my intentions. And it was my freedom from life-long servitude that was at stake. So I did not give back the money in person, but placed it in an envelope, wrote upon it " For the Brazilian Mission," and left it, on my departure, with all the rest of my papers, in the open drawer of my writing table.*

I now had the means for attaining freedom. But how could I hasten on its hour? The third accident came to my aid.

A few days before Christmas, 1892, I received a commission to render assistance to the pastor of a parish not far from München-Gladbach. This was the desired opportunity for leaving Exaeten openly. To escape secretly in the night, perhaps through a window, was repugnant to me; not to mention that I might easily have been discovered, and then my fate would have been sealed. So on the 16th December, 1892 (I think this was the day, but am not quite certain), I stepped across the threshold

* Ultramontane Jesuit calumny many years ago spread the report that I had taken away the money and failed to return it. It is possible this lie may again be revived. It is, of course, impossible for me to refute it, if the Jesuits assert that after my departure the money was not found among my papers. Those who can believe me capable of stealing a few hundred marks will not be convinced by me. But two facts may be adduced: 1. As soon as I obtained possession of my property I sent the Procurator of the Order, the Jesuit Caduff, 150 marks from Berlin, as compensation for the old clothes I was wearing, and obliged to take away with me from Exaeten. 2. In 1896, three years after I left the Order, the Jesuit Fäh wrote me a very friendly letter from Brazil, in which he thanked me for collecting money for his mission, and said that it had been spent on books for him.

The Tertiate and the End 421

of Exaeten in broad daylight, apparently on a commission for the Order—in reality trampling it and its laws underfoot.

I went to Cologne. I revealed myself to a lawyer there. I gave him letters to the Order, and to my mother, in which I declared the irrevocability of my step, since I had lost my faith in the truth of the Catholic doctrine; bound him over to keep my address in a foreign country secret; and, after exchanging the garb of a secular priest for a suit of lay clothes, bought ready-made, set out for Paris. But, first of all, I had to set the mind of the priest, to whom I had been sent, at rest about my non-appearance, so that he might not perhaps send a telegram to Exaeten, and thus make known my flight before I had crossed the frontier and the letters handed to the lawyer for delivery had reached their destination. So I telegraphed to the priest that the promised supply could not come, and in order to arouse no suspicion, I signed the telegram with the name of the Jesuit Superior Fischer, who had promised to send the supply.

The crime of forging the telegram I gladly admit, and rejoice, even at this day, that I boldly tore through a little wire thread (the consideration of sending off such a telegram with a false signature), else this thread might easily have grown into an iron fetter.

I remained in Paris under an *alias* taken from one of my father's estates until I received the news that my family was ready to arrange the money matters. The provisional settlement took place at the beginning of January, 1893, in Cologne, with the assistance of the Bank of Deichmann.

I took up my residence at first at Frankfort-on-the-Main. There the final settlement of property took place, when I handed over to my younger brother a capital of forty thousand marks (£2,000), which he declared he could no longer do without. He had owned it ever since my entrance into the Order, with my consent, on the assumption that I should remain permanently in the Order, and regarded and treated it as his own property.

The terrible excitement of this last period brought on a long and serious illness, of which I was only cured by a residence of some months in Heligoland, from May to August, 1893. Returned from Heligoland, I took up my permanent residence in Berlin.

How often have I been reproached, publicly and privately, by Catholic Ultramontanes, who say: "You broke your vows; you committed perjury." Even evangelical circles have manifested their disapproval of the "apostate Jesuit," the "recreant priest."

It is surely more than obvious that after fourteen years of conscientious life in the Order and six years' priesthood, the questions of apostasy, recreancy, and perjury should have occurred seriously to myself. But I took little time to decide them, so simple are they.

The vows of an Order, and the state of the priesthood, are adopted in the belief of serving God and thus entering into a specially close relation to Him. When this belief is recognised to be erroneous, in that same moment the vows of the Order and the priesthood are cancelled. They were errors, just as the foundation on which they were based was itself an error, and a man is fully entitled to cast such errors away.

That evangelical circles too are often subject to such prejudices, is due to their contemptible traditional dependence on the Catholic ultramontane point of view. The fact of the apostate monk and recreant priest, Luther, strangely enough, seems to make no impression on such evangelicals.

CHAPTER XXIX

GENERAL VERDICT ON THE JESUIT ORDER

AN appreciation of the Jesuit Order must proceed from two different standpoints: the Order as a religious ultramontane institution must be judged from the religious point of view, and the association of men to attain certain ends here on earth independent of religion, must be judged from the human point of view. To distinguish sharply between the two is not easy, but as far as possible it should be done. Since the whole ultramontane Catholic system of orders, with its vows and its special state of an order, must be designated as a departure from Christianity and a distortion of its religious outlines, this general verdict applies also to the Jesuit Order. Indeed, it applies specially here, for the Jesuit Order has peculiarities which are reprehensible even from the Catholic standpoint.

Its blind obedience, its "Statement of Conscience," its system of espionage and levelling, its training to denunciation, its misuse of confession, and many other peculiarities, are immoral institutions which Catholic Christianity too should repudiate, and in former times would doubtless have repudiated. That the Jesuit Order, which came into being in the sixteenth century, was not so repudiated, that, on the contrary, its Constitutions, though abounding in such immoralities, were approved by the Popes, is a proof to what extent at that time and, indeed, much earlier, the Papacy and Church were infected and dominated by Ultramontanism.

The monasticism of the Theban and Libyan deserts knew none of these things, nor yet did Benedict of Nursia, the first founder of the Western convents. The more recent founders of orders, St. Dominic and St. Francis, did not introduce into their foundations this intellectual and religious slavery and bondage, enveloped in a garb of religious Christianity. To make these the basis of Christian perfection was left to the Jesuit Order. By its example and agency the innumerable later foundations of male and, above all, female orders were equipped with these monstrous excrescences. The plague of an anti-Christian dependence, which rages there in devastating fashion, and deprives many thousands of their inherited and divinely appointed freedom, the "freedom of Christianity," is of Jesuit origin.

In another essential point too the Jesuit Order differs in religious matters unfavourably from the old Catholic Orders, the Benedictines, Augustinians, Franciscans, and Dominicans.

While among these the original religious enthusiasm mounted upwards in a brightly flaming fire to heaven at their foundation, while evangelical poverty and evangelical chastity—their celebrated triumphs, which surpassed human nature and violated Christianity, but for all that were heroic—were maintained for decades, almost centuries, in a state of "first youth," while their ecstatic zeal never grew cold, and the "first fruits of the Spirit," even though falsely understood, never ceased to mature, in the Jesuit Order from the very beginning everything was attuned to sobriety and calculation; there was no "first youth," no "first fruits of the Spirit."

The founder of the Jesuit Order, Ignatius Loyola, though as a man and a saint he was a visionary and hysterical enthusiast, was prudence personified as the founder of an order. The Constitutions, written, at any

General Verdict on the Jesuit Order

rate for the greater part, by him, are calculated from beginning to end for temporal success, power, and influence over men. Ecstatic impetus, inward enthusiasm and religious warmth are lacking. Where they appear to be present, they are merely external adornment, applied in order to disguise the calculated sobriety.

The Scripture saying, "By their fruits ye shall know them," condemns the Jesuit Order as a religious institution. The blessing of God, which according to the faithful Catholic conception—the conception which is decisive in judging the religious side of the Jesuit Order—must rest on the work of a divinely sanctioned Order, does not rest on the work of the Society of Jesus.

I have already, in the chapter on the Jesuit System of Education, referred to the absence of permanent results—a proof, surely, of the absence of God's blessing—in the main activity of the Order, the education of youth. Outward splendour and useless show are the main fruits of Jesuit activity, but, like everything external, the splendour and show soon fade away. The words of Piaget's criticism* should be read, too, for it shows clearly the fiasco of the Jesuit Order.

Again, the words of the Jesuit Cordara, already quoted,

* *Essai sur l'Organisation de la Compagnie de Jésus* (Paris, 1893), pp. 235 *et seq.* After commenting on the failure of the Jesuits to achieve any lasting results in their missions to the heathen, and their efforts to check the spread of Protestantism, Piaget asks this question : "What is the cause of this failure at the end of so much apparent success ? I may be mistaken, but it seems to me that Jesuitism was nowhere a true religious awakening, a revival of sincere piety, which alone could have supplied a lasting foundation for its work." In regard to the revival of pious works, to be attributed to the influence of Jesuit confessors, he asks: " But did the overwhelming influence they attained lessen or even check the loose morality of the seventeenth and eighteenth centuries ? Must we not rather say that immorality made way in those very classes of the population which were trained in their schools ? Strangely enough, it was the very generation that was trained up by the Jesuits which rose against them and procured their suppression." The complete passage is quoted in the chapter on the " Suppression of the Order " in the German edition of this book.

on the arrogance of the Order are a strong indictment of the chief cause of Jesuit failure.

Cordara's criticism was written at the end of the eighteenth century, when the Order had had two hundred and fifty years of work, including its best period, and he designated the suppression of the Society of Jesus as a Divine judgment on the pride which is so hateful to God. It would be impossible to bring a more serious indictment against the worth of a religious order. And from a purely human standpoint it is natural that the Jesuits should in part suppress and in part falsify the words of their distinguished fellow-Jesuit. For their undeniable failure they can find other causes than the rejection by God as a punishment for arrogance. The malice of men! It is just because the Jesuit Order is so holy, so well-pleasing to God, that it suffers in a special degree the fate of all saints, "the hatred and persecution of godless men." The Society of Jesus fares as did Jesus Himself—how often have I heard this said!—"The servant is not greater than his master. If they have persecuted Me, they will also persecute you."

Not one single *Mea Culpa* is to be found in the four hundred years' history of the Jesuit Order. For that uttered by Cordara was not official, nor meant for publicity, not even for the Order itself. It was recorded after the suppression of the Order in the secrecy of a document intended only for his brother.

The very fact that the Jesuit Order proclaims its absolute immaculacy in so bombastic and boastful a fashion, transcending the bounds of the permissible (as shown, for instance, in the work *Imago primi saeculi*), as though it were enunciating a dogma, is so un-Christian, so irreligious, that it alone would suffice to condemn the Order as a religious and Christian institution. For the words placed by Christ in the mouth of the Pharisee,

General Verdict on the Jesuit Order

"God, I thank thee that I am not as other men are, or even as this publican," should express the strongest contrast to the religious and moral conception of Christ. Yet these very words are the fundamental note of all the manifestations of the Society of Jesus.

Strong contrasts to the teaching of Jesus are also to be found in other important points, particularly in the domain of morals. Some of these I have discussed in the chapter on Jesuit Morality.

Further, what could be more irreligious and, therefore, unchristian than the Jesuit piety of the Exercises, which sets aside the individual and substitutes for it a mechanical type? This is one of the greatest crimes which the Jesuit Order commits against the human being, as I have already shown.

Thus Jesus and the Society of Jesus, religion and the Jesuit Order, stand in sharpest contrast to one another. Only the ignorance of Catholics, and their bias in favour of ultramontane Jesuit views, explain the fact that the strong contrasts are not recognised. The light which has dawned on individual Catholics must dawn on all. But the first condition of this is to subdue Ultramontanism in the hierarchy. For this ultramontanised Papacy and Episcopacy supply the strongest support for Jesuitism, because in its turn Jesuitism is also the bulwark of Ultramontanism and its hierarchy; and this brings us to the consideration of the Jesuit Order as an association of human beings destined to pursue here on earth purely human aims which, however much they may be embellished by religion and Christianity, are in reality far removed from both.

When the Jesuit Order came into being, a fatal hour had struck for the Papacy. The movement originated by Luther, in connection with other causes, had caused the ship of St. Peter to rock dangerously. A world with a new philosophy of life was coming into view, which no longer recognised the Pope-God of the Middle Ages, the sovereign Lord of the whole world in that capacity. Ultramontanism which, since Gregory VII., had been firmly established in its seat, and was ruling the world, in particular the political world, from Rome, under religious forms, felt the onset of the new age, whence the cry, "Free from Rome," was already resounding.

Then the threatened Papacy found in the Jesuit Order an ultramontane auxiliary regiment of extraordinary power and pertinacity. The Papal dominion was to be re-established. The ultramontane system, with its secular and political kernel disguised under a garb of religion, was concentrated, as it were, in the Constitutions of the Jesuit Order, and even more in its well calculated labours directed from central points. Words and deeds, teaching and example, of the new Order, were a single great propaganda for the ultramontane Papacy. The doctrine of the "direct"—that is, the immediate dominion of the Vicar of Christ over the whole world—had become untenable; the Jesuit Order (*e.g.* Bellarmin and Suarez) replaced it completely by the doctrine of the "indirect" power.

There is not the least fraction of religion in this doctrine. Everything in it is irreligious and anti-Christian, but it is quite specially calculated for religious display, for it makes a pretence of God's Kingdom, which embraces this world and the next, which tolerates only one supreme ruler—God and His Vicar—and thus makes this comprehensive political universal dominion an acceptable, even desirable, religious demand in the eyes of Catholics. The love of dominion implanted in the Jesuit Order finds the greatest possibility of development in this doctrine, hence its never-resting zeal in trying to raise the indirect power of the Papacy to a fundamental dogma of Church policy. The Order, as such, cannot openly aspire to universal dominion; however powerful its equipment may be, it must always appear as a mere auxiliary member, a subordinate part of the Catholic whole, the Papal Church; the more it furthers the temporal political power of Rome and extends the religious belief in its justification among men, the more political power will it attain itself; the Papacy and its indirect power serve but as a screen behind which are concealed the Jesuit Order and its aspirations for power. By its zeal and skill it becomes an indispensable servant of the Papacy, and thus acquires direct dominion over the wearers of the Papal crown, and through them indirect dominion over the whole world.

Hence the continuous and detailed occupation with politics, forbidden by the Constitutions as unreligious, but which became its most comprehensive sphere of activity by the religious road of confession.

It was this very political activity of the Order which let loose the storm against it. And, as I have already shown, it was in the first instance the Catholic courts, at which the Jesuit confessor had carried on his religious activity for centuries, which demanded more and more eagerly the suppression of the Order, and finally attained it from Clement XIV. They felt that here, in the Jesuit Order, a power was rising which would gain the mastery over them. Claudius Acquaviva, the fifth General, gave to this political power, working in the religious atmosphere of the confessional, the form still valid at the present day, by means of a secret Instruction, which, as its discoverer, the Benedictine Dudik says, "shows quite clearly the ultimate aim the Jesuits tried to attain through their confessors—dominion over the Catholic Church, such as Gregory and Innocent and Boniface strove to attain."

But has the Jesuit Order not performed conspicuous

services for the Catholic religion ? Are not the successes of the counter-Reformation in the main its work ? There, surely, it was not a question of universal dominion, but of universal religion.

Doubtless the counter-Reformation was in the main the work of the Jesuit Order, but for that very reason it also bears the stamp of its spirit, and is characterised by measures of violence, even by blood and iron. The lost Papal dominion was to be restored. Religion took a second place, or rather supplied the cloak which was to conceal the craving for rule, and to sanctify the use of violent measures. We need only remember the words of the Jesuit Bobadilla,* one of the trusted comrades of Ignatius Loyola, to understand the nature and goal of the counter-Reformation, as conducted by the Jesuit Order.

The Jesuit Order, therefore, stands before us as the embodiment of a system which aims at temporal political dominion through temporal political means, embellished by religion, which assigns to the head of the Catholic religion—the Roman Pope—the rôle of a temporal overlord, and under shelter of the Pope-King, and using him as an instrument, desires itself to attain the dominion over the whole world.

That opinion is not only mine—that of the renegade, the apostate Jesuit—good Catholics too, who otherwise praise the Jesuit Order, advocate it strongly.

Thus, for instance, Reinhold Baumstark says: " For beyond all facts stands the decisive circumstance that Jesuitism cannot rise above one point of view, that of the temporal political power and external compulsion."†

From these efforts, directed for its own benefit and

---

* P. 383.

† *Schicksale eines deutschen Katholiken* (Strassburg, 1885), Second Ed., p. 91. Baumstark was for many years Leader of the Baden Catholics in the Second Chamber at Karlsruhe. He died in 1900 as President of the Provincial Court at Mannheim.

towards its own power, may be explained the twofold attitude of the Jesuit Order towards the Papacy; loudly emphasised submission which even takes the form of a special vow,* and harsh insubordination as soon as the Papacy opposes the special interests of the Order, above all, its attempt at rule. Then, as a matter of course, the reverence for bishops and cardinals also disappears. If the Vicar of Christ be set on one side, how should any regard be paid to the "successors of the Apostles"?

The Jesuit greed for power also explains another phenomenon, conspicuous through the whole history of the Order—its incessant quarrels with other religious organisations. Wherever the Order sets its foot, there peace ends and the struggle for existence begins. Its own churches are to be full, its own confessionals besieged, its own teachings in dogma and morality are to give the lead—in short, it desires to rule alone. The immeasurable arrogance, the inconsiderate and contemptible attitude towards other orders, those truly irreligious peculiarities of the Order which the Jesuit Cordara designated as the causes of its rejection by God, are the natural consequences of its unbridled greed for dominion.

The Jesuit Order has attained many successes by its temporal political efforts. The courts of Vienna, Munich, Paris, Madrid, Lisbon, and for a time of London too, to say nothing of smaller ones, were for a long time completely subject to it. But even these purely worldly successes lacked endurance and magnitude. Through the Jesuit confessors of the German Emperor and the French, Spanish and Portuguese Kings in the sixteenth and seventeenth centuries, and their almost unlimited influence, the whole of Europe might have been subjected for generations to the Order. Instead of this, the political influence of the confessors is frittered away in a variety

* In the vow taken by the Professed of four vows.

of intrigues, in small disputes which, though all directed to the increase of Jesuit power and dominion, still universally lack statesmanship on a large scale and effective unity. The Jesuit confessors have always been political intriguers, never and nowhere statesmen. Therefore, in influential positions held continuously for several centuries, they have caused disturbance, confusion, and breaches of peace; they have increased the outward splendour and glory of their Order and filled its coffers, but they cannot point to a single political action with an effect on the present and the future, nor a single far-reaching successful undertaking in the domain of universal politics, in the centre of which they carried on their labours. The Jesuit Order has always fished in troubled waters, and harvested the small gains connected with small undertakings; the results that can only be attained in the clearness of great endeavour are completely missing in its political ledger, although the most powerful rulers of their day are entered there as its devoted and politically obedient penitents.

Whence comes this failure? In the first place, from the same cause which led to its religious failures.

The politics of the Order did not penetrate far enough. They were directed too much towards securing quickly attainable momentary successes which should shed fresh glory around the external position of the Order. Here too it was appearance, and not reality. But the deeper reason is the following, which at the same time reveals the weakness and strength of the Order in general.

The Jesuit Order does not train men to independent thought and independent action. It trains machines, which let themselves be used without reason and will, like corpses and sticks. The Jesuit aim, in the education of the members of its Order and others, is the destruction of the individual, the levelling away of all originality. Its Exercises, to which it subjects men of all classes, are

General Verdict on the Jesuit Order

the great planing machines through which human beings are enslaved in their minds and made dependent. The sinew of individuality there receives a fatal blow, and that not only in religious respects, but in general.

I have already described the effect of the Jesuit educational system on the Jesuit himself, and shown how it produces mechanical routine and easy mobility, and thus turns the individual into a smoothly gliding ball which yields silently to every impulse. But this deprives the Jesuit of the first condition for successful and permanent work—the impetus of his individual peculiarity. His work is all on the surface. Smoothly gliding balls trace no deep furrows, they leave only light, easily effaceable marks. The possibility of enormous activity in the most varied fields, of quick movement hither and thither, of incessant beginning and ceasing, now here, now there, is supplied by the pliable routine of the individual Jesuit. And as the history of the Order shows, this possibility has, in the most conspicuous manner, become a fact. No other institution has given so much cause for discussion in so comparatively short a time, nor been active in so many different directions. All Europe, half Asia and America, have become the field of its activity. In all possible positions and offices we see Jesuits employed. But nowhere has even a single Jesuit shown himself a truly great man, with a far-seeing outlook and enduring activity. And for this reason—because every Jesuit lacks personality—he is a wheel of a machine, not a human being thinking freely, acting freely, and creating values of his own.

This is true of all ranks of the Order, of the General and the Superiors as well as the lower spiritual and temporal coadjutors.

This complete lack of personality, the deliberate and necessary consequence of Jesuit education, is not balanced by the heroic devotion to definite tasks, which is certainly not lacking in the Jesuit. For Jesuit devotion and self-sacrifice is and remains the devotion and self-sacrifice of a machine, which also wears itself out, which does its duty and lets itself be used to the very last of its powers, but which in all this performs no individual, but only a mechanical task. The Jesuit does not devote himself to his allotted labours in the first instance from the interest he feels in them—the ascetic discipline of his Order enjoins on him sacred indifference in regard to every kind of work—no, he acts, and acts in this particular way, because he constitutes this particular wheel in the great machine which perhaps in the very next hour will be changed for another by the hand of the Superior; he works zealously, because obedience for the moment has set him at this particular point of the machine's activity, which he will perhaps have to exchange to-morrow for another. "One foot in the air," as my Novice-Master, the Jesuit Meschler, used to characterise the fundamental attitude of a Jesuit at work, does not assist us to accomplish anything great and permanent in any domain. For this we require permanence of place and the possibility of striking root, absorption in the occupation and, above all, the consciousness of being set tasks for life, not merely temporary experiments which at any moment if it seem good to the Superior, must be exchanged for another occupation.

As a Jesuit is unfitted even by his education in the Order to become a powerful implement for lasting and individual labours, the lack of aptitude is transferred, if not in so marked a degree, to all who submit to his influence, all whom he educates. They too suffer more or less in their individuality, lose a good part of their independence and power of decision. The many thousands who, in all classes and professions, are attached to the Jesuit Order, are pliant implements in its hand, but for that very reason lack the requisites for great and enduring results—initiative and independence.

It is undeniable that we here meet with the weakness of the Order, and it appears conspicuously in the notorious lack of enduring success, in spite of favourable opportunities, in the history of the Order.

But here also lies the strength of the Jesuit Order. Its education produces a similarity among its members, a uniformity of activity which cannot be surpassed, and which is a guarantee for those results which can be attained through its mechanical and automatic methods.

The ball can roll in any direction, into any corner, however small; the Jesuit, with no will of his own, but obeying blindly, can adapt himself without difficulty; he changes his place again and again, and brings to all the same trained and superficial skill. I have often spoken of the Jesuit mass; here we find it. Human beings with their individual differences have vanished; a light and mobile army, battalions drawn up in rank and file, march in equal step in their place. The persons who stand outside the Order but submit to its guidance belong also to the Jesuit mass—they are a column that can be directed by a single word.

Thus the Jesuit mass permeates the whole world, young and old, men and women, untold, innumerable "congregations." It is clear that this is a cause of strength, in spite of the weakness which in another direction is combined with it. Indeed the strength is far greater than the weakness. For mankind cannot tolerate continuous violent rule and violent impressions for ever. For them the commonplace is the rule, controlled by the smooth working of small events and impressions. Those who understand how to guide men silently and quietly, to put them in leading strings without their noticing it, become their masters more certainly than the revolutionary warrior or statesman.

That brings us to the question: Is the Jesuit Order dangerous, and to what extent?

Here is my answer: For the individual human being, for State and Religion (I purposely do not say "Church," for it is not only not harmful to the Church, but even very useful), the Jesuit Order is one of the most dangerous institutions which has ever existed. For it destroys that which is most valuable in men—moral and intellectual independence. After what I have already said, there is no need to explain this in further detail.

In this system of dependence lies the danger that threatens true religion and genuine Christianity from the Jesuit Order. The reproach that is brought against the Romish Church in general, that it sets its official hierarchical personages and its sacraments and sacramental offices and ceremonies between God and man, that it has elevated religious tutelage into a dogma—in short, tries to check free intercourse between man and God as far as possible: this worst of all religious reproaches is incurred in the strongest manner by the Jesuit system. The Jesuit and the man who submits to Jesuit direction are in reality slaves, who approach the world beyond and God—that is, may only take part in religion—in the way in which the piety and asceticism of the Order permits. They must renounce even the last remnant of religious freedom. They must be accessible, to the very depths of their soul, not to God, but to the Superior of their Order, and to him alone. This too requires no further proof after the detailed expositions I have given on the subject.

What about the danger of the Jesuit Order to the State? It is many-sided and far-reaching.

In the first place, we must remember the fundamental constitutional dogma of the Jesuit Order—complete dependence of the State on the Church; its obligation to fashion itself and its life according to the laws of the Church. Numerous quotations from Jesuit authorities,* and among them the present General of the Order, go to prove that from this fundamental dogma may be deduced the doctrine that it is permissible and meritorious to disobey the laws of the State which are opposed to the laws of the Church, and in case of punishment for such breaches of law to be indemnified from the State Treasury.

Even active resistance to Government officials is permitted. And the most simple circumstance which throws a strong light on the danger to the State of such doctrines is, that they are to be found in books which expressly serve as directions for attending the confessional. The fact that their chief advocate is the German Jesuit Lehmkuhl, the political theological councillor of the Centre Party, gives them an increased importance for Germany.†

---

* Some of these are given in the chapter on Jesuit Morality.

† It is right, however, to emphasise the fact that Lehmkuhl's theses are the hereditary doctrines of the Jesuit Order: the twentieth century in them meets the sixteenth and seventeenth. I have already referred to the Jesuits Bellarmin and Suarez as the most celebrated theoretical advocates of the indirect power of the Church over the State. Two other Jesuits, also belonging to the early days of the Order, and among the members most actively concerned in politics, whom we have already encountered in this activity—Parsons and Garnet—may also be mentioned, because the teaching of one almost coincides with that of Lehmkuhl.

" One necessary condition required in every law is that it be just; for, if this condition be wanting, that the law be unjust, then it is, *ipso facto*, void and of no force, neither hath it any power to oblige any. . . . Hereupon ensueth that no power on earth can forbid or punish any action, which we are bound unto by the law of God, so that the laws against recusants [the English Oath of Allegiance was in question], against receiving of priests, against mass, and other rites of Catholic religion are to be esteemed as no laws by such as steadfastly believe these to be necessary observances of the true religion. Being asked what I meant by ' true treason,' I answer, that is a true treason which is made treason by any just law; and that is no treason at all which is made treason by an unjust law."—Jardine, p. 235.

And the Jesuit Parsons, of many names and devices, in his book, *Elizabethae Angliae Reginae haeresim Calvinianum propugnantis saevissimum in Catholicos sui regni edictum*, says: " The universal school of Catholic theologians and canonists hold (and it is certain and of faith) that any Christian prince who manifestly

But even this attitude towards the authority and sovereignty of the State does not satisfy them. The Jesuit Order is the sworn foe of the modern State and all its educational functions.

This is surely and strikingly demonstrated in the 12th decree of the 23rd General Congregation, of the year 1883. Here the Order asserts that it abides by the Encyclical of Pius IX., *Quanta cura,* of December 8th, 1864, and the Syllabus of the same date, and emphatically designates as " plagues " the " errors " condemned in these two documents. But this Encyclical *Quanta cura* and the Syllabus are the most comprehensive declarations of war against all the foundations and achievements of the modern State education and civilisation. Since, then, the Jesuit Order does not content itself with giving its silent assent to the Papal ultramontane declaration of war, " which would be a matter of course for every ultramontane Catholic," but gives it in the most solemn manner through its General Congregation, it expresses its deadly hatred towards the modern State in a specially ostentatious manner, within twenty years after the publication of the Encyclical and Syllabus. Like the ultramontane Papacy in the Syllabus, the Jesuit Order too says : " I cannot be reconciled, nor agree with, progress, liberalism, and modern civilisation."

True, the Jesuit Order makes use of the attainments of progress, liberalism, and civilisation. True, it clothes itself in modern garb, and apparently takes part in all domains of civilisation ; but under its modern garb is

swerves from the Catholic religion, and wishes to call others from it, falls at once from all power and dignity, both by divine right, and before any sentence can be passed against him by the supreme pastor and judge (the Pope) ; and his subjects are free from the obligation of any oath of allegiance which they had taken to him as a legitimate prince ; they may and should (if they have power), expel from his sovereignty over Christians such a man as an apostate, a heretic. . . . Now this, the certain, defined and undoubted opinion of the most learned is clearly conformable and in agreement with the apostolic doctrine."—Taunton, 148, 149.

General Verdict on the Jesuit Order

hidden the bitter opponent, who hates with intensity that progress the advantages of which he utilises for his own purposes. So deep, so universal, is the Jesuit hatred for our modern civilisation that we encounter it even where we should least expect it, and sometimes in the most grotesque form. Here is an instance:

The Jesuit Meschler, a former Novice-Master, Rector, Provincial, and Assistant to the General, consequently a prominent Jesuit, in the *Stimmen aus Maria-Laach*, for October, 1909 (page 568), publishes an article on St. Ludgerus, first Bishop of Münster, in the eighth century. His article ends with this characteristic sentiment:

"The civilisation of St. Ludger built hospitals, churches, and convents; the civilisation of our day builds barracks, lunatic asylums, and prisons." Away then with the civilisation of the twentieth and let us return to that of the eighth century!

Special hostility is shown by the Jesuit Order to one of the sources of civilisation, and one of the most important institutions of the State as a civilising agent—I mean the State school.

The Jesuits Wernz (the present General), Laurentius, Cathrein, von Hammerstein, etc., in their widely read books and articles, set up the most unlimited demands in regard to the suzerainty of the Church over the State schools, and in so doing pour the most opprobrious abuse on the State and its schools. Thus, for instance, the Jesuit von Hammerstein writes:

"The idea of State and school, as conceived and handled by the modern State and embodied for the last centuries in a large amount of legislation, is unjust, and that not only in the most general sense of unfairness, but unjust in the truest signification of the word—that is, the laws in question lack the foundation of justice in a great part of their content. They are null and void, just as a Socialistic decree, issued by a democratic State, abolishing all private property, would be null and void. Not only does the modern school idea deserve the designations 'unpractical' and 'unjust'—it also unquestionably merits the further reproach of being un-Christian. . . . On closer examination, we are indeed actually compelled to bring the reproach of immorality and dishonesty against the modern school." "If the State abides in future by its modern school idea, we do not know how we can acquit it of the reproach of inaugurating a system of hypocrisy on a large scale. Such a system must in time become the grave of fidelity, faith, and morality for our youth and the whole people." "The apex of the Prussian school pyramid is the ministry and minister of public worship and instruction (*Kultusminister*). Even the mere notion of a minister for spiritual affairs on the lines of the modern school idea is felt to be a declaration of war against the Catholic Church, and a manifesto in favour of Protestantism."*

Four sections are devoted by Hammerstein to the question: "Can Catholics be expected to entrust their sons to Prussian State Gymnasia?" Of course, he answers "No." †

Thus writes the same Jesuit in another book: "We should like to set over the gateway of every school which is not genuinely a Church school these words as the brand of Cain:

> 'Through me the way is to the city dolent;
> Through me the way is to eternal dole;
> Through me the way among the people lost.' ‡
> Hate of the Godhead called me into being."

Side by side with this school hatred goes denominational hatred.§

The fundamental condition of civilisation is peaceful dwelling together, and tolerant collaboration among

---

* *Das preussische Schulmonopol*, pp. 127, 139, 162, 163.
† *Ibid.*, pp. 165–224.
‡ Longfellow's translation of the *Inferno*.
§ *Die Schulfrage*, p. 125.

General Verdict on the Jesuit Order

different denominations, which the modern State has admitted into its constitutions as toleration and religious equality;* but this is regarded by the Jesuit Order as an "abuse," a "disease." I have already given many proofs of this Jesuit quarrelsomeness. They show that "the seeds of hatred are inborn" [in the Jesuit Order towards those of other faith], as the *Imago primi saeculi* so characteristically expresses it.

Then, finally, there is the docrine of Tyrannicide which, as is proved by numerous writings of individual members approved by the Order, has gained a firm footing in the Jesuit Order. Even the very ambiguous attitude of General Acquaviva towards these doctrines gives cause for serious consideration.

My assertion is therefore justified: The constitutional and political educational doctrines of the Jesuit Order are the destruction of the modern State, and its destruction is intended by the Jesuit Order.

Now the danger from such teaching and intention would in itself not be so very great. What dangerous theories and intentions has the world not witnessed, and yet it has continued to proceed on its own course! But here, when the Jesuit Order represents these ideas, matters are entirely different. Here the danger is imminent because it is founded on the dangerousness of the Order as such.

Very erroneous ideas are held as to this dangerousness. It has been sought where it is non-existent, or in but a small degree; where it is actually present it has been overlooked.

The dangerousness of the Order, and its powerful influence, do not consist in the prominent intelligence of its members, not even in that of its leaders, the Superiors. Fourteen years' intimate acquaintance with members and

* *Parität.*

leaders has taught me that neither class exceeds the average. Indeed, in some of the Superiors (Rectors and Provincials) I learned to know men of but moderate intelligence who, had they stood alone and not been supported and guided by the traditions and ordinances, and by an organisation spread over the whole world, would of themselves have achieved nothing worthy of note.

I have already characterised in detail the deliberately fostered dependence of the individual Jesuit as the main weakness of the Order. But I have shown that this weakness also constitutes its strength, and this strength is essentially increased by the manner in which the Order exercises its activity. This manner, combined with the marvellous organisation of the Order, is the nucleus of its power and also of its dangerousness.

In the first instance, the Order utilises the same most effective means as Ultramontanism. "Religion" is the fair wide cloak with which Jesuitism covers everything, in which it clothes everything, and which wins for it easy admission into the heads and hearts of Catholics. By means of this illusion, the Jesuit Order has reached an unexampled mastery. There is nothing so earthly, so worldly, so political, there is no attack on State and civilisation, which the Jesuit system does not represent, plausibly too, as "religious," as "lying within the sphere of religion." By means of this untruth it replaces its own weakness, due to its mechanical methods, by the gigantic force of these religious passions of its adherents. Jesuits need then only fan the flame which has been already kindled. But this can be done even by men of inferior gifts, who have lost their individuality, especially if they are assisted by a well-planned and far-reaching organisation.

This is greatly assisted by the secrecy of Jesuit activity.

General Verdict on the Jesuit Order

It is excessively cunning, and by no means confined to the secrecy of the confessional, in which Ultramontanism too possesses a mighty lever for work in politics and against enlightenment, carried on under the shelter of darkness.

True, the Jesuit Order has, more than any other ultramontane institution, contrived to make confession subserve its own ends; it has succeeded in attaching troops of the faithful to its own confessionals. But its furtive activity extends far beyond the Church and the confessional.

The Jesuit has become a popular, indispensable spiritual director in the families of the upper classes, above all with the women. In this position the most secret activity becomes easy and safe for him. If we asked the Catholic families among the nobility of Germany, France, England, Austria, Spain, Portugal, Italy, as well as numerous families of the upper ten thousand, which of them has not a Jesuit as a permanent or occasional spiritual director, we shall find the number of these to be extremely small. Although from my youth upwards I was accustomed to "domestic Jesuits," yet when I myself belonged to the Order and had an insight into its activity, even I was surprised at the extent of this "domestic" activity of the Order.

In this must also be included its educational activity, although this apparently is not carried on in secret, since the numerous "German" educational establishments (Feldkirch, Kalksburg, Freinberg, Stonyhurst, Ordrupshoj, etc.) stand broad and clear in the light of day, and although the Jesuit boarding-school presupposes the separation from home and family, yet a strong and secret influence penetrates thence into both home and family. For the Jesuit boarding-schools transform their pupils into the "Jesuit mass," which continues to work silently and imperceptibly in the families themselves. In the Jesuit boarding-schools the pupils are planed and polished who, when they grow up, extend the Jesuit spirit and thought. Here too a circular letter to ultramontane editors, members of Parliament, writers, officials, and so on, would produce the remarkable result that about 80 per cent. among them are old Jesuit pupils. The same applies to numerous landed proprietors in the Rhinelands, Westphalia, Silesia, Bavaria, Baden, and Würtemberg. Many officers, too, have been educated in Jesuit institutions, especially at Feldkirch and Kalksburg (both in Austria).

If we add to these the many thousands of Congreganists in all classes and professions, these genuinely and organically co-ordinated "affiliates" of the Order, we see the gigantic nexus of circles spread over the whole world, from the centres of which the Jesuit Order pursues its activity silently, but with certainty of success. And in this activity, which sets in motion a pliable mass, permeated with Jesuit conceptions, lies the power of the Order.

This power is the greater, because the Jesuit Order is surrounded by a special halo, since it clothes itself in an atmosphere of glory which raises it in the estimation of the Catholic masses far above all similar religious institutions. For the Catholic outside the orders knows even less than the Jesuit himself of the true history of the Order. He only knows the bright immaculate picture which he encounters in the innumerable books and writings published, *in majorem Societatis Jesu gloriam*. Therefore he honours in the Jesuit Order, and in the individual Jesuits, the acme and the highest attainment of Christianity. The Jesuit Order works by fascination—that is the right word to use. And this gives it one of the most effective means for the maintenance and increase of its influence. Sober consideration certainly deprives the Order of the false adornments and pretended glory with which it has surrounded itself. Unfalsified history repre-

General Verdict on the Jesuit Order

sents it as an organisation injurious to religion, politics, society, and civilisation, which endeavours with inconsiderate egotism to make mankind serviceable to its selfish ends, and is directed towards their material exploitation and intellectual suppression. But there are great difficulties in the way of introducing the sober historical points of view into those circles where the truth about Jesuitism is most needed, *i.e.* the Catholic circles; and the Jesuit Order has succeeded in transforming these difficulties into almost insuperable obstacles.

The method employed for the purpose reveals the whole extent of its unscrupulousness, its cunning, and therefore its dangerousness.

The belief in the almost immaculate excellence of all institutions of religious orders and the like, sanctioned by the Church, is still unshaken among Catholics. This belief is utilised unscrupulously by the Jesuit Order for its own advantage, by systematically falsifying history, and also all the products of free thought. For it is sure of its public. In these circles everything which the Jesuit Order sends into the world marked with its stamp is regarded as indubitable truth—as good and true.

Thus the Order can boldly add calumny to falsification. Perhaps the only saying of Jesus which the Society of Jesus realises is this: "He who is not with Me is against Me." It shrinks from no means for making its opponents harmless. Falsehood and physical violence, calumny and cunning, are its weapons, which deal fatal blows from its ambush.

By depriving all kinds of critics and opponents of their power to injure, unhindered by any qualms of conscience, the Jesuit Order in the course of centuries has piled up a discreditable account such as could not be rivalled in the whole history of Christian civilisation: it tramples under foot truth and right; it steps over the lives, the happiness and the freedom of men, and goes on its way, thus proving itself to be one of the most dangerous enemies of mankind in the realm of truth and justice and of civilisation.

The Jesuit Order is an international organisation which most profoundly and skilfully, in hundreds of disguises, excavates religion and State, knowledge and civilisation, in order to fill the gap with its own spirit. And this spirit is a spirit of lust and power, of lying and deceit, of immoderate self-seeking, of greed for the possessions of mankind, and even more for their freedom and independence—the spirit of irreligion and anti-Christianity.

CHAPTER XXX

FROM THEN TILL NOW

My account of the past is ended. But a few lines must still be given to the present and the road by which I reached it.

If a tree uprooted by the storm could speak, it would express what I felt after the breach with the Church and the Order was accomplished. I had been torn away from soil that had supplied the origin and sustenance of my whole being, physical, moral and religious. In a sense I was face to face with nothingness, and my blood seemed to be flowing from a thousand open wounds, just as the tangled roots of the tree would also pour forth their sap.

What was to become of me? I had formed no definite plan when I left the old world behind. My step, so weighty with consequences, had been a leap in the dark, for I had burnt my ships behind me. Should I succeed in reaching with new ships a better shore that I dreamed of rather than saw, enveloped in mist and clouds? Not even these thoughts presented themselves to me at that time clearly and distinctly. To escape from bondage, from the yoke which threatened to suffocate my independence and my individuality, to be rid of fetters which held my soul tightly compressed—this was all that I then desired. All else was but one mighty question.

The separation from the Order could have been endured with comparative ease. This wound, if wound indeed I may call it, was soon closed, for, in spite of my fourteen years of membership, I had never been a true Jesuit. My mind never assimilated the Jesuit spirit.

But the separation from my religion! It was flesh and blood to me; I was united to it by the bonds of centuries; every human possession that had hitherto been mine was included in it—father, mother, brothers and sisters. I could not even imagine them except in and with my religion; my thoughts and feelings had for nearly forty years been permeated by Catholicism. And now! Such deeply rooted conceptions cannot be cast aside like a coat. True, my outward connection with the Catholic Church had been sundered by a single blow, for I had recognised the erroneousness of some of the fundamental dogmas of the Catholic faith. And I had deliberately thrown aside the priestly cassock and the Jesuit's garb because I could no longer regard the priesthood and the Order as Christian and religious.

But these violent steps did not avail to set aside and destroy the innumerable Catholic feelings, emotions, sentiments and opinions which in a life of forty years had grown along with the innermost parts of my being, with my whole body and soul. True, I felt that they too must go. But for the present they were still there, torturing, troubling, frightening me. My whole being was in a state of chaos. I no longer believed in the God of ultramontane Catholic dogma. That Church in which I had been born and educated, in which I had lived for more than a generation, had fallen to ruins in my sight, and I never even thought of any other Church. My soul resembled a vessel without mast, sail or rudder, tossed hither and thither by mountainous waves, and I, its pilot, had no compass, saw no star shining overhead.

Nor could I tell what to do, or how to find occupation. I have now been for several years occupied in a definite and systematic fight against the most dangerous and strongest of all powers—ultramontane Rome. To-day I know what I want; at that time I never thought of taking up such a position, and knew neither what I wanted nor what I ought to do, a state of torture which several times suggested to me the thought of suicide.

Then a chance occurrence helped to disperse the clouds. I had imagined that my secession from the Jesuit Order, and my breach with the Church, had attracted no attention; for my part I did nothing to make them known. And yet they were known. A hand was extended to me from a side to which I am now almost as sharply opposed as to Ultramontanism.

I received a letter from the Court Chaplain, Dr. Adolf Stöcker, inviting me to write something about—*i.e.* against—the Jesuit Order for the *Kreuzzeitung* of his friend, Baron von Hammerstein. I wrote a short feuilleton article, but did not sign it, so little did I at that time think of publicity and attack. The little article aroused interest. The editor of the *Preussische Jahrbücher*, Professor Delbrück, placed his review at my disposal. And so, in the spring of 1893, I wrote for the *Preussische Jahrbücher* my first series of long articles above my own name. They bore the title "*Mein Austritt aus dem Jesuitenorden,*" and were afterwards reprinted as a pamphlet.

Thus was the road opened to me which was to lead me to my life's work: the enlightening of men on the ultramontane danger. My first steps along this road were but timid, probably because I was not yet fully conscious of that work. Anyone who should compare that first pamphlet with this book would notice no inconsiderable differences. In spite of the condemnation of the Jesuit Order expressed in the pamphlet, I was comparatively mild in this first work of mine. There is some uncertainty about it; it utters no direct challenge. With each fresh book this has gradually changed and improved, because knowledge has arisen or been strengthened in me, bringing about a clarity and certainty of will which could only find expression in blows of the hammer.

In Heligoland I made the acquaintance of a member of the Upper House, Count Karl von Finckenstein. I paid frequent visits to his estate of Madlitz. The Master of Madlitz was a thoroughly orthodox Protestant and Conservative. Through him I was brought into touch with his religious and political circles, and this contact gradually matured in me a distinct religious and political attitude, though opposed to his.

My inborn inclination towards political liberalism and religious free thought, which had been the point of departure for my liberation from ultramontane Catholic servitude, revolted against the orthodox and conservative routine mould. Truly I had not broken with Rome in order to cast myself into the arms of the Chief Consistory or the *Kreuzzeitung*. But here too, I had slowly and gradually to feel my way towards my new point of view, for it must be remembered that after fourteen years' seclusion from the world I was an absolute stranger to the religious and political currents of its life. I re-entered them at the age of forty with almost child-like inexperience. How could I have come quickly and easily to a decision?

There was one person who helped my views to mature, but who afterwards took little pleasure in the fruits.

Scarcely had I settled down in Berlin when Dr. Adolf Stöcker, who had suggested the writing of my first anti-Jesuit article, tried to bring me over to his side. He often visited me, and also invited me. Only on one occasion did I accept his invitation, in order to avoid the appearance of discourtesy; and then I met, among a fairly large party, his " friend," Baron Wilhelm von

Hammerstein. At our very first meeting Stöcker made an unpleasant impression on me. He appeared to me the type of the domineering and—with all his gifts— narrow-minded parson. With and for him: never! Of that I was determined at the outset. There are " Jesuits," too, among the " orthodox " Protestants, and Stöcker was their General. What I found particularly repugnant in Stöcker was his hatred of Catholicism (which was afterwards modified through his greed for political power), combined with a boundless ignorance of the subject. I had left the Catholic religion, but I did not hate it then, nor do I now. How, indeed, would it have been possible, when throughout my life I had found in it so much that was fair and good? It was absolutely revolting to my feelings to find such hatred, inflamed by ignorance, poured forth by a weighty representative of Christianity.

Yet Stöcker's ignorance of Catholicism is a fundamental fault of all Protestant circles, in particular of the " Orthodox " section.

Once I was visiting one of our leading Protestant dignitaries. The late Provost von der Göltz was also present. The two men discussed their experiences at Bonn, and the conversation turned on the Catholic Church. Their statements could have been proved by any Catholic schoolboy in the Second Class to be foolish distortion and misunderstanding. At that time I was still very reserved and shy, though happily I have since thrown off my shyness, and therefore I did not undertake to play the schoolboy's part, but entered into an animated conversation with the hostess, a charming lady, whom death unfortunately claimed all too soon.

These people do not know how injurious are the effects of ignorance, how greatly it widens the gulf between the denominations. Things are beginning to improve in this respect in Liberal Protestant circles. But even they are still overshadowed by a dense cloud of ignorance. And the worst of it is that both Orthodox Protestants and Liberals are as convinced of their accurate knowledge of Catholicism as the Pope of his infallibility. I have often observed this with sorrow and dismay at the central committee meetings of the "Evangelischer Bund." There I saw leaders of the Liberal and Orthodox theology, who thought themselves much better informed about Catholicism than I, who had belonged to the Roman Church for forty years. The ignorance of Protestantism among Catholics is not nearly so great. The saying, *Catholica non leguntur*, is unfortunately often true; while, on the other side, *Protestantica* are very carefully studied.

In February, 1895, I joined the Protestant State Church. Dr. Dryander, at that time pastor of the Holy Trinity Church, admitted me to communion. I had also attended his preparatory course, but found little satisfaction in it. Dryander's diplomatic theological manner, which gives no decided answer to any question, neither was nor is congenial to me.

What was it that induced me to join the Protestant community? Certainly not my love of the State Church. After living for forty years in a Church community, I was growing weary of my religious wanderings, which had continued since the end of 1892, and as the delusion that Church and religion were necessarily connected was not yet extinguished in me, I was easily induced, by the gentle pressure brought by various acquaintances, to formal and outward adhesion. But I never left Dryander in doubt as to my want of enthusiasm for the step.

At this day I should no longer take the step, but neither do I retract it.

Church and religion—Church and Christianity—are different, often antagonistic, ideas. This I have learnt with certainty. All Churches are merely the work of man;

in the fewest cases are they the outcome of religious needs; far oftener they spring from a greed for power. And further, the Prussian State Church is a very imperfect human institution which, both inwardly and outwardly, has lost much of its religious Christian character, and assumed instead that of bureaucratic formalism combined with dependence on State and Court.

The "religious" Head of the State Church, its *summus episcopus*, is the lord of the land, who at the same time is Head of the Army and Navy, and commander of such and such foreign regiments; the dignitaries of the State Church (the Head of the Consistory, the Consistories, General Superintendents, Superintendents, Pastors), are State officials in the pay of the State. A mere glance at the Scriptures, and the position there occupied by the Christian dignitaries, the "episcopi" and "presbyters," must show that the Archbishop and the authorities of the State Church have not the slightest connection with Christianity. State and religion, State and Christianity, are eccentric circles; they can only be made concentric through the sacrifice of religion and Christianity.

But its unnatural relation to the State is not the only thing in the State Church which is unchristian and unreligious. Their dependence on the Court is as much to be condemned. The whole system of Court chaplains is —to speak openly for once—a system of Court flunkeyism, far removed from the point of view of the Christian religion. Of course, I do not speak of the Court preachers in their character as men. I refer to Court chaplains and Court chaplaincies as conceptions and State institutions.

The Court chaplains are part of the *staffage* at Court ceremonies; they bear courtly titles such as Your Excellency; they have to preach at the time and place prescribed by the wearer of the crown, and from texts chosen by him, often at festivals, such as the Conferment of Orders, which are absolutely opposed to the essence of Christianity—and, indeed, of religion.* What room is there left for a trace of religion and Christianity ?

State and Church, bureaucracy and formalism, have almost completely estranged the State Church from the people, and that is another of its fundamental abuses. It is believed that by elaborate Church edifices "the religion of the people will be maintained," that Christianity can be supported and popularised by meaningless externalities (such as an elaborate consecration ceremony of the Cathedral and a ceremonious expedition to Palestine), but the recognition seems lacking that such things have very little to do with popularising, and nothing at all with Christianity and religion. In the midst of the numerous unchristian externalities of the State Church, God, religion and Christianity have become a mere cover to hide a mass of vanity and self-glorification. And it is a serious delusion to imagine that the "people" are not aware of it.

The more a Church is built up, both within and without, on sincerity and simplicity, the closer it adheres to the impressive simplicity of the model afforded by the community of Christ and the Apostles as depicted in the Bible, the larger will be the circles of the masses it encompasses, the deeper its impression on humanity and its power to ennoble and raise them.

In addition to all this, there is in the State Church an unevangelical lack of freedom, which takes the form of compulsory belief, trials for heresy, laws against heresy, and all the other fine things which call themselves Christian, and yet are so human that they must be included among the darker aspects of human activity, those which owe

* The right text for a sermon on the occasion of conferring orders was once suggested by the old Court Chaplain Büchsel with delightful outspokenness and ironical reflection on himself: "When they saw the star, they rejoiced with exceeding great joy."

their origin not to religion, but to a truly unreligious lust for power and dominion.

Such a Church cannot inspire love, nor even much respect. For the good it does in the social or educational domain, to balance its failure in the domain of religion and Christianity, cannot be taken into account when estimating its value as a Christian Church and community. This is done much better by other non-religious associations.

And yet, as I have said, I shall not retract the step I took in February, 1895, for by leaving a Church we forfeit the right to share in its deliberations and help in the work of reform.

Again and again have I been asked, often in most indiscreet fashion, " What is your religious standpoint ? " The question is quite unjustifiable, for religion is an absolutely private matter which concerns no one, least of all the general public or the curious and sensation-mongers. "When thou prayest," thus spoke the most religious of all men, Jesus Christ, " enter into thy closet," *i.e.* keep the public out. And in my view prayer is not *one* of the main functions of religion, but *the* main function.

The inquiry as to my religious attitude is, therefore, unjustifiable; but still in this, the book of my life, I will say a few words in answer.

The point at which I now stand has been reached by a process of slow development, a road of curves and spirals. The development is, strictly speaking, as old as my power of thinking. Vague doubts dawned even in my childish soul ; in later years they often became tormenting temptations, until at last Catholic faith and Catholic Christianity collapsed within me. The result was my secession from the Church and the Jesuit Order.

What new edifice did I erect on these gigantic ruins of

religion and Christianity? A small one, for I have learnt to be modest in my religious demands.

First of all, I do not include in religion such externals as dogmas, sacraments, creeds, symbols, liturgies, ceremonies. They may be of less or greater religious value to individuals, but in themselves they are not part of religion; at most and at best they supply to many thousands useful, perhaps even necessary, outward manifestations of their religious impulses and feelings. But religion is the inward relation of the individual, based on subjective and individual recognition and the personal conscience, to God, that Being beyond this world, Whose existence is demanded by reason as the origin and final aim of the physical and spiritual world.*

Now, what is the character of this relation of man to God? This question is answered by Christ, Who thus steps into the foreground as the founder, even creator, of a religion.

It is He Who has set mankind in the filial relation to God, Who gave him God as a Father. The age of religious servitude which saw in God and gods only lords, kings and tyrants, who worshipped God and gods in fear and trembling, has gone by. From henceforth the wondrous saying of Christ has become the basis of religion: " Our Father, which art in Heaven."

The proclamation of the Fatherhood of God by Christ is not without precedent in the history of religion. Buddha had already set mankind on the road of heartfelt love and communion with God, but never yet had the relation of father and child, between God and man, been so clearly expressed and so comprehensively represented as by Christ.

This is the characteristic of the whole of Christianity;

---

* The man whose reason does not demand the existence of such a supernatural Being possesses no religion, but is not on that account bad, if his life is in harmony with innate natural laws and the ethical principles universally recognised in civilised countries; and sooner or later he, too, will attain to God.

it comprises its whole contents as a religion. Everything else which the Scriptures lay down as the teaching of Christ is either a development of this fundamental idea or an injunction for the conduct of men towards one another. Dogmas and creeds (the divine humanity of Christ, the Trinity, etc.) are the products of a subtilising theology which has lost the immediate characteristic of religious feeling—are systems more or less subtle which satisfy the desire of men for abstract sophistry, for fashioning according to types and by means of catalogues, but which are entirely opposed to the notion of religion. It is on the recognition of this fact that my Christianity is based, and in this I find the satisfaction of my religious needs.

Not that there are not a number of world riddles and obscure questions—as, for instance, What is the nature of God ? (Even the fact of His existence cannot be mathematically demonstrated.) What happens after death ? and many other problems.

But such questions and riddles have nothing to do with religion. Religion and its true meaning consist in the saying: "I am God's child and God is my Father." Those who cannot fashion their religion and their religious attitude out of this thought will not be furthered in their religion by creeds, symbols, dogmas, liturgies, and sermons.

In the thought of God's Fatherhood lies also the impulse to that religious activity which I regard as the main sinew of religion, without which all religious apparatus lacks religion, and with which everything is religion, even without any apparatus—I mean, our intercourse with God the Father in prayer.

The idea of God's Fatherhood is an endless source of immeasurable confidence. The Being Whom I call God, the final Aim and End of the world and its happenings, must be endlessly wise, good, powerful, just. And this unending Being is my Father. There is neither weakness nor sin nor error which does not vanish into nothingness in the face of such unending nature. God my Father is the Author of my being; He has placed me in the world, unasked, therefore He must also, some time—when, where and how I know not—become the Perfecter of my happiness. The saying, often frivolously applied, *Tout comprendre, c'est tout pardonner*, has the deepest religious and genuine God-like meaning.

This religious meaning has been revealed to me by Christ, and, therefore, it is the foundation and cornerstone of my religion. Therefore I am a Christian.

Would this recognition have been impossible without Christ? Certainly not. Therefore Christ is, to speak, theoretically, not the indispensable founder of religion. But because He actually drew forth this recognition from the existing religious confusion, and placed it before our eyes in its grand simplicity, therefore, in the light of history, He is the greatest religious founder.

Thus Christianity is also the world-religion, for thus it comprises all religions, and leads them, as long as they are not opposed to natural laws, upwards into a higher unity. Divine Manhood, and the doctrine of the Two Natures, transform Christ into an unnatural hybrid, and plunge Him so deeply into the heathen mythology of demigods and the offspring of gods as to remove Him entirely from healthy human comprehension, which must be at the basis of every religious sentiment.

And thus Christ, Who on the cross became a martyr to His religious ideas, has arisen from the grave, not in the body, but in the Spirit; He lives, not in flesh and blood, but in Spirit and in Truth, in Power, and in the effects of His teachings and works.

The small and limited literary activity described above by no means satisfied my desire for work. In particular, I missed a regular fixed occupation, which was the natural result of the training I had had ever since my childhood. I hoped to find it in the Government service. Before I entered the Jesuit Order I had been a Royal Prussian *Referendar*, and, as an irreproachable citizen, I thought that I had the right to re-appointment. How greatly was I to be undeceived!

What I am about to write here is not stated from any sensational motives. I register facts which constitute a piece of not uninteresting contemporary history, and which, under the stage direction of the Centre Party, were enacted behind the scenes.

Count Finckenstein-Madlitz, whom I have already mentioned, had been kind enough, in the summer of 1894, to go to the Imperial Chancellor, Count Caprivi, and ask him to re-appoint me to the Prussian State service. Caprivi, with a movement of distinct alarm, gave the remarkable answer: "What would the Holy Father in Rome and the Centre Party say, if we were to employ Count Hoensbroech in the State service?" That settled the request of a German and Prussian citizen for a State appointment, as far as the German Imperial Chancellor and Prussian Minister-President was concerned. But there was a sequel to that story.

In February, 1895, I suddenly, without any action on my part, received "by Imperial command" an invitation to a small Court ball. The Kaiser desired to make my acquaintance. For more than half an hour on the evening of February 13th, 1895, William II. conversed with me in the White Hall of the Berlin Castle, to the great annoyance of the Centre leader, Lieber, who was also present and, because the Kaiser was so long conversing with me, missed the opportunity of being presented. To the Kaiser's question as to what I intended to do, I replied that it was my wish to re-enter the State service, but there were great difficulties in the way of its fulfilment. And I informed him about the utterance of Caprivi. The Kaiser took a step back, put his hand on his sword, and said excitedly: "What! Did Caprivi say that to you?" "Yes, your Majesty." "Well, my dear Count, then I assure you that from this time forward I shall take your affairs into my own hands."

I asked him for a private audience, to enable me to give him further information, for the long conversation with the Kaiser was causing universal sensation—Miquel was circling fox-like round the Kaiser and me—and therefore it appeared to me undiplomatic. The Kaiser graciously consented, with the remark that I was to inform Lukanus, saying: "There he stands." Then he dismissed me with a friendly and hearty handshake. I immediately informed Lukanus of the granting of the private audience, and asked him to assign a time for it. Lukanus received my communication with an expression of ill-concealed annoyance, but in face of the wish of his master he could not avoid assuring me that he would "in due time" inform me of the day and hour of the audience.

For the next few days the leading organs of the Centre Party (*Germania* and *Kölnische Volkszeitung*) contained violent articles inspired by the Centre leader, Lieber, about the "extraordinary circumstance" of the Kaiser's invitation to me, and the distinction he conferred on me by our long interview.

The whole attitude of the Kaiser had convinced me that the promised audience would soon be granted. Weeks and months went by, but I saw and heard nothing. Several questions addressed in letters to Lukanus were answered evasively. As the Kaiser had promised me a post as Head of a District (*Landrat*), and only a province with a preponderance of Protestants could be under consideration, the then Minister of the Interior, von Köller, had advised me to take up my residence in Kiel, in order to become acquainted with the conditions there. Therefore, in October, 1895, I migrated to Kiel with my wife, for I had married in August of that year. But her severe illness, which necessitated an operation, forced me to return to Berlin in December.

During my residence in Kiel, I several times visited the General Field-Marshal, Count Waldersee, with whom I was acquainted, who at that time was General in command of the 9th Army Corps at Altona. On one of these occasions I informed Waldersee of my still unsatisfied claim for an audience. I had long ago given up all hope of it, on account of the information I had in the meantime received about the influence of the Centre Party on the Kaiser; but I did not want to be so curtly set aside. I desired that my right to an audience, founded on the Imperial promise, should be recognised.

Waldersee said, with a peculiar expression on his face, "Yes, yes; that fox Lukanus," and proposed that I should give him a memorial to the Kaiser, who was expected at Altona in the next few days for an inspection and would be lunching with him. He would choose a favourable moment for presenting my memorial to the Kaiser and enforcing its claim. "Then we shall have disposed of Lukanus." I sat down at Waldersee's writing-table, and wrote the petition, and after a little while I was informed by Waldersee: "Everything has gone off satisfactorily; I hope you will soon get your audience." Again weeks went by; then, at the end of January, 1896, when I lay ill in bed with influenza, I received a telegram, signed by the Chief Court-Marshal Eulenberg, from the New Palace, which invited me to an audience, "to-morrow at 11 o'clock." One of the Imperial carriages would fetch me from Wildpark.

My first impulse was to telegraph a refusal on account

of my illness, but then I thought, "The opportunity may never recur"; and so I put in an appearance punctually at the New Palace, in a high state of fever, without even considering that I was exposing the Kaiser to the risk of infection. Lukanus conducted me to the Kaiser, and remained present during the audience, which lasted for more than an hour. The Kaiser received me very graciously. After a sympathetic inquiry about the health of my wife, who was ill in a nursing-home, he opened the conversation with the words: "I have asked you here to learn your opinion about the attitude of my Government to the Centre Party." Of course, I cannot repeat the contents of our interview; it gave me the opportunity for an interesting insight into the Kaiser's psychology and into public affairs. But there was not a word about personal matters, of a State appointment, nor of his promise to take my affairs into his own hands. Only, quite at the end, when he dismissed me in a friendly manner, the Emperor said: "Everything else Lukanus will tell you"; but after the audience I informed Lukanus that I set little value on "everything else" which he would have to tell me; that I should only come to him in order to carry out the wish of the Kaiser. In the interview which then took place with Lukanus I curtly rejected his proposals, which contained next to nothing tangible: a position as *Landrat* or anything else of the kind had become "impossible," but there was nothing to prevent my returning to the State service as *Referendar* at Frankfort-on-the-Oder!

Soon afterwards I was told by a well-informed authority that the Centre had told the Minister of War that if I received a State appointment, the Party would close its ranks, and vote against the next naval estimates. And when the Minister reported this to the Kaiser, he let fall the remark: "If matters stand thus, I shall let the man drop." In this way I and my affairs slipped through the fingers of his Majesty which, according to his Imperial promise, were to hold and lead me on. The pressure from the Centre Party had compelled the Imperial hand to let me go.

Of course it was not the matter of my own personality which induced the Centre Party to take up this attitude. It was a fundamental principle for which it was fighting: the rebel against the Roman Church must not make his way in Prussia. And yet the Centre emphatically advocates " civic toleration " and " religious equality."

A good friend of mine in the Ministry of Public Instruction, the late Count Andreas Bernsdorff, had suggested to me the idea of taking up an academic career, and settling down at the University of Berlin, or some other Prussian University, as a lecturer (*Privatdozent*) on Church history. He procured me an interview with the Minister of Public Instruction, Dr. Bosse.

Bosse received me with overwhelming amiability : that was an excellent idea, and quite in accordance with his own wishes, etc., etc., but the consideration which he was obliged to take for the powerful Centre Party unfortunately rendered the execution of this excellent plan impossible. " What a storm the Centre would raise in Parliament were I to consent to your appointment as lecturer, or even advocate it ! " This panic-mongering caused my gall to overflow; I rose and took my leave with the words : " Your Excellency, until to-day I should not have thought that a Minister in a land of religious equality like Prussia, would thus give way before the troops of Rome."*

In Prussia accordingly the doors of all appointments were closed to me. Would they stand open in the Empire ?

---

* Bosse was speechless at the time ; it was not till years later that he recovered his voice, when he happened once to sit next me at dinner after his resignation. Then he said to me: " At that time you treated me very badly " ; to which I replied : " And you treated me and yourself even worse."

A request to the Imperial Chancellor, Prince Hohenlohe, for admission to the diplomatic service met with a polite refusal.

These are some reminiscences from the dark days of my rebellion against the Church, whose arm is long. They belong to the same time when I was warned by the Foreign Office only to go there after dark, and with great precautions (I used often to go there to visit one of the Reporting Councillors), for the Centre Party had set detectives to watch my goings to and fro.*

Still, I regard it as providential that everything turned out thus. How could I, as a State official or a diplomat, have carried on my life's task: to spread enlightenment about Ultramontanism, and stir up a conflict against it?

In the fulfilment of this difficult task I have found contentment and success, but also many a disappointment.

It is impossible in this place to develop my ultramontane programme. For this I refer to my writings: *Ultramontanism: its Nature and how to Attack It*;† *The Modern State and the Romish Church*; *Rome and the Centre*.‡

I will say only a few words about my disappointments, because they are characteristic of our internal politics.

The wrongly conducted *Kulturkampf* of the 'seventies, with its unfortunate issue, had greatly damped the desire to attack Ultramontanism, and also increased immeasurably the political force which Ultramontanism possesses in the Centre. The Government parties and the Press,

---

* I do not propose to enter into the violent personal attacks to which I and my family were exposed. My book, *In eigener Sache und Anderes*, gives information on the subject.

† It afforded me great satisfaction that Bismarck had read this book with considerable interest. It stood among other much-used books in his reference library. There I saw it, full of book-markers, when I visited Friedrichsruhe soon after the death of the great man.

‡ *Der Ultramontanismus, sein Wesen und seine Bekämpfung* (Leipzig, Breitkopf und Härtel), *Moderner Staat und Römische Kirche* (Berlin, E. N. Schwetschke und Sohn), *Rom und das Zentrum* (Leipzig, Breitkopf und Härtel).

unable to distinguish the wrongful methods of the old struggle from its rightful aims, were powerless in face of their great antagonist. On the other hand, the Centre had offered its Parliamentary collaboration. The Government parties and the Press were overcome by the desire for compromise; they forgot that in the Centre is embodied the ultramontane view of life, that it is the deadly enemy of the modern State and the development of its civilisation, and saw in it only the party whose numerous members could give decisive votes for their legislation. Added to this was their fear of social democracy. " Better black than red," they used to say at that time!

Each year the Centre became a more convenient ally. Shallow opportunism and Miquel's "collective policy" did their part. No one would hear of a new and better conducted *Kulturkampf*. The circles that set the tone regarded a *Kulturkampf* as a struggle between denominational passions. The recognition that Ultramontanism is historically and actually separable from the Catholic religion, that therefore the struggle against it must be, not a denominational but a political struggle on behalf of civilisation—this recognition, which is the alpha and omega of a *Kulturkampf* with any prospect of success, had not yet dawned upon them. Therefore my rallying cry against Ultramontanism fell on deaf ears. I was included among the stirrers up of denominational strife.*

---

* Every association with a distinctly denominational tendency (such as the " Evangelischer Bund," the " Gustav Adolf Verein," etc.) is, as far as its tendency is anti-ultramontane, harmful, for it arouses denominational counter-passions, and thus supplies Ultramontanism with a weapon which makes it invincible, the calling of religion into the field for its own purposes. The only right method in combating Ultramontanism is pursued by the " Anti-ultramontaner Reichsverband " (President, Admiral von Knorr; Office, Berlin, S.W., Wilhelmstrasse 122a). Here denominationalism and religion are excluded by the constitutions. It attacks its opponents on those domains where alone it is open to attack and capable of defeat—that is, politics and education. All who recognise the threatening danger of ultramontane Jesuitism should join this Association.

2 E

In spite of the greatest hindrances, and often of the severest disappointments, increased by ultramontane attacks and accusations, I held out, in the consciousness that I was on the right road. And my work of enlightenment, in spoken words and in writings, has not been in vain. Slowly the wheel began to swing round, and a characteristic proof of this is that, in great part through my labours on behalf of enlightenment, the saying, "Rather black than red" has been changed for the opposite, "Rather red than black." Still there is an immense deal yet to be done. Above all, the highest standpoint is still lacking: the consciousness that the struggle with Ultramontanism has a background and a significance in universal history; that in reality the existence or non-existence of a modern state of civilisation depends on the result of this struggle. And only this recognition can produce the joy and determination for combat which are guarantees of victory.

This book proves beyond refutation that at the present moment the driving force of Ultramontanism is Jesuitism. In Jesuitism are concentrated all the intolerance, reaction, fanaticism, irreligion, and hostility to progress which in the course of centuries have sprung from ultramontane soil. And these forces, with their hostility to human nature, have been set in motion by Jesuitism with a cunning and unscrupulous daring unexampled in the history of the Christian era. Thus the sum total of my book may be compressed into the saying of the great French statesman and patriot, Gambetta, with an addition, "*Le Cléricalisme*" —Clericalism is Ultramontanism—"*et le Jésuitisme, voilà l'ennemi!*"

Yet my book shall close with a more peaceful note and a happier outlook.

Those who fight against Jesuitism and Ultramontanism fight for the religious liberation of many, many millions of Catholics. But the Catholic religion conceals, in spite of terrible human weaknesses—and in what creed are these lacking?—forcible and profound elements of edification and civilisation. They are held down and misused by the violation of their true nature through ultramontane Jesuit tyranny. What a task for a liberator, after subduing Ultramontanism and Jesuitism, to allow these seeds to germinate!

Wide horizons and possibilities of religious and educational development open up before us. We seem to hear the bells ringing for peace, and their sound proclaims the coming of a better day.

For humanity needs religion, and will always need it. But men must refrain from religious strife and denominational bitterness.

Let us allow religions to develop themselves, only let us root out ignorance from them, and destroy it!

Concord—and unity too—comprehension and toleration will result and bring blessing.

THROUGH CONFLICT TO PEACE.

INDEX

achen, relics at the Cathedral of, i. 324.5; author's pilgrimage to, ii. 212
albeck, Jesuit villa at, ii. 77
biturienten at Berlin University, ii. 403 (*note*)
bsolution, question of, in reserved cases, i. 363
cademy, purpose of the Jesuit, i, 125; exclusion from, as a means of pressure, 177
colyte, misuse of the post of, in Jesuit schools, i. 161
cquaviva, Claudius, drafts the *Ratio Studiorum*, i. 63; condemns Jesuit neglect of Latin, 101.2; approves Marian Congregations, 176; Commission of Studies in Germany instituted by, 190; on the unchastity of the Order, 204, ii. 71, 107 (*note*); enjoins the reading of Loyola's letter on obedience, i. 337; deprecates the reluctance to make a "statement" of conscience, 347; advises the omission of references to confession from annual reports, 366; concerning women and the Exercises, 383-4; completes the organisation of the Society of Jesus, 407; advises reserve in political matters, ii. 10; his instructions as to the confessing of women, 124, 125, 126; enjoins surveillance of priests and the size of confessionals, 127.8; his crafty hint to confessors of princes, 137; his Ordinance on the confessing of sovereigns, 169.70; his secret Instructions touching the confessing of sovereigns, 172-3, 429; sanctions the publication of Mariana's book approving tyrannicide, 328; obliged to condemn this doctrine, 333.4
dmonitor, duties of, i. 352, 420, 422, 424
dultery, Jesuit condonation of, ii. 305, 309; on sinning to avoid, 323-5
Advocatus Diaboli, duties of, ii. 86 (*note*)
Aehrenthal, Baron Luis von, i. 244
Æsthetics, Jesuit conception of, i. 124
Affiliates of the Society of Jesus, ii. 13-21; Loyola's recognition of, 16-17
Agnus Dei, as used by Jesuit students, i. 182; in Bavaria, 319
Agricola, Father, records the existence of some curious relics, i. 313; gives an instance of demoniac possession, 322
Aguirre, Cardinal, on Jesuit morals, ii. 291.2
Aix-la-Chapelle, great relics at, i. 324-5; author's pilgrimage to, ii. 212
Alexander III , Tsar, ii. 167
Alexander VII , Pope, the *Exercitium spirituale* of, used at Jesuit schools, i. 181; supports the designs of the Jesuits in Hungary, ii. 145; condemns Jesuit teaching on morals, 292
Alexander VIII., Pope, condemns Jesuit teaching on morals, ii. 292
Algiers, author visits, i. 261-2
Allen, Cardinal, ii. 151
Aloysius of Gonzaga, an objectionably "angelic" boy, i. 208, 386, 400; an example to the young, ii. 111; supports the Virgin in a vision of her Descent, 112
Aloysius, St., Congregations of, i. 164
Altona, Count Waldersee at, ii. 461
Alvarez, Father Balthasar, i. 370
Alvarez, Emanuel, "Latin Grammar" of, i. 70-2
Ambiguity, Jesuit doctrine of, ii. 304.7
America, Province of, Bishop Palafox's report of Jesuit wealth in, ii. 87-8
Anatomia anatomiae Societatis Jesu, ii. 9
Anderledy, General of the Jesuit Order, influence of, over the Marchioness of Hoensbroech, i. 33; admits the Jesuit control of the Marian Congregations, 171; examples of his mental dexterity, 174; approves of the author's conduct during novitiate, 403; declines to stop the ostracism of Leo XIII., ii. 67; his diploma to the Marchioness of Hoensbroech, 129; attitude of, towards General Boulanger, 165; unpopularity of, among Jesuits, 414
André on Jesuit morality, ii. 299
Angelic Doctor (Aquinas), ii. 253
Angelita, Canon John Marcell, on the death of Cardinal Tournon, ii. 54
Angelus Bell, Jesuit students and, i. 121
Angelus Custos, the duties of, i. 271, 355
Anti-ultramontaner Reichsverband, ii. 465 (*note*)
Antonio, Father Francisco, on the post of princes' confessor, ii. 195.
Apparitions, Catholic belief in, encouraged, i. 26 *et seqq.*; instances of pseudo-mystical, 299 *et seqq.*
Appiani, Antonio, alleges that Cardinal Tournon was poisoned, ii. 54-5; persecuted by the Jesuits, 61, 63
Aquinas, Thomas, authority of, in theology, ii. 253.6
Arcana Societatis Jesu, ii. 10
Aristocracy, Jesuit subservience to, i. 145.6, ii. 372
Aristotle, supremacy of, in the Jesuit philosophy schools, ii. 250.3
Arminia, the Catholic Students' Union at Bonn, i. 245
Arnauld, Antoine, Jesuit forgeries in the name of, ii 315.7

Index

rnoux, Father, Confessor of Louis XIII., intrigues of, ii. 183, 184 (*note*) rrogance of the Society of Jesus, ii. 105-23

Art, doctrine of the Catholic Church concerning, i. 46.7; Jesuit teaching about, 124.5

Artaut, Adrien, ii. 93

Asceticism of the Jesuit Order, i. 326 *et seqq.*; as distinct from piety, 295; Jesuit ascetic discipline considered, 326-90; Jesuit asceticism compared with Christian, 326; its end and the means to it, ιο.; maintained by blind obedience, 326.40; how it compels to sin, 335.6; dependence on the Superior the rule of practice of, 341; the Statement of Conscience as a mainstay of, 342.8; fostered by denunciation, espionage and uniformity, 348.61; greatly supported by confession, 361.9; observances of the Exercises complete the discipline of, 369.84; fruits of, 384.90; instances of what has been done as a result of, 386-90

Assistancies of the Jesuit Order, i. 416

Assistants to the General of the Society of Jesus, i. 422

Attrition, doctrine of, ii. 300, 381-2

Auersperg, Prince, ii. 146-7

Austria, education in, shaped by the Jesuits, i. 70-2; the El Dorado of the Jesuits, 93; the Jesuits and the war with Prussia in 1866, 210-14, ii. 37-8; wealth of the Jesuits in, at the date of the suppression of the Order, 85

vaux, Claude Mesmes, Count d', ii. 160

'Ave, Maria," Latin and German texts, i. 5

Aveiro, Duke of, ii. 336

Bachem, A., on the Marian Congregations, i. 170

Bachem, Karl, on the German Centre Party's indebtedness to Jesuit guidance, ii. 344 (*note*)

aexem, Suicide's grave at, ii. 398

Bagshawe, Christopher, on Jesuits of Elizabeth's reign, ii. 46

Balde, Jacob, Jesuit poet, ii. 160; held up to admiration, 229

Ballerini on the use of equivocations, ii. 307

Bamberg, the Jesuit gymnasium in, in 1742, i. 114

Barat, Madeleine, Mother, foundress of the female Congregation of the Sacred Heart, i. 307

Bartoli, Father, on the necessity of blind obedience, i. 339

Baumgartner, his criticism of Schiller, ii. 234.6; his tirade on Goethe, 236.45; his real literary convictions, 244; required to alter his monograph on Goethe, 244.5; his character transformed, 245 (*note*), 372

Baumstark, Reinhold, on Jesuit morality, ii. 294; on Jesuit influence through confession, 387; his condemnation of the Order, 430; death of, 430 (*note*)

Bavaria, Jesuit schools in, condemned by Government, i. 193.4; effects of Jesuit piety in, 319; wealth of the Jesuit Order in, ii. 83.4

Bazaine, Marshal, i. 232

Beauty, perverted Catholic ideas of, i. 46-8

Becanus, Father, activity of, in Austrian public affairs, ii. 181; on the doing of a lesser sin to avoid a greater, 321

Beck, Chief District Judge, and the Jesuit designs against the Hohenzollerns, ii. 384.5

Beck, Theoderich, i. 207, ii. 71

Beckx, Peter, General of the Jesuit Order, maintains the reactionary system of education in Austria, i. 71; the author visits, at Rome, 263; his advice, 264; approves of the author's conduct during novitiate, 403; provides for the supremacy of the General Congregation, 423; a confessor of princes, ii. 135 (*note*), pleased with the author's " progress in virtue," 209; on modern philosophy, 251.2; instruction of, establishing literary censorship, 264-6

Bedburg, the Catholic aristocratic academy at, i. 229

Behrens, Provincial Superior of the German Jesuit province, character of, i. 33; his influence over the author's sister Antonia, 211; misrepresents the facts of the Franco-German war, 233; his power paramount with the author's mother, 234 and *note*; disciplinary notions of, 389

Beissel, Stephan, and the relics at Aix-la-Chapelle, i. 324.5; edits the *Stimmen aus Maria-Laach*, 345

Bellarmin, Cardinal, saves Loyola's letter from condemnation by the Inquisition, i. 336; a famous Jesuit theologian, ii. 111; on the supremacy of Church over State, 338; teaches the " indirect " power of the Pope, 428

Benedict, St., the founder of monachism, ii. 424

Benedict XIII., Pope, and the Jesuit Memorial touching the Chinese Mission, ii. 60-1 (*note*), refrains from publishing Innocent XI.'s decree against the Jesuits, 65

Benedict XIV., Pope, and the Marian Congregations, i. 165; asserts the Jesuit right to control them, 170; repealed the decree of Innocent X. as to the holding of General Congregations, 424; reminds the Jesuits of the obedience they owe the Pope, ii. 66

Benedictines, Jesuit opposition to, at Magdeburg, ii. 98; free from the stains of the Jesuits, 424

Bennigsen, Rudolf, and the suspension of the German laws against the Jesuits, ii. 345 (*note*)

Berchmanns, Johannes, wonders wrought by, i. 308, 309.10; canonised by Leo XIII., 309; legends of, ii. 111.2

Berge-Borbeck, railway accident at, i. 250

Berlin, author joins the First Dragoon Guards at, i. 253.4; author prepares for the Jesuit settlement at, ii. 399 411; author attends university at, 403; result of the author's studies

Index

in, 407; author makes his residence in, 422
Berling, Jesuits convert the wealthy widow of, ii. 166-7
Berlingske Tidende, ii. 167
Bermudez, Father, character of, ii. 188
Bernard, St., his contempt of the human body, i. 391-2
Bernsdorff, Count Andreas, ii. 463
Berruyer, Father Joseph, the Pope condemns the book by, ii. 52
Berti, Giovanni, on Jesuit versatility, ii. 291
Bethmann-Hollweg, Von, German Chancellor, ii. 85 (*note*)
Beyschlag, Professor, ridiculed by the Jesuit Pesch, ii. 361; his private life to be investigated, 375
Bible, Catholic neglect of the, i. 14; disregarded in Jesuit education, 318; neglect of, in the Exercises, 382
Bieczynski, Father Stanislaus, i. 140-1
Biedermann, influence of, on the author, ii. 406
Biedermann, Father Jacob, celebrates the pity and love of Father Rem, i. 311
Bien Public, Le, i. 6; supports Papal infallibility, 222
Billet, Father Karl, tries to induce the author to enter the Jesuit Order, i. 217
Bishops, Catholic, status of, i. 272
Bismarck, Prince, as a sort of Diocletian, i. 16; antagonism of the author's parents to, 16-7; Cohen-Blind's and Kullmann's attempts on the life of, 212; "not wanted even by the devil," *ib.*; his blunder over the Kulturkampf, 255-6; forged documents to be used against, ii. 167; a student of the author's book on Ultramontanism, 464 (*note*)
Bissel, Father, ii. 160-1
Blasius, St., feast of, at Kevelaer, i. 32
Blessed (*Beatus*), a title preliminary to Saint (*Sanctus*), i. 310 (*note*)
Blyenbeck Castle, offered to exiled German Jesuits, i. 248; ceremonial reception of exiles at, 249; set aside for the students in philosophy, 287; a "magister" meal at, ii. 76; the author's residence at, 214-6; the author reads his first Mass at, 222; becomes the seat of the novitiate, 369
Blyssem, Father, on Jesuit political activity at Graz, ii. 140; equivocation of his report to General Acquaviva, 141-2; his use of pseudonyms, 142
Boarding-house system advocated by the Jesuits, i. 130; lack of supervision in, 185
Bobadilla, ii. 383
Bodler, John, on Jesuit wirepulling in Poland, ii. 146-8
Boeselager, Baron Karl von, urges the author to join the Jesuits, i. 248
Böger, Dr., pronounces the author consumptive, i. 254
Bohemia, Jesuits support the war against, ii. 159-60
Bollandists, the compilers of the *Acta Sanctorum*, i. 300 (*note*); library of, ii. 390; a literary republic, 390 (*note*)
Bollandus, John, ii. 114
Bombay, German Jesuit mission at, i. 85
Bone, Heinrich, anthologies compiled by, favoured of the Jesuits, i. 108; Director of the Mayence Gymnasium, 220; teacher at the Catholic Academy at Bedburg, 229
Bongart, Baron von dem, gives the Jesuits the use of his estate of Wynandsrade, i. 287
Boniface VIII., Pope, on the relation between Church and State, ii. 339, 340
Bonn University, the author attends, i. 122, 243; the Arminia at, 245; the Union boycotted by German high-class students, 246
Bonucci on the persecution of Gonzalez, ii. 295 (*note*)
Borgia, Francis, i. 400; canonised, ii. 16, 111
Bosse, Dr., surrenders to Rome, ii. 463 and *note*
Bossuet attacked by Father La Chaise, ii. 185
Boulanger, General, supported by the Jesuits, ii. 164-5
Bourdaloue, Father, duplicity of, ii. 185, 186 (*note*)
Bracamonte y Guzman, Gaspar de, Count of Peñaranda, Catholic ambassador at Munster, ii. 160
Brazil, German Jesuit mission at, i. 85; Father Fah transferred to, ii. 411 (*note*), the author collects money for, 419
Breitung, work of, on the Deluge condemned, ii. 268; is rusticated to Ordrupshoj, *ib.*
Breisgau, in the Austrian Borderlands, ii. 40
Brentano, as a German classic, i. 108
Bresciani, Antonio, novels of, approved by Jesuit teachers, i. 153-4
Brischar, Father, Professor of History at Wynandsrade, ii. 121
Britto, Father, ii. 64-5
Bruhl, Pastor of Guelders, i. 43
Brussels, the De Buck lawsuit at, ii. 99-100; the author's studies in, 390-1
Buchberger, Professor, ii. 311
Buchsel, Court Chaplain, ii. 454 (*note*)
Buchum, General Assembly of Catholics at, ii. 393
Buck, De, lawsuit at Brussels, i. 99-100
Buddha and his teaching, ii. 456
Buffalo, German Jesuit mission at, i. 85
Bulls: *Omnipotentis Dei*, i. 165; *Regimini militantis ecclesiae*, 407, 413; *Exposcit debitum*, 413; *Ascendente Domino*, 417; of Urban VIII., canonising Ignatius Loyola, ii. 21-2; of Clement XI., excommunicating the Bishop of Macao, 59; *unigenitus*, 189; *Unam sanctam*, 312, 340
Buonvisi, Francisco, Cardinal, on Jesuit morality, ii. 291
Busch, Father, i. 121
Busenbaum, a leading Jesuit casuist, ii. 287; on calumniation, 308

Cabarassi, Sebastian, ii. 164
Cabrallius, Jesuit ambassador of Portugal to the Pope, ii. 144
Caduff, Procurator, the author's lie to,

ii. 419; the author restores the money to, 420
alumniation from the Jesuit standpoint, ii. 308
amargo on Jesuit morality, ii. 298-9
ampian, Father Edmund, the English Jesuit preacher, ii. 111; and the excommunication of Queen Elizabeth, 312
ampmuller, Father, violates the confession of Maria Theresa, ii. 175-6
anada, lay members of the Society of Jesus in, ii. 19
anaye, French Ambassador at Venice, on Jesuits and confession, i. 367
andlemas Day, why so named, i. 402 (note)
anisius, Peter, the "Hammer of Heretics," ii. 111
nossa, the Kulturkampf sends Germany to, i. 256
anrobert, Marshal, i. 232
anterbury, Boulangist activity in the Jesuit College at, ii. 164.5
aprivi, Count, ii. 459
apuchins, Jesuit opposition to, at Colmar, ii. 97
arafla, Vincent, enjoins teaching on all Jesuit students, i. 87.8; intervenes on behalf of the other Orders at Vienna University, ii. 45; his crafty device of the "Conscience" formula, 170-1
ardeñas on justifiable equivocation, ii. 304-5
arissimus, the use of this title in a Jesuit society, i. 271
asaubon, Isaac, on the Mayence reprint of Mariana's book, ii. 332-3
astropalao on the justifiable connivance at sin, ii. 322.6
asuists, the chief, among the Jesuits, ii. 288
atalogues, the two Jesuit, i. 354; character of the second, 354.5
atherine of Alexandria, St., ii. 397
atholic League and the German Jesuits, ii. 161
atholic Students' Unions boycotted by Catholics of " blood," i. 246
atholicism, force of tradition in, i. 4.6; grandeur of and superstition in, 12-13; neglect of the Bible by, 14; character of the German Catholic priests, 23; teaches faith in guardian angels, ghosts and devils, 26.7; requires early confession, and why, 34 et seqq.; " morality " of, 39, 40; the three fundamental practices of piety compulsory, 159; erroneously alleged to have been beaten at Königgratz and Sedan, 233; affected by the force of Christian idealism, 277 et seqq.; morality of, dominated by Jesuitism, 286.8; dogma of, dominated by Ultramontanism, 287-8; condemned by its toleration of Jesuitism, 423; the only hope for, 467
Jathrein reflects on Leo XIII., ii. 67; his appearance of scholarship, 277; juggles with the Jesuit approval of Mariana's book on tyrannicide, 328 (note), 331 (note); his view of religious toleration, 353.4; his hostility to State schools, 439
Jaussin, Nicholas, on Jesuit influence in politics, ii. 170; protests against violation of confession of sovereigns, 174
Celibacy, the question of, i. 275
Censorship, Jesuit, ii. 264.9
Centre Party in German politics, a strong ultramontane force, i. 246; created by the Kulturkampf, 256; Jesuit leaders of, ii. 165.6; under Jesuit guidance, 344 and note; involved in the Jesuit settlement in Berlin, 401, 402; power of, in Parliament, 459; hostility of, to the author, 460, 464; influence of, with the Kaiser, 461.3; the predominant force in German politics of the day, 463.4; " better black than red," 465; " rather red than black," 466
Chanones, Loyola's confessor at Montserrat, i. 371
Charity, commercial aspect of, ii. 413
Chastity, the vow of, i. 273; the counsel of chastity examined, 275; violation of, by the Jesuits, ii. 67-71; Jesuit boastfulness of their, 109
Chatel, John, attempts to murder Henry IV. of France, ii. 335
Cheminet, Father, discreditable conduct of, ii. 190
China, wealth of the Jesuits in, ii. 88.9
Chinese rites and missions, the struggle between Rome and the Jesuits about, ii. 53-66
" Chocolate " for the General of the Society of Jesus, ii. 104
Christ, the work He accomplished for humanity, ii. 456.8
Christ, or Anti-Christ," the author's pamphlet, ii. 394
Christianity, the real nature of, ii. 406; the root idea of, 456.8
Christians, classification of, by the Ultramontane Catholic Church, i. 272
Christmas crèche before the High Altar, i. 160.1; midnight Mass on Christmas Eve at Feldkirch, 201.2
Church and State considered, ii. 452.5; a National Church a branch of the Civil Service, 453
Churches, Jesuit, decoration of, i. 160; music in, ib.; theatrical representations in, ib.
Cienfuegos, Cardinal, relates how the Virgin interceded for a dead Jesuit, i. 404.5; extravagance of, ii. 78
Cilicium, use of i. 395
Circulus (Circle) disputation, ii. 248.9
Cisneros, Garcia de, i. 371
Cistercians, Jesuit opposition to, at Magdeburg, ii. 98
Civilta cattolica, the mouthpiece of the Vatican, ii. 340 and note; on the subordination of the State to the Church, 340.2
Cleanliness not always next to godliness, i. 289; lack of, during the novitiate, 392.3
Clement VIII., Pope, and the Marian Congregations, i. 165; on abuse of confession, ii. 387
Clement IX., Pope, prohibits the Orders from carrying on commerce, ii. 99 and note
Clement XI., Pope, Gonzalez appeals to, ii. 51; flagrantly scouted by the Jesuits, 53.65

Index 473

lement XIII., Pope, confirms the condemnation of Berruyer's book, i. 52
lement XIV., Pope, suppresses the Jesuit Order, ii. 22, 66
lément, Jacques, murders Henry III. of France, ii. 328.9
lermont, the Jesuit College authorities at, and the attempt to murder Henry IV. of France, ii. 335
leves, the author takes the State oath at, i. 265
oadjutors. (See Formed Coadjutors)
oblence, anecdote of a nunnery at, i. 8
ohen-Blind attempts the life of Bismarck, i. 212
olleges of Jesuits, i. 78 (note), 79, 80
olmar, trading practices of the Jesuits of, ii. 94.8
ologne, the Jesuits settle at, i. 33; Archbishop Melchers in his cell at, 257; the author studies for the law at, 261; ascetic practices at, 387; the author visits, ii. 421
ommerce and trade, Jesuit success in, ii. 91-9
ommunion, compulsory, in Jesuit schools, i. 159; the author's first communion, 197-200
ompositio loci in the Exercises, i. 373
oncertation, nature of, i. 97; conduct of, 143
oncina, Daniel, on Jesuit morality, ii. 292.3; Jesuit plot against, 317
onfession, mischief of early, i. 34 et seqq., how it destroys the young conscience, 36.9; the monstrosity of early confession, 43; frequency of confession enjoined, and why, 44; mechanical and compulsory, 137, 159; detrimental effect of general confession in Jesuit schools, 162, 163; as practised at Jesuit schools, 183, 198-9; wickedness of confession in the confessor's bedroom, 202.3; as an essential of ascetic discipline, 361.9; freedom of confession denied to the Jesuit, 361; used as a disciplinary scourge, 362; disregarders of Jesuit commands as to, may be starved, 362.3; of reserved sins, 363.4; impropriety of a repeated confession, 364; seal of, violated, 365.7; aided by the practice of conscience-searching, 368-9; the Particular Examination, ib., Jesuit instructions on the confession of women and nuns, ii. 124.5; Jesuit violation of the confession of sovereigns, 174.8; priestly qualification to hear, 192 (note); how abused, 197, 387; veiled under the term Moral Theology, 286; Jesuit exploitation of 386.7; real object of, 388
Confession-Book for Children," cited, i. 36 et seqq.
onfessionals, General Acquaviva's instructions as to the position and size of, for women, ii. 128
ongregations, Marian, i. 163-180; of the Guardian Angels, 164; of St. Aloysius (see Marian Congregations); of the Society of Jesus, 423-5 (see also General Congregation, Procuratorial Congregation, Provincial Congregation); Lazarist Missionary Congregation, ii. 55; Mémoires de la Congrégation de la Mission, 55, 56, 57, 58, 59-65

Conscience weakened and destroyed by confession, i. 36 et seqq.; what the "Statement of Conscience" implies, 228; the sense of personal responsibility ruined by the "statement," 296-7; the "statement" of first rate importance, 342.8; how the "statement" is effected, 344.5; frequency of the "statement," 345; abuses of the "statement," 346.8; degradation of, by the Jesuits in their dealings with sovereigns, 170.1; the use of "conscience cases," 346 (note); liberty of, an absurd doctrine, 351
Conscience-searching, ordinary and particular, i. 368-9
Consecration, the power of, 221.2
Constance, university at, established, ii. 42
Constitutions of the Society of Jesus, touching scholars and other such matters, i. 78; concerning the final importance of obedience, 326 et seqq.; on the "Statement of Conscience," 342.4; on denunciation, 348.9; on the means of reporting (espionage), 352; on compulsory frequent confession to specified confessors, 362; sanction violation of confession, 366; on the use of, 383; experiments prescribed by, 392-3; on penances, 395; authorship of, 407.8; summary of the ten parts of, 408.11; quintessence of, contained in the Formula Instituti, 413; are the Constitutions complete? ii. 1 et seqq.; obscurity respecting, intentional, 3; non-Christian character of, 30.2; cosmopolitanism of, 32; on the vow of chastity, 67; on the scope of the vow of poverty, 71.2; the theory and practice of, compared and contrasted, 105-32; on the confessing of women, 124.5; forbid interference in politics and State affairs, 133.4; prohibit Jesuits from acting as the confessors of statesmen, 168; on the Humanities, 229; on tyrannicide, 334; on keeping the Jesuit lay brother in ignorance, 388-9; approved by the Papacy, 423; cold and calculating regulations, 424-5
Consultors, the duties of, i. 352, 353, 424
Contemplation, a great feature of Jesuit upbringing, i. 297
Contemplations of the Exercises, i. 373-5; effect of, on sensitive natures, 381
Contzen, Professor Adam, ii. 314
Convents, the spirit that fills, i. 278; difficulties which prevent adherents from leaving, 279
Cordara, Julius Cæsar, on the Chinese and Indian Mission, ii. 58, 65; on the Jesuit "cooking" of accounts, 89; on the avarice imputed to Jesuits, 102; his conversation with the King of Sardinia on the boundless wealth of the Jesuits, 103; on Jesuit effeminacy, 103.4; on the overweening pride of the Jesuit Society, 106.9, 426; on Jesuit influence at the Courts of Europe, 168; his Memoirs under a ban at Ditton Hall, 225.6
Cornely, Father, and the affair Tournon, ii. 56, 57
Cornova on the compulsory teaching of Jesuits, i. 86.7; on Jesuit neglect

Index

of German, 110; condemns neglect of poor scholars, 147; admits that Jesuits proselytise at their schools, 158; defends the Jesuit system of education, 192
orporal punishment, futility of, i. 45.6; how Jesuits inflict, 148.50
rrespondence of pupils, mischievous supervision of, at Jesuit schools, i. 141.2; grossly abused, 145
smopolitanism of the Jesuit Order, ii. 32 *et seqq.*, the heart of, 38
ton, Father, ii. 183
ourt chaplains, the *status* of, ii. 453
ourt confessors, Jesuit, ii. 172-98; the salaries of, 193
rasset, Jean, ii. 198
reighton, accomplice in the Jesuit plot against Queen Elizabeth, ii. 149; confessions of, 149-50; his book in favour of the succession of the King of Scotland, 313-4
étineau-Joly on the discovery of MSS. of the *Monita* at Prague and Paderhorn, ii. 9 (*note*); admits Jesuit hostility to heresy, 22; admits the enormous wealth of the Jesuits in France in 1773, 89; on the political activity of Edward Petre, 157; justifies Jesuit activity in politics, 197-8; on Liguori's teaching, 287
Jross of Ashes at Kevelaer, ceremony of, i. 32
Crucifix, as used by Jesuit students, i. 182
Cyprian, Father Francis, the strange case of, i. 303-4

Dackazat, John, i. 87
Dasbach, his safe challenge, ii. 320
D'Aubanton, betrayal of a confession of Philip V.'s by, ii. 178; alleged author of the Bull *unigenitus*, 189; his evil influence at the Spanish Court, *ib.*; salary of, as confessor to the King, 193
Declarations of the Constitutions, i. 73 (*note*), 80
Decurio, duties of, i. 138-41
Deger's "Madonnas," i. 124, ii. 397
Delatio, or Denunciation, i. 348 *et seqq.*
Delbruck, Professor, commissions the author to write for the *Preussische Jahrbücher*, ii. 449
Delrio, Professor, on permissible falsehood, ii. 302-3
Deluge, Jesuit view of the, ii. 268
Demoniac possession, how to exorcise it, i. 320-1; instances of, 321-3
Denbigh, the Earl of, i. 242
Denmark, Jesuit activity in, ii. 166-7
Denunciation in the Jesuit system of education, i. 139-41; expounded by the Constitutions, 348-9; a wholesale secret detective agency, 349-51; underband method of securing the consent of young students to, 350; training in, 351-2; system of secret reporting used in, 352-4; misery entailed by the practice of, ii. 378-9
"Deo gratias" at the Stella Matutina, i. 55
Deposition of Bishops, i. 257
Desertion from the Army, Jesuit opinion of, ii. 346
Devil, Jesuit belief in the, i. 226; the Devil at Babylon, 375; in Romish dogma, 381, ii. 208-9
Devils, belief in, a feature of Jesuit piety, i. 319-23; how to exorcise them, 320-1; instances of possession, 321-3; names of the chief possessing devils, 322
Dickens, Charles, as a classic at Stonyhurst, i. 242
Diel, Father, i. 120
Diest, the asylum at, ii. 418
Discipline, the Master of, at Jesuit schools, i. 149-50, thoroughness of, within the Jesuit Order, ii. 379
Discretion, doctrine of, i. 34
Disputation, importance of, in the scheme of Jesuit study, ii. 248-50; various kinds of, 248-9; form of, 249; use of Latin in, compulsory, 250; specimen of the conduct of a, 258-60; examples of subjects chosen for, at Freiburg, 280-1
Ditton Hall, set aside for Jesuit students of theology, i. 287; an experience of the author's at, 323; the "table" at, ii. 75; mysterious messages from, 101; the author's stay at, for theology, 216-22, 413; the terrible environment of the Hall, 216; the author is consecrated to the priesthood at, 222
Dogma, falseness of the Jesuit conception of, ii. 406
Döllinger, Dr., records instances of grotesque miracles, i. 312-13; discovers documents reproaching the Jesuits with their great wealth, ii. 102; Vol. III. of his "Beiträge" creates a temporary sensation at Ditton Hall, 225; his "History of the Moral-Theological Disputes" in the Catholic Church, 396-7
Domenech, Abbot, ii. 16
Dominic, St., ii. 424
Dominican Orders, i. 164 and *note*; Jesuit dealings with the Dominicans at Colmar, ii. 96; alleged tyranny of, 103 (*note*), arrogance of the Jesuits towards, 108-9; Dominican nuns and the Jesuit Order, 131; clear of the flaws of the Jesuits, 424
Donat, Professor Josef, ii. 272.4
Donnés, a class of affiliate Jesuits, ii 20
Doss, von Adolf, compositions of, preferred by Jesuits in Church service i. 160; Superior of the Jesuit settlement at Mayence, 220; his appearance, 225; becomes the author's confessor, 226; his foolish views about Goethe and the German classics 227-8; force of his influence, 229 terrible interview with, at Marxheim 249-50
Douai, Jesuit plot against the Catholi College at, ii. 315-16
Drecker, Father, i. 121
Dreves, Guido Maria, ii. 371 (*note*)
Droste-Vischering-Erbdroste, Count, an Catholic students' unions, i. 246
Dryander, Dr., receives the author int the Protestant State Church, ii. 452
Dudik on the confessing of sovereigns ii. 172
Dufrene, Father Maximilian, ii. 111
Duhr, B., explains how the Jesuit syste of education resembles that of th

Index 475

"Brothers of the Common Life" at Liège, i. 63; misleading criticism of, anent Jesuit scholars and externs, 84; approves of use of Latin for ordinary conversation, 99; disingenuous assertions of, as to free education of the Jesuits, 115-17; tries to minimise the effect of the publication of the Daily Routine, 183 (note); his "Studienordnung der Gesellschaft Jesu," 184; on witch persecution by the Jesuits, 319 and note; on the genuineness of the Monita, ii. 8, 9; on the existence of affiliates, 20; defends the Jesuits in the affair Tournon, 56, 57; his insinuations against Bishop Palafox, 86-7; defends Jesuit political activity against the Protestants of Graz in the sixteenth century, 142-3; his defence of Edward Petre, 155-7; on the violation of the confession of Maria Theresa, 175-6; instances of his untrustworthiness, 283-5

u Lac, supports Boulanger, ii. 164-5.
uplicia feasts among the Jesuits, ii. 75 (note)

benhoch, Karl, the tragedy of, ii. 100-2
bner, R., answers Kelle's criticism of the standard of Latin Grammar in Jesuit schools, i. 69 (note), tries to depreciate the Declarations of the Jesuit Constitutions, 78; praises the practice of Latin composition, 98; his views about German classics, 110; ineffective reply to Jesuit strictures on Jesuit education, 189 (note), his notions of modern philosophy, ii. 252; a surprise for, 281

ducation, Jesuit, international, to destroy patriotism and nationality, i. 50-1; produces a "common" type of man and woman, ib., crushes independence of thought and keeps the mind in bondage, 51-2; quality of actual instruction behind the times, 52; description of the administration and routine at the Stella Matutina, Feldkirch, 54-60; eulogy of Jesuit teaching greatly overdone, 61; lacks the creative spirit, 63; practically unchanged during three centuries, 64; the Ratio Studiorum, 63-111; reactionary methods in Austria, 70-2; the teachers poorly equipped, 72-4; grudging concessions to public opinion, 74; retrograde features of the Scheme of Study, 75; the lost chances of Jesuit education, 76-7; egotism and selfishness of the system, 77-84; Nostri considered always, the externs casually, 77, 79-80; limited attention to externs, 81; one brand of teaching for all countries, 83; a system to last for centuries, ib.; cardinal defect in Jesuit conception of teaching as a profession, 84-6; the end of teaching, 85; regulations as to training of teachers disregarded, 95-6; special favour shown to the study of Latin, 96-114; an educational farce, 99; neglect of the German tongue, 104; disregard of the world's classics, 107; can show no world classic in German and other tongues, 114; on the alleged gratuitous teaching of the Jesuits, 115-6; why Jesuit teaching fails, 117; weighed by the author and found wanting, 126; its real aim, 129; number of educational establishments in the Order in 1762, 129 (note), the so-called celebrated pupils, 130; represses family life, 130-1; as authorised by the Ratio Studiorum, 135 et seqq., police-like supervision, 137-42; espionage and tale-bearing encouraged, 138-41; worship of wealth and aristocracy, 145-6; treatment of poor scholars, 147; likeness and unlikeness between Jesuit schools and English public schools, 148 (note), Jesuits and corporal punishment, 148-50; and expulsion from school, 151; on the prohibition of friendships, 151-2; "good" pupils make bad scholars, 152; encourages superstition, 154-5; proselytising at school, 157-8; piety in the school, 158-63; use and influence of Marian Congregations, 163-80; the daily routine at a Jesuit school, 181-4; espionage enjoined, 183; Jesuit strictures on the systems of instruction and education, 184-95; the question of unchastity, 203-8; why their education always must fail, ii. 432-4

Eichendorf as a German classic, i. 108
Elizabeth, Queen, Parsons' plot to murder, ii. 149-53; excommunicated by Pius V., 311
Elizalde, Michael de, on Jesuit morality, ii. 297-8; his work on Probabilism rejected by the Order, 298; threatened by General Oliva, ib.
Encyclicals, Papal, the real source of, ii. 255
Encyclopædists in France overcome Jesuitism, i. 128
"End sanctifies the means, the," ii. 320-7; Jesuit attitude to the maxim, 320; lawsuits regarding it, ib.
England, Parsons' plot to depose Elizabeth from the throne of, ii. 149-53
Epping's lectures on astronomy at Blyenbeck, ii. 248
Equivocation, use of, ii. 302-3; Jesuit justification of, 304-5
Erfurt, how the French prisoner at, made his peace with the Church, ii. 381
Espionage. (See Denunciation)
Esseiva, Father Joseph, illustrates General Anderledy's mental gymnastics, i. 174
Etiquette in the Jesuit Order, i. 356-7
Eulenberg, Court Marshal, ii. 461
Evangelical Alliance of Germany, as seen through Jesuit glasses, ii 361; ignorance of Catholicism among the members of, 452; mistaken tactics of, against Ultramontanism, 465 (note)
Exaeten, the author enters the novitiate at, for a few days, i 259; enters again, 270; reserved originally for the novices, 288; hardship and discomfort of life at, 288-9; seclusion of, 292; devils at, 323; reading aloud at meals, 394; the author leaves, 406; its villa at Oosen, ii. 77; the author appointed

Index

Scriptor at, 244, 270; becomes the seat of the Philosophate, 369.70; headquarters of the *Stimmen aus Maria-Laach* and *Die Katholischen Missionen*, 369, 370; the structural improvements at, 369-70; the author quits, for Portico, 411; the author leaves, for ever, 420

xamen generale, craft of the, i. 351; summary of the, 411; *E. rigorosum*, ii. 369

xamination, Particular, i. 368.9; pulling the "particular examination chain," 369

xercises, spiritual, effect of, on Jesuit pupils, i. 162.3; nervous excitement caused by, 162; the end and aim of, 163; used to win recruits for the Jesuit priesthood, 214.5; terror in the young inspired by melodramatic addresses in the, 227; the authorship of, ascribed to the Virgin and to God, 370; duration of, 371; summary of the contents of, 371-6; criticism of, 377.84; actual object of, 378; two main characteristics ot, 378-82; make every Jesuit everywhere of a uniform pattern, 379; Director of, and his duties, 380; pseudo-mysticism of, 380-2; high fees charged for the Exercises, etc., ii. 80; value of the Exercises in popular missions, 382; utilised for political purposes, 384.5

xperiments during the novitiate, i. 392-3

xpulsion from school, how effected by Jesuits, i. 151

xternals, attention paid to, in Jesuit labours, ii. 381.2

yre, Father, i. 240-1

aber, Frederick William, ii. 31

ah, Father Jacob, i. 171; consults with Windthorst in Berlin, ii. 165; editor-in-chief of the *Stimmen aus Maria-Laach* and *Die Katholischen Missionen*, 244, 370; character of, 371; sends the author to Brussels for research work in history, 390; ignores the author's hints as to the effect of his studies, 391; is despatched to Berlin to prepare for a Jesuit settlement there, 399-400; is transferred to Brazil, 411 (*note*)

alk, Dr., ii. 231

aller, Father, General Prefect at Feldkirch, i. 197; his attempts to induce the author to enter the Jesuit Order, 217; annoyance at their temporary failure, 218

alsification of the text, a Jesuit method of embellishment, ii. 284 (*note*), 285

amily life and the Jesuit system of education, i. 130.1

arnese, Margaret Duchess of, ii. 129

atherhood of God the basis of true religion, ii. 456.8

eldkirch, the Jesuit school at, i. 49; description of the buildings, administration, daily routine, 54.60; fees at, 116; Government grants at, *ib.*, why the system of education at, was a failure, 117.9; teachers at, in the author's time, 118; improvement in teaching at, due to State pressure, 119; negative results of the education at, 129; mixed nationality of the teaching staff at, 132; jubilee of, 133, 148; how wealth and rank were favoured at, 146; punishment at, 150; the best scholars were the day boys, 152; the library at, 153; curious "atmosphere" at, 155-7; gluttony tacitly encouraged, 156; sports at, *ib.*, game of "running the gauntlet," 156.7; Marian observances at, 161; foolish rites in honour of the Virgin at, 179; midnight Mass on Christmas Eve at, 201.2; the author's confessors and teachers at, 202.10; atmosphere of, 208

Fénélon denounces Father La Chaise, ii. 183-4

Ferdinand I. and the Jesuit Professors of Theology at Vienna, ii. 32-3

Ferdinand II., under the influence of the Jesuits, ii. 40; and the Chancellorship of Prague University, 52.3; a ready tool of the Jesuits, 159; an instance in which he withstood his confessor, 182

Fessler, Ignatius, and the discovery of the confessions of eminent persons, ii. 177

Fessler, Joseph, i. 200

Feuerbach, Anselm, records a priest's confession of murder, ii. 366.7

Fiesole, Jesuit headquarters at, i. 264

Filling, Father Jacob, his fondness for the author, i. 205; his feats in prevarication, 213; tries to persuade the author to become a Jesuit, 217

Finckenstein, Count Karl von, on the author's recantation, i. 6; introduces the author to Orthodoxy and Conservatism, ii. 450; applies for a post in the State service for the author, 459

Flores mariani, i. 161

Flugschriften zur Wehr und Lehr, ii. 361

Foley, his free and easy manner of dealing with history, ii. 284 (*note*)

Forer, ᵉ u ia ion of the *Monita* by, ii. 9-p d t

Formed coadjutors of the Society of Jesus, i. 415; simple vows of, 417; final vows of, 418

Formula Instituti, text of, i. 413.4; contents of, ii. 3-4

Formula scribendi, i. 352 *et seqq*.

Forsler, Emerich, on Jesuit political activity at Graz, ii. 178

Fox's Commentary on Demosthenes' *de Corona*, a "classic" of Jesuit scholarship, ii. 229

France, favoured by the Jesuits in the war of 1870-1, i. 233.4; Cardinal Reisach's prophecy regarding, 238; the "patriotism" of German Jesuits as evidenced in the war of 1870-1, ii. 36.8; Boulanger's plot against, supported by the Jesuits, 164.5

Francis, St., how he assisted justice, ii. 304, 305; a wiser man than Loyola, 424

Franciscan Orders, i. 164 and *note*; Jesuit *hauteur* towards, ii. 108; Franciscan nuns and the Jesuit Order, 131; cannot be condemned as can the Jesuits, 424

Franco-German war of 1870-1, i. 232-3;

Jesuit hatred of Prussia, *ib.*; the Prussian victories, 232; the war misrepresented, 232.3

'rankfort - on - the - Main, the author's residence at, ii. 421

rankfort - on - the - Oder, County Court judgeship at, offered to the author, ii. 462

ranzelin, Cardinal, on mental reservation, i. 264.5

rederick, Cardinal, of Hesse, the immoral confessor of, i. 207

rederick II., the Great, as seen through Jesuit glasses, i. 122

rederick William IV. and the author's father, i. 7

reemasonry, denounced and misrepresented by Jesuits, i. 154; attitude of Ultramontanes to, 224

reethinker, the, who is governed by morals is not far from God, ii. 456 (*note*)

rehner's revolt, ii. 281

reiburg, Latin Grammar in the Jesuit College of St. Michael at, i. 69; Jesuit intrigues at the University of, ii. 40.2; low state of Jesuit learning at, 280.1

rench League supported by the Jesuits, ii. 161-2

rick's "Manual on Logic for the use of Schools," ii. 257.8

riday, specially sacred to the Heart of Jesus, i. 307

riedrich, Professor J., on the soul-destroying effect of Jesuit teaching on the German students at Rome, i. 342; and the report of the poisoning of Cardinal Tournon, ii. 55

riendships at school, Jesuit objections to, i. 151.2; Father Link recognises their value, 210; friendship forbidden within the Jesuit Order, ii. 378-9

rins, Professor Victor, a constant adviser of Windthorst, ii. 166, 411 (*note*); his opinion about Protestant girls, 367; succeeds the author in Berlin, 411 (*note*)

roment, Chancellor of the University of Paris, on Jesuit self-aggrandisement, ii. 47-8

urstenberg, Baron Klemens von, on the German Jesuits and the war of 1870.1, i. 233

urstenberg, Count Wratislaw von, intrigues of, ii. 183

alen, Count Ferdinand von, i. 238

alen, Count Max von, i. 227

arnet, Father Henry, involved in Jesuit activity in England, ii. 46, 111; friendship with Lady Anne Vaux, 128; concerned in Parsons' plot against Queen Elizabeth, 152; freely employs equivocation, 309-11; a learned and saintly man, 311; his views touching the killing of the king, 336; on just and unjust laws, 437 (*note*)

astel, Johannes, on effective Jesuit vengeance, ii. 382

Gauntlet-running at Jesuit schools, i. 156-7

Gelsenkirchen, scenes during the mission at, ii. 380.1

Genelli, opinion of, as to Jesuit chastity, ii. 67

General Congregation, the highest court of the Society of Jesus, i. 422.3; how often held, 423; powers of, *ib.*, summoned by, *ib.*, composition of, *ib.*, voting power of, *ib.*; the Decrees of, carefully edited for publication, ii. 5

General of the Society of Jesus, Head of the Order, i. 419; elected *aut vitam aut culpam*, 419.20; qualifications for, *ib.*, powers of, *ib.*, supervision over, 420.1; deposition of, 421.2; activity of, 422; subordination of, to the General Congregation, 422.3

Gerard, Father John, secures money for the Order, ii. 11-2, 90.1; how he acknowledged Elizabeth as Queen of England, 311

German tongue, Jesuit neglect of the, i. 104; nominally adopted as a subject of study, 105; this reform compulsory, 106; Jesuit ordinance anent German classics, 109; great German classics denounced by von Doss, 227.8; by von Hammerstein, ii. 230.4; by Baumgartner, 234.45

Germania, character of, ii. 376; organ of the Centre Party, 411 (*note*), attacks the author, 460

Germany, unity of, the real object of the war of 1870-1, i. 232.3; Jesuit hatred of the idea, 233.4; strong ultramontane sentiment in the Centre Party, 246.7; sent to Canossa by the Kulturkampf, 256; Jesuit scheme to subjugate, ii. 158-9; return of the Jesuits to, 166; activity of Jesuits in, 384; dominated by the Centre Party, 462; unfortunate results to, of the Kulturkampf, 464.5; danger of Jesuitism to, 466

Gertt, Reinhold, condemns the secret drinking in Jesuit settlements, i. 188

Gfrörer ascribes the Thirty Years' War to the Jesuits, ii. 158-9

Ghosts, Catholic belief in, and fear of, i. 26-8; cruelty of the doctrine to the young, 28; haunted houses at Zeil and Muffendorf, 27-8

Gindely's account of the Jesuit proceedings against Wallenstein, ii. 179-80; records an instance of Ferdinand II.'s resistance to the Jesuits, 182; as garbled by Duhr, 283

Ginzel, Canon, anent the violation of the confession of Maria Theresa, ii. 175-6

Giphanius, Professor, on Jesuit intrigue at Ingolstadt, ii. 39

Goch, the author's momentous discourse at, ii. 419

"God" as conceived by Catholic theology and in part also by Protestant, ii. 408.9; the Fatherhood of God the basis of true religion, 456.8

Goethe, Jesuit opinion of, i 109; Jesuit ordinance concerning German classics issued in the year of Goethe's death, *ib.*, Von Doss on the overrated renown of, 227; "Behold the man whom thou didst worship!" 228; von Hammerstein's appreciation of, ii. 230.2; Baumgartner's tirade on, 236.45

Goldie, Francis, records Alonzo Rodriguez's senseless literalism, i. 329

oltz, Provost von der, shares the too common Protestant ignorance of things Catholic, ii. 451
onzalez, Thyrsus, author of a missing Decree, ii. 5; Pope approves of his work against Probabilism, 50.1; forbids the teaching of modern philosophy, 253; condemns Jesuit teaching on morals, 292; Jesuit persecution of, 295 and *note*, his statement of the position, 296; real reason why Jesuits attack him, 297
ossler, von, ii. 231
otthein, wrongs of, concerning Loyola's asceticism and piety, i. 299 (*note*)
öttingen, author attends lectures at, i. 122; parents' reluctance to allow him, 251; complexion of his stay tnere, 252; studies for the Law at, 251
ottlieb, the pen-name of Tilmann Pesch, ii. 357
rand National at Liverpool, Stonyhurst students at, i. 241
randerath defends capital punishment for heretics, ii. 356
raz, Jesuit political activity at, ii. 140.3, 179
reenway, connection of, with the Gunpowder Plot, ii. 310
regorovius, influence of, on the author, ii. 406
regory XIII., Pope, confirms the Marian Congregation at Rome, i. 165, 169; sanctions purchases for profit by the Society of Jesus, 413; ordains that the Jesuit's simple vows constitute an impediment to marriage, 417; concerned in Parsons' plot against Queen Elizabeth, ii. 149; confirms the deposition of Elizabeth, 312
regory XV., Pope, and the Marian Congregations, i. 165
regory XVI., Pope, canonises Liguori, ii. 286
retser is instructed to refute the *Monita*, ii. 7
rimm, Father Leopold, on the custom of confessing boys in the confessor's bedroom, i. 203
Juardian angels, Catholic teaching about, i. 26; Congregations of the, 164; use of the guardian angel (*angelus custos*) in the novitiate, 355
Juignard hanged for complicity in the attempt to murder Henry IV. of France, ii. 335
Guise, Duke of, involved in Parsons' plot against Queen Elizabeth, ii. 149.51
Gunpowder Plot, Duhr's tenderness for the, i. 284; Garnet's connection with the, ii. 309, 310
ury, prevalence of his textbook of Moral Theology, ii. 288; his teaching on adultery, ii. 309
Gustav Adolf Verein, mistaken tactics of, against Ultramontanism, ii. 465 (*note*)
u a u Adolphus, the three "L's" who he wished to see hanged, ii. 183 m
na iu , superiority of the education at the State, over that of the Jesuits, i. 118.9, 124

Haag Castle, i. 1
Habsburg, inordinate ambition of the House of, ii. 159
Hahn-Hahn, Countess Ida, novels by, approved by the Jesuits, i. 153; composes the "Cradle Song of a Polish Mother," 211
Hahn's book on Saint Teresa censored, ii. 269
Haller, Father, the dangers of Jesuit political activity in Austria, ii. 139
Hammerstein, Baron Ludwig von, on the German classics, ii. 230.4; his appreciation of Goethe, 230-2; of Schiller, 232; of Lessing, 232.3; on the predominance of the Church over the State, 342.4; on the evil of religious toleration, 352; his hostility to State schools, 439.40
Hammerstein, Baron Wilhelm von, proprietor of the *Kreuzzeitung*, ii. 449; the author meets him, 450.1
Harnack, Adolf, and the genuineness of the *Monita*, ii. 7; his lectures on dogma at Berlin University, 403; what his influence lacks, 403.4
Harrach, Cardinal von, struggle of, at Prague, against the Jesuits, ii. 52-3
Hartmann, Father, lawsuit at Straubing, ii. 100-2
Hatzfeld, Countess Sophie, i. 245
Hausherr, Father, becomes confessor of the author's mother, i. 234 (*note*); his influence, 249
Helfert, Alexander von, reproaches the Jesuits for their addiction to a dead language not properly understood, i. 104; condemns Jesuit neglect of German literature, 110; criticises the abuses of the Jesuit system of education, 192-3
Heligoland, the author's stay in, ii. 422; his acquaintance with Count Karl von Finckenstein in, 450
Hell, Abbé, as a Professor of Astronomy, ii. 280
Hell, as portrayed in the Exercises, i. 372.3; monstrosity of the belief in, ii. 407; the hell dogma a priest's dogma, 409
Helten, Father, considers Goethe a heathen, i. 109; Professor of Greek, German and Æsthetics at Wynandsrade, 121; astonished at his pupils' excellent Greek exercises, 123-4
Henry III. of France, murder of, approved by the Jesuit Mariana, ii. 144; demands the support of the Jesuits, 161-2; murder of, justified by the Jesuit Mariana and the Society, 328.9
Heresy, especially attacked by Jesuits, flict with the Jesuits, ii. 191; murder of, by Ravaillac, 333; public fury at the murder, and its effect on the Jesuit Society, *ib.*; Chatel's attempt to murder, 335
Heresy, especially attacked by Jesuits, ii. 21 *et seqq.*; absolutely condemned by the *Imago*, 350; Jesuit defence of the capital punishment of heretics, 354.7; the various punishments for, 356
Heroism of the Jesuits, ii. 379; of humanity, 380
Hertling, Baron von, president of the Görresgesellschaft, i. 224

Index

ilgers on the need for and usefulness of the Index Expurgatorius, ii. 274-5
oensbroech Castle, i. 2
oensbroech, Adrian, Count of, the author's brother, attends the Jesuit school at Feldkirch, i. 49; death of, 253
oensbroech, Antonia von, the author's sister, bitterly hostile to Prussia, i. 211; her anger with the author about the German victories in 1870, i. 233; marriage to Count Franz Xavier Korff-Schmising-Kerssenbrock, i. 252; death of, ib., entirely subjugated by her Jesuit confessors, ii. 130
oensbroech, Clement, Count of, the author's brother, attends Feldkirch and the State Gymnasium, i. 118; marriage of, ii. 400
oensbroech, Franz Egon, Marquis of, the author's father, character of, i. 3; his blindness, ib.; his view of religion, 4-5; his politics, 6-7; relations to the king, 7-8; his career, 10; makes a pilgrimage to La Salette, but is not cured, 28-9; before the shrine at Kevelaer, 31; induced to sanction Jesuit influence in his home, 33; his coldness to Prussia in the war with Austria, 210; death of, 252
oensbroech, Lothar, Count von, the author's brother, death of, i. 253
oensbroech, Luise, Countess of, the author's sister, takes the veil, i. 48; urges the author to join the Jesuit Order, 247
oensbroech, Marie, Countess von, the author's sister, engagement of, to Count Franz zu Stolberg-Stolberg, i. 242-3; a marriage of *convenance*, 243; urges the author to enter into the Jesuit Order, 247; leads the first German pilgrimage to Lourdes, 253; goes to Algiers for her health, 261; birth of her daughter, Monica, 265; death of, 269
oensbroech, Matilda, Marchioness of, the author's mother, i. 3; nobility of her character, 10-11; devotion to her husband, 10; in religion a "whole" Catholic, 12-14; depth of her credulity, 13-14; her curious indifference to the Bible, 14; her fervour and fanaticism, 15; her dislike of the Protestant dynasty of Prussia, 15-17; her hatred of Prince Bismarck, 16-17; undertakes a pilgrimage to La Salette, 28; her faith superior to her disappointment, 29; her frequent devotions at the shrine at Kevelaer, 31; comes wholly under Jesuit influence, 33. ii. 129-30; her anti-Prussian bitterness, i. 210-2; quarrels with her brother about Prince Bismarck, 212; her fanatical faith in infallibility, 222; coolness with the Bishop of Mayence, ib.; punishes the author for defending the Bishop, ib; entirely under the control of Father Behrens, her confessor, 234; makes over part of her fortune to the Jesuits, ib. (*note*), lives in widowed seclusion at Rackelwitz, 234 (*note*); strongly opposes the author's delay to enter into the Jesuit Order, 236; hands over Blyenbeck Castle in Holland as a retreat for the exiled Jesuits, 248; is endowed with all the graces and dispensations of the Order, ii. 129

Hoensbroech, Paul, Count of, the author, birth of, i. 3; parentage of, 3-17; anecdote about the Latin and German text of the "Ave, Maria," 5; routine of home life, 18-20; religion the dominant note of his education, 20-1; suffered from denominational exclusiveness, 20; taught to minister at Mass, 22; plays the Mass-game, 22-3; how his early piety was fostered, 24 *et seqq.*; steeped in sham mysticism and asceticism, 25 *et seqq.*, terrified by ghosts, 28; his frequent visits to the shrine at Kevelaer, 29 *et seqq.*; degrading effect of the superstition, 32; comes under Jesuit influence, 34; his first confession, ib., realises the horrors of ultramontane "morality," 36 *et seqq.*; the general run of his education, 45; doubts and criticism repelled, ib., is subjected to corporal punishment, 45-6; defects of his education, 46-8; is sent to Feldkirch, 49, 53; account of his school, 54-60; describes the "O Sanctissima," 57; nearly loses his life, 58; concludes that the Jesuit system of instruction is bad, 61; discovers the Jesuit teachers were poorly equipped, 73; learns how Latin verses were composed, 99; his "guardian angel," 100; on the scant attention paid at school to German, ib., never saw a Latin play at Feldkirch, 106; rebuked for admiring Goethe, 109; why his education at Feldkirch was comparatively a failure, 117-9; the entrance examination at Mayence Gymnasium, 118; attends the college at Wynandsrade, 119-24; had already practised law, 120; his course at Bonn and Gottingen, 122; is reprimanded for plain speaking, 123; his summary of Jesuit instruction as he found it, 126; is sent to arrange a difficulty concerning a Marian Congregation at Cologne, 171-2; his years as a member of the Marian Congregation, 179; reminiscences of Feldkirch, 196-218; cured of home-sickness, 197; his first Communion, 197-200; how midnight Mass was celebrated at Feldkirch on Christmas Eve, 201-2; his confessors at, 202-6, 208-10; offends his family by his sympathies with Prussia, 211-3; efforts made to entice him into the Jesuit Order, 216-8; attends the Gymnasium at Mayence, 219-20; defends the Bishop of Mayence and incurs his mother's censure, 222; under the strange spell of Adolf von Doss, 226-7; German essay and its fateful motto, 230; a change silently at work in his mind, 231; his invincible patriotism, 232-3; his youthful love for his cousin and its effect on him, 235-6; postpones entering on his novitiate, 236; interviews Manning, 239; attends Stonyhurst College, 240-2; disgusted at the laxity of the students' morals, 240.1; the courses in Latin and philosophy both poor, 240.2; studies law at Bonn, 243.4; some of his fellow-students, 244; abets the Jesuit insolence towards the Old Catholics, 244.5; joins the Catholic Students' Union, 246; his cousin takes the veil, 250; he is haunted with the thought, "End of my love; entrance into the Order," ib., narrow escape from death in a railway accident, ib.; a dilemma of Divine Providence, 250.1; is disqualified purposely for the army, 253.4; the reason why, 254; disastrous effect of the Kulturkampf, 256; he joins the German pilgrimage to Lourdes, 258.9; enters the novitiate at Exaeten, 259; the mental agony he suffered, 260-1; visits Algiers, 261.2; visits Rome, 262.3; acquires some of the Pope's cast-off garments as relics, 263; as county court judge takes the oath at Cleves with mental reservation, 265; beseeches the intercession of Leo XIII. for his sister Marie, 268; sees his cousin at Frankfort and his love for her is revived, 269; enters Exaeten again, 270; is examined as a postulant, 282; becomes a novice, 285; gratitude to Jesuits for teaching him self-control, 385; his practical duties during novitiate, 392.3; examples of his self-mortification, 393.4; how he acquired clear enunciation, 394; his experience of penitential practices, 394.5; his sense of repugnance to the Jesuit Order, 395 et seqq., his simple faith in the system, 396-7; he is repelled by the rule requiring separation from and renunciation of parents, 398 et seqq., how he trod his mother underfoot, 401; his zealous effort to become a complete Jesuit, 402; may take the devotional vows, 402.3; he receives a belated letter before leaving Exaeten, 405; becomes a scholastic, 406; extract from *Austritt* to show how the Jesuits crush patriotism, ii. 34.6; his experience of the effects of poverty, 73.80; tells the painful story of Karl Ebenhoch's deathbed, 100-2; is intended to be the confessor of aristocratic women because of his social rank, 130; is the victim of Tilmann Pesch's jealousy, 131.2; discovers that the Jesuits support Boulanger's designs on France, 164.5; years at Wynandsrade for Humanity and Rhetoric, 201-14; assailed by doubts about the Order and the Church, 202-9; his Parthian victory, 209; ascetic life at Wynandsrade, 210.11; sufferings at Aix-la-Chapelle, 212; goes to Blyenbeck for Philosophy, 214.6; renounces his property, 215; takes the first step to the priesthood, 215; goes to Ditton Hall for Theology, 216.22; is consecrated to the priesthood, 222; his mental agony on the occasion of the reading of his first Mass, 222.3; his experience of swallowing the host, 223; is troubled by the doctrines of the Trinity and Original Sin, 224;

becomes Scriptor at Exaeten, 244, 270, his progress in Philosophy and Theology officially approved, 269; his insanity hinted at, ib., his discussion about the Creation, 281-2; is shocked at the atmosphere of falsehood in which the Jesuit students are trained, 318-19; tests at law the maxim "The end sanctifies the means," 320.1; his sentiments on taking up residence at Exaeten as Scriptor, 370; assistant editor of the *Stimmen aus Maria-Laach* and *Die Katholischen Missionen*, ib., his relations with Fah, the chief editor, 371; his intimacy with the Provincial of the German Province and its close, 372.4; declines the post of tutor to the sons of the Austrian Ambassador, 374; assists at the Mayence Conference that founded the National Union for Catholic Germany, 375; undertakes all manner of pastoral work, 380, 384.6; how he absolved a murderess, 386 and *note*; his practice in the matter of confession, 388; specialises in the history of the Church and the Papacy, 390; the consequences of his studies of this subject, ib., visits Brussels for research, 390.1; learns that there are two sides to the Papacy, 391; is instructed to defend the Papacy, 392; success of his pamphlet on Church and State, 393; is commissioned to write in defence of the Jesuit Order, 393; his pamphlet "Why should the Jesuits not return to Germany?" 393-4; his pamphlet "Christ, or Anti-Christ," 394; declines to collaborate with Tilmann Pesch, 394.5; his literary labours appreciated and depreciated by the same people, 395; is despatched to Berlin to prepare for a Jesuit settlement, 399; his instructions how to act as a Jesuit ambassador, 399.400; marries his brother, 400; attends lectures in Berlin University, 403.4; Treitschke's influence on, 405; patriotism reawakes, ib., the liberators of the mind of, 405.7; revolts at the chief Catholic dogmas, 407.9; agony of his mental conflict, 409.11; decides to enter the tertiate, 411; is ill with diphtheria, ib., experience as a tertiary, 412-5; his mental sufferings as the tertiate closed, 414.5; takes the final decision and leaves the Order and the Church, 416.22; the accidents that enabled him to leave the Order undetected, 419.22; the question of his temporary use of the money he collected for Brazil, 419.20, 420 (*note*), sojourns at Cologne, Paris and Frankfort-on-Main, 421; falls ill, 422; takes up his permanent residence in Berlin, ib.; the question of apostacy, ib.; the wrench from Catholicism, 448; his first commissions for the Press, 449; discovers his life-work in exposing Ultramontanism, ib.; gravitates towards Liberalism and freethought, 450; joins the Protestant State Church, 452; his objections to any connection between State and

Index

Church, 452-5; statement of his present religious position, 455-8; unconsciously alarms Count Caprivi, 459; his long conversation with Wilhelm II., 459; the Kaiser's promise, 460; goes to Kiel to qualify for the post of *Landrat*, 460-1; is married, 461; his wife's severe illness, 461-2; Count Waldersee intervenes on his behalf, 461; further interview with the Kaiser and what came of it, 462-3; is refused a lectureship at a University, 463; and also denied the diplomatic service, 464; develops his future life-work, 464; his labours not in vain, 466; encouraged by hope for the future of the race, 467

Hoensbroech, William, Count of, the author's brother, at Feldkirch, 1. 49; found the equipment imperfect compared with that at the State Gymnasium, 118; visits Algiers, 261; marriage of, 266; how the death of a daughter of William's affects the author, ii. 410-11

Hoffaus, Paul, on Jesuit vice in the Upper German Province, ii. 69-70; deplores the growing luxury of the Order, 81; deplores Jesuit interference in politics, 193-4

Hohenlohe, Prince, refuses the author admission into the diplomatic service, ii. 464

Hohenzollerns, Jesuit designs against, ii. 385

Homonna, ascetic practices at the College of, i. 386

Hompesch, Count, i. 8

Hospitieren at Berlin University, ii. 403 (*note*), 405

Houses of Jesuits, i. 78 (*note*)

Hovel, Father, receives the author at Exaeten, i. 259, 270; approves of the author's conduct as a novice, 403; Rector at Ditton Hall, ii. 217

Humanistic studies of the scholasticate, ii. 228-45

Humility of the Jesuit Order, ii. 105-6

Hungary, Jesuit political activity in 1655 in, ii. 144-6

Ibañez on the Jesuits in Paraguay, ii. 6

Ignatius Day, St., i. 291

Imago primi saeculi Societatis Jesu on the authorship of the Constitutions. i. 408; on the Jesuits' undying hatred of heretics and heresy, ii. 24-5; a centennial memorial of the work of the Order, 112, 113; its boastfulness an annoyance to the Order, *ib*., the Jesuits' attempt to ascribe it to "young scholastics," 112-14; alleged to have been written by Bollandus, 114; description of the pictures in, 115-18; summary of the contents of the six books, 119-22; its self-glorification revolting, 122-3; on Jesuit morality, 301; explicitly condemns heresy, 350

'Immaculate Conception, The," at Lourdes, i. 258

Imprimatur, the Jesuit, ii. 266

Index of Forbidden Books, Jesuit plea for, ii. 274-5

Indies, East, Jesuit trading in the, ii. 91

Indifferents of the Society of Jesus, i. 416

Individuality rigorously repressed by Jesuit discipline, 1. 296 *et seqq.*; effaced by asceticism. 326; the instruments whereby Jesuitism murders the will, 342-84

Infallibility of the Pope, i. 221; the doctrine the occasion of controversy in the author's family, 222; German bishops' unconditional acceptance of, 223-4

Informations, based on espionage, obtained about nominees to posts in the Society of Jesus, i. 425-7

Ingolstadt, morbid excesses of Jesuit scholars at, i. 178; Jesuit intrigues at University of, ii. 38-40

Innocent III , Pope, and the apparition of a virgin, 1. 305

Innocent X., Pope, attempts to reform the practice of appointing Superiors, i. 367; fixed the intervals of the session of the General Congregation of the Jesuit Society, 424; letter of, touching reforms of the Order, ii. 5; letter to, on the wealth of the Order in America, 86-8, requires the Jesuits to refrain from political activity, 144

Innocent XI, Pope, sanctions Gonzalez's work against Probabilism, ii. 51, 295; requires the Society of Jesus to submit to the Pope, *ib.*, severely censures the Jesuits for their conduct in the Indian and Chinese Mission, 65; condemns Jesuit teaching on morals, 292; sees the dangers of Probabilism, 296; on the use of ambiguity, 304

Innocent XIII., Pope, receives a memorial from the Jesuits touching the Indian Mission, ii. 60 (*note*), receives a report from Tournon about his persuasion by the Jesuits in China, 63

Inquisition, and Loyola's letter on obedience, 336-7; founded by Loyola, ii. 23

Insinuation as a means of obtaining wealth, ii. 82

Institute of the Society of Jesus, contents of the, i. 142; *Formula Instituti*, 413-4; *Substantialia Instituti*, 414; difficulty of procuring copies of the *Institute*, ii. 1 (*note*)

Instruction as compared with education, i. 127. (*See* Education)

Instructor, the official Director of the tertiate, ii. 412

Intellect, Jesuit regulations to hamper and stifle the working of, ii. 262-4

Internationalism, the hall-mark of Jesuit education, i. 50-2; and of the Order in all its works, 90; sedulously fostered, 131-3; the proper use of, at a proper age, 133

Intrigue, love of, the ruin of Jesuit power, ii. 432

Jahnel, Catholic Provost, the author's host in Berlin, ii. 399; character of, 401; he visits the author after the latter's marriage, *ib* (*note*)

James II. of England, alleged to be an affiliate of the Jesuit Society, ii. 17; the Jesuit Petre and, 153

2 F

aniszewski, Dr., i. 257
anitor in Jesuit schools, duty of, i. 144
ansenism, Jesuit plot against, ii. 315, 316
apan, Jesuits' policy in, ii. 365
ardine, D., his " Narrative of the Gunpowder Pot" cited, ii. 128, 284, 309-11; his criticism of Garnet's equivocation, 310-11
erome, St., on the renunciation of his mother, i. 401; on opposition to heretics, ii. 25
esuits, influence of, established at Hoensbroech, i. 33; expulsion of, from Germany, 53; school management of, 61-2; value of their teaching overrated, 61, 63; their control of education in Austria, 70-2; their lost chances in teaching, 76-7; terminology of Jesuit dwellings, 78 (note); their belauded altruism nonexistent, 79-82; how they push the use of Jesuit textbooks, 82-3; suppression of, by Clement XIV., 86; obedience the first Jesuit law, 88; international in all their activities, 90; and the study of Latin, 96-114; untruthfulness sanctioned by the Order, i. 100, ii. 301-19; neglect of the German language, i. 104; German classics contemned, 108; their estimate of Goethe, 109; have produced no great classic, 114; have no system of free education, 116; greed of the Order, ib., in face of attack, 128; their adroit advertising, 130; why Jesuits can never become good teachers, 134-5; their attitude to rank and riches, 145-6; and to poverty, 147-8; corporal punishment among, 148-50; and expulsion from school, 151; reasons why friendships at school are forbidden, 151-2; and freemasonry, witchcraft and magic, 154-5; and proselytism, 157-8; various aspects of Jesuit piety, 158-63; really control the Marian Congregations, 163-80; allow of no Order but one, 166; suppression and resuscitation of the Order, 168; daily routine at a Jesuit school, 181-4; charged with trying to destroy or remove incriminating documents in public libraries, 189; alleged unchastity of, 203-8; their constant hatred of heresy, 213; hoped for the success of France in the war of 1870-1, 233-4; their singular notions of patriotism, ib.; excellent haters, 240; though legally prohibited in England their settlements numerous and churches fine, ib.; lax supervision of the students' morals at Stonyhurst, 240-1; expelled from Germany, 248; their philosophy of clothes, 284-5; good preachers, 292; piety of the Order, 295 et seqq.; the grotesque or blasphemous miracles recounted in Jesuit literature, 299-325; ascetic disciple of the Order considered in full, 326 et seqq.; abuse of confession, 361-9; their famous motto, 365; flout the Pope, 367, 368 (note); subtly supported by the Exercises, 378; their power of enduring physical pain, 385; the inner constitution of the Order, 407-27; foundation of the Society, 407; summary of the Constitutions, 408-11; privileges extended to the Society, 412-3; the *Formula Instituti*, 413; *Substantialia Instituti*, 414; degrees of the Society, 414-6; distribution of the Order, 416; number of members in 1773 and at present, ib., various kinds of vows, 416-8; government of, 418-27; the head of the Order, 418-23; concealed statutes of, ii. 5-7; their activity in England, 11-2, 17; how dismissed members are treated, 12-3; affiliates of the Society, 13-21; bitter hostility of, to heresy, 21-30; the non-Christian spirit of the Order, 30 et seqq., cosmopolitanism of, 32-8; their intrigues at various universities, 40-8; their attitude to the secular clergy, 44-8; nature of their self-sacrifice, 48; their violation of the vow of obedience, 50-67; their violation of the vow of chastity, 67-71; their wholesale breach of the vow of poverty, 71-104; their arrogance, 105-23; the *Imago* and its contents, 112-22; every Jesuit goes to heaven, 121; relation of the Order to women, 123-32; activity of Jesuits in politics, 133-98; their political ability vastly overrated, 136 and *note*; responsible for the fall of the Stuarts, 155, 157; Thirty Years' War partly financed by German Jesuits, 161; support Boulanger's designs on France, 164-5; Jesuits only allowed to know the "official" history of their Order, 224-6; barrenness of Jesuit scholarship, 228; literary censorship established by, 264-6; their attitude to learning and research, 270-85; their inevitable literary barrenness, 275-6; popular delusion regarding the, 278; their morality, 286-337; the doctrine that "the end sanctifies the means," 320-7; their teaching as to tyrannicide, 327-37; their teaching as to the subordination of the State to the Church, 338-68; on the impossibility of religious equality, 349-54; on the capital punishment of heretics, 354-7; account of the common daily life within the Order, 376-80; review of the success and failure of the Order, 423-46; price at which the Order saved the Papacy, 428-9; political activity of the Order its undoing, 429; their counter-reformation, 430; their attitude to the Papacy, 431; their lust of power, ib.; their successes and failures, 431-2; they make machines not men, 432-4; secret of their strength, 435; their danger to religion and the State, 436-41; their hostility to State schools, 439-40; under the cloak of religion, 442; their subterranean methods of working, 443; their falsified history, 444; the fascination of the Order, ib.; essentially anti-Christian character of the Order, 446; the driving force of Ultramontanism, 466
Jewish disabilities, removal of, and the Jesuits, ii. 352
Joanna ab Alexandro beholds Jesus as in a vision, i. 340, ii. 110

Index 483

John III. of Sweden and Jesuit influence, ii. 138, 139

John IV. of Portugal attains the throne through Jesuit support, ii. 162

Joller, Father, the author's confessor at Feldkirch, i. 202; his detestable character, 202, 204

o e , King of Portugal, attempted murder of, at Jesuit instigation, ii. 336

Joseph II., Emperor, on the Jesuits, ii. 85

Jouvancy, Father Joseph de, and the study of the mother tongue, i. 113

Julius III., Pope, issues the Bull *Exposcit debitum*, i. 413; confirms the *Formula Instituti*, ii. 3-4

Jungmann as an authority on æsthetics, i. 124

Kant, Jesuit boycott of, ii. 251; the author's first acquaintance with the real teaching of, 405-6

Katholischer Missionen, Die, headquarters of, at Exaeten, ii. 369, 370

Kelle, Professor Johann, on Alvarez's "Latin Grammar," i. 69 (*note*), states there is no great German classic in the Jesuit College at Prague, 114; discoveries of, in the archives of the Vienna Library, 184 *et seqq.*; accuses the Jesuits of attempting to do away with incriminating documents in public libraries, 189; quotes Viennese MS. as to blind obedience, 338; opposed by Ebner, ii. 252

Kempis, Thomas à, his "Imitation of Christ" must be read by all novices, i. 313, 318

Kerr, Father, Under-Prefect at Stonyhurst, i. 241

Ketteler, Baron Otto von, death of, ii. 400

Ketteler, Baron Wilhelm Emanuel von, advice of, to the author on the subject of his entering the Jesuit Order, i. 217-8; his remarkable personality, 220-5; leader of the Minority party at the Vatican Council, 220; author's mother's quarrel with, 222; his submission to the Vatican Council, 223-4; his extraordinary credulity, 224; his death, 225; on the question whether Jesuits can be compelled to sin, 335-6

evelaer, the Madonna's shrine at, i. 5; description of the scenes of pilgrimage, 30; the exorcism at the feast of St. Blasius at, 31-2; the ceremony of the cross of ashes at, 32; e author's fruitless appeal to, 252-3 h

Kiel, the author migrates to, ii. 461

Kink shows why Jesuit teaching can never be national, ii. 32; his opinion of van Swieten, 43; his account of Jesuit arrogance towards other Orders, 44-5; expounds the evils of scholasticism, 278-9

ladderadatsch on Jesuit greed and acquisitiveness, i. 248

leutgen, Joseph, ii. 255

luckhohn, August, account of the daily routine at a Jesuit school by, i. 181-4; on Jesuit unchastity, 207, ii. 69

Kneller, Father, on the death of his mother when he was a novice, i. 401

Knorr, Admiral von, ii. 465 (*note*)

Knox, Thomas Francis, his "Records of English Catholics," ii. 149

Köller, von, advises the author to reside in Kiel, ii. 460-1

Kolnische Blatter (now *Volkszeitung*), i. 6, ii. 340 (*note*)

Königgratz, Jesuit lies after the battle of, i. 213; misrepresentation concerning, 233

Kopp, Cardinal, on Marian Congregations, i. 172; his goodwill to be conciliated, ii. 399; his alleged anti-Jesuitism, 400; appointed Cardinal, 403

Korff-Schmising-Kerssenbrock, Count Franz Xavier, marriage of, to the author's sister Antonia, i. 252

Korum, Dr., Bishop of Trèves, ii. 375

Kostka, Stanislaus, an undesirably "angelic" boy, i. 208; festival of, 285; an example to the young, ii. 111

Kreutzer, Joseph, dismissal of, ii. 397; driven to suicide, 398

Kreuzzeitung, burning of the, i. 7; the author's first articles in, ii. 449

Krones on real aim of Jesuit activity in Hungary in 1655, ii. 145-6

Kropf, Francis Xavier, supports Latin against German, i. 112

Kubeck, Baron von, i. 17

Kullmann attempts the life of Bismarck, i. 212

Kulturkampf, incident in the, i. 8; feeling aroused by the, 16; outbreak of, 244; the fundamental blunder of, 255-6; Leo XIII. brings the, to a close, ii. 67; unfortunate effects of, 464-5; the only possible form of, 465

"L's," three, that deserved hanging, ii. 183

La Chaise, Father, denounced by Fénelon, ii. 183-4; Madame de Maintenon on, 185-6; on the power of the Jesuits, 191; his country house, 193; the cemetery of Père La Chaise, *ib.*; shows how the Jesuits may run with the hare and hunt with the hounds, 313-4

Lacroix, a Jesuit casuist, ii. 287

Lallemand, author of the Douai forgeries, ii. 315, 316

Lallemant, Father, on lay members of the Jesuit Order in Canada, ii. 19

Lamormaini, Father, Rector of the Jesuit College at Graz, Confessor to Ferdinand II., ii. 159; procures the election of Ferdinand III., 179; his share in Wallenstein's fate, 179-80; frequent interference of, in Austrian politics, 180-2; his tyranny over Ferdinand II., 182; how to produce an erroneous impression of, 283

Landrat, post of, promised to the author, ii 460; the post had become "impossible," 462

Lang, Karl Heinrich von, inquires into the charge of immorality among Jesuits, i. 206-7; examples of vicious practices cited by, ii. 68-9

Index

Langen, Professor, decree of excommunication against, i. 244
Lapidatio, a system of fault-finding in the novitiate, i. 355
La Salette, the miraculous spring at, i. 28-9
Lassaulx, Amalie von, a nun who refused to subscribe the dogma of infallibility, i. 245
Lateran, the author climbs the Scala Santa at the Church of St. John of, i. 268
Lateran Council, Decree of, as to confession, i. 34
Latin, Jesuits and the study of, i. 96-114; dog-Latin of the Jesuit scholastics, 98; novice's Latin more barbarous still, 99-100, the Latin of the Order condemned by Oliva, 100-1; Latin always used for ceremonial purposes, 106; imperfectly taught by Jesuits, 193; use of Latin compulsory in lectures and disputations, ii. 250, 261-2
Latin grammar as taught by Jesuits, i. 68-70
Laurentius on the supremacy of Church over State, ii. 344; on the death sentence for heretics, 356; his hostility to State schools, 439
Lavalette, a Jesuit trader, ii. 92-3
Lawsuits touching Jesuit misappropriation of money: the De Buck process at Brussels, ii. 99-100; the Hartmann process at Straubing, 100-2
Layman in the Catholic Church, status of, i. 272; demeanour enjoined as lay Jesuits, 358; the custom of keeping the lay brother in ignorance, ii. 388-9
Laymann favours permissible ambiguities, ii. 305-7
Laynez, Father Jacob (James), ascribes the authorship of the Exercises to God and the Virgin, i. 370; advised to adopt the practice of insinuation, ii. 82; as a theologian, 111
Lazarist Missionary Congregation, ii. 55; founded by St. Vincent de Paul, 57 (note)
Leaders in Jesuit schools, duties of, i. 144
Le Bret's Magazine of Church and political history and law, ii. 196 (note); on Jesuit doings in Scio, 364
Ledochowski, Cardinal, receives the author at Rome, i. 262
Lehmkuhl's *Theologia moralis*, ii. 248; his view of the Creation, 282; justifies the use of mental reservation, 307-8; adviser of the German Centre Party, 344; on the non-observance of civil oaths 345-6; when civil laws may be disregarded, 346-9; condemns religious toleration, 351-2; his personal character, 368
Leibnitz (Leibniz), Godfrey William, Baron, on the dangers of Jesuit activity in politics, ii. 196; on Jesuit morality, 294; on the Douai forgeries, 315-6
Leo XII., Pope, detested by the Jesuit Order, ii. 373-4, 374 (note)
Leo XIII., Pope, sanctions the Lourdes pilgrimages, i. 258; intercedes for the restoration of the author's sister

Marie, 268; canonises Johannes Bechmanns, 309; provokes the hostility of the Jesuits, ii. 66; effects an end to the Kulturkampf, 67; his manifestoes against modern research and learning, 270, 271; on the supremacy of Church over State, 338
Leon, John, i. 164
Le Roux on the deathbed repentance of the wicked, ii. 300-1
Lessing, L. von Hammerstein's appreciation of, ii. 232-3
Libellus exercitiorum, i. 380
Liberalism of thought and research, Jesuit attitude to, ii. 270-85
Libraries at Jesuit schools, character of, i. 152-3
Lieber, Leader of the German Centre, in consultation with the Jesuits, ii. 165 character of, 402; his annoyance at the Kaiser's interview with the author, 459; attacks the author, 460
Liège, the schools of the "Brothers of the Common Life" at, i. 63; the unjust judge and the witch at, ii. 302, 303
Liguières, De, Father, how he confessed Louis XV., ii. 192
Ligny, Professor, entrapped into a sham correspondence at Douai, ii. 315
Liguori, Alfonso Maria di, canonised by Gregory XVI., ii. 286; his teaching implicitly accepted, 287; on calumniation, 308; on adultery, 309
Link, Father, the author's confessor at Feldkirch, i. 202; nobility of his character, 208-10; his sympathy with boys, 209; on the question of school-boy friendship, 210; counsels the author when efforts are being made to induce him to enter the Jesuit Order, 217
"Little Table," penalty of the, i. 203
Liverpool, terrible social conditions of, ii. 413
Loë, Baron Felix von, intensity of his dislike of Protestant Prussia, i. 212; a surprise visit to Blyenbeck, ii. 76
Loe, Matilda, Baroness von. (See Hoensbroech, Matilda, Marchioness of)
Loe, Max, Count von, on priestly pride, i. 24; quarrels with his sister about Prince Bismarck, 212
Loë, Walther, Baron von, Field-Marshal, resides at Bonn, i. 245; connives at the disqualification of the author for military service, 253-4; regrets the author's entrance into the Jesuit Order, 405; change of his views in old age, 406; opinion of Longridge's gun, ii. 218
Löffler, Father, eulogises the Marian Congregations, i. 166; claims Jesuit direction for them, 167-8; describes their foes, 176; extols the fruits of their piety, 178; arrogance of his praise, 180
Lohmann, Father, as an art critic, ii 397; harshness of, towards Kreutzer, 398
Longridge, Cecil, and his new gun, ii 218
Louis XIII., Jesuits and, ii. 183
Louis XVI. and Father La Chaise, ii 183-4; his fear of the Jesuits, 191-2; his present to Father La Chaise, 192

ouis XV., how he was confessed by Father de Lignières, ii. 192
ourdes, the author undertakes a journey to, i. 253, 257; the miracle at, 258; the wonder-working spring at, ib., revenue derived from the pilgrimages to, ib. (note), intoxication of the "atmosphere" at, 258-9
ove, Jesuit degradation of, ii. 289
oyola, Ignatius, putative enlightenment of, i. 76, denunciation enjoined by, 140; originated Spiritual Exercises, 162; examples of his hysterical mysticism, 299-302, on the virtue of obedience, 323-30, the non-morality of his commands exposed, 330-6; author of the Exercises at the dictation of the Virgin and God, 370; how the composition was actually suggested to him, 371; original intention of, in writing the Exercises, 379; founder of the Society of Jesus, 407; author of the Constitutions, ib., recognises affiliates, ii. 16-17; canonisation of, 21-2, 111; founder of the Inquisition, 23; advises how the Order may acquire wealth, 82; enjoins intercourse only with women of very high rank, 127; rebuffs Elisabeth Roser, 129, his consideration for the Duchess of Farnese, ib., appoints confessors to sovereigns, 169; the incarnation of prudence and calculation, 424-5
uca, De, on capital punishment for heretics, ii. 355
udger, St., the civilisation of, ii. 439
ugo favours the use of ambiguity, ii. 305
ukanus thwarts the Kaiser's wishes, ii. 460; Waldersee's attempt to checkmate, 461; the author declines the proposals of, 462
umina, character of, i. 297-8
'Univers, i. 6; supports Papal infallibility, 222
uther, that "horrible monster," ii. 21; his "blasphemous tongue," 72; the "Epicurean swine," 24; scurrilous account of, 358-63; Luther's suicide! 360 and note, views on polygamy, 362
Lutheranism, an object of Jesuit hostility, ii. 21-4
Lutherisch," Jesuit pronunciation of the word, ii. 29-30
Lying made easy, ii. 302-3

Macao, death of Cardinal-Legate Tournon at, ii. 54; Bishop of, excommunicated, 59; the Jesuit church and seminary at, ib.
Macaulay, Lord, his criticism of Edward Petre, ii. 153; on the versatility of Jesuits, 197
MacMahon, Marshal, i. 232
Magdeburg, Jesuit greed at, ii. 98
aggio, Father, confessor of Rudolf II., ii. 178
Magister meals of Jesuits, ii. 75-7
Magistri, Jesuit fathers who had charge of the lessons at Feldkirch, i. 57; no prospects for, 85; their loathing of teaching, 86
Maigrot, Bishop, banished at the instigation of the Jesuits, ii. 59; decrees against, issued by the Emperor of China, 64
Maintenon, Madame de, on the activities of Father La Chaise, ii. 185-6
Mairhofer, M., Rector of the Jesuit college at Munich, ii. 143.
Malagrida advises the murder of King Joseph of Portugal, ii. 336
Malta, apparitions of the Madonna at the Jesuit college at, i. 323
Malvasia, Monsignore, on the attempt to restore by force Catholicism in Scotland, ii. 148-9
Mamachi's theory of crime, ii. 366
Manáraus, Oliverius, approves Delrio's work in favour of untruthfulness, ii. 303
Manchester, terrible social conditions of, ii. 413
Manning, Cardinal-Archbishop, author's interview with, i. 239; hostility to Jesuits, 239-40; on Jesuit mischiefmaking in politics, ii. 163-4, calumniated by the Jesuits, 299
Manresa, Loyola's stay at, i. 371
Mansonius, Father Ludovicus, relates an apparition of Jesus sanctioning blind obedience, i. 340; the same apparition also requires all to love his society, ii. 110
Manuductor, the duties of, i. 271, 393
Maréchal, disclosures of, as to the influence of the Jesuits over Louis XIV., ii. 191-2
Marellus, Jacobus, the loves of, i. 206, ii. 68
Maria-Laach, i. 230
Maria Theresa, Empress, intervenes on behalf of German in the Jesuit schools, i. 114; supports Gerhard van Swieten against the Jesuits, ii. 43 and note, betrayal by the Jesuits of her confession, 174-6; her scruples as to the partition of Poland, 176; her opinion of Jesuit learning, 279-80
Marian Congregations considered, i. 163-80; significance of, 164; the founders of, ib., controlled by the Jesuits, 165-72; pliability of, 166; aim of, 168; tercentenary of, 170; administration of, 174; power of the president, 175; vow taken by all congreganists, ib., alleged educational purpose of, 177; supervision effected by, ib., doubtful value of, 179; extravagant claims on behalf of, 180
Mariana, Juan, on Jesuit neglect of Latin, i. 103; applauds the murder of Henry III. of France, ii. 144; his De Rege et Regis Institutione, 327; the book licensed by the Society of Jesus, 328; Mariana's teaching as to the killing of tyrants and princes 328-31; the Mayence reprint of his book, 332; book burned at the order of the Sorbonne, 333
Marks, reading out of, at Jesuit schools, mischief of, i. 144-5
Marpingen, the alleged apparition of the Virgin at, i. 266-7
Marriage, the simple vows of scholastics and spiritual and temporal coadjutors in the Society of Jesus, an impediment to, i. 273, 417; Jesuit degradation of, ii 289
Marseilles, Jesuit trading scandal in, ii. 92-3

Index

Martin, Dr., escapes from Wesel, i. 257
Martin, Joseph, on the Marian Congregations, i. 170-1
Martin, Luiz, and the control of the Marian Congregations, i. 172; mental reservation of his statements, 173
Martinique, Jesuit trading in, ii. 92-3
Marxheim, i. 249
Mary, Mouth of, i. 161; Flowers of, *ib.* (*See* Virgin)
Mary Queen of Scots, ii. 149-53
Mass, character of the ceremony of the, i. 22; midnight Mass on Christmas Eve at Feldkirch, 201-2
Mass-game, i. 22-3
Matthieu, Jesuit, chief promoter of the League of the Guises, ii. 144; involved in Parsons' plot against Queen Elizabeth, 150
May Laws, Jesuit casuistry respecting, i. 264
May meditations in Jesuit education, i. 161
Mayence, the Gymnasium teaching at, i. 118; the Gymnasium at, 220; von Ketteler, Bishop of, and his character, 220-5; the "trinity" of, 221; von Doss, Superior of the Jesuit settlement at, and his influence, 225-9; Heinrich Bone, Director of the Gymnasium, 229-30, excitement at, during the Franco-German War, 232; the National Union for Catholic Germany founded at, ii. 375
Meals, daily, of the Jesuits, ii. 75; "magister" meals, 75-7; *duplicia* feasts, 75 (*note*)
Mecklenburg, Friedrich Franz III., Grand Duke of, i. 244
Meditations of the Exercises, i. 375-6
Mein Austritt aus dem Jesuitenorden, ii. 449
Mejer, Otto, lectures of, at Göttingen, i. 122
Melchers, Archbishop, arrest and imprisonment of, i. 257
Mémoires de la Congrégation de la Mission, official character of, ii. 55, 57; charges against, 56; its statements in the matter of the Legation and death of Cardinal Tournon unassailable, 58; some of the documents it published, 59-65
Memorie Storiche dell' Eminentissimo Monsignore Cardinale di Tournon, ii. 54 *et seqq.*
Mendoza, Cardinal, on Jesuit political activity against England, ii. 150-1
Mendoza, Hernando de, on the evil of reserved cases of sin, i. 364-5; denounced by Jesuits, 364 (*note*)
Menstruae Disputationes, ii. 248-9
Mental reservation, uses of, i. 173, 174; Cardinal Franzelin on, 264-5; Jesuit justifications of, ii. 304-5, 306, 307-8
Mercurian, General of the Jesuit Society, on matters outside of pastoral functions, ii. 137-8
Meschler, Father, on the uncertainty of the Jesuit's calling and location, i. 88; becomes confessor of the author's mother, 234 (*note*); guarantees the authenticity of the apparition of the Madonna at Marpingen, 266; applauds the extravagances at Lourdes, *ib.*, examines the author before his admission into the Jesuit Order, 282;

ascetic practices encouraged by, 389-90; travels in comfort, ii. 132
Meulen, Fraulein von, her influence o the author, i. 25; her faith in gro supernaturalism, 26 *et seqq.*
Mezzafalce, Papal Legate to China, persecuted by the Jesuits, ii. 58; banished through their means, 59
Migazzi, Cardinal, on Jesuit flouting o the Pope, ii. 52
Miller, Father, approves of the author' progress, ii. 215; experiences an em barrassment, 225
Minoux, Father, Rector at Feldkirch, i 197
Miquel and the author's interview wit the Kaiser, ii. 460; his "collectiv policy," 465
Miracle "cures," i. 13
Miranda, on the difficulty of learnin all about the Society, ii. 6
Missions of the Jesuit Order, i. 416; in stances of the missionary spirit, ii 382-3
Missions, popular, exercises for th masses, i. 384; excitement during th continuance of, ii. 380-1; instances o the organisation of, 383-4; carrie on in Germany, 384
Modernism, Jesuit denunciation of, i 271-4
Modesty, false, and its bane, i. 40-2
Mohler, Professor Johann Adam, o Jesuit morality, ii. 293-4
Molinism, the doctrine of, ii. 187; synonym for Jesuitism, 290
Mommsen asserts that Jesuits attemp to do away with incriminating docu ments in public libraries, i. 189
Monita privata Societatis Jesu, ii. 7; th question of its genuineness, 7-9 examples of the Secret Instructions 10-13
Monod, Father, his influence in France ii. 189
Monsperger, Professor, confessions o eminent persons discovered by, ii. 177
Monte, Cardinal, avows Jesuit opposi tion to Lutheranism, ii. 22
Montezon on the moral teaching of th Jesuits, ii. 287
Montserrat, Benedictine Convent at, i 370
Monumenta Germaniae paedagogica, i 63 (*note*); purpose with which it wa compiled, 184; spirit in which the compilers did their work, 191 (*note*)
Moral theology, a variant of the con fessional, ii. 286; irretrievabl damaged by the Jesuits, 289, 293 Döllinger and Reusch's great wor on the "Moral-Theological Di putes" in the Catholic Church, 396-7
Morality, Jesuit, ii. 286-337; unwhole someness of Jesuit teaching regard ing, 327; and the State, 338-68; ap plication of, 363-8
Moretus, Balthasar, ii. 112
Müffendorf, exorcising a ghost at, i. 27-8
Munchen-Gladbach, the author commis sioned to help the pastor of a parish near, ii. 420-21
Munich, Jesuit documents lodged in the library at, i. 189; revelations of the secret Jesuit documents, 206, 207; documents in, concerning the Jesuits and miracles, 312; and about the

Index 487

Jesuits and witchcraft, 320; memorial of the Jesuit College at, touching blind obedience, 338; evidence at, of the use of secret reports by Jesuit officials, 353; MS. of the *Monita* at, ii. 9; luxury of the Jesuit College at, 81; endowment of the Jesuit College in, 83-4
ünster, political activity of the Jesuits of, ii. 160
usic, sensuousness of, affected by Jesuits, i. 160
Mysteries of the Exercises, i. 376
Mysticism, false, warmly approved by the Jesuits, i. 299 *et seqq.*; true, strongly antipathetic to them, 299

amur, Jesuit activity at, in 1692, ii. 162
atalis, Father, on permissible subjects of talk among Jesuit novices, i. 292-3
ational Union for Catholic Germany, ii. 375
ationality, sense of, obliterated under the Jesuit education, i. 131-3; destruction of, required by the Jesuit spirit of cosmopolitanism, ii. 34-8
aumann, Dr. Friedrich, his error respecting Thomas Aquinas, ii. 256 (*note*)
ewnham Paddox, i. 242
icasius Grammaticus on the barbarous Latinity of Spanish Jesuits, i. 103
ickel, Goswin, General, supports Jesuit activity in Hungary in 1655, ii. 145; one of the two German Generals of the Order, 145 (*note*), his ordinance touching the confessing of sovereigns, 173
Vickes, compositions by, i. 160
idhard, Eberhard, ii. 158
iemoller, deathbed confession of, ii. 318
imeguen, Peace of, ii. 42
ix, Hermann, takes the Wynandsrade scholastics to view the relics at Aix-la-Chapelle, i. 323; receives the author as a member of the Jesuit Order, 407; involved in the Hartmann trial, ii. 100-2; character of, 201; the author's indebtedness to, 202; Nix's reverence for the Virgin, 208; his eulogy of the Jesuit Order, 213-4
oailles, Cardinal-Archbishop of Paris, and the Jesuits, ii. 192
oris, H., Cardinal, and Probabilism, ii. 297
ovenae, value of, i. 306-7; "novena of grace" in honour of St. Francis Xavier, 323
ovice Master, duties of, i. 271, 284, 285, 286, 287, 290, 291, 297, 298, 318, 355, 393
ovitiate, ignorance during, i. 99; novice's Latin, 99-100; the novice's garb, 284, 285; the novice's patron saint, 285-6; daily routine of, 286-7; hardship and discomfort of life at Exaeten, 288-9; fare of novices, 289; recreations of, 290; oratory, practice of, during, 291; seclusion during, 292-4; permissible subjects of conversation during, 292-3; meditation imperative, 297; object of the *Lumina*, 297-8; tale-bearing and fault-finding encouraged, 355-6; the novice's all-seeing eye, 357; deadly monotony of life of, 358-61; full course of the Exercises during, 371; manual work during, 392-3; modes of self-humiliation during, 394; penitential practices in, 394-5; the cruelty of renunciation of parents in, 398-402; expulsion from, 403
Noyelle, Charles de, Jesuit General, on illiterate teachers, i. 186
Noyers, Louis XIII.'s secretary, a lay member of the Jesuit Society, ii. 19
Nun, the confessions of a, i. 260; Jesuits forbidden to undertake the regular cure of nuns, ii. 124; avoidance of nuns, though enjoined, only ostensible, 131; a nunnery more comfortable than a convent, 132; Jesuits supposed to exist for men, not women, *ib.*; really women and nuns exist for Jesuits, *ib.*
Nursing Orders, self-sacrifice of the, ii. exist for Jesuits, *ib.*

Oaths, Jesuit attitude to non-observance of civil, ii. 345-6, when oath of allegiance may be ignored, 437-8 (*note*)
Obedience, the first law of Jesuits, i. 88; the vow of, 273; the dominant note in Jesuit ascetic discipline, 326 *et seqq.*; the three degrees of, 328; Jesuit obedience absolutely non-moral, 330-6; as enjoined by Jesus, 333-4; how the Jesuit doctrine compels to sin, 335-6; Jesuit defence of the doctrine of, 336; testimony of history to breach of the vow, ii. 50-67
Observator, duties of, i. 138-9
Old Catholics, Jesuit attitude towards, i. 244-5
Oldenburg, Grand Duke of, i. 244
Oliva, Paul, on poor quality of Jesuit Latin, i. 100, 101; condones breach of the "Statement of Conscience," 346; condemns Gonzalez's work on Probabilism, ii. 50; disobeys the Papal injunction, 51
Omnia ad majorem Dei gloriam, motto of the Jesuit Order, i. 365, ii. 106
Oncken, Hermann, his *Rudolf von Bennigsen*, ii. 344 (*note*)
Oosen, the Jesuit villa at, ii. 77; equivocation associated with its purchase, 319
Oppelt, Johannes, an approved German classic in Jesuit eyes, ii. 110 (*note*)
Orders in the Catholic Church, status of monastic, i. 272; essentials of an Order, 273; wealth of the French Orders, 274 (*note*), artificial basis of, 276-7; why they are filled, 278; the disillusionment, 279; the steps of membership of an Order, 280 *et seqq.*; the impediments to membership, 280-1; the garb of the Jesuit Order, 284-5; exaggerated opinions of the perfection of the members of various Orders, ii. 377-8; the common life within the Jesuit Order, 376 80; heroism of the nursing Orders, 378 (*note*), most Orders free from the gross defects of the Jesuit Order, 424
Ordinations, the four minor, ii. 215
Ordrupshoj, Denmark, Jesuit school at, i. 53; the benefactress of, ii. 167;

Index

"harmless" place for men of thought, 268
Original sin, doctrine of, ii. 224
Orlandinus on the authorship of the Constitutions, i. 408
Oswald, Augustine, ii. 413

Pachtler, Georg Michael, defends the Jesuit system of education, i. 63 (note); attacks freemasonry, 64 (note), one of the only two professional teachers at Feldkirch, 72; approves a crystallised scheme of education, 83; tries to veil the selfishness of Jesuit education, 84; admits the centralisation of the Jesuit Order, 92; his lack of the historic conscience, 191; examined the author before his admission to the Order, 282; attacks Leo XIII., ii. 67
Paderborn, MS. copy of the *Monita* at, ii. 9, 10
Palafox, Don Juan de, Bishop of Los Angeles, protest of, against the secret statutes of the Jesuits. ii. 6-7; persecuted by the Jesuits, 6; calumniated by the Jesuits, 86-7 (note), proposed beatification of, *ib.*
Palestrina, Masses by, in Jesuit worship, i. 160
Palmieri, Domenico, in conflict with the censorship, ii. 269; on the use of equivocation, 307
Papacy, the character of, ii. 392; a purely human institution, 406. (See Pope)
Papal States, independence of, ii. 166; attempt to galvanise the question, 391-2. (See Pope)
Paris, the author's sojourn at, ii. 421
Parsons, Father Robert, engaged in Jesuit activity in England, ii. 46, 111; his plot against Queen Elizabeth, 149-53; his many pseudonyms, 151 (note), his political pamphlets, 151, 152; and the deposition of Queen Elizabeth, 312; object of his book against the succession of the King of Scotland, 313-4; on the repudiation of the oath of allegiance, 437-8 (note)
Passau, endowment of the Jesuit College at, ii. 84
Passionei, Cardinal, author of the *Memorie storiche Tournon*, ii. 56; annotates the Jesuit memorial to Innocent XIII., 60-1 (note)
Passow's Lexicon, uses of, i. 123-4
Patriotism, Christian view of, ii. 34; what the Jesuits put in its place, 35; essential characteristics of real, 35-6; "two-faced" patriotism, 37
Paul III., Pope, issues the Bull founding the Society of Jesus, i. 407, 413
Paul V., Pope, canonises Loyola, ii. 111; at war with Venice, 364
Paul the Hermit, the questions asked by, i. 293
Paulsen, Friedrich, lectures on Modern Philosophy at Berlin University, ii. 404
Peking, usurious practices of the Jesuits in, ii. 88, 89
Pemble, Father, on the undergarment and seamless cloak of Jesus and the wood of the Cross, i. 304-5; his booklet about the Virgin, ii. 207
Penitential practices in the novitiate, i. 394-5
Père La Chaise cemetery, ii. 193
Pereyra, Thomas, Superior of the Portuguese Jesuits, and Cardinal Tournon, ii. 60 *et seqq.*
Perfection, counsel of, i. 273-6
Pergen, Count, memorial to the Empress Maria Theresa on the imperfect study of German in the Jesuit curriculum, i. 114; deplores the neglect of poor scholars, 146-7; animadverts on the deficiences of Jesuit education, 194-5
Perjury, Jesuit notion of, ii. 305-6
Pesch, Tilmann, gives way to jealousy and abuse, ii. 131-2; how he enjoys the appearance of scholarship, 277; his "Christ oder Anti-Christ," 357; defames Protestantism and slanders Luther, 358-63; favours an extremist policy against non-Catholic Christians, 375; is refused the author's collaboration, 394-5
Petre, Edward, the evil counsellor of James II., ii. 153-5; attitude of the Jesuit Order towards, 155-8
Petri, Dr., and Jesuit designs against the Hohenzollerns, ii. 384-5
Pfeil, Aloysius, on the effective conversion of the heathen, ii. 382-3
Pfulf, Father, and A. von Doss's lecture and article on German classics, i. 227, 228
Philip II. of Spain implicated in Parsons' plot against Queen Elizabeth, ii. 149-53
Philip V. of Spain, violation of a confession of, by his confessor, ii. 178; the victim of Jesuit intrigues, 189
Philosophy in the Jesuit sense, ii. 246; the course of the study of, in the scholasticate, 246-7; what is comprehended by, 247-8; Aristotle supreme in, 250-3
Piaget on the Jesuit Order, ii. 425 and note
Piccolomini, General, and the study of Aristotle, ii. 252-3
Piety, in Jesuit education, various phases of, i. 158-63; of the Jesuit Order, 295 *et seqq.*; objects of the *Lumina*, 297-8; battens on mawkish mysticism, 299 *et seqq.*; disregard of the Scriptures as a means of edification, 318; the sole use of the New Testament in, *ib.*; belief in devils and witchcraft a feature of, 319-23; the part played by relics in, 324-5
Pilgrimages, wickedness and degradation of, ii. 212
Pingsmann, Dr., on the return of the Jesuits to Germany, ii. 47
Pius V., Pope, excommunication of Queen Elizabeth by, ii. 311
Pius VII., Pope, restores the Jesuit Order, ii. 135
Pius IX., Pope, overcome by the secrets at La Salette, i. 28; alleged hopes respecting France, 238; sanctions the Lourdes pilgrimages, 258; unattractive personality of, 262; his cast-off clothes as relics, 263; his manifestoes anent modern research and learning,

Index

ii. 270, 271; on the supremacy of Church over State, 339
Pius X., Pope, enjoins absolute docility, i. 51; sanctions the Lourdes pilgrimages, 258; his syllabus against Modernism, ii. 270; on the supremacy of Church over State, 338
Plantin Press produces the *Imago*, ii. 112-3
Plautus as a theologian, i. 102
Poland, Jesuit political intrigues in, ii. 138, 139; the candidature for the throne of, 146-8; Maria Theresa and the partition of, 176
Politics and the Jesuit Order, ii. 133-98; Jesuit political ability greatly overrated, 136 and *note*; the "conscience" formula in, 170-1; Hoffaus on the evils of Jesuit interference in temporal affairs, 193-4
Pombal, Marquis of, his scheme to unite Portugal to England thwarted by the Jesuits, ii. 163
Pondicherry, Jesuit trading at, ii. 91
Pontan (Spanmuller), Jacob, on the abuses in the Jesuit system of instruction, i. 189-91
Ponte, Father Louis de, on the authorship of the Exercises, i. 370
Pope, the relations of the Society of Jesus to, i. 412; the Jesuits claim to be the bodyguard of, ii. 50; Jesuit resistance, active or passive, to, 51, 52, 53, 53-66, 66-7; on the supreme power of the Pope in civil matters, 339; is the Pope the Vicar of Christ? 392; the price the Pope has had to pay for Jesuit support, 428; the "direct" power of the Pope, no longer tenable, replaced by the "indirect," 428. (*See* Papal, Papacy)
Porquet, Father, on the Chinese rites adopted by the Jesuits, ii. 64; excommunicated by the Cardinal Legate Tournon, *ib.*
Porsch, Dr., and the author's Church and State pamphlet, ii. 393
Portico, the residence for theology students at, i. 287; the author enters, ii. 411; his experiences at, 413-4
Portugal, political activity of the Jesuits in, ii. 162-3
Possevin, Anton, Jesuit political agent at Stockholm, ii. 138; receives John III. into the Catholic Church, *ib.*, intervenes in the affairs of Poland, 139
Postulancy, the stage preceding the novitiate, i. 228; the period of probation, 280; the preliminary examination for, 280-2
Pottgeisser, Julius, General Prefect at Feldkirch, i. 145; introduces the game of "running the gauntlet," 156-7; a narrow-minded martinet, 210
Poverty, the Jesuit attitude to, i. 147-8; the vow of, 273; the counsel of poverty examined, 273-5; scope of the vow of, ii. 71-4; habitual disregard of, 74-104
Praetor, duties of, i. 138-41
Prague, the Jesuit College at, contained no German classic in 1772, i. 114; MS. of the *Monita* at, ii. 9; Jesuits secure the control of the University of, 52-3; Jesuits and the Carolinian Academy at, 110

Prantl, his account of Jesuit intrigues in the Ludwig-Maximilian University at Ingolstadt, ii. 38-40
Prat on the dealings of the Jesuits and the French League, ii. 161-2; on Father Coton's interference in French politics, 183
Pray's, Father, calumnious work on the Chinese Missions, ii. 66 (*note*)
Prayer, the chief function of true religion, ii. 455, 457
Predestination, Jesuit view of, i. 251; security of salvation and probability of damnation, 403-5
Prefects, Jesuit Fathers who superintended pupils at Feldkirch, i. 57; no prospects for, 85; prefects of the novices at Exaeten, 290
Prelection, i. 94
Preludes of the Exercises, i. 373
Premonstrants, Jesuit opposition to, at Magdeburg, ii. 98
Preussische Jahrbucher, the author's articles in the, ii. 449
Pride of the Society of Jesus, ii. 105-23
Priest in the Catholic Church, status of, i. 272; his part in the Mass, ii. 219-21; course of studies and discipline necessary for, i. 271-390, ii. 227-69
Priests, German Catholic, i. 23-4
Princes' confessors, influence in politics of, ii. 135; the salaries of, 193
Privatdozent, the post of, ii. 463
Probabilism, the Pope's order respecting works on, ii. 50-1; the mischief of, 293
Procuratorial Congregation of the Society of Jesus, i. 424
Procurator, status of, in the Jesuit Order, i. 354 (*note*), two classes of, 424
Professed members of the Society of Jesus, qualifications for, i. 414-5; vow of, 417-8; five minor vows of, 418
Promotor Fidei, duties of, ii. 86 (*note*)
Property, renunciation of, by intending priests, ii. 215
Proselytising at Jesuit schools, i. 157-8
Protestantism, qualified by tradition, i. 6; relations of Ultramontanism towards, 9; weakness of its view respecting art, 46-7; antagonism with Catholicism after the close of the Franco-German War, 232-3; travesty of, ii. 358-63; the Jesuits of Protestantism, 451; ignorance of Catholicism too common in the ranks of, *ib.*
Provinces of the Jesuit Order, i. 416; how they are governed, 424
Provincial Congregation of the Society of Jesus, i. 424
Prussia, Catholic dislike of Protestantism of, i. 8-9; boycott of history of, at Feldkirch, 122
Purgatory, suffering souls in, the counterpart of ghosts, i. 26
Pütz, Father, singular conduct of, ii. 398

Questor in Jesuit schools, duty of, i. 144
Quintinye, La, on Jesuit morality, ii. 300

Index

acke's attack on Lieber, ii. 402
tackelwitz, in Saxony, i. 234 (*note*); the author's brother-in-law buried at, 267
agusa, Latin and Greek in the Jesuit high school at, i. 69
ncé, Armand de, Abbé, on Jesuit morals, ii. 290; treatment of, by the Jesuits, 291, 299
anke, why the "History of the Popes" by, is forbidden, ii. 273; influence of, on the author, 406
atgeb, Father Jacob, justifies the alleged removal from public libraries of documents incriminating Jesuits, i. 189; about the doubts concerning the completeness of the Constitutions, ii. 2; on the return of the Jesuits to Germany, 47; consults with the leaders of the German Centre, 165; approves of the author's progress in philosophy and theology, 269; termination of the author's intimacy with, 372-4; commissions the author to write in defence of the Jesuit Order, 393; on Döllinger and Reusch's book on the "Moral-Theological Disputes," 396-7; commissions the author to go to Berlin to prepare for a Jesuit settlement there, 399-400; consents to the author's tertiate, 411
atio conscientiae, i. 342 *et seqq.*
atio Studiorum Societatis Jesu, the be-all and end-all of the Jesuit system of education, i. 63-111; its prescription as to Physics, 65-6; as to Mathematics, 67; as to History, *ib.*; as to the Natural Sciences, *ib.*; as to Theology and Philosophy, 68; as to Scholarship and Philology, 68-70; fulsome and ridiculous praise of, 74-6; egotism of, 82; the system of education authorised by, 135 *et seqq.*; on hostility to heretics, ii. 24-5; considers the execution of heretics an edifying sight, 356-7
availlac, murder of Henry IV. of France by, ii. 333
tavignan on Jesuit support of the revolution in Portugal, ii. 162-3; on the struggle of the Order with Gonzalez and the Pope, 295-6
teal Presence, doctrine of the, i. 199; the essence of the Catholic priesthood, ii. 219; the dogmatic teaching of the Church respecting the, 219-22
egulae Communes, ii. 2
teferendar, or county court judge, i. 264; the author appointed to the office at Cleves, 265; difficulty of his reappointment to, ii. 459; is offered the post of, at Frankfort-on-the-Oder, 462
teformation, Jesuit scheme to undo the, ii. 159
egulae Communes, ii. 2
teichensperger, August, on Jesuit political activity, ii. 166
eichmann, his praise of Tilmann Pesch, ii. 357; how he dealt with the calumny of Luther's suicide, 360 (*note*); collaborates with Tilmann Pesch, 395 (*note*)
teinhold, Professor Karl Leonard, on the Jesuit rule commanding renunciation of parents, i. 399-400

Reinkens, Bishop, Bonn students' rudeness towards, i. 245
Reisach, Cardinal Count, once Archbishop of Munich and afterwards President of the Vatican Council, i. 237; his prediction about France speedily falsified, 238
Relics, Pope's cast-off clothes utilised as, i. 263; at the Church of St. John of Lateran, 268; at Aix-la-Chapelle described, 324-5; the author's misery at Aix-la-Chapelle, ii. 212
Religion, the chief function of true, ii. 455; what constitutes true, 456; the only basis of true, 456-8
Rem, Father Jacob, visited by the souls of the dead, i. 310-1; his pity immortalised by Biedermann, 311
Remigius, the strange case of, ii. 346-9
Renewal of vows, ii. 389
Reports, the method and character of, in the Jesuit Order, i. 352-5
Residences of Jesuits, i. 78
Retz, Francis, General, laments the decay of the zeal for knowledge, i. 185
Reusch, Professor, decree of excommunication against, i. 244; accepts as probable the report of the poisoning of Cardinal Tournon, ii. 55; his "History of the Moral-Theological Disputes" in the Catholic Church, 396-7
Reutsch, Father Karl, forbids the admittance of boys to the bedroom of his brotherhood, i. 203
Rhenish-Westphalia, Catholics of, and their hatred of Prussia, i. 8-9; defective education in, 10; their strong pro-Austrian attitude in the war with Prussia, 211; fanaticism of, concerning the doctrine of infallibility, 221-2
Rhetoric, studies of, during the scholasticate, ii. 230-45
Ribadeneira on the authorship of the Constitutions, i. 408
Riembauer, Father Franz, confesses to the murder of a woman, ii. 367-8
Riezler, Sigmund, on Loyola's piety and asceticism, i. 299 (*note*); on the effect of Jesuit piety in Bavaria, 319; on Duhr's untrustworthiness, ii. 283
Rist, M., illustrates the Jesuit notions of patriotism, ii. 37; relates how peace may be made with the Church, 381
Rivalry in Jesuit schools, unwholesome, i. 143-4
Rodriguez, Alonzo, on simplicity in Jesuit garb, i. 285; sanctity attached to his "Practice of Christian Perfection," 313-4; quotations from this work as examples of credulity, 314-8; on blind obedience, 339-40; his excessive literalism, 389; is assured that no Jesuit will be damned, 404; on the authorship of the Constitution, 408
Roermond, i. 283
Roh, Father, teaches the author, i. 34; proposes a safe bet, ii. 320; alleged statement of, about the Jesuit designs against the Hohenzollerns, 385
Roller, John, deplores the laziness of Jesuit teachers, i. 187
Rom und das Zentrum, ii. 402

Index

Rome, external show at, i. 262; visit to the miraculous image of Mary at, 263
Roothaan, John, General, re-edits the *Ratio Studiorum*, i. 63; relates how a dismissed Jesuit missed salvation, 405; declares the Jesuit Order is strictly non-political, ii. 133; holds a conference to establish missions in Germany, 383-4
Rosary as used by Jesuit students, i. 182
Roser, Elisabeth, rebuffed by Loyola, ii. 129
Rosetti, Professor Costa, avows that it is very probable all Jesuits go to heaven, i. 405
Rosignoli, Father, extracts from his "Pity the Souls in Purgatory," i. 305-6
Roth, Hugo, ii. 314
Rothe, influence of, on the author, ii. 406
Roux, Le, on the deathbed repentance of the godless, ii. 300-1, 381-2
Ruga, Father, ii. 17-8
Rules concluding the Exercises, i. 376
Rumer, Rector of the Jesuit College at Passau, ii. 159-60
Ryswick, peace of, ii. 42

Sabbatina disputation, ii. 248-9
Saint (*Sanctus*), the title of the canonised, i. 310 (*note*)
St. Hedwig's Infirmary, the headquarters of the Jesuits in Berlin, ii. 411 (*note*)
Saint-Simon, the Duke de, recognises the existence of lay members of the Jesuit Society, ii. 19; his anecdote about chocolate for the General, 104; of the Jesuits at Namur, 162 and *note*, on Jesuit influence at the courts of Europe, 167-8; his portrait of Tellier, 186-8; his note about Father Bermudez, 188; his opinion of Father D'Aubanton, 189; on the pressure brought to bear by the Jesuits on Louis XIV., 191-2
Salmeron, Alphonso, a famous Jesuit theologian, ii. 111
Sanchez, disgraceful character of his writings, ii. 289-90; favours the use of ambiguity, 304
Santarelli's *Tractatus de Haeresi* approved by the Jesuit Society, and condemned by the Sorbonne, ii. 312
Sarasa, Antonius de, on blind obedience, i. 338-9
Sardinia, King of (Charles Emmanuel), on the wealth and arrogance of the Jesuits, ii. 103
Sarpi, Paolo, on Jesuit intrigues in politics, ii. 196; on Jesuit approval of the murder of Henry IV. of France, 336; on the conduct of the Jesuits towards Venice, 364-5
Sarrazin effects a deathbed repentance, ii. 381
Sattenwolf, Father Wenzel, enjoined to take steps to raise the standard of Latinity, i. 101
Scapulars, wearing of, i. 21 (*note*)
Schaffer, Father Karl, i. 132-3
Schall, Adam, ii 60 (*note*)
Scheeben, Professor, on the genuineness of the sham apparition at Marpingen, i. 266
Schiller, a false ideal in von Doss's opinion, i. 227; the author's bodeful motto from Schiller's *Piccolomini*, 230; L. von Hammerstein's estimate of, ii. 232-3; Baumgartner's criticism of, 234-6
Schleiermacher, influence of, on the author, ii. 406
Schneider, Father Joseph, how his "magister" meal was interrupted, ii. 76
Scholastic, the garb of a, i. 284 (*note*); is kept in ignorance of the history of the Order of Jesuits, ii. 224-5
Scholasticate, meditation during the, i. 237; study of the Exercises during the, 371; when the scholasticate begins, 407; duration of, *ib.* and *note*, simple vows of, 417; uniformity of the routine during the, ii. 199-200; ignorance of the Order a peculiarity of the, 224-5; scheme of study during the, 227-69; humanistic studies during the, 228-9; rhetoric studies during the, 229-45; philosophy and theology studies of the, 246-9
Scholasticism, Jesuit, perfect sterility of, ii. 260; Kink on the evils of, 278-9
Schreiber's specimens of subjects selected for disputation at Freiburg, ii. 280-1
Schwarzenberg, Prince, and the German Empire's indebtedness to the Jesuits, ii. 85
Scio, how the Jesuits Christianised the Mohammedans of, ii. 364
Scotland, Jesuit designs touching the restoration of the Catholic religion in, ii. 148; Parsons' plot in favour of Mary, Queen of, 149-53
Scott, Sir Walter, as a classic at Stonyhurst, i. 242
Scourge, use of, i. 395
Scriptor, duties of, ii. 370, 389-90
Secrecy enjoined in the Jesuit Order, i. 353; use of a cipher, *ib.*
Secret instructions of the Jesuit Society. (*See Monita*)
Secrets at La Salette, the, i. 28
Secular clergy, relations of the Jesuits with, ii. 44-8
Sedan, prisoners taken at, i. 233; misrepresentation of the results of, 234
Sendbote des göttlichen Herzens, examples of the grotesque cures recorded in the, i. 306-8
Sergardi, Ludovico, on Jesuit morals, ii. 289-90
Sermon on the Mount, the true Christian code, i. 274; why the Jesuits set it aside, 277
Servi Mariae in Jesuit-schools, duties of, i. 144
Settlements of Jesuits, i. 78 (*note*); constitution of, 424
Seuse, the mysticism of, repugnant to the Jesuits, i 299
Sexuality, teaching of the Christian Church regarding, i. 40-1; attitude of Jesuits towards, in schools, 202-8; delicacy of the question, 209
Simple vows of scholastics and spiritual and temporal coadjutors, i. 417; constitute an impediment to marriage, 273, 417

Index

Sixtus V., Pope, favours the Marian Congregations, i. 165, 169; condemns Loyola's letter on obedience, 336; death of, ii. 110 (note)
Slaughter, Father, on the deathbed repentance of the wicked, ii. 382
Smet, de, character of, ii. 391
Snuff-taking, a habit of Jesuits, i. 205, Pius IX.'s "snuffy" appearance, 262
Socialism has a link with Jesuitism, ii. 371 (note)
Societas Jesu, or Society of Jesus, *Monita* of, ii. 7; *Anatomia* of, 9; *Arcana* of, 10; name of, 110 and notes, 119-20; *Imago* of, 112-23. (See Imago, Institute, Jesuits)
Socius, the post of, in a Jesuit Society, i. 271; and in a Province, 424
Solms-Braunfels, Prince Alexander of, turns Catholic, i. 20, widow of, entertains von Doss as her spiritual director at Marxheim, 249
Sorbonne, the, condemns Santarelli's *Tractatus de Haeresi*, ii. 312; orders Mariana's book to be burned, 333
Sotelo, Louis, Franciscan Bishop, records the conduct of the Jesuits towards him, ii. 365
Soubirous, Bernadotte, i. 253
Soullier, Father, ii. 92
Southwell, Father Robert, equivocation of, ii. 312
Sovereigns, Jesuits and the confession of, ii. 168-98; secret instructions for the confessing of, 172; purpose of the confessing of, 172-3
Spalatro, Jesuit trading in the district of, ii. 98
Spee, Friedrich von, on the Jesuits and witchcraft, i. 319, 320
Spichern, incident of the news of the German victory at, i. 233
Sprenger on legitimate equivocations, ii. 302
Stanislaus' Day, St., i. 285; author preaches the sermon on, 291. (See Kostka)
Stapleton, Lady, and the use of Ditton Hall as a Jesuit college, i. 287
State, the, in its relations to the Church, ii. 338-68; Jesuitism a standing menace to, 436.41; Jesuit hostility to the schools of the, 439,40; the connection between Church and State considered, 452.5
Stattler, Father Benedict, his theory of justifiable murder, ii. 366 and note
Steer, Father Norbert, on the evil of confessing children in the confessor's bedroom, i. 203
Stella Matutina, Jesuit school at Feldkirch, i. 54-60
Stentrup, Professor, ii. 367
Stern, Dr. Jacob, anent the violation of Maria Theresa's confession, ii. 175-6
Stessl, Jac., condemns the ignorance of Greek amongst Jesuits, i. 187
Stieger," meaning of the new verb "to," i. 150
Stimmen aus Maria-Laach, i. 325; headquarters of, at Exaeten, ii. 369, 370
Stitzing, Professor von, ultramontane students' demonstration against, i. 244-5
Stöcker, Dr. Adolf, invites the author to write for the *Kreuzzeitung*, ii. 449; character of, 451

Stolberg, Count Alfred, on Kullmann' attempt on Bismarck's life, i. 212
Stolberg-Stolberg, Count Caius zu, hi antipathy to Protestantism, i. 6-7 the author's godfather, 7, 243
Stolberg-Stolberg, Count Franz zu, e gaged to the author's sister Mari i. 243; death of, 267
Stolberg-Stolberg, Count Friedrich Le pold zu, i. 7, 243
Stonyhurst, fees at, i. 116; character the buildings at, 240; laxity supervision, 240.1; pursuits of th students, 241; inadequacy of th instruction at, 241.2; the "table at, ii. 75
Straubing, the Hartmann lawsuit a ii. 100-2
Strauss, Father Karl, Music Prefect a Feldkirch, i. 213
Streicher, Father, exposes the Spanis Jesuits' ignorance of Latin, i. 102 how members dismissed from th Order are treated, ii. 12-13
Stuarts, the Jesuits and the downfall the, ii. 153, 155
Studt sanctions the right of gymnasiu to a part in Marian Congregation i. 172
Sturm, Johannes, scholastic scheme o copied by the Jesuits, i. 63
Suarez, Francis, the greatest theologia of the Jesuit Order, i. 408, ii. 111 thesis in his *De Religione* touchin the authorship of the Constitution i. 407-8; condones the use of amb guity, ii. 305; on adultery, 309; o the supremacy of Church over Stat 338; allows that heretics may b sentenced to death, 355; teache the "indirect" power of the Pop 428
Substantialia Instituti, "the essenti contents of the Institute," are ke strictly secret, i. 414; supposed de nition of, ii. 3-4
Sulkow, Demetrius, Archbishop of Le berg, on persons dismissed the S ciety of Jesus, ii. 13
Summa theologica, ii. 255
Summarium Constitutionum, ii. 2
Superior, subordination to, must b complete, i. 134; the Constitution on the supremacy of the, 326 *et seqq*. head of Province and of Settlemen 424; secret routine before the a pointment of a Provincial Superio 425-7
Superstitious observances in Cathol cism, i. 12-14
Suppression of the Jesuit Order, i. 8 168, ii. 22, 66; Cordara discusses wh God permitted it, ii. 106-9
Sweden, Jesuit political intrigues in, i 138
Swieten, Gerhard van, summoned t Vienna by Maria Theresa, ii. 43; h struggle with the Jesuits, 43.4; sla dered by the Jesuits, 43 (*note*); i forms Maria Theresa of Jesuit a noyance at the *Imago*, 112; on th decay of those universities wher the Jesuits ruled, 279
Sybel, Heinrich von, lectures of, i. 122

Tamburini, General, prohibits certai propositions from Descartes an

Index

Leibnitz, ii. 253; on the persecution of, by the Order, 295 (*note*)
Tanner, Father Matthias, recommends scourging for Jesuits who fondle young persons, i. 206
Tauler, the mysticism of, repugnant to the Jesuits, i. 299
Taunton, E. L., his "Jesuits in England" cited, ii. 46, 150, 152, 153, 154; his review of Edward Petre's conduct, 155; ascribes the fall of the Stuarts to the Jesuits, *ib.*, on Foley's habit of garbling the text, 284.5 (*note*), on 's notion of allegiance, 311-2 Gerard
Taunus, an all-night sitting in the, i. 226, 249
Taxil hoax, the, i. 267
Teaching, why Jesuits must fail in, i. 134 (*See* Education *and* Jesuits)
Tellier succeeds La Chaise as Confessor to Louis XIV., ii. 186; Saint-Simon's pen portrait of, 187-8
Teresa, Saint, vision of, i. 404; unwittingly gets Hahn into trouble, ii. 269
Terrien, Father, i. 404
Tertiaries, a class of Jesuit affiliates, ii. 19
i e, full course of the Exercises during the, i. 371; final stage of probation for the priesthood, ii. 369; course of study during, 412-5; chief feature of, 412
Theology, importance of, to Jesuits, ii. 248; course of study of, 248-250; authority of Thomas Aquinas supreme in, 253-6
Thirty Years' War, Jesuit selfishness during the, ii. 41; Jesuits' share in the, 158-9; partly financed by the Jesuits, 160-1
Thomism" and "Thomistic," ii. 256 (*note*)
Thorn, the massacre of, ii. 25-29
Toleration, religious, Jesuit attitude towards, ii. 349-354
Toni, or the practice in oratory, i. 291
Torres, Miguel, ii. 16
curnay, Convent, an old vest of the Pope's sent to, as a relic, i. 263
ournon, Charles, sent by Clement XI. to settle the disputes about the Chinese rites and missions, ii. 53; opposed by the Jesuits, 54; Jesuits accused of poisoning him, 54-6; letters and reports from Tournon complaining how the Jesuits obstructed him, 59-64; condemns their usury in China, 89
rade and commerce, Jesuits' success in, ii. 91-9
ransubstantiation, the process of, ii. 220
reitschke, Heinrich von, as a lecturer, ii. 404-5; influence on the author, 405
Triduum, the nature of the, ii. 389
Trinity, doctrine of the, ii 224
urmae, the system of, i. 290
yannicide, Jesuit teaching about, ii. 327-337; approval of Mariana's doctrine in favour of the killing of princes, 328; attempt of the Order to meet the public indignation caused by their approval, 332-3

Ultramontanism, certain journals of, i. 6; heresy-hunting spirit of, 7; how it colours loyalty and patriotism, 9; tyranny of, over the mind, 12; superstitious observances of, 12, 13; the essence of, 21; unscrupulous fondness for theatricality, 22.3; the supernatural world of, 26; teaches belief in guardian angels, ghosts and devils, 26-7; why it insists on early confession, 34; evil of its teaching respecting sexuality, 39; its attitude towards the liberal arts, 46-78; internationalism in its system of education, 49-51; complete subserviency of the laity to, 142; wholehearted selfishness of, 222.3; attitude of towards freemasonry, 224; in the political arena, 231, 246.7; pomp and splendour of and their object, 237-8; resistance to its arrogance would help undo it, 238; insolence of, towards the Old Catholics, 244-5; consolidated by the Kulturkampf, 255.6, the bondage of Ultramontanism, 260-1; doctrine as to the Catholic taking of the oath of allegiance in Germany, 264-5; the willing dupe of hoaxes and sham apparitions, 266-7; its classification of Christians of its own Church, 272; its doctrine of the Orders, 273; puts on one side the Sermon on the Mount in favour of its own artificial basis for the Orders, 277; governed also by Christian idealism, 278; its handling of confession, 361.9; doctrine of, touching God, Christ and the world, 377; the Exercises the main prop of, 377-8; its view of woman, ii. 125; its reason for inventing the system of princes' confessors, 135; its faith in the devil a vital matter, 209; has dominated dogma within the Catholic church, 287-8; insists on the supremacy of Church over State, 338-368; uses confession as a lever to move the world, 386-7; an abuse of the Catholic religion, 406-7; the Order fatal to the Papacy, 427; historically and actually a separable force from Catholicism, 465; the proper method of combating it, in Germany, 465 (*note*)
Uniformity in the Jesuit Order, i. 356-361
Universities, Jesuit intrigues at the, of Ingolstadt, ii. 38-40; of Freiburg in Breisgau, 40.2; of Vienna, 42.5; of Paris, 47.8
Untruthfulness, an all-pervading Jesuit failing, ii. 49; considered in detail, 302-319
Urban VIII., Pope, canonises Ignatius Loyola, ii. 21.2; forbids the Orders to carry on commerce, 99 and *note*; favours the annexation of Lusatia to France, 182
Ursula, St., the virgins of, ii. 207

Vatican Council of 1870, incidents at, i. 220.4; the minority party at, 220.1; surrender of the German bishops at, 223-4; its President, 237
Vatican Palace, non-Christian character of, i. 263

Index

aughan, Father Bernard, in great request for charity sermons, ii. 413
aux, Lady Anne, letters of, to Father Garnet, ii. 128
enerable (*Venerabilis*), a title preliminary to Saint (*Sanctus*), i. 310 (*note*)
enice, conquest of Scio by, ii. 364; Paul V. at war with, *ib.*, Jesuits driven out of, 364-5
ergara, secretly a Jesuit, ii. 16
erjus, Father Antoine, ii. 198
ervaux, Father, ii. 190-1
icar-General of the Society of Jesus, duties of, i. 421-3
icecomes, Jesuit General, on the competition of secular schools, i. 187
icious practices alleged of Jesuits, i. 206-7, ii. 68-9
ienna, important Jesuit documents in the library at, i. 184 *et seqq.*; how they came to be placed there, 189; ignorance of German on the part of Jesuit Professors at the University of, ii. 32-3; Jesuit intrigues at the University of, 42-5
illas of the Jesuit Order, ii. 77
iller, Father, an active political agent in Austria, ii. 139; deprecates Jesuit jealousy, 195
incent, Julian, i. 336
Vincent de Paul, St., ii. 57 (*note*)
Virgin, the adoration of the, ii. 204-5; extravagances of the worship of the, 205-7
Visitator, status of, in the Jesuit Order, ii. 33 (*note*)
Vitelleschi, Mutius, General, requires the *Monita* to be refuted, ii. 7; ordinance of, anent the confessing of sovereigns, 173; approves Santarelli's *Tractatus de Haeresi*, 312
Vocation, choice of, ii. 215; gains students for the Jesuit priesthood, 216; disregard of the, and the mental torture it entails, 260-1
Voit on the advice to avoid a greater sin by perpetrating a lesser, ii. 326-7
Voltaire mentions an instance of a betrayed confession, ii. 177-8
Vow, Jesuits by, ii. 17-20. (*See* Affiliates)
Vows of poverty, chastity and obedience, i. 273; devotional or votive vows, 402-3; constitutional vows of the Society, 416-8; simple vows of scholastics and spiritual and temporal coadjutors, 417; vow of the professed, 417-8; five minor vows of the professed, 418; final vows of the spiritual and temporal coadjutors, *ib.*, Jesuit violation of the vow of obedience, ii. 50-67; Jesuit violation of the vow of chastity, 67-71; Jesuit violation of the vow of poverty, 71-104; the renewal of vows, 389

Wagner, Franz, on a uniform timetable for use in Jesuit schools, i. 93
Waitz, Georg, lectures of, at Göttingen, i. 122
Waldburg-Zeil, Georg, ii. 383-4
Waldemar of Denmark, the Princess, under the influence of the Jesuits, ii. 167
Waldersee, Count, ii. 461

Waldthauser, Ferdinand, Bohemian Provincial, on secret drinking among Jesuits, i. 183
Wallenstein, fall of, the work of the Jesuits, ii. 159; Jesuits assist in procuring the doom of, 179-80
Warner, Jesuit Confessor of James II., ii. 153
Wars: Austro-Prussian of 1866, i. 210-3; Franco-German of 1870-1, 232-3; Jesuit hostility to Prussia in both cases, *ib.*, Jesuit conduct during the Thirty Years' War, ii. 41, 158-9
Warsewicz, Stanislaus, ii. 138
Wasmann, Erich, ii. 266
Wealth of the Jesuit Order, ii. 82-90; acquired in trade and commerce, 91-9; revenue of the Jesuits in the Upper German Province from 1620 to 1700, 82-3; vast landed property of the Jesuits in the Upper German Province in 1773, 84-5; wealth of the Order in, at the date of its suppression, 85; in the Province of America, 87-8; in China, 88-9; in France at date of the suppression, 89-90
Wendt-Gevelinghausen, Baron von, ii. 393
Wenig, Professor J. L., on the death sentence for heretics, ii. 354; cries "God bless the Inquisition!" 355
Wernz, Francis Xavier, General, a teacher at Feldkirch, i. 118; one of the two German Generals of the Order, ii. 145 (*note*); insists on the supremacy of Church over State, 338-40; holds that non-Catholic Christians are beyond the pale, 350-1; his hostility to State schools, 439
Wertenberg, Father, i. 264
Weston, Father, records instances of the exorcism of devils, i. 321-2
"Why should the Jesuits not return to Germany?" the author's pamphlet in defence of the Order, ii. 393-4; why it is superficial and untrue, 395-6
Wiedemann, Father, character of, ii. 217-8; interested in a new gun, 218
Wilhelm, Balthasar, ii. 277
William I. and the Empress Augusta, i. 8; reception of the Emperor at Mayence, 232
William II., German Emperor, has a long conversation with the author, ii. 459; the Kaiser's promise, 460; Count Waldersee's memorial to, 461; the author has another interview with, 461-2; the Kaiser "lets the man drop," 462-3
William V. of Bavaria, Duke, ii. 83
Windthorst, Herr, in frequent consultation with the Jesuits, ii. 165-6; not in favour of extreme measures against non-Catholic Christians, 375; decides to make capital out of the Papal States question, 391-2; approves of the author's Church and State pamphlet, 393; approves of the Jesuit settlement in Berlin, 400; Lieber's relations with, 402; extraordinary statement alleged to have been made by, *ib.*
Winfridian Students' Union at Göttingen, i. 246

isbeach (Wisbech), Jesuit activity at, in Elizabeth's reign, ii. 46

iseman, Cardinal Nicholas, "Hidden Gem" by, the type of a safe drama in Jesuit eyes, i. 125; deplores the lack of Jesuit zeal in London, ii. 31-2

itchcraft and magic, Jesuit procedure in cases of, i. 154-5; how to exorcise witches, 320-1; instance of bewitchment, 322

Wolff-Metternich, Count Paul, i. 261

Woman, place of, in the Jesuit scheme, in theory and in practice, i. 384, ii. 123; easily led by Jesuit guile, ii. 11, 12, 18; relation of the Order to, 123-32; instructions to Jesuits respecting women and confession permeated with suspicion and suggestion, 124-5; women of rank may enter Jesuit Colleges, 126; the status of the women who may be visited by Jesuits, 126-7; woman as regarded by Loyola, 127; every attention paid by Jesuits to wealthy women, 128-9

Würzburg, the author studies for the Law at, i. 261

Wynandsrade, the professional staff at the College at, i. 119-24; the Rhetoric curriculum at, 120; the History course at, 121-2; set aside for the students of Humanity, 287; the author migrates to Wynandsrade for his scholasticate, 406, 407; its villa at Aalbeek, ii. 77; the author's residence at, for Humanity and Rhetoric, 201-14; the Virgin held in special honour at, 208

Xavier, St. Francis, successful invocation to, i. 304; miraculous portrait of, 312; "novena of grace" in honour of, 323; universal fame of, ii. 111

Zahorowski, editor of the first edition of the *Monita privata*, ii. 7

Zeil, the haunted wing in the Castle of, i. 27

Zeno, Antonio, and the renegade Mohammedans of Scio, ii. 364

Zorell, Francis, on the clockwork system of Jesuit education, i. 93

Zorzi, Marino, ii. 158

Zottowski, Ladislaus, Jesuit Provincial, on the indifference shown by teachers, i. 186